T0236766

Lecture Notes in Computer Science 10508

Commenced Publication in 1973
Founding and Former Series Editors:
Gerhard Goos, Juris Hartmanis, and Jan van Leeuwen

Editorial Board

David Hutchison
  Lancaster University, Lancaster, UK
Takeo Kanade
  Carnegie Mellon University, Pittsburgh, PA, USA
Josef Kittler
  University of Surrey, Guildford, UK
Jon M. Kleinberg
  Cornell University, Ithaca, NY, USA
Friedemann Mattern
  ETH Zurich, Zurich, Switzerland
John C. Mitchell
  Stanford University, Stanford, CA, USA
Moni Naor
  Weizmann Institute of Science, Rehovot, Israel
C. Pandu Rangan
  Indian Institute of Technology, Madras, India
Bernhard Steffen
  TU Dortmund University, Dortmund, Germany
Demetri Terzopoulos
  University of California, Los Angeles, CA, USA
Doug Tygar
  University of California, Berkeley, CA, USA
Gerhard Weikum
  Max Planck Institute for Informatics, Saarbrücken, Germany

More information about this series at http://www.springer.com/series/7407

Gabriele Fici · Marinella Sciortino
Rossano Venturini (Eds.)

String Processing
and Information Retrieval

24th International Symposium, SPIRE 2017
Palermo, Italy, September 26–29, 2017
Proceedings

 Springer

Editors
Gabriele Fici ⓘ
Università di Palermo
Palermo
Italy

Rossano Venturini ⓘ
Università di Pisa
Pisa
Italy

Marinella Sciortino ⓘ
Università di Palermo
Palermo
Italy

ISSN 0302-9743   ISSN 1611-3349 (electronic)
Lecture Notes in Computer Science
ISBN 978-3-319-67427-8   ISBN 978-3-319-67428-5 (eBook)
DOI 10.1007/978-3-319-67428-5

Library of Congress Control Number: 2017952852

LNCS Sublibrary: SL1 – Theoretical Computer Science and General Issues

© Springer International Publishing AG 2017
This work is subject to copyright. All rights are reserved by the Publisher, whether the whole or part of the material is concerned, specifically the rights of translation, reprinting, reuse of illustrations, recitation, broadcasting, reproduction on microfilms or in any other physical way, and transmission or information storage and retrieval, electronic adaptation, computer software, or by similar or dissimilar methodology now known or hereafter developed.
The use of general descriptive names, registered names, trademarks, service marks, etc. in this publication does not imply, even in the absence of a specific statement, that such names are exempt from the relevant protective laws and regulations and therefore free for general use.
The publisher, the authors and the editors are safe to assume that the advice and information in this book are believed to be true and accurate at the date of publication. Neither the publisher nor the authors or the editors give a warranty, express or implied, with respect to the material contained herein or for any errors or omissions that may have been made. The publisher remains neutral with regard to jurisdictional claims in published maps and institutional affiliations.

Printed on acid-free paper

This Springer imprint is published by Springer Nature
The registered company is Springer International Publishing AG
The registered company address is: Gewerbestrasse 11, 6330 Cham, Switzerland

Preface

This volume contains the papers presented at SPIRE 2017, the 24th International Symposium on String Processing and Information Retrieval, held September 26–28, 2017, in Palermo, Italy. Following the tradition of previous symposia, the focus of SPIRE this year was on fundamental studies on string processing and information retrieval, as well as on computational biology.

The call for papers resulted in 71 submissions. Each submitted paper was reviewed by at least three Program Committee members. Based on the thorough reviews and discussions by the Program Committee members and additional subreviewers, the Program Committee decided to accept 26 papers. The main conference featured three keynote speeches by Flavio Chierichetti (Sapienza Università di Roma), Moshe Lewenstein (Bar Ilan University), and Stéphane Vialette (CNRS & Université Paris-Est Marne-la-Vallée), together with presentations by authors of the 26 accepted papers. Just after the main conference, a satellite workshop was held: the 12th Workshop on Compression, Text, and Algorithms (WCTA 2017), held on September 29, 2017, in Palermo. WCTA was coordinated by Simon Gog and Giovanna Rosone. WCTA this year featured two keynote speeches by Knut Reinert (Freie Universität Berlin) and Sebastiano Vigna (Università degli Studi di Milano).

We would like to thank the SPIRE Steering Committee for giving us the opportunity to host this wonderful event. Also, many thanks go to the Program Committee members and the additional subreviewers for their valuable contribution ensuring the high quality of this conference. We are grateful to Springer for their professional publishing work and for sponsoring the Best Paper Award for SPIRE 2017. We finally thank the Local Organizing Committee for the smooth running of the event.

September 2017

Gabriele Fici
Marinella Sciortino
Rossano Venturini

Organization

Program Committee

Aris Anagnostopoulos	Sapienza University of Rome, Italy
Golnaz Badkobeh	University of Warwick, UK
Djamal Belazzougui	CERIST (Research Centre for Scientific and Technical Information), Algeria
Philip Bille	Technical University of Denmark, Denmark
Timothy Chan	University of Illinois at Urbana-Champaign, USA
Gianluca Della Vedova	DISCo, Univ. degli Studi Milano-Bicocca, Italy
Riccardo Dondi	Università degli Studi di Bergamo, Italy
Nadia El-Mabrouk	University of Montreal, Canada
Gabriele Fici	Università di Palermo, Italy
Travis Gagie	Diego Portales University, Chile
Leszek Gasieniec	University of Liverpool, UK
Pawel Gawrychowski	University of Haifa, Israel
Szymon Grabowski	Technical University of Lodz, Poland
Danny Hermelin	Ben Gurion University of the Negev, Israel
Jan Holub	Czech Technical University in Prague, Czech Republic
Tomohiro I	Kyushu Institute of Technology, Japan
Shunsuke Inenaga	Kyushu University, Japan
Giuseppe F. Italiano	University of Rome "Tor Vergata", Italy
Artur Jeż	University of Wroclaw, Poland
Tomasz Kociumaka	University of Warsaw, Poland
Daniel Lemire	LICEF Research Center, Université du Québec, Canada
Zsuzsanna Liptak	University of Verona, Italy
Stefano Lonardi	UC Riverside, USA
Florin Manea	Christian-Albrechts-Universitätzu Kiel, Germany
Giovanni Manzini	University of Eastern Piedmont, Italy
Robert Mercas	Loughborough University, UK
Laurent Mouchard	University of Rouen, France
Gonzalo Navarro	University of Chile, Chile
Patrick K. Nicholson	Bell Labs Ireland, Ireland
Kunsoo Park	Seoul National University, South Korea
Solon Pissis	King's College London, UK
Simon Puglisi	University of Helsinki, Finland
Jakub Radoszewski	University of Warsaw, Poland
Rajeev Raman	University of Leicester, UK
Eric Rivals	LIRMM - UMR 5506 CNRS UM2, France
Kunihiko Sadakane	The University of Tokyo, Japan
Marinella Sciortino	Università di Palermo, Italy

Fabrizio Silvestri	Facebook, London, UK
Tatiana Starikovskaya	Université Paris-Diderot - Paris 7, France
Jens Stoye	Bielefeld University, Germany
Alexandru I. Tomescu	University of Helsinki, Finland
Rossano Venturini	Università di Pisa, Italy

Additional Reviewers

Alanko, Jarno	Karimi, Sarvnaz
Atassi, Reem	Kempa, Dominik
Ayad, Lorraine	Kosolobov, Dmitry
Baisya, Dipankar Ranjan	Larsson, N. Jesper
Bannai, Hideo	Nakashima, Yuto
Beretta, Stefano	Nie, Jian-Yun
Billerbeck, Bodo	Noutahi, Emmanuel
Burcsi, Péter	Patterson, Murray
Castelli, Mauro	Previtali, Marco
Cazaux, Bastien	Prezza, Nicola
Charalampopoulos, Panagiotis	Rizzi, Raffaella
Christiansen, Anders Roy	Roayaei Ardakany, Abbas
Cunial, Fabio	Rosone, Giovanna
Day, Joel	Sebastiani, Fabrizio
Denti, Luca	Shapira, Dana
Doerr, Daniel	Sikora, Florian
Faro, Simone	Smyth, William F.
Fujishige, Yuta	Sugimoto, Shiho
Gańczorz, Michał	Takabatake, Yoshimasa
Hasan, Md Abid	Walen, Tomasz
Heliou, Alice	Weimann, Oren
Hucke, Danny	Wittler, Roland
Ionescu, Radu Tudor	Yamanaka, Katsuhisa

Abstracts of Invited Talks

Locality Sensitive Hashing, Similarities, and Distortion

Flavio Chierichetti

Dipartimento di Informatica, Sapienza University of Rome

Abstract. Locality sensitive hashing (LSH) is a key algorithmic tool that lies at the heart of many information retrieval systems [1, 2, 8]. In a nutshell, LSH schemes are used to sketch dense objects (e.g., Web pages, fields of flowers, cells) into small fingerprints; the fingerprints are then used to approximately reconstruct some similarity relation between the objects.

LSH schemes can significantly improve the computational cost of many algorithmic primitives — thus, for the last two decades, theoretical researchers have tried to understand the conditions under which similarities can admit efficient LSH schemes: such schemes were obtained for many similarities [1–3, 7–9], while the non-existence of LSH schemes was proved for a number of other similarities [3].

In this talk, we will first introduce the class of LSH-preserving transformations [4] (functions that, when applied to a similarity that admits a LSH scheme, return a similarity that also admits such a scheme). We will give a characterization of this class of functions: they are precisely the probability generating functions, up to scaling. We will show how this characterization was used to construct LSH schemes for a number of well-known similarities.

Then, we will discuss a notion of similarity distortion [6], in order to deal with similarities which are known to not admit LSH schemes — this notion aims to determine the minimum distortions that these similarities have to be subject of, before starting to admit a LSH scheme. We will introduce a number of theoretical tools that can be used to determine the optimal distortions of some important classes of similarities.

Finally, we will analyze the computational problem of checking whether a similarity admits a LSH scheme [5]. We will show that, unfortunately, this problem is computationally hard in a very strong sense.

References

1. Andoni, A., Indyk, P.: Near-optimal hashing algorithms for approximate nearest neighbor in high dimensions. In: FOCS, pp. 459–468 (2006)
2. Broder, A.Z.: On the resemblance and containment of documents. In: Proceedings of SEQUENCES, pp. 21–29 (1997)

Supported in part by the ERC Starting Grant DMAP 680153, by a Google Focused Research Award and by the SIR Grant RBSI14Q743.

3. Charikar, M.: Similarity estimation techniques from rounding algorithms. In: Proceedings of STOC, pp. 380–388 (2002)
4. Chierichetti, F., Kumar, R.: LSH-preserving functions and their applications. J. ACM **62**(5), 33:1–33:25 (2015)
5. Chierichetti, F., Kumar, R., Mahdian, M.: The complexity of LSH feasibility. Theor. Comput. Sci. **530**, 89–101 (2014)
6. Chierichetti, F., Kumar, R., Panconesi, A., Terolli, E.: The distortion of locality sensitive hashing. In: ITCS (2017)
7. Christiani, T., Pagh, R.: Set similarity search beyond minhash. In Proceedings of the 49th Annual ACM SIGACT Symposium on Theory of Computing, STOC 2017, pp. 1094–1107, New York, NY, USA. ACM (2017)
8. Gionis, A., Indyk, P., Motwani, R., et al.: Similarity search in high dimensions via hashing. In: VLDB, pp. 518–529 (1999)
9. Indyk, P., Motwani, R.: Approximate nearest neighbors: towards removing the curse of dimensionality. In: STOC, pp. 604–613 (1998)

Conditional Lower Bounds
for String Problems

Moshe Lewenstein

Bar-Ilan University

Abstract. In recent years, intensive research has been dedicated to proving conditional lower bounds of algorithmic problems in order to reveal the inner structure of the class P. These conditional lower bounds are based on many popular conjectures on well-studied problems. For example, one popular conjecture is the celebrated Strong Exponential Time Hypothesis (SETH). Another is a conjecture of hardness for the well-known 3SUM problem. There are several other popular conjectures that are widely used.

The field of string matching and indexing is no exception. The celebrated algorithms for LCS and edit distance algorithms are of quadratic time, up to log factors. For many years the challenge of obtaining a better running time was a lofty goal within the stringology community. However, lately, almost matching conditional lower bounds were shown [1, 4, 6] for these problems.

Likewise, close upper bounds and conditional lower bounds [3, 8, 11] are shown for histogram indexing [7, 9, 15], for constant-sized alphabets of size greater than two. The CGL data structure for indexing with errors [10] can be closely matched, for certain instances, with conditional lower bounds.

These examples are supported by even more conditional lower bounds for string matching, e.g. [2, 5, 14].

In this talk we will survey the world of conditional lower bounds within the framework of stringology. Specifically, we will look at some popular conjectures and their implications. We will follow an example of a string-problem conditional lower bound and its relation to the best-known upper bound. Given sufficient time, we will speak about new implications of conditional lower bound time-space tradeoffs [12, 13].

References

1. Abboud, A., Backurs, A., Vassilevska Williams, V.: Tight hardness results for LCS and other sequence similarity measures. In: Proceedings of the Symposium on Foundations of Computer Science, FOCS 2015, pp. 59–78 (2015)
2. Abboud, A., Vassilevska Williams, V., Weimann, O.: Consequences of faster alignment of sequences. In: Proceedings of the International Colloquium on Automata, Languages, and Programming, ICALP 2014, pp. 39–51 (2014)
3. Amihood, A., Chan, T.M., Lewenstein, M., Lewenstein, N.: On hardness of jumbled indexing. In: Proceedings of the International Colloquium on Automata, Languages, and Programming, ICALP 2014, pp. 114–125 (2014)

4. Backurs, A., Indyk, P.: Edit distance cannot be computed in strongly subquadratic time (unless SETH is false). In: Proceedings of the Symposium on Theory of Computing, STOC 2015, pp. 51–58 (2015)
5. Bringmann, K., Gawrychowski, P., Mozes, S., Weimann, O.: Tree edit distance cannot be computed in strongly subcubic time (unless APSP can). CoRR, abs/1703.08940 (2017)
6. Bringmann, K., Künnemann, M.: Quadratic conditional lower bounds for string problems and dynamic time warping. In: Proceedings of the Symposium on Foundations of Computer Science, FOCS 2015, pp. 79–97 (2015)
7. Butman, A., Eres, R., Landau, G.: Scaled and permuted string matching. Inf. Process. Lett. **92**(6), 293–297 (2004)
8. Chan, T.M., Lewenstein, M.: Clustered integer 3sum via additive combinatorics. In: Proceedings of the ACM Symposium on Theory of Computing, STOC 2015, pp. 31–40 (2015)
9. Cicalese, F., Fici, G., Lipták, Z.: Searching for jumbled patterns in strings. In: Prague Stringology Conference, pp. 105–117 (2009)
10. Cole, R., Gottlieb, L.A., Lewenstein, M.: Dictionary matching and indexing with errors and don't cares. In: Proceedings of the Annual ACM Symposium on Theory of Computing, STOC 2004, pp. 91–100 (2004)
11. Goldstein, I., Kopelowitz, T., Lewenstein, M., Porat, E.: How hard is it to find (honest) witnesses? In: 24th Annual European Symposium on Algorithms, ESA 2016, pp. 45:1–45:16 (2016)
12. Goldstein, I., Kopelowitz, T., Lewenstein, M., Porat, E.: Conditional lower bounds for space/time tradeoffs. In: Proceedings of Algorithms and Data Structures, WADS 2017, pp. 421–436 (2017)
13. Goldstein, I., Lewenstein, M., Porat, E.: Orthogonal vectors indexing (2017, In submitted)
14. Kopelowitz, T., Pettie, S., Porat, E.: Higher lower bounds from the 3SUM conjecture. In: Proceedings of the Annual ACM-SIAM Symposium on Discrete Algorithms, SODA 2016, pp. 1272–1287 (2016)
15. Moosa, T.M., Sohel Rahman, M.: Indexing permutations for binary strings. Inf. Process. Lett. **110**(18–19), 795–798 (2010)

Permutationology: Stringology for Permutations

Stéphane Vialette

Université Paris-Est, LIGM (UMR 8049), CNRS, UPEM,
ESIEE Paris, ENPC, F-77454, Marne-la-Vallée, France
stephane.vialette@u-pem.fr

Abstract. A permutation τ is said to *contain* the permutation π if there exists a subsequence of (not necessarily consecutive) entries of τ that has the same relative order as π, and in this case π is said to be a *pattern* of τ, written $\pi \leq \tau$. Otherwise, τ is said to *avoid* the permutation π. For example, the permutation $\tau = 543621$ contains the pattern $\pi = 3241$, as can be seen in the highlighted subsequence of $\tau = 543621$. However, since the permutation $\tau = 543621$ contains no increasing subsequence of length three, τ avoids 123. The introduction of the area of permutation patterns is traditionally attributed to D. Knuth is his first volume of "*The Art of Computer Programming*".

The term *stringology* is a popular nickname for string algorithms. In this talk, we shall focus on *permutationology* by revisiting some classical fundamental string algorithms such as pattern matching, (un-)shuffling and finding longest common subsequences in the realm of permutation patterns (with a particular emphasis of pattern avoiding permutations).

Contents

Greedy Shortest Common Superstring Approximation in Compact Space

Jarno Alanko$^{(\boxtimes)}$ and Tuukka Norri

Department of Computer Science, University of Helsinki,
Gustaf Hällströmin katu 2b, 00560 Helsinki, Finland
{jarno.alanko,tuukka.norri}@helsinki.fi

Abstract. Given a set of strings, the shortest common superstring problem is to find the shortest possible string that contains all the input strings. The problem is NP-hard, but a lot of work has gone into designing approximation algorithms for solving the problem. We present the first time and space efficient implementation of the classic greedy heuristic which merges strings in decreasing order of overlap length. Our implementation works in $O(n \log \sigma)$ time and bits of space, where n is the total length of the input strings in characters, and σ is the size of the alphabet. After index construction, a practical implementation of our algorithm uses roughly $5n \log \sigma$ bits of space and reasonable time for a real dataset that consists of DNA fragments.

Keywords: Greedy · Approximation · Compact · Space-efficient · Burrows-Wheeler transform · BWT · Shortest common superstring · SCS

1 Introduction

Given a set of strings, the shortest common superstring is the shortest string which contains each of the input strings as a substsring. The problem is NP-hard [4], but efficient approximation algorithms exist. Perhaps the most practical of the approximation algorithms is the greedy algorithm first analyzed by Tarhio, Ukkonen [14] and Turner [15]. The algorithm greedily joins together the pairs of strings with the longest prefix-suffix overlap, until only one string remains. In case there are equally long overlaps, the algorithm can make an arbitrary selection among those. The remaining string is an approximation of the shortest common superstring. The algorithm has been proven to give a superstring with length at most $3\frac{1}{2}$ times the optimal length [6]. It was originally conjectured by Ukkonen and Tarhio [14] that the greedy algorithm never outputs a superstring that is more than twice as long as the optimal, and the conjecture is still open.

Let m be the number of strings, n be the sum of the lengths of all the strings, and σ the size of the alphabet. In 1990 Ukkonen showed how to implement the greedy algorithm in $O(n)$ time and $O(n \log n)$ bits of space using the Aho-Corasick automaton [16]. Since then, research on the problem has focused on finding algorithms with better provable approximation ratios (see e.g. [9] for a summary).

© Springer International Publishing AG 2017
G. Fici et al. (Eds.): SPIRE 2017, LNCS 10508, pp. 1–13, 2017.
DOI: 10.1007/978-3-319-67428-5_1

Currently, algorithm with the best proven approximation ratio in peer reviewed literature is the one by Mucha with an approximation ratio of $2\frac{11}{23}$ [9], and there is a preprint claiming an algorithm with a ratio of $2\frac{11}{30}$ [11]. However, we are not aware of any published algorithm that solves the problem in better than $O(n \log n)$ bits of space. Improving the factor $\log n$ to $\log \sigma$ is important in practice. Many of the largest data sets available come from DNA strings which have an alphabet of size only 4, while n can be over 10^9.

We present an algorithm that implements the greedy heuristic in $O(n \log \sigma)$ time and bits of space. It is based on the FM-index enhanced with a succinct representation of the topology of the suffix tree. The core of the algorithm is the iteration of prefix-suffix overlaps of input strings in decreasing order of length using a technique described in [8,13], combined with Ukkonen's bookkeeping [16] to keep track of the paths formed in the overlap graph of the input strings. The main technical novelty of this work is the implementation of Ukkonen's bookkeeping in $O(n \log \sigma)$ space. We also have a working implementation of the algorithm based on the SDSL-library [5]. For practical reasons the implementation differs slightly from the algorithm presented in this paper, but the time and space usage should be similar.

2   Preliminaries

Let there be m strings $s_1, \ldots, s_m$ drawn from the alphabet Σ of size σ such that the sum of the lengths of the strings is $\sum_{i=1}^{m} |s_i| = n$. We build a single string by concatenating the m strings, placing a separator character $\$ \notin \Sigma$ between each string. We define that the separator is lexicographically smaller than all characters in Σ. This gives us the string $S = s_1 \$ s_2 \$ \cdots s_m \$$ of length $n + m$. Observe that the set of suffixes that are prefixed by some substring α of S are adjacent in the lexicographic ordering of the suffixes. We call this interval in the sorted list of suffixes the *lexicographic range* of string α. All occurrences of a substring α can be uniquely represented as a triple $(a_\alpha, b_\alpha, d_\alpha)$, where $[a_\alpha, b_\alpha]$ is the lexicographic range of α, and d_α is the length of α. A string α is *right maximal* in S if and only if there exist two or more distinct characters $y, z \in \Sigma \cup \{\$\}$ such that the strings αy and αz are substrings of S. Our algorithm needs support for two operations on substrings: left extensions and suffix links. A left extension of string α with character x is the map $(a_\alpha, b_\alpha, d_\alpha) \mapsto (a_{x\alpha}, b_{x\alpha}, d_{x\alpha})$. A suffix link for the right-maximal string $x\alpha$ is the map $(a_{x\alpha}, b_{x\alpha}, d_{x\alpha}) \mapsto (a_\alpha, b_\alpha, d_\alpha)$.

3   Overview of the Algorithm

We use Ukkonen's 1990 algorithm [16] as a basis for our algorithm. Conceptually, we have a complete directed graph where vertices are the input strings, and the weight of the edge from string s_i to string s_j is the length of the longest suffix of s_i which is also a prefix of s_j. If there is no such overlap, the weight of the edge is zero. The algorithm finds a Hamiltonian path over the graph, and merges the strings in the order given by the path to form the superstring. We define the merge of strings $s_i = \alpha\beta$ and $s_j = \beta\gamma$, where β is the longest prefix-suffix overlap of s_i and s_j, as the string $\alpha\beta\gamma$. It is known that the string formed by merging the strings in the order given by the maximum weight Hamiltonian path gives a superstring of optimal length [14]. The greedy algorithm tries to heuristically find a Hamiltonian path with a large total length.

Starting from a graph G where the vertices are the input strings and there are no edges, the algorithm iterates all prefix-suffix overlaps of pairs of strings in decreasing order of length. For each pair (s_i, s_j) we add an edge from s_i to s_j iff the in-degree of s_j is zero, the out-degree of s_i is zero, and adding the edge would not create a cycle in G. We also consider overlaps of length zero, so every possible edge is considered and it is easy to see that in the end the added edges form a Hamiltonian path over G.

4   Algorithm

Observe that if an input string is a proper substring of another input string, then any valid superstring that contains the longer string also contains the shorter string, so we can always discard the shorter string. Similarly if there are strings that occur multiple times, it suffices to keep only one copy of each. This preprocessing can be easily done in $O(n \log \sigma)$ time and space for example by backward searching all the input strings using the FM-index.

After the preprocessing, we sort the input strings into lexicographic order, concatenate them placing dollar symbols in between the strings, and build an index that supports suffix links and left extensions. The sorting can be done with merge sort such that string comparisons are done $O(\log(n))$ bits at a time using machine word level parallelism, as allowed by the RAM model. This works in $O(n \log \sigma)$ time and space if the sorting is implemented so that it does not move the strings around, but instead manipulates only pointers to the strings.

For notational convenience, from here on s_i refers to the string with lexicographic rank i among the input strings.

We iterate in decreasing order of length all the suffixes of the input strings s_i that occur at least twice in S and for each check whether the suffix is also a prefix of some other string s_j, and if so, we add an edge from s_i to s_j if possible. To enumerate the prefix-suffix overlaps, we use the key ideas from the algorithm for reporting all prefix-suffix overlaps to build an overlap graph described in [8] and [13], adapted to get the overlaps in decreasing order of length.

We maintain an iterator for each of the input strings. An iterator for the string s_i is a quadruple (i, ℓ, r, d), where $[\ell, r]$ is the lexicographic range of the current suffix α of s_i and d is the length of α, i.e. the depth of the iterator. Suffixes of the input strings which are not right maximal in the concatenation $S = s_1\$ \ldots s_m\$$ can never be a prefix of any of the input strings. The reason is that if α is not right-maximal, then α is always followed by the separator $\$$. This means that if α is also a prefix of some other string s_j, then $s_j = \alpha$, because the only prefix of s_j that is followed by a $\$$ is the whole string s_j. But then s_j is a substring of s_i, which can not happen because all such strings were removed in the preprocessing stage. Thus, we can safely disregard any suffix α of s_i that is not right maximal in S. Furthermore, if a suffix α of s_i is not right maximal, then none of the suffixes $\beta\alpha$ are right-maximal either, so we can disregard those, too.

We initialize the iterator for each string s_i by backward searching s_i using the FM-index for as long as the current suffix of s_i is right-maximal. Next we sort these quadruples in the decreasing order of depth into an array iterators. When this is done, we start iterating from the iterator with the largest depth, i.e. the first element of iterators. Suppose the current iterator corresponds to string i, and the current suffix of string s_i is α. At each step of the iteration we check whether α is also a prefix of some string by executing a left extension with the separator character \$. If the lexicographic range $[\ell', r']$ of \$$\alpha$ is non-empty, we know that the suffixes of S in the range $[\ell', r']$ start with a dollar and are followed by a string that has α as a prefix. We conclude that the input string with lexicographic rank i among the input strings has a suffix of length d that matches a prefix of the strings with lexicographic ranks $\ell', \ldots, r'$ among the input strings. This is true because the lexicographic order of the suffixes of S that start with dollars coincides with the lexicographic ranks of the strings following the dollars in the concatenation, because the strings are concatenated in lexicographic order.

Thus, according to the greedy heuristic, we should try to merge s_i with a string from the set $s_{\ell'}, \ldots, s_{r'}$, which corresponds to adding an edge from s_i to some string from $s_{\ell'}, \ldots, s_{r'}$ in the graph G. We describe how we maintain the graph G in a moment. After updating the graph, we update the current iterator by decreasing d by one and taking a suffix link of the lexicographic range $[\ell, r]$. The iterator with the next largest d can be found in constant time because the array iterators is initially sorted in descending order of depth. We can maintain a pointer to the iterator with the largest d. If at some step iterators$[k]$ has the largest depth, then in the next step either iterators$[k+1]$ or iterators$[1]$ has the largest depth. The pseudocode for the main iteration loop is shown in Algorithm 1.

Now we describe how we maintain the graph G. The range $[\ell', r']$ now represents the lexicographical ranks of the input strings that are prefixed by α among all input strings. Each string s_j in this range is a candidate to merge to string s_i, but some bookkeeping is needed to keep track of available strings. We use essentially the same method as Tarhio and Ukkonen [14]. We have bit vectors leftavailable$[1..m]$ and rightavailable$[1..m]$ such that leftavailable$[k] = 1$ if and only if string s_k is available to use as the left side of a merge, and rightavailable$[k] = 1$ if and only if string s_k is available as the right side of a merge. Equivalently, leftavailable$[k] = 1$ iff the out-degree of s_k is zero and rightavailable$[k] = 1$ if the in-degree of s_k is zero. Also, to prevent the formation of a cycle, we need arrays leftend$[1..m]$, where leftend$[k]$ gives the leftmost string of the chain of merged strings to the left of s_k, and rightend$[1..m]$, where rightend$[k]$ gives the rightmost string of the chain of merged strings to the right of s_k. We initialize leftavailable$[k] = $ rightavailable$[k] = 1$ and leftend$[k] = $ rightend$[k] = k$ for all $k = 1, \ldots, m$.

Algorithm 1. Iterating all prefix-suffix overlaps

$k \leftarrow 1$
while iterators$[k].d \geq 0$ **do**
    $(i, [\ell, r], d) \leftarrow$ iterators$[k]$
    $[\ell', r'] \leftarrow$ leftextend$([\ell, r], \$)$
    if $[l', r']$ *is non empty* **then**
      | trymerge$([l', r'], i)$
    end
    iterators$[k] \leftarrow (i, \text{suffixlink}(\ell, r), d - 1)$
    if $i = m$ *or* (iterators$[1].d >$ iterators$[i+1].d$) **then**
      | $k \leftarrow 1$
    else
      | **else** $k \leftarrow k + 1$
    end
end

When we get the interval $[\ell', r']$ such that leftavailable$[j] = 1$, we try to find an index $j \in [\ell_{\$\alpha}, r_{\$\alpha}]$ such that rightavailable$[i] = 1$ and leftend$[j] \neq i$. Luckily we only need to examine at most two indices j and j' such that rightavailable$[j] = 1$ and rightavailable$[j'] = 1$ because if leftend$[j] = i$, then leftend$[j'] \neq i$, and vice versa. This procedure is named trymerge$([l', r'], i)$ in Algorithm 1.

The problem is now to find up to two ones in the bit vector rightavailable in the interval of indices $[\ell_{\$\alpha}, r_{\$\alpha}]$. To do this efficiently, we maintain for each index k in rightavailable the index of the first one in rightavailable$[k + 1..m]$, denoted with next_one(k). If there are two ones in the interval $[\ell_{\$\alpha}, r_{\$\alpha}]$, then they can be found at next_one$(\ell_{\$\alpha} - 1)$ and next_one(next_one$(\ell_{\$\alpha} - 1)$). The question now becomes, how do we maintain this information efficiently? In general, this is the problem of indexing a bit vector for dynamic successor queries, for which there does not exist a constant time solution using $O(n \log \sigma)$ space in the literature. However, in our case the vector rightavailable starts out filled with ones, and once a one is changed to a zero, it will not change back for the duration of the algorithm, which allows us to have a simpler and more efficient data structure.

Initially, next_one$(k) = k + 1$ for all $k < m$. The last index does not have a successor, but it can easily be handled as a special case. For clarity and brevity we describe the rest of the process as if the special case did not exist. When we update rightavailable$(k) := 0$, then we need to also update next_one$[k'] :=$ next_one(k) for all $k' < k$ such that rightavailable$[k' + 1..k]$ contains only zeros. To do this efficiently, we store the value of next_one only once for each sequence of consecutive zeros in rightavailable, which allows us to update the whole range at once. To keep track of the sequences of consecutive zeros, we can use a union-find data structure. A union-find data structure maintains a partitioning of a set of elements into disjoint groups. It supports the operations find(x), which returns the representative of the group containing x, and $\texttt{union}(x, y)$, which takes two representatives and merges the groups containing them.

We initialize the union-find structure such that there is an element for every index in $\texttt{rightavailable}$, and we also initialize an array $\texttt{next}[1..m]$ such that $\texttt{next}[k] := k+1$ for all $k = 1, \ldots m$. When a value at index k is changed to a zero, we compute $q := \texttt{next}[\texttt{find}(k)]$. Then we will do $\texttt{union}(\texttt{find}(k), \texttt{find}(k-1))$ and if $\texttt{rightavailable}[k+1] = 0$, we will do $\texttt{union}(\texttt{find}(k), \texttt{find}(k+1))$. Finally, we update $\texttt{next}[\texttt{find}(k)] = q$. We can answer queries for $\texttt{next\_one}(k)$ with $\texttt{next}[\texttt{find}(k)]$.

Whenever we find a pair of indices i and j such that $\texttt{leftavailable}[i] = 1$, $\texttt{rightavailable}[j] = 1$ and $\texttt{leftend}[j] \neq i$, we add an edge from s_i to s_j by recording string j as the successor of string i using arrays $\texttt{successor}[1..m]$ and $\texttt{overlaplength}[1..m]$. We set $\texttt{successor}[j] = i$ and $\texttt{overlaplength}[j] = d_i$, where d_i is the length of the overlap of s_i and s_j, and do the updates:

$$\texttt{leftavailable}[i] := 0$$
$$\texttt{rightavailable}[j] := 0$$
$$\texttt{leftend}[\texttt{rightend}[j]] := \texttt{leftend}[i]$$
$$\texttt{rightend}[\texttt{leftend}[i]] := \texttt{rightend}[j]$$

Note that the arrays $\texttt{leftend}$ and $\texttt{rightend}$ are only up to date for the end points of the paths, but this is fine for the algorithm. Finally we update the $\texttt{next}$ array with the union-find structure using the process described earlier. We stop iterating when we have done $m - 1$ merges. At the end, we have a Hamiltonian path over G, and we form a superstring by merging the strings in the order specified by the path.

5   Time and Space Analysis

The following space analysis is in terms of number of bits used. We assume that the strings are binary encoded such that each character takes $\lceil \log_2 \sigma \rceil$ bits. A crucial observation is that we can afford to store a constant number of $O(\log n)$ bit machine words for each distinct input string.

Lemma 1. *Let there be* m ***distinct*** *non-empty strings with combined length* n *measured in* ***bits*** *from an alphabet of size* $\sigma > 1$. *Then* $m \log n \in O(n \log \sigma)$.

Proof. Suppose $m \leq \sqrt{n}$. Then the Lemma is clearly true, because:

$$m \log n \leq \sqrt{n} \log n \in O(n \log \sigma)$$

We now consider the remaining case $m \geq \sqrt{n}$, or equivalently $\log n \leq 2 \log m$. This means $m \log n \leq 2m \log m$, so it suffices to show $m \log m \in O(n \log \sigma)$.

First, note that at least half of the strings have length at least $\log(m)-1$ bits. This is trivially true when $\log(m) - 1 \leq 1$. When $\log(m) - 1 \geq 2$, the number of distinct binary strings of length at most $\log(m) - 2$ bits is

$$\sum_{i=1}^{\lfloor \log(m)-2 \rfloor} 2^i \leq 2^{\log(m)-1} = \frac{1}{2}m$$

Therefore indeed at least half of the strings have length of at least $\log m - 1$ bits. The total length of the strings is then at least $\frac{1}{2}m(\log m - 1)$ bits. Since the binary representation of all strings combined takes $n\lceil \log_2 \sigma \rceil$ bits, we have $n\lceil \log_2 \sigma \rceil \geq \frac{1}{2}m(\log m - 1)$, which implies $m \log m \leq 2n\lceil \log_2 \sigma \rceil + 1 \in O(n \log \sigma)$. □

Next, we describe how to implement the suffix links and left extensions. We will need to build the following data structures for the concatenation of all input strings separated by a separator character:

- The Burrows-Wheeler transform, represented as a wavelet tree with support for rank and select queries.
- The C-array, which has length equal to the number of characters in the concatenation, such that $C[i]$ is the number of occurrences of characters with lexicographic rank strictly less than i.
- The balanced parenthesis representation of the suffix tree topology with support for queries for leftmost leaf, rightmost leaf and lowest common ancestor.

Note that in the concatenation of the strings, the alphabet size is increased by one because of the added separator character, and the total length of the data in characters is increased by m. However this does not affect the asymptotic size of the data, because

$$(n + m)\log(\sigma + 1) \leq 2n(\log \sigma + 1) \in \Theta(n \log \sigma)$$

The three data structures can be built and represented in $O(n \log \sigma)$ time and space [1]. Using these data structures we can implement the left extension for lexicographic interval $[\ell, r]$ with the character c by:

$$([\ell, r], c) \mapsto [C[c] + \text{rank}_{BWT}(\ell, c), C[c] + \text{rank}_{BWT}(r, c)]$$

We can implement the suffix link for the right maximal string $c\alpha$ with the lexicographic interval $[\ell, r]$ by first computing

$$v = \text{lca}(\text{select}_{BWT}(c, \ell - C[c]), \text{select}_{BWT}(c, r - C[c]))$$

and then

$$[\ell, r] \mapsto [\text{leftmostleaf}(v), \text{rightmostleaf}(v)]$$

This suffix link operation works as required for right-maximal strings by removing the first character of the string, but the behaviour on non-right-maximal strings is slightly different. The lexicographic range of a non-right-maximal string is the same as the lexicographic range of the shortest right-maximal string that has it as a prefix. In other words, for a non-right-maximal string $c\alpha$, the operation maps the interval $[\ell_{c\alpha}, r_{c\alpha}]$ to the lexicographic interval of the string $\alpha\beta$, where β is the shortest right-extension that makes $c\alpha\beta$ right-maximal. This behaviour allows us to check the right-maximality of a substring $c\alpha$ given the lexicographic ranges $[\ell_\alpha, r_\alpha]$ and $[\ell_{c\alpha}, r_{c\alpha}]$ in the iterator initialization phase of the algorithm as follows:

Lemma 2. *The substring $c\alpha$ is right maximal if and only if the suffix link of $[\ell_{c\alpha}, r_{c\alpha}]$ is $[\ell_\alpha, r_\alpha]$.*

Proof. As discussed above, the suffix link of $[\ell_{c\alpha}, r_{c\alpha}]$ maps to the lexicographic interval of the string $\alpha\beta$ where β is the shortest right-extension that makes $c\alpha\beta$ right-maximal. Suppose first that $c\alpha$ is right-maximal. Then $[\ell_{\alpha\beta}, r_{\alpha\beta}] = [\ell_\alpha, r_\alpha]$, because β is an empty string. Suppose on the contrary that $c\alpha$ is not right-maximal. Then $[\ell_{\alpha\beta}, r_{\alpha\beta}] \neq [\ell_\alpha, r_\alpha]$, because $\alpha\beta$ and α are distinct right-maximal strings. $\square$

Now we are ready to prove the time and space complexity of the whole algorithm.

Theorem 3. *The algorithm in Sect. 4 can be implemented in $O(n \log \sigma)$ time and $O(n \log \sigma)$ bits of space.*

Proof. The preprocessing to remove contained and duplicate strings can be done in $O(n \log \sigma)$ time and space for example by building an FM-index, and backward searching all input strings.

The algorithm executes $O(n)$ left extensions and suffix links. The time to take a suffix link is dominated by the time do the select query, which is $O(\log \sigma)$, and the time to do a left extension is dominated by the time to do a rank-query which is also $O(\log \sigma)$. For each left extension the algorithm does, it has to access and modify the union-find structure. Normally this would take amortized time related to the inverse function of the Ackermann function [2], but in our case the amortized complexity of the union-find operations can be made linear using the construction of Gabow and Tarjan [3], because we know that only elements corresponding to consecutive positions in the array `rightavailable` will be joined together. Therefore, the time to do all left extensions, suffix links and updates to the union-find data structure is $O(n \log \sigma)$.

Let us now turn to consider the space complexity. For each input string, we have the quadruple (i, ℓ, r, d) of positive integers with value at most n. The quadruples take space $3m \log m + m \log n$. The union-find structure of Gabow and Tarjan can be implemented in $O(m \log m)$ bits of space [3]. The bit vectors `leftavailable` and `rightavailable` take exactly $2m$ bits, and the arrays `successor`, `leftend`, `rightend` and `next` take $m \log m$ bits each. The array `overlaplength` takes $m \log n$ bits of space. Summing up, in addition to the data structures for the left extensions and contractions, we have only $O(m \log n)$ bits of space, which is $O(n \log \sigma)$ by Lemma 1. $\square$

6   Implementation

The algorithm was implemented with the SDSL library [5]. A compressed suffix tree that represents nodes as lexicographic intervals [10] was used to implement the suffix links and left extensions. Only the required parts of the suffix tree were built: the FM-index, balanced parentheses support and a bit vector that indicates the leftmost child node of each node. These data structures differ slightly from the description in Sect. 5, because they were chosen for convenience as they were readily available in the SDSL library, and they should give very similar performance compared to those used in the aforementioned Section. In particular, the leftmost child vector was needed to support suffix links, but we could manage without it by using the operations on the balanced parenthesis support described in Sect. 5. Our implementation is available at the URL https://github.com/tsnorri/compact-superstring

The input strings are first sorted with quicksort. This introduces a $\log n$ factor to the time complexity, but it is fast in practice. The implementation then runs in two passes. First, exact duplicate strings are removed and the stripped compact

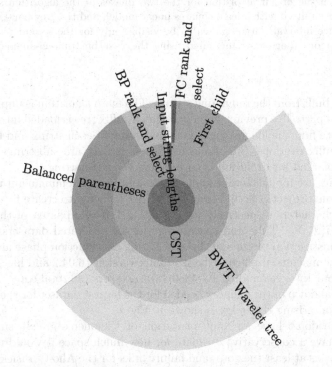

Fig. 1. Memory breakdown of the data structures used by our implementation. The plot was generated using the SDSL library. Each sector angle represents the portion of the memory taken by the data structure of the total memory of the inner data structure; areas have no special meaning. Abbreviations: CST = compressed suffix tree, BWT = Burrows-Wheeler Transform, BP = balanced parenthesis, FC = first child.

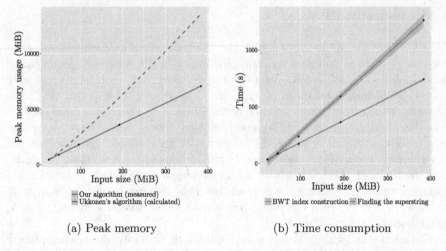

(a) Peak memory   (b) Time consumption

Fig. 2. (a) The peak memory usage of our algorithm plotted against a conservative estimate of $4n \log n$ bits of space needed by Ukkonen's Aho-Corasick based method. (b) the time usage of our algorithm for the two phases of the algorithm. The data points have been fitted with a least-squares linear model, and the grey band shows the 95% confidence interval (large enough to be visible only for the second phase). The time and memory usage were measured using the /usr/bin/time command and the RSS value.

suffix tree is built from the remaining strings. The main algorithm is implemented in the second part. The previously built stripped suffix tree is loaded into memory and is used to find the longest right-maximal suffix of each string and to iterate the prefix-suffix overlaps. Simultaneously, strings that are substrings of other strings are marked for exclusion from building the superstring.

For testing, we took a metagenomic DNA sample from a human gut microbial gene catalogue project [12], and sampled DNA fragments to create five datasets with 2^{26+i} characters respectively for $i = 0, \ldots, 4$. The alphabet of the sample was $\{A, C, G, T, N\}$. Time and space usage for all generated datasets for both the index construction phase and the superstring construction phase are plotted in Fig. 2. The machine used run Ubuntu Linux version 16.04.2 and has 1.5 TB of RAM and four Intel Xeon CPU E7-4830 v3 processors (48 total cores, 2.10 GHz each). A breakdown of the memory needed for the largest dataset for the different structures comprising the index is shown in Fig. 1.

While we don't have an implementation of Ukkonen's greedy superstring algorithm, have a conservative estimate for how much space it would take. The algorithm needs at least the goto- and failure links for the Aho-Corasick automaton, which take at least $2n \log n$ bits total. The main algorithm uses linked lists named L and P, which take at least $2n \log n$ bits total. Therefore the space usage is at the very least $4n \log n$. This estimate is plotted in Fig. 2.

Figure 3 shows the space usage of our algorithm in the largest test dataset as a function of time reported by the SDSL library. The peak memory usage

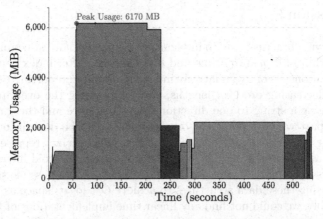

(a) Index construction

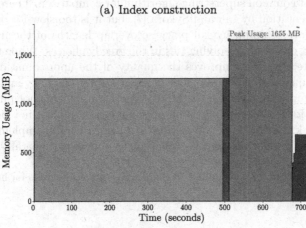

(b) Superstring construction

Fig. 3. Subfigures (a) and (b) show the memory usage as a function of time for index construction and superstring construction, respectively. The peak in Figure (a) occurs during suffix array construction, and the peak in Figure (b) occurs during the iteration of prefix-suffix overlaps.

of the whole algorithm occurs during index construction, and more specifically during the construction of a compressed suffix array. The SDSL library used this data structure to build the BWT and the balanced parenthesis representation, which makes the space usage unnecessarily high. This could be improved by using more efficient algorithms to build the BWT and the balanced parenthesis representation of the suffix tree topology [1]. These could be plugged in to bring down the index construction memory. At the moment index constructions takes roughly 19 times the size of the input in bits. The peak memory of the part of the algorithm which constructs the superstring is only approximately 5 times the size of the input in bits.

7 Discussion

We have shown a practical way to implement the greedy shortest common superstring algorithm in $O(n \log \sigma)$ time and bits of space. After index construction, the algorithm consists of two relatively independent parts: reporting prefix-suffix overlaps in decreasing order of lengths, and maintaining the overlap graph to prevent merging a string to one direction more than once and the formation of cycles. The part which reports the overlaps could also be done in other ways, such as using compressed suffix trees or arrays, or a succinct representation of the Aho-Corasick automaton. The only difficult part is to avoid having to hold $\Omega(n)$ integers in memory at any given time. We believe it is possible to engineer algorithms using these data structures to achieve $O(n \log \sigma)$ space as well.

Regrettably, we could not find any linear time implementations of Ukkonen's greedy shortest common superstring algorithm for comparison. There is an interesting implementation by Liu and Sýkora [7], but it is too slow for our purposes because it involves computing all pairwise overlap lengths of the input strings to make better choices in resolving ties in the greedy choices. While their experiments indicate that this improves the quality of the approximation, the time complexity is quadratic in the number of input strings. Zaritsky and Sipper [17] also have an implementation of the greedy algorithm, but it's not publicly available, and the focus of the paper is on approximation quality, not performance. As future work, it would be interesting to make a careful implementation of Ukkonen's greedy algorithm, and compare it to ours experimentally.

Acknowledgements. We would like to thank anonymous reviewers for improving the presentation of the paper.

References

1. Belazzougui, D.: Linear time construction of compressed text indices in compact space. In: Proceedings of the 46th Annual ACM Symposium on Theory of Computing, pp. 148–193. ACM (2014)
2. Cormen, T.H., Leiserson, C.E., Rivest, R.L., Stein, C.: Introduction to Algorithms, vol. 6. MIT Press, Cambridge (2001)
3. Gabow, H.N., Tarjan, R.E.: A linear-time algorithm for a special case of disjoint set union. J. Comput. Syst. Sci. **30**(2), 209–221 (1985)
4. Gallant, J., Maier, D., Astorer, J.: On finding minimal length superstrings. J. Comput. Syst. Sci. **20**(1), 50–58 (1980)
5. Gog, S., Beller, T., Moffat, A., Petri, M.: From theory to practice: plug and play with succinct data structures. In: Gudmundsson, J., Katajainen, J. (eds.) SEA 2014. LNCS, vol. 8504, pp. 326–337. Springer, Cham (2014). doi:10.1007/978-3-319-07959-2_28
6. Kaplan, H., Shafrir, N.: The greedy algorithm for shortest superstrings. Inf. Process. Lett. **93**(1), 13–17 (2005)
7. Liu, X., Sýkora, O.: Sequential and parallel algorithms for the shortest common superstring problem. In: Proceedings of the International Workshop on Parallel Numerics, pp. 97–107 (2005)

8. Mäkinen, V., Belazzougui, D., Cunial, F., Tomescu, A.I.: Genome-Scale Algorithm Design. Cambridge University Press, New York (2015)
9. Mucha, M.: Lyndon words and short superstrings. In: Proceedings of the Twenty-Fourth Annual ACM-SIAM Symposium on Discrete Algorithms, pp. 958–972. Society for Industrial and Applied Mathematics (2013)
10. Ohlebusch, E., Fischer, J., Gog, S.: CST++. In: Chavez, E., Lonardi, S. (eds.) SPIRE 2010. LNCS, vol. 6393, pp. 322–333. Springer, Heidelberg (2010). doi:10.1007/978-3-642-16321-0_34
11. Paluch, K.: Better approximation algorithms for maximum asymmetric traveling salesman and shortest superstring. arXiv preprint (2014). arXiv:1401.3670
12. Qin, J., Li, R., Raes, J., Arumugam, M., Burgdorf, K.S., Manichanh, C., Nielsen, T., Pons, N., Levenez, F., Yamada, T., et al.: A human gut microbial gene catalogue established by metagenomic sequencing. Nature 464(7285), 59–65 (2010)
13. Simpson, J.T., Durbin, R.: Efficient construction of an assembly string graph using the fm-index. Bioinformatics 26(12), i367–i373 (2010)
14. Tarhio, J., Ukkonen, E.: A greedy approximation algorithm for constructing shortest common superstrings. Theoret. Comput. Sci. 57(1), 131–145 (1988)
15. Turner, J.S.: Approximation algorithms for the shortest common superstring problem. Inf. Comput. 83(1), 1–20 (1989)
16. Ukkonen, E.: A linear-time algorithm for finding approximate shortest common superstrings. Algorithmica 5(1–4), 313–323 (1990)
17. Zaritsky, A., Sipper, M.: The preservation of favored building blocks in the struggle for fitness: the puzzle algorithm. IEEE Trans. Evol. Comput. 8(5), 443–455 (2004)

Longest Common Factor After One Edit Operation

Amihood Amir[1], Panagiotis Charalampopoulos[2], Costas S. Iliopoulos[2],
Solon P. Pissis[2], and Jakub Radoszewski[2,3(✉)]

[1] Department of Computer Science, Bar-Ilan University, Ramat Gan, Israel
amir@esc.biu.ac.il
[2] Department of Informatics, King's College London, London, UK
{panagiotis.charalampopoulos,costas.iliopoulos,solon.pissis}@kcl.ac.uk
[3] Institute of Informatics, University of Warsaw, Warsaw, Poland
jrad@mimuw.edu.pl

Abstract. It is well known that the longest common factor (LCF) of two strings over an integer alphabet can be computed in time linear in the total length of the two strings. Our aim here is to present an algorithm that preprocesses two strings S and T in order to answer the following type of queries: Given a position i on S and a letter α, return an LCF of T and S', where S' is the string resulting from S after substituting $S[i]$ with α. In what follows, we present an algorithm that, given two strings of length at most n, constructs in $\mathcal{O}(n \log^4 n)$ expected time a data structure of $\mathcal{O}(n \log^3 n)$ space that answers such queries in $\mathcal{O}(\log^3 n)$ time per query. After some trivial modifications, our approach can also support the case of single letter insertions or deletions in S.

Keywords: Longest common factor · Dynamic data structure · Suffix tree · Heavy-path decomposition · Orthogonal range searching

1 Introduction

In this work we consider strings over an integer alphabet. The longest common factor (LCF), also known as longest common substring, of two strings S and T, each of length at most n, can be computed in $\mathcal{O}(n)$ time [5,11,12,15]. The LCF with k-mismatches problem has received much attention recently, in particular due to its applications in computational molecular biology [13,17]. We refer the interested reader to [3,8,10,14,16].

A. Amir—Partially supported by the ISF grant 571/14 and the Royal Society.
C.S. Iliopoulos—Partially supported by the Onassis Foundation and the Royal Society.
J. Radoszewski—Supported by the "Algorithms for text processing with errors and uncertainties" project carried out within the HOMING programme of the Foundation for Polish Science co-financed by the European Union under the European Regional Development Fund.

© Springer International Publishing AG 2017
G. Fici et al. (Eds.): SPIRE 2017, LNCS 10508, pp. 14–26, 2017.
DOI: 10.1007/978-3-319-67428-5_2

Our motivation comes mainly from [14]; the author mentions that the solution to the LCF problem "is not robust and can vary significantly when the input strings are changed even by one letter". Somewhat surprisingly, however, dynamic instances of the LCF problem have not yet been studied thoroughly to the best of our knowledge. In this paper, we aim at initiating a line of research on this general version of the problem, by presenting a solution for the restricted case, where any single edit operation is allowed. In what follows, we focus on the case of a letter substitution; insertions and deletions can be handled analogously.

Given two strings S and T over an integer alphabet, each of length at most n, one may ask the following question: How fast can we find an LCF of S and T after a single letter substitution? For instance, after substituting $S[i]$ with letter α. The goal is to preprocess S and T so that we do not need $\Omega(n)$ time to compute an LCF for each such query. A naïve solution is to precompute an LCF for all $\Theta(\sigma n)$ possible substitutions in $\Theta(\sigma n^2)$ time and then be able to answer any such query in $\mathcal{O}(1)$ time per query, where σ is the size of the alphabet.

Hence, for q such queries, computations can be done trivially in either $\mathcal{O}(qn)$ time (directly) or in $\mathcal{O}(\sigma n^2 + q)$ total time—this includes the $\mathcal{O}(\sigma n^2)$ time for preprocessing. We thus aim at an algorithm that will require $t_p = o(\sigma n^2)$ preprocessing time and $t_q = o(n)$ querying time. We will then be able to answer q such queries in $\mathcal{O}(t_p + q t_q)$ time, hence being more efficient than the aforementioned solutions, depending on the number q of queries to be answered.

Our Contribution. We present a data structure for solving the problem of LCF after a single letter substitution for two strings, each of length at most n, over an integer alphabet. Specifically, our construction requires $t_p = \mathcal{O}(n \log^4 n)$ expected preprocessing time and $\mathcal{O}(n \log^3 n)$ space. After this preprocessing, the answer to any subsequent query for i and α is computed in $t_q = \mathcal{O}(\log^3 n)$ time.

2   Preliminaries

We begin with basic definitions and notation generally following [6]. Let $S = S[1]S[2]\ldots S[n]$ be a *string* of length $|S| = n$ over a finite ordered alphabet. We consider *integer alphabets*, i.e. Σ of size $|\Sigma| = \sigma = n^{\mathcal{O}(1)}$. By ε we denote an *empty string*. For two positions i and j on S, we denote by $S[i\mathinner{.\,.}j] = S[i]\ldots S[j]$ the *factor* (sometimes called substring) of S that starts at position i and ends at position j (it equals ε if $j < i$). We recall that a *prefix* of S is a factor that starts at position 1 ($S[1\mathinner{.\,.}j]$) and a *suffix* is a factor that ends at position n ($S[i\mathinner{.\,.}n]$). We denote the *reverse string* of S by S^R, i.e. $S^R = S[n]S[n-1]\ldots S[1]$.

Let Y be a string of length m with $0 < m \le n$. We say that there exists an *occurrence* of Y in S, or, more simply, that Y *occurs in* S, when Y is a factor of S. Every occurrence of Y can be characterised by a starting position in S. We thus say that Y occurs at the *starting position* i in S when $Y = S[i\mathinner{.\,.}i+m-1]$.

Given two strings S and T, a string Y that occurs in both is a *longest common factor* (LCF) of S and T if there is no longer factor of T that is also a factor of S; note that S and T can have multiple LCFs. We introduce a natural representation of an LCF of S and T as a triple (m, p, q) such that

$S[p \mathinner{\ldotp\ldotp} p+m-1] = T[q \mathinner{\ldotp\ldotp} q+m-1]$ is an LCF of S and T. The problem in scope can be formally defined as follows; see also Table 1 for an example.

LCF AFTER ONE SUBSTITUTION
Input: Two strings S and T.
Query: $\mathsf{LCF}(i, \alpha)$ that represents an LCF of S' and T, where $S'[i] = \alpha$ and $S'[j] = S[j]$, for all $1 \leq j \leq |S|$, $j \neq i$.

Table 1. Answers to all $\mathsf{LCF}(i, \alpha)$ queries for $S = \mathtt{baccb}$ and $T = \mathtt{baacca}$ over alphabet $\Sigma = \{\mathtt{a, b, c}\}$. In each case the corresponding LCF string is shown.

α	i				
	1	2	3	4	5
a	(4,1,2) aacc	(3,2,3) acc	(4,1,1) baac	(2,3,5) ca	(4,2,3) acca
b	(3,2,3) acc	(2,3,4) cc	(2,1,1) ba	(2,2,3) ac	(3,2,3) acc
c	(3,2,3) acc	(2,3,4) cc	(3,2,3) acc	(3,2,3) acc	(3,2,3) acc

Suffix Tree and Suffix Array. The *suffix tree* $\mathcal{T}(S)$ of a non-empty string S of length n is a compact trie representing all suffixes of S. The *branching* nodes of the trie as well as the *terminal* nodes, that correspond to suffixes of S, become *explicit* nodes of the suffix tree, while the other nodes are *implicit*. Each edge of the suffix tree can be viewed as an upward maximal path of implicit nodes starting with an explicit node. Moreover, each node belongs to a unique path of that kind. Thus, each node of the trie can be represented in the suffix tree by the edge it belongs to and an index within the corresponding path. We let $\mathcal{L}(v)$ denote the *path-label* of a node v, i.e., the concatenation of the edge labels along the path from the root to v. We say that v is path-labelled $\mathcal{L}(v)$. Additionally, $\mathcal{D}(v) = |\mathcal{L}(v)|$ is used to denote the *string-depth* of node v. A terminal node v such that $\mathcal{L}(v) = S[i \mathinner{\ldotp\ldotp} n]$ for some $1 \leq i \leq n$ is also labelled with index i. It should be clear that each factor of S is uniquely represented by either an explicit or an implicit node of $\mathcal{T}(S)$, called its *locus*. In standard suffix tree implementations, we assume that each node of the suffix tree is able to access its parent. Once $\mathcal{T}(S)$ is constructed, it can be traversed in a depth-first manner to compute the string-depth $\mathcal{D}(v)$ for each node v. It is known that the suffix tree of a string of length n, over an integer ordered alphabet, can be computed in time and space $\mathcal{O}(n)$ [7]. In the case of integer alphabets, in order to access the child of an explicit node by the first letter of its edge label in $\mathcal{O}(1)$ time, perfect hashing [9] can be used.

The *suffix array* of a non-empty string S of length n, denoted by $\mathsf{SA}(S)$, is an integer array of size $n+1$ storing the starting positions of all (lexicographically) sorted suffixes of S, i.e. for all $1 < r \leq n+1$ we have $S[\mathsf{SA}(S)[r-1] \mathinner{\ldotp\ldotp} n] < S[\mathsf{SA}(S)[r] \mathinner{\ldotp\ldotp} n]$. Note that we explicitly add the empty suffix to the array. The suffix array $\mathsf{SA}(S)$ corresponds to a pre-order traversal of all terminal nodes of the suffix tree $\mathcal{T}(S)$. The inverse $\mathsf{iSA}(S)$ of the array $\mathsf{SA}(S)$ is defined by $\mathsf{iSA}(S)[\mathsf{SA}(S)[r]] = r$, for all $1 \leq r \leq n+1$.

Algorithmic Tools for Trees. Let $\mathcal{T}$ be a rooted tree with integer weights on nodes. We require that the weight of the root is zero and the weight of any other node is strictly greater than the weight of its parent. We say that a node v is a *weighted ancestor* of a node u at depth ℓ if v is the highest ancestor of u with weight of at least ℓ.

Lemma 1 ([2]). *After $\mathcal{O}(n)$-time preprocessing, weighted ancestor queries for nodes of a tree $\mathcal{T}$ of size n can be answered in $\mathcal{O}(\log \log n)$ time per query.*

The following corollary applies Lemma 1 to the suffix tree.

Corollary 2. *The locus of any factor $S[i..j]$ in $\mathcal{T}(S)$ can be computed in $\mathcal{O}(\log \log n)$ time after $\mathcal{O}(n)$-time preprocessing.*

Let us also recall the notion of heavy-path decomposition. Consider a rooted tree $\mathcal{T}$. For each non-leaf node u of $\mathcal{T}$, the *heavy edge* (u, v) is an edge for which the subtree rooted at v has the maximal number of leaves (in case of several such subtrees, we fix one of them). A *heavy path* is a maximal path of heavy edges.

Let π be a heavy path and u be its topmost node. Assume that u contains m leaves in its subtree. We then denote by $L(\pi)$ the level of the path π, which is equal to $\log m$[1]. The crucial property of heavy-path decompositions can be stated as follows.

Observation 1. *For any leaf v of $\mathcal{T}$, the levels of all heavy paths visited on the path from v to the root of $\mathcal{T}$ are distinct.*

Range Maxima in 2-d. Assume we are given a collection $\mathcal{P}$ of n points in a 2-d grid with integer weights of magnitude $\mathcal{O}(n)$. In a 2-d range maximum query $\mathsf{RMQ}(\mathcal{P}, [a, b] \times [c, d])$, given a rectangle $[a, b] \times [c, d]$, we are to report the maximum weight of a point from $\mathcal{P}$ in the rectangle. We assume that the point that attains this maximum is also computed.

Lemma 3 ([1]). *Range maximum queries over a set of n weighted points in 2-d can be answered in $\mathcal{O}(\log n)$ time with a data structure of size $\mathcal{O}(n \log n)$ that can be constructed in $\mathcal{O}(n \log^2 n)$ expected time.*

Among orthogonal range searching problems one can also consider the so-called *range emptiness queries*, in which we are only to check if any of the n points is located inside a query rectangle. Such queries are obviously a special case of 2-d range maximum queries.

---

[1] Throughout the paper we assume that $\log m$ denotes the binary logarithm of m rounded down to the nearest integer.

3 Two Auxiliary Problems

We assume throughout the paper that both strings S and T are over an integer alphabet Σ and that each of them has length at most n. We can decompose the problem in scope into the following two subproblems; we then only need to take the maximum. See also Tables 2 and 3 for an example.

LCF AVOIDING i

Input: Two strings S and T.

Output: An array LCF_1 of size $|S|$ such that $\mathsf{LCF}_1[i]$ represents a longest factor Y common to S and T such that Y occurs in S at some position p, where $p \leq i - |Y|$ or $p > i$.

Table 2. The $\mathsf{LCF}_1[i]$ array for $S = \mathtt{baccb}$ and $T = \mathtt{baacca}$. The auxiliary arrays that are used to compute it in Sect. 4 are also presented.

i	1	2	3	4	5
$\mathsf{LCF}_1[i]$	(3,2,3) acc	(2,3,4) cc	(2,1,1) ba	(2,2,3) ac	(3,2,3) acc
$\overleftarrow{\mathsf{LCF}_1}[i]$	(1,1,1) b	(2,1,1) ba	(2,2,3) ac	(3,2,3) acc	
$\overrightarrow{\mathsf{LCF}_1}[i]$		(3,2,3) acc	(2,3,4) cc	(1,5,1) b	(1,5,1) b

---

LCF INCLUDING $S[i]:=\alpha$

Input: Two strings S and T.

Query: $\mathsf{LCF}_2(i,\alpha)$ that represents an LCF Y of S' and T, where $S'[i] = \alpha$ and $S'[j] = S[j]$, for all $1 \leq j \leq |S|$, $j \neq i$, such that Y occurs in S' at some position $p \in \{i - |Y| + 1, \ldots, i\}$.

Table 3. Answers to all $\mathsf{LCF}_2(i,\alpha)$ queries for $S = \mathtt{baccb}$ and $T = \mathtt{baacca}$.

α \ i	1	2	3	4	5
a	(4,1,2) aacc	(3,2,3) acc	(4,1,1) baac	(2,3,5) ca	(4,2,3) acca
b	(2,1,1) ba	(1,2,1) b	(1,3,1) b	(1,4,1) b	(1,5,1) b
c	(2,1,5) ca	(2,2,4) cc	(3,2,3) acc	(3,2,3) acc	(2,4,4) cc

Observation 2. *Suppose that we replace $S[i]$ by α. If this gives us a longer common factor than an LCF of S and T, this has to contain position i of S.*

We first build $\mathcal{T}(X)$, where $X = T\#S$ and $\# \notin \Sigma$ is a letter that is lexicographically smaller than all the letters of Σ. We then store for every node of $\mathcal{T}(X)$ whether it has descendants from S, T, or both and a starting position in each case; we can do this by performing a depth-first traversal. We further preprocess $T(X)$ in $\mathcal{O}(n)$ time so that we can answer *lowest common ancestor* (LCA) queries for any pair of explicit nodes in $\mathcal{O}(1)$ time per query [4]. We construct and preprocess in the same manner the suffix tree $T(X^R)$, where $X^R = S^R \# T^R$. There will be more preprocessing that will be described later.

4   LCF Avoiding i

In this section we present an algorithm for determining an LCF of S and T avoiding position i in S. It is clear that this is the longest between an LCF of $S[1..i-1]$ and T and an LCF of $S[i+1..|S|]$ and T. Let us denote the representation of the former by $\overleftarrow{\mathsf{LCF}}_1[i-1]$ and the representation of the latter by $\overrightarrow{\mathsf{LCF}}_1[i+1]$; see also Table 2 for an example. We will show how to efficiently compute $\overrightarrow{\mathsf{LCF}}_1[i]$ for all $i = |S|, \ldots, 2$.

We denote the length of the *longest common prefix* of two strings W and Y by $\mathsf{lcp}(W, Y)$. Further we will also use the notation $\mathsf{lcs}(W, Y)$ to denote the length of the longest common suffix of W and Y. Let us make the following observation.

Observation 3. *If for a pair* (p, q) *with* $i \leq p \leq |S|$ *and* $1 \leq q \leq |T|$ *we have*

$$m = \mathsf{lcp}(S[p..|S|], T[q..|T|]) = \max_{\substack{i \leq j \leq |S| \\ 1 \leq k \leq |T|}} \{\mathsf{lcp}(S[j..|S|], T[k..|T|])\},$$

then $S[p..p+m-1] = T[q..q+m-1]$ *is an LCF of* $S[i..|S|]$ *and* T.

We first traverse $T(X)$ in a depth-first manner in order to store, for every explicit node u, the maximal length $\ell(u)$ of the longest common prefix of $\mathcal{L}(u)$ and any suffix of T and a position $t(u)$ of T where the maximum is attained. If a node u has descendants from T, then clearly $\ell(u) = \mathcal{D}(u)$ and $t(u)$ is already stored. Whenever we reach a node u that does not have descendants from T, we set the values $\ell(u)$ and $t(u)$ equal to these of u's explicit parent.

To compute the array $\overrightarrow{\mathsf{LCF}}_1$, we go through the terminal nodes of $T(X)$ that represent suffixes of S in increasing order with regards to the length of the suffix they represent. We initialize variables $lcf = p = q = 0$. When processing node u, with $\mathcal{L}(u) = S[i..|S|]$, we first check whether $\ell(u) > lcf$; if so, we set $lcf = \ell(u)$, $p = i$ and $q = t(u)$. Then, based on Observation 3, we set $\overrightarrow{\mathsf{LCF}}_1[i] = (lcf, p, q)$.

The computation of $\overleftarrow{\mathsf{LCF}}_1[i]$ for $i = 1, \ldots, |S| - 1$ can be done in a symmetric way by employing $T(X^R)$. Finally, we compare $\overleftarrow{\mathsf{LCF}}_1[i-1]$ with $\overrightarrow{\mathsf{LCF}}_1[i+1]$ and store the longer one as $\mathsf{LCF}_1[i]$. We thus arrive at the following result.

Lemma 4. *Problem* LCF AVOIDING i *can be solved in* $\mathcal{O}(n)$ *time and space.*

5   LCF Including $S[i] := \alpha$

We first compute two factors, P and Q, of T:

- P is the longest factor of T that is equal to a suffix of $S[1 .. i-1]\alpha$;
- Q is the longest factor of T that is equal to a prefix of $S[i+1 .. |S|]$.

In addition to P and Q, we will also compute the locus p of P^R in $\mathcal{T}(X^R)$ and the locus q of Q in $\mathcal{T}(X)$. Note that q is an explicit node of $\mathcal{T}(X)$, however, p need not be an explicit node of $\mathcal{T}(X^R)$. We first compute the locus p' of P in $\mathcal{T}(X)$ (which may be implicit as well).

The locus p' is computed by performing binary search on $S[1 .. i-1]$. We first identify the locus of $S[\lfloor i/2 \rfloor .. i-1]$ in $\mathcal{T}(X)$. If it is explicit, we check whether it has an outgoing edge with label α and if the explicit node we obtain by following this edge has descendants in T. If it is implicit, we check if the next letter on the path-label of the edge is α and whether the explicit node to which this edge points has descendants in T. If the corresponding check succeeds, we look at the locus of $S[\lfloor i/4 \rfloor .. i-1]$, otherwise we look at the locus of $S[\lfloor 3i/4 \rfloor .. i-1]$; and so on. The whole binary search works in $\mathcal{O}(\log n \log \log n)$ time using Corollary 2.

Recall that for the closest explicit descendant of p' we store the starting position of some occurrence of the corresponding factor in X. We can then use this information to find the locus p of P^R in $\mathcal{T}(X^R)$ in $\mathcal{O}(\log \log n)$ time using Corollary 2.

Finally, the locus q of Q in $\mathcal{T}(X)$ can be analogously computed by binary search on $S[i+1 .. |S|]$ in $\mathcal{O}(\log n \log \log n)$ time.

Let us note that $\mathsf{LCF}_2(i, \alpha)$ corresponds to the longest factor of T that is composed by concatenating a suffix of P with a prefix of Q. We say that a node u of $\mathcal{T}(X^R)$ with path-label U and a node v of $\mathcal{T}(X)$ with path-label V are T-attached if and only if $U^R V$ is a factor of T. We thus aim at finding an ancestor u of p in $\mathcal{T}(X^R)$ and an ancestor v of q in $\mathcal{T}(X)$ such that u and v are T-attached and the sum $\mathcal{D}(u) + \mathcal{D}(v)$ of string-depths is maximal.

5.1 $\tilde{\mathcal{O}}(|P|)$-Time Query

In this section we show how to find the desired pair of T-attached nodes (u, v) in $\tilde{\mathcal{O}}(\mathcal{D}(p)) = \tilde{\mathcal{O}}(|P|)$ time[2]. We improve this solution in the next subsection.

Recall that $\mathsf{SA}(T)$ and $\mathsf{SA}(T^R)$ are the suffix arrays of T and T^R, respectively. Note that $\mathsf{SA}(T)$ (resp. $\mathsf{SA}(T^R)$) corresponds to a pre-order traversal of all the terminal nodes of $\mathcal{T}(X)$ ($\mathcal{T}(X^R)$) that are loci of suffixes of T concatenated with $\#S$ (loci of suffixes of T^R). For each explicit node v of $\mathcal{T}(X)$ we precompute a range $range_T(v)$ of $\mathsf{SA}(T)$ that corresponds to suffixes of T that start with $\mathcal{L}(v)$. Similarly, for each explicit node u of $\mathcal{T}(X^R)$ we precompute a range $range_{T^R}(u)$ of $\mathsf{SA}(T^R)$ that corresponds to suffixes of T^R that start with $\mathcal{L}(u)$. The precomputations can be done via bottom-up traversals of $\mathcal{T}(X)$ and $\mathcal{T}(X^R)$ in $\mathcal{O}(n)$ time. For $\mathcal{T}(X)$, the range of every explicit node is computed by summing the

---

[2] Throughout the paper $\tilde{\mathcal{O}}$ notation suppresses $\log^{\mathcal{O}(1)} n$ factors.

ranges of its explicit children. Additionally, for a terminal node being a locus of a suffix $T[j \mathrel{..} |T|]\#S$ we extend its range by the element $\mathsf{iSA}(T)[j]$. The computations for $T(X^R)$ are analogous. The ranges of implicit nodes of $T(X)$ and $T(X^R)$ are defined as the corresponding ranges of their closest explicit descendants.

We can use the ranges to state an equivalent condition on when two nodes are T-attached:

Observation 4. *Node u of $T(X^R)$ and node v of $T(X)$ are T-attached if and only if there exist integers $i \in range_{TR}(u)$ and $j \in range_T(v)$ such that $SA(T^R)[i] = |T| + 2 - SA(T)[j]$.*

It turns out that the problem of checking if two nodes are T-attached can be reduced to a 2-d range emptiness query. Indeed, let us consider a $(|T| + 1) \times (|T| + 1)$ grid. We create a collection $\mathcal{P}$ of $|T| + 1$ points from the grid; for each position j in T, $j \in \{1, \ldots, |T| + 1\}$, we select the point:

$$(\,\mathsf{iSA}(T^R)[|T| + 2 - j],\ \mathsf{iSA}(T)[j]\,).$$

Intuitively, the dimensions of the grid correspond to $SA(T^R)$ and $SA(T)$ and the points that are selected correspond to pairs of suffixes: $T^R[|T| + 2 - j \mathrel{..} |T|] = (T[1 \mathrel{..} j - 1])^R$ and $T[j \mathrel{..} |T|]$. Observation 5 is a reformulation of Observation 4 in terms of range emptiness queries in $\mathcal{P}$.

Observation 5. *Node u of $T(X^R)$ and node v of $T(X)$ are T-attached if and only if the rectangle $range_{TR}(u) \times range_T(v)$ contains a point from $\mathcal{P}$.*

Example 5. Consider the string $T = \mathtt{baacca}$ from Tables 1, 2 and 3. Then:

$$SA(T^R) = 7\ (\varepsilon),\ 4\ (\mathtt{aab}),\ 5\ (\mathtt{ab}),\ 1\ (\mathtt{accaab}),\ 6\ (\mathtt{b}),\ 3\ (\mathtt{caab}),\ 2\ (\mathtt{ccaab})$$
$$SA(T) = 7\ (\varepsilon),\ 6\ (\mathtt{a}),\ 2\ (\mathtt{aacca}),\ 3\ (\mathtt{acca}),\ 1\ (\mathtt{baacca}),\ 5\ (\mathtt{ca}),\ 4\ (\mathtt{cca})$$

The points from the set $\mathcal{P}$ on the 7×7 grid are shown on the figure below.

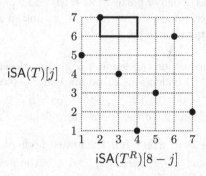

Consider node u of $T(X^R)$ such that $\mathcal{L}(u) = \mathtt{a}$ and node v of $T(X)$ such that $\mathcal{L}(v) = \mathtt{c}$. Then $range_{TR}(u) = [2, 4]$ and $range_T(v) = [6, 7]$. The corresponding rectangle $range_{TR}(u) \times range_T(v)$ contains a single point $(2, 7)$ from $\mathcal{P}$ which corresponds to the second suffix in $SA(T^R)$, which is $Y = \mathtt{aab}$, and the seventh suffix in $SA(T)$, which is $Z = \mathtt{cca}$. Note that, indeed, Y starts with an $\mathtt{a}$, Z starts with a $\mathtt{c}$ and $Y^R Z = T$. Hence, u and v are T-attached.

From the previous subsection we know that we need to find an ancestor u of p in $\mathcal{T}(X^R)$ and an ancestor v of q in $\mathcal{T}(X)$ such that u and v are T-attached and $\mathcal{D}(u) + \mathcal{D}(v)$ is maximal. To find the desired nodes, we examine each node u on the path from p to the root of $\mathcal{T}(X^R)$ and apply binary search to find the deepest node v on the path from q to the root of $\mathcal{T}(X)$ such that u and v are T-attached. There are $|P|$ binary searches to perform, each of which has $\mathcal{O}(\log n)$ steps. In each such step we first locate the required node in $\mathcal{O}(\log \log n)$ time by Corollary 2 and then check if the two nodes are T-attached via Observation 5 using a range emptiness query which takes $\mathcal{O}(\log n)$ time by Lemma 3. In total, we arrive at an $\mathcal{O}(|P| \log^2 n)$-time computation of $\mathsf{LCF}_2(i, \alpha)$.

5.2 $\tilde{\mathcal{O}}(1)$-Time Query

Main Idea. In order to drop the $|P|$ factor from the complexity, we make use of the heavy-path decompositions of $\mathcal{T}(X^R)$ and $\mathcal{T}(X)$. For each heavy path, we store its level. Moreover, each explicit node w of $\mathcal{T}(X^R)$ and $\mathcal{T}(X)$ stores the topmost node $top(w)$ of its heavy path. For simplicity we first assume that p is explicit in $\mathcal{T}(X^R)$ (recall that q is explicit in $\mathcal{T}(X)$); we then discuss how to tackle the case of p being implicit. By Observation 4, the sought node v is always explicit and u may be implicit only if p is implicit and u is on the same edge of $\mathcal{T}(X^R)$ as p.

The path from p to the root of $\mathcal{T}(X^R)$ is composed of *prefix fragments* of at most $\log n + 1$ heavy paths interleaved by single non-heavy (compact) edges. Here a prefix fragment of a path π is a path connecting the topmost node of π with any of its explicit nodes. We denote this decomposition by $H(p)$; note that it can be computed in $\mathcal{O}(\log n)$ time by using the *top*-pointers of nodes, starting from p. Similarly, we can decompose the path from q to the root of $\mathcal{T}(X)$ into a collection $H(q)$ of at most $\log n + 1$ prefix fragments of heavy paths in $\mathcal{O}(\log n)$ time. For each of the $\mathcal{O}(\log^2 n)$ pairs of prefix fragments of heavy paths $\pi_1' \in H(p)$ and $\pi_2' \in H(q)$ we will check if there are any T-attached nodes $u \in \pi_1'$ and $v \in \pi_2'$ and, if so, find the maximum value of $\mathcal{D}(u) + \mathcal{D}(v)$ among such pairs.

Precomputations. We consider the same 2-d grid as described in the previous subsection with $\mathcal{O}(\log^2 n)$ collections of points being copies of the collection $\mathcal{P}$; they are denoted by $\mathcal{P}_{a,b}^{(I)}$, $\mathcal{P}_a^{(II)}$, $\mathcal{P}_b^{(III)}$, $\mathcal{P}^{(IV)}$ for $a, b = 0, \dots, \log n$. The points in the respective collections have the following weights:

- $(j, k) \in \mathcal{P}_{a,b}^{(I)}$: $\mathcal{D}(u) + \mathcal{D}(v)$ where u is the lowest node on a heavy path of level a in $\mathcal{T}(X^R)$ such that $j \in range_{T^R}(u)$ and v is the lowest node on a heavy path of level b in $\mathcal{T}(X)$ such that $k \in range_T(v)$;
- $(j, k) \in \mathcal{P}_a^{(II)}$: $\mathcal{D}(u)$ where u is the lowest node on a heavy path of level a in $\mathcal{T}(X^R)$ such that $j \in range_{T^R}(u)$;
- $(j, k) \in \mathcal{P}_b^{(III)}$: $\mathcal{D}(v)$ where v is the lowest node on a heavy path of level b in $\mathcal{T}(X)$ such that $k \in range_T(v)$;
- each point in $\mathcal{P}^{(IV)}$ has a unit weight.

By Observation 1, the heavy paths in each case, if they exist, are determined in a unique way by j and k. If any of the nodes u or v does not exist, we set its depth $\mathcal{D}$ to $-\infty$. Note that each of the nodes u and v, if it exists, is explicit in $\mathcal{T}(X^R)$ and $\mathcal{T}(X)$, respectively.

The total size of the collections of points is $\mathcal{O}(n \log^2 n)$. We further have:

Lemma 6. *Weights of the points from the collections* $\mathcal{P}_{a,b}^{(I)}$, $\mathcal{P}_a^{(II)}$, $\mathcal{P}_b^{(III)}$, $\mathcal{P}^{(IV)}$ *for* $a, b = 0, \ldots, \log n$ *can be computed in* $\mathcal{O}(n \log^2 n)$ *time.*

Proof. First, for each $b = 0, \ldots, \log n$ and $k = 1, \ldots, |T|+1$ we compute $D[b][k] = \mathcal{D}(v)$ where v is the lowest node on a heavy path of level b in $\mathcal{T}(X)$ such that $k \in range_T(v)$. For each explicit node w of $\mathcal{T}(X)$ we consider its heavy edge (if exists) that leads to its explicit child w' and for each $k \in range_T(w) \setminus range_T(w')$, we set $D[b][k] = \mathcal{D}(w)$ where b is the level of the heavy path that contains the node w. This computation works in $\mathcal{O}(n \log n)$ time.

In the same way we can compute a symmetric array $D'[a][j] = \mathcal{D}(u)$ where u is the lowest node on a heavy path of level a in $\mathcal{T}(X^R)$ such that $j \in range_{T^R}(u)$. The two arrays allow us to compute the weights of all points. For example, the weight of the point $(j, k) \in \mathcal{P}_{a,b}^{(I)}$ is $D'[a][j] + D[b][k]$. □

Queries. Let us consider a heavy path π_1 of level a in $\mathcal{T}(X^R)$ and a heavy path π_2 of level b in $\mathcal{T}(X)$. Let π_1' be a prefix fragment of π_1 that leads from node x_1 down to node y_1 and π_2' be a prefix fragment of π_2 that leads from node x_2 down to node y_2. Let A_1, B_1, C_1 be intervals such that

$$range_{T^R}(y_1) = B_1 \quad \text{and} \quad range_{T^R}(x_1) \setminus B_1 = A_1 \cup C_1.$$

Similarly, we define the intervals A_2, B_2, C_2 so that:

$$range_T(y_2) = B_2 \quad \text{and} \quad range_T(x_2) \setminus B_2 = A_2 \cup C_2;$$

see Fig. 1 for an illustration. Then the maximum of $\mathcal{D}(u) + \mathcal{D}(v)$ over all T-attached pairs of nodes $u \in \pi_1'$ and $v \in \pi_2'$ is the maximum of the following nine values:

(1) $\mathsf{RMQ}(\mathcal{P}_{a,b}^{(I)}, A_1 \times A_2)$

(2) $\mathsf{RMQ}(\mathcal{P}_{a,b}^{(I)}, A_1 \times C_2)$

(3) $\mathsf{RMQ}(\mathcal{P}_{a,b}^{(I)}, C_1 \times A_2)$

(4) $\mathsf{RMQ}(\mathcal{P}_{a,b}^{(I)}, C_1 \times C_2)$

(5) $\mathsf{RMQ}(\mathcal{P}_a^{(II)}, A_1 \times B_2) + \mathcal{D}(y_2)$

(6) $\mathsf{RMQ}(\mathcal{P}_a^{(II)}, C_1 \times B_2) + \mathcal{D}(y_2)$

(7) $\mathcal{D}(y_1) + \mathsf{RMQ}(\mathcal{P}_b^{(III)}, B_1 \times A_2)$

(8) $\mathcal{D}(y_1) + \mathsf{RMQ}(\mathcal{P}_b^{(III)}, B_1 \times C_2)$

(9) $\mathcal{D}(y_1) + \mathcal{D}(y_2)$ if $\mathsf{RMQ}(\mathcal{P}^{(IV)}, B_1 \times B_2) \neq -\infty$.

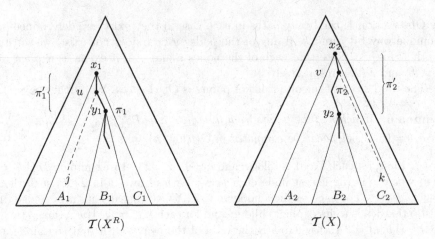

Fig. 1. Illustration of the notations used to handle a pair of prefix fragments $\pi_1' \in H(p)$ and $\pi_2' \in H(q)$. Assume that the sought pair of T-attached nodes $u \in \pi_1'$ and $v \in \pi_2'$ are located as shown. Here $j \in \{1, \ldots, |T|+1\}$ is an index for which u is the lowest node on π_1 such that $j \in range_{TR}(u)$; same holds for k and $v \in \pi_2$. Then $\mathcal{D}(u) + \mathcal{D}(v)$ is computed by value (2): $\mathsf{RMQ}(\mathcal{P}_{a,b}^{(I)}, A_1 \times C_2)$.

Values (1)–(4) correspond to the situation when the sought nodes u and v are located strictly above y_1 and y_2, respectively. Values (5)–(6) assume the case that $v = y_2$; values (7)–(8) assume the case that $u = y_1$; finally, value (9) assumes that $u = y_1$ and $v = y_2$.

The maximum of the values of the form (1)–(9) is computed for all pairs of prefix fragments of heavy paths $\pi_1' \in H(p)$ and $\pi_2' \in H(q)$. The global maximum is the length of an LCF with $S[i]{:=}\alpha$. Its example occurrence can be retrieved from the coordinates (j, k) of the point for which the range maximum is obtained. Indeed, let $r = \mathsf{SA}(T)[k]$. Then an LCF occurs in S' and T at positions $i - d$ and $r - 1 - d$, respectively, where $d = \mathsf{lcs}(S[1\mathinner{..}i-1], T[1\mathinner{..}r-2])$. Note that d can be computed via an LCA query in $\mathcal{T}(X^R)$ in $\mathcal{O}(1)$ time.

The Case of Implicit p. If p is not explicit, we make the above computations for the nearest explicit ancestor of p. We need to consider separately the case that u is an implicit node located between p and this ancestor. In this case $range_{TR}(u) = range_{TR}(p)$; we denote this interval by F. Hence, we take $u = p$. We consider every prefix fragment $\pi_2' \in H(q)$ of a heavy path with level b, endpoints x_2, y_2, and implied intervals A_2, B_2, C_2 and pick the maximum of:

- $\mathcal{D}(p) + \mathsf{RMQ}(\mathcal{P}_b^{(III)}, F \times A_2)$
- $\mathcal{D}(p) + \mathsf{RMQ}(\mathcal{P}_b^{(III)}, F \times C_2)$
- $\mathcal{D}(p) + \mathcal{D}(y_2)$ if $\mathsf{RMQ}(\mathcal{P}^{(IV)}, F \times B_2) \neq -\infty$.

Lemma 7. *After $\mathcal{O}(n \log^4 n)$ expected time and $\mathcal{O}(n \log^3 n)$ space preprocessing, LCF* INCLUDING *$S[i]{:=}\alpha$ queries can be answered in $\mathcal{O}(\log^3 n)$ time.*

Proof. The suffix trees $\mathcal{T}(X^R)$ and $\mathcal{T}(X)$ with heavy-path decompositions and ranges $range_{TR}$ and $range_T$, respectively, take $\mathcal{O}(n)$ space and $\mathcal{O}(n)$ time to construct. The $\mathcal{O}(\log^2 n)$ weighted collections of points can be constructed in $\mathcal{O}(n \log^2 n)$ time by Lemma 6. Then the data structures for range maximum queries in 2-d (Lemma 3) in total take $\mathcal{O}(n \log^3 n)$ space and require $\mathcal{O}(n \log^4 n)$ expected time to construct.

To compute $\mathsf{LCF}_2(i, \alpha)$, we perform the following steps. First, we compute the loci p and q in $\mathcal{O}(\log n \log \log n)$ time. Then, in $\mathcal{O}(\log n)$ time we compute the collections $H(p)$ and $H(q)$ of prefix fragments of heavy paths. Finally, for each pair $\pi'_1 \in H(p)$ and $\pi'_2 \in H(q)$, we answer range maximum queries of the form (1)–(9), each in $\mathcal{O}(\log n)$ time. This gives $\mathcal{O}(\log^3 n)$ total query time.   □

Lemmas 4 and 7 lead to the main result of this paper.

Theorem 8. LCF AFTER ONE SUBSTITUTION *can be computed in* $\mathcal{O}(\log^3 n)$ *time, after* $\mathcal{O}(n \log^4 n)$ *expected time and* $\mathcal{O}(n \log^3 n)$ *space preprocessing.*

Corollary 9. *Given two strings S and T over a constant-sized alphabet, the answers to all $\Theta(n)$ possible* LCF AFTER ONE SUBSTITUTION *queries can be computed in* $\mathcal{O}(n \log^4 n)$ *expected time and* $\mathcal{O}(n \log^3 n)$ *space.*

6   Conclusions

We have presented an $\tilde{\mathcal{O}}(n)$-space data structure that can be constructed in $\tilde{\mathcal{O}}(n)$ expected time and supports $\tilde{\mathcal{O}}(1)$-time computation of an LCF of two strings S and T, each of length at most n, over an integer alphabet after one letter substitution in S. Notably, our algorithm can be easily modified to work if we also allow for single letter insertions or deletions in S.

An open question is to extend this result to a fully dynamic case; that is, to propose a data structure that allows for *subsequent* edit operations in one or in both strings supporting fast computation of an LCF after each such operation.

References

1. Alstrup, S., Brodal, G.S., Rauhe, T.: New data structures for orthogonal range searching. In: FOCS, pp. 198–207. IEEE Computer Society (2000)
2. Amir, A., Landau, G.M., Lewenstein, M., Sokol, D.: Dynamic text and static pattern matching. ACM Trans. Algorithms **3**(2), 19 (2007)
3. Babenko, M.A., Starikovskaya, T.A.: Computing the longest common substring with one mismatch. Probl. Inf. Transm. **47**(1), 28–33 (2011)
4. Bender, M.A., Farach-Colton, M.: The LCA problem revisited. In: Gonnet, G.H., Viola, A. (eds.) LATIN 2000. LNCS, vol. 1776, pp. 88–94. Springer, Heidelberg (2000). doi:10.1007/10719839_9
5. Chi, L., Hui, K.: Color set size problem with applications to string matching. In: Apostolico, A., Crochemore, M., Galil, Z., Manber, U. (eds.) CPM 1992. LNCS, vol. 644, pp. 230–243. Springer, Heidelberg (1992). doi:10.1007/3-540-56024-6_19

6. Crochemore, M., Hancart, C., Lecroq, T.: Algorithms on Strings. Cambridge University Press, Cambridge (2007)
7. Farach, M.: Optimal suffix tree construction with large alphabets. In: FOCS, pp. 137–143. IEEE Computer Society (1997)
8. Flouri, T., Giaquinta, E., Kobert, K., Ukkonen, E.: Longest common substrings with k mismatches. Inf. Process. Lett. **115**(6–8), 643–647 (2015)
9. Fredman, M.L., Komlós, J., Szemerédi, E.: Storing a sparse table with $O(1)$ worst case access time. J. ACM **31**(3), 538–544 (1984)
10. Grabowski, S.: A note on the longest common substring with k-mismatches problem. Inf. Process. Lett. **115**(6–8), 640–642 (2015)
11. Gusfield, D.: Algorithms on Strings, Trees, and Sequences: Computer Science and Computational Biology. Cambridge University Press, New York (1997)
12. Kociumaka, T., Starikovskaya, T., Vildhøj, H.W.: Sublinear space algorithms for the longest common substring problem. In: Schulz, A.S., Wagner, D. (eds.) ESA 2014. LNCS, vol. 8737, pp. 605–617. Springer, Heidelberg (2014). doi:10.1007/978-3-662-44777-2_50
13. Leimeister, C., Morgenstern, B.: kmacs: the k-mismatch average common substring approach to alignment-free sequence comparison. Bioinformatics **30**(14), 2000–2008 (2014)
14. Starikovskaya, T.: Longest common substring with approximately k mismatches. In: CPM. LIPIcs, vol. 54, pp. 21:1–21:11. Schloss Dagstuhl-Leibniz-Zentrum fuer Informatik, Dagstuhl (2016)
15. Starikovskaya, T., Vildhøj, H.W.: Time-Space trade-offs for the longest common substring problem. In: Fischer, J., Sanders, P. (eds.) CPM 2013. LNCS, vol. 7922, pp. 223–234. Springer, Heidelberg (2013). doi:10.1007/978-3-642-38905-4_22
16. Thankachan, S.V., Apostolico, A., Aluru, S.: A provably efficient algorithm for the k-mismatch average common substring problem. J. Comput. Biol. **23**(6), 472–482 (2016)
17. Thankachan, S.V., Chockalingam, S.P., Liu, Y., Apostolico, A., Aluru, S.: ALFRED: a practical method for alignment-free distance computation. J. Comput. Biol. **23**(6), 452–460 (2016)

Distinct Squares in Circular Words

Mika Amit[1,2] and Paweł Gawrychowski[2,3(✉)]

[1] IBM Research, Haifa, Israel
[2] University of Haifa, Haifa, Israel
[3] Institute of Computer Science, University of Wrocław, Wrocław, Poland
gawry@cs.uni.wroc.pl

Abstract. A circular word, or a necklace, is an equivalence class under conjugation of a word. A fundamental question concerning regularities in standard words is bounding the number of distinct squares in a word of length n. The famous conjecture attributed to Fraenkel and Simpson is that there are at most n such distinct squares, yet the best known upper bound is $1.84n$ by Deza et al. [Discr. Appl. Math. 180, 52–69 (2015)]. We consider a natural generalization of this question to circular words: how many distinct squares can there be in all cyclic rotations of a word of length n? We prove an upper bound of $3.14n$. This is complemented with an infinite family of words implying a lower bound of $1.25n$.

Keywords: Squares conjecture · Circular words

1 Introduction

Combinatorics on words is mostly concerned with regularities in words. The most basic example of such a regularity is a square, that is, a substring of the form uu. We might either want to create words with no such substrings, called square-free, or show that there cannot be too many distinct squares for an arbitrary word of length n. Fraenkel and Simpson proved that $2n$ is an upper bound on the number of distinct squares contained in a word of length n, and also constructed an infinite family of words of length n containing $n - \Theta(\sqrt{n})$ distinct squares [12]. Their upper bound uses a combinatorial lemma of Crochemore and Rytter [6], called the Three Squares Lemma. Later, Ilie provided a short and self-contained argument [16]. The Three Squares Lemma is concerned with the rightmost occurrence of every distinct square, and says that, for any position in the word, there do not exist three such rightmost occurrences starting at that position (hence the name of the lemma). It is widely believed that the example given by Frankel and Simpson is the worst possible, and the right bound is n instead of $2n$. The best known upper bound was $2n - \Theta(\log n)$ [17] until recently Deza, Franek and Thierry improved the upper bound to $11/6n$ through a somewhat involved argument [9]. All these bounds are based on the idea of looking at three rightmost occurrences of squares starting at the same position. It is known that two such occurrence already imply a certain periodic structure [2,10,13,18,23], and that it is enough to consider binary words [20].

© Springer International Publishing AG 2017
G. Fici et al. (Eds.): SPIRE 2017, LNCS 10508, pp. 27–37, 2017.
DOI: 10.1007/978-3-319-67428-5_3

Regularities are commonly considered in more general contexts than standard words, such as partial words [1] or trees [5,14]. Another natural generalization of standard words, motivated by the circular structure of some biological data, are circular words (also known as necklaces). A circular word (w) is defined as an equivalence class under conjugation of a word w, that is, it corresponds to all possible rotations of w. Both algorithmic [3,4,15] and combinatorial aspects of such words have been studied. The latter are mostly motivated by an old result of Thue [25], who showed that there is an infinite square-free word over $\{0, 1, 2\}$. This started a long line of research of pattern avoidance. Currie and Fitzpatrick [8] generalized this to circular words, and then Currie [7] showed that for any $n \geq 18$ there exists a circular square-free word of length n (see also a later proof by Shur [22]). Recently, Simpson [24] considered bounding the number of distinct palindromes in a circular word of length n. It is well-known (and easy to prove) that the number of distinct palindromes in a standard word of length n is at most n. Interestingly, this increases to $5/3n$ for circular words. Also equations on circular words have been studied [21].

We consider the following question: how many distinct squares can there be in a circular word of length n? Note that due to how we have defined a circular word, we are interested in squares of length at most n. Recall that the $2n$ bound of Fraenkel and Simpson [12] is based on the notion of rightmost occurrences. The improved $11/6n$ bound of Deza et al. [9] is also based on this concept. For a circular word, it is not clear what the rightmost occurrence might mean, and indeed the proofs seem to completely break. Of course, to bound the number of distinct squares in a circular word w of length n, one can simply bound the number of distinct squares in a word ww of length $2n$, thus immediately obtaining an upper bound of $4n$ (by invoking the simple proof of Ilie [16]) or $3.67n$ (by invoking the more involved proof of Deza et al. [9]). This, however, completely disregards the cyclic nature of the problem.

We start with exhibiting an infinite family of circular words of length n containing $1.25n - \Theta(1)$ distinct squares. Therefore, it appears that the structure of distinct squares in circular words is more complex than in standard words. We then continue with a simple and self-contained upper bound of $3.75n$ on the number of distinct squares in a circular word of length n. Then, by invoking some of the machinery used by Deza et al. [9], we improve this to $3.14n$.

2   Preliminaries

Let $|w|$ denote the length of a string w, $w[i]$ is the i-th character of w, and $w[i..j]$ is a shortcut for $w[i]w[i+1]\ldots w[j]$. A natural number p is a period of w iff $w[i] = w[i+p]$ for every $i = 1, 2, \ldots, |w| - p$. The smallest such p is called the period of w. We say that w is periodic if its period is at most $|w|/2$, otherwise w is aperiodic. The well-known periodicity lemma says that if p and q are both periods of w and furthermore $p + q \leq |w| + \gcd(p, q)$ then $\gcd(p, q)$ is also a period of w [11].

$w^{(i)}$ denotes the cyclic rotation of w by i, that is, $w[i..|w|]w[1..(i-1)]$. A circular word (w) is an equivalence class under conjugation of w, that is, all cyclic rotations $w^{(i)}$. A word uu is called a square, and we say that it occurs in (w) if it occurs in $w^{(i)}$ for some i. We are interested in bounding the number of distinct squares occurring in a circular word of length n.

3   Lower Bound

We define an infinite family of words $f_k = \mathsf{a(ba)}^{k+1}\mathsf{a(ba)}^{k+2}\mathsf{a(ba)}^{k+1}\mathsf{a(ba)}^{k+2}$. See Fig. 1 for an example. Observe that $|f_k| = 8k + 16$. We claim that cyclic rotations of f_k contain many distinct squares.

k	f_k	#squares / $|f_k|$
1	ababaababababaababaababababa	25/24
2	ababababaabababababaababababaababababa	36/32
3	abababababaababababababaababababababaababababababa	45/40
4	ababababababaabababababababababaababababababababaababababababababa	56/48
5	abababababababaababababababababababaababababababababababaababababababababababababa	65/56

Fig. 1. The number of distinct squares in f_k, for $k = 1, 2, 3, 4, 5$.

Lemma 1. *For any $k \geq 0$, the circular word (f_k) contains $10k + 16 - (k \bmod 2)$ distinct squares.*

Proof. To count distinct squares uu occurring in (f_k), we consider a few disjoint cases. We first count uu such that aa occurs at most once inside:

1. Any uu such that aa does not occur inside must be be fully contained in an occurrence of $\mathsf{a(ba)}^{k+2}$ or $\mathsf{a(ba)}^{k+1}$ in f_k. Thus, to count such uu we only have to find all distinct squares in $\mathsf{a(ba)}^{k+2}$. For any $i = 1, 2, \ldots, \lfloor (k+2)/2 \rfloor$, $(\mathsf{ab})^i(\mathsf{ab})^i$ and $(\mathsf{ba})^i(\mathsf{ba})^i$ appear there, and it can be seen that there are no other squares. Thus, the number of such uu is exactly $2\lfloor (k + 2)/2 \rfloor$.
2. Any uu such that aa occurs exactly once inside must have the property that u starts and ends with a. It follows that such uu must be be fully contained in an occurrence of $\mathsf{a(ba)}^{k+1}\mathsf{a(ba)}^{k+1}$ in f_k. For any $i = 0, 1, \ldots, k+1$, $\mathsf{a(ba)}^i\mathsf{a(ba)}^i$ appears there, and it can be seen that there are no other squares containing exactly one occurrence of aa, so there are exactly $k + 2$ such uu.

Then we count uu such that aa occurs exactly twice inside. Then, aa must occur once in u and furthermore, by analyzing the distances between the occurrences of aa in f_k, we obtain that $|u| = 2k + 5$ or $|u| = 2k + 3$. We analyze these two possibilities:

1. If $|u| = 2k + 3$ then uu appears in an occurrence of $(\mathsf{ba})^k\mathsf{baa(ba)}^k\mathsf{baa(ba)}^k\mathsf{b}$ in f_k. There are $2k + 2$ such uu.
2. If $|u| = 2k + 5$ then uu appears in an occurrence of $\mathsf{a(ba)}^k\mathsf{baaba(ba)}^k$ $\mathsf{baaba(ba)}^k$ in f_k. There are $2k + 2$ such uu.

Finally, we count uu such that aa occurs at least three times inside. By analyzing the distances between the occurrences of aa in f_k, we obtain that in such case $|u| = 4k + 8$, so $|uu| = |f_k|$. We claim that there are exactly $|f_k|/2 = 4k + 8$ such uu. To prove this, write $f_k = x_k x_k$ with $x_k = a(ba)^{k+1}a(ba)^{k+2}$. x_k cannot be represented as a nontrivial power y^p with $p \geq 2$, because aa occurs only once inside x_k, so it would mean that y starts and ends with a, but then $p = 2$ is not possible due to $|a(ba)^{k+1}| \neq |a(ba)^{k+2}|$, and $p \geq 3$ would generate another occurrence of a. Clearly, every cyclic shift of f_k is a square occurring in (f_k), because a cyclic shift of a square is still a square. It remains to count distinct cyclic shifts of f_k. Assume that two of these shifts are equal, that is, $(f_k)^{(i)} = (f_k)^{(j)}$ for some $0 \leq i < j < |f_k|$, so $x_k = (x_k)^{(j-i)}$. Then $\gcd(|x_k|, j-i)$ is a period of x_k. But x_k is not a nontrivial power, so $j - i = 0 \bmod |x_k|$. Consequently, every $i = 0, 1, \ldots, |x_k| - 1$ generates a distinct square.

All in all, the number of distinct squares occurring in (f_k) is

$$k + 2 + 2\lfloor (k+2)/2 \rfloor + 2(2k+2) + 4k + 8 = 9k + 16 + 2\lfloor k/2 \rfloor$$

or, in other words, $10k + 16 - (k \bmod 2)$.   □

By Lemma 1, for any n_0 there exists a circular word of length $n \geq n_0$ containing at least $1.25n - \Theta(1)$ distinct squares.

4   Upper Bound

Our goal is to upper bound the number of distinct squares occurring in a circular word (w) of length n. Each such square occurs in ww, hence clearly there are at most $4n$ such distinct squares by plugging in the known bound on the number of distinct squares. However, we want a stronger bound.

Recall that the bound on the number of distinct squares is based on the notion of the rightmost occurrence. For every distinct square uu occurring in a word, we choose its rightmost occurrence. Then, we have the following property.

Lemma 2 ([12]). *For any position i, there are at most two rightmost occurrences starting at i.*

Consider the rightmost occurrences of distinct squares of length up to n in ww. We first analyze the rightmost occurrences starting at positions $1, 2, \ldots, \frac{1}{4}n$.

Lemma 3. *If $w[\frac{1}{4}n..\frac{1}{2}n]$ is aperiodic then every rightmost occurrence starting at position $i \in \{1, 2, \ldots, \frac{1}{4}n\}$ is of the same length.*

Proof. Assume otherwise, that is, $w[\frac{1}{4}n..\frac{1}{2}n]$ is aperiodic, but there are two rightmost occurrences uu and $u'u'$ starting at positions $i, i' \in \{1, 2, \ldots, \frac{1}{4}n\}$, respectively, in ww such that $|u| > |u'|$. Then, $i + 2|u| > n$ and $i' + 2|u'| > n$, as otherwise we could have found the same square in the second half of ww. Because $|u|, |u'| \leq \frac{1}{2}n$, this implies $i + |u| > \frac{1}{2}n$ and $i' + |u'| > \frac{1}{2}n$. So $w[\frac{1}{4}n..\frac{1}{2}n]^1$

---

[1] Formally, we need to appropriately round both $\frac{1}{4}n$ and $\frac{1}{2}n$. We chose not to do so explicitly as to avoid cluttering the presentation.

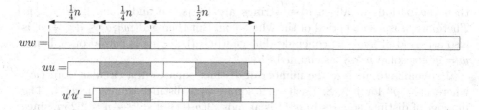

Fig. 2. Two rightmost occurrences of squares uu and $u'u'$ in ww.

is fully inside the first half of both uu and $u'u'$. But then it also appears starting at positions $\frac{1}{4}n + |u|$ and $\frac{1}{4}n + |u'|$, see Fig. 2. The distance between these two distinct (due to $|u| > |u'|$) occurrences is

$$(\frac{1}{4}n + |u|) - (\frac{1}{4}n + |u'|) = |u| - |u'|$$

We know that $|u| \leq \frac{1}{2}n$ and $|u'| > \frac{1}{2}n - i' \geq \frac{1}{2}n - \frac{1}{4}n = \frac{3}{8}n$. Thus, the distance is less than $\frac{1}{2}n - \frac{3}{8}n = \frac{1}{8}n$ and we conclude that the period of $w[\frac{1}{4}n..\frac{1}{2}n]$ is at most $\frac{1}{8}n$, which is a contradiction. $\square$

By Lemm 3, assuming that $w[\frac{1}{4}n..\frac{1}{2}n]$ is aperiodic, for every $i = 1, 2, \ldots, \frac{1}{4}n$ there is at most one rightmost occurrence starting at i. For all the remaining i, there are at most two rightmost occurrences starting at i, making the total number of distinct squares at most $\frac{1}{4}n + 2(2n - \frac{1}{4}n) = 3\frac{3}{4}n$.

It might be the case that $w[\frac{1}{4}n..\frac{1}{2}n]$ is periodic. However, the number of distinct squares occurring in (w) is the same as the number of distinct squares occurring in any $(w^{(i)})$, so we are free to replace w with any of its cyclic shifts. We claim that if, for any $i = 0, 1, \ldots, n - 1$, $w^{(i)}[\frac{1}{4}n..\frac{1}{2}n]$ is periodic, then the whole w is a nontrivial power y^p with $p \geq 8$. To show this, we need an auxiliary lemma that is a special case of Lemma 8.1.2 of [19]. We provide a proof for completeness.

Lemma 4. *For any word w and characters a, b, if both aw and wb are periodic then their periods are in fact equal.*

Proof. We assume that the period of aw is $p \leq |aw|/2$ and the period of wb is $q \leq |wb|/2$. Then p and q are both periods of w. By symmetry, we can assume that $p \geq q$. $p + q \leq (|aw| + |wb|)/2 = 1 + |w|$, so by the periodicity lemma $\gcd(p, q)$ is a period of w. We claim that $\gcd(p, q)$ is also a period of aw. To prove this, it is enough to show that $a = w[\gcd(p, q)]$. $\gcd(p, q)$ is a period of w and, for $n \geq 2$, $p \leq |w|$, so this is equivalent to showing that $a = w[p]$. But this holds due to p being a period of aw. Hence $\gcd(p, q)$ is a period of aw, but p is the period of aw and $p \geq q$, therefore $p = q$. $\square$

We observe that the substrings $w^{(i)}[\frac{1}{4}n..\frac{1}{2}n]$ correspond to all substrings of length $\frac{1}{4}n$ of ww. By Lemma 4, if every substring of length $\frac{1}{4}n$ of ww is periodic, then the periods of all such substrings are the same and equal to $d \leq \frac{1}{8}n$. Therefore, d is also a period of the whole ww. But then $\gcd(|w|, d) \leq d \leq \frac{1}{8}|w|$ is also a period of ww. We conclude that $\gcd(|w|, d) \leq \frac{1}{8}|w|$ is period of w, hence $w = y^p$ for some $p \geq 8$, as claimed.

It remains to analyze the number of distinct squares in a circular word (w), where $w = y^p$ for $p \geq 8$. Each such square is a distinct square in y^{p+1}. The number of distinct squares in y^{p+1} is at most $2(p+1)|y| = 2\frac{p+1}{p}n \leq 2.25n$, since $p \geq 8$.

Theorem 5. *The number of distinct squares in a circular word of length n is at most $3.75n$.*

To improve on the above upper bound, we need some of the machinery used by Deza et al. [9]. Two occurrences of squares uu and UU starting at the same position such that $|u| < |U|$ are called a double square and denoted (u, U). If both are the rightmost occurrences, this is an FS-double square. An FS-double square is identified with the starting position of the two occurrences.

Lemma 6 (see proof of Theorem 32 in [9]). *If (u, U) is the leftmost FS-double square of a string x and $|x| \geq 10$, then the number of FS-double squares in x is at most $\frac{5}{6}|x| - \frac{1}{3}|u|$.*

We again consider the rightmost occurrence of every distinct square of length up to n in ww and assume that $w[\frac{1}{4}n..\frac{1}{2}n]$ is aperiodic (as otherwise we already know there are at most $2.25n$ distinct squares). We need to consider two cases: either there are no rightmost occurrences starting at $i = 1, 2, \ldots, \frac{1}{4}n$, or there is at least one such occurrence.

No Rightmost Occurrences Starting at $i = 1, 2, \ldots, \frac{1}{4}n$. In this case, it is enough to bound the number of distinct squares in $\hat{w} = w[(\frac{1}{4}n + 1)..n]w$. Let i be the starting position of the leftmost FS-double square (u, U) in $\hat{w}$. If $i > \frac{3}{4}n$ then the total number of distinct squares is at most $\frac{3}{4}n + 2n = 2\frac{3}{4}n$, so we assume $i \leq \frac{3}{4}n$. Then, the total number of distinct squares can be bounded by applying Lemma 6 on $w[(\frac{1}{4}n + i)..n]w$ to show that the number of FS-double squares is at most

$$\frac{5}{6}(\frac{7}{4}n - i + 1) - \frac{1}{3}|u|$$

We know that $i + 2|u| > \frac{3}{4}n$, as otherwise uu would occur later in w. Therefore, the maximum number of distinct squares is

$$\frac{7}{4}n + \frac{5}{6}(\frac{7}{4}n - i + 1) - \frac{1}{3}\frac{1\frac{3}{4}n - i + 1}{2} = (\frac{7}{4} + \frac{35}{24} - \frac{1}{8})n - (\frac{5}{6} - \frac{1}{6})i + \frac{4}{6} \leq 3\frac{1}{12}n \quad (1)$$

At Least One Rightmost Occurrence Starting at $i \in \{1, 2, \ldots, \frac{1}{4}n\}$. We now move to the more interesting case where there are some rightmost occurrences starting at $i = 1, 2, \ldots, \frac{1}{4}n$. We then know by Lemma 3 that they all correspond to squares of the same length 2ℓ. Let $i \in \{1, 2, \ldots, \frac{1}{4}n\}$ be the starting position of one of these rightmost occurrences. Then, $i + 2\ell > n$ as otherwise the square would occur later in the second w, so $\ell > (n - \frac{n}{4})/2 = \frac{3}{8}n$. We also know that $\ell < \frac{1}{2}n$, as otherwise $w = y^2$ and there are only $3n$ distinct squares. To conclude, $\ell \in (\frac{3}{8}n, \frac{1}{2}n)$. Observe that, due to the square starting at position i, the aperiodic substring $s = w[\frac{1}{4}n..\frac{1}{2}n]$ also occurs at position $\frac{1}{4}n + \ell$ in ww. Therefore, we can rotate w by ℓ and repeat the whole reasoning. We either obtain that the number of distinct squares is at most $3\frac{1}{12}n$ (if, in $w^{(\ell)}w^{(\ell)}$, there are no rightmost occurrences starting at $i = 1, 2, \ldots, \frac{1}{4}n$), or there is another occurrence of s at position $\frac{1}{4}n + \ell + \ell' - n$ in w, where $\ell, \ell' \in (\frac{3}{8}n, \frac{1}{2}n)$. Because s is aperiodic and $\ell + \ell' > \frac{3}{4}n$, the other occurrence must actually be at position $\frac{1}{4}n - \Delta$, where $\Delta \in (\frac{1}{8}n, \frac{1}{4}n)$. By repeating this enough times (and recalling that two occurrences of s cannot be too close to each other, as otherwise s is not aperiodic), we either obtain that there are at most $3\frac{1}{12}n$ distinct squares or all occurrences of s in (w) are at positions $\frac{1}{4}n + \sum_{j=1}^{i-1} \Delta_j$ (recall that (w) denotes the circular word, so we calculate positions modulo n) for $i = 1, 2, \ldots, d$, where $\sum_{j=1}^{d} \Delta_j = n$ and $\Delta_j \in (\frac{1}{8}n, \frac{1}{4}n)$ for every $j = 1, 2, \ldots, d$. That is, the whole (w) is covered by the occurrences of s, and because s is aperiodic these occurrences overlap by less than $\frac{1}{8}n$. Observe that there cannot be any other occurrences of s in (w), because the additional occurrence would overlap with one of the already found occurrences by at least $\frac{1}{8}n$, thus contradiction the assumption that s is aperiodic. By the constraints on Δ_j, $d \in \{5, 6, 7\}$. See Fig. 3 for an illustration with $d = 7$. We further consider three possible subcases.

$d = 5$. In such case, we have $\Delta_j \geq \frac{1}{5}n$ for some j. By rotating w, we can assume that $j = 1$. Recall that then all squares starting at $i = 1, 2, \ldots, \frac{1}{4}n$ have the same length 2ℓ (and there is at least one such square), so there is another occurrence of s starting at position $\frac{1}{4}n + \ell$, and then by repeating the reasoning at position $\frac{1}{4}n + \ell + \ell'$, where $\ell + \ell' = n - \Delta_1$ (due to $\ell, \ell' \in (\frac{3}{8}n, \frac{1}{2}n)$). Combining this with $\Delta_1 \geq \frac{1}{5}n$, we obtain that $\min\{\ell, \ell'\} \leq \frac{2}{5}n$. By again rotating w, we can assume that in fact $\ell \leq \frac{2}{5}n$. Let $i \in \{1, 2, \ldots, \frac{1}{4}n\}$ be the starting position of a rightmost occurrence of a square of length 2ℓ. Then $i + 2\ell > n$ as otherwise it would not be a rightmost occurrence, so $i > \frac{1}{5}n$ and we obtain that there are less than $\frac{1}{4}n - \frac{1}{5}n = \frac{1}{20}n$ rightmost occurrences starting at $i = 1, 2, \ldots, \frac{1}{4}n$. By the previous calculation (1) the number of remaining rightmost occurrences is at most $3\frac{1}{12}n$, making the total number of distinct squares at most $3\frac{2}{15}n$.

$d = 6$. We will show that this is, in fact, not possible. Recall that, for every $i = 1, 2, \ldots, 6$, after rotating w by $r = \sum_{j=1}^{i-1} \Delta_j$ we obtain that there is at least one rightmost occurrence starting in the prefix of length $\frac{1}{4}n$ of $w^{(r)}w^{(r)}$, and in fact, by Lemma 3, all such rightmost occurrences correspond to squares of the same length $2\ell_i$, where $\ell_i \in (\frac{3}{8}n, \frac{1}{2}n)$. Thus, for every occurrence of s starting at position $\frac{1}{4}n + \sum_{j=1}^{i-1} \Delta_j$, there is another occurrence at position $\frac{1}{4}n + \sum_{j=1}^{i-1} \Delta_j + \ell_i$ in (w) (recall that the positions are taken modulo n). We claim that $\ell_i = \Delta_i + \Delta_{i+1}$ or $\ell_i = \Delta_i + \Delta_{i+1} + \Delta_{i+2}$, where the indices are taken modulo 6. Certainly, $\ell_i = \Delta_i + \Delta_{i+1} + \ldots + \Delta_{i+k}$ for some k. We cannot have

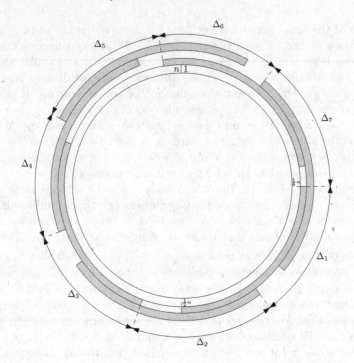

Fig. 3. Seven occurrences of an aperiodic s of length $\frac{1}{4}n$ inside (w).

$k = 0$ because $\ell_i > \frac{3}{8}n$ and $\Delta_i < \frac{3}{8}n$. We also cannot have $k \geq 3$, because $\ell_i < \frac{1}{2}n$ and $\Delta_i + \Delta_{i+1} + \Delta_{i+2} + \Delta_{i+3} > \frac{1}{2}n$. So, $k = 1$ or $k = 2$. For every $i = 1, 2, \ldots, 6$, we define $\mathsf{succ}(i) \in \{1, 2, \ldots, 6\}$ as follows. If $\ell_i = \Delta_i + \Delta_{i+1}$ then we set $\mathsf{succ}(i) = i + 2$, and otherwise (if $\ell_i = \Delta_i + \Delta_{i+1} + \Delta_{i+2}$) $\mathsf{succ}(i) = i + 3$. Intuitively, every occurrence of s in (w) points to another such occurrence. Due to $\ell_i \in (\frac{3}{8}n, \frac{1}{2}n)$ holding for every $i = 1, 2, \ldots, 6$, the difference between the starting positions of the i-th and the $\mathsf{succ}(i)$-th occurrence of s belongs to $(\frac{3}{8}n, \frac{1}{2}n)$, so the difference between the starting position of the i-th and the $\mathsf{succ}(\mathsf{succ}(i))$-th occurrence of s belongs to $(\frac{3}{4}n, n)$. In fact, due to s being aperiodic, the latter difference must belong to $(\frac{3}{4}n, \frac{7}{8}n)$. Consequently, there are no other occurrences of s between the $\mathsf{succ}(\mathsf{succ}(i))$-th and the i-th, so $\mathsf{succ}(\mathsf{succ}(i)) = i - 1$. Now, we consider two cases:

1. $\mathsf{succ}(1) = 3$, then $\mathsf{succ}(3) = 6$, so $\mathsf{succ}(6) = 2$, $\mathsf{succ}(2) = 5$ and $\mathsf{succ}(5) = 1$.
2. $\mathsf{succ}(1) = 4$, then $\mathsf{succ}(4) = 6$, so $\mathsf{succ}(6) = 3$, $\mathsf{succ}(3) = 5$, $\mathsf{succ}(5) = 2$, $\mathsf{succ}(2) = 4$.

In both cases, we obtain that $\mathsf{succ}(i) = \mathsf{succ}(j)$ for some $i \neq j$. But this is a contradiction, because then there are two occurrences of s within distance less than $\frac{1}{8}n$, so s is not aperiodic.

$d = 7$. We define $\mathsf{succ}(i)$ for every $i = 1, 2, \ldots, 7$ as in the previous case. Because $\mathsf{succ}(i) \in \{i+2, i+3\}$ and $\mathsf{succ}(\mathsf{succ}(i)) = i - 1$ still holds, we obtain that in fact

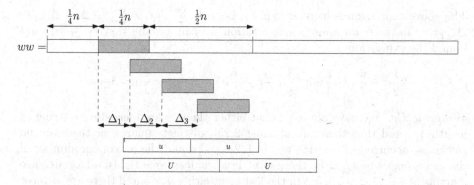

Fig. 4. The leftmost FS-square starting at position $j \le \frac{1}{4}n + \Delta_1$.

$\text{succ}(i) = i + 3$ for every $i = 1, 2, \ldots, 7$. This means that $\ell_i = \Delta_i + \Delta_{i+1} + \Delta_{i+2}$. Consider all rightmost occurrences starting at $i = 1, 2, \ldots, \frac{1}{4}n$. We must have that $i + 2\ell_1 > n$ for each of them, so $i > n - 2(\Delta_1 + \Delta_2 + \Delta_3)$, making the total number of such occurrences at most $\min\{\frac{1}{4}n, 2(\Delta_1 + \Delta_2 + \Delta_3) - \frac{3}{4}n\}$. Because $\Delta_1 + \Delta_2 + \Delta_3 \le \frac{1}{2}n$ due to $\Delta_i > \frac{1}{8}n$ holding for every $i = 1, 2, \ldots, 7$ and $\sum_{i=1}^{7} \Delta_i = n$, this number is actually $2(\Delta_1 + \Delta_2 + \Delta_3) - \frac{3}{4}n$.

Now we must account for the remaining distinct squares. Let j be the starting position of the leftmost FS-double square (u, U) in ww. Note that $j > \frac{1}{4}n$ because there is at most one rightmost occurrence starting at $i = 1, 2, \ldots, \frac{1}{4}n$. We lower bound j by considering two possible cases:

1. $j > \frac{1}{4}n + \Delta_1$.
2. $j \le \frac{1}{4}n + \Delta_1$, then the occurrences of s starting at $\frac{1}{4}n + \Delta_1$ and $\frac{1}{4}n + \Delta_1 + \Delta_2 + \Delta_3$ are disjoint and both fully inside the first w, because $\Delta_1 + \Delta_2 + \Delta_3 \le \frac{1}{2}n$. Thus, both u and U contain s as a substring. See Fig. 4. Then, because all occurrences of s start at positions of the form $\frac{1}{4}n + \sum_{j=1}^{i-1} \Delta_j$, we conclude that $|u| = \Delta_2 + \Delta_3$ and $|U| = \Delta_2 + \Delta_3 + \Delta_4$. So, $j > n - 2(\Delta_2 + \Delta_3)$.

We now know that $j > \min\{\frac{1}{4}n + \Delta_1, n - 2(\Delta_2 + \Delta_3)\}$. Using $j + 2|u| > n$ we obtain that the number of remaining distinct squares is at most

$$1\frac{3}{4}n + \frac{5}{6}(2n - j) - \frac{1}{3}|u| \le 3\frac{5}{12}n - \frac{5}{6}j - \frac{1}{3}\frac{n-j}{2} = 3\frac{1}{4}n - \frac{2}{3}j$$

so the total number of squares is

$$\le 3\frac{1}{4}n + 2(\Delta_1 + \Delta_2 + \Delta_3) - \frac{3}{4}n - \frac{2}{3}j$$

$$\le 2\frac{1}{2}n + 2(\Delta_1 + \Delta_2 + \Delta_3) - \frac{2}{3}\min\{\frac{1}{4}n + \Delta_1, n - 2(\Delta_2 + \Delta_3)\}$$

We rewrite the above in terms of ℓ_1 and Δ_1:

$$2\frac{1}{2}n + 2\ell_1 - \frac{2}{3}\min\{\frac{1}{4}n + \Delta_1, n - 2\ell_1 + 2\Delta_1\} \le 2\frac{1}{2}n + 2\ell_1 - \frac{2}{3}\min\{\frac{3}{8}n, \frac{5}{4}n - 2\ell_1\}$$

The above expression is increasing in ℓ_1. Because $\sum_{i=1}^{7} \ell_i = \sum_{i=1}^{7}(\Delta_i + \Delta_{i+1} + \Delta_{i+2}) = 3n$, after an appropriate rotation we can assume that $\ell_1 \leq \frac{3}{7}n$, and bound the expression:

$$2\frac{1}{2}n + \frac{6}{7}n - \frac{2}{3}\min\{\frac{3}{8}n, \frac{5}{4}n - \frac{6}{7}n\} = 3\frac{5}{14}n - \frac{1}{4}n = 3\frac{3}{28}n$$

Wrapping Up. We have obtained that either there is an aperiodic substring of length $\frac{1}{4}n$, and thus there are at most $2.25n$ distinct squares, or there are no rightmost occurrences starting at $i = 1, 2, \ldots, \frac{1}{4}n$ and the maximum number of distinct squares is $3\frac{1}{12}n$, or there is at least at least one rightmost occurrence starting at $i \in \{1, 2, \ldots, \frac{1}{4}n\}$. In the last case, either $d = 5$ and there are at most $3\frac{2}{15}n$ distinct squares, or $d = 7$ and there are at most $3\frac{3}{28}n$ distinct squares. The maximum of these upper bounds is $3\frac{2}{15}n$.

Theorem 7. *The number of distinct squares in a circular word of length n is at most $3.14n$.*

5   Conclusions

We believe that it should be possible to show an upper bound of $3n$, possibly without using the machinery of Deza et al., but it seems to require some new combinatorial insights. A computer search seems to suggest that the right answer is $1.25n$, but showing this is probably quite difficult. Another natural direction for a follow-up work is to consider higher powers in circular words.

References

1. Blanchet-Sadri, F., Mercas, R., Scott, G.: Counting distinct squares in partial words. Acta Cybern. **19**(2), 465–477 (2009)
2. Bland, W., Smyth, W.F.: Three overlapping squares: the general case characterized and applications. Theor. Comput. Sci. **596**, 23–40 (2015)
3. Castiglione, G., Restivo, A., Sciortino, M.: Circular Sturmian words and Hopcroft's algorithm. Theor. Comput. Sci. **410**(43), 4372–4381 (2009)
4. Crochemore, M., Fici, G., Mercaş, R., Pissis, S.P.: Linear-time sequence comparison using minimal absent words & applications. In: Kranakis, E., Navarro, G., Chávez, E. (eds.) LATIN 2016. LNCS, vol. 9644, pp. 334–346. Springer, Heidelberg (2016). doi:10.1007/978-3-662-49529-2_25
5. Crochemore, M., Iliopoulos, C.S., Kociumaka, T., Kubica, M., Radoszewski, J., Rytter, W., Tyczyński, W., Waleń, T.: The maximum number of squares in a tree. In: Kärkkäinen, J., Stoye, J. (eds.) CPM 2012. LNCS, vol. 7354, pp. 27–40. Springer, Heidelberg (2012). doi:10.1007/978-3-642-31265-6_3
6. Crochemore, M., Rytter, W.: Squares, cubes, and time-space efficient string searching. Algorithmica **13**(5), 405–425 (1995)
7. Currie, J.D.: There are ternary circular square-free words of length n for $n \geq 18$. Electron. J. Comb. **9**(1), N10 (2002)

8. Currie, J.D., Fitzpatrick, D.S.: Circular words avoiding patterns. In: Ito, M., Toyama, M. (eds.) DLT 2002. LNCS, vol. 2450, pp. 319–325. Springer, Heidelberg (2003). doi:10.1007/3-540-45005-X_28

9. Deza, A., Franek, F., Thierry, A.: How many double squares can a string contain? Discrete Appl. Math. **180**, 52–69 (2015)

10. Fan, K., Puglisi, S.J., Smyth, W.F., Turpin, A.: A new periodicity lemma. SIAM J. Discrete Math. **20**(3), 656–668 (2006)

11. Fine, N., Wilf, H.: Uniqueness theorems for periodic functions. Proc. Am. Math. Soc. **16**, 109–114 (1965)

12. Fraenkel, A.S., Simpson, J.: How many squares can a string contain? J. Comb. Theory Ser. A **82**(1), 112–120 (1998)

13. Franek, F., Fuller, R.C.G., Simpson, J., Smyth, W.F.: More results on overlapping squares. J. Discrete Algorithms **17**, 2–8 (2012)

14. Gawrychowski, P., Kociumaka, T., Rytter, W., Waleń, T.: Tight bound for the number of distinct palindromes in a tree. In: Iliopoulos, C., Puglisi, S., Yilmaz, E. (eds.) SPIRE 2015. LNCS, vol. 9309, pp. 270–276. Springer, Cham (2015). doi:10.1007/978-3-319-23826-5_26

15. Hegedüs, L., Nagy, B.: Representations of circular words. AFL. EPTCS **151**, 261–270 (2014)

16. Ilie, L.: A simple proof that a word of length n has at most $2n$ distinct squares. J. Comb. Theory **112**(1), 163–164 (2005)

17. Ilie, L.: A note on the number of squares in a word. Theor. Comput. Sci. **380**(3), 373–376 (2007)

18. Kopylova, E., Smyth, W.F.: The three squares lemma revisited. J. Discrete Algorithms **11**, 3–14 (2012)

19. Lothaire, M. (ed.): Algebraic Combinatorics on Words, Encyclopedia of Mathematics and its Applications, vol. 90. Cambridge University Press, Cambridge (2002)

20. Manea, F., Seki, S.: Square-density increasing mappings. In: Manea, F., Nowotka, D. (eds.) WORDS 2015. LNCS, vol. 9304, pp. 160–169. Springer, Cham (2015). doi:10.1007/978-3-319-23660-5_14

21. Massé, A.B., Brlek, S., Garon, A., Labbé, S.: Equations on palindromes and circular words. Theor. Comput. Sci. **412**(27), 2922–2930 (2011)

22. Shur, A.M.: On ternary square-free circular words. Electron. J. Comb. **17**(1), R140 (2010)

23. Simpson, J.: Intersecting periodic words. Theor. Comput. Sci. **374**(1–3), 58–65 (2007)

24. Simpson, J.: Palindromes in circular words. Theor. Comput. Sci. **550**, 66–78 (2014)

25. Thue, A.: Über unendliche zeichenreihen. Norske Vid. Selsk. Skr. I Mat.-Nat. Kl. Christiania **7**, 1–22 (1906)

LZ78 Compression in Low Main Memory Space

Diego Arroyuelo[1], Rodrigo Cánovas[2], Gonzalo Navarro[3(✉)],
and Rajeev Raman[4]

[1] Departamento de Informática, Universidad Técnica Federico Santa María,
Vicuña Mackenna 3939, San Joaquín, Santiago, Chile
darroyue@inf.utfsm.cl
[2] LIRMM and IBC, 161 rue Ada, 34095 Montpellier Cedex 5, France
yigorc@gmail.com
[3] Deptartment of Computer Science, University of Chile,
Beauchef 851, Santiago, Chile
gnavarro@dcc.uchile.cl
[4] Department of Informatics, University of Leicester,
F33 Computer Science Building, University Road, Leicester, UK
r.raman@mcs.le.ac.uk

Abstract. We present the first algorithms that perform the LZ78 compression of a text of length n over alphabet $[1..\sigma]$, whose output is z integers, using only $O(z \lg \sigma)$ bits of main memory. The algorithms read the input text from disk in a single pass, and write the compressed output to disk. The text can also be decompressed within the same main memory usage, which is unprecedented too. The algorithms are based on hashing and, under some simplifying assumptions, run in $O(n)$ expected time. We experimentally verify that our algorithms use 2–9 times less time and/or space than previously implemented LZ78 compressors.

1 Introduction

The Ziv-Lempel algorithm of 1978 [19] (known as LZ78) is one of the most famous compression algorithms. Its variants (especially LZW [17]) are used in software like Unix's Compress and formats like GIF. Compared to the stronger LZ77 format [18], LZ78 has a more regular structure, which has made it the preferred choice for compressed sequence representations supporting optimal-time access [16] and compressed text indexes for pattern matching [3,7,15] and document retrieval [5,6].

Compared to LZ77, the LZ78 compressed output is also easier to build. For example, a simple and classical implementation compresses a text of length n over an alphabet $[1..\sigma]$ into z integers, where $\sqrt{n} \leq z = O(n/\lg_\sigma n)$, in $O(n \lg \sigma)$ deterministic or $O(n)$ randomized time, using $O(z \lg n) = O(n \lg \sigma)$ bits of space. A comparable result for LZ77 was obtained only recently [11] and it required sophisticated compressed suffix array construction algorithms.

This collaboration started during the Dagstuhl Seminar 16431, "Computation over Compressed Structured Data". We also acknowledge the funding from Millennium Nucleus Information and Coordination in Networks ICM/FIC RC130003 (G.N.).

© Springer International Publishing AG 2017
G. Fici et al. (Eds.): SPIRE 2017, LNCS 10508, pp. 38–50, 2017.
DOI: 10.1007/978-3-319-67428-5_4

The time and main memory space required by compression algorithms is important. Building the compressed file within less main memory allows us compressing larger files without splitting them into chunks, yielding better compression in general. The fastest deterministic LZ78 compression algorithms require $O(n)$ time, but $O(n \lg n)$ bits of main memory [8]. If the main memory is limited to $O(n \lg \sigma)$ bits (*i.e.*, proportional to the input text size), then the time increases to $O(n \lg \lg \sigma)$ [11]. Finally, if we limit the main memory to $O(z \lg n)$ bits (*i.e.*, proportional to the compressed text size, like the classic scheme), then the compression time becomes $O(n(1 + \lg \sigma / \lg \lg n))$ [1], which improves the classic $O(n \lg \sigma)$ time. If we allow randomization, then the classic scheme yields $O(n)$ expected time and $O(z \lg n)$ bits of space.

In this paper we show that the LZ78 compression can be carried out within just $O(z \lg \sigma)$ bits of main memory, which is less than any other previous scheme, and asymptotically less than the size of the compressed file, $z(\lg z + \lg \sigma)$ bits. Ours are randomized and streaming algorithms. They read the text once from disk, and output the compressed file to disk as well, and therefore they may run within memory sizes unable to fit even the compressed file. One of our algorithms requires $O(n)$ expected compression time, but may rewrite the output multiple times, whereas the other takes $O(n \lg \sigma)$ expected time but writes the output only once. Both are able to decompress the file in a single $O(n)$-time pass on disk and using $O(z \lg \sigma)$ bits of main memory, where previous decompression algorithms need to store the whole compressed text in main memory.

Our results hold under some simplifying assumptions on randomness. Nevertheless, our experimental results demonstrate that these assumptions do not affect the practical competitiveness of the new algorithms, which outperform current alternatives in space and/or time by a factor from 2 to 9.

To obtain the result, we build on a hash-based trie representation [14], which has the advantage that the addresses of the nodes do not change as we insert new leaves, and that $O(\lg \sigma)$ bits are sufficient to encode the trie nodes since some of the information is implicit in their hash addresses. The main challenge is to design schemes so that the hash tables can grow as the LZ78 parsing progresses, so as to ensure that they have only $O(z)$ cells without knowing z in advance.

2   LZ78 Compression

The LZ78 compression algorithm [19] parses the text into a sequence of phrases. Assume we are compressing a text $T[1..n]$ and we have already processed $T[1..i-1]$ into r phrases $B_0 B_1 B_2 \cdots B_{r-1}$, where phrase B_0 represents the empty string. Then, to compute B_r we find the longest prefix $T[i..j-1]$ (with $j-1 < n$) that is equal to some B_q, with $q < r$. Then we define $B_r = B_q . T[j]$, which is represented as the pair $(q, T[j])$, and we continue the parsing from $T[j+1]$.

If we add a unique terminator character to T, then every phrase represents a different text substring. We call z the final number of phrases generated. It is known that $\sqrt{n} \leq z = O(n/\lg_\sigma n)$, where σ is the size of the alphabet of T.

The usual way to carry out the parsing efficiently is to use the so-called LZTRIE. This is a trie with one node per phrase, where the root node corresponds to B_0, and the node of $B_r = B_q . T[j]$ is the child of the node of phrase B_q with the edge labeled by $T[j]$. Since the set of phrases is prefix-closed, LZTRIE has z nodes. Then, to process $T[i..j-1]$, we traverse LZTRIE from the root downwards, following the characters $T[i], T[i+1] \ldots$ until falling out of the tree at a node representing phrase B_q. Then we create a new node for B_r, which is the child of B_q labelled by $T[j]$. Since the trie has z nodes, it requires $O(z(\lg n + \lg \sigma)) = O(n \lg \sigma)$ bits for the parsing, which can be done in $O(n \lg \sigma)$ deterministic time (using binary search on the children) or $O(n)$ randomized time (using hash tables to store the children, whose sizes double when needed).

The usual way to represent the LZ78 parsing in the compressed file consists of two (separate or interlaced) arrays, $S[1..z]$ of $z \lg \sigma$ bits, and $A[1..z]$ of $z \lg z$ bits. If $B_r = B_q . T[j]$ is a phrase, then we represent it by storing $A[r] = q$ and $S[r] = T[j]$. For decompressing a given phrase B_r, we follow the referencing chain using array A, obtaining the corresponding symbols from array S, until we read a 0 in A. Thus $S[r]$, $S[A[r]]$, $S[A[A[r]]]$, $\ldots$ obtains B_r in reverse order in $O(|B_r|)$ time, and the complete text is decompressed in $O(n)$ time.

An alternative way to represent the LZ78 parsing [3] uses a succinct encoding of LZTRIE, which uses just $2z + z \lg \sigma + o(z)$ bits, $2z + o(z)$ for the topology and $z \lg \sigma$ for the labels. It also stores an array $L[1..z]$, such that $L[r]$ stores the preorder number of the LZTRIE node corresponding to phrase B_r. This array requires $z \lg z$ bits. To extract the text for phrase B_r, we start from the node with preorder $L[r]$ in LZTRIE, and obtain the symbols labeling the upward path up to the root, by going successively to the parent in the trie. Using succinct tree representations that support going to the parent in constant time, this procedure also yields $O(n)$ total decompression time.

This second representation is more complex and uses slightly more space than the former, more precisely, the $2z + o(z)$ bits for the tree topology. Yet, it is sometimes preferred because it allows for operations other than just decompressing T. For instance, Sadakane and Grossi [16] show how to obtain any substring of length ℓ of T in optimal $O(\ell/\lg_\sigma n)$ time (i.e., in time proportional to the number of machine words needed to store ℓ symbols). In this work, a different representation of LZTRIE will allow us carrying out the compression within $O(z \lg \sigma)$ bits of main memory.

3   Previous Work on LZ78 Construction

A classic pointer-based implementation of LZTRIE, with balanced binary trees to handle the children of each node, carries out the compression in $O(n \lg \sigma)$ time and $O(z \lg n)$ bits of space.

Jansson et al. [10] introduce a particular trie structure to represent LZTRIE, which still uses $O(z \lg n)$ bits of space but reduces the construction time to $O\left(n \lg \sigma \cdot \frac{(\lg \lg n)^2}{\lg n \lg \lg \lg n}\right)$. The algorithm needs two passes on the text, each of which involves $n \lg \sigma$ bits of I/O if it is stored on disk.

Arroyuelo and Navarro [2] manage to perform a single pass over the text, in exchange for $2z \lg z$ additional bits of I/O, and a total time of $O(n(\lg \sigma + \lg \lg n))$.

Table 1. Previous and new LZ78 compression algorithms. Times with a star mean expected time of randomized algorithms. We first list the classic schemes, then the deterministic methods, from fastest and most space-consuming to slowest and least space-consuming. At the end, our randomized method uses less space than all the others, and also matches the fastest ones in expectation.

Reference	RAM space in bits	Compression time
Classic [19]	$O(z \lg n)$	$O(n \lg \sigma)$
	$O(z \lg n)$	$O(n)^*$
Fischer et al. [8]	$(1 + \epsilon)n \lg n + O(n)$	$O(n/\epsilon^2)$
Köppl and Sadakane [11]	$O(n \lg \sigma)$	$O(n \lg \lg \sigma)$
Jansson et al. [10]	$O(z \lg n)$	$O\left(n \lg \sigma \cdot \frac{(\lg \lg n)^2}{\lg n \lg \lg \lg n}\right)$
Arroyuelo et al. [1]	$z(\lg n + \lg \sigma + 2)$	$O\left(n \lg \sigma \cdot \frac{1}{\lg \lg n}\right)$
Arroyuelo and Navarro [2]	$z(\lg n + \lg \sigma + 2)$	$O(n \lg \sigma + n \lg \lg n)$
This paper	$O(z \lg \sigma)$	$O(n)^*$

The peak memory usage is $z(\lg n + \lg \sigma + 2)$ bits. They use the compact LZTRIE representation described in the previous section. An obstacle to further reducing the space is that they need to build the whole LZTRIE before they can build the array L, because preorder numbers vary as new leaves are inserted. Later improvements on dynamic tries introduced by Arroyuelo et al. [1] reduce the time to $O\left(n \frac{\lg \sigma}{\lg \lg n}\right)$. Notice that this is $O(n)$ for small alphabets, $\sigma = \mathrm{polylog}(n)$. However, the peak space usage remains the same.

Fischer et al. [8] finally obtained linear worst-case time. They construct the LZ78 parsing using $(1 + \epsilon)n \lg n + O(n)$ bits of space in $O(n/\epsilon^2)$ time.

Recently, Köppl and Sadakane [11] showed how to construct the parsing in $O(n \lg \lg \sigma)$ time, using $O(n \lg \sigma)$ bits of working space; note this is $\Omega(z \lg n)$.

Table 1 shows all these previous results, and our contribution in context. Our results hold under some simplifying assumptions that are described in Sect. 8.

4 Dynamic Compact Tries

We will make use of the following data structure to maintain a dynamic trie of up to t nodes that uses $O(t \lg \sigma)$ bits, while supporting insertion of edges, and navigation upwards and downwards from nodes, within constant randomized time [14]. The structure has two components:

1. A closed hash table $H[0..M - 1]$, where $M = m/\alpha$, m is an upper bound to the number of nodes, and the constant $\alpha < 1$ is the load factor to use. Table H is a simple array that stores information on the nodes of the trie, using only $\lg \sigma + O(1)$ bits per entry.
2. An array $D[0..M - 1]$ to store information about the collisions (all entries initialized with value -1).

Each trie node y is identified with the position where it is stored in H; sometimes we will write $p(y)$ explicitly to refer to this position. This position will not change with time. The root is placed at an arbitrary position, say $H[0]$. Every other node y is represented by a pair (x, c), where x is (the position in H of) the parent of y and c is the character labeling the edge between x and y.

The hash function used to place y in H is $h(y) = ((a \cdot w(y)) \bmod P) \bmod M$, where a is an integer chosen at random in $[1, P - 1]$, P is the first prime such that $P > M \cdot \sigma$, and $w(y) = p(x) \cdot \sigma + (c - 1)$. The value we store in the cell of H associated with y is $v(y) = ((a \cdot w(y)) \bmod P) \operatorname{div} M$.

With this mechanism, since $P = O(M\sigma)$ [9, p. 343], it holds $v(y) = O(\sigma)$, and thus the values stored in H require $\lg \sigma + O(1)$ bits. With this information we can still reconstruct $(a \cdot w(y)) \bmod P = v(y) \cdot M + h(y)$, and then $w(y) = a^{-1} \cdot (a \cdot w(y)) \bmod P$, where $a^{-1} \bmod P$ is easily computed from a and stored with the index. From $w(y)$ we recover the pair (x, c), which allows us traversing the trie upwards.

On the other hand, to insert a new child $y = (x, c)$ from the position $p(x)$, we compute $h(y)$ and try to write $v(y)$ at $H[h(y)]$. If the cell is free (which we signal with $D[h(y)] = -1$), then we write $H[h(y)] \leftarrow v(y)$ and $D[h(y)] \leftarrow 0$. If the cell is not free, we probe consecutive positions $H[p]$ with $p = (h(y) + k) \bmod M$, for $k = 1, 2, \ldots$. The following cases may occur:

1. $D[p] = -1$, in which case we terminate with $H[p] \leftarrow v(y)$ and $D[p] \leftarrow k$, so that $D[p]$ indicates the number of probes between $h(y)$ and the final position p where y is finally written. Note that p will become $p(y)$, and from $p(y)$ we can recover $h(y)$ without knowing y, with $h(y) = (p(y) - D[p(y)]) \bmod M$.
2. $D[p] \neq -1$, $H[p] = v(y)$, and $(p - D[p]) \bmod M = h(y)$, thus node y is already stored in H, so we should not insert it.
3. $D[p] \neq -1$, but $H[p] \neq v(y)$ or $(p - D[p]) \bmod M \neq h(y)$, thus the cell is occupied by another node and we must continue with the next value of k.

Case 2 also shows how to traverse the trie downwards, from the current node towards its child labeled by c, to find the node $y = (x, c)$.

Note that the values stored in D are constant in expectation, as they record the insertion time for each element. Poyias et al. [14] show how D can be represented with a data structure using $O(z)$ bits and constant amortized-time operations. We refer the reader to their article for further details.

5   Using a Fixed Hash Table

In this section we show how to do the parsing of $T[1..n]$ within $O(n \lg \sigma / \lg_\sigma n)$ bits of main memory. This space is already $O(z \lg \sigma)$ on incompressible texts; we will later achieve it for all texts.

We use a compact dynamic trie to build the LZTRIE associated with the LZ78 parse of T, and to compress T accordingly. We set m to an upper bound on the number of LZTRIE nodes: m is the smallest number with $m(\lg_\sigma m - 3) \geq n$. Thus $m = \Theta(n / \lg_\sigma n)$. Further, we will use an array $L[0..z]$ to store in $L[r]$ the position in H where the LZTRIE node of block B_r is stored. Each entry of L takes $\lceil \lg M \rceil = \lg n + O(1)$ bits, but the array is generated directly on disk.

To perform the parsing of a new phrase $T[i..j]$, we start from the trie root (say, x_0, with $p(x_0) = 0$), and use the mechanism described in the previous section to compute $x_1 = (x_0, T[i])$, $x_2 = (x_1, T[i+1])$, and so on until $x_{j-i+1} = (x_{j-i}, T[j])$ does not exist in the trie. At this point we insert $x_{j-i+1} = (x_{j-i}, T[j])$, write to disk the next value $L[r] \leftarrow p(x_{j-i+1})$, and continue with $T[j+1..n]$.

Overall, compression is carried out within the $O(n \lg \sigma / \lg_\sigma n)$ bits of main memory used by H and D, in $O(n)$ expected time if H is chosen from a universal family of hash functions, and T and L are read/written from/to disk in streaming mode. When we finish the parsing, we write H and D at the end of L in the file, and add some header information including n, σ, M, P, a, a^{-1}.

Decompression can also be made in streaming mode and using memory space only for H and D, which is not possible in classical schemes where each phrase is stored as a pointer to its earlier position in the file. We load the LZTRIE into memory (i.e., tables H and D). Now we read the consecutive entries of $L[1..z]$ in streaming mode. For each new entry $L[r] = p$, we start from $H[p]$ and decode $x_0 = (x_{-1}, c_{-1})$ from it; then we decode $x_{-1} = (x_{-2}, c_{-2})$, and so on, until we reach the root $x_{-s} = L[0]$. Then we append $c_{-s}c_{-s+1} \ldots c_{-2}c_{-1}$ to the decompressed text in streaming mode. The stack may require up to $z \lg \sigma$ bits in extreme cases, but this is still within our main memory budget. Its use can also be avoided in standard ways, at the expense of increased I/Os.

Note that this structure permits retrieving the contents of any individual block B_r, by traversing the LZTRIE upwards from $L[r]$, just as done for decompression. This can make it useful as a succinct data structure as well.

The obvious disadvantage of this simple scheme is that it uses more than $O(z \lg \sigma)$ bits of space when T is highly compressible, $z = o(n/\lg_\sigma n)$ (that is, when it is most interesting to compress T!). A simple workaround is to start assuming that $z = O(\sqrt{n})$, since $\sqrt{n}$ is the smallest possible value for z. If, during the parsing, this limit is exceeded, we double the value of z and repeat the whole process. Since we may rerun the process $O(\lg z)$ times, the total expected time is $O(n \lg z) = O(n \lg n)$ (in LZ78, $\lg z = \Theta(\lg n)$). In exchange, the main memory space is now always $O(z \lg \sigma)$ bits. Further, the extra space added to the compressed file due to the tables H and D is just $O(z \lg \sigma)$. Apart from the increased time, a problem with this scheme is that it reads T several times from disk, and thus it is not a streaming algorithm. In the next sections we explore two faster solutions that in addition scan T only once.

6   Using a Growing Table

We can obtain $O(z \lg \sigma)$ bits of space for any text by letting H and D grow as more blocks are produced along the parsing. We start with a hash table of size $\sqrt{n}/\alpha^2$, since $\sqrt{n}$ is a lower bound on z. Then, whenever the load factor in H reaches α, we allocate a new table H' (and D') with size multiplied by $1/\alpha$, and load them with all the current trie nodes. We will read T only once, but we will still perform multiple rewriting passes on L.

The main challenge is how to remap all the nodes x from H to H', since their position $p(x)$ in H are their identity, which is mentioned not only in L but also in their children $y = (p(x), c)$. That is, in order to map y to its new position $p'(y)$ in H', we need to know the mapped position $p'(x)$ of its parent x, that is, we must map the LZTRIE nodes top-down. Yet, we cannot simply perform a DFS traversal on LZTRIE, because we cannot efficiently enumerate the children of a node x in less than $O(\sigma)$ time.

We remap the nodes as follows. We traverse L from left to right (on disk), and traverse upwards from each position $L[r]$ in H up to the root. All the nodes from the parent of $L[r]$ must already exist in H', so we stack the symbols traversed in the upward path on H and use them to traverse downwards in H' from the root. Then we insert in H' (and D') the new node that corresponds to $L[r]$, and rewrite $L[r]$ with the new position in H'. If B_r corresponds to $T[i..j]$, then our retraversal costs $O(j-i)$ time, so the expected time to retraverse $T[1..n']$ is $O(n')$. Since we perform $O(\lg z)$ passes, the total cost may reach $O(n \lg z) = O(n \lg n)$.

We can reduce the time to $O(z \lg_\sigma n) = O(n)$ by storing, when we have to load H', $O(z/\lg_\sigma n)$ sampled nodes of H in a (classic) hash table W, which stores the position in H' of each sampled position in H. Table W uses $O(z \lg \sigma)$ bits, which is within our budget. We will guarantee that every node of LZTRIE whose depth is a multiple of $\lg_\sigma n$ and whose height is at least $\lg_\sigma n$ will be sampled. This ensures that $O(z/\lg_\sigma n)$ nodes are sampled and that we traverse less than $2 \lg_\sigma n$ nodes of H from any cell $L[r]$ before reaching a sampled node, from which we can descend in H' and insert $L[r]$ in time $O(\lg_\sigma n)$. Thus we do the translation in $O(|L| \lg_\sigma n)$ time. Since the size of L grows by a factor of $1/\alpha$ each time we create a larger table, the total work amounts to $O(z \lg_\sigma n)$. To obtain the sampling invariant, we start by sampling the root. Then, every time we traverse from the node of $L[r]$ upwards, if we traverse $\lg_\sigma n$ cells or more before finding a sampled node, we sample the node we traversed that is at distance $\lg_\sigma n$ from the sampled node we reached.

Once H' and D' are built, we continue with them and discard H and D. The peak space usage of the tables, when old and new ones are active, is $(1/\alpha^2 + 1/\alpha)z \lg \sigma + O(z) = O(z \lg \sigma)$ bits. Note that we can always keep the entries of L within $\lg z + O(1)$ bits, slightly expanding them when we retraverse L to rewrite the new positions in H'. At the end, L may need to point to a table H whose size is z/α^2, thus using $z \lg z + O(z)$ bits. To store H and D, we first write a bitvector B of length at most z/α^2 indicating which entries are $\neq -1$ in D. This requires $O(z)$ bits. Only the z filled entries of H and D are then written to the compressed file. The final compressed file size is then $z(\lg z + \lg \sigma) + O(z)$ bits.

Note that the $O(z)$ bits spent in L can be eliminated with a final pass on L replacing $L[r]$ by $rank_1(B, L[r])$, which is the number of 1s in B up to position $L[r]$. This can be computed in $O(z)$ time, and the values can be recovered in $O(z)$ time at decompression time using the complementary query $select_1(B, L[r])$ [4].

7   Using Multiple Hash Tables

A way to avoid rebuilding the hash table is to create additional hash tables apart from the original one, $H_0 = H$. When the load factor of H reaches α, we allocate a new table H_1, with $|H_1| = 2|H_0|$, where all the subsequent insertions will take place. When H_1 becomes full enough, we create H_2, with $|H_2| = 2|H_1|$, and so on, each time doubling the previously allocated space. Each table H_h has its own value M_h, prime P_h, and so on.

To properly address the nodes, we need to build a global address that can point to entries in any table. We regard the tables as their concatenation, that is, $H_0 H_1 H_2 \ldots$ The addresses within table H_h are built by adding $|H_0 H_1 \ldots H_{h-1}|$ to the normal address computation within H_h. The prime P_h must then be larger than $(M_0 + M_1 + \ldots + M_h) \cdot \sigma$, so as to store any element $(p(x), c)$ where $p(x)$ is a global address. This requires only $O(1)$ extra bits per cell to store $P_h/M_h \le 2\sigma$.

Assume we are at a node x in a table H_g and want to add a child $y = (x, c)$ in the current table H_h. The entry $(p(x), a)$ will be inserted in H_h, leaving no indication in H_g of the existence of y. This means that, if we want to descend from x by c, we must probe tables $H_g, H_{g+1}, \ldots, H_h$ to see if it was inserted in later tables. Therefore, the cost of traversing towards a child grows to $O(\lg z)$, as we can build that many tables during the parsing. However, since the children are inserted later than their parents, the current table index does not decrease as we move down from the root towards the node where we will insert the new block, and thus we do these $O(\lg z)$ probes once per inserted block, for a total time of $O(z \lg z) = O(n \lg \sigma)$.

Instead, the parent x is decoded immediately from $y = (p(x), a)$, since $p(x)$ is a global address, and this allows decompressing in $O(n)$ time. Finding the table H_g from $p(x)$ is a matter of dividing $p(x)$ by $\sqrt{n}$ and then finding the logarithm in base 2, which is done in constant time in most architectures (and in theory, using constant precomputed tables of small size).

This technique has the advantage that it treats T and L in streaming mode, as it does not have to retraverse them. The values written on L are final (note that their width grows along the process, each time we start using a new table). These can be compacted as in the previous section if we are willing to perform a second pass on L.

8   Simplifying Assumptions

Our expected-case analysis inherits some simplifications from Poyias et al. [14], when it assumes constant expected time for hashing with linear probing.

A first one is that analyses usually assume that the hash function is chosen independently of the set of values to hash. In our scheme, however, the values $(p(x), c)$ to hash depend on the hash function $h(x)$ itself. So, at least in principle, the typical assumptions to prove 2-independence do not hold, even if we changed our function to the standard $((a_0 + a_1 \cdot w(y)) \bmod M) \bmod P$ for randomly chosen a_0 and a_1.

Another issue is that 2-independence may not be sufficient to assume randomness in the case of linear probing. This has only been proved assuming 5-independence [12,13]. To make it 5-independent, the component $a \cdot w(y)$ of our hash function should become $a_0 + a_1 w(y) + a_2 w(y)^2 + a_3 w(y)^3 + a_4 w(y)^4$. We do not know how to invert such a function in order to find $w(y)$ given $h(y)$ and $v(y)$.

In the next section we show, however, that those theoretical reservations do not have a significant impact on the practical performance of the scheme.

9   Experimental Results

In this section we experimentally evaluate our new algorithms with some previous implemented alternatives. We measure compression and decompression time, RAM usage and overhead of the final file size compared with the standard LZ78 format. All the experiments were performed on an Intel(R) Core(TM) i7-5500U CPU at 2.40 GHz. The operating system was Ubuntu 16.04.2 LTS, version 4.4.0-72-generic Linux kernel. Our compressors were implemented in C++11, using g++ version 4.8.4.

The texts considered are a highly compressible XML text, an English text, and a less compressible Protein file, all obtained from the Pizza&Chili Corpus[1]. We also used a DNA file generated by extracting a prefix of a human genome[2]. Table 2 lists the test files used and their main statistics. For the compression ratio we assume that each of the z phrases gives the parent phrase number and the symbol. For the former, the next 2^i phrases use $i + 1$ bits, starting from the second with $i = 0$. For the latter, we use $\lceil \lg \sigma \rceil$ bits.

Table 2. Text files used in the experiments.

File name	Size n (Megabytes)	σ	Number z of phrases	Avg. phrase length (n/z)	Compr. ratio
XML	282.42	97	16,205,171	18.27	20.50%
English	1,024.00	237	96,986,744	11.07	37.96%
Proteins	1,129.20	27	147,482,019	8.03	48.55%
Human Genome	3,182.00	51	227,419,107	14.67	27.96%

Figure 1 shows the maximum RAM used by each structure during compression, and the resulting compression time. Our approaches are labeled HLZ (fixed hash table of maximum size, no rebuilding), MHLZ (multiple hash tables) and GHLZ (growing hash tables, no sampling). We obtain tradeoffs by using various load factors for the hash tables, $1/\alpha = 1.05, 1.10, 1.20, 1.40, 1.60$.

---

[1] http://pizzachili.dcc.uchile.cl/texts.
[2] http://hgdownload.cse.ucsc.edu/goldenPath/hg18/bigZips/est.fa.gz.

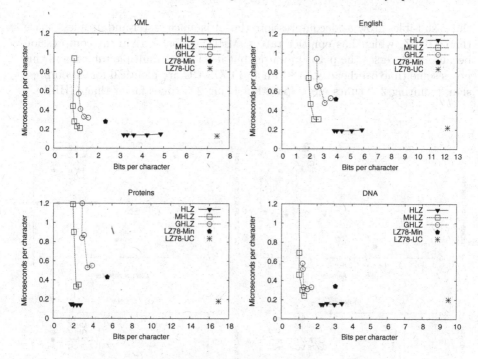

Fig. 1. Maximum RAM and time used during compression.

As previous work, we include LZ78-Min, the compact representation of Arroyuelo and Navarro [2], and LZ78-UC, their uncompressed baseline, both implemented in C.

It can be seen that MHLZ always outperforms GHLZ in space/time, using 1.0–2.2 bits and 0.2–0.3 μs per symbol with $1/\alpha = 1.40$. For the same space, the overhead of using multiple tables is lower than that of rebuilding the table, which implies rereading the L array from disk. In general, the time of MHLZ is very sensitive to high load factors, without significantly improving the space. With a sufficiently low load factor, instead, it outperforms all the others in time and space. It even gets close to the time of HLZ, always below 0.2 μs, with much less space (with the exception of Proteins, where the final-size guess of HLZ is nearly optimal). The maximum space usage of GHLZ occurs when it has to expand the table, at which moment it has the old and new tables in RAM. This requires more space than MHLZ even when the MHLZ tables are emptier on average. LZ78-Min, instead, requires 2–3 times more space and is up to 4 times slower. Finally, LZ78-UC requires 6–9 times more space than MHLZ, and is not faster than HLZ.

Figure 2 shows the RAM used by each structure during decompression. This time GHLZ always obtains the best time of MHLZ but using slightly less space. GHLZ uses 0.9–1.8 bits and 0.1–0.2 μs per symbol, even outperforming HLZ, which uses much more space (except on Proteins). GHLZ does not need to make the hash tables grow at decompression, thus it is much faster and uses less space than MHLZ, which has emptier tables. MHLZ is faster than for compression because it traverses the paths upwards, but it still uses multiple tables, and this poses some time overhead. LZ78-Min and LZ78-UC are identical for decompression, requiring 2–3 times more space but being 2–3 times faster than GHLZ.

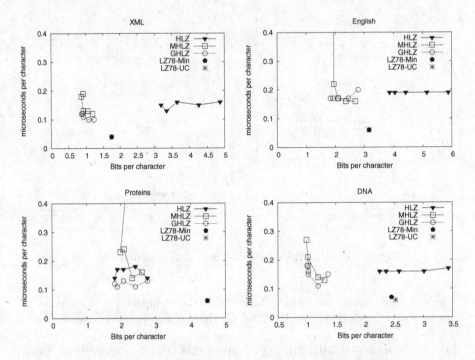

Fig. 2. Maximum RAM and time used during decompression.

Finally, Fig. 3 shows the ratio between the actual compressed file size and the output of a classical LZ78 compressor (see Table 2). We exclude the HLZ baseline because it does not really compress. While MHLZ poses 30%–40% of overhead, GHLZ requires 25%–35%. We note that, to reach this overhead, we need to use $1/\alpha = 1.1$ or less, that is, almost the slowest. In this case, it is preferable to use GHLZ, which uses 1–3 bits and 0.5–0.8 μs per symbol for compression and 0.1–0.2 μs for decompression. If we want to have the fastest MHLZ compression times, we must accept an overhead of 40%–45%. On the other hand, LZ78-Min has an overhead of 4%–15%.

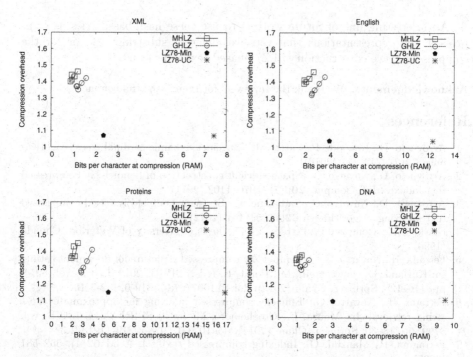

Fig. 3. Maximum RAM used at compression versus ratio of the final file size over the classical output size.

10   Conclusions

We have presented new LZ78 compression/decompression algorithms based on hashing, which under some simplifying assumptions use $O(z \lg \sigma)$ bits of main memory in expectation, while running in $O(n \lg \sigma)$ time for compression and $O(n)$ time for decompression, where n is the text length, z the number of LZ78 phrases, and σ the alphabet size. Our algorithms read the text once, in streaming mode, and write the output to disk. There exists no previous algorithm using so little main memory.

Our experiments show that our new methods use 2–3 times less space for compression than the most space-efficient implemented compressor in the literature, while being up to 4 times faster. Compared to a classical baseline, our compressor uses 6–9 times less space and is only 50% slower. Our decompressor uses 2–3 times less space than both baselines, but it is 2–3 times slower.

For example, our compressor can use up to 3 bits and $0.8\,\mu s$ per symbol and our decompressor up to 2 bits and $0.2\,\mu s$ per symbol, posing a space overhead around 30% over the optimally compressed file.

Our compressors and the competing algorithms are publicly available at https://github.com/rcanovas/Low-LZ78.

An interesting line of future work is to use these hash-based tries as compressed text representations that retrieve any text substring [16], or for the compressed-space construction of LZ78-based text indexes [2].

Acknowledgements. We thank the reviewers for their insightful comments.

References

1. Arroyuelo, D., Davoodi, P., Satti, S.R.: Succinct dynamic cardinal trees. Algorithmica **74**(2), 742–777 (2016)
2. Arroyuelo, D., Navarro, G.: Space-efficient construction of Lempel-Ziv compressed text indexes. Inf. Comput. **209**(7), 1070–1102 (2011)
3. Arroyuelo, D., Navarro, G., Sadakane, K.: Stronger Lempel-Ziv based compressed text indexing. Algorithmica **62**(1), 54–101 (2012)
4. Clark, D.R.: Compact PAT trees. Ph.D. thesis, University of Waterloo, Canada (1996)
5. Ferrada, H., Navarro, G.: A Lempel-Ziv compressed structure for document listing. In: Kurland, O., Lewenstein, M., Porat, E. (eds.) SPIRE 2013. LNCS, vol. 8214, pp. 116–128. Springer, Cham (2013). doi:10.1007/978-3-319-02432-5_16
6. Ferrada, H., Navarro, G.: Efficient compressed indexing for approximate top-k string retrieval. In: Moura, E., Crochemore, M. (eds.) SPIRE 2014. LNCS, vol. 8799, pp. 18–30. Springer, Cham (2014). doi:10.1007/978-3-319-11918-2_3
7. Ferragina, P., Manzini, G.: Indexing compressed texts. J. ACM **52**(4), 552–581 (2005)
8. Fischer, J., I, T., Köppl, D.: Lempel Ziv Computation in Small Space (LZ-CISS). In: Cicalese, F., Porat, E., Vaccaro, U. (eds.) CPM 2015. LNCS, vol. 9133, pp. 172–184. Springer, Cham (2015). doi:10.1007/978-3-319-19929-0_15
9. Hardy, G.H., Wright, E.M.: An Introduction to the Theory of Numbers, 6th edn. Oxford University Press, Oxford (2008)
10. Jansson, J., Sadakane, K., Sung, W.: Linked dynamic tries with applications to LZ-compression in sublinear time and space. Algorithmica **71**(4), 969–988 (2015)
11. Köppl, D., Sadakane, K.: Lempel-Ziv Computation in Compressed Space (LZ-CICS). In: Proceedings of 26th Data Compression Conference, pp. 3–12 (2016)
12. Pagh, A., Pagh, R., Ruzic, M.: Linear probing with 5-wise independence. SIAM Rev. **53**(3), 547–558 (2011)
13. Patrascu, M., Thorup, M.: On the k-independence required by linear probing and minwise independence. ACM Trans. Algorithms **12**(1) (2016). Article 8
14. Poyias, A., Puglisi, S.J., Raman, R.: m-Bonsai: a practical compact dynamic trie. In: Preliminary Version Proceedings of SPIRE 2015. LNCS, vol. 9309 (2017). CoRR abs/1704.05682. http://arxiv.org/abs/1704.05682,
15. Russo, L.M.S., Oliveira, A.L.: A compressed self-index using a Ziv-Lempel dictionary. Inf. Retrieval **11**(4), 359–388 (2008)
16. Sadakane, K., Grossi, R.: Squeezing succinct data structures into entropy bounds. In: Proceedings of 17th Annual ACM-SIAM Symposium on Discrete Algorithms (SODA), pp. 1230–1239 (2006)
17. Welch, T.A.: A technique for high performance data compression. IEEE Comput. **17**(6), 8–19 (1984)
18. Ziv, J., Lempel, A.: A universal algorithm for sequential data compression. IEEE Trans. Inf. Theory **23**(3), 337–343 (1977)
19. Ziv, J., Lempel, A.: Compression of individual sequences via variable length coding. IEEE Trans. Inf. Theory **24**(5), 530–536 (1978)

On Two LZ78-style Grammars: Compression Bounds and Compressed-Space Computation

Golnaz Badkobeh[1], Travis Gagie[2], Shunsuke Inenaga[3], Tomasz Kociumaka[4], Dmitry Kosolobov[5(✉)], and Simon J. Puglisi[5]

[1] Department of Computer Science, University of Warwick, Coventry, England
g.badkobeh@warwick.ac.uk
[2] CeBiB, EIT, Diego Portales University, Santiago, Chile
travis.gagie@mail.udp.cl
[3] Department of Informatics, Kyushu University, Fukuoka, Japan
inenaga@inf.kyushu-u.ac.jp
[4] Institute of Informatics, University of Warsaw, Warsaw, Poland
kociumaka@mimuw.edu.pl
[5] Department of Computer Science, University of Helsinki, Helsinki, Finland
dkosolobov@mail.ru, puglisi@cs.helsinki.fi

Abstract. We investigate two closely related LZ78-based compression schemes: LZMW (an old scheme by Miller and Wegman) and LZD (a recent variant by Goto et al.). Both LZD and LZMW naturally produce a grammar for a string of length n; we show that the size of this grammar can be larger than the size of the smallest grammar by a factor $\Omega(n^{\frac{1}{3}})$ but is always within a factor $O((\frac{n}{\log n})^{\frac{2}{3}})$. In addition, we show that the standard algorithms using $\Theta(z)$ working space to construct the LZD and LZMW parsings, where z is the size of the parsing, work in $\Omega(n^{\frac{5}{4}})$ time in the worst case. We then describe a new Las Vegas LZD/LZMW parsing algorithm that uses $O(z \log n)$ space and $O(n + z \log^2 n)$ time w.h.p.

Keywords: LZMW · LZD · LZ78 · Compression · Smallest grammar

1 Introduction

The LZ78 parsing [18] is a classic dictionary compression technique, discovered by Lempel and Ziv in 1978, that gained wide use during the 1990s in, for example, the Unix compress tool and the GIF image format. Not written about until much later was that LZ78 actually produces a representation of the input string as a context-free grammar. In recent years, grammar compressors have garnered immense interest, particularly in the context of compressed text indexing: it is now

G. Badkobeh—Supported by the Leverhulme Trust's Early Career Scheme.

T. Kociumaka—Supported by Polish budget funds for science in 2013–2017 under the 'Diamond Grant' program.

S.J. Puglisi—Supported by the Academy of Finland via grant 294143.

© Springer International Publishing AG 2017
G. Fici et al. (Eds.): SPIRE 2017, LNCS 10508, pp. 51–67, 2017.
DOI: 10.1007/978-3-319-67428-5_5

possible to efficiently execute many operations directly on grammar-compressed strings, without resorting to full decompression (e.g., see [3,4,6,7,10,16]).

A wide variety of grammar compressors are now known, many of them analyzed by Charikar et al. [5] in their study of the smallest grammar problem, which is to compute the smallest context-free grammar that generates the input string (and only this string). Charikar et al. show that this problem is NP-hard, and further provide lower bounds on approximation ratios for many grammar compressors. LZ78 is shown to approximate the smallest grammar particularly poorly, and can be larger than the smallest grammar by a factor $\Omega(n^{\frac{2}{3}}/\log n)$ (in [9] this bound was improved to $\Omega((\frac{n}{\log n})^{\frac{2}{3}}))$, where n is the input length.

Our focus in this paper is on the LZD [8] and LZMW [14] grammar compression algorithms, two variants of LZ78 that usually outperform LZ78 in practice. Despite their accepted empirical advantage over LZ78, no formal analysis of the compression performance of LZD and LZMW in terms of the size of the smallest grammar exists. This paper addresses that need. Moreover, we show that the standard algorithms for computing LZD and LZMW have undesirable worst case performance, and provide an alternative algorithm that runs in log-linear randomized time. In particular the contributions of this article are as follows:

1. We show that the size of the grammar produced by LZD and LZMW can be larger than the size of the smallest grammar by a factor $\Omega(n^{\frac{1}{3}})$ but is always within a factor $O((\frac{n}{\log n})^{\frac{2}{3}})$. To our knowledge these are the first non-trivial bounds on compression performance known for these algorithms.
2. Space usage during compression is often a concern. For both LZD and LZMW, parsing algorithms are known that use $O(z)$ space, where z is the size of the final parsing. We describe strings for which these algorithms require $\Omega(n^{\frac{5}{4}})$ time. (The only previous analysis is an $O(n^2/\log n)$ upper bound [8].)
3. We describe a Monte-Carlo parsing algorithm for LZD/LZMW that uses a z-fast trie [2] and an AVL-grammar [15] to achieve $O(z \log n)$ space and $O(n + z \log^2 n)$ time for inputs over the integer alphabet $\{0, 1, \ldots, n^{O(1)}\}$. This algorithm works in the streaming model and computes the parsing with high probability. Using the Monte-Carlo solution, we obtain a Las Vegas algorithm that, with high probability, works in the same space and time.

In what follows we provide formal definitions and examples of LZD and LZMW parsings. Section 2 then establishes bounds for the approximation ratios for the sizes of the LZD/LZMW grammars. In Sect. 3 we consider the time efficiency of current space-efficient parsing schemes for LZD/LZMW. Section 4 provides an algorithm with significantly better (albeit randomized) performance. Conclusions and reflections are offered in Sect. 5.

Preliminaries. We consider strings drawn from an alphabet Σ of size $\sigma = |\Sigma|$. The *empty string* is denoted by ϵ. The ith letter of a string s is denoted by $s[i]$ for i such that $1 \leq i \leq |s|$, and the substring of s that begins at position i and ends at position j is denoted by $s[i..j]$ for $1 \leq i \leq j \leq |s|$. Let $s[i..j] = \epsilon$ if $j < i$. For any i, j, the set $\{k \in \mathbb{Z} \colon i \leq k \leq j\}$ (possibly empty) is denoted by $[i..j]$.

For convenience, we assume that the last letter of the input string s is \$, where \$ is a special delimiter letter that does not occur elsewhere in the string.

Definition 1. The *LZD (LZ–Double) parsing* [8] of a string s of length n is the parsing $s = p_1 p_2 \cdots p_z$ such that, for $i \in [1..z]$, $p_i = p_{i_1} p_{i_2}$ where p_{i_1} is the longest prefix of $s[k..n]$ and p_{i_2} is the longest prefix of $s[k + |p_{i_1}|..n]$ with $p_{i_1}, p_{i_2} \in \{p_1, \ldots, p_{i-1}\} \cup \Sigma$ where $k = |p_1 \cdots p_{i-1}| + 1$. We refer to the set $\Sigma \cup \bigcup_{i \in [1..z]} \{p_i\}$ as the *dictionary of LZD*.

Definition 2. The *LZMW (LZ–Miller–Wegman) parsing* [14] of a string s of length n is the parsing $s = p_1 p_2 \cdots p_z$ such that, for $i \in [1..z]$, p_i is the longest prefix of $s[k..n]$ with $p_i \in \{p_j p_{j+1} : 1 \leq j \leq i-2\} \cup \Sigma$ where $k = |p_1 \cdots p_{i-1}| + 1$. We refer to the set $\bigcup_{i \in [2..z]} \{p_{i-1} p_i\}$ as the *dictionary of LZMW*.

Example. The LZD parsing of the string $s = abbaababaaba\$$ is $p_1 = ab$, $p_2 = ba$, $p_3 = abab$, $p_4 = aab$, and $p_5 = a\$$. This can be represented by $(a, b), (b, a), (1, 1), (a, 1), (a, \$)$. The LZMW parsing of s is the following: $p_1 = a$, $p_2 = b$, $p_3 = b$, $p_4 = a$, $p_5 = ab$, $p_6 = ab$, $p_7 = aab$, $p_8 = a$, and $p_9 = \$$. This can be represented by $(a, b, b, a, 1, 1, 4, a, \$)$.

Notice that the LZD/LZMW parsing of string s can be seen as a grammar that only generates s, with production rules of form $p_i \rightarrow p_j p_k$ $(j < i, k < i)$ or $p_i \rightarrow a$ $(\in \Sigma)$ for each phrase p_i, and the start rule $S \rightarrow p_1 p_2 \cdots p_z$. The *size* of a grammar is the total number of symbols in the right-hand side of the production rules. Thus, the size of the LZD (resp., LZMW) grammar is only by a constant factor larger than the number of phrases in the LZD (resp., LZMW) parsing.

2   Approximating the Smallest Grammar

The following theorem shows that, although LZD and LZMW have good compression performance in practice on high-entropy strings, their performance on low-entropy strings can be very poor.

Theorem 1. *For arbitrarily large n, there are strings s of length n for which the size of the grammars produced by the LZD and LZMW parsings is larger than the size of the smallest grammar generating s by a factor $\Omega(n^{\frac{1}{3}})$.*

Proof. Our proof is inspired by [5, Sect. 6, C]. Let $k \geq 4$ be an integer that is a power of 2. We will construct a string s of length $n = \Theta(k^3)$ that can be encoded by a grammar of size $O(k) = O(n^{\frac{1}{3}})$, but for which the LZMW parsing produces a grammar of size $\Omega(k^2) = \Omega(n^{\frac{2}{3}})$. The input alphabet is $\{a, b, c, d\}$; the letters c and d serve as separators. Denote $\delta_i = a^i b b a^{k-i}$ and $\gamma_i = ba^i \, a \, a^i b \, c \, ba \, ba^2 \, ba^3 \cdots ba^i$. The string s is as follows:

$$x = \delta_k \delta_{k-1} \, \delta_k \delta_{k-2} \, \delta_k \delta_{k-3} \cdots \delta_k \delta_{k/2+1} \, \delta_k a^{k-1},$$
$$s = \gamma_0 \gamma_1 \cdots \gamma_{k-1} \delta_0 d \delta_1 d \cdots \delta_k d \, caa \, caa^2 a^2 \cdots ca^{2^i-1} a^{2^i} a^{2^i} \cdots ca^{\frac{k}{2}-1} a^{\frac{k}{2}} a^{\frac{k}{2}} dc \, x^{\frac{k}{2}} \ .$$

We have $|s| = \Theta(k^3)$. Consider the prefix $\gamma_0\gamma_1\cdots\gamma_{k-1}\,\delta_0 d\delta_1 d\cdots d\delta_k d$, which will ensure the strings δ_i are in the LZMW dictionary.

We will show by induction on i that each substring γ_i of the prefix $\gamma_0\gamma_1\cdots\gamma_{k-1}$ is composed of the phrases ba^i, a, $a^i b$, $cbaba^2\cdots ba^i$ in the parsing of the string s. It is trivial for $i = 0$. Suppose that $i > 0$ and the assertion holds for all $\gamma_{i'}$ and $i' < i$. It follows from the inductive hypothesis that ba^i is the longest prefix of γ_i that is equal to a concatenation of two adjacent phrases introduced before the starting position of γ_i. Hence, by the definition of LZMW, the string γ_i starts with the phrase ba^i. In the same way we deduce that the phrase ba^i is followed by the phrases a, $a^i b$, and $cbaba^2\cdots ba^i$.

By an analogous inductive argument, one can show that each substring $\delta_i d$ of the substring $\delta_0 d\delta_1 d\cdots\delta_k dc$ is composed of the phrases $a^i b$, ba^{k-i}, d. Since the phrases $a^i b$ and ba^{k-i} are adjacent, the LZMW dictionary now contains the strings $\delta_i = a^i bba^{k-i}$ for all $i = 0, 1, \ldots, k$.

Similarly, the substring $caacaa^2 a^2\cdots ca^{2^i-1}a^{2^i}a^{2^i}\cdots ca^{\frac{k}{2}-1}a^{\frac{k}{2}}a^{\frac{k}{2}}dc$ is parsed as $c, a, a, ca, a^2, a^2, \ldots, ca^{2^i-1}, a^{2^i}, a^{2^i}, \ldots, ca^{\frac{k}{2}-1}, a^{\frac{k}{2}}, a^{\frac{k}{2}}, dc$. In what follows we need only the string a^k introduced to the dictionary by the pair of phrases $a^{\frac{k}{2}}$.

Finally, consider the substring $x^{\frac{k}{2}}$. Observe that the first occurrence of x is parsed in (almost) the way it is written, i.e., it is parsed as $\delta_k, \delta_{k-1}, \delta_k, \delta_{k-2}, \ldots, \delta_k, \delta_{k/2+1}, \delta_k$. But the last phrase is a^k instead of a^{k-1}. In other words, the parsing of the second occurrence of x starts from the second position of x and, therefore, the first phrases of this parsing are as follows:

$$\delta_{k-1}, \delta_{k-2}, \delta_{k-1}, \delta_{k-3}, \ldots, \delta_{k-1}, \delta_{k/2}, \delta_{k-1}.$$

Again, the last phrase is a^k and, hence, the parsing of the third occurrence of x starts with the third position of x, and so on.

The LZMW parsing of s, therefore, consists of $\Omega(k^2)$ phrases and the size of the LZMW grammar is $\Omega(k^2)$. But there is a grammar of size $O(k)$ producing s:

$$S \to \Gamma_0\Gamma_1\cdots\Gamma_{k-1}\Delta_0 d\Delta_1 d\cdots\Delta_k dcA_2 cA_5 cA_{11}\cdots cA_{k/2+k-1}dcX^{k/2},$$
$$A_0 \to \epsilon, \quad B_0 \to c, \quad A_i \to A_{i-1}a, \quad B_i \to B_{i-1}bA_i \quad \text{for } i \in [1..2k],$$
$$\Gamma_i \to bA_{2i+1}bB_i, \quad \Delta_i \to A_i bbA_{k-i} \quad \text{for } i \in [0..k],$$
$$X \to \Delta_k\Delta_{k-1}\Delta_k\Delta_{k-2}\cdots\Delta_k\Delta_{k/2+1}\Delta_k A_{k-1}.$$

Using similar ideas we can describe a troublesome string for the LZD scheme:

$$s = (a^2 c^2 a^3 c^3\cdots a^k c^k)(bb\,abb\,a^2 bb\,a^3\cdots bba^{k-1}bb)(\delta_0 d^2\delta_1 d^3\cdots\delta_k d^{k+2})x^{\frac{k}{2}}\;.$$

As above, the size of the grammar corresponding to the LZD parsing of s is $\Omega(k^2)$ whereas the size of the smallest grammar is $O(k)$; hence, the result follows.

$$S \to A_2 C_2 A_3 C_3\cdots A_k C_k bbA_1 bbA_2\cdots bbA_{k-1}bb\Delta_0 D_2\Delta_1 D_3\cdots\Delta_k D_{k+2}X^{k/2},$$
$$A_0 \to \epsilon, C_0 \to \epsilon, D_0 \to \epsilon, A_i \to A_{i-1}a, C_i \to C_{i-1}c, D_i \to D_{i-1}d \text{ for } i \in [1..k+2],$$
$$\Delta_i \to A_i bbA_{k-i} \text{ for } i \in [0..k], \quad X \to \Delta_k\Delta_{k-1}\Delta_k\Delta_{k-2}\cdots\Delta_k\Delta_{k/2+1}\Delta_k A_{k-1}.$$

The analysis is similar to the above but simpler, so, we omit it. To additionally verify the correctness of both constructions, we conducted experiments on small k and, indeed, observed the described behavior; the code can be found in [1]. □

We can also show that the upper bound for the approximation ratio of the LZ78 parsing given in [5] also applies to the LZD and LZMW parsings. For this, we will use the following known results.

Lemma 2 ([5]). *If there is a grammar of size m generating a given string, then this string contains at most mk distinct substrings of length k.*

Lemma 3 ([8]). *All phrases in the LZD parsing of a given string are distinct.*

Lemma 4. *Let $p_1 p_2 \cdots p_z$ be the LZMW parsing of a given string. Then, for any $i \in [2..z]$ and $j \in [i+2..z]$, we have $p_{i-1}p_i \neq p_{j-1}p_j$.*

Proof. If $p_{i-1}p_i = p_{j-1}p_j$ for $i < j - 1$, then, by the definition of LZMW, the phrase p_{j-1} either is equal to $p_{i-1}p_i$ or contains $p_{i-1}p_i$ as a prefix, which is a contradiction.   □

Now we are ready to show an upper bound on the approximation ratio of the LZD and LZMW parsings.

Theorem 5. *For all strings s of length n, the size of the grammar produced by the LZD/LZMW parsing is larger than the size of the smallest grammar generating s by at most a factor $O((n/\log n)^{2/3})$.*

Proof. The theorem can be shown by an analogous way as for the upper bound of the LZ78 parsing against the smallest grammar [5] (which is especially straightforward for LZD due to Lemma 3), but we provide a full proof for completeness.

Let us consider LZMW. Suppose that s is a string of length n and m^* is the size of the smallest grammar generating s. Let $p_1, p_2, \ldots, p_z$ be the LZMW parsing of s. It suffices to evaluate the number z of phrases since the total size of the grammar produced by LZMW is only by a constant factor larger than z.

Consider the multiset $S = \{p_1 p_2, p_2 p_3, \ldots, p_{z-1} p_z\}$ (recall that a multiset can contain an element more than one time). Let $p_{i_1}p_{i_1+1}, p_{i_2}p_{i_2+1}, \ldots, p_{i_{z-1}}p_{i_{z-1}+1}$ be a sequence of all strings from S sorted in increasing order of their lengths (again, some strings may occur more than once in the sequence). We partition the sequence by grouping the first $2 \cdot m^*$ strings, then the next $2 \cdot 2m^*$ strings, the next $2 \cdot 3m^*$ strings, and so forth. Let r be the minimal integer satisfying $2(1m^* + 2m^* + \cdots + rm^* + (r+1)m^*) > z$. This implies that $z = O(r^2 m^*)$.

By Lemma 4, any string has at most two occurrences in the multiset S. Also, it follows from Lemma 2 that s contains at most km^* distinct substrings of length k. Thus, for any $k \geq 1$, there are at most $2km^*$ strings from S that generate substrings of length k. This implies that each string in the kth group generates a substring of length at least k. Hence, we have that

$$2n \geq |p_{i_1}p_{i_1+1}| + |p_{i_2}p_{i_2+1}| + \cdots + |p_{i_{z-1}}p_{i_{z-1}+1}| \geq 2(1^2 m^* + 2^2 m^* + \cdots + r^2 m^*),$$

which implies that $r = O((n/m^*)^{1/3})$. By plugging this into $z = O(r^2 m^*)$, we obtain $z = O((n/m^*)^{2/3} m^*)$ and thus the approximation ratio of the grammar produced by LZMW is $O((n/m^*)^{2/3})$. Since $m^* = \Omega(\log n)$, we finally get the desired bound $O((n/\log n)^{2/3})$.

Let us sketch the analysis of LZD, which is very similar. In this case, we consider the set S' of all phrases $p_1, p_2, \ldots, p_z$ (not pairs as in LZMW) of the LZD parsing. Let $p_{i_1}, \ldots, p_{i_z}$ be the sequence of all strings from S' sorted by the increasing order of lengths. We partition the sequence into groups of size $1m^*, 2m^*, 3m^*, \ldots$ (without the factor 2 as in LZMW). It follows from Lemma 3 that any string occurs in S' at most once. Therefore, similar to the case of LZMW, we obtain $n = |p_{i_1}| + |p_{i_2}| + \cdots + |p_{i_z}| \geq 1^2 m^* + 2^2 m^* + \cdots + r^2 m^*$, which implies the result in the same way as above.   □

3   Small-Space Computation

In this section we analyze the time required to compute the LZD and LZMW parsings using the $O(z)$-space algorithms described by Goto et al. [8] and Miller and Wegman [14], where z is the number of phrases. We focus on LZD throughout, but a very similar algorithm and analysis applies for LZMW. Goto et al. upperbound the runtime at $O(z(m + \min(z, m) \log \sigma))$, where m is the length of the longest LZD (or LZMW) phrase and σ is the size of the input alphabet. Because $m = O(n)$ and $z = O(n)$, the runtime is upper bounded by $O(n^2)$. Below we provide a lower bound of $\Omega(n^{5/4})$ on the worst-case runtime, but before doing so we provide the reader with a description of Goto et al.'s algorithm [8].[1]

Naive Parsing Algorithms. In the compacted trie for a set of strings, each edge label ℓ is represented as a pair of positions delimiting an occurrence of ℓ in the set. In this way we can store the trie for $s_1, \ldots, s_k$ in $O(k)$ space. During parsing Goto et al. [8] maintain the dictionary of LZD phrases in a compacted trie. The trie is of size $O(z)$, but read-only random access to the input string is also required in order to determine the actual values of the strings on the edge labels.

Initially the trie is empty, consisting of only the root. At a generic step during parsing, when we go to compute the phrase $p_i = p_{i_1} p_{i_2}$ starting at position $j = |p_1 p_2 \ldots p_{i-1}| + 1$, the trie contains nodes representing the phrases $p_1, p_2, \ldots, p_{i-1}$ and all the distinct symbols occurring in $s[1..j-1]$, and all these nodes (corresponding to phrases and symbols) are marked. Note that there may also be some nodes in the trie that do not correspond to any phrase, i.e., branching nodes. Let $s[j..k]$ be the longest prefix of $s[j..n]$ that can be found by traversing the trie from the root. If $s[j..k]$ cannot be matched even for $k = j$, then $s[j]$ is the leftmost occurrence of symbol $c = s[j]$ in s, and we add a child node of the root labelled with c, mark the node, and set it as the first element of the new phrase, i.e., $p_{i_1} = c$. Otherwise, the first element of p_i, p_{i_1}, is the string written on the path connecting the root and the lowest marked node on the path that spells $s[j..k]$. The second element, p_{i_2}, of the phrase is computed in a similar manner, by searching for $s[j + |p_{i_1}| + 1..n]$ in the trie.

After computing p_i we modify the trie by a standard procedure so that there is a marked node representing p_i: first, we traverse the trie from the root finding

---

[1] We concern ourselves here with LZD parsing, but it should be easy for the reader to see that the algorithms are trivially adapted to instead compute LZMW.

the longest prefix of p_i present in the trie, then, possibly, create one or two new nodes, and, finally, mark the node (which, probably, did not exist before) corresponding to p_i (the details can be found in any stringology textbook).

The time taken to compute a new phrase and update the trie afterwards is bounded by $O(m + \min(z, m) \log \sigma)$, where $m = O(n)$ is the length of the longest phrase (and therefore an upper bound on the length of the longest path in the trie), $\min(z, m)$ is an upper bound on the number of branching nodes, and $\log \sigma$ is the time taken to find the appropriate outgoing edge at each branching node during downward traversal. Over all z phrases the runtime is thus $O(z(m + \min(z, m) \log \sigma))$.

The LZMW construction algorithm of Miller and Wegman [14] is analogous but, unlike the LZD algorithm, when we go to compute the phrase p_i, the trie contains the strings $p_1 p_2, p_2 p_3, \ldots, p_{i-2} p_{i-1}$ and the nodes corresponding to these strings are marked. One can easily show that the running time of this algorithm is $O(z(m + \min(z, m) \log \sigma))$, where z and m are defined analogously as for LZD.

We call both these algorithms *naïve*.

Worst-Case Time of the Naïve Algorithms. Now let us investigate the worst-case time complexity of the naïve LZD and LZMW construction algorithms.

Theorem 6. *The naïve LZD and LZMW construction algorithms take time $\Omega(n^{\frac{5}{4}})$ in the worst case.*

Proof. Let $k \geq 8$ be an integer that is a power of two. We will describe a string s of length $n = \Theta(k^4)$ for which the basic LZD construction algorithm (see the above discussion) spends $\Theta(n^{\frac{5}{4}})$ time to process. The string s is composed of pairwise distinct letters $a_{i,j}$, for $i, j \in [1..k]$, and "separator" letters, all of which are denoted $\diamond$ and supposed to be distinct. We will first construct a prefix s' of s that forces the algorithm to fill the dictionary with a set of strings that are used as building blocks in further constructions. To this end, denote (with parentheses used only for convenience):

$$w_i = a_{i,1} a_{i,2} \cdots a_{i,k} \text{ for } i = 1, 2, \ldots, k \text{ and } w = w_1 w_2 \cdots w_k,$$
$$s_{pre,i} = w_i[1..2] w_i[1..3] \cdots w_i[1..k] \text{ for } i = 1, 2, \ldots, k,$$
$$s_{suf,i} = w_i[k-1..k] w_i[k-2..k] \cdots w_i[2..k] \text{ for } i = 1, 2, \ldots, k,$$
$$p = (s_{pre,1} s_{pre,2} \cdots s_{pre,k})(s_{suf,1} s_{suf,2} \cdots s_{suf,k}),$$
$$q = (w_{k-2} w_{k-1})(w_{k-3} w_{k-2} w_{k-1}) \cdots (w_1 w_2 \cdots w_{k-1})(w),$$
$$s' = pq \cdot w^{2^1} w^{2^2} \cdots w^k (w_k[2..k] w^k)(w_k[3..k] w^k) \cdots (w_k[k..k] w^k).$$

Analyzing the prefix p of s', it is clear that the LZD construction algorithm adds to the dictionary exactly all prefixes and suffixes of the strings w_i for $i = 1, 2, \ldots, k$; parsing the string q, the algorithm adds the strings $w_{k-2} w_{k-1}, w_{k-3} w_{k-2} w_{k-1}, \ldots, w_1 w_2 \cdots w_{k-1}$, and $w_1 w_2 \cdots w_k = w$; then, processing the string $w^{2^1} w^{2^2} \cdots w^k$, the algorithm adds $w^{2^1}, w^{2^2}, \ldots, w^k$ (we are interested only in w^k); finally, the strings $w_k[2..k] w^k, w_k[3..k] w^k, \ldots, w_k[k..k] w^k$ are added. So, the algorithm adds to the dictionary exactly the following strings:

- all prefixes and suffixes of w_i (including w_i itself) for $i = 1, 2, \ldots, k$;
- $w_{k-2}w_{k-1}, w_{k-3}w_{k-2}w_{k-1}, \ldots, w_1 w_2 \cdots w_{k-1}$, and w;
- w^k along with $w^{k/2}, \ldots, w^{2^2}, w^2$ (we use only w^k in what follows);
- $w_k[2..k]w^k, w_k[3..k]w^k, \ldots, w_k[k..k]w^k$.

It is easy to verify that $|w| = k^2$, $|w^k| = k^3$, and $|s'| = \Theta(k^4)$. (The string $w_k[2..k]w^k w_k[3..k]w^k \cdots w_k[k..k]w^k$ contributes the most to the length.)

We first provide an overview of our construction. The main load on the running time of the algorithm is concentrated in the following strings z_i:

$$z_i = w_i[2..k]w_{i+1} \cdots w_k w^{k-2} w_1 \cdots w_i \text{ for } i = 1, 2, \ldots, k-2.$$

Put $s = s' x_1 z_1 \infty x_2 z_2 \infty \cdots x_{k-2} z_{k-2} \infty$, where $x_1, \ldots, x_k$ are auxiliary strings defined below. Before processing of z_i, the algorithm processes x_i and adds the strings $w_i[j..k]w_{i+1} \cdots w_{k-1}w_k[1..j-1]$ and $w_k[j..k]w_1 \cdots w_{i-1}w_i[1..j]$ for $j \in [2..k]$ to the dictionary (see below). So, analyzing z_i, the algorithm consecutively "jumps", for $j = 2, 3, \ldots, k$, from the string $w_i[j..k]w_{i+1} \cdots w_{k-1}w_k[1..j-1]$ to $w_k[j..k]w_1 \cdots w_{i-1}w_i[1..j]$ and so on. The crucial point is that, while analyzing the string $w_k[j..k]w_1 \cdots w_{i-1}w_i[1..j]$, the algorithm does not know in advance that the string $w_k[j..k]w^k$ from the dictionary does not occur at this position and, since the length of the longest common prefix of the strings $w_k[j..k]w^k$ and $w_k[j..k]w^{k-j}w_1 \cdots w_i \infty$ is $\Theta(k - j + 1 + |w^{k-j}|)$, spends $\Theta(|w^{k-j}|) = \Theta((k - j)k^2)$ time verifying this. Therefore, the analysis of the string s takes $\Theta((k - 2)\sum_{j=2}^{k}(k - j)k^2) = \Theta(k^5)$ time overall. Since $|z_i| = O(k^3)$ and, as it is shown below, $|x_i| = O(k^3)$, we have $n = |s| = \Theta(k^4)$ and the processing time is $\Theta(n^{\frac{5}{4}})$ as required. We now describe this in more detail.

We prove by induction that the following invariant is maintained: when the algorithm starts the processing of the suffix $x_i z_i \infty \cdots x_{k-2} z_{k-2} \infty$ of the string s (x_i are defined below), the dictionary contains the following set of strings:

- "building blocks" constructed during the processing of s';
- pairs of separators ∞ (recall that all separators are distinct);
- for each $i' \in [1..i-1]$ and $j \in [2..k]$:
  - $w_{i'}[j..k]w_{i'+1} \cdots w_{k-1}w_k[1..j-1]$ and $w_k[j..k]w_1 \cdots w_{i'-1}w_{i'}[1..j]$,
  - $w_{i'}[j..k]w_{i'+1} \cdots w_{k-1}$ and $w_k[j..k]w_1 \cdots w_{i'-1}$,
  - $w_{i'}[j..k]w_{i'+1} \cdots w_k w_1 \cdots w_{i'-1}w_{i'}[1..j]$.

The strings from the last two lines in the above list are not used and appear as byproducts. (But it is still important to have them in mind to verify that the algorithm works as expected.) So, assume that, by inductive hypothesis, the invariant holds for all $i' \in [1..i-1]$ (it is trivial for $i = 1$).

Define x_i as follows (the parentheses are only for visual ease):

$$u'_{i,j} = (w_k[j..k]w_1 \cdots w_{i-1}w_i[1..j]),$$
$$u_{i,j} = (w_k[j..k]w_1 \cdots w_{i-2}w_{i-1}[1..j])(w_{i-1}[j+1..k])u'_{i,j},$$
$$v_{i,j} = (w_i[j..k]w_{i+1} \cdots w_{k-1})(w_i[j..k]w_{i+1} \cdots w_{k-1}w_k[1..j-1]),$$
$$x_1 = (u'_{1,2} \infty u'_{1,3} \infty \cdots u'_{1,k-1} \infty u'_{1,k} \infty)(v_{1,2} \infty v_{1,3} \infty \cdots v_{1,k} \infty),$$
$$x_i = (u_{i,2} \infty u_{i,3} \infty \cdots u_{i,k-1} \infty u'_{i,k} \infty)(v_{i,2} \infty v_{i,3} \infty \cdots v_{i,k} \infty), \text{ for } i \neq 1.$$

Clearly $|x_i| = O(k^3)$. Using the hypothesis, one can show that the algorithm adds the strings $w_k[j..k]w_1 \cdots w_{i-1}$ $(j \neq k)$, $w_k[j..k]w_1 \cdots w_{i-1}w_i[1..j]$, $w_i[j..k]w_{i+1} \cdots w_{k-1}$, $w_i[j..k]w_{i+1} \cdots w_{k-1}w_k[1..j-1]$ for $j \in [2..k]$ to the dictionary after the processing of x_i (plus several pairs $\diamond\diamond$). It remains to show that the algorithm adds exactly the strings $w_i[j..k]w_{i+1} \cdots w_k w_1 \cdots w_{i-1}w_i[1..j]$, for $j \in [2..k]$, to the dictionary when processing z_i.

Observe that, for $j \in [2..k]$, $w_i[j..k]w_{i+1} \cdots w_{k-1}w_k[1..j-1]$ is the longest string from the dictionary that has prefix $w_i[j..k]$, and $w_k[j..k]w_1 \cdots w_{i-1}w_i[1..j]$ is the longest string from the dictionary that has prefix $w_k[j..k]$ and does not coincide with $w_k[j..k]w^k$. Hence, the algorithm consecutively "jumps" over the substrings w of the string z_i adding after each such "jump" the string $w_i[j..k]w_{i+1} \cdots w_k w_1 \cdots w_{i-1}w_i[1..j]$ to the dictionary (for $j = 2, 3, \ldots, k$). No other strings are added.

Each time the algorithm processes a substring $w_k[j..k]w_1 \cdots w_{i-1}w_i[1..j]$, it also verifies in $\Theta(ki + |w^{k-j}|)$ time whether the string $w_k[j..k]w^k$ occurs at this position. Therefore, by the above analysis, processing takes $\Theta(|s|^{\frac{5}{4}})$ time.

An analogous troublesome string for the naïve LZMW construction algorithm is as follows (again, all separators $\diamond$ are assumed to be distinct letters):

$$w_i = a_{i,1}a_{i,2} \cdots a_{i,k} \text{ and } w = w_1 w_2 \cdots w_k,$$
$$s_{pre,i} = w_i[1..2]\diamond w_i[1..3]\diamond \cdots \diamond w_i[1..k]\diamond,$$
$$s_{suf,i} = w_i[k-1..k]\diamond w_i[k-2..k]\diamond \cdots \diamond w_i[2..k]\diamond,$$
$$p = s_{pre,1}s_{pre,2} \cdots s_{pre,k}s_{suf,1}s_{suf,2} \cdots s_{suf,k},$$
$$q = w_{k-2}w_{k-1}\diamond w_{k-3}w_{k-2}w_{k-1}\diamond \cdots \diamond w_1 w_2 \cdots w_{k-1}\diamond w\diamond,$$
$$s' = pqw^{2^1}\diamond w^{2^2}\diamond \cdots \diamond w^k \diamond w_k[2..k]w^k \diamond w_k[3..k]w^k \diamond \cdots \diamond w_k[k..k]w^k \diamond,$$
$$y_j = w_k[j..k]w_1 \diamond w_k[j..k]w_1 w_2[1..j]\diamond,$$
$$t_{i,j} = w_{i-2}[j+1..k]w_{i-1}[1..j]\diamond w_{i-1}[j+1..k]w_i[1..j],$$
$$u_{i,j} = (w_k[j..k]w_1 \cdots w_{i-3}w_{i-2}[1..j])(w_{i-2}[j+1..k]w_{i-1}[1..j]),$$
$$v_{i,j} = w_i[j..k]w_{i+1} \cdots w_{k-1}\diamond w_i[j..k]w_{i+1} \cdots w_{k-1}w_k[1..j-1],$$
$$x_i = t_{i,2}\diamond t_{i,3}\diamond \cdots \diamond t_{i,k-1}\diamond u_{i,2}u_{i,3}\diamond \cdots \diamond u_{i,k}\diamond v_{i,2}\diamond v_{i,3}\diamond \cdots \diamond v_{i,k}\diamond,$$
$$z_i = w_i[2..k]w_{i+1} \cdots w_k w^{k-2}w_1 \cdots w_i \diamond,$$
$$s = s'y_2 y_3 \cdots y_k x_4 z_4 x_6 z_6 \cdots x_{2j} z_{2j} \cdots x_{k-2}z_{k-2}.$$

Let us explain on a high level why the LZMW algorithm works slowly on s. While analyzing the prefix $s'y_2 y_3 \cdots y_k$, the algorithm adds a number of "building block" strings into the LZMW dictionary, including the strings $w[j..k]w^k$ for $j = 2, 3, \ldots, k$ (recall that, unlike the LZD dictionary containing phrases, the LZMW dictionary contains pairs of adjacent phrases). Before the processing of z_i, the algorithm processes x_i and adds the strings $w_i[j..k]w_{i+1} \cdots w_{k-1}w_k[1..j-1]$ (from $v_{i,j}$), $w_k[j..k]w_1 \cdots w_{i-2}w_{i-1}[1..j]$ (from $u_{i,j}$), and $w_{i-1}[j+1..k]w_i[1..j]$ (from $t_{i,j}$) to the dictionary. The concatenation of these three strings is $w_i[j..k]w_{i+1} \cdots w_k w_1 \cdots w_{i-1}w_i[1..j]$, so, analyzing z_i, the algorithm consecutively "jumps", for $j = 2, 3, \ldots, k$, from the string $w_i[j..k]w_{i+1} \cdots w_{k-1}w_k[1..j-1]$ to $w_k[j..k]w_1 \cdots w_{i-2}w_{i-1}[1..j]$ and then to $w_{i-1}[j+1..k]w_i[1..j]$, thus producing three new phrases (and then moves on to $j+1$). The point is that, while analyzing the string $w_k[j..k]w_1 \cdots w_{i-2}w_{i-1}[1..j]$,

the algorithm does not know in advance that the string $w_k[j..k]w^k$ from
the dictionary does not occur at this position and, since the length of the
longest common prefix of the strings $w_k[j..k]w^k$ and $w_k[j..k]w^{k-j}w_1 \cdots w_i \diamond$ is
$\Theta(k - j + 1 + |w^{k-j}|)$, spends $\Theta(|w^{k-j}|) = \Theta((k - j)k^2)$ time verifying this.
Therefore, the analysis of the string s takes $\Theta((k/2) \sum_{j=2}^{k} (k - j)k^2) = \Theta(k^5)$
time overall. Since $n = |s| = \Theta(k^4)$, the processing time is $\Theta(n^{\frac{5}{4}})$ as required.
We omit the detailed proof since it is very similar to the LZD case.

To additionally verify the correctness of both constructed examples, we performed the naïve LZD and LZMW algorithms (with some diagnostics to track
their execution) on the examples for small k and, indeed, observed the expected
"bad" behavior in the special positions described above. Our verifying code (it
can be found in [1]) thoroughly checks the correspondence of the behavior of the
parsers in the special positions to the behavior discussed in the above text. Thus,
we hope that the correctness of both our constructions is well supported.   □

We now explain how to decrease the alphabet size in the examples of
Theorem 6. The construction for both parsing schemes relies on the following
reduction.

Lemma 7. *Consider the parsing scheme LZD or LZMW and a string $s \in \Sigma^*$.
There exists a string $t \in \{0, 1\}^*$ of length $\Theta(|\Sigma| \log |\Sigma|)$ and a morphism ϕ with
$\phi(\Sigma) \subseteq \{0, 1\}^\ell$ for $\ell = \Theta(\log |\Sigma|)$ such that the parsing of $t \cdot \phi(s)$ consists of the
parsing of t followed by the image with respect to ϕ of the parsing of s.*

Proof. We analyze the two parsing schemes separately. For LZD, we recursively
define $A_L \subseteq \{0, 1\}^{2^L}$, setting $A_0 = \{0, 1\}$ and $A_L = \{xy : x, y \in A_{L-1} \wedge x \le y\}$
for $L > 0$. Let $(\alpha_i)_{i=1}^{\infty}$ be the infinite sequence of all elements of A_L, for all $L \ge$
1, with members of each set A_L listed in the lexicographic order; e.g., $\alpha_1, \ldots, \alpha_{12}$
$= 00, 01, 11, 0000, 0001, 0011, 0101, 0111, 1111, 00000000, 00000001, 00000011$. We
will define $t = \alpha_1 \cdots \alpha_m$ for some m. Let us characterize parsings of such strings.

Claim. For any non-negative integer m and any string $w \in \{0, 1\}^*$, the first m
phrases of the LZD parsing of the binary string $\alpha_1 \cdots \alpha_m \cdot w$ are $\alpha_1, \ldots, \alpha_m$.

Proof. We proceed by induction on m; the base case of $m = 0$ is trivial.

For $m > 0$, the inductive assumption implies that the first $m - 1$ phrases are
$\alpha_1, \ldots, \alpha_{m-1}$. Our goal is to prove that the mth phrase is α_m. Before processing
α_m, the LZD dictionary is $D = \{0, 1, \alpha_1, \ldots, \alpha_{m-1}\}$. Suppose that $\alpha_m = xy \in$
A_L with $x, y \in A_{L-1}$. Recall that $x \le y$; consequently, $D \cap (y \cdot \{0, 1\}^*) = \{y\}$
and
$$D \cap (x \cdot \{0, 1\}^*) = \{x\} \cup \{xy' : y' \in A_{L-1} \wedge x \le y' < y\}.$$
Thus, the longest prefix of $\alpha_m \cdot w$ contained in D is x, and the longest prefix of
$y \cdot w$ contained in D is y. This means that the mth phrase is indeed $\alpha_m = xy$.   □

Consider a string $s \in \Sigma^n$. We choose the smallest L with $|A_L| \ge |\Sigma|$ and
define $t = \alpha_1 \cdots \alpha_m$ so that t is shortest possible and the LZD dictionary after

processing t contains at least $|\Sigma|$ elements of A_L. The morphism ϕ is then defined by injectively mapping Σ to these dictionary strings from A_L.

Note that $|A_{L-1}| \leq |\Sigma|$ and $m \leq |\Sigma| + \sum_{\ell=1}^{L-1} |A_\ell|$, so we have $m = \Theta(|\Sigma|)$, $\ell = 2^L = \Theta(\log|\Sigma|)$, and $|t| = \Theta(|\Sigma|\log|\Sigma|)$, as desired.

We are to prove that the LZD parsing of $t \cdot \phi(s)$ is $\alpha_1, \ldots, \alpha_m, \phi(p_1), \ldots, \phi(p_z)$, where $p_1, \ldots, p_z$ is the LZD parsing of s. For this, we inductively prove that the LZD dictionary D after parsing $p_1 \cdots p_i$ is related to the LZD dictionary $\hat{D}$ after parsing $t \cdot \phi(p_1 \cdots p_i)$ by the following invariant: $\hat{D} \cap (\phi(\Sigma) \cdot \{0,1\}^*) = \phi(D)$. The base case follows from the claim $(\hat{D} \cap (\phi(\Sigma) \cdot \{0,1\}^*) = \phi(\Sigma) = \phi(D))$, and the inductive step is straightforward. This completes the proof for the LZD scheme.

The construction for LZMW is more involved, but the idea is the same. We recursively define $B_L \subseteq \{0,1\}^{2^L}$, setting $B_0 = \{0,1\}$ and $B_L = \{xy : x, y \in B_{L-1} \wedge xy \neq 1^{2^{L-1}} 0^{2^{L-1}}\}$ for $L > 0$. Let $(\beta_i)_{i=1}^\infty$ be the infinite sequence that lists all elements of B_L consecutively for all $L \geq 0$, with members of each B_L listed in the lexicographic order (i.e., $(\beta_i)_{i=1}^\infty$ is defined by analogy with $(\alpha_i)_{i=1}^\infty$ for LZD but starting with $L = 0$). For $\beta_m \in B_L$, define $b(\beta_m) = \beta_M \beta_m \cdot \beta_{M+1}\beta_m \cdots \beta_{m-1}\beta_m \cdot \beta_m$, where $\beta_M = 0^{2^L}$ is the first element of B_L in $(\beta_i)_{i=1}^\infty$. For example, $b(\beta_1) \cdots b(\beta_6) = 0 \cdot 0 \ 1 \ 1 \cdot 00 \cdot 00 \ 01 \ 01 \cdot 00 \ 11 \ 01 \ 11 \ 11 \cdot 0000$.

Claim. For $m \geq 1$, consider a binary string $b(\beta_1) \cdots b(\beta_m) \cdot 0^{|\beta_m|} \cdot w$ for $w \in \{0,1\}^*$. The LZMW parsing decomposes its fragments $b(\beta_i)$ into phrases of length $|\beta_i|$.

Proof. We proceed by induction on m. The base case $m = 1$ is straightforward: it suffices to note that the first phrase of $0 \cdot 0 \cdot w$ is 0. Below, we consider $m > 1$.

First, suppose that $\beta_m = 0^{2^L}$, i.e., $\beta_{m-1} = 1^{2^{L-1}} \in B_{L-1}$. Note that $b(\beta_m)$ starts with $0^{2^{L-1}}$, so the inductive hypothesis yields that the prefix $b(\beta_1) \cdots b(\beta_{m-1})$ is parsed as desired. Observe that after parsing this prefix, the LZMW dictionary is $D = \{1^{2^{\ell-1}} 0^{2^\ell} : 0 < \ell < L\} \cup \bigcup_{\ell=0}^L B_\ell$. Consequently, we obtain $D \cap (B_L \cdot \{0,1\}^*) = B_L$ and, therefore, $b(\beta_m) = \beta_m$ is parsed as claimed.

Finally, suppose that $\beta_m \in B_L \setminus \{0^{2^L}\}$. In this case, $\beta_{m-1} \in B_L$ and $\beta_M = 0^{2^L}$ for some $M < m$. Since $b(\beta_m)$ starts with $\beta_M = 0^{2^L}$, the inductive hypothesis lets us assume that the prefix $b(\beta_1) \cdots b(\beta_{m-1})$ is parsed as desired. Due to $1^{2^{L-1}} 0^{2^L-1} \notin B_L$, after parsing this prefix, the LZMW dictionary D satisfies:

$$D \cap (B_L \cdot \{0,1\}^*) = B_L \cup \{\beta_k \beta_{k'} : M \leq k, k' < m \wedge (k, k') \neq (m-1, M)\}.$$

Let us consider the parsing of $b(\beta_m) 0^{2^L} w = \beta_M \beta_m \cdot \beta_{M+1}\beta_m \cdots \beta_{m-1}\beta_m \cdot \beta_m \cdot 0^{2^L} w$. One can inductively prove that before parsing $\beta_k \beta_m \cdot \beta_{k+1} \cdots$, for $M \leq k < m$, we have $D \cap (\beta_k \cdot \{0,1\}^*) = \{\beta_k\} \cup \{\beta_k \beta_{k'} : M \leq k' < m\}$, so the subsequent phrase is β_k. Next, before parsing $\beta_m \cdot \beta_{k+1} \cdots$, for $M \leq k < m$, we have $D \cap (\beta_m \cdot \{0,1\}^*) = \{\beta_m\} \cup \{\beta_m \beta_{k'} : M < k' \leq k\}$, so the subsequent phrase is β_m. Finally, before parsing $\beta_m \cdot 0^{2^L} w$, we have $D \cap (\beta_m \cdot \{0,1\}^*) = \{\beta_m\} \cup \{\beta_m \beta_{k'} : M < k' < m\}$, so the last phrase is also β_m. Thus, $b(\beta_m)$ is parsed as claimed. $\square$

Consider a string $s \in \Sigma^n$. We choose the smallest L with $|B_L| \geq |\Sigma|$ and define $t = b(\beta_1) \cdots b(\beta_m)$ so that t is shortest possible and the LZMW dictionary after processing t contains at least $|\Sigma|$ members of B_L (note that $\beta_m \in B_{L-1}$ in this case). The morphism ϕ is then defined by injectively mapping Σ to these dictionary strings from B_L. Moreover, we put $\phi(s[1]) = 0^{2^L}$ so that the claim is applicable for $t \cdot \phi(s)$. The remaining proof is analogous to the LZD counterpart. We only need to observe that the LZMW dictionary additionally contains $\beta_m 0^{2^L}$, but $\beta_m 0^{2^{L-1}} \notin \phi(\Sigma)$ and, hence, this does not affect the parsing of $t \cdot \phi(s)$. $\square$

The hard binary examples are now straightforward to derive.

Theorem 8. *The naïve LZD and LZMW parsing algorithms take time $\Omega(n^{5/4}/\log^{1/4} n)$ in the worst case even on a binary alphabet.*

Proof. We apply Lemma 7 for a string $s \in \Sigma^*$ of length n constructed in the proof of Theorem 6 for the appropriate parsing algorithm, which results in a binary string $\hat{s} := t \cdot \phi(s)$. Without loss of generality, we may assume $|\Sigma| \leq n$, so $\hat{n} := |\hat{s}| = \Theta(|\Sigma| \log |\Sigma| + n \log |\Sigma|) = \Theta(n \log |\Sigma|)$. Recall that the naïve parsing algorithm traverses at least $\Omega(n^{5/4})$ trie edges while parsing s. Since the parsing of the suffix $\phi(s)$ of $\hat{s}$ is the ϕ-image of the parsing of s, this algorithm traverses at least $\Omega(n^{5/4} \log |\Sigma|)$ trie edges while parsing $\hat{s}$. In terms of $\hat{n}$, the running time is at least $\Omega(\hat{n}^{5/4}/\log^{1/4} |\Sigma|)$, which is $\Omega(\hat{n}^{5/4}/\log^{1/4} \hat{n})$ due to $|\Sigma| \leq n < \hat{n}$. $\square$

4   Faster Small-Space Computation

In this section we describe a new parsing algorithm that works in $O(n + z \log^2 n)$ time (randomized, in expectation) and uses $O(z \log n)$ working space to parse the input string over the integer alphabet $\{0, 1, \ldots, n^{O(1)}\}$. Before getting to the algorithm itself, we review four tools that are essential for it: Karp–Rabin hashing [11], AVL-grammars of Rytter [15], the dynamic z-fast trie of Belazzougui et al. [2], and the dynamic marked ancestor data structure of Westbrook [17].

Karp–Rabin Hashing. A Karp–Rabin [11] hash function ϕ has the form $\phi(s[1..n]) = \sum_{i=1}^{n} s[i]\delta^{i-1} \bmod p$, where p is a fixed prime and δ is a randomly chosen integer from the range $[0..p{-}1]$ (this is a more popular version of the original hash proposed in [11]). The value $\phi(s)$ is called s's Karp–Rabin hash. It is well-known that, for any $c > 3$, if $p > n^c$, then the probability that two distinct substrings of the given input string of length n have the same hash is less than $\frac{1}{n^{c-3}}$.

We extensively use the property that the hash of the concatenation $s_1 s_2$ of two strings s_1 and s_2 can be computed as $(\phi(s_1) + \delta^{|s_1|}\phi(s_2)) \bmod p$. Therefore, if the values $\phi(s_1)$ and $\phi(s_2)$ are known and $p \leq n^{O(1)}$, then $\phi(s_1 s_2)$ can be calculated in $O(1)$ time provided the number $(\delta^{|s_1|} \bmod p)$ is known.

AVL-Grammars. Consider a context-free grammar G that generates a string s (and only s). Denote by $Tree(G)$ the derivation tree of s. We say that G is an *AVL-grammar* (see [15]) if G is in the Chomsky normal form and, for every internal node v of $Tree(G)$, the heights of the trees rooted at the left and right children of v differ by at most 1. The following result straightforwardly follows from the algorithm of Rytter described in [15].

Lemma 9 (see [15, Theorem 2]). *Let G be an AVL-grammar generating a prefix $s[1..i-1]$ of a string s. Suppose that the string $s[i..k]$ occurs in $s[1..i-1]$; then one can construct an AVL-grammar generating the string $s[1..k]$ in $O(\log i)$ time modifying at most $O(\log i)$ rules in G.*

Let G be an AVL-grammar generating a string s. It is well-known that, for any substring $s[i..j]$, one can find in $O(\log n)$ time $O(\log n)$ non-terminals $A_1, \ldots, A_k$ such that $s[i..j]$ is equal to the string generated by $A_1 \cdots A_k$. Hence, if each non-terminal A of G is augmented with the Karp–Rabin hash $\phi(t)$ of the string t generated by A and with the number $\delta^{|t|} \bmod p$, then we can compute $\phi(s[i..j])$ in $O(\log n)$ time. One can show that, during the reconstruction of the AVL-grammar in Lemma 9, it is easy to maintain the described integers augmenting the non-terminals (see [15]).

Z-Fast Tries. Let x be a string such that one can compute the Karp–Rabin hash of any prefix of x in $O(t_x)$ time. The z-fast trie [2] is a compacted trie containing a dynamic set of variable-length strings that supports the following operations:

- we can find (w.h.p.) in $O(t_x \log |x|)$ time the highest explicit node v such that the longest prefix of x present in the trie is written on the root-v path;
- we can insert x into the trie in $O(|x| + t_x \log |x|)$ randomized time.

The space occupied by the z-fast trie is $\Theta(k)$, where k is the number of strings inserted in the trie.

Dynamic Marked Ancestor. Let T be a dynamic compacted trie (or just tree) with k nodes. The dynamic marked ancestor data structure of [17] supports the following two operations on T (both in $O(\log k)$ time): for a given node v, (1) mark v, (2) find the nearest marked ancestor of v (if any).

Algorithm. Our faster parsing algorithm computes the LZD phrases from left to right one by one, spending $O(\log^{O(1)} n)$ time on each phrase. We maintain an AVL-grammar G for the prefix $s[1..i-1]$ of s we have already parsed, and a z-fast trie T containing the first phrases $p_1, p_2, \ldots, p_r$ of the LZD parsing of s such that $s[1..i-1] = p_1 p_2 \cdots p_r$. We augment T with the dynamic marked ancestor data structure and mark all nodes corresponding to phrases (i.e., all nodes v such that the string written on the path from the root to v is equal to $t \in \{p_1, \ldots, p_r\}$). We augment each non-terminal of G with the Karp–Rabin hash $\phi(t)$ of this non-terminal's expansion t and with the number $\delta^{|t|} \bmod p$, so that the hash of any substring of $s[1..i-1]$ can by calculated in $O(\log n)$ time.

Suppose we are looking for the first part of the next phrase and that, in addition to having parsed $s[1..i-1]$, we have already read $s[i..j-1]$ without parsing it—but we have found the endpoints of an occurrence of $s[i..j-1]$ in $s[1..i-1]$. (Notice $s[i..j-1]$ can be empty, i.e., $i = j$.) Denote by x the longest prefix of $s[i..j-1]$ that is also a prefix of some of the phrases $p_1, \ldots, p_r$. Since we can compute quickly with G the hash of any prefix of $s[i..j-1]$, we can use the z-fast search to find in $O(\log^2 n)$ time a node v of T such that x is written on the path connecting the root and v. Let $s[\ell_v..r_v]$ be a substring of $s[1..i-1]$ corresponding to v (the numbers ℓ_v and r_v are stored with the node v). Using hashes and the binary search, we find the longest common prefix of the strings $s[i..j-1]$ and $s[\ell_v..r_v]$ (with high probability) in $O(\log^2 n)$ time; this prefix must be x.

If $s[i..j-1] \neq x$, then we perform a marked-ancestor query on the vertex corresponding to x (which can be found in $O(\log^2 n)$ time in the same way as v) and thus find the longest phrase that is a prefix of $s[i..j-1]$. We take that phrase as the first part of the next phrase and start over, looking for the second part, with the remainder of $s[i..j-1]$ now being what we have read but not parsed (of which we know an occurrence in $s[1..i-1]$). On the other hand, if $s[i..j-1] = x$, then we read $s[j..n]$ in blocks of length $\log^2 n$, stopping when we encounter an index k such that $s[i..k]$ is not a prefix of a phrase $p_1, \ldots, p_r$; the details follow.

Suppose that we have read q blocks and the concatenation $s[i..j+q\log^2 n-1]$ of $s[i..j-1]$ and the q previous blocks is a prefix of a phrase $t \in \{p_1, \ldots, p_r\}$. We compute in $O(\log^2 n)$ time the hashes of all the prefixes of the block $s[j + q\log^2 n..j + (q+1)\log^2 n - 1]$, which allows us to compute the hash of any prefix of $s[i..j + (q+1)\log^2 n - 1]$ in $O(\log n)$ time. Therefore, again using z-fast search and binary search, we can check in $O(\log^2 n)$ time if the block $s[j + q\log^2 n..j + (q+1)\log^2 n - 1]$ contains such a k—and, if so, find it. If k is not found, then using information from the search, we can find a phrase $t' \in \{p_1, \ldots, p_r\}$—which may or may not be equal to t—such that $s[i..j + (q+1)\log^2 n - 1]$ is a prefix of t'; we then proceed to the $(q+2)$nd block.

Once we have found such a k, we conceptually undo reading the characters from $s[k]$ onwards (which causes us to re-read later those $O(\log^2 n)$ characters), then perform a search and marked-ancestor query in T, which returns the longest phrase that is a prefix of $s[i..k-1]$. We take that longest phrase as the first part of the next phrase and start over, looking for the second part, with the remainder of $s[i..k-1]$ now being what we have read but not parsed (of which we know an occurrence in $s[1..i-1]$).

Once we have found both the first and second parts of the next phrase—say, p_1' and p_2'—we add the next phrase $p_{r+1} = p_1' p_2'$ to G (by Lemma 9) and to T, which takes $O(|p_{r+1}| + \log^2 n)$ time. In total, since processing each block takes $O(\log^2 n)$ time and the algorithm processes at most $z + \frac{n}{\log^2 n}$ blocks, we parse s in $O(n + z\log^2 n)$ time. Our space usage is dominated by G, which takes $O(z \log n)$ space. Finally, we verify in a straightforward manner in $O(n)$ time whether the constructed parsing indeed encodes the input string. If not (which can happen with probability $\frac{1}{n^{c-3}}$, where $p > n^c$), we choose a different random $\delta \in [0..p-1]$ for the Karp–Rabin hash and execute the whole algorithm again.

The computation of the LZMW parsing in $O(n + z \log^2 n)$ expected time and $O(z \log n)$ space is similar: the z-fast trie stores pairs $p_1 p_2, p_2 p_3, \ldots, p_{z-1} p_z$ of adjacent phrases in this case and the nodes corresponding to these pairs are marked. We omit the details as they are straightforward.

5   Concluding Remarks

We believe that our new parsing algorithms can be implemented efficiently, and we leave this as future work. Perhaps a more interesting question is whether there exists an LZD/LZMW parsing algorithm with better working space and the same (or better) runtime. We note that the algorithmic techniques we have developed here can also be applied to, e.g., develop more space-efficient parsing algorithms for LZ-End [13], a variant of LZ77 [19] with which each phrase $s[i..j]$ is the longest prefix of $s[i..n]$ such that an occurrence of $s[i..j-1]$ in $s[1..i-1]$ ends at a phrase boundary. Kempa and Kosolobov [12] very recently gave an LZ-End parsing algorithm that runs in $O(n \log \ell)$ expected time and $O(z + \ell)$ space, where ℓ is the length of the longest phrase and z is the number of phrases.

To reduce Kempa and Kosolobov's space bound, we keep an AVL-grammar (again augmented with the non-terminals' Karp–Rabin hashes, meaning our algorithm Monte-Carlo) of the prefix of s we have processed so far; a list of the endpoints of the phrases so far, in the right-to-left lexicographic order of the prefixes ending at the phrases' endpoints; and an undo stack of the phrases so far. For each character $s[k]$ in turn, for $1 \leq k \leq n$, in $O(\log^{O(1)} n)$ time we use the grammar and the list to find the longest suffix $s[j..k]$ of $s[1..k]$ such that an occurrence of $s[j..k-1]$ in $s[1..j-1]$ ends at a phrase boundary. We use the undo stack to remove from the grammar, the list, and the stack itself, all the complete phrases lying in the substring $s[j..k-1]$, and then add the phrase consisting of the concatenation of those removed phrases and $s[k]$. By [12, Lemma 3], we remove at most two phrases while processing $s[k]$, so we still use a total of $O(\log^{O(1)} n)$ worst-case time for each character of s. Again, the space bound is dominated by the grammar, which takes $O(z \log n)$ words. We leave the details for the full version of this paper.

Regarding compression performance, we have shown that like their ancestor, LZ78, both LZD and LZMW sometimes approximate the smallest grammar poorly. This, of course, does not necessarily detract from their usefulness in real compression tools; now however, practitioners have a much clearer picture of these algorithms' possible behavior. The future work includes closing the gap between the lower bound $\Omega(n^{\frac{1}{3}})$ and the upper bound $O((n/\log n)^{\frac{2}{3}})$ for the approximation ratio and designing parsing algorithms with better guarantees.

Acknowledgements. We thank H. Bannai, P. Cording, K. Dabrowski, D. Hücke, D. Kempa, L. Salmela for interesting discussions on LZD at the 2016 StringMasters and Dagstuhl meetings. Thanks also go to D. Belazzougui for advice about the z-fast trie and to the anonymous referees.

References

1. Supplementary materials for the present paper: C++ code for described experiments. https://bitbucket.org/dkosolobov/lzd-lzmw
2. Belazzougui, D., Boldi, P., Vigna, S.: Dynamic Z-Fast tries. In: Chavez, E., Lonardi, S. (eds.) SPIRE 2010. LNCS, vol. 6393, pp. 159–172. Springer, Heidelberg (2010). doi:10.1007/978-3-642-16321-0_15
3. Belazzougui, D., Cording, P.H., Puglisi, S.J., Tabei, Y.: Access, rank, and select in grammar-compressed strings. In: Bansal, N., Finocchi, I. (eds.) ESA 2015. LNCS, vol. 9294, pp. 142–154. Springer, Heidelberg (2015). doi:10.1007/978-3-662-48350-3_13
4. Bille, P., Landau, G.M., Raman, R., Sadakane, K., Satti, S.R., Weimann, O.: Random access to grammar-compressed strings and trees. SIAM J. Comput. 44(3), 513–539 (2015)
5. Charikar, M., Lehman, E., Liu, D., Panigrahy, R., Prabhakaran, M., Sahai, A., Shelat, A.: The smallest grammar problem. IEEE Trans. Inf. Theor. 51(7), 2554–2576 (2005)
6. Claude, F., Navarro, G.: Self-indexed grammar-based compression. Fundamenta Informaticae 111(3), 313–337 (2011)
7. Gagie, T., Gawrychowski, P., Kärkkäinen, J., Nekrich, Y., Puglisi, S.J.: A faster grammar-based self-index. In: Dediu, A.-H., Martín-Vide, C. (eds.) LATA 2012. LNCS, vol. 7183, pp. 240–251. Springer, Heidelberg (2012). doi:10.1007/978-3-642-28332-1_21
8. Goto, K., Bannai, H., Inenaga, S., Takeda, M.: *LZD Factorization*: simple and practical online grammar compression with variable-to-fixed encoding. In: Cicalese, F., Porat, E., Vaccaro, U. (eds.) CPM 2015. LNCS, vol. 9133, pp. 219–230. Springer, Cham (2015). doi:10.1007/978-3-319-19929-0_19
9. Hucke, D., Lohrey, M., Reh, C.P.: The smallest grammar problem revisited. In: Inenaga, S., Sadakane, K., Sakai, T. (eds.) SPIRE 2016. LNCS, vol. 9954, pp. 35–49. Springer, Cham (2016). doi:10.1007/978-3-319-46049-9_4
10. I, T., Nakashima, Y., Inenaga, S., Bannai, H., Takeda, M.: Efficient Lyndon factorization of grammar compressed text. In: Fischer, J., Sanders, P. (eds.) CPM 2013. LNCS, vol. 7922, pp. 153–164. Springer, Heidelberg (2013). doi:10.1007/978-3-642-38905-4_16
11. Karp, R.M., Rabin, M.O.: Efficient randomized pattern-matching algorithms. IBM J. Res. Devel. 31(2), 249–260 (1987)
12. Kempa, D., Kosolobov, D.: LZ-End parsing in compressed space. In: Proceedings of Data Compression Conference (DCC), pp. 350–359. IEEE (2017)
13. Kreft, S., Navarro, G.: On compressing and indexing repetitive sequences. Theoret. Comput. Sci. 483, 115–133 (2013)
14. Miller, V.S., Wegman, M.N.: Variations on a theme by Ziv and Lempel. In: Apostolico, A., Galil, Z. (eds.) Proceedings of NATO Advanced Research Workshop on Combinatorial Algorithms on Words, NATO ASI, vol. 12, pp. 131–140. Springer, Heidelberg (1985)
15. Rytter, W.: Application of Lempel-Ziv factorization to the approximation of grammar-based compression. Theoret. Comput. Sci. 302(1–3), 211–222 (2003)
16. Tanaka, T., I, T., Inenaga, S., Bannai, H., Takeda, M.: Computing convolution on grammar-compressed text. In: Proceedings of Data Compression Conference (DCC), pp. 451–460. IEEE (2013)

17. Westbrook, J.: Fast incremental planarity testing. In: Kuich, W. (ed.) ICALP 1992. LNCS, vol. 623, pp. 342–353. Springer, Heidelberg (1992). doi:10.1007/3-540-55719-9_86
18. Ziv, J., Lempel, A.: Compression of individual sequences via variable-rate coding. IEEE Trans. Inf. Theor. **24**(5), 530–536 (1978)
19. Ziv, J., Lempel, A.: A universal algorithm for sequential data compression. IEEE Trans. Inf. Theor. **23**(3), 337–343 (1977)

On Suffix Tree Breadth

Golnaz Badkobeh[1], Juha Kärkkäinen[2(✉)], Simon J. Puglisi[2], and Bella Zhukova[2]

[1] Department of Computer Science, University of Warwick, Conventry, UK
g.badkobeh@warwick.ac.uk
[2] Department of Computer Science, Helsinki Institute for Information Technology, University of Helsinki, Helsinki, Finland
{juha.karkkainen,puglisi,bzhukova}@cs.helsinki.fi

Abstract. The suffix tree—the compacted trie of all the suffixes of a string—is the most important and widely-used data structure in string processing. We consider a natural combinatorial question about suffix trees: for a string S of length n, how many nodes $\nu_S(d)$ can there be at (string) depth d in its suffix tree? We prove $\nu(n, d) = \max_{S \in \Sigma^n} \nu_S(d)$ is $O((n/d) \log n)$, and show that this bound is almost tight, describing strings for which $\nu_S(d)$ is $\Omega((n/d) \log(n/d))$.

1 Introduction

The *suffix tree*, T_S, of a string S of n symbols is a compacted trie containing all the suffixes of S. Since its discovery by Weiner 44 years ago [6]—as an optimal solution to the longest common substring problem—the suffix tree has emerged as perhaps the most important abstraction in string processing [1], and now has dozens of applications, most notably in bioinformatics [5].

Consequently, combinatorial properties of suffix trees are of great interest, and have been exploited in various ways to obtain faster construction algorithms, succinct representations, and efficient pattern matching and discovery algorithms.

Our focus in this article is a natural combinatorial question about suffix trees: how many nodes $\nu_S(d)$ can there be at (string) depth d in the suffix tree of a string S? We prove that $\nu(n, d) = \max_{S \in \Sigma^n} \nu_S(d)$ is $O((n/d) \log n)$, and show that this bound is almost tight, describing strings for which $\nu_S(d)$ is $\Omega((n/d) \log(n/d))$.

In the following section we lay down notation and formally define basic concepts. Sections 3 and 4 deal with the upper bound and lower bound in turn, and we close with a discussion of the results.

G. Badkobeh—Supported by a Leverhulme Early Career Fellowship.

S.J. Puglisi and B. Zhukova—Supported by the Academy of Finland via grant 294143.

© Springer International Publishing AG 2017
G. Fici et al. (Eds.): SPIRE 2017, LNCS 10508, pp. 68–73, 2017.
DOI: 10.1007/978-3-319-67428-5_6

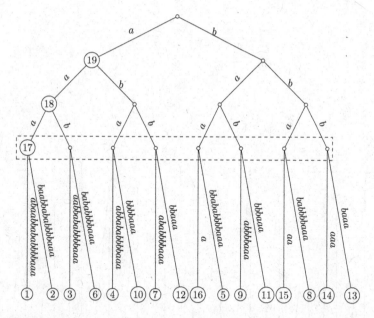

Fig. 1. The suffix tree of string β_4 = *aaaabaabbababbbbaaa*, the binary de Bruijn sequence of order 4. The dashed rectangle contains internal nodes at depth 3.

2   Preliminaries

Throughout we consider a string $S = S[1..n] = S[1]S[2]\ldots S[n]$ of n symbols drawn from an ordered alphabet Σ of size σ. For $i = 1, \ldots, n$ we write $S[i..n]$ to denote the *suffix* of S of length $n - i + 1$, that is $S[i..n] = S[i]S[i + 1] \cdots S[n]$. For convenience we will frequently refer to suffix $S[i..n]$ simply as "suffix i".

The suffix tree of S is a compact trie representing all the suffixes of S. Every suffix tree node either represents a suffix or is a branching node. Each branching node represents a string that occurs at least twice in S and has at least two distinct symbols following those occurrences. The string depth—or simply depth—of a node is the length of the string it represents. Figures 1 and 2 show examples of suffix trees.

The *suffix array* of S, denoted SA, is an array $SA[1..n]$ which contains a permutation of the integers $1..n$ such that $S[SA[1]..n] < S[SA[2]..n] < \cdots < S[SA[n]..n]$. In other words, $SA[j] = i$ iff $S[i..n]$ is the jth suffix of S in ascending lexicographical order. We use SA^{-1} to denote the inverse permutation. For convenience, we also define $SA[0] = n + 1$ to represent the empty suffix.

The *lcp array* LCP = $LCP[1..n]$ is an array defined by S and SA. Let $lcp(i, j)$ denote the length of the longest common prefix of suffixes i and j. For every $j \in 1..n$,

$$LCP[j] = lcp(SA[j - 1], SA[j]),$$

that is, LCP contains the length of the longest common prefix for each pair of lexicographically adjacent suffixes.

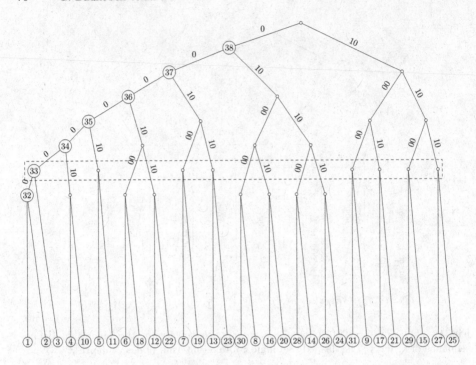

Fig. 2. The suffix tree of string $W_{2,4}$ = 00000000100000101000100010101010000000. The dashed rectangle contains internal nodes at depth 6.

The *permuted lcp array*—PLCP[1..n]—has the same contents as LCP but in a different order. Specifically, for every $j \in 1..n$,

$$\text{PLCP}[\text{SA}[j]] = \text{LCP}[j]. \tag{1}$$

Then $\text{PLCP}[i] = \text{lcp}(i, \phi(i))$ when we define $\phi(i) = \text{SA}[\text{SA}^{-1}[i] - 1]$.

A binary de Bruijn sequence of order k, denoted by β_k, is a binary word of length $2^k + k - 1$ where each of the 2^k words of length k over the binary alphabet appears as a factor exactly once. As an example, $\beta_4 = aaaabaabbababbbbaaa$ is a de Bruijn sequence of order 4, see Fig. 1.

3   Upper Bound

We are interested in the quantity $\nu(n, d)$, which is the maximum number of branching nodes at depth d over any string of length n.

A trivial upper bound on $\nu(n, d)$—relevant for shallow levels—is $\nu(n, d) \leq \sigma^d$ for strings over an alphabet of size σ. Another easy upper bound is $\nu(n, d) \leq (n - d)/2$, since there are $n - d$ suffixes longer than d and each branching node at depth d must represent a prefix of at least two such suffixes. In particular, $\nu(2^k + k - 1, k - 1) = 2^{k-1}$ since the upper bound is matched by a binary de Bruijn sequence of order k, as shown in Fig. 1.

Based on the above, $\nu(n,d)$ increases with d up to level $d \approx \log_\sigma n$ and then starts to go down. The main result of this section is a much tighter upper bound for larger d showing a quick decrease after level $\log n$.

Our upperbound proof makes use of the concept of *irreducible* lcp values, first defined in [3]. We say that $\text{PLCP}[i] = \text{lcp}(i, \phi(i))$ is *reducible* if $S[i{-}1] = S[\phi(i){-}1]$ and *irreducible* otherwise. In particular, it is irreducible if $i = 1$ or $\phi(i) = 1$. Reducible values are easy to compute via the next lemma.

Lemma 1 ([3]). *If* $\text{PLCP}[i]$ *is reducible, then* $\text{PLCP}[i] = \text{PLCP}[i-1] - 1$.

We also need an upper bound on the sum of irreducible lcp values.

Lemma 2 ([2,3]). *The sum of all irreducible lcp values is* $\leq n \log n$.

Theorem 3. *The number of branching nodes at depth d in the suffix tree for a string of length n is* $\leq (n/d) \log n$.

Proof. Let S be a string with $\nu(n,d)$ branching nodes at depth d in the suffix tree of S. Every such branching node corresponds to one or more values d in the lcp array, each of which in turn corresponds to a position in the PLCP array with value d. In other words, the number of d's in the PLCP array of S is an upper bound on $\nu_S(d)$. Let $i_1, \ldots, i_r$ be the positions of irreducible values in the PCLP array in ascending order, and let $i_{r+1} = n + 1$. Since $i_1 = 1$, the intervals $\text{PLCP}[i_j..i_{j+1} - 1]$, $j = 1..n$, form a partitioning of the PLCP array. Due to Lemma 1, for every $j = 1..n$, $\text{PLCP}[i_j..i_{j+1} - 1]$ contains at most one d and only if $\text{PLCP}[i_j] \geq d$. Therefore, each occurrence of d can be mapped to a unique irreducible lcp value $\geq d$. Using Lemma 2, $d\nu(n,d) \leq n \log n$ so the upper bound follows. □

4 Lower Bound

This section is devoted to proving the following result.

Theorem 4. *For any positive integers $j \geq 1$ and $k \geq 3$, there exists a string of length $n = j(2^k + k - 1)$ such that its suffix tree has $\geq \frac{1}{2} \left(\frac{n}{d} - 1 \right) \log \left(\frac{n}{d} - 1 \right)$ branching nodes at depth $d = j(k - 1)$.*

Proof. Our proof is based on a construction of the following string, $W_{j,k}$. Let β_k be a binary de Bruijn sequence of order k. Clearly, the suffix tree of β_k is full up to depth $k - 1$, and has 2^{k-1} nodes at depth $k - 1$. Now, let $W_{j,k} = w_j(\beta_k)$ where morphism w_j is the following

$$\begin{cases} w_j(a) = 0^j \\ w_j(b) = 10^{j-1} \end{cases}$$

It is clear that $|W_{j,k}| = n = j(2^k + k - 1)$. Let $m = \nu_{W_{j,k}}(j(k-1))$ denote the number of branching nodes of the suffix tree of string $W_{j,k}$ at depth $d = j(k-1)$. We claim that $m \geq 2^{k-1}$. If both ya and yb occur in β_k for some string y, then both $x0$ and $x1$ occur in $W_{i,j}$ for $x = w_j(y)$. Thus every branching node representing y in the suffix tree of β_k is uniquely mapped to a branching node representing $x = w_j(y)$ in the suffix tree of $W_{i,j}$. Since the suffix tree of β_k has 2^{k-1} branching nodes at depth $k - 1$, the claim $m \geq 2^{k-1}$ follows.

What remains is to show the steps for the calculation of the lower bound. Since $m \geq 2^{k-1}$ and $d = j(k-1) = \frac{n(k-1)}{(2^k+k-1)}$, we have $\frac{n}{d} = \frac{2^k}{k-1} + 1 \leq \frac{2m}{k-1} + 1$, which implies

$$m \geq \frac{1}{2}\left(\frac{n}{d} - 1\right)(k-1) \geq \frac{1}{2}\left(\frac{n}{d} - 1\right)\log\left(\frac{2^k}{k-1}\right) = \frac{1}{2}\left(\frac{n}{d} - 1\right)\log\left(\frac{n}{d} - 1\right).$$

$\square$

5   Discussion

Notice that the lowerbound construction implies $d = \Omega(\log n)$; thus it does not contradict the upper bounds for small d discussed in Sect. 3.

The upper and lower bounds of Theorems 3 and 4 are asymptotically equal when $d = O(n^{1-\epsilon})$ for any constant $\epsilon > 0$. We conjecture that the lower bound is asymptotically tight even for larger d, but proving a matching upper bound remains an open problem.

Essentially the same bounds hold for all variants and generalizations. We have counted only branching nodes but including leaves (and unary nodes representing suffixes) too would not change much as there can be only one leaf (or unary node) at each level. Similarly, adding a unique terminator symbol to the end of the string adds at most one node per level. Considering a suffix tree of multiple strings (containing all suffixes of all strings) could add more leafs to a level but no more than n/d leafs at a level d; thus the asymptotic results do not change. Another variant considers the string to be cyclic—replacing suffixes with rotations—and even suffix trees for collections of cyclic strings have been considered [2,4]. All the results hold in this case too: the key result for the upper bound, Lemma 2, was proved for collections of cyclic strings [2], and de Bruijn sequences are naturally defined as cyclic strings. Finally, notice that Theorems 3 and 4 hold for any alphabet size.

References

1. Apostolico, A., Crochemore, M., Farach-Colton, M., Galil, Z., Muthukrishnan, S.: 40 years of suffix trees. Commun. ACM **59**(4), 66–73 (2016)
2. Kärkkäinen, J., Kempa, D., Piatkowski, M.: Tighter bounds for the sum of irreducible LCP values. Theor. Comput. Sci. **656**, 265–278 (2016). https://doi.org/10.1016/j.tcs.2015.12.009
3. Kärkkäinen, J., Manzini, G., Puglisi, S.J.: Permuted longest-common-prefix array. In: Kucherov, G., Ukkonen, E. (eds.) CPM 2009. LNCS, vol. 5577, pp. 181–192. Springer, Heidelberg (2009). doi:10.1007/978-3-642-02441-2_17

4. Kärkkäinen, J., Piatkowski, M., Puglisi, S.J.: String inference from longest-common-prefix array. In: 44th International Colloquium on Automata, Languages, and Programming, ICALP 2017, pp. 62:1–62:14 (2017). https://doi.org/10.4230/LIPIcs.ICALP.2017.62
5. Mäkinen, V., Belazzougui, D., Cunial, F., Tomescu, A.I.: Genome-Scale Algorithm Design: Biological Sequence Analysis in the Era of High-Throughput Sequencing. Cambridge University Press, Cambridge (2015). http://www.genome-scale.info/
6. Weiner, P.: Linear pattern matching algorithms. In: 14th Annual Symposium on Switching and Automata Theory, pp. 1–11. IEEE Computer Society (1973)

Pattern Matching on Elastic-Degenerate Text with Errors

Giulia Bernardini[1], Nadia Pisanti[2,3], Solon P. Pissis[4],
and Giovanna Rosone[2(✉)]

[1] Department of Mathematics, University of Pisa, Pisa, Italy
[2] Department of Computer Science, University of Pisa, Pisa, Italy
giovanna.rosone@unipi.it
[3] Erable Team, INRIA, Villeurbanne, France
[4] Department of Informatics, King's College London, London, UK

Abstract. An elastic-degenerate string is a sequence of n sets of strings of total length N. It has been introduced to represent a multiple alignment of several closely-related sequences (e.g. pan-genome) compactly. In this representation, substrings of these sequences that match exactly are collapsed, while in positions where the sequences differ, all possible variants observed at that location are listed. The natural problem that arises is finding all matches of a deterministic pattern of length m in an elastic-degenerate text. There exists an $\mathcal{O}(nm^2 + N)$-time algorithm to solve this problem on-line after a pre-processing stage with time and space $\mathcal{O}(m)$. In this paper, we study the same problem under the edit distance model and present an $\mathcal{O}(k^2mG + kN)$-time and $\mathcal{O}(m)$-space algorithm, where G is the total number of strings in the elastic-degenerate text and k is the maximum edit distance allowed. We also present a simple $\mathcal{O}(kmG + kN)$-time and $\mathcal{O}(m)$-space algorithm for Hamming distance.

Keywords: Uncertain sequences · Elastic-degenerate strings · Degenerate strings · Pan-genome · Pattern matching

1 Introduction

There is a growing interest in the notion of *pan-genome* [20]. In the last ten years, with faster and cheaper sequencing technologies, re-sequencing (that is, sequencing the genome of yet another individual of a species) became more and more a common task in modern genome analysis workflows. By now, a huge amount of genomic variations within the same population has been detected (e.g. in humans for medical applications, but not only), and this is only the beginning. With this, new challenges of functional annotation and comparative analysis have been raised. Traditionally, a single annotated *reference genome* is used as a control sequence. The reference genome is a representative example of the genomic sequence of a species. It serves as a reference text to which, for example, fragments of newly sequenced genomes of individuals are mapped. Although a single reference genome provides a good approximation of any individual genome,

© Springer International Publishing AG 2017

G. Fici et al. (Eds.): SPIRE 2017, LNCS 10508, pp. 74–90, 2017.
DOI: 10.1007/978-3-319-67428-5_7

in loci with polymorphic variations, mapping and sequence comparison often fail their purposes. This is where a multiple genome, i.e. a pan-genome, would be a better reference text [10].

In the literature, many different (compressed) representations and thus algorithms have been considered for pattern matching on a set of similar texts [3–6,12,16,21]. A natural representation of pan-genomes, or fragments of them, that we consider here are elastic-degenerate texts [11]. An *elastic-degenerate text* is a sequence which compactly represents a multiple alignment of several closely-related sequences. In this representation, substrings that match exactly are collapsed, while in positions where the sequences differ (by means of substitutions, insertions, and deletions of substrings), all possible variants observed at that location are listed. Elastic-degenerate texts correspond to the Variant Call Format (VCF), that is, the *standard* for storing gene sequence variations [19].

Consider, for example, the following *multiple sequence alignment* of three closely-related sequences:

$$\text{GAAAGTGAGCA}$$
$$\text{GAGACAAA-CA}$$
$$\text{G--A-ACAGCA}$$

These sequences can be compacted into the single elastic-degenerate string:

$$\tilde{T} = \{G\} \cdot \begin{Bmatrix} \text{AA} \\ \text{AG} \\ \varepsilon \end{Bmatrix} \cdot \{A\} \cdot \begin{Bmatrix} \text{GTG} \\ \text{CAA} \\ \text{AC} \end{Bmatrix} \cdot \{A\} \cdot \begin{Bmatrix} \text{G} \\ \varepsilon \end{Bmatrix} \cdot \{\text{CA}\}.$$

The total number of segments is the *length* of $\tilde{T}$ and the total number of letters is the *size* of $\tilde{T}$. The natural problem that arises is finding all matches of a deterministic pattern P in text $\tilde{T}$. We call this the ELASTIC-DEGENERATE STRING MATCHING (*EDSM*) problem. The simplest version of this problem assumes that a degenerate (sometimes called indeterminate) segment can contain only single letters [9].

Due to the application of cataloguing human genetic variation [19], there has been ample work in the literature on the *off-line* (indexing) version of the pattern matching problem [10,14,15,17,18]. The *on-line*, more fundamental, version of the *EDSM* problem has not been studied as much as indexing approaches. Solutions to the on-line version can be beneficial for a number of reasons: (a) efficient on-line solutions can be used in combination with partial indexes as practical trade-offs; (b) efficient on-line solutions for exact pattern matching can be applied for fast average-case approximate pattern matching similar to standard strings [2]; (c) on-line solutions can be useful when one wants to search for a few patterns in many degenerate texts similar to standard strings [1].

Previous Results. Let us denote by m the length of pattern P, by n the length of $\tilde{T}$, and by $N > m$ the size of $\tilde{T}$. A few results exist on the (exact) *EDSM* problem. In [11], an algorithm for solving the *EDSM* problem in time $\mathcal{O}(\alpha\gamma mn + N)$ and space $\mathcal{O}(N)$ was presented; where α and γ are parameters, respectively representing the maximum number of strings in any degenerate segment of the text and the maximum number of degenerate segments spanned by any occurrence of the pattern in the text. In [7], two new algorithms to solve the same problem in an on-line manner[1] were presented: the first one requires time $\mathcal{O}(nm^2 + N)$ after a pre-processing stage with time and space $\mathcal{O}(m)$; the second requires time $\mathcal{O}(N \cdot \lceil \frac{m}{w} \rceil)$ after a pre-processing stage with time and space $\mathcal{O}(m \cdot \lceil \frac{m}{w} \rceil)$, where w is the size of the computer word in the RAM model.

Our Contribution. Since genomic sequences are endowed with polymorphisms and sequencing errors, the existence of an exact occurrence can result into a strong assumption. The aim of this work is to generalize the studies of [7,11] for the exact case, allowing some approximation in the occurrences of the input pattern. We suggest a simple on-line $\mathcal{O}(kmG + kN)$-time and $\mathcal{O}(m)$-space algorithm, G being the total number of strings in $\tilde{T}$ and $k > 0$ the maximum number of allowed substitutions in a pattern's occurrence, that is nonzero *Hamming distance*. Our main contribution is an on-line $\mathcal{O}(k^2mG + kN)$-time and $\mathcal{O}(m)$-space algorithm where the type of edit operations allowed is extended to insertions and deletions as well, that is nonzero *edit distance*. These results are *good* in the sense that for *small* values of k the algorithms incur (essentially) no increase in time complexity with respect to the $\mathcal{O}(nm^2 + N)$-time and $\mathcal{O}(m)$-space algorithm presented in [7] for the exact case.

Structure of the Paper. Section 2 provides some preliminary definitions and facts as well as the formal statements of the problems we address. Section 3 describes our solution under the edit distance model, while Sect. 4 describes the algorithm under the Hamming distance model.

2   Preliminaries

An *alphabet* Σ is a non-empty finite set of letters of size $|\Sigma|$. We consider the case of a constant-sized alphabet, i.e. $|\Sigma| = \mathcal{O}(1)$. A *string* S on an alphabet Σ is a sequence of elements of Σ. The set of all strings on an alphabet Σ, including the *empty string* ε of length 0, is denoted by Σ^*. For any string S, we denote by $S[i \dots j]$ the *substring* of S that *starts* at position i and *ends* at position j. In particular, $S[0 \dots j]$ is the *prefix* of S that ends at position j, and $S[i \dots |S| - 1]$ is the *suffix* of S that begins at position i, where $|S|$ denotes the *length* of S.

Definition 1 ([7]). *An* elastic-degenerate (ED) string $\tilde{T} = \tilde{T}[0]\tilde{T}[1] \dots \tilde{T}[n-1]$ *of length n on alphabet Σ, is a finite sequence of n degenerate letters. Every degenerate letter $\tilde{T}[i]$ is a finite non-empty set of strings $\tilde{T}[i][j] \in \Sigma^*$, with $0 \le j < |\tilde{T}[i]|$. The size N of $\tilde{T}$ is defined as*

$$N = \sum_{i=0}^{n-1} \sum_{j=0}^{|\tilde{T}[i]|-1} |\tilde{T}[i][j]|$$

assuming (for representation purposes only) that $|\varepsilon| = 1$.

---

[1] On-line refers to the fact that the algorithm reads the elastic-degenerate text set-by-set in a serial manner.

Definition 2. *The total number of strings in $\tilde{T}$ is defined as* $G = \sum_{i=0}^{n-1} |\tilde{T}[i]|$.

Notice that $n \leq G \leq N$. A *deterministic string* is simply a string in Σ^*. The *Hamming distance* is defined between two deterministic strings of equal length as the number of positions at which the two strings have different letters. The *edit distance* between two deterministic strings is defined as the minimum total cost of a sequence of edit operations (that is, substitution, insertion, or deletion of a letter) required to transform one string into the other. Here we only count the number of edit operations, considering the cost of each to be 1. In [7] the authors give a definition of a match between a deterministic string P and an ED string $\tilde{T}$; here we extend their definition to deal with errors.

Definition 3. *Given an integer $k > 0$, we say that a string $P \in \Sigma^m$ k_H-matches (resp. k_E-) an ED string $\tilde{T} = \tilde{T}[0]\tilde{T}[1]\ldots\tilde{T}[n-1]$ of length $n > 1$ if all of the following hold:*

- *there exists a non-empty suffix X of some string $S \in \tilde{T}[0]$;*
- *if $n > 2$, there exist strings $Y_1 \in \tilde{T}[1],\ldots,Y_t \in \tilde{T}[t]$, for $1 \leq t \leq n-2$;*
- *there exists a non-empty prefix Z of some string $S \in \tilde{T}[n-1]$;*
- *the Hamming (resp. edit) distance between P and $XY_1 \ldots Y_t Z$ (note that $Y_1 \ldots Y_t$ can be ε) is no more than k.*

We say that P has a k_H-*occurrence* (resp. k_E-) ending at position j in an ED string $\tilde{T}$ of length n if either there exists a k_H-match (resp. k_E-) between P and $\tilde{T}[i \ldots j]$ for some $0 \leq i < j \leq n-1$ or P is at Hamming (resp. edit) distance of at most k from a substring of some string $S \in \tilde{T}[j]$.

Example 4. Consider $P =$ GAACAA of length $m = 6$. The following ED string has $n = 7$, $N = 20$, and $G = 12$. An 1_H-occurrence is underlined, and an 1_E-occurrences is overlined.

$$\tilde{T} = \{\underline{\text{G}}\} \cdot \left\{ \begin{array}{c} \overline{\text{AA}} \\ \text{AG} \\ \underline{\varepsilon} \end{array} \right\} \cdot \{\underline{\text{A}}\} \cdot \left\{ \begin{array}{c} \overline{\text{GTG}} \\ \overline{\text{CAA}} \\ \underline{\text{AC}} \end{array} \right\} \cdot \{\underline{\text{A}}\} \cdot \left\{ \begin{array}{c} \text{G} \\ \varepsilon \end{array} \right\} \cdot \{\underline{\text{CA}}\}$$

A *suffix tree* ST_X for a string X of length m is a tree data structure where edge-labels of paths from the root to the (terminal) node labelled i spell out suffix $X[i \ldots m-1]$ of X. ST_X can be built in time and space $\mathcal{O}(m)$. The suffix tree can be generalized to represent the suffixes of a set of strings $\{X_1,\ldots,X_n\}$ (denoted by $GST_{X_1,\ldots,X_n}$) with time and space costs still linear in the length of the input strings (see [8], for details).

Given two strings X and Y and a pair (i,j), with $0 \leq i \leq |X| - 1$ and $0 \leq j \leq |Y| - 1$, the *longest common extension* at (i,j), denoted by $lce_{X,Y}(i,j)$, is the length of the longest substring of X starting at position i that matches a substring of Y starting at position j. For instance, for $X =$ CGCGT and $Y =$ ACG, we have that $lce_{X,Y}(2,1) = 2$, corresponding to the substring CG.

Fact 1 ([8]). *Given a string X and its ST_X, and a set of strings $W = \{Y_1, \ldots, Y_l\}$, it is possible to build the generalized suffix tree $GST_{X,W}$ extending ST_X, in time $\mathcal{O}(\sum_{h=1}^{l} |Y_h|)$. Moreover, given two strings X and Y of total length q, for each index pair (i,j), $lce_{X,Y}(i,j)$ queries can be computed in constant time per query, after a pre-processing of $GST_{X,Y}$ that takes time and space $\mathcal{O}(q)$.*

We will denote by $GST^*_{X,Y}$ such a pre-processed tree for answering *lce* queries. The time is ripe now to formally introduce the two problems considered here.

[k_E-**EDSM**] ELASTIC-DEGENERATE STRING MATCHING WITH EDIT DISTANCE:

Input: A deterministic pattern P of length m, an ED text $\tilde{T}$ of length n and size $N \geq m$, and an integer $0 < k < m$.
Output: Pairs (i,d), i being a position in $\tilde{T}$ where at least one k_E-occurrence of P ends and $d \leq k$ being the minimal number of errors (substitutions, insertions, and deletions) for occurrence i.

[k_H-**EDSM**] ELASTIC-DEGENERATE STRING MATCHING WITH HAMMING DISTANCE:

Input: A deterministic pattern P of length m, an ED text $\tilde{T}$ of length n and size $N \geq m$, and an integer $0 < k < m$.
Output: Pairs (i,d), i being a position in $\tilde{T}$ where at least one k_H-occurrence of P ends and $d \leq k$ being the minimal number of substitutions for occurrence i.

3   An Algorithm for k_E-EDSM

In [7] the exact *EDSM* problem (that is, for $k = 0$) was solved in time $\mathcal{O}(nm^2 + N)$. Allowing up to k substitutions, insertions, and deletions in the occurrences clearly entails a time-cost increase, but the solution proposed here manages to keep the time-cost growth limited, solving the k_E-EDSM problem in time $\mathcal{O}(k^2mG + kN)$, G being the total number of strings in the ED text. At a high level, the k_E-EDSM algorithm (pseudocode shown below) works as follows.

Pre-processing phase: the suffix tree for the pattern P is built (line 1 in pseudocode).
Searching phase: in an on-line manner, the text $\tilde{T}$ is scanned from left to right and, for each $\tilde{T}[i]$:

(1) It finds the prefixes of P that are at distance at most k from any suffix of some $S \in \tilde{T}[i]$; if there exists an $S \in \tilde{T}[i]$ that is long enough, it also searches for k_E-occurrences of P that start and end at position i (lines 6 and 16);
(2) It tries to extend at $\tilde{T}[i]$ each partial k_E-occurrence of P which has started earlier in $\tilde{T}$ (lines 23 and 30);
(3) In both previous cases, if a full k_E-occurrence of P also ends at $\tilde{T}[i]$, then it outputs position i; otherwise it stores the prefixes of P extended at $\tilde{T}[i]$ (lines 7–9, 17–19, 24–26, 31–32).

---

k_E-EDSM($P,m,\tilde{T},n,k$)

---

1 Build ST_P;
2 **for** $j = 0$ **to** $m - 1$ **do** $V_c[j] \leftarrow \infty$;
3 $L_c \leftarrow \emptyset$;
4 Build $GST^*_{P,\tilde{T}[0]}$;
5 **forall** $S \in \tilde{T}[0]$ **do**
6      $L' \leftarrow \emptyset$; $L' \leftarrow k_E$-BORDERS($P, m, S, |S|, GST^*_{P,\tilde{T}[0]}, k$);
7   **forall** $(j, d) \in L'$ **do**
8   **if** $j = m - 1 \wedge d < V_c[m - 1]$ **then** $V_c[m - 1] = d$;
9   **else** INSERT($L_c,(j,d),V_c$);
10 **if** $V_c[m - 1] \neq \infty$ **then report** $(0, V_c[m - 1])$;
11 **for** $i = 1$ **to** $n - 1$ **do**
12     $L_p \leftarrow L_c$; $L_c \leftarrow \emptyset$;
13     $V_p \leftarrow V_c$; **for** $j = 0$ **to** $m - 1$ **do** $V_c[j] \leftarrow \infty$;
14   Build $GST^*_{P,\tilde{T}[i]}$;
15   **forall** $S \in \tilde{T}[i]$ **do**
16         $L' \leftarrow \emptyset$; $L' \leftarrow k_E$-BORDERS($P, m, S, |S|, GST^*_{P,\tilde{T}[i]}, k$);
17   **forall** $(j, d) \in L'$ **do**
18   **if** $j = m - 1 \wedge d < V_c[m - 1]$ **then** $V_c[m - 1] = d$;
19   **else** INSERT($L_c,(j,d),V_c$);
20   **if** $|S| < m$ **then**
21   **forall** $p \in L_p$ **do**
22                 $L' \leftarrow \emptyset$;
23                 $L' \leftarrow k_E$-EXTEND($p + 1, P, m, S, |S|, GST^*_{P,\tilde{T}[i]}, k - V_p[p]$);
24   **forall** $(j, d) \in L'$ **do**
25   **if** $j = m - 1 \wedge d + V_p[p] < V_c[m - 1]$ **then**
                        $V_c[m - 1] = d + V_p[p]$;
26   **else** INSERT($L_c,(j, d + V_p[p]), V_c$);
27   **if** $|S| \geq m$ **then**
28   **forall** $p \in L_p$ **do**
29                 $L' \leftarrow \emptyset$;
30                 $L' \leftarrow k_E$-EXTEND($p + 1, P, m, S, |S|, GST^*_{P,\tilde{T}[i]}, k - V_p[p]$);
31   **forall** $(j, d) \in L'$ **do**
32   **if** $j = m - 1 \wedge d + V_p[p] < V_c[m - 1]$ **then**
                        $V_c[m - 1] = d + V_p[p]$;
33   **if** $V_c[m - 1] \neq \infty$ **then report** $(i, V_c[m - 1])$;

Step (1) of algorithm k_E-EDSM is implemented by algorithm k_E-BORDERS described in Sect. 3.1. Step (2) is implemented by algorithm k_E-EXTEND described in Sect. 3.2.

The following lemma follows directly from Fact 1.

Lemma 5. *Given P of length m and $\tilde{T}$ of length n and size N, building $GST^*_{P,\tilde{T}[i]}$, for all $i \in [0, n-1]$, takes total time $\mathcal{O}(mn + N)$.*

Besides ST_P (built once as a pre-processing step) and $GST^*_{P,\tilde{T}[i]}$ (built for all $\tilde{T}[i]$'s), the algorithm uses the following data structures:

L' A list re-initialized to $\emptyset$ for each $S \in \tilde{T}[i]$: contains pairs (j, d) storing the rightmost position j of P such that $P[0 \ldots j]$ is at distance d from a suffix of S. L' is filled in by k_E-BORDERS and k_E-EXTEND.

V_c A vector of size $|P|$ re-initialized to $V_c[j] = \infty$ for each $\tilde{T}[i]$ (c stands for *current*) for all j's: $V_c[j]$ contains the lowest number of errors for a partial k_E-occurrence of $P[0 \ldots j]$. For each pair (j, d) in L', if $V_c[j] < d$ then $V_c[j]$ is updated with d by the function INSERT. $V_c[j] = \infty$ denotes that a partial k_E-occurrence of $P[0 \ldots j]$ has not yet been found.

L_c A list re-initialized to $\emptyset$ for each $\tilde{T}[i]$: contains the rightmost positions of the prefixes of P found in L'. It is filled in by function INSERT for each rightmost position j where $V_c[j]$ turns into a value $\neq \infty$.

L_p A list where at the beginning of each iteration i for $\tilde{T}[i]$, the L_c list for $i-1$ is copied. L_p thus stores prefixes of P found in L' during the previous iteration (p stands for *previous*).

V_p Similarly, in V_p the vector V_c of the previous position is copied.

Algorithm k_E-EDSM needs to report each position i in $\tilde{T}$ where some k_E-occurrence of P ends with edit distance $d \leq k$, d being the minimal such value for position i. To this aim, the last position of V_c can be updated with the following criterion: each time an occurrence of P ending at $\tilde{T}[i]$, $(m-1, d)$, is found, if $V_c[m-1] > d$ then we set $V_c[m-1] = d$. After all $S \in \tilde{T}[i]$ have been examined, if $V_c[m-1] \neq \infty$, the algorithm outputs the pair $(i, V_c[m-1])$.

3.1 Algorithm k_E-BORDERS

For each i and for each $S \in \tilde{T}[i]$, Step (1) of the algorithm needs to find the prefixes of P that are at distance at most k from any suffix of S, as well as k_E-occurrences of P that start and end at position i if S is long enough. To this end, we use and modify the Landau-Vishkin algorithm [13]. We first recall some relevant definitions concerning the dynamic programming table [8].

Given an $m \times q$ dynamic programming table (m rows, q columns), the *main diagonal* consists of cells (h, h) for $0 \leq h \leq \min\{m-1, q-1\}$. The diagonals above the main diagonal are numbered 1 through $(q-1)$; the diagonal starting in cell $(0, h)$ is diagonal h. The diagonals below the main diagonal are numbered -1 through $-(m-1)$; the diagonal starting in cell $(h, 0)$ is diagonal $-h$. A *d-path* in the dynamic programming table is a path that starts in row zero and specifies a total of exactly d errors (substitutions, insertions, and deletions). A d-path is *farthest reaching in diagonal h* if it is a d-path that ends in diagonal h and the index of its ending column c is $\geq$ to the ending column of any other d-path ending in diagonal h.

Algorithm k_E-BORDERS takes as input a pattern P of length m, a string $S \in \tilde{T}[i]$ of length q, the $GST^*_{P,\tilde{T}[i]}$ and the upper bound k for edit distance; it outputs pairs (j, d), where j is the rightmost position of the prefix of P that is at distance $d \leq k$ from a suffix of S, with the minimal value of d reported for each j. In order to fulfill this task, at a high level, the algorithm executes the following steps on a table having P at the rows and S at the columns:

(1a) For each diagonal $0 \leq h \leq q - 1$ it finds $lce_{P,S}(0, h)$. This specifies the end column of the farthest reaching 0-path on each diagonal from 0 to $q - 1$.

(1b) For each $1 \leq d \leq k$, it finds the farthest reaching d-path on diagonal h, for each $-d \leq h \leq q - 1$. This path is found from the farthest reaching $(d - 1)$-paths on diagonals $(h - 1)$, h and $(h + 1)$.

(1c) If a d-path reaches the last row of the dynamic programming table, then a k_E-occurrence of P with edit distance d that starts and ends at position i has been found, and the algorithm reports $(m - 1, d)$; if a d-path reaches the end of S in row r, then the prefix of P ending at $P[r]$ is at distance d from a suffix of S, and the algorithm reports (r, d).

In Step (1b), the farthest reaching d-path on diagonal h can be found by computing and comparing the following three particular paths that end on diagonal h:

R_1 Consists of the farthest reaching $(d - 1)$-path on diagonal $h + 1$, followed by a vertical edge to diagonal h, and then by the maximal extension along diagonal h that corresponds to identical substrings. Function R_1 takes as input the length $|X|$ of a string X, whose letters spell the rows of the dynamic programming table, the length $|Y|$ of a string Y, whose letters spell the columns, $GST^*_{X,Y}$ and the pair row-column (r, c) where the farthest reaching $(d - 1)$-path on diagonal $h + 1$ ends. It outputs pair (r_1, c_1) where path R_1 ends. This path represents a letter insertion in X.

R_2 Consists of the dual case of R_1 with a horizontal edge representing a letter deletion in X.

R_3 Consists of the farthest reaching $(d - 1)$-path on diagonal h followed by a diagonal edge, and then by the maximal extension along diagonal h that corresponds to identical substrings. Function R_3 takes as input the length $|X|$ of a string X, whose letters spell the rows of the dynamic programming table, the length $|Y|$ of a string Y, whose letters spell the columns, $GST^*_{X,Y}$ and the pair row-column (r, c) where the farthest reaching $(d - 1)$-path on diagonal h ends. It outputs pair (r_3, c_3) where path R_3 ends. This path represents a letter substitution.

Fact 2 ([8]). *The farthest reaching path on diagonal h is the path among R_1, R_2 or R_3 that extends the farthest along h.*

INSERT(L,(j,d),V)

1 **if** $V[j] > d$ **then**
2   **if** $V[j] = \infty$ **then** Insert j in L;
3      $V[j] \leftarrow d$;

$R_1(|X|, |Y|, GST^*_{X,Y}, r, c)$

1 **if** $-1 \leq r \leq |X| - 1 \wedge -1 \leq c \leq$ $|Y| - 1$ **then**
2      $l \leftarrow lce_{X,Y}(r + 2, c + 1)$;
3      $c_1 \leftarrow c + l$;
4      $r_1 \leftarrow r + 1 + l$;
5   **return** (r_1, c_1)
6 **else return** (r, c);

$R_2(|X|, |Y|, GST^*_{X,Y}, r, c)$

1 **if** $-1 \leq r \leq |X| - 1 \wedge -1 \leq c \leq$ $|Y| - 1$ **then**
2      $l \leftarrow lce_{X,Y}(r + 1, c + 2)$;
3      $c_2 \leftarrow c + 1 + l$;
4      $r_2 \leftarrow r + l$;
5   **return** (r_2, c_2)
6 **else return** (r, c);

$R_3(|X|, |Y|, GST^*_{X,Y}, r, c)$

1 **if** $-1 \leq r \leq |X| - 1 \wedge -1 \leq c \leq$ $|Y| - 1$ **then**
2      $l \leftarrow lce_{X,Y}(r + 2, c + 2)$;
3      $c_3 \leftarrow c + 1 + l$;
4      $r_3 \leftarrow r + 1 + l$;
5   **return** (r_3, c_3)
6 **else return** (r, c);

In each one of the iterations in k_E-BORDERS, a diagonal is associated with two variables $pFRP$ and $cFRP$, storing the column reached by the farthest reaching path (FRP) in the previous and in the current iteration, respectively. Notice that at most $k + q$ diagonals need to be taken into account: the algorithm first finds the lce's between $P[0]$ and $S[j]$, for all $0 \leq j \leq q - 1$, and hence it initializes q diagonals; after this, for each successive step (there are at most k of them), it widens to the left one diagonal at a time because an initial deletion can be added; therefore, it will consider at most $k + q$ diagonals.

Lemma 6. *Given P of length m, $\tilde{T}$ of length n and size N, the $GST^*_{P,\tilde{T}[i]}$, for all $i \in [0, n - 1]$, and an integer $0 < k < m$, k_E-BORDERS finds the minimal edit distance $\leq k$ between the prefixes of P and any suffix of $S \in \tilde{T}[i]$, as well as the k_E-occurrences of P that start and end at position i, in time $\mathcal{O}(k^2 G + kN)$, G being the total number of strings in $\tilde{T}$.*

Proof. For a string $S \in \tilde{T}[i]$, for each $0 \leq d \leq k$ and each diagonal $-k \leq h \leq |S| - 1$, the k_E-BORDERS algorithm must retrieve the end of three $(d - 1)$-paths (constant-time operations) and compute the path extension along the diagonal via a constant-time lce query (Fact 1). It thus takes time $\mathcal{O}(k^2 + k|S|)$ to find the prefixes of P that are at distance at most k from any suffix of S; the k_E-occurrences of P that start and end at position i are computed within the same complexity. The total time is $\mathcal{O}(k^2|\tilde{T}[i]| + k \sum_{j=0}^{|\tilde{T}[i]|-1} |S|)$, for all $S \in \tilde{T}[i]$. Since the size of $\tilde{T}$ is N and the total number of strings in $\tilde{T}$ is G, the result follows. $\square$

3.2 Algorithm k_E-EXTEND

In Step (2), algorithm k_E-EDSM tries to extend each partial k_E-occurrence that has started earlier in $\tilde{T}$. That is, at position i, for each $p \in L_p$ and for each string $S \in \tilde{T}[i]$, we try to extend $P[0 \dots p]$ with S. Once again, we modify the Landau-Vishkin algorithm [13] to our purpose: it suffices to look for the FRPs starting at the desired position only.

---

k_E-BORDERS$(P, m, S, q, GST^*_{P,\tilde{T}[i]}, k)$

---

1 **for** $h = -(k+1)$ **to** -1 **do** $cFRP(h) \leftarrow h - 1$;
2 **for** $h = 0$ **to** $q - 1$ **do**
3      $l \leftarrow lce_{P,S}(0, h)$;
4      $cFRP(h) \leftarrow l - 1 + h$;
5   **if** $l + h = q$ **then report** $(l - 1, 0)$;
6   **else**
7   **if** $l = m$ **then report** $(m - 1, 0)$;
8 **for** $d = 1$ **to** k **do**
9   **for** $h = -(k+1)$ **to** $q - 1$ **do** $pFRP(h) \leftarrow cFRP(h)$;
10   **for** $h = -d$ **to** $q - 1$ **do**
11         $(r_1, c_1) \leftarrow R_1(|P|, |S|, GST^*_{P,\tilde{T}[i]}, pFRP(h+1) - (h+1), pFRP(h+1))$;
12         $(r_2, c_2) \leftarrow R_2(|P|, |S|, GST^*_{P,\tilde{T}[i]}, pFRP(h-1) - (h-1), pFRP(h-1))$;
13         $(r_3, c_3) \leftarrow R_3(|P|, |S|, GST^*_{P,\tilde{T}[i]}, pFRP(h) - h, pFRP(h))$;
14         $cFRP(h) \leftarrow \max\{c_1, c_2, c_3\}$;
15   **if** $\max\{r_1, r_2, r_3\} = m - 1$ **then report** $(m - 1, d)$;
16   **if** $\max\{c_1, c_2, c_3\} = q - 1$ **then report** $(q - 1 - h, d)$;

---

k_E-EXTEND takes as input a pattern P of length m, a string $S \in \tilde{T}[i]$ of length q, the $GST^*_{P,\tilde{T}[i]}$, the upper bound k for edit distance and the position j in P where the extension should start; it outputs a list of distinct pairs (h, d), where h is the index of P where the extension ends, and d is the minimum additional number of errors introduced by the extension. Algorithm k_E-EXTEND performs a similar task to that of k_E-BORDERS: (i) it builds a $q \times (m - j)$ DP table (rather than an $m \times q$ table) and (ii) instead of searching for occurrences of P starting anywhere within S, k_E-EXTEND checks whether the whole of S can extend the prefix $P[0 \dots j - 1]$ detected at the previous text position or whether a prefix of S matches the suffix of P starting at $P[j]$ (and hence a k_E-occurrence of P has been found). In order to fulfill this task, at a high level, the algorithm executes the following steps on a table having S at the rows and $P[j \dots m - 1]$ at the columns:

(2a) It finds $lce_{S,P}(0, j)$ specifying the end column of the farthest reaching 0-path on diagonal 0 (the table is built for S and $P[j \dots m - 1]$).

(2b) For each $1 \leq d \leq k$, it finds the farthest reaching d-path on diagonal h, for each $-d \leq h \leq d$. This path is found from the farthest reaching $(d - 1)$-paths on diagonals $(h - 1)$, h and $(h + 1)$.

---

k_E-EXTEND$(j, P, m, S, q, GST^*_{P,\tilde{T}[i]}, k)$

---

1 **if** $S = \varepsilon$ **then**
2   **for** $d = 0$ **to** k **do report** $(j + d, d)$;
3 **else**
4   **for** $h = -(k+1)$ **to** $k+1$ **do** $cFRP(h) \leftarrow h - k - 1$;
5      $l \leftarrow lce_{S,P}(0, j)$;
6      $cFRP(0) \leftarrow l - 1$;
7   **if** $l = q$ **then report** $(l + j - 1, 0)$;
8   **for** $d = 1$ **to** k **do**
9   **for** $h = -(k+1)$ **to** d **do** $pFRP(h) \leftarrow cFRP(h)$;
10   **for** $h = -d$ **to** d **do**
11              $(r_1, c_1) \leftarrow R_1(|S|, m - j, GST^*_{P,\tilde{T}[i]}, pFRP(h+1) - (h+1), pFRP(h+1))$;
12              $(r_2, c_2) \leftarrow R_2(|S|, m - j, GST^*_{P,\tilde{T}[i]}, pFRP(h-1) - (h-1), pFRP(h-1))$;
13              $(r_3, c_3) \leftarrow R_3(|S|, m - j, GST^*_{P,\tilde{T}[i]}, pFRP(h) - h, pFRP(h))$;
14              $cFRP(h) \leftarrow \max\{c_1, c_2, c_3\}$;
15   **if** $\max\{r_1, r_2, r_3\} = q - 1$ **then report** $(cFRP(h) + j, d)$;
16   **if** $\max\{c_1, c_2, c_3\} = m - j - 1$ **then report** $(m - 1, d)$;

(2c) If a d-path reaches the last row of the dynamic programming table in column c, then an occurrence of the whole S with edit distance d has been found, and the algorithm reports $(c + j, d)$, $c + j$ being the position in P where the occurrence ends; if a d-path reaches the end of P, then a prefix of S is at distance d from a suffix of P starting at position j, and the algorithm reports $(m - 1, d)$.

Lemma 7. *Given a prefix of P, a string $S \in \tilde{T}[i]$, the $GST^*_{P,\tilde{T}[i]}$, and an integer $0 < k < m$, k_E-EXTEND extends the prefix of P with S in time $\mathcal{O}(k^2)$.*

Proof. The k_E-EXTEND algorithm does k iterations: at iteration d, for each diagonal $-d \leq h \leq d$, the end of three paths must be retrieved (constant-time operations) and the path extension along diagonal h must be computed via a constant-time lce query (Fact 1). The overall time for the extension is then bounded by $\mathcal{O}(1 + 2 + \cdots + (2k + 1)) = \mathcal{O}(k^2)$.   □

The following lemma summarizes the time complexity of k_E-EDSM.

Lemma 8. *Given P of length m, $\tilde{T}$ of length n and total size N, and an integer $0 < k < m$, algorithm k_E-EDSM solves the k_E-EDSM problem, in an on-line manner, in time $\mathcal{O}(k^2 mG + kN)$, G being the total number of strings in $\tilde{T}$.*

Proof. At the i-th iteration, algorithm k_E-EDSM tries to extend each $p \in L_p$ with each string $S \in \tilde{T}[i]$. By Lemma 5, building $GST^*_{P,\tilde{T}[i]}$, for all $i \in [0, n-1]$, requires time $\mathcal{O}(mn + N)$. By Lemma 7, extending a single prefix with a string S costs time $\mathcal{O}(k^2)$; in L_p there are at most $|P| = m$ prefixes; then to extend all of them with a single string S requires time $\mathcal{O}(mk^2)$. In $\tilde{T}[i]$ there are $|\tilde{T}[i]|$ strings, so the time cost rises to $\mathcal{O}(|\tilde{T}[i]|mk^2)$ for each $\tilde{T}[i]$, leading to an overall time cost of $\mathcal{O}(k^2mG)$ to perform extensions. By Lemma 6, the prefixes of P that are at distance at most k from any suffix of S as well as the k_E-occurrences of P that start and end at position i can be found in time $\mathcal{O}(k^2G + kN)$; the overall time complexity for the whole k_E-EDSM algorithm is then $\mathcal{O}(mn + N + k^2mG + k^2G + kN) = \mathcal{O}(k^2mG + kN)$. The algorithm is on-line in the sense that any occurrence of the pattern ending at position i is reported before reading $\tilde{T}[i+1]$. $\qquad\square$

Theorem 9. *The k_E-EDSM problem can be solved on-line in time $\mathcal{O}(k^2mG + kN)$ and space $\mathcal{O}(m)$.*

Proof. In order to obtain the space bound $\mathcal{O}(m)$, it is necessary to modify algorithm k_E-EDSM. The proposed method works as follows: each string $S \in \tilde{T}[i]$ is (conceptually) divided into windows of size $2m$ (except for the last one, whose length is $\leq m$) overlapping by m. Let W_j be the j-th window in S, $1 \leq j \leq \frac{|S|}{m}$. Instead of building $GST^*_{P,\tilde{T}[i]}$ for each degenerate letter $\tilde{T}[i]$, the algorithm now builds GST^*_{P,W_j} for each $1 \leq j \leq \frac{|S|}{m}$ and for each $S \in \tilde{T}[i]$: since the windows are of size $2m$, this can be done in both time and space $\mathcal{O}(m)$. Both algorithms k_E-BORDERS and k_E-EXTEND require space linear in the size of the string that spell the columns of the dynamic programming table, that is either P (in extensions) or a window of size $2m$ (in borders). Each list (L_c, L_p, L') and each vector (V_c, V_p) requires space $\mathcal{O}(m)$, so the overall required space is actually $\mathcal{O}(m)$.

The time bound is not affected by these modifications of the algorithm: the maximum number of windows in $\tilde{T}[i]$, in fact, is $\max\{|\tilde{T}[i]|, \frac{N_i}{m}\}$, where $N_i = \sum_{j=0}^{|\tilde{T}[i]|-1} |\tilde{T}[i][j]|$. This means that it takes time $\mathcal{O}(m|\tilde{T}[i]|)$ or $\mathcal{O}(m\frac{N_i}{m}) = O(N_i)$ to build and pre-process every suffix tree for $\tilde{T}[i]$. Algorithm k_E-BORDERS requires time $\mathcal{O}(k^2 + km) = \mathcal{O}(km)$ (because $k < m$) for each window: again, this must be multiplied by the number of windows in $\tilde{T}[i]$, so the time is $\max\{\mathcal{O}(km|\tilde{T}[i]|), \mathcal{O}(kN_i))\}$ for $\tilde{T}[i]$. Coming to algorithm k_E-EXTEND, nothing changes, as prefixes of P can only be extended by prefixes of S, so it suffices to consider one window for each S: it still requires time $\mathcal{O}(k^2mG)$ over the whole ED text. Summing up all these considerations, it is clear that the overall time is

$$\mathcal{O}(\sum_{i=0}^{n-1}[\max\{m|\tilde{T}[i]|, N_i\} + \max\{km|\tilde{T}[i]|, kN_i\}] + k^2mG)$$

$$= \mathcal{O}(\sum_{i=0}^{n-1}[\max\{km|\tilde{T}[i]|, kN_i\}] + k^2mG)$$

which is clearly bounded by $\mathcal{O}(k^2mG + kN)$. $\qquad\square$

4 An Algorithm for k_H-EDSM

The overall structure of algorithm k_H-EDSM (pseudocode not shown) is the same as k_E-EDSM. The two algorithms differ in the functions used to perform Step (1) (k_H-BORDERS rather than k_E-BORDERS) and Step (2) (k_H-EXTEND rather than k_E-EXTEND). The new functions take as input the same parameters as the old ones and, like them, they both return lists of pairs (j, d) (pseudocode shown below). Unlike k_E-BORDERS and k_E-EXTEND, with k_H-BORDERS and k_H-EXTEND such pairs now represent partial k_H-occurrences of P in $\tilde{T}$.

---

k_H-BORDERS$(P, m, S, q, GST^*_{P, \tilde{T}[i]}, k)$

---

1 **for** $h = 0$ **to** $q - 1$ **do**
2    $count \leftarrow 0$;
3    $j \leftarrow 0$;
4    $h' \leftarrow h$;
5   **while** $count \leq k$ **do**
6      $l \leftarrow lce_{P,S}(j, h')$;
7   **if** $h' + l = q$ **then** **report** $(q - h - 1, count)$;
8   **else**
9   **if** $h' + l + 1 = q \wedge count + 1 \leq k$ **then** **report** $(q - h, count + 1)$;
10   **else**
11   **if** $j + l = m$ **then** **report** $(m - 1, count)$;
12   **else**
13   **if** $j + l + 1 = m \wedge count + 1 \leq k$ **then** **report** $(m - 1, count + 1)$;
14   **else**
15             $count \leftarrow count + 1$;
16             $j \leftarrow j + l + 1$;
17             $h' \leftarrow h' + l + 1$;

At the i-th iteration, for each $S \in \tilde{T}[i]$ and any position h in S, k_H-BORDERS determines whether a prefix of P is at distance at most k from the suffix of S starting at position h via executing up to $k+1$ lce queries in the following manner: computing $l = lce_{P,S}(0, h)$, it finds out that $P[0 \ldots l - 1]$ and $S[h \ldots h + l - 1]$ match exactly and $P[l] \neq S[h + l]$. It can then skip one position in both strings (the mismatch $P[l] \neq S[h + l]$), increasing the error-counter by 1, and compute the $lce_{P,S}(l+1, h+l+1)$. This process is performed up to $k+1$ times, until either (i) the end of S is reached, and then a prefix of P is at distance at most k from the suffix of S starting at h (lines 7–12 in pseudocode); or (ii) the end of P is reached, then a k_H-occurrence of P has been found (lines 13–17 in pseudocode). If the end of S nor the end of P are reached, then more than k substitutions are required, and the algorithm continues with the next position (that is, $h+1$) in S.

The following lemma gives the total cost of all the calls of algorithm k_H-BORDERS in k_H-EDSM.

Lemma 10. *Given P of length m, $\tilde{T}$ of length n and size N, the $GST^*_{P,\tilde{T}[i]}$, for all $i \in [0, n-1]$, and an integer $0 < k < m$, k_H-BORDERS finds the minimal Hamming distance $\leq k$ between the prefixes of P and any suffix of $S \in \tilde{T}[i]$, as well as the k_H-occurrences of P that start and end at position i, in time $\mathcal{O}(kN)$.*

Proof. For any position h in S, the k_H-BORDERS algorithm finds the prefix of P that is at distance at most k from the suffix of S starting at position h in time $\mathcal{O}(k)$ by performing up to $k+1$ lce queries (Fact 1). Over all positions of S, the method therefore requires time $\mathcal{O}(k|S|)$. Doing this for all $S \in \tilde{T}[i]$ and for all $i \in [0, n-1]$ leads to the result.   □

---

k_H-EXTEND$(j, P, m, S, q, GST^*_{P,\tilde{T}[i]}, k)$

---

1 **if** $S = \varepsilon$ **then** report $(j, 0)$;
2 **else**
3      $count \leftarrow 0$;
4      $h \leftarrow 0$;
5      $j' \leftarrow j$;
6   **while** $count \leq k$ **do**
7          $l \leftarrow lce_{P,S}(i', j)$;
8   **if** $h + l = q$ **then** report $(j' + l - 1, count)$;
9   **else**
10   **if** $h + l + 1 = q \wedge count + 1 \leq k$ **then** report $(j' + l, count + 1)$;
11   **else**
12   **if** $j' + l = m$ **then** report $(m - 1, count)$;
13   **else**
14   **if** $j' + l + 1 = m \wedge count + 1 \leq k$ **then** report $(m - 1, count + 1)$;
15   **else**
16                        $count \leftarrow count + 1$;
17                        $h \leftarrow h + l + 1$;
18                        $j' \leftarrow j' + l + 1$;

At the i-th iteration, for each partial k_H-occurrence of P started earlier (represented by $p \in L_p$ similar to algorithm k_E-EDSM) k_H-EXTEND tries to extend it with a string from the current text position. To this end, for each string $S \in \tilde{T}[i]$, it checks whether some partial k_H-occurrence can be extended with the whole S starting from position $j = p + 1$ of P, or whether a full k_H-occurrence can be obtained by considering only a prefix of S for the extension. The algorithm therefore executes up to $k + 1$ lce queries with the same possible outcomes and consequences mentioned for k_H-BORDERS.

The following lemma gives the total cost of all the calls of algorithm k_H-EXTEND in k_H-EDSM.

Lemma 11. *Given P of length m, $\tilde{T}$ of length n and size N, the $GST^*_{P,\tilde{T}[i]}$, for all $i \in [0, n-1]$, and an integer $0 < k < m$, k_H-EXTEND finds all the extensions of prefixes of P required by k_H-EDSM in time $\mathcal{O}(kmG)$, G being the total number of strings in $\tilde{T}$.*

Proof. Algorithm k_H-EXTEND determines in time $\mathcal{O}(k)$ whether a partial k_H-occurrence of P can be extended by S by performing up to $k+1$ constant-time *lce* queries (Fact 1); checking whether a full k_H-occurrence is obtained by considering only a prefix of S for the extension can be performed within the same complexity. Since P has m different prefixes, extending all of them costs $\mathcal{O}(km)$ per each string S. Given that there are G such strings, the overall time is $\mathcal{O}(kmG)$. □

Lemma 12. *Given P of length m, $\tilde{T}$ of length n and total size N, and an integer $0 < k < m$, algorithm k_H-EDSM solves the k_H-EDSM problem, in an on-line manner, in time $\mathcal{O}(kmG + kN)$, G being the total number of strings in $\tilde{T}$.*

Proof. At the i-th iteration, algorithm k_H-EDSM tries to extend each $p \in L_p$ with each string $S \in \tilde{T}[i]$. By Lemma 5, building $GST^*_{P,\tilde{T}[i]}$, for all $i \in [0, n-1]$, requires time $\mathcal{O}(mn + N)$. By Lemma 11, extending prefixes of P stored in L_p with each string $S \in \tilde{T}[i]$ has an overall time cost of $\mathcal{O}(kmG)$. By Lemma 10, the prefixes of P that are at distance at most k from any suffix of S as well as the k_H-occurrences of P that start and end at position i can be found in time $\mathcal{O}(kN)$ in total. Summing up, the overall time complexity for the whole k_H-EDSM algorithm is then $\mathcal{O}(mn + N + kmG + kN) = \mathcal{O}(kmG + kN)$, as $G \geq n$. The algorithm is on-line in the sense that any occurrence of the pattern ending at position i is reported before reading $\tilde{T}[i+1]$. □

The proof of Theorem 9 suggests a way in which algorithm k_E-EDSM can be run on-line in space $\mathcal{O}(m)$; it should be straightforward to see that a similar modification of algorithm k_H-EDSM leads to the following result.

Theorem 13. *The k_H-EDSM problem can be solved on-line in time $\mathcal{O}(kmG + kN)$ and space $\mathcal{O}(m)$.*

Acknowledgements. NP and GR are partially supported by the project MIUR-SIR CMACBioSeq ("Combinatorial methods for analysis and compression of biological sequences") grant n. RBSI146R5L. GB, NP, and GR are partially supported by the project UniPi PRA_2017_44 ("Advanced computational methodologies for the analysis of biomedical data"). NP, SPP, and GR are partially supported by the Royal Society project IE 161274 ("Processing uncertain sequences: combinatorics and applications").

References

1. Altschul, S.F., Gish, W., Miller, W., Myers, E.W., Lipman, D.J.: Basic local alignment search tool. J. Mol. Biol. **215**(3), 403–410 (1990)
2. Baeza-Yates, R.A., Perleberg, C.H.: Fast and practical approximate string matching. Inf. Process. Lett. **59**(1), 21–27 (1996)
3. Barton, C., Liu, C., Pissis, S.P.: On-line pattern matching on uncertain sequences and applications. In: Chan, T.-H.H., Li, M., Wang, L. (eds.) COCOA 2016. LNCS, vol. 10043, pp. 547–562. Springer, Cham (2016). doi:10.1007/978-3-319-48749-6_40
4. Bille, P., Landau, G.M., Raman, R., Sadakane, K., Satti, S.R., Weimann, O.: Random access to grammar-compressed strings. In: SODA, pp. 373–389. SIAM (2011)
5. Gagie, T., Gawrychowski, P., Puglisi, S.J.: Faster approximate pattern matching in compressed repetitive texts. In: Asano, T., Nakano, S., Okamoto, Y., Watanabe, O. (eds.) ISAAC 2011. LNCS, vol. 7074, pp. 653–662. Springer, Heidelberg (2011). doi:10.1007/978-3-642-25591-5_67
6. Gagie, T., Puglisi, S.J.: Searching and indexing genomic databases via kernelization. Front. Bioeng. Biotechnol. **3**, 12 (2015)
7. Grossi, R., Iliopoulos, C.S., Liu, C., Pisanti, N., Pissis, S.P., Retha, A., Rosone, G., Vayani, F., Versari, L.: On-line pattern matching on similar texts. In: CPM. LIPIcs, vol. 78, pp. 9:1–9:14. Schloss Dagstuhl-Leibniz-Zentrum fuer Informatik (2017)
8. Gusfield, D.: Algorithms on Strings, Trees, and Sequences. Cambridge University Press, New York (1997)
9. Holub, J., Smyth, W.F., Wang, S.: Fast pattern-matching on indeterminate strings. J. Discrete Algorithms **6**(1), 37–50 (2008)
10. Huang, L., Popic, V., Batzoglou, S.: Short read alignment with populations of genomes. Bioinformatics **29**(13), 361–370 (2013)
11. Iliopoulos, C.S., Kundu, R., Pissis, S.P.: Efficient pattern matching in elastic-degenerate texts. In: Drewes, F., Martín-Vide, C., Truthe, B. (eds.) LATA 2017. LNCS, vol. 10168, pp. 131–142. Springer, Cham (2017). doi:10.1007/978-3-319-53733-7_9
12. Kociumaka, T., Pissis, S.P., Radoszewski, J.: Pattern matching and consensus problems on weighted sequences and profiles. In: ISAAC. LIPIcs, vol. 64, pp. 46:1–46:12. Schloss Dagstuhl-Leibniz-Zentrum fuer Informatik (2016)
13. Landau, G., Vishkin, U.: Introducing efficient parallelism into approximate string matching and a new serial algorithm. In: STOC, pp. 220–230. ACM (1986)
14. Maciuca, S., de Ojo Elias, C., McVean, G., Iqbal, Z.: A natural encoding of genetic variation in a Burrows-Wheeler transform to enable mapping and genome inference. In: Frith, M., Storm Pedersen, C.N. (eds.) WABI 2016. LNCS, vol. 9838, pp. 222–233. Springer, Cham (2016). doi:10.1007/978-3-319-43681-4_18
15. Na, J.C., Kim, H., Park, H., Lecroq, T., Léonard, M., Mouchard, L., Park, K.: FM-index of alignment: a compressed index for similar strings. Theor. Comput. Sci. **638**, 159–170 (2016)
16. Navarro, G.: Indexing highly repetitive collections. In: Arumugam, S., Smyth, W.F. (eds.) IWOCA 2012. LNCS, vol. 7643, pp. 274–279. Springer, Heidelberg (2012). doi:10.1007/978-3-642-35926-2_29
17. Rahn, R., Weese, D., Reinert, K.: Journaled string tree - a scalable data structure for analyzing thousands of similar genomes on your laptop. Bioinformatics **30**(24), 3499–3505 (2014)
18. Sirén, J.: Indexing variation graphs. In: ALENEX, pp. 13–27. SIAM (2017)

19. The 1000 Genomes Project Consortium: A global reference for human genetic variation. Nature **526**(7571), 68–74 (2015)
20. The Computational Pan-Genomics Consortium: Computational pan-genomics: status, promises and challenges. Briefings Bioinform. 1–18 (2016). bbw089. https://academic.oup.com/bib/article-lookup/doi/10.1093/bib/bbw089
21. Wandelt, S., Leser, U.: String searching in referentially compressed genomes. In: KDIR, pp. 95–102. SciTePress (2012)

Succinct Partial Sums and Fenwick Trees

Philip Bille, Anders Roy Christiansen, Nicola Prezza[⊠],
and Frederik Rye Skjoldjensen

Technical University of Denmark, DTU Compute, Kgs. Lyngby, Denmark
{phbi,aroy,npre,fskj}@dtu.dk

Abstract. We consider the well-studied *partial sums* problem in succint space where one is to maintain an array of n k-bit integers subject to updates such that partial sums queries can be efficiently answered. We present two succint versions of the Fenwick Tree – which is known for its simplicity and practicality. Our results hold in the encoding model where one is allowed to reuse the space from the input data. Our main result is the first that only requires $nk + o(n)$ bits of space while still supporting sum/update in $\mathcal{O}(\log_b n)$ / $\mathcal{O}(b \log_b n)$ time where $2 \leq b \leq \log^{\mathcal{O}(1)} n$. The second result shows how optimal time for sum/update can be achieved while only slightly increasing the space usage to $nk + o(nk)$ bits. Beyond Fenwick Trees, the results are primarily based on bit-packing and sampling – making them very practical – and they also allow for simple optimal parallelization.

Keywords: Partial sums · Fenwick tree · Succinct · Parallel

1 Introduction

Let A be an array of k-bits integers, with $|A| = n$. The *partial sums* problem is to build a data structure maintaining A under the following operations.

- sum(i): return the value $\sum_{t=1}^{i} A[t]$.
- search(j): return the smallest i such that sum(i) $\geq j$.
- update(i, Δ): set $A[i] \leftarrow A[i] + \Delta$, for some Δ such that $0 \leq A[i] + \Delta < 2^k$.
- access(i): return $A[i]$.

Note that access(i) can implemented as sum(i) − sum($i − 1$) and we therefore often do not mention it explicitly.

The partial sums problem is one of the most well-studied data structure problems [1–4,6–9]. In this paper, we consider solutions to the partial sums problem that are *succinct*, that is, we are interested in data structures that use space close to the information-theoretic lower bound of nk bits. We distinguish between *encoding data structures* and *indexing data structures*. Indexing data structures are required to store the input array A verbatim along with additional information to support the queries, whereas encoding data structures have to support operations without consulting the input array.

© Springer International Publishing AG 2017
G. Fici et al. (Eds.): SPIRE 2017, LNCS 10508, pp. 91–96, 2017.
DOI: 10.1007/978-3-319-67428-5_8

In the indexing model Raman et al. [8] gave a data structure that supports
sum, update, and search in $\mathcal{O}(\log n/\log\log n)$ time while using $nk+o(nk)$ bits of
space. This was improved and generalized by Hon et al. [6]. Both of these papers
have the constraint $\Delta \leq \log^{\mathcal{O}(1)} n$. The above time complexity is nearly optimal
by a lower bound of Patrascu and Demaine [7] who showed that sum, search,
and update operations take $\Theta(\log_{w/\delta} n)$ time per operation, where $w \geq \log n$ is
the word size and δ is the number of bits needed to represent Δ. In particular,
whenever $\Delta = \log^{\mathcal{O}(1)} n$ this bound matches the $\mathcal{O}(\log n/\log\log n)$ bound of
Raman et al. [8].

Fenwick [2] presented a simple, elegant, and very practical encoding data
structure. The idea is to replace entries in the input array A with partial sums
that cover A in an implicit complete binary tree structure. The operations are
then implemented by accessing at most $\log n$ entries in the array. The Fenwick
tree uses $nk + n\log n$ bits and supports all operations in $O(\log n)$ time. In this
paper we show two succinct b-ary versions of the Fenwick tree. In the first version
we reduce the size of the Fenwick tree while improving the sum and update time.
In the second version we obtain optimal times for sum and update without using
more space than the previous best succinct solutions [6,8]. All results in this
paper are in the RAM model.

Our results. We show two encoding data structures that gives the following
results.

Theorem 1. *We can replace A with a succinct Fenwick tree of $nk + o(n)$
bits supporting sum, update, and search queries in $\mathcal{O}(\log_b n)$, $\mathcal{O}(b\log_b n)$, and
$\mathcal{O}(\log n)$ time, respectively, for any $2 \leq b \leq \log^{\mathcal{O}(1)} n$.*

Theorem 2. *We can replace A with a succinct Fenwick tree of $nk + o(nk)$ bits
supporting sum and update queries in optimal $\mathcal{O}(\log_{w/\delta} n)$ time and search
queries in $\mathcal{O}(\log n)$ time.*

2 Data Structure

For simplicity, assume that n is a power of 2. The Fenwick tree is an implicit
data structure replacing a word-array $A[1, \ldots, n]$ as follows:

Definition 1. *Fenwick tree of A [2]. If $n = 1$, then leave A unchanged. Otherwise, divide A in consecutive non-overlapping blocks of two elements each
and replace the second element $A[2i]$ of each block with $A[2i - 1] + A[2i]$, for
$i = 1, \ldots, n/2$. Then, recurse on the sub-array $A[2, 4, \ldots, 2i, \ldots, n]$.*

To answer $sum(i)$, the idea is to write i in binary as $i = 2^{j_1} + 2^{j_2} + \cdots + 2^{j_k}$
for some $j_1 > j_2 > \cdots > j_k$. Then there are $k \leq \log n$ entries in the Fenwick
tree, that can be easily computed from i, whose values added together yield
$sum(i)$. In Sect. 2.1 we describe in detail how to perform such accesses. As per
the above definition, the Fenwick tree is an array with n indices. If represented
compactly, this array can be stored in $nk+n\log n$ bits. In this section we present
a generalization of Fenwick trees taking only succinct space.

2.1   Layered b-ary Structure

We first observe that it is easy to generalize Fenwick trees to be b-ary, for $b \geq 2$: we divide A in blocks of b integers each, replace the first $b-1$ elements in each block with their partial sum, and fill the remaining n/b entries of A by recursing on the array A' of size n/b that stores the sums of each block. This generalization gives an array of n indices supporting sum, update, and search queries on the original array in $\mathcal{O}(\log_b n)$, $\mathcal{O}(b \log_b n)$, and $\mathcal{O}(\log n)$ time, respectively. We now show how to reduce the space of this array.

Let $\ell = \log_b n$. We represent our b-ary Fenwick tree $T_b(A)$ using $\ell + 1$ arrays (layers) $T_b^1(A), \ldots, T_b^{\ell+1}(A)$. For simplicity, we assume that $n = b^e$ for some $e \geq 0$ (the general case is then straightforward to derive). To improve readability, we define our layered structure for the special case $b = 2$, and then sketch how to extend it to the general case $b \geq 2$. Our layered structure is defined as follows. If $n = 1$, then $T_2^1(A) = A$. Otherwise:

- $T_2^{\ell+1}(A)[i] = A[(i-1) \cdot 2 + 1]$, for all $i = 1, \ldots, n/2$. Note that $T_2^{\ell+1}(A)$ contains $n/2$ elements.
- Divide A in blocks of 2 elements each, and build an array $A'[j]$ containing the $n/2$ sums of each block, i.e. $A'[j] = A[(j-1) \cdot 2 + 1] + A[(j-1) \cdot 2 + 2]$, for $j = 1, \ldots, n/2$. Then, the next layers are recursively defined as $T_2^{\ell}(A) \leftarrow T_2^{\ell}(A'), \ldots, T_2^1(A) \leftarrow T_2^1(A')$.

For general $b \geq 2$, $T_b^{\ell+1}(A)$ is an array of $\frac{n(b-1)}{b}$ elements that stores the $b-1$ partial sums of each block of b consecutive elements in A, while A' is an array of size n/b containing the complete sums of each block. In Fig. 1 we report an example of our layered structure with $b = 3$. It follows that elements of $T_b^i(A)$, for $i > 1$, take at most $k + (\ell - i + 2) \log b$ bits each. Note that arrays $T_b^1(A), \ldots, T_b^{\ell+1}(A)$ can easily be packed contiguously in a word array while preserving constant-time access to each of them. This saves us $\mathcal{O}(\ell)$ words that would otherwise be needed to store pointers to the arrays. Let $S_b(n, k)$ be the space (in bits) taken by our layered structure. This function satisfies the recurrence

$$S_b(1, k) = k$$
$$S_b(n, k) = \frac{n(b-1)}{b} \cdot (k + \log b) + S_b(n/b, k + \log b)$$

Which unfolds to $S_b(n, k) = \sum_{i=1}^{\log_b n + 1} \frac{n(b-1)}{b^i} \cdot (k + i \log b)$. Using the identities $\sum_{i=1}^{\infty} 1/b^i = 1/(b-1)$ and $\sum_{i=1}^{\infty} i/b^i = b/(b-1)^2$, one can easily derive that $S_b(n, k) \leq nk + 2n \log b$.

We now show how to obtain the time bounds stated in Theorem 1. In the next section, we reduce the space of the structure without affecting query times.

Answering sum. Let the notation $(x_1 x_2 \ldots x_t)_b$, with $0 \leq x_i < b$ for $i = 1, \ldots, t$, represent the number $\sum_{i=1}^{t} b^{t-i} x_i$ in base b. $sum(i)$ queries on our structure are a generalization (in base b) of $sum(i)$ queries on standard Fenwick trees. Consider the base-b representation $x_1 x_2 \ldots x_{\ell+1}$ of i, i.e. $i = (x_1 x_2 \ldots x_{\ell+1})_b$ (note that we have at most $\ell + 1$ digits since we enumerate indexes starting from 1). Consider now all the positions $1 \leq i_1 < i_2 < \cdots < i_t \leq \ell+1$ such that $x_j \neq 0$, for $j = i_1, \ldots, i_t$. The idea is that each of these positions $j = i_1, \ldots, i_t$ can be used to compute an offset o_j in $T_b^j(A)$. Then, $sum(i) = \sum_{j=i_1,\ldots,i_t} T_b^j(A)[o_j]$. The offset o_j relative to the j-th most significant (nonzero) digit of i is defined as follows. If $j = 1$, then $o_j = x_1$. Otherwise, $o_j = (b-1) \cdot (x_1 \ldots x_{j-1})_b + x_j$. Note that we scale by a factor of $b-1$ (and not b) as the first term in this formula as each level $T^j(A)$ stores only $b-1$ out of b partial sums (the remaining sums are passed to level $j-1$). Note moreover that each o_j can be easily computed in constant time and *independently from the other offsets* with the aid of modular arithmetic. It follows that sum queries are answered in $\mathcal{O}(\log_b n)$ time. See Fig. 1 for a concrete example of sum.

Answering update. The idea for performing $update(i, \Delta)$ is analogous to that of $sum(i)$. We access all levels that contain a partial sum covering position i and update at most $b-1$ sums per level. Using the same notation as above, for each $j = i_1, \ldots, i_t$ such that $x_j \neq 0$, we update $T_b^j(A)[o_j + l] \leftarrow T_b^j(A)[o_j + l] + \Delta$ for $l = 0, \ldots, b - x_j - 1$. This procedure takes $\mathcal{O}(b \log_b n)$ time.

Answering search. To answer $search(j)$ we start from $T_b^1(A)$ and simply perform a top-down traversal of the implicit B-tree of degree b defined by the layered structure. At each level, we perform $\mathcal{O}(\log b)$ steps of binary search to find the new offset in the next level. There are $\log_b n$ levels, so search takes overall $\mathcal{O}(\log n)$ time.

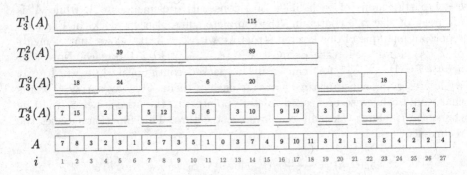

Fig. 1. Example of our layered structure with $n = 27$ and $b = 3$. Horizontal red lines show the portion of A covered by each element in $T_3^j(A)$, for $j = 1, \ldots, \log_b n + 1$. To access the i-th partial sum, we proceed as follows. Let, for example, $i = 19 = (0201)_3$. The only nonzero digits in i are the 2-nd and 4-th most significant. This gives us $o_2 = 2 \cdot (0)_3 + 2 = 2$ and $o_4 = 2 \cdot (020)_3 + 1 = 13$. Then, $sum(19) = T_3^2(A)[2] + T_3^4(A)[13] = 89 + 3 = 92$. (Color figure online)

2.2   Sampling

Let $0 < d \leq n$ be a sample rate, where for simplicity we assume that d divides n. Given our input array A, we derive an array A' of n/d elements containing the sums of groups of d adjacent elements in A, i.e. $A'[i] = \sum_{j=1}^{d} A[(i-1) \cdot d + j]$, $i = 1, \ldots, d$. We then compact A by removing $A[j \cdot d]$ for $j = 1, \ldots, n/d$, and by packing the remaining integers in at most $nk(1 - 1/d)$ bits. We build our layered b-ary Fenwick tree $T_b(A')$ over A'. It is clear that queries on A can be solved with a query on $T_b(A')$ followed by at most d accesses on (the compacted) A. The space of the resulting data structure is $nk(1 - 1/d) + S_b(n/d, k + \log d) \leq nk + \frac{n \log d}{d} + \frac{2n \log b}{d}$ bits. In order to retain the same query times of our basic layered structure, we choose $d = (1/\epsilon) \log_b n$ for any constant $\epsilon > 0$ and obtain a space occupancy of $nk + \epsilon \left(\frac{n \log \log_b n}{\log_b n} + \frac{2n \log b}{\log_b n} \right)$ bits. For $b \leq \log^{\mathcal{O}(1)} n$, this space is $nk + o(n)$ bits. Note that—as opposed to existing succinct solutions—the low-order term does not depend on k.

3   Optimal-Time sum and update

In this section we show how to obtain optimal running times for sum and update queries in the RAM model. We can directly apply the word-packing techniques described in [7] to speed-up queries; here we only sketch this strategy, see [7] for full details. Let us describe the idea on the structure of Sect. 2.1, and then plug in sampling to reduce space usage. We divide arrays $T_b^j(A)$ in blocks of $b - 1$ entries, and store one word (w bits) for each such block. We can pack $b - 1$ integers of at most $w/(b - 1)$ bits each (for an opportune b, read below) in the word associated with each block. Since blocks of $b - 1$ integers fit in a single word, we can easily answer sum and update queries on them in constant time. sum queries on our overall structure can be answered as described in Sect. 2.1, except that now we also need to access one of the packed integers at each level j to correct the value read from $T_b^j(A)$. To answer update queries, the idea is to perform update operations on the packed blocks of integers in constant time exploiting bit-parallelism instead of updating at most $b - 1$ values of $T_b^j(A)$. At each update operation, we transfer one of these integers on $T_b^j(A)$ (in a cyclic fashion) to avoid overflowing and to achieve worst-case performance. Note that each packed integer is increased by at most Δ for at most $b - 1$ times before being transferred to $T_b^j(A)$, so we get the constraint $(b - 1) \log((b - 1)\Delta) \leq w$. We choose $(b - 1) = \frac{w}{\log w + \delta}$. Then, it is easy to show that the above constraint is satisfied. The number of levels becomes $\log_b n = \mathcal{O}(\log_{w/\delta} n)$. Since we spend constant time per level, this is also the worst-case time needed to answer sum and update queries on our structure. To analyze space usage we use the corrected formula

$$S_b(1, k) = k$$
$$S_b(n, k) = \frac{n(b-1)}{b} \cdot (k + \log b) + \frac{nw}{b} + S_b(n/b, k + \log b)$$

yielding $S_b(1, k) \leq nk + 2n \log b + \frac{nw}{b-1}$. Replacing $b - 1 = \frac{w}{\log w + \delta}$ we achieve $nk + \mathcal{O}(n\delta + n \log w)$ bits of space.

We now apply the sampling technique of Sect. 2.2 with a slight variation. In order to get the claimed space/time bounds, we need to further apply bit-parallelism techniques on the packed integers stored in A: using techniques from [5], we can answer sum, search, and update queries in $\mathcal{O}(1)$ time on blocks of w/k integers. It follows that we can now use sample rate $d = \frac{w \log n}{k \log(w/\delta)}$ without affecting query times. After sampling A and building the Fenwick tree above described over the sums of size-d blocks of A, the overall space is $nk(1 - 1/d) + S_b(n/d, k + \log d) = nk + \frac{n \log d}{d} + \mathcal{O}(\frac{n\delta}{d} + \frac{n \log w}{d})$. Note that $d \leq \frac{w^2}{k \log(w/\delta)} \leq w^2$, so $\log d \in \mathcal{O}(\log w)$ and space simplifies to $nk + \mathcal{O}(\frac{n\delta}{d} + \frac{n \log w}{d})$. The term $\frac{n\delta}{d}$ equals $\frac{n\delta k \log(w/\delta)}{w \log n}$. Since $\delta \leq w$, then $\delta \log(w/\delta) \leq w$, and this term therefore simplifies to $\frac{nk}{\log n} \in o(nk)$. Finally, the term $\frac{n \log w}{d}$ equals $\frac{n \log w \cdot k \log(w/\delta)}{w \log n} \leq \frac{nk}{(w \log n)/(\log w)^2} \in o(nk)$. The bounds of Theorem 2 follow.

Parallelism. Note that sum and update queries on our succinct Fenwick trees can be naturally parallelized as all accesses/updates on the levels can be performed independently from each other. For sum, we need $\mathcal{O}(\log \log_b n)$ further time to perform a parallel sum of the $\log_b n$ partial results. It is not hard to show that—on architectures with $\log_b n$ processors—this reduces sum/update times to $\mathcal{O}(\log \log_b n)/\mathcal{O}(b)$ and $\mathcal{O}(\log \log_{w/\delta} n)/\mathcal{O}(1)$ in Theorems 1 and 2, respectively.

References

1. Dietz, P.F.: Optimal algorithms for list indexing and subset rank. In: Dehne, F., Sack, J.-R., Santoro, N. (eds.) WADS 1989. LNCS, vol. 382, pp. 39–46. Springer, Heidelberg (1989). doi:10.1007/3-540-51542-9_5
2. Fenwick, P.M.: A new data structure for cumulative frequency tables. Softw. Pract. Exp. **24**(3), 327–336 (1994)
3. Fredman, M., Saks, M.: The cell probe complexity of dynamic data structures. In: Proceedings of 21st STOC, pp. 345–354 (1989)
4. Fredman, M.L.: The complexity of maintaining an array and computing its partial sums. J. ACM (JACM) **29**(1), 250–260 (1982)
5. Hagerup, T.: Sorting and searching on the word RAM. In: Morvan, M., Meinel, C., Krob, D. (eds.) STACS 1998. LNCS, vol. 1373, pp. 366–398. Springer, Heidelberg (1998). doi:10.1007/BFb0028575
6. Hon, W.K., Sadakane, K., Sung, W.K.: Succinct data structures for searchable partial sums with optimal worst-case performance. Theor. Comput. Sci. **412**(39), 5176–5186 (2011)
7. Patrascu, M., Demaine, E.D.: Logarithmic lower bounds in the cell-probe model. SIAM J. Comput. **35**(4), 932–963 (2006)
8. Raman, R., Raman, V., Rao, S.S.: Succinct dynamic data structures. In: Dehne, F., Sack, J.-R., Tamassia, R. (eds.) WADS 2001. LNCS, vol. 2125, pp. 426–437. Springer, Heidelberg (2001). doi:10.1007/3-540-44634-6_39
9. Yao, A.C.: On the complexity of maintaining partial sums. SIAM J. Comput. **14**(2), 277–288 (1985)

Tight Bounds for Top Tree Compression

Philip Bille[✉], Finn Fernstrøm, and Inge Li Gørtz

DTU Compute, Technical University of Denmark,
Richard Petersens Plads, 2800 Kgs. Lyngby, Denmark
{phbi,inge}@dtu.dk, finnfernstroem@gmail.com

Abstract. We consider compressing labeled, ordered and rooted trees using DAG compression and top tree compression. We show that there exists a family of trees such that the size of the DAG compression is always a logarithmic factor smaller than the size of the top tree compression (even for an alphabet of size 1). The result settles an open problem from Bille et al. (Inform. and Comput., 2015).

1 Introduction

Let T be a labeled, ordered, and rooted tree. The overall idea in *top tree compression* [3] is to first construct the *top tree* $\mathcal{T}$ for T [1,2], which is a balanced binary tree representing a hierarchical decomposition of T into overlapping connected subgraphs of T. The top tree $\mathcal{T}$ is then *DAG compressed*, i.e., converted into the minimal DAG representation [4], into the *top DAG*, which we then output as the final compressed representation of T. Top tree compression has several attractive properties. For instance, it achieves almost optimal worst-case compression, supports navigational queries in logarithmic time, and is highly competitive in practice [3,5].

An interesting open question from Bille et al. [3] is how top tree compression compares to classical DAG compression. Let n_G denote the size (vertices plus edges) of the graph G. From Bille et al. [3, Thm. 2] we have that for any tree T, the size of the top DAG $\mathcal{TD}$ of T is always at most a factor $O(\log n_T)$ larger than the size of DAG $\mathcal{D}$ of T. However, it is not known if this bound is tight and answering this question is stated as an open problem. Our main result in this paper is to show that there exists a family of trees such that the DAG is always a factor $\Omega(\log n_T)$ smaller than the top DAG and that this bound can be achieved even for an alphabet of size 1 (i.e. unlabeled trees). This settles this open question and proves that the $O(\log n_T)$ factor is tight.

Due to lack of space we omit a detailed discussion of the related work.

2 Top Trees and Top DAGs

We briefly review top tree compression [3]. Let T be a tree with n_T nodes. Let v be a node in T with children $v_1, \ldots, v_k$ in left-to-right order. Define $T(v)$ to be the

P. Bille and I.L. Gørtz—Partially supported by the Danish Research Council (DFF - 4005-00267).

© Springer International Publishing AG 2017
G. Fici et al. (Eds.): SPIRE 2017, LNCS 10508, pp. 97–102, 2017.
DOI: 10.1007/978-3-319-67428-5_9

subtree induced by v and all proper descendants of v and define $F(v)$ to be the forest induced by all proper descendants of v. For $1 \leq s \leq r \leq k$ let $T(v, v_s, v_r)$ be the tree pattern induced by the nodes $\{v\} \cup T(v_s) \cup T(v_{s+1}) \cup \cdots \cup T(v_r)$.

A *cluster* with *top boundary node* v is a tree pattern of the form $T(v, v_s, v_r)$, $1 \leq s \leq r \leq k$. A *cluster* with *top boundary node* v and *bottom boundary node* u is a tree pattern of the form $T(v, v_s, v_r) \backslash F(u)$, $1 \leq s \leq r \leq k$, where u is a node in $T(v_s) \cup \cdots \cup T(v_r)$. Nodes that are not boundary nodes are called *internal nodes*. Two edge disjoint clusters A and B whose vertices overlap on a single boundary node can be *merged* if their union $C = A \cup B$ is also a cluster using various type of merges (see details in Bille et al. [3]).

A *top tree* $\mathcal{T}$ of T is a hierarchical decomposition of T into clusters. It is an ordered, rooted, labeled, and binary tree defined as follows.

- The nodes of $\mathcal{T}$ correspond to clusters of T.
- The root of $\mathcal{T}$ corresponds to the cluster T itself.
- The leaves of $\mathcal{T}$ correspond to the edges of T. The label of each leaf is the pair of labels of the endpoints of its corresponding edge (u, v) in T. The two labels are ordered so that the label of the parent appears before the label of the child.
- Each internal node of $\mathcal{T}$ corresponds to the merged cluster of its two children. The label of each internal node is the type of merge it represents (out of the five merging options from [3]). The children are ordered so that the left child is the child cluster visited first in a preorder traversal of T.

We construct the top tree $\mathcal{T}$ of height $O(\log n_T)$ for top tree compression bottom-up in $O(\log n_T)$ iterations. At each iteration we maintain an auxiliary rooted ordered tree $\widetilde{T}$ initialized as $\widetilde{T} := T$. The edges of $\widetilde{T}$ will correspond to the nodes of $\mathcal{T}$ and to the clusters of T. The internal nodes of $\widetilde{T}$ will correspond to boundary nodes of clusters in T and the leaves of $\widetilde{T}$ will correspond to a subset of the leaves of T. In each iteration, a constant fraction of $\widetilde{T}$'s edges (i.e., clusters of T) are merged as described below. The precise sequence of merges is essential for obtaining the compression guarantees of top tree compression and enabling efficient navigation.

Step 1: Horizontal Merges . For each node $v \in \widetilde{T}$ with $k \geq 2$ children $v_1, \ldots, v_k$ for $i = 1$ to $\lfloor k/2 \rfloor$, merge the edges (v, v_{2i-1}) and (v, v_{2i}) if v_{2i-1} or v_{2i} is a leaf. If k is odd and v_k is a leaf and both v_{k-2} and v_{k-1} are non-leaves then also merge (v, v_{k-1}) and (v, v_k).

Step 2: Vertical Merges . For each maximal path $v_1, \ldots, v_p$ of nodes in $\widetilde{T}$ such that v_{i+1} is the parent of v_i and $v_2, \ldots, v_{p-1}$ have a single child: If p is even merge the following pairs of edges $\{(v_1, v_2), (v_2, v_3)\}, \ldots, \{(v_{p-2}, v_{p-1})\}$. If p is odd merge the following pairs of edges $\{(v_1, v_2), (v_2, v_3)\}, \ldots, \{(v_{p-3}, v_{p-2})\}$, and if (v_{p-1}, v_p) was not merged in Step 1 then also merge $\{(v_{p-2}, v_{p-1}), (v_{p-1}, v_p)\}$.

Since each iteration shrinks the tree by a constant factor the resulting top tree $\mathcal{T}$ has height $O(\log n_T)$. The top DAG $\mathcal{TD}$ is the minimal DAG representation of $\mathcal{T}$.

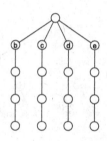 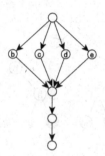

Fig. 1. An example of the labeled construction with $h = 4$ and $\sigma = 5$. On the right is the minimal DAG representation of the tree. Only labels different from a are shown.

2.1 Top DAG Properties

We show a few basic properties of top DAGs that we need for our construction. Let $\widehat{T}$ be a subtree of T. If there are no merges in the first k iterations of the top tree construction algorithm, which include edges from both $\widehat{T}$ and $T \backslash \widehat{T}$, we define $\widehat{T}$ to be k-*local*. A path $v_0, \ldots, v_\ell$ such that v_ℓ is a leaf, v_{i+1} is a child of v_i, and v_i has no other children for $i > 0$, is an *isolated path*. The following results follow directly from the top DAG construction.

Lemma 1. *Any k-local isolated path of length $2^{k-1} < j \le 2^k$ will be merged into a single cluster in exactly k iterations of the top tree construction algorithm.*

Lemma 2. *Any k-local isolated path of length 2^k, where all nodes except one have identical labels is represented by a subgraph in the top DAG of size $\Theta(k)$, where each node is contained in atleast one path of clusters of length k.*

Lemma 3. *Let $\widehat{T}$ be a k-local subtree of T, which after $j > 0$ iterations of the construction algorithm is an isolated path p in $\widetilde{T}$ of length 2^{k-j}, where all clusters except two are identical. The part of $T\mathcal{D}$, which represents $\widehat{T}$ above level j, then has size $\Theta(k - j)$, and each cluster in $\widetilde{T}$ is contained in a path of clusters of length $k - j$.*

3 Bounds for Large Alphabets

As a warm-up we first consider large alphabets and show the following result.

Theorem 4. *There exists a family of rooted, ordered, and labeled trees, for which $n_{T\mathcal{D}} = \Theta(\log n_T) \cdot n_D$ for alphabets of size $\Omega(\sqrt{n_T})$.*

Proof. Given positive integers k, w, and an alphabet $\Sigma = \{a, b, c, \ldots\}$ of size σ, construct a tree T as the union of w isolated paths of length $h = 2^k$ with a shared root. The second node of each path has its own unique label, $b, c, d, \ldots$. All other nodes are labeled a. We have $n_T = \Theta(wh)$ and $n_D = \Theta(w + h)$ (see Fig. 1).

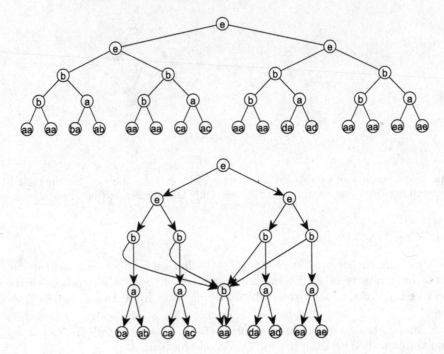

Fig. 2. Top tree and top DAG of the tree in Fig. 1. The label of the leaves corresponding to an edge $(v, p(v))$ in T, where $p(v)$ is the parent of v, is the label of $p(v)$ followed by the label of v. The labels of the internal nodes are the merge types as defined in [3].

Next consider the top DAG. We show that $n_{TD} = \Theta(w \log h)$. It is easy to verify that the paths are k-local. By Lemma 1 the edges of each path p will be merged into one cluster in the first k iterations. Subsequently these clusters are merged together. By Lemma 2 each path p is represented in TD by a subgraph of size $\Theta(\log h)$, where the second node v_1 of p is contained in a path of clusters of length $\Theta(\log h)$. These clusters cannot be shared by another path p', since the label of v_1 is unique. We have w paths, so in total this part of the top DAG has size $\Theta(w \log h)$. The merging of the clusters containing the w paths is represented by $\Theta(w)$ clusters in TD. Hence in total $n_{TD} = \Theta(w \log h)$ (see Fig. 2).

We choose $w = \Theta(\sqrt{n_T})$ and $h = \Theta(\sqrt{n_T})$. Hence we get $n_D = \Theta(\sqrt{n_T})$ and $n_{TD} = \Theta(\sqrt{n_T} \log n_T)$, which implies $n_{TD} = \Theta(\log n_T) \cdot n_D$. We need $w + 1$ different characters, hence $\sigma = \Omega(\sqrt{n_T})$. $\square$

4   Bounds for Unlabeled Trees

We now modify the construction from Sect. 3, such that it works for unlabeled trees, and show the following result.

Theorem 5. *There exists a family of rooted, ordered, and unlabeled trees, for which $n_{TD} = \Theta(\log n_T) \cdot n_D$.*

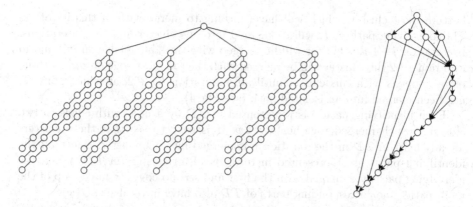

Fig. 3. An example of the unlabeled construction with $w = 4$ and $h = 4$. On the right is the minimal DAG representation of the tree.

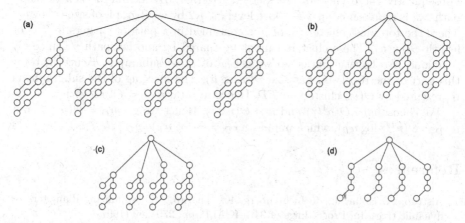

Fig. 4. The auxiliary tree $\tilde{T}$ of the tree from Fig. 3 after the first 4 iterations: (a) iteration 1, (b) iteration 2, (c) iteration $3 = k_w + 1$, (d) iteration $4 = k_w + 2$.

Proof. Given integers $k_h > 1$ and $k_w > 0$, construct a rooted tree T as the union of $w = 2^{k_w}$ subtrees, $T_1, \ldots, T_w$, connected only at the root of T. Each T_i has a path of length $h = 2^{k_h}$, denoted its *main path* m_i. The second node on m_i has a path on its left side of length i, denoted the *identifying path* of T_i. All other nodes on m_i have a path on their left side of length $2w$, denoted a *side path*. We have $n_T = \Theta(w^2 h)$ and $n_D = \Theta(w + h)$ (see Fig. 3).

We now show that $n_{\mathcal{TD}} = \Theta(w \log h)$. By definition $w = 2^{k_w}$, so all of the side paths have length 2^{k_w+1}. They are all isolated and $(k_w + 1)$-local, so by Lemma 1 each of them will be merged into one cluster in $k_w + 1$ iterations, and by Lemma 2 they are represented in $\mathcal{TD}$ by a subgraph of size $\Theta(\log w)$. Consider now a subtree T_i. In iteration $k_w + 2$ each of the clusters containing the side paths of T_i will be merged with the sibling edge on m_i, except for the bottom most cluster, which will have nothing to merge with in this iteration. The identifying path of T_i will be merged into one cluster in $j \leq k_w$ iterations. In iteration $j+1$ this cluster will be merged with the sibling edge on m_i, and in iteration $j+2$ this cluster will be merged with the top most edge on m_i. Nothing more happens with this cluster until after iteration $k_w + 2$, at which point T_i has been merged into an isolated path (see Fig. 4).

Each identifying path p is represented in $\mathcal{TD}$ by a node with edges to two clusters, which merged together gives p. It is easy to see that these clusters already exist in $\mathcal{TD}$ in the iteration p is merged into one cluster. Hence all the identifying paths are represented in total by $\Theta(w)$ clusters in $\mathcal{TD}$. When the identifying paths are merged with the first and second edges from the top of the main paths, the corresponding parts of $\mathcal{TD}$ also have in total size $\Theta(w)$.

After $k_w + 2$ iterations $\widetilde{T}$ will consist of w isolated paths (of clusters) of length $h = 2^{k_h}$. It is easy to verify that they are $(k_w + 2 + k_h)$-local. By Lemma 1 the clusters of each path p will be merged into one cluster in the next k_h iterations. Subsequently these clusters are merged together. By Lemma 3 each of these paths, p, is represented in $\mathcal{TD}$ above level $k_w + 2$ by a subgraph of size $\Theta(\log h)$, where the top most cluster C_0 of p is contained in a path of clusters in $\mathcal{TD}$ of length $\Theta(\log h)$. These clusters cannot be shared by another path p', since C_0 is unique. We have w paths, so we get w of these subgraphs. Hence in total this part of the top DAG has size $\Theta(w \log h)$. The merging of the subgraphs is represented by $\Theta(w)$ clusters in $\mathcal{TD}$. Hence in total $n_{\mathcal{TD}} = \Theta(w \log h)$.

We choose $w = \Theta(n^{1/3})$ and $h = \Theta(n^{1/3})$. Hence we get $n_D = \Theta(n^{1/3})$ and $n_{\mathcal{TD}} = \Theta(n^{1/3} \log n_T)$, which implies $n_{\mathcal{TD}} = \Theta(\log n_T) \cdot n_D$. □

References

1. Alstrup, S., Holm, J., de Lichtenberg, K., Thorup, M.: Minimizing diameters of dynamic trees. In: Proceedings of 24th ICALP, pp. 270–280 (1997)
2. Alstrup, S., Holm, J., Thorup, M.: Maintaining center and median in dynamic trees. In: Proceedings of 7th SWAT, pp. 46–56 (2000)
3. Bille, P., Gørtz, I.L., Landau, G.M., Weimann, O.: Tree compression with top trees. Inform. Comput. **243**, 166–177 (2015)
4. Downey, P.J., Sethi, R., Tarjan, R.E.: Variations on the common subexpression problem. J. ACM **27**(4), 758–771 (1980)
5. Hübschle-Schneider, L., Raman, R.: Tree compression with top trees revisited. In: Proceedings of 14th SEA, pp. 15–27 (2015)

Efficient Compression and Indexing
of Trajectories

Nieves R. Brisaboa[1], Travis Gagie[2], Adrián Gómez-Brandón[1(✉)],
Gonzalo Navarro[3], and José R. Paramá[1]

[1] Computer Science Deparment, Universidade da Coruña, A Coruña, Spain
{brisaboa,adrian.gbrandon,jose.parama}@udc.es
[2] School of Informatics and Telecommunications, Diego Portales University,
Santiago, Chile
travis.gagie@mail.udp.cl
[3] Department of Computer Science, University of Chile, Santiago, Chile
gnavarro@dcc.uchile.cl

Abstract. We present a new compressed representation of free trajectories of moving objects. It combines a partial-sums-based structure that retrieves in constant time the position of the object at any instant, with a hierarchical minimum-bounding-boxes representation that allows determining if the object is seen in a certain rectangular area during a time period. Combined with spatial snapshots at regular intervals, the representation is shown to outperform classical ones by orders of magnitude in space, and also to outperform previous compressed representations in time performance, when using the same amount of space.

1 Introduction

With the appearance of cheap devices, such as smartphones or GPS trackers, which record the position of moving objects, the need to efficiently store and manage information on trajectories has become commonplace. Although storage, network, and processing capacities are rapidly increasing, the available data grows faster, and demands reduced-size representations [20]. The first option is to lose precision and discard points of the acquired trajectories, with more or less sophisticated procedures. A second choice is to keep all the points of the trajectories and use differential compression [6,12]. These methods store for each coordinate (x, y) the difference with the previous point. The problem is that, to obtain the coordinates of the ith point, we must add up all the preceding differences. This is a variant of the *partial sums problem* where the values can be positive or negative.

Funded in part by European Union Horizon 2020 Marie Skłodowska-Curie grant agreement No. 690941; MINECO (PGE and FEDER) [TIN2016-78011-C4-1-R;TIN2013-46238-C4-3-R]; CDTI, MINECO [ITC-20161074;IDI-20141259;ITC-20151305;ITC-20151247]; Xunta de Galicia (co-founded with FEDER) [ED431G/01]; and Fondecyt Grants 1-171058 and 1-170048, Chile.

© Springer International Publishing AG 2017
G. Fici et al. (Eds.): SPIRE 2017, LNCS 10508, pp. 103–115, 2017.
DOI: 10.1007/978-3-319-67428-5_10

Our new method, called Constant Time Access Compressed Trajectories (ContaCT), uses an Elias-Fano-based [8,9] representation of the differences that allows computing the partial sums in constant time while using space comparable to other differential encoding methods. In addition to constant-time access to the trajectory data, ContaCT provides a hierarchical structure that allows efficiently answering time-interval queries [14] (i.e., determine if an object is seen inside a rectangular area during a time interval) without the need to follow all the movements of the object in the queried interval. We use ContaCT to represent the trajectories of a large set of objects. At regular time instants, ContaCT includes a spatial snapshot with a structure that supports range queries, which is useful to bound the objects that must be tracked to answer time-interval queries.

Our experiments on a set of real trajectories of ships shows that, while there exist techniques based on grammar-compression that use less space than ContaCT [3], our index is up to 2.7 times faster when using about the same amount of space. Our index is also much faster than a baseline differentially compressed representation, for about the same space. We also compared ContaCT with a classical MVR-tree, where trajectories are stored as sets of points and time-interval queries reduce to 3D range queries. It turns out that ContaCT required 1,300 times less space, and it was still faster in time-interval queries spanning more than 14 instants.

2   Background

A trajectory is a sequence of timestamped geographic positions in the two-dimensional space. We assume that the recorded timestamps are regularly placed over time, possibly with periods of time without values. We also assume that the recorded timestamps are exactly the same for all the objects.

Apart from the basic functionality of returning the whole trajectory of an object or its position at some time instant, we deal with the following, more elaborate queries [14]: *time-slice* returns all the objects in a given query region at a given timestamp, and *time-interval* returns all the objects that overlap the query region at any time instant of an interval.

Bitmaps. A *bitmap* is a binary sequence $B[1,n]$ that supports the following operations: (i) $access(B,i)$ returns the bit $B[i]$, (ii) $rank_b(B,i)$ returns the number of occurrences of bit $b \in 0,1$ in $B[1,i]$, and (iii) $select_b(B,j)$ returns the position in B of the jth occurrence of bit $b \in 0,1$. There exist representations using $n + o(n)$ bits that answer all those queries in constant time [5]. When the bitmap has $m \ll n$ 1s, it is possible to use compressed representations that use $m \log(n/m) + O(m)$ bits [8,9]. This representation still performs $select_1$ queries in constant time, whereas $access$ and $rank$ require time $O(\log(n/m))$ [13].

Partial Sums. Given values $0 < x_1 < x_2 < \ldots < x_m \leq n$, we can define the differences $d_i = x_i - x_{i-1}$ and $d_1 = x_1$, so that $x_i = \sum_{j=1}^{i} d_i$. An Elias-Fano representation of the partial sums is a bitmap $B[1..n]$ with all $B[x_i] = 1$ and all the rest zero, or which is the same, the concatenation of the d_i values written in unary. Therefore, we can retrieve $x_i = select_1(B, i)$ in constant time, and the space of the representation is $\log(n/m) + O(m)$ bits, close to a differential representation of the d_i values.

3 Related Work

Reducing the Size of Trajectories. A lossy way to reduce size is to generate a new trajectory that approximates the original one, by keeping the most representative points. The best known method of this type is the Douglas-Peucker algorithm [7]. Other strategies record speed and direction, discarding points that can be reasonably predicted with this data [17]. A lossless way to reduce space is to use differential encodings of the consecutive values x, y, and time [6,12,19].

Spatio-Temporal Indexes. Spatio-temporal indexes can be classified into three types. The first is a classic multidimensional spatial index, usually the R-tree, augmented with a temporal dimension. For example, the 3DR-tree [18] uses three-dimensional Minimum Bounding Boxes (MBBs), where the third dimension is the time, to index segments of trajectories. A second approach is the multiversion R-trees, which creates an R-tree for each timestamp and a B-tree to select the relevant R-trees. The best known index of this family is the MV3R-tree [16]. The third type of index partitions the space statically, and then a temporal index is built for each of the spatial partitions [4].

3.1 GraCT

The closest predecessor of our work, GraCT [3], assumes regular timestamps and stores trajectories using two components. At regular time instants, it represents the position of all the objects in a structure called *snapshot*. The positions of objects between snapshots are represented in a structure called *log*.

Let us denote Sp_k the snapshot representing the position of all the objects at timestamp k. Between two consecutive snapshots Sp_k and Sp_{k+d}, there is a log for each object, which is denoted $\mathcal{L}_{k,k+d}(id)$, being id the identifier of the object. The log stores the differences of positions compressed with *RePair* [11], a grammar-based compressor. In order to speed up the queries over the resulting sequence, the nonterminals are enriched with additional information, mainly the MBB of the trajectory segment encoded by the nonterminal.

Each snapshot is a binary matrix where a cell set to 1 indicates that one or more objects are placed in that position of the space. To store such a (generally sparse) matrix, it uses a k^2-tree [2]. The k^2-tree is a space- and time- efficient version of a region quadtree [15], and is used to filter the objects that may be relevant for a time-instant or time-interval query.

3.2 ScdcCT

ScdcCT was implemented as a classical compressed baseline to compare against GraCT [3]. It uses the same components, snapshots and logs, but the logs are compressed with differences and not with grammars. The differences are compressed using (s, c)-Dense Codes [1], a fast-to-decode variable-length code that has low redundancy over the zero-order empirical entropy of the sequence. This exploits the fact that short movements to contiguous cells are more frequent than movements to distant cells.

4 ContaCT

ContaCT uses snapshots and logs, just like GraCT. The main differences are in the log. As explained, in GraCT the log stores the differences of the consecutive positions. In order to know the position of an object at a given timestamp i, we access the closest previous snapshot and add up the differences until reaching the desired timestamp. GraCT speeds up this traversal by storing the total differences represented by nonterminals, so that they can be traversed in constant time. This makes GraCT faster than a differential representation that needs to add up all the individual differences, but still it has to traverse a number of symbols that grows proportionally to the distance d between consecutive snapshots. ContaCT completely avoids that sequential traversal of the log.

4.1 The Log

ContaCT represents each $\mathcal{L}_{k,k+d}(id)$ with components $time(id)$, $\Delta_X(id)$, $\Delta_Y(id)$.

Time (id) tells the timestamps for which object id has (x, y) coordinates. It stores the $first$ and $last$ positions with data in $\mathcal{L}_{k,k+d}(id)$, and a bitmap $T(id)$ of $last - first + 1$ bits indicating with a 0 that there is data at that time instant.

$\Delta_X(id)$ stores the differences of the x coordinate using three bitmaps: $X(id)_t$ indicates, for each position having a 0 in $T(id)$, whether the difference is positive or negative; and $X(id)_p$ and $X(id)_n$ store the positive and negative differences, respectively, using Elias-Fano. $\Delta_Y(id)$ is analogous.

Given the log $\mathcal{L}_{k,k+d}(id)$ and a local timestamp $i \in [1, d - 1]$, we compute the x coordinate of the object id at that timestamp as follows (analogous for y):

1. $dis = rank_1(T(id), i - first + 1)$ returns the number of timestamps for which we have no data (the object was missing) until position i, counting from the first timestamp with data.
2. $pos = rank_1(X(id)_t, i - dis - first + 1)$ and $neg = i - dis - first - pos + 1$, are the number of positive and negative differences until position i, respectively.
3. $select_1(X(id)_p, pos) - pos - (select_1(X(id)_n, neg) - neg)$ returns the x coordinate at timestamp i.

We use the sparse bitmap representation for $X(id)_p$ and $X(id)_n$, and the plain version for $X(id)_t$ and $T(id)$. The size of the complete structure is $n \log N/n + O(d)$ bits, where N is the sum of the differences in x, and $n \le d$ is the number of positions where the object has coordinate information.

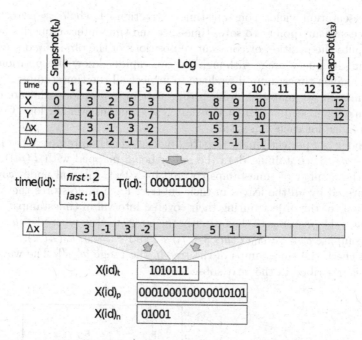

Fig. 1. The log of ContaCT for a given object id.

Example. The top of Fig. 1 shows the coordinates of a trajectory. There is no data about the position of the object at timestamps 1, 6, 7, 11, and 12. Timestamps 0 and 13 are represented with snapshots. Arrays X and Y contain the absolute coordinates of the trajectory, and ΔX and ΔY the corresponding differences (the arrays are not stored in this form, they are included for clarity).

Below those arrays, we have the data structure $time(id)$: *First* and *last* store the first and last timestamps of $\mathcal{L}_{0,13}(id)$ that have data, and bitmap $T(id)$ has a bit for each timestamp in between. A bit 1 means no data for its timestamp.

The bottom of the figure shows the three bitmaps that represent $\Delta X(id)$. $X(id)_t$ has a bit for each bit set to 0 in $T(id)$, that is, for each position of $\Delta X(id)$ with a value. Each bit of $X(id)_t$ indicates whether the corresponding difference is positive or negative. For each bit of $X(id)_t$ set to 1, $X(id)_p$ stores that value in unary. $X(id)_n$ stores, in the same way, the negative differences.

Let us extract the x coordinate at timestamp 9. First, we obtain the number of disappearances until timestamp 9: $dis = rank_1(T(id), i - first + 1) = 2$. Next, we obtain the number of positive and negative differences until timestamp 9: $pos = rank_1(X(id)_t, i - dis - first + 1) = 4$ and $neg = i - dis - first - pos + 1 = 2$.

Finally, the x coordinate is $select_1(X(id)_p, pos) - pos - (select_1(X_n, neg) - neg) =$
$select_1(X(id)_p, 4) - 4 - (select_1(X(id)_n, 2) - 2) = 16 - 4 - (5 - 2) = 12 - 3 = 9.$ □

4.2   Indexing the Logs

Our representation yields constant-time extraction of whole trajectories and
direct access to any point. To solve time-slice and time-interval queries, we may
just compute the position or consecutive positions of the object and see if they
fall within the query area. Although we can rapidly know the position of an
object in a given timestamp, if we have to inspect all the timestamps of a given
queried interval, we may spend much time obtaining positions that are outside
the region of interest. In order to accelerate these queries over the logs, ContaCT
stores an index for each $\mathcal{L}_{k,k+d}(id)$.

The index is a perfect binary tree that indexes the timestamps of the interval
$[k+1, k+d-1]$ containing data (i.e., after being mapped with $T(id)$). Let C
indicate the number of timestamps covered by a leaf. Internal nodes cover the
ranges covered by all the leaves in their subtree. Each node stores the MBR of
the positions of the object during their covered interval of timestamps.

To check the positions of the object in the interval $[b, e]$, where $1 \leq b \leq e < d$,
we first compute $b' = rank_0(T(id), b - first)$ and $e' = rank_0(T(id), e - first)$,
and then check the timestamps of the tree in the range $[b', e']$. The way to use
this tree is described in the next subsection.

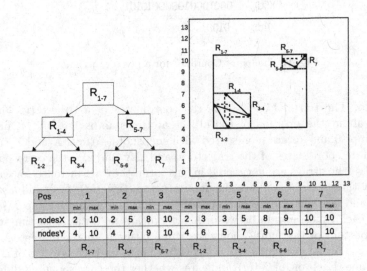

Fig. 2. The index of a log.

Example. Figure 2 shows the index for the trajectory of Fig. 1. C is 2, so the
leaves cover at most 2 timestamps. In $\mathcal{L}_{0,13}(id)$, there are 7 time instants with
values, at timestamps 2, 3, 4, 5, 8, 9, and 10. Therefore the leftmost leaf of

the tree covers the positions at timestamps 2 and 3, the next leaf covers the timestamps 4 and 5, and so on.

The root contains the MBR that encloses all the positions in the interval covered by $\mathcal{L}_{0,13}(id)$. Since there are 7 timestamps with values, we labeled it R_{1-7}. At the top right, that MBR is drawn as a rectangle with a solid line. The left child, R_{1-4}, covers the positions of the first 4 timestamps. The right child, R_{5-7}, covers the timestamps from the 5th to the 7th, and so on. The second-level MBRs are shown at the top right as rectangles with densely dotted lines, whereas the third level MBRs are drawn with scattered dotted lines.   □

Observe that each log stores the movements of one object between two snapshots, therefore there will be a considerable number of trees. To save space, we store the perfect trees in heap order, avoiding pointers. Each tree is then stored as two arrays, $nodesX$ and $nodesY$, storing the extremes of the MBRs in each dimension. The children of a node at position p are at $2p$ and $2p + 1$.

Further, the arrays $nodesX$ and $nodesY$ are compressed by storing the values of the nodes below the root as differences with respect to their parent. For example, the values at position 2 (corresponding to R_{1-4}) of $nodeX$ are stored as the values of the parent (2,10) minus the values at position 2 (2,5), that is, (0,5). As a result, the numbers are smaller, and we use $\lfloor \log m \rfloor + 1$ bits for each number, being m the largest difference (the root MBRs are stored separately).

4.3   Queries

To answer a time-slice or a time-interval query, we use the closest previous snapshot to filter the objects that cannot possibly make it to the query region within the given time frame, by exploiting the maximum speed at which objects can move. Let $r = [x_1, x_2] \times [y_1, y_2]$ be a rectangular region in the two-dimensional space, and $b < e$ be two timestamps. Let s be the maximum speed, in our dataset, of any object. We denote $ER(r, q)$, the *expanded region* of r at timestamp q, the area that contains the points that must be considered from the preceding snapshot. If the timestamp of the preceding snapshot is k, then $ER(r, q) = [x_1 - s \cdot (q - k), x_2 + s \cdot (q - k)] \times [y_1 - s \cdot (q - k), y_2 + s \cdot (q - k)]$.

Time-Slice. A time-slice query specifies a region r and a timestamp q. Assume q is between snapshots Sp_k and Sp_{k+d}. We perform a range query on Sp_k to retrieve all the objects id in $ER(r, q)$. If $q = k$, we simply return all those objects id. Otherwise, we access the log $\mathcal{L}_{k,k+d}$ of each such object id to find, in $O(1)$ time, its position at (local) time $q - k$, and report id if the position is within r.

Time-Interval. A time-interval query specifies a region r and an interval $[b, e]$. It can be solved as a sequence $e' - b' + 1$ time-slice queries (where b' and e' are described previously), but we exploit the tree of MBRs to speed up the query.

Each object that is within $ER(r, q)$ must be tracked along the timestamps b to e, to determine if it has a position inside r. We compute b' and e' as described previously and use the MBR tree to quickly filter out the elements that do not qualify. We start at the tree root, and check if (1) the timestamps of the node intersect $[b', e']$ and (2) the root MBR intersects r. If not, we abandon the search at that node. Otherwise, we recursively enter its left and right children. When we reach a leaf, we extract all the positions one by one, looking for the first that falls within r. We develop specialized procedures to extract the next point faster than a random access in our Elias-Fano representation.

We further prune the search by continuously considering the maximum speed of the objects. Assume $[b', e']$ is within the right child of a node since the left one covers only $[b'_1, e'_1]$. If the minimum distance between the MBR of the left and r, along any coordinate, is $p > s \cdot (b - e_1)$, then there is no need to examine the right child. Here e_1 is the original timestamp corresponding to e'_1, which is obtained with $select_0(T(id), e'_1) + first - 1$. The same argument holds symmetrically with the left child. Finally, as we traverse the positions in a leaf, we verify this condition continuously to preempt the scan as soon as possible (we use a special "select-next" method on $T(id)$ to speed up consecutive $select$ queries).

Example. Let us run the time-interval query for the area $r = [4, 5] \times [4, 10]$ and (mapped) time interval $[b', e'] = [2, 4]$ in the log of Fig. 2. We start at the root, which covers the time range $[1, 7]$ and has MBR $[2, 10] \times [4, 10]$. Since both intersect the query, we continue. Since the tree is perfect, we know that the left subtree covers the timestamps $[1, 4]$ and the right one covers $[5, 7]$. Since the right child does not intersect the query time interval, we only descend by the left one, $R_{1,4}$. Its MBR is $[2, 5] \times [4, 7]$, which intersects r, so we continue. Its left child, $R_{1,2}$, covers the time interval $[1, 2]$, which intersects $[b', e']$, so we enter it. However, its MBR is $[2, 3] \times [4, 6]$, which does not intersect r and thus we abandon it. The right child of $R_{1,4}$, $R_{3,4}$, also intersects the time interval of the query. Its MBR is $[3, 5] \times [5, 7]$, which intersects r. Finally, since $R_{3,4}$ is a leaf, we access the 3rd and 4th positions in the log, finding that the object was in r at time instant 4.   □

5   Experimental Results

ContaCT was coded in C++ and uses several data strucures of the SDSL library [10]. As baselines, we include GraCT and ScdcCT [3], also C++ programs, and the MVR-tree from the spatialindex library (`libspatialindex.github.io`). We used a real dataset storing the movements of 3,654 ships on a grid of size $2,723 \times 367,775$ and 44,642 time instants, whose plain representation requires 395.07 MB; we measure our compression ratios against that size. Appendix A gives more details on the dataset.

The experiments ran on an Intel® Core™ i7-3820 CPU @ 3.60 GHz (4 cores) with 10 MB of cache and 64 GB of RAM, over Ubuntu 12.04.5 LTS with kernel 3.2.0-115 (64 bits), using gcc 4.6.4 with -O9. We tested six types of queries:

- *Object* searches for the position of a specific object at a given timestamp.
- *Trajectory* returns the positions of an object between two timestamps.

- *Slice S* and *Slice L* are time-slice queries for small regions (272×367 cells) and large regions (2723×3677 cells), respectively.
- *Interval S* are time-interval queries specifying a small region on small intervall (36 timestamps), and *Interval L* are time-interval queries specifying large regions on large intervals (90 timestamps).

We measure elapsed times. Each data point averages 20,000 Object queries, 10,000 Trajectory queries, or 1,000 of Slice/Interval queries.

Compressed Representations. We built ContaCT, ScdcCT and GraCT with different snapshot distances, namely every 120, 240, 360, and 720 timestamps. ContaCT was also built with different values of C (the number of timestamps covered by the leaves of the MBR trees), specifically 20, 40, 80, 160, 320, and 640. We used Elias-Fano on the bitmaps $T(id)$, which were sparse, but turned to plain bitmaps to represent $X(id)$ and $Y(id)$, as they were not sufficiently sparse after mapping from $T(id)$.

Figure 3(a) shows the size with the different settings. All the structure sizes decrease as the distances between snapshots increase, and ContaCT also decreases as C increases. Thanks to its grammar-compression, the densest snapshot sampling of GraCT still uses 11% less space than the sparsest sampling of

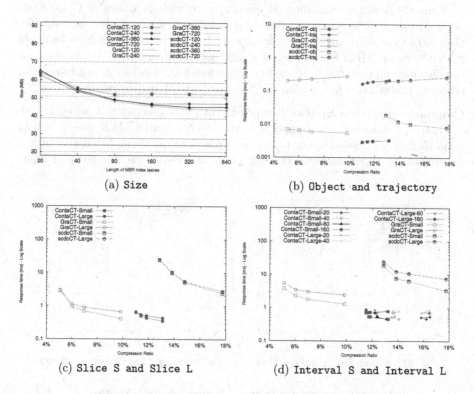

(a) Size

(b) Object and trajectory

(c) Slice S and Slice L

(d) Interval S and Interval L

Fig. 3. Compressed representations comparison; beware of logarithmic y axes.

ContaCT. In turn, ContaCT is smaller than the other differentially compressed representation, ScdcCT, for example by 14% in their sparsest configurations.

Figure 3(b) shows the average answer times for Object and Trajectory queries. ContaCT is especially fast on Object queries, thanks to its constant-time extraction mechanism. This makes it mostly independent of the snapshot sampling, and twice as fast as GraCT and three times faster than ScdcCT, even with their fastest configurations. GraCT is faster than ScdcCT, because it can traverse nonterminals of the grammar in constant time. For Trajectory queries, ContaCT is still faster by 20%. The difference decreases because sequential access to trajectories is not comparatively that slow with the other methods. The reason why some curves actually improve with a sparser snapshot sampling is that some extra work is needed when the query goes through various snapshots.

Figure 3(c) shows time-slice queries. The snapshot sampling is now crucial, since it affects the number of candidates that must be considered from the preceding snapshot (the computation of $ER(r, q)$). Since ContaCT can access the desired time instant in constant time, it is considerably faster than the others for a given snapshot sampling. However, GraCT matches ContaCT (and outperforms it for more selective queries) for a similar space usage, because GraCT can use a denser sampling thanks to its better compression of the log. ContaCT, on the other hand, outperforms ScdcCT by far.

Figure 3(d) shows time-interval queries, with various values of C for ContaCT. Even with the nearly smallest-space configuration (snapshot interval 360, $C = 160$), ContaCT outpeforms the largest GraCT configuration by a factor of 2, thanks to the MBR trees that index the logs. Using smaller C values does not significantly improve the time, on the other hand, thanks to our optimized leaf traversal procedure. Once again, the baseline ScdcCT is much slower.

Comparison with a Spatio-Temporal Index. We compare ContaCT with MVR-tree, a classic spatio-temporal index. We configured MVR-tree to run in main memory. To avoid space problems, we had to build the MVR-tree over a quarter of the input dataset. The size of the MVR-tree on this reduced input

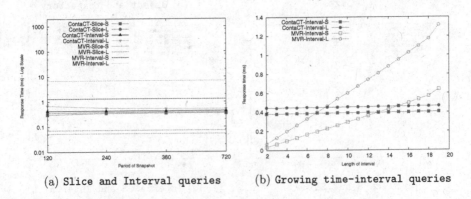

(a) Slice and Interval queries   (b) Growing time-interval queries

Fig. 4. Comparison with spatio-temporal index MVR-tree.

was 15.41 GB (including the data), while the maximum-space configuration of ContaCT uses 11.61 MB, three orders of magnitude less.

The MVR-tree can only solve time-slice and time-interval queries. We built ContaCT with different snapshot samplings and $C = 80$. Figure 4(a) shows that our structure is faster on time time-interval queries, but slower on our time-slice queries. Figure 4(b) studies the turning point, by increasing the time span of time-interval queries, using the smallest-space configuration of ContaCT (snapshot period of 720). Note that MVR-tree times increase linearly whereas ContaCT stays essentially constant. ContaCT outperforms MVR-tree on interval lengths over 8 on large-region queries and over 14 in small-region ones.

6   Conclusions

We have presented ContaCT, a structure to index trajectories of sets of moving objects in compressed form. ContaCT can efficiently retrieve points or segments of individual trajectories, and answer spatio-temporal range queries on the set of objects. ContaCT combines sampled two-dimensional snapshots compressed with k^2-trees, with logs differentially compressed and represented with Elias-Fano, which gives constant-time access to trajectory points. It also includes a hierarchical MBR mechanism that, combined with a pruning done on the snapshots, efficiently answers spatio-temporal queries.

Our experiments show that ContaCT compresses the data by a factor of almost 10 and outperforms by far, in space and time, a baseline alternative based on compressing small consecutive differences. ContaCT is also more than 1,000 times smaller than a classical spatio-temporal index, while being faster on all but very time-narrow queries. Compared with GraCT, the smallest existing representation based on grammar-compressing the trajectories, ContaCT uses more space. However, when both indexes are set to use the same amount of space, ContaCT generally makes better use of it, outperforming GraCT in most queries, by a factor of up to 3.

Future work involves extending ContaCT to more sophisticated queries, such as nearest-neighbor spatio-temporal queries.

A   Dataset Details

The dataset used in our experimental evaluation corresponds to a real dataset storing the movements of 3,654 boats sailing in the UTM Zone 10 during one month of 2014. It was obtained from MarineCadastre.[1] Every position emitted by a ship is discretized into a matrix where the cell size is 50×50 meters. With this data normalization, we obtain a matrix with 1,001,451,325 cells, 2,723 in the x-axis and 367,775 in the y-axis. As our structure needs the position of the objects at regular timestamps, we preprocessed the signals every minute, sampling the time into 44,642 min in one month.

---

[1] http://marinecadastre.gov/ais/.

To filter out some obvious GPS errors, we set the maximum speed of our dataset to 55 cells per minute (over 234 km/h) and deleted every movement faster than this speed. In addition, we observe that most of the boats sent their positions frequently when they were moving, but not when they were stopped or moving slowly. This produced logs of boats with many small periods without signals (absence period). Taking into account that an object cannot move too far away during a small interval of time, we interpolated the signals when the absence period was smaller than 15 min, filling the periods of absence with these interpolated positions.

With these settings the original dataset occupies 974.43 MB in a plain text file with four columns: *object identifier, time instant, coordinate x* and *coordinate y*. Every value of these columns are stored as a string. However, to obtain a more precise compression measure, we represent this information in a binary file using two bytes to represent object identifiers (max value 3,653), two bytes for the instant column (max value 44,641), two bytes for the x-axis (max value 2,723) and three bytes for the y-axis (max value 367,775). Therefore, the binary representation of our dataset occupies 395.07 MB.

References

1. Brisaboa, N.R., Fariña, A., Navarro, G., Param, J.R.: Lightweight natural language text compression. Inf. Retrieval **10**(1), 1–33 (2007)
2. Brisaboa, N.R., Ladra, S., Navarro, G.: Compact representation of web graphs with extended functionality. Inf. Syst. **39**(1), 152–174 (2014)
3. Brisaboa, N.R., Gómez-Brandón, A., Navarro, G., Paramá, J.R.: GraCT: a grammar based compressed representation of trajectories. In: Inenaga, S., Sadakane, K., Sakai, T. (eds.) SPIRE 2016. LNCS, vol. 9954, pp. 218–230. Springer, Cham (2016). doi:10.1007/978-3-319-46049-9_21
4. Chakka, V.P., Everspaugh, A., Patel, J.M.: Indexing large trajectory data sets with SETI. In: CIDR (2003)
5. Clark, D.: Compact Pat Trees. Ph.D. thesis, Univ. Waterloo (1996)
6. Cudre-Mauroux, P., Wu, E., Madden, S.: Trajstore: an adaptive storage system for very large trajectory data sets. In: ICDE, pp. 109–120 (2010)
7. Douglas, D.H., Peuker, T.K.: Algorithms for the reduction of the number of points required to represent a line or its caricature. Can. Cartogr. **10**(2), 112–122 (1973)
8. Elias, P.: Efficient storage and retrieval by content and address of static files. J. ACM **21**, 246–260 (1974)
9. Fano, R.: On the number of bits required to implement an associative memory. Memo 61, Computer Structures Group, Project MAC, Massachusetts (1971)
10. Gog, S., Beller, T., Moffat, A., Petri, M.: From theory to practice: plug and play with succinct data structures. In: Gudmundsson, J., Katajainen, J. (eds.) SEA 2014. LNCS, vol. 8504, pp. 326–337. Springer, Cham (2014). doi:10.1007/978-3-319-07959-2_28
11. Larsson, N.J., Moffat, A.: Off-line dictionary-based compression. Proc. IEEE **88**(11), 1722–1732 (2000)
12. Nibali, A., He, Z.: Trajic: an effective compression system for trajectory data. IEEE Trans. Knowl. Data Eng. **27**(11), 3138–3151 (2015)

13. Okanohara, D., Sadakane, K.: Practical entropy-compressed rank/select dictionary. In: ALENEX, pp. 60–70 (2007)
14. Pfoser, D., Jensen, C.S., Theodoridis, Y.: Novel approaches to the indexing of moving object trajectories. In: VLDB, pp. 395–406 (2000)
15. Samet, H.: Foundations of Multimensional and Metric Data Structures. Morgan Kaufmann, Burlington (2006)
16. Tao, Y., Papadias, D.: MV3R-tree: A spatio-temporal access method for timestamp and interval queries. In: VLDB. pp. 431–440 (2001)
17. Trajcevski, G., Cao, H., Scheuermann, P., Wolfson, O., Vaccaro, D.: On-line data reduction and the quality of history in moving objects databases. In: MobiDE, pp. 19–26 (2006)
18. Vazirgiannis, M., Theodoridis, Y., Sellis, T.K.: Spatio-temporal composition and indexing for large multimedia applications. ACM Multimedia Syst. J. 6(4), 284–298 (1998)
19. Wang, H., Zheng, K., Xu, J., Zheng, B., Zhou, X., Sadiq, S.: Sharkdb: an in-memory column-oriented trajectory storage. In: CIKM, pp. 1409–1418 (2014)
20. Zheng, Y., Zhou, X. (eds.): Computing with Spatial Trajectories. Springer, New York (2011)

Fast Construction of Compressed Web Graphs

Jan Broß[1]([⊠]), Simon Gog[2], Matthias Hauck[1,3], and Marcus Paradies[1]

[1] SAP SE, Dietmar-Hopp-Allee 16, 69190 Walldorf, Germany
{jan.bross,matthias.hauck,marcus.paradies}@sap.com
[2] Institute of Theoretical Informatics, Karlsruhe Institute of Technology,
Am Fasanengarten 5, 76131 Karlsruhe, Germany
gog@kit.edu
[3] Institute of Computer Engineering, Ruprecht-Karls Universität Heidelberg,
B6, 26, 68159 Mannheim, Germany

Abstract. Several compressed graph representations were proposed in the last 15 years. Today, all these representations are highly relevant in practice since they enable to keep large-scale web and social graphs in the main memory of a single machine and consequently facilitate fast random access to nodes and edges.

While much effort was spent on finding space-efficient and fast representations, one issue was only partially addressed: developing resource-efficient construction algorithms. In this paper, we engineer the construction of regular and hybrid k^2-trees. We show that algorithms based on the Z-order sorting reduce the memory footprint significantly and at the same time are faster than previous approaches. We also engineer a parallel version, which fully utilizes all CPUs and caches. We show the practicality of the latter version by constructing partitioned hybrid k-trees for Web graphs in the scale of a billion nodes and up to 100 billion edges.

Keywords: Web graphs · Compact data structures · Graph compression

1 Introduction

Processing large graphs, e.g., social networks or the structure of the World Wide Web (WWW), is challenging since these structures usually do not fit into main memory in their traditional representation. As a consequence, algorithms designed for in-memory computations cannot be executed efficiently. While it is possible to tackle the problem by designing distributed or external memory data structures and algorithms (as implemented in Pregel/Giraph [15], GraphX [17], and Gradoop [13] or GraphChi [14]), it is often better to use a space-efficient representation of the graph. Existing algorithms work directly on the space-efficient data structure without the need of modification and in-memory computing is often faster and more energy efficient than distributed or external processing. While there are many proposals for more space-efficient graph representations

© Springer International Publishing AG 2017
G. Fici et al. (Eds.): SPIRE 2017, LNCS 10508, pp. 116–128, 2017.
DOI: 10.1007/978-3-319-67428-5_11

(e.g. in [1,5,8,9,11]), there was less effort on optimizing the construction of these representations. However, this is of paramount importance in real-world applications where the static, space-efficient representation is built on-the-fly out of a graph store. For instance, in SAP HANA, graphs are stored in a relational format and transformed into other formats more suitable for query execution during runtime.

An attractive graph representation based on the adjacency matrix was recently proposed by Brisaboa et al. [8]: the succinct k^2-tree. It efficiently supports three basic operations – test if a link exits (CHECKLINK) and reporting all outgoing/incoming links of a page (PREDECESSORS/SUCCESSORS) – and takes only little space: typically 1.3–3.0 bits per link for web graphs while CHECKLINK can be answered in 100 ns and one element of PREDECESSORS/SUCCESSORS can be retrieved in 2–8 µs. Brisaboa et al. [8] report that adjacency list-based structures, such as the WebGraph framework by Boldi and Vigna [5], are typically one order of magnitude faster on the latter operations and one order of magnitude slower for CHECKLINK, but also require twice the space. In this paper, we present, implement, and empirically evaluate several optimizations to the succinct k^2-tree structure.

2 Preliminaries

We are given a graph G of n nodes and m directed edges. For web graphs a page corresponds to a node and a link between two pages is represented as an edge. Nodes are numbered from 0 to $n - 1$. One representation of G is a $n \times n$ adjacency matrix A, where each cell $a_{i,j}$ indicates whether an edge runs from node i to j. Figure 1 depicts an example. To simplify the presentation, we will assume in the following that n is a power of k, e.g. $n = k^h$. The k^2-tree is recursively defined for A as follows: A node with k^2 children is generated. The r-th child ($0 \leq r < k^2$) represents the sub-matrix A_r which is formed by all

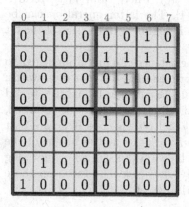
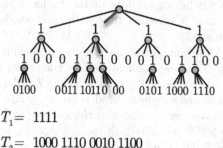

Fig. 1. Left: Adjacency matrix A of an example graph G. Right: k^2-tree of G and succinct representation with binary vectors T_1, T_2, and L

elements $a_{i,j}$ with $np \leq i \cdot k < n(p+1)$ and $nq \leq j \cdot k < n(q+1)$, where $p = \lfloor \frac{r}{k} \rfloor$ and $q = r \bmod k$. Each child is marked with a bit indicating whether the corresponding sub-matrix contains at least one non-zero entry. For those sub-matrices, the k^2-tree is constructed, and appended to the corresponding child. We call a node marked by a one (resp. zero) also 1-node (resp. 0-node). Figure 1 illustrates the k^2-tree for our running example and $k = 2$. The tree's height is $h = \log_k n$. Note that the children are ordered according to the top-left corner of the corresponding sub-matrix from left to right and top to bottom. This ordering is known as *Z-order* or *Morton order*. The Z-order corresponds to the lexicographic order of the strings which are generated by concatenating the binary representations of size $\lceil \log_2 k \rceil$ of the x- and y-coordinate of the sub-matrices, with $0 \leq x, y < k$. The Morton number of a link (p, q) is constructed by concatenating the Z-order strings from the root to the corresponding leaf in the k^2 tree. For example, link $(2, 5)$ lies in quadrant $(0, 1)$ on the first level, quadrant $(1, 0)$ on the second, and $(0, 1)$ on the last level. The Morton number is therefore $011001_2 = 25$. Figure 2 depicts the Morton numbers of all points in our example graph.

Tree representation. Brisaboa et al. [6] proposed a compact representation for the k^2-tree, which is an adapted version of the LOUDS (Level-Ordered Unary Degree Sequence) [12] succinct tree structure. It is generated by traversing the k^2-tree level by level and by concatenating the indicator bits of all children of the visited inner nodes on each level (cf. Fig. 1).

Bit vector T_1 and T_2 contain the concatenation of the first two levels and L of the leaf level. It is possible to efficiently navigate in this representation. Let x be the position of a 1-node v on level ℓ; then the position of the children of v on level $\ell + 1$ can be computed easily as all 1-nodes on level ℓ left of v have exactly k^2 children on level $\ell + 1$. These children are located left of the first child of node v. With *rank*, a fundamental operation of succinct structures, we can therefore express the operation of finding the position of the j-th child at level $\ell + 1$ as follows: $child_j(x, T_i) = rank(T_i, x) \cdot k^2 + j$, where $rank(T_i, x)$ returns the number of set bits in the prefix $T_i[0, x-1]$. The latter operation can be executed in constant time with an index, which is sublinear in the size of the bit vector [12].

More complex operations, e.g., checking the existence of a link from page p to page q, can be implemented by traversing the k^2-tree from the root downwards; see Algorithm 1. On each level the Z-order is calculated (Line 1) and it is tested if the corresponding child is empty (Line 1). If it is empty, **false** is returned, otherwise we recurse into the subtree in Line 1 and return **true** if we are past the leaf level. The runtime is in $\mathcal{O}(h)$, where $h = \log_k n$ is the height of the tree. Related queries, as reporting all outgoing links (SUCCESSORS) or incoming links (PREDECESSORS), can be solved similarly; as we do not focus on those operations, we refer the interested reader to Brisaboa et al. [8] for details.

Hybrid k^2-trees. Motivated by the observation that there are no empty subtrees close to the root of the k^2-tree, Brisaboa et al. [8] suggested to vary k dependent

Procedure checkLink(p, q, x, ℓ):

> **if** $\ell > h$ **then**
>> | return true ;
>
> **else**
>> $z_\ell \longleftarrow (p/k^{h-\ell}) \cdot k + (q/k^{h-\ell})$;   /* Z-order on level ℓ */
>>
>> **if** $T_\ell[x + z_\ell] = 1$ **then**
>>> | $x' \longleftarrow child_{z_\ell}(x, T_\ell)$;   /* succinct op for child position */
>>> | return checkLink$(p \bmod k^{h-\ell}, q \bmod k^{h-\ell}, x', \ell + 1)$;
>>
>> **else**
>>> | return false ;
>>
>> **end**
>
> **end**

end

Algorithm 1. Recursive method to determine whether there is a link from page p to q. The method is initially called with arguments p, q, $x = 0$, and $\ell = 1$.

on the level. They specify three k values: k_1, k_2, and k_l. Value k_1 is used for the first k_1^{size} levels, where k_1^{size} is configurable. Value k_2 is used for the remaining levels up to the second to last and k_l is used for the last level. Choosing a k value is a trade-off between access time and compressed size. A smaller k value leads to a smaller representation as fewer zeros are stored but also leads to higher access times as the tree height increases. By varying the k value, it is possible to use larger k values for the top levels where it is unlikely that a large sub-matrix only contains zeros. This reduces the tree height and therefore improves the speed of the access operations. Furthermore, by using a smaller k value for the following levels where it is more likely that complete sub-matrices are empty it is possible to reduce the memory needed for the compressed representation. Using a larger k_l value reduces the tree height and improves access times. Brisaboa et al. [8] also suggest a separate compression for the last level nodes. Instead of storing fixed k_l^2 bits for the last level nodes, these k_l^2 bit wide words are dictionary-encoded and the dictionary entry is stored. These entries are then compressed with a variable bit-length encoding scheme allowing for fast, direct access; e.g., Direct Accessible Codes (DAC) [7].

Top-level partitioned. k^2-trees Another option to lower the height of the tree is to partition the adjacency matrix into sub-matrices of fixed size $S^2 = n^2/k_0^2$ and building separate k^2-trees for each tree. While this complicates some operations, it can be used to reduce the space overhead during construction.

Construction. The most practical construction method for k^2-trees described by Brisaboa et al. [8] is based on counting sort. The graph is given as an array E of m edges. E is then partitioned into k^2 sub-ranges as follows. A queue is initialized with a state consisting of the tree level ℓ, the upper left corner (x, y) of the matrix, and the range in E: $\langle 1, (0, 0), [0, m-1] \rangle$. After extracting a state, the edges in the range are partitioned into k^2 ranges as follows. An edge (p, q) belongs to the z_ℓth sub-range iff $z_\ell = \lfloor (p-x)/k^{h-\ell} \rfloor \cdot k + \lfloor (q-y)/k^{h-\ell} \rfloor$. For each range a 1-bit (resp. 0-bit) is appended to T_ℓ if the sub-range is non-empty (resp. empty), and for every non-empty range $[a, b]$ a new state $\langle \ell + 1, (x + \lceil z_\ell/k \rceil, y + z_\ell \bmod k), [a, b] \rangle$ is added. On the second-to-last level, the states are not pushed to the queue but value z_ℓ is dictionary-encoded as described before.

The construction process takes $\mathcal{O}(m \log_k n)$ time in the worst case and the queue can use up to $\mathcal{O}(m)$ words of space. The latter is potentially much larger than the output, which can be upper bounded by $k^2 m \left(\log_{k^2} \frac{n^2}{m} + \mathcal{O}(1) \right)$ bits. In the following, we present a construction process, which requires less additional memory, avoids the costly divisions, and can also be parallelized.

3   Basic Optimizations

The practical performance of the described k^2-tree operations and construction can be improved by choosing k as a power of two, e.g. $k = 2^r$. Costly division $(x/2^r)$ and modulo $(x \bmod 2^r)$ operations can be replaced by shifts $(x \gg r)$ and bitwise AND $(x \,\&\, ((1 \ll r) - 1))$ operations[1]. In Algorithm 1 the expression in Line 1 is simplified to

$$((p \gg r(h - \ell)) \ll r) | (q \gg r(h - \ell))$$

and the modulo operations in Line 1 are replaced by a bitwise AND with mask $(1 \ll r(h - \ell)) - 1$, where $2^{r(h-\ell)}$ is the size of the sub-matrix on level ℓ. This optimization can be adapted for hybrid k^2-trees, where the value of k varies with the level in the tree. Let $k_i = 2^{r_i}$ be the k-value on level i. Then the size of the sub-matrix on level ℓ is 2 to the prefix sum $R[\ell] = \sum_{i=\ell+1}^{h} r_i$ and Line 1 in Algorithm 1 is changed to

$$z_\ell \leftarrow ((p \gg R[\ell])) \ll r_\ell) | (q \gg R[\ell]) \tag{1}$$

and Line 1 to a bitwise AND and with mask $(1 \ll R[\ell]) - 1$, where the $\log_k n$ entries of array R are precomputed once for each tree. In Sect. 5 we will observe that this optimization already halves the time for the counting sort-based construction of hybrid k^2-trees. We further improve this in the next section.

4   Z-Order Based Construction

Instead of calculating and sorting according to z_ℓ level by level it is also possible to first generate the Morton numbers of all links, sort those numbers, and then construct the k^2-tree from left to right. The idea of sorting the Morton numbers originates from Bern et al. [2]. The virtue of this approach is that all those steps can be done efficiently and also be split up into equal-sized parts for parallelization.

---

[1] We use the notation and precedence and associativity rules of the C programming language for shift left "$\ll$", shift right "$\gg$", bitwise AND "$\&$", and bitwise OR "$|$".

Morton number calculation. For a hybrid k^2-tree with k-values $\langle 2^{r_1}, 2^{r_2}, \ldots, 2^{k_\ell} \rangle$ the Morton number of a link (p, q) is generated by splitting the binary representation of p and q into blocks of $r_1, r_2, \ldots, r_\ell$ bits and interleaving these blocks, e.g., given $\langle 4, 4, 2, 8 \rangle$ and a link $(152, 43)$. The binary representation of p and q is $(\underline{10011001}_2, \overline{00101011}_2)$, and the Morton number representation is $\underline{1000}\overline{0110}\underline{1011}\overline{00101011}_2$. We underlined (resp. overlined) blocks originating from p (resp. q) for illustration purposes. On modern CPUs calculating the Morton number can be reduced to a bitwise OR and the Parallel Bit Deposit (PDEP[2]) operation. The PDEP operation takes a word of size w and a mask of the same size with b bits set. The operation spreads the last b bits of w to the positions of the set bits in the mask. In our example we would use the mask 1100110010111000_2 for p and 0011001101000111_2 for q and use a bitwise OR to combine the two PDEP results.

Serial construction. Dependent on m and the depth of the k^2-tree, we either apply a comparison based or radix sorting algorithm to sort in $\mathcal{O}(m \log m)$ or $\mathcal{O}(m \log_k n)$ time. Now, let $z(p_i, q_i) = z_{i,1} z_{i,2} \ldots z_{i,\ell}$ be the Morton number of the i-th smallest link (p_i, q_i), which consists of ℓ concatenated blocks of $2r_1, \ldots, 2r_\ell$ bits. We start building the k^2-tree by appending the $2r_{1,j}$-bit binary representation of $z_{1,j}$ to T_j. For all following elements (p_i, q_i) we first determine the smallest index s such that $z_{i-1,s} \neq z_{i,s}$. This can be done in constant time on modern CPUs[3]. Bit vectors $T_1, \ldots, T_{s-1}$ do not have to be changed, as the two links share the same path up to level $s - 1$. On level s, we add the new child by ORing the last $2r_s$ bits of T_s with $z_{i,s}$. For all levels $j > s$, we generate a new path under the new node at level s by appending $z_{i,j}$ to T_j. The total time complexity is $\mathcal{O}(m \log_k n)$.

Parallel construction. We note that calculating the Morton number for the edge array can be implemented embarrassingly parallel. There is no dependency between the Morton number calculation of different links. By splitting the input into p parts of size at most $\lceil m/p \rceil$ and using one thread per part the time is bounded by $\mathcal{O}(m/p)$. Parallel sorting can be done by employing multi-way merge sort [16] in $\mathcal{O}\left(\frac{m \log m}{p} + p \log p \cdot \log \frac{m}{p}\right)$ time. Next, we divide the sorted input into p parts of at most $\lceil m/p \rceil$ elements and calculate p separate k^2-trees. Applying the serial construction to each part results in a running time of $\mathcal{O}\left(\frac{m}{p} \log_k n\right)$. Figure 2 depicts an example for $p = 3$ on our running example. In a final step, we merge the p trees into a single tree. For each tree, we check which nodes on the path to the leftmost leaf are shared with the nodes on the path to the rightmost leaf in the previous tree. Shared nodes are marked with a pentagon in Fig. 2, while non-shared nodes are marked by a circle. The runtime to determine this information is $\mathcal{O}(\log_k n)$ per thread. The k^2 bits of shared nodes are subtracted from the length of the L bit vectors on the different levels. In Fig. 2

---

[2] See e.g. http://www.agner.org/optimize/instruction_tables.pdf.
[3] Via a combination of XOR and count leading zeros (clz).

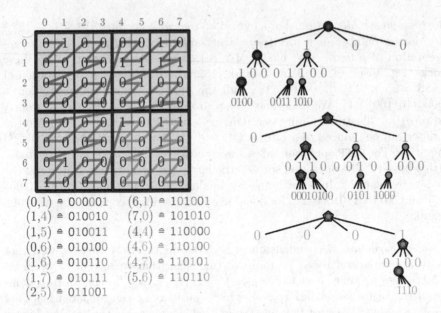

Fig. 2. Top left: Z-order curve in the adjacency matrix of our running example. Bottom left: Links and corresponding Morton numbers. Right: Three separate k^2-trees produced independently by three threads.

we get lengths $4, 8$, and 12 for the first tree, $0, 8$, and 12 for the second, and $0, 0$, and 4 for the third tree. The exclusive prefix sums for each level – in our example $0, 0, 0$ for level one, $0, 8, 20$, for level two, and $0, 12, 24$ – determine the offsets where the bit vectors of each thread have to be copied in the final tree. This can done in $\mathcal{O}\left(\log_k n + p\right)$ using p threads. After copying the non-colliding regions, we merge (using bitwise OR) the colliding nodes one after another and copy the result into the final representation. This takes $\mathcal{O}\left(p \cdot \log_k n\right)$ time. The total running time of the last steps is therefore $\mathcal{O}\left(\frac{m}{p}\log_k n + p\log_k n\right)$ and we can conclude that the initial sort dominates in realistic cases where $m > n$.

5   Experimental Study

We evaluate our proposals[4] in an empirical study and compare them against two state-of-the-art implementations: the code of Brisaboa et al. [8] and the well-known WebGraph framework of Boldi and Vigna [3–5]. The WebGraph project also provides graphs which are used in our experiments (cf. Table 1). For experiments on a very large graph, we added a web graph originating from the CommonCrawl project.

Experimental setup. We use two experimental platforms. Machine **A** is equipped with 2 Intel Xeon E5–2660 v3 (Haswell) processors and has 128 GB memory

---

[4] The code is available at https://github.com/Jabro/sdsl-lite.

Table 1. Data sets used for the performance evaluation. Graphs are stored as set of adjacency lists. Each list entry occupies 4 bytes (8 bytes in case of `CommonCrawl`). We use the partitioned sizes S of the last column when constructing partitioned k^2-trees. `UK-07-05-BFS` is the BFS-ordered version of `UK-2007-05` provided by Susana Ladra.

Graph (Year)	Nodes (n)	Edges (m)	m/n	File size	S
EU-2005 (2005)	862 664	19 235 140	22.30	77.0 MB	2^{18}
Indochina (2002)	7 414 866	194 109 311	26.18	769.0 MB	2^{20}
UK-2002 (2002)	18 520 486	298 113 762	16.10	1.2 GB	2^{22}
Arabic (2005)	22 744 080	639 999 458	28.14	2.5 GB	2^{22}
UK-07-05-BFS (2007)	105 218 569	3 733 873 648	35.49	14.3 GB	2^{22}
UK-2014 (2014)	787 801 471	47 614 527 250	60.44	189.3 GB	2^{26}
EU-2015 (2015)	1 070 557 254	91 792 261 600	85.74	363.1 GB	2^{26}
CommonCrawl (2012)	3 563 666 998	128 736 914 864	36.12	1033.6 GB	2^{28}

attached. Each processor has 10 cores with 2 threads running at 2.6 GHz. The Haswell architecture provides the `PDEP` operation, which showed to speed up the Morton number calculation by about 30%. Machine **B** is equipped with 4 Intel Xeon E7–4870 processors and has 1 TB of main memory attached. Each processor has 10 cores running at 2.4 GHz. As the system does not support the `PDEP` instruction we use several lookup tables to generate Morton numbers. All benchmarks for small graphs – up to `UK-07-05-BFS`– were executed on machine **A** while large graphs were processed on machine **B**. As some of the large graphs are loaded from a network storage, we exclude I/O times for a fair comparison. All programs were compiled with GCC 4.9.3 with full optimizations and all hardware-specific optimizations (`-march=native`).

K^2-*tree construction.* Figure 3 depicts construction space and time of the counting sort approach of Brisaboa et al. [8] (BLN), our optimized variant (COUNT), and the presented serial and parallel Z-order implementation (SZORD/PZORD). We show results for unpartitioned hybrid k^2-trees and partitioned ones. For the latter, we split the input into squares of size S^2 as denoted in Table 1. We choose to focus on the results for `UK-07-05-BFS` as they show the typical trade-off between the implementations. We observe that COUNT, which replaced the costly division operations in BLN, takes less than half of the time to construct the partitioned k^2-tree and is also more space-efficient. The excessive space requirement of BLN prohibits the construction for the unpartitioned k^2-tree. For smaller graphs, we observed that the same improvements of COUNT also appear for the construction of unpartitioned k^2-trees. The Z-order implementation SZORD uses more space than COUNT as we are not using in-place sorting algorithm. However, we note that the space usage of COUNT depends on the space of its state queue, which can be larger for other node orderings of the graph; for instance the space consumption of COUNT was worse than that of SZORD on the natural ordering of `UK-2007-05`. In the following, the space

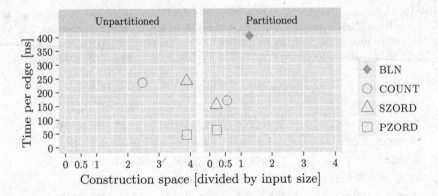

Fig. 3. Construction of hybrid (left) and partitioned hybrid (right) k^2-trees with $k_1 = 4$, $k_1^{size} = 6$, $k_2 = 2$, $k_h = 8$ for UK-07-05-BFS. BLN refers to the counting sort construction of Brisaboa et al. and COUNT to our optimized variant. SZORD and PZORD are our serial and parallel Z-order sort construction, the latter uses 20 threads.

consumption of the unpartitioned variant is not a concerning issue, as in practice it is more attractive to build and use the partitioned graph. We also observe that SZORD, which first calculates the Morton numbers and uses a general-purpose, comparison-based algorithm, is faster than the specialized counting sort approach COUNT. By using all CPU resources with PZORD, the construction time is further reduced to an eighth of the initial time of BLN.

Parallel construction. We examine the properties of PZORD in more details in Fig. 4 on a larger graph, which was constructed on machine **B**, which has twice the number of cores of machine **A**. The black line in the left plot marks the serial construction time of SZORD. The time is slower than in the previous plot,

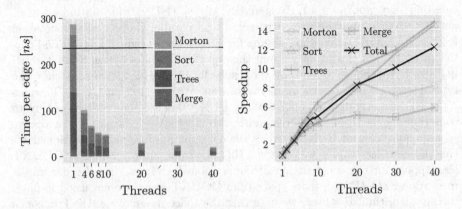

Fig. 4. Left: Breakdown of the construction time per edge for PZORD on UK-2014. We vary the amount of used threads. Right: Speedup of the total construction and the components compared to the serial construction SZORD.

as the machine runs on a lower clock speed and also does not feature the PDEP instruction. We can observe that the runtime is dominated by the sorting of the Morton numbers and the construction of the trees. Note that the merge phase for one thread just consists of copying the bit vectors. While the calculation of the Morton numbers and the merge phase are cheap compared to sorting and building the trees, we observe in the right plot that their parallelization does only scale well up to 10 or 20 threads. For the merge phase this can be explained by the fact that with a growing amount of threads, the memory bandwidth will be reached and more conflicts have to be resolved by ORing parts of the vectors. For the Morton numbers we are inspecting NUMA-effects. The sorting of the Multi-Core Standard Library (MCSTL) and the tree construction exhibit good scalability.

Construction time and space for huge graphs. Our implementation allows processing large-scale graphs. Table 2 shows the results for the construction of partitioned hybrid k^2-trees. We use the same ks as in the first experiment. This time we also include our parallel DAC compression for the last level and also report the average time to check a link, and report all outgoing (resp. incoming) links of a page. Different to the methodology of Brisaboa et al. [8], we benchmark the CHECKLINK by querying $5 \cdot 10^5$ existing edges and $5 \cdot 10^5$ randomly generated edges instead of only querying randomly generated edges. The latter method results in faster query times as the search in the k^2-tree can often be terminated early for non-existing edges and is therefore much faster compared to adjacency list-based indices, such as WebGraph.

Table 2. Performance of PZORD with 40 threads on large-scale data sets.

File	UK-2014	EU-2015	CommonCrawl
Construction time [min]	13	23	73
DAC compression time [sec]	197	210	1018
Compressed size [bpe]	1.05	0.78	4.1
W.o. DAC compression [bpe]	4.03	2.96	11.8
CHECKLINK [μs]	1.5	1.9	9.8
SUCCESSORS [μs]	1.9	2.4	11.8
PREDECESSORS [μs]	1.7	2.5	16.9

Comparison to WebGraph. Following Brisaboa et al. [8], we configure WebGraph with three choices of window size (w) and maximal number of backward references (m) for both directions. We refer to $\langle w, m \rangle = \langle 3, 3 \rangle$ as $\mathrm{BV}_{(d+r)}{}^a$, resp. $\mathrm{BV}_{(d+r)}{}^b$ and $\mathrm{BV}_{(d+r)}{}^c$ for $\langle 70, 100 \rangle$ and $\langle 70, 1000 \rangle$. Table 3 shows that our new implementation does not only allow for fast construction but also significantly reduces query times. We observed a factor of seven for CHECKLINK compared

Table 3. Comparison of different graph compression techniques on UK-07-05-BFS. In the parallel version PZORD (20 threads) operations PREDECESSORS/SUCCESSORS are solved by merging the results of multiple partitions. Those results are computed concurrently.

	$BV_{(d+r)}$			BLN	NEW	
	a	b	c		SZORD	PZORD
Construction time [s]	4281	6988	7355	1468	641	220
Construction space [MB]	188	3825	4251	18270	8280	8793
Compressed size [bpe]	4.53	3.66	3.58	1.45	1.49	1.49
CHECKLINK [μs]	2.01	63.04	291.06	6.21	0.86	0.84
SUCCESSORS [μs]	0.06	1.71	5.58	2.45	1.91	1.08
PREDECESSORS [μs]	0.05	0.30	0.65	2.31	1.82	0.72

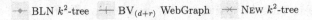

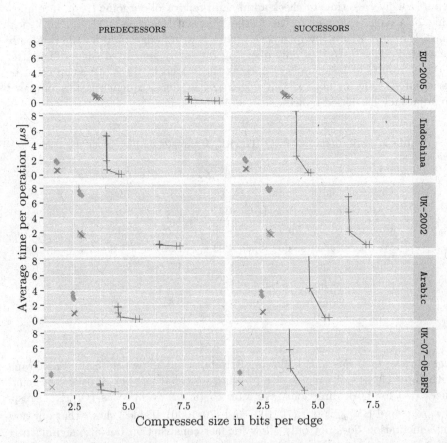

Fig. 5. Comparison space/time trade-off for successor and predecessor queries with other compression techniques

to BLN. We also observed consistent query time improvements on the remaining datasets. Figure 5 shows that the optimizations scale with the graph size. While the serial construction of WebGraph is space-efficient, we note that we also implemented an external version of Z-order-based construction using the STXXL library [10], which enables to build k^2-trees on machines with restricted memory capacity.

6 Conclusion

We proposed a Z-order sorting based construction for partitioned hybrid k^2-trees and its parallel version. We showed that a careful implementation, which leverages new CPU features and/or bit-level optimizations, results in significantly faster construction and query times.

References

1. Apostolico, A., Drovandi, G.: Graph compression by BFS. Algorithms **2**(3), 1031–1044 (2009)
2. Bern, M., Eppstein, D., Teng, S.-H.: Parallel construction of quadtrees and quality triangulations. In: Dehne, F., Sack, J.-R., Santoro, N., Whitesides, S. (eds.) WADS 1993. LNCS, vol. 709, pp. 188–199. Springer, Heidelberg (1993). doi:10.1007/3-540-57155-8_247
3. Boldi, P., Codenotti, B., Santini, M., Vigna, S.: UbiCrawler: a scalable fully distributed web crawler. Softw. Pract. Exp. **34**(8), 711–726 (2004)
4. Boldi, P., Marino, A., Santini, M., Vigna, S.: BUbiNG: massive crawling for the masses. In: Proceedings of WWW, pp. 227–228 (2014)
5. Boldi, P., Vigna, S.: The webgraph framework I: compression techniques. In: Proceedings of WWW, pp. 595–601 (2004)
6. Brisaboa, N.R., Ladra, S., Navarro, G.: k²-trees for compact web graph representation. In: Karlgren, J., Tarhio, J., Hyyrö, H. (eds.) SPIRE 2009. LNCS, vol. 5721, pp. 18–30. Springer, Heidelberg (2009). doi:10.1007/978-3-642-03784-9_3
7. Brisaboa, N.R., Ladra, S., Navarro, G.: DACs: bringing direct access to variable-length codes. Inf. Process. Manag. **49**(1), 392–404 (2013)
8. Brisaboa, N.R., Ladra, S., Navarro, G.: Compact representation of web graphs with extended functionality. Inf. Syst. **39**, 152–174 (2014)
9. Claude, F., Navarro, G.: Fast and compact web graph representations. ACM Trans. Web **1**(1), 77–91 (2009)
10. Dementiev, R., Kettner, L., Sanders, P.: STXXL: standard template library for XXL data sets. Softw. Pract. Exper. **38**(6), 589–637 (2008)
11. Hernández, C., Navarro, G.: Compressed representations for web and social graphs. Knowl. Inf. Syst. **40**(2), 279–313 (2014)
12. Jacobson, G.: Space-efficient static trees and graphs. In: Proceedings of FOCS, pp. 549–554 (1989)
13. Junghanns, M., Petermann, A., Gómez, K., Rahm, E.: GRADOOP: scalable graph data management and analytics with Hadoop. CoRR abs/1506.00548 (2015)
14. Kyrola, A., Blelloch, G., Guestrin, C.: GraphChi: large-scale graph computation on just a PC. In: Proceedings of USENIX, pp. 31–46 (2012)

15. Malewicz, G., Austern, M.H., Bik, A.J.C., Dehnert, J.C., Horn, I., Leiser, N., Czajkowski, G.: Pregel: a system for large-scale graph processing. In: Proceedings of SIGMOD, pp. 135–146 (2010)
16. Singler, J., Sanders, P., Putze, F.: MCSTL: the multi-core standard template library. In: Kermarrec, A.-M., Bougé, L., Priol, T. (eds.) Euro-Par 2007. LNCS, vol. 4641, pp. 682–694. Springer, Heidelberg (2007). doi:10.1007/978-3-540-74466-5_72
17. Xin, R.S., Crankshaw, D., Dave, A., Gonzalez, J.E., Franklin, M.J., Stoica, I.: GraphX: unifying data-parallel and graph-parallel analytics. CoRR abs/1402.2394 (2014)

Constructing a Consensus Phylogeny from a Leaf-Removal Distance (Extended Abstract)

Cedric Chauve[1], Mark Jones[2(✉)], Manuel Lafond[3], Céline Scornavacca[4], and Mathias Weller[5]

[1] Department of Mathematics, Simon Fraser University, Burnaby, Canada
cedric.chauve@sfu.ca
[2] Delft Institute of Applied Mathematics, Delft University of Technology,
P.O. Box 5, 2600 AA Delft, The Netherlands
M.E.L.Jones@tudelft.nl
[3] Department of Mathematics and Statistics, University of Ottawa, Ottawa, Canada
mlafond2@uOttawa.ca
[4] Institut des Sciences de l'Evolution, Université de Montpellier, CNRS, IRD,
EPHE, Montpellier, France
Celine.Scornavacca@umontpellier.fr
[5] Laboratoire d'Informatique, de Robotique et de Microélectronique de Montpellier,
Université de Montpellier, IBC, Montpellier, France
mathias.weller@lirmm.fr

Abstract. Understanding the evolution of a set of genes or species is a fundamental problem in evolutionary biology. The problem we study here takes as input a set of trees describing possibly discordant evolutionary scenarios for a given set of genes or species, and aims at finding a single tree that minimizes the leaf-removal distance to the input trees. This problem is a specific instance of the general consensus/supertree problem, widely used to combine or summarize discordant evolutionary trees. The problem we introduce is specifically tailored to address the case of discrepancies between the input trees due to the misplacement of individual taxa. Most supertree or consensus tree problems are computationally intractable, and we show that the problem we introduce is also NP-hard. We provide tractability results in form of a 2-approximation algorithm and a parameterized algorithm with respect to the number of removed leaves. We also introduce a variant that minimizes the maximum number d of leaves that are removed from any input tree, and provide a parameterized algorithm for this problem with parameter d.

Keywords: Computational biology · Phylogenetics · Parameterized algorithms · Approximation · Consensus trees · Leaf deletion

1 Introduction

In the present paper, we consider a very generic computational biology problem: given a collection of trees representing, possibly discordant, evolutionary

---

All missing proofs are provided in [6].

© Springer International Publishing AG 2017
G. Fici et al. (Eds.): SPIRE 2017, LNCS 10508, pp. 129–143, 2017.
DOI: 10.1007/978-3-319-67428-5_12

scenarios for a set of biological entities (genes or species – also called *taxa* in the following), we want to compute a single tree that agrees as much as possible with the input trees. Several questions in computational biology can be phrased in this generic framework. For example, for a given set of homologous gene sequences that have been aligned, one can sample *evolutionary trees* for this gene family according to a well defined posterior distribution and then ask how this collection of trees can be combined into a single gene tree, a problem known as *tree amalgamation* [16]. In phylogenomics, one aims at *inferring a species tree* from a collection of input trees obtained from whole-genome sequence data. A first approach considers gene families and proceeds by computing individual *gene trees* from a large set of gene families, and then combining this collection of gene trees into a unique species tree for the given set of taxa; this requires handling the discordant signal observed in the gene trees due to evolutionary processes such as gene duplication and loss [13], lateral gene transfer [17], or incomplete lineage sorting [15]. Another approach concatenates the sequence data into a single large multiple sequence alignment, that is then partitioned into overlapping subsets of taxa for which partial evolutionary trees are computed, and a unique species tree is then inferred by combining the resulting collection of partial trees [14].

For example, the Maximum Agreement Subtree (MAST) problem considers a collection of input trees[1], all having the same leaf labels and looks for a tree of maximum size (number of leaves), which agrees with each of the input trees. This problem is tractable for trees with bounded degree but NP-hard generally [2]. The MAST problem is a *consensus problem*, because the input trees share the same leaf labels set, and the output tree is called a *consensus* tree. In the *supertree framework*, the input trees might not all have identical label sets, but the output is a tree on the whole label set, called a *supertree*. For example, in the Robinson-Foulds (RF) supertree problem, the goal is to find a supertree that minimizes the sum of the RF-distances to the individual input trees [18]. One way to compute consensus trees and supertrees that is closely related to our work is to modify the collection of input trees minimally in such a way that the resulting modified trees all agree. For example, in the MAST problem, modifications of the input trees consist in removing a minimum number of taxa from the whole label set, while in the Agreement Supertree by Edge Contraction (AST-EC) problem, one is asked to contract a minimum number of edges of the input trees such that the resulting (possibly non-binary) trees all agree with at least one supertree [10]; in the case where the input trees are all triplets (rooted trees on three leaves), this supertree problem is known as the Minimum Rooted Triplets Inconsistency problem [5]. The SPR Supertree problem considers a similar problem where the input trees can be modified with the Subtree-Prune-and-Regraft (SPR) operator [19].

In the present work, we introduce a new consensus problem, called LR-Consensus. Given a collection of input trees having the same leaf labels set, we want to remove a minimum number of leaves – an operation called a

---

[1] All trees we consider here are uniquely leaf-labeled, rooted (*i.e.* are out-trees) and binary; see next section for formal definitions.

Leaf-Removal (LR) – from the input trees such that the resulting pruned trees all agree. Alternatively, this can be stated as finding a consensus tree that minimizes the cumulated *leaf-removal distance* to the collection of input trees. This problem also applies to tree amalgamation and to species tree inference from one-to-one orthologous gene families, where the LR operation aims at correcting the misplacement of a single taxon in an input tree. This may occur particularly in the case of 'rogue taxa' [1], for example when a sequence from a taxon has mistakenly been put in a gene family where it does not belong.

In the next section, we formally define the problems we consider, and how they relate to other supertree problems. Next we show that the LR-Consensus problem is NP-hard and that in some instances, a large number of leaves need to be removed to lead to a consensus tree. We then provide a 2-approximation algorithm, and show that the problem is fixed-parameter tractable (FPT) when parameterized by the total number of LR. However, these FPT algorithms have impractical time complexity, and thus, to answer the need for practical algorithms, we introduce a variant of the LR-Consensus problem, where we ask if a consensus tree can be obtained by removing at most d leaves from each input tree, and describe an FPT algorithm with parameter d.

2   Preliminary Notions and Problem Statements

Trees. All trees in the rest of the document are assumed to be rooted and binary. If T is a tree, we denote its root by $r(T)$ and its leaf set by $\mathcal{L}(T)$. Each leaf is labeled by a distinct element from a *label set* $\mathcal{X}$, and we denote by $\mathcal{X}(T)$ the set of labels of the leaves of T. We may sometimes use $\mathcal{L}(T)$ and $\mathcal{X}(T)$ interchangeably. For some $X \subseteq \mathcal{X}$, we denote by $lca_T(X)$ the *least common ancestor* of X in T. The subtree rooted at a node $u \in V(T)$ is denoted T_u and we may write $\mathcal{L}_T(u)$ for $\mathcal{L}(T_u)$. If T_1 and T_2 are two trees and e is an edge of T_1, grafting T_2 on e consists of subdividing e and letting the resulting degree 2 node become the parent of $r(T_2)$. Grafting T_2 above T_1 consists of creating a new node r, then letting r become the parent of $r(T_1)$ and $r(T_2)$ (note that grafting T_2 above T_1 is equivalent to grafting T_1 above T_2). Grafting T_2 on T_1 means grafting T_2 either on an edge of T_1 or above T_1.

The Leaf Removal Operation. For a subset $L \subseteq \mathcal{X}$, we denote by $T - L$ the tree obtained from T by removing every leaf labeled by L, contracting the resulting non-root vertices of degree two, and repeatedly deleting the resulting root vertex while it has degree one. The *restriction* $T|_L$ of T to L is the tree $T - (\mathcal{X} \setminus L)$, *i.e.* the tree obtained by removing every leaf *not* in L. A *triplet* is a rooted tree on 3 leaves. We denote a triplet R with leaf set $\{a, b, c\}$ by $ab|c$ if c is the leaf that is a direct child of the root (the parent of a and b being its other child). We say $R = ab|c$ is a triplet of a tree T if $T|_{\{a,b,c\}} = R$. We denote $tr(T) = \{ab|c : ab|c$ is a triplet of $T\}$.

We define a *distance function* d_{LR} between two trees T_1 and T_2 on the same label set $\mathcal{X}$ consisting in the minimum number of labels to remove from $\mathcal{X}$ so that the two trees are equal. That is,

$$d_{LR}(T_1, T_2) = \min\{|X| : X \subseteq \mathcal{X} \text{ and } T_1 - X = T_2 - X\}$$

Note that d_{LR} is closely related to the Maximum Agreement Subtree (MAST) between two trees on the same label set $\mathcal{X}$, which consists in a subset $X' \subseteq \mathcal{X}$ of maximum size such that $T_1|_{X'} = T_2|_{X'}$: $d_{LR}(T_1, T_2) = |\mathcal{X}| - |X'|$. The MAST of two binary trees on the same label set can be computed in time $O(n \log n)$, where $n = |\mathcal{X}|$ [8], and so d_{LR} can be found within the same time complexity.

Problem Statements. In this paper, we are interested in finding a tree T on $\mathcal{X}$ minimizing the sum of d_{LR} distances to a given set of input trees.

LR-Consensus
Given: a set of trees $\mathcal{T} = \{T_1, \ldots, T_t\}$ with $\mathcal{X}(T_1) = \ldots = \mathcal{X}(T_t) = \mathcal{X}$.
Find: a tree T on label set $\mathcal{X}$ that minimizes $\sum_{T_i \in \mathcal{T}} d_{LR}(T, T_i)$.

We can reformulate the LR-Consensus problem as the problem of removing a minimum number of leaves from the input trees so that they are *compatible*. Although the equivalence between both formulations is obvious, the later formulation will often be more convenient. We need to introduce more definitions in order to establish this equivalence.

A set of trees $\mathcal{T} = \{T_1, \ldots, T_t\}$ is called *compatible* if there is a tree T such that $\mathcal{X}(T) = \bigcup_{T_i \in \mathcal{T}} \mathcal{X}(T_i)$ and $T|_{\mathcal{X}(T_i)} = T_i$ for every $i \in [t]$. In this case, we say that T *displays* $\mathcal{T}$. A list $\mathcal{C} = (\mathcal{X}_1, \ldots, \mathcal{X}_t)$ of subsets of $\mathcal{X}$ is a *leaf-disagreement* for $\mathcal{T}$ if $\{T_1 - \mathcal{X}_1, \ldots, T_t - \mathcal{X}_t\}$ is compatible. The *size* of $\mathcal{C}$ is $\sum_{i \in [t]} |\mathcal{X}_i|$. We denote by $AST_{LR}(\mathcal{T})$ the minimum size of a leaf-disagreement for $\mathcal{T}$, and may sometimes write $AST_{LR}(T_1, \ldots, T_t)$ instead of $AST_{LR}(\mathcal{T})$. A subset $\mathcal{X}' \subseteq \mathcal{X}$ of labels is a *label-disagreement* for $\mathcal{T}$ if $\{T_1 - \mathcal{X}', \ldots, T_t - \mathcal{X}'\}$ is compatible. Note that if $\mathcal{T} = \{T_1, T_2\}$, then the minimum size of a leaf-disagreement and label-disagreement for $\mathcal{T}$ are the same, namely $d_{LR}(T_1, T_2)$. Note however that this does not hold in general (see Fig. 1 for an example). We may now define the AST-LR problem.

Agreement Subtrees by Leaf-Removals (AST-LR)
Given: a set of trees $\mathcal{T} = \{T_1, \ldots, T_t\}$ with $\mathcal{X}(T_1) = \ldots = \mathcal{X}(T_t) = \mathcal{X}$.
Find: a leaf-disagreement $\mathcal{C}$ for $\mathcal{T}$ of minimum size.

Lemma 1. *Let $\mathcal{T} = \{T_1, \ldots, T_t\}$ be a set of trees on the same label set $\mathcal{X}$, with $n = |\mathcal{X}|$. Given a supertree T such that $v := \sum_{T_i \in \mathcal{T}} d_{LR}(T, T_i)$, one can compute in time $O(tn \log(n))$ a leaf-disagreement $\mathcal{C}$ of size at most v. Conversely, given a leaf-disagreement $\mathcal{C}$ for $\mathcal{T}$ of size v, one can compute in time $O(tn \log^2(tn))$ a supertree T such that $\sum_{T_i \in \mathcal{T}} d_{LR}(T, T_i) \leq v$.*

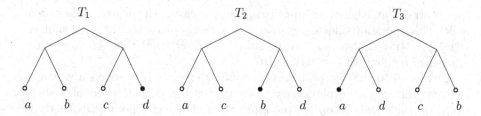

Fig. 1. Example instance $\mathcal{T} = \{T_1, T_2, T_3\}$ of AST-LR with label set $\mathcal{X} = \{a, b, c, d\}$. The list $(\mathcal{X}_1 = \{d\}, \mathcal{X}_2 = \{b\}, \mathcal{X}_3 = \{a\})$ is a leaf-disagreement for $\mathcal{T}$ of size 3. The set $\mathcal{X}' = \{a, b\}$ is a label-disagreement of size 2. Note that there is no leaf-disagreement for $\mathcal{T}$ of size 2.

Proof. In the first direction, for each $T_i \in \mathcal{T}$, there is a set $X_i \subseteq \mathcal{X}$ of size $d_{LR}(T, T_i)$ such that $T_i - X_i = T - X_i$. Moreover, X_i can be found in time $O(n \log n)$. Thus $(X_1, \ldots, X_t)$ is a leaf-disagreement of the desired size and can be found in time $O(tn \log n)$. Conversely, let $\mathcal{C} = (X_1, \ldots, X_t)$ be a leaf-disagreement of size v. As $\mathcal{T}' = \{T_1 - X_1, \ldots, T_t - X_t\}$ is compatible, there is a tree T that displays $\mathcal{T}'$, and it is easy to see that the sum of distances between T and $\mathcal{T}'$ is at most the size of $\mathcal{C}$. As for the complexity, it is shown in [9] how to compute in time $O(tn \log^2(tn))$, given a set of trees $\mathcal{T}'$, a tree T displaying $\mathcal{T}'$ if one exists. □

From Lemma 1, both problems share the same optimality value, the NP-hardness of one implies the hardness of the other, and approximating one problem within a factor c implies that the other problem can be approximated within a factor c. We conclude this subsection with the introduction of a parameterized variant of the AST-LR problem.

AST-LR-d
Input: a set of trees $\mathcal{T} = \{T_1, \ldots, T_t\}$ with $\mathcal{X}(T_1) = \ldots = \mathcal{X}(T_t) = \mathcal{X}$, and an integer d.
Question: are there $\mathcal{X}_1, \ldots, \mathcal{X}_t \subseteq \mathcal{X}$ such that $|\mathcal{X}_i| \leq d$ for each $i \in [t]$, and $\{T_1 - \mathcal{X}_1, \ldots, T_t - \mathcal{X}_t\}$ is compatible?

We call a tree T^* a *solution* to the AST-LR-d instance if $d_{LR}(T_i, T^*) \leq d$ for each $i \in [t]$.

Relation to Other Supertree/Consensus Tree Problems. The most widely studied supertree problem based on modifying the input trees is the SPR Supertree problem, where arbitrarily large subtrees can be moved in the input trees to make them all agree (see [19] and references there). The interest of this problem is that the SPR operation is very general, modelling lateral gene transfer and introgression. The LR operation we introduce is a limited SPR, where the displaced subtree is composed of a single leaf. An alternative to the SPR operation to move subtrees within a tree is the Edge Contraction (EC) operation, that contracts an edge of an input tree, thus increasing the degree of the parent node. This operation allows correcting the local misplacement of a full subtree. AST-EC is NP-complete but can be solved in $O((2t)^p tn^2)$ time where p is the number of required EC operations [10].

Compared to the two problems described above, an LR models a very specific type of error in evolutionary trees, that is the misplacement of a single taxon (a single leaf) in one of the input trees. This error occurs frequently in reconstructing evolutionary trees, and can be caused for example by some evolutionary process specific to the corresponding input tree (recent incomplete lineage sorting, or recent lateral transfer for example). Conversely, it is not well adapted to model errors, due for example to ancient evolutionary events that impact large subtrees. However, an attractive feature of the LR operation is that computing the LR distance is equivalent to computing the MAST cost and is thus tractable, unlike the SPR distance which is hard to compute. This suggests that the LR-Consensus problem might be easier to solve than the SPR Supertree problem, and we provide indeed several tractability results. Compared to the AST-EC problem, the AST-LR problem is naturally more adapted to correct single taxa misplacements as the EC operation is very local and the number of EC required to correct a taxon misplacement is linear in the length of the path to its correct location, while the LR cost of correcting this is unitary. Last, LR-Consensus is more flexible than the MAST problem as it relies on modifications of the input trees, while with the way MAST corrects a misplaced leaf requires to remove this leaf from all input trees. This shows that the problems AST-LR and AST-LR-d complement well the existing corpus of gene tree correction models.

3   Hardness and Approximability of AST-LR

In this section, we show that the AST-LR problem is NP-hard, from which the LR-Consensus hardness follows. We then describe a simple factor 2 approximation algorithm. The algorithm turns out to be useful for analyzing the worst case scenario for AST-LR in terms of the required number of leaves to remove, as we show that there are AST-LR instances that require removing about $n - \sqrt{n}$ leaves in each input tree.

NP-Hardness of AST-LR

We assume here that we are considering the decision version of AST-LR, *i.e.* deciding whether there is a leaf-disagreement of size at most ℓ for a given ℓ. We use a reduction from the MinRTI problem: given a set $\mathcal{R}$ of rooted triplets, find a subset $\mathcal{R}' \subset \mathcal{R}$ of minimum cardinality such that $\mathcal{R} \setminus \mathcal{R}'$ is compatible. The MinRTI problem is NP-Hard (and furthermore $W[2]$-hard) [5], and hard to approximate within a $O(2^{\log^{1-\epsilon} n})$ factor [7]. Denote by $MINRTI(\mathcal{R})$ the minimum number of triplets to remove from $\mathcal{R}$ to attain compatibility. We describe the reduction here.

Let $\mathcal{R} = \{R_1, \ldots, R_t\}$ be an instance of MinRTI, with the label set $L := \bigcup_{i=1}^{t} \mathcal{X}(R_i)$. For a given integer m, we construct an AST-LR instance $\mathcal{T} = \{T_1, \ldots, T_t\}$ such that $MINRTI(\mathcal{R}) \leq m$ if and only if $AST_{LR}(\mathcal{T}) \leq t(|L| - 3) + m$.

We first construct a tree Z with additional labels which will serve as our main gadget. Let $\{L_i\}_{1 \leq i \leq t}$ be a collection of t new label sets, each of size $(|L|t)^{10}$, all disjoint from each other and all disjoint from L. Each tree in our AST-LR instance will be on label set $\mathcal{X} = L \cup L_1 \cup \ldots \cup L_t$. For each $i \in [t]$, let X_i be any tree with label set L_i. Obtain Z by taking any tree on t leaves $l_1, \ldots, l_t$, then replacing each leaf l_i by the X_i tree (i.e. l_i is replaced by $r(X_i)$). Denote by $r_Z(X_i)$ the root of the X_i subtree in Z.

Then for each $i \in [t]$, we construct T_i from R_i as follows. Let $L' = L \setminus \mathcal{X}(R_i)$ be the set of labels not appearing in R_i, noting that $|L'| = |L| - 3$. Let $T_{L'}$ be any tree with label set L', and obtain the tree Z_i by grafting $T_{L'}$ on the edge between $r_Z(X_i)$ and its parent. Finally, T_i is obtained by grafting R_i above Z_i. See Fig. 2 for an example. Note that each tree T_i has label set $\mathcal{X}$ as desired. Also, it is not difficult to see that this reduction can be carried out in polynomial time. This construction can now be used to show the following.

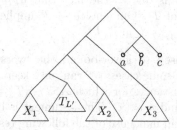

Fig. 2. Construction of the tree T_1 for an instance $\mathcal{R} = \{R_1, R_2, R_3\}$ of MinRTI in which $R_1 = ab|c$.

Theorem 2. *The AST-LR and LR-Consensus problems are NP-hard.*

The idea of the proof is to show that in the constructed AST-LR instance, we are "forced" to solve the corresponding MinRTI instance. In more detail, we show that $MINRTI(\mathcal{R}) \leq m$ if and only if $AST_{LR}(\mathcal{T}) \leq t(|L| - 3) + m$. In one direction, given a set $\mathcal{R}'$ of size m such that $\mathcal{R} \setminus \mathcal{R}'$ is compatible, one can show that the following leaf removals from $\mathcal{T}$ make it compatible: remove, from each T_i, the leaves $L' = L \setminus \mathcal{X}(R_i)$ that were inserted into the Z subtree, then for each $R_i \in \mathcal{R}'$, remove a single leaf in $\mathcal{X}(R_i)$ from T_i. This sums up to $t(|L| - 3) + m$ leaf removals. Conversely, it can be shown that there always exists an optimal solution for $\mathcal{T}$ that removes, for each T_i, all the leaves $L' = L \setminus \mathcal{X}(R_i)$ inserted in the Z subtree, plus an additional single leaf l from m trees $T_{i_1}, \ldots, T_{i_m}$ such that $l \in L$. The corresponding triplets $R_{i_1}, \ldots, R_{i_m}$ can be removed from $\mathcal{R}$ so that it becomes compatible.

Approximating AST-LR and Bounding Worst-Case Scenarios

Given the above result, it is natural to turn to approximation algorithms in order to solve AST-LR or LR-Consensus instances. It turns out that there is a simple factor 2 approximation for LR-Consensus which is achieved by interpreting the problem as finding a median in a metric space. Indeed, it is not hard to see that d_{LR} is a metric (over the space of trees on the same label set $\mathcal{X}$). A direct consequence, using an argument akin to the one in [12, p. 351], is the following.

Theorem 3. *The following is a factor 2 approximation algorithm for LR-Consensus: return the tree $T \in \mathcal{T}$ that minimizes $\sum_{T_i \in \mathcal{T}} d_{LR}(T, T_i)$.*

Proof. Let T^* be an optimal solution for LR-Consensus, *i.e.* T^* is a tree minimizing $\sum_{T_i \in \mathcal{T}} d_{LR}(T_i, T^*)$, and let T be chosen as described in the theorem statement. Moreover let T' be the tree of $\mathcal{T}$ minimizing $d_{LR}(T', T^*)$. By the triangle inequality,

$$\sum_{T_i \in \mathcal{T}} d_{LR}(T', T_i) \leq \sum_{T_i \in \mathcal{T}} (d_{LR}(T', T^*) + d_{LR}(T^*, T_i)) \leq 2 \sum_{T_i \in \mathcal{T}} d_{LR}(T^*, T_i)$$

where the last inequality is due to the fact that $d_{LR}(T', T^*) \leq d_{LR}(T^*, T_i)$ for all i, by our choice of T'. Our choice of T implies $\sum_{T_i \in \mathcal{T}} d_{LR}(T, T_i) \leq \sum_{T_i \in \mathcal{T}} d_{LR}(T', T_i) \leq 2 \sum_{T_i \in \mathcal{T}} d_{LR}(T_i, T^*)$. □

Theorem 3 can be used to lower-bound the 'worst' possible instance of AST-LR. We show that in some cases, we can only keep about $\sqrt{|\mathcal{X}|}$ leaves per tree. That is, there are instances for which $AST_{LR}(\mathcal{T}) = \Omega(t(n - \sqrt{n}))$, where t is the number of trees and $n = |\mathcal{X}|$. The argument is based on a probabilistic argument, for which we will make use of the following result [4, Theorem 4.3.iv].

Theorem 4 ([4]). *For any constant $c > e/\sqrt{2}$, there is some n_0 such that for all $n \geq n_0$, the following holds: if T_1 and T_2 are two binary trees on n leaves chosen randomly, uniformly and independently, then $\mathbb{E}[d_{LR}(T_1, T_2)] \geq n - c\sqrt{n}$.*

Corollary 5. *There are instances of AST-LR in which $\Omega(t(n - \sqrt{n}))$ leaves need to be deleted.*

The above is shown by demonstrating that, by picking a set $\mathcal{T}$ of t random trees, the expected optimal sum of distances $\min_T \sum_{T_i \in \mathcal{T}} d_{LR}(T, T_i)$ is $\Omega(t(n - \sqrt{n}))$. This is not direct though, since the tree T^* that minimizes this sum is not itself random, and so we cannot apply Theorem 4 directly on T^*. We can however, show that the tree $T' \in \mathcal{T}$ obtained using the 2-approximation, which is random, has expected sum of distances $\Omega(t(n - \sqrt{n}))$. Since T^* requires, at best, half the leaf deletions of T', the result follows. Note that finding a non-trivial upper bound on $AST_{LR}(\mathcal{T})$ is open.

4   Fixed-Parameter Tractability of AST-LR and AST-LR-d

An alternative way to deal with computational hardness is parameterized complexity. In this section, we first show that AST-LR is fixed-parameter-tractable with respect to $q := AST_{LR}(\mathcal{T})$. More precisely, we show that AST-LR can be solved in $O(12^q t n^3)$ time, where $n := |\mathcal{X}|$. We then consider an alternative parameter d, and show that finding a tree T^*, if it exists, such that $d_{LR}(T_i, T^*) \leq d$ for every input tree T_i, can be done in $O(c^d d^{3d}(n^3 + tn \log n))$ time for some constant c.

4.1   Parameterization by q

The principle of the algorithm is the following. It is known that a set of trees $\mathcal{T} = \{T_1, \ldots, T_t\}$ is compatible if and only if the union of their triplet decomposition $tr(\mathcal{T}) = \bigcup_{T_i \in \mathcal{T}} tr(T_i)$ is compatible [3]. In a step-by-step fashion, we identify a conflicting set of triplets in $tr(\mathcal{T})$, each time branching into the (bounded) possible leaf-removals that can resolve the conflict. We stop when either $tr(\mathcal{T})$ is compatible after the performed leaf-removals, or when more than q leaves were deleted.

We employ a two-phase strategy. In the first phase, we eliminate direct conflicts in $tr(\mathcal{T})$, *i.e.* if at least two of $ab|c, ac|b$ and $bc|a$ appear in $tr(\mathcal{T})$, then we recursively branch into the three ways of choosing one of the 3 triplets, and remove one leaf in each T_i disagreeing with the chosen triplet (we branch into the three possible choices, either removing a, b or c). The chosen triplet is locked in $tr(\mathcal{T})$ and cannot be changed later.

When the first phase is completed, there are no direct conflicts and $tr(\mathcal{T})$ consists of a *full set of triplets* on $\mathcal{X}$. That is, for each distinct $a, b, c \in \mathcal{X}$, $tr(\mathcal{T})$ contains exactly one triplet on label set $\{a, b, c\}$. Now, a full set of triplets is not necessarily compatible, and so in the second phase we modify $tr(\mathcal{T})$, again deleting leaves, in order to make it compatible. Only the triplets that have not been locked previously can be modified. This second phase is analogous to the FPT algorithm for *dense* MinRTI presented in [11]. The dense MinRTI is a variant of the MinRTI problem, introduced in Sect. 3, in which the input is a full set of triplets and one has to decide whether p triplets can be deleted to attain compatibility.

Theorem 6 ([11]). *A full set of triplets $\mathcal{R}$ is compatible if and only if for any set of four labels $\{a, b, c, d\}$, $\mathcal{R}$ does not contain the subset $\{ab|c, cd|b, bd|a\}$ nor the subset $\{ab|c, cd|b, ad|b\}$.*

One can check, through an exhaustive enumeration of the possibilities, that given a conflicting set of triplets R_1, R_2, R_3 where $R_1 = ab|c, R_2 = cd|b, R_3 \in \{bd|a, ad|b\}$, any tree on a set $\mathcal{X}$ containing $\{a, b, c, d\}$ must have at least one of the following triplets: (1) $bc|a$; (2) $ac|b$; (3) $bd|c$; (4) $ab|d$. Note that each of these conflicts with one of R_1, R_2, R_3. This leads to a $O(4^p n^3)$ algorithm for solving dense MinRTI: find a conflicting set of four labels, and branch on the four possibilities, locking the selected triplet each time.

For the second phase of AST-LR, we propose a slight variation of this algorithm. Each time a triplet R is chosen and locked, say $R = ab|c$, the trees containing $ac|b$ or $bc|a$ must lose a, b or c. We branch into these three possibilities. Thus for each conflicting 4-set, there are four ways of choosing a triplet, then for each such choice, three possible leaves to delete from a tree. This gives 12 choices to branch into recursively. Algorithm 1 summarises the procedure and its analysis yields the following.

Theorem 7. *AST-LR can be solved in time* $O(12^q tn^3)$.

Data: $\mathcal{T}$ is the set of input trees, q is the maximum number of leaves to delete, F is the set of locked triplets so far.

if $q < 0$ *or F contains conflicting triplets* **then**
  | **return** False;
else if *there are $ab|c \in F$ and $T_i \in \mathcal{T}$ with $ac|b \in tr(T_i)$ or $bc|a \in tr(T_i)$* **then**
  | Branching: If one of the following calls returns True:
  | $\text{MASTRL}((\mathcal{T} \setminus \{T_i\}) \cup \{T_i - \{a\}\}, q - 1, F)$;   /* remove a from T_i */
  | $\text{MASTRL}((\mathcal{T} \setminus \{T_i\}) \cup \{T_i - \{b\}\}, q - 1, F)$;   /* remove b from T_i */
  | $\text{MASTRL}((\mathcal{T} \setminus \{T_i\}) \cup \{T_i - \{c\}\}, q - 1, F)$;   /* remove c from T_i */
  | then **return** True, otherwise **return** False;
else if *there are $a, b, c \in \mathcal{X}$ such that $|\{ab|c, ac|b, bc|a\} \cap tr(\mathcal{T})| \geq 2$* **then**
  | Branching: If one of the following calls returns True:
  | $\text{MASTRL}(\mathcal{T}, q, F \cup \{ab|c\})$
  | $\text{MASTRL}(\mathcal{T}, q, F \cup \{ac|b\})$
  | $\text{MASTRL}(\mathcal{T}, q, F \cup \{bc|a\})$
  | then **return** True, otherwise **return** False;
else if *there is a conflicting set $\{a, b, c, d\}$ in $tr(\mathcal{T}) \cup F$* **then**
  | Branching: If one of the following calls returns True:
  | $\text{MASTRL}(\mathcal{T}, q, F \cup \{ac|b\})$
  | $\text{MASTRL}(\mathcal{T}, q, F \cup \{bc|a\})$
  | $\text{MASTRL}(\mathcal{T}, q, F \cup \{bd|c\})$
  | $\text{MASTRL}(\mathcal{T}, q, F \cup \{ab|d\})$
  | then **return** True, otherwise **return** False;
else
  | **return** True ;   /* There are no conflicts $\Rightarrow tr(\mathcal{T}) \cup F$ is compatible */
end

Algorithm 1. $\text{MASTRL}(\mathcal{T}, q, F)$ — Recursive AST-LR FPT algorithm.

Although Theorem 7 is theoretically interesting as it shows that AST-LR is in FPT with respect to q, the 12^q factor might be too high for practical purposes, motivating the alternative approach below.

4.2 Parameterization by Maximum Distance d

We now describe an algorithm for the AST-LR-d problem, running in time $O(c^d d^{3d}(n^3 + tn \log n))$ that, if it exists, finds a solution (where here c is a constant not depending on d nor n). We employ a branch-and-bound strategy. Taking $T = T_1$ as our initial solution, we transform a candidate solution T until we have $d_{LR}(T, T_i) \leq d$ for every input tree T_i.

The type of transformations we use are *leaf prune-and-regraft (LPR)* moves, which provide another way of characterising the distance function d_{LR}. Informally speaking, an LPR move prunes a leaf from a tree and then regrafts it another location. We now give a more formal definition:

Definition 8. *Let T be a tree on label set $\mathcal{X}$. An LPR move on T is a pair (ℓ, e) where $\ell \in \mathcal{X}$ and $e \in \{E(T - \{\ell\}), \bot\}$. Applying (ℓ, e) consists of grafting ℓ on the e edge of $T - \{\ell\}$ if $e \neq \bot$, and above $T - \{\ell\}$ if $e = \bot$.*

An LPR sequence $L = ((\ell_1, e_1), \dots, (\ell_k, e_k))$ is an ordered tuple of LPR moves, where for each $i \in [k]$, (ℓ_i, e_i) is an LPR move on the tree obtained after applying the first $i - 1$ LPR moves of L.

Lemma 9. *Given two trees T_1 and T_2 on label set $\mathcal{X}$, there is a subset $X \subseteq \mathcal{X}$ such that $T_1 - X = T_2 - X$ if and only if there exists an LPR sequence $((x_1, e_1), \dots, (x_k, e_k))$ turning T_1 into T_2 such that $X = \{x_1, \dots, x_k\}$. Furthermore, if such a sequence exists then for each $i \in [k]$, there also exists an LPR sequence $L' = ((x'_1, e'_1), \dots, (x'_k, e'_k))$ turning T_1 into T_2 such that $X = \{x'_1, \dots, x'_k\}$ and $x'_1 = x_i$.*

Lemma 9 implies that in order for our algorithm to find a solution, it is enough to choose the correct LPR move on T at each stage. In order to get the desired running time, we need to bound the number of possible transformations to try on T.

This can be done as follows. Given a tree T_i with $d_{LR}(T, T_i) > d$, let us call a leaf x *interesting* if there is a solution T^*, and minimal sets $X', X_i \subseteq \mathcal{X}$ of size at most d, such that (a) $T - X' = T^* - X'$, (b) $T_i - X_i = T^* - X_i$, (c) $x \in X' \setminus X_i$. (Roughly speaking, x is in the 'wrong place' in T but not T_i.)

The following lemma shows that if a solution T^* exists, then T^* can always be reached by moving an interesting leaf at each stage.

Lemma 10. *Suppose that $d < d_{LR}(T_1, T_2) \leq d' + d$ with $d' \leq d$, and that there is a tree T^* and subsets $X_1, X_2 \subseteq \mathcal{X}$ such that $T_1 - X_1 = T^* - X_1$, $T_2 - X_2 = T^* - X_2$ and $|X_1| \leq d', |X_2| \leq d$. Then, there is a minimal label-disagreement X for $\{T_1, T_2\}$ with $|X| \leq d + d'$, and there exists $x \in X$ such that $x \in X_1 \setminus X_2$.*

Moreover, we can in polynomial time construct a set S of size $O(d^2)$ containing all interesting leaves:

Lemma 11. *Suppose that $d_{LR}(T_1, T_2) \leq d$ for some integer d. Then, there is some $S \subseteq \mathcal{X}$ such that $|S| \leq 8d^2$, and for any minimal label-disagreement X for $\{T_1, T_2\}$ with $|X| \leq d$, $X \subseteq S$. Moreover S can be found in time $O(n^2)$.*

The idea behind the proof of Lemma 11 is as follows: In polynomial time, we can find a set $X' \subseteq \mathcal{X}$ for which $T_1 - X' = T_2 - X'$. Letting X_1 and X_2 be disjoint copies of X, it is easy to construct a tree T_J with label set $(\mathcal{X} \setminus X') \cup X_1 \cup X_2$, such that $T_J - X_2 = T_1$ and $T_J - X_1 = T_2$. Such a tree therefore represents the structure of T_1 and T_2 at the same time. Moreover, by letting T^* be the subtree of T_J spanning $X_1 \cup X_2$, we have that T_J can be derived from T^* by grafting trees (on subsets of $\mathcal{X} \setminus X'$) onto edges of T_J. We call these subtrees *dangling clades*.

It can be shown that for any dangling clade, any minimal label-disagreement for $\{T_1, T_2\}$ either contains all labels from that clade or contains none of them. Moreover, if there are multiple dangling clades grafted onto the same edge of T^*, then a minimal label-disagreement for $\{T_1, T_2\}$ either contains the labels of every such dangling clade, or every such dangling clade except one, or none of them.

As a result, we can construct our set S by taking X' together with any combination of clades as described above that has total size at most d. It can be shown that S in fact has at most $2d$ labels for each edge of T^*, and as T^* has $O(d)$ edges, we get the desired bound on $|S|$.

The last ingredient needed for Theorem 13 is Lemma 12, which shows that if a leaf x of T_1 as described in Lemma 10 has to be moved, then there are not too many ways to regraft it in order to get closer to T^*. This gives us a bound of $O(d^3)$ on the number of branches at each step of our search tree, which in turn implies that there are at most $O(c^d d^{3d})$ steps.

Lemma 12. *Suppose that $d < d_{LR}(T_1, T_2) \leq d' + d$ with $d' \leq d$, and that there are $X_1, X_2 \subseteq \mathcal{X}$, and a tree T^* such that $T_1 - X_1 = T^* - X_1, T_2 - X_2 = T^* - X_2, |X_1| \leq d', |X_2| \leq d$, and let $x \in X_1 \setminus X_2$. Then, there is a set P of trees on label set $\mathcal{X}$ that satisfies the following conditions:*

- *for any tree T' such that $d_{LR}(T', T^*) < d_{LR}(T_1, T^*)$ and T' can be obtained from T_1 by pruning a leaf x and regrafting it, $T' \in P$;*
- *$|P| \leq 18(d + d') + 8$;*
- *P can be found in time $O(n(\log n + 18(d + d') + 8))$.*

The idea behind the proof of Lemma 12 is as follows: by looking at a subtree common to T_1 and T_2, we can identify the location that T_2 "wants" x to be positioned. This may not be the correct position for x, but we can show that if x is moved too far from this position, we will create a large number of conflicting triplets between T_2 and the solution T^*. As a result, we can create all trees in P by removing x from T_1 and grafting it on one of a limited number of edges.

Putting everything together, we have the procedure outlined in Algorithm 2. (In this algorithm, the subroutines DISAGREEMENT-KERNEL and CANDIDATE-TREES refer to the algorithms described in Lemmas 11 and 12, respectively.) Analysing this algorithm gives the desired running time.

Theorem 13. *AST-LR-d can be solved in time $O(c^d d^{3d}(n^3 + tn \log n))$, where c is a constant not depending on d or n.*

Data: $\mathcal{T}$ is the set of input trees (represented as a sequence to distinguish T_1 from the other trees), d is the maximum number of leaves we can remove in a tree, d' is the maximum number of leaves we can move in T_1, which should be initially set to d.

if $d_{LR}(T_1, T_i) \leq d$ *for each* $T_i \in \mathcal{T}$ **then**
| **return** T_1;
else if *there is some* $T_i \in \mathcal{T}$ *such that* $d_{LR}(T_1, T_i) > d' + d$ **then**
| **return** False ;   /* handles the $d' \leq 0$ case */
else
| /* Here we 'guess' a leaf prune-and-regraft move on T_1 */
| Choose $T_i \in \mathcal{T}$ such that $d_{LR}(T_1, T_i) > d$;
| Set $S = \text{DISAGREEMENT-KERNEL}(d + d', T_1, T_i)$;
| **for** $x \in S$ **do**
| | /* We are 'guessing' that x should go where T_i wants
| | it.   */
| | Set $P = \text{CANDIDATE-TREES}(T_1, T_i, x, d, d')$;
| | $T^* = False$;
| | **for** $T \in P$ **do**
| | | $T' = \text{MASTRL}-\text{DISTANCE}((T, T_2, \ldots, T_t), d, d' - 1)$;
| | | If T' is not $False$, let $T^* := T'$;
| | **end**
| | **return** T^*;
| **end**
end

Algorithm 2. MASTRL$-$DISTANCE$(\mathcal{T} = (T_1, T_2, \ldots, T_t), d, d')$ $-$ FPT algorithm for parameter d.

5 Conclusion

To conclude, we introduced a new supertree/consensus problem, based on a simple combinatorial operator acting on trees, the Leaf-Removal. We showed that, although this supertree problem is NP-hard, it admits interesting tractability results, that compare well with existing algorithms. Future research should explore if various simple combinatorial operators, that individually define relatively tractable supertree problems (for example LR and EC) can be combined into a unified supertree problem while maintaining approximability and fixed-parameter tractability.

Acknowledgements. MJ was partially supported by Labex NUMEV (ANR-10-LABX-20) and Vidi grant 639.072.602 from The Netherlands Organization for Scientific Research (NWO). CC was supported by NSERC Discovery Grant 249834. CS was partially supported by the French Agence Nationale de la Recherche Investissements d'Avenir/Bioinformatique (ANR-10-BINF-01-01, ANR-10-BINF-01-02, Ancestrome). ML was supported by NSERC PDF Grant. MW was partially supported by the Institut de Biologie Computationnelle (IBC).

References

1. Aberer, A.J., Krompass, D., Stamatakis, A.: Pruning rogue taxa improves phylogenetic accuracy: an efficient algorithm and webservice. Syst. Biol. **62**(1), 162–166 (2013). http://dx.doi.org/10.1093/sysbio/sys078

2. Amir, A., Keselman, D.: Maximum agreement subtree in a set of evolutionary trees: metrics and efficient algorithms. SIAM J. Comput. **26**, 1656–1669 (1997). http://dx.doi.org/10.1137/S0097539794269461

3. Bryant, D.: Building trees, hunting for trees, and comparing trees. Ph.D. thesis, Bryant University (1997)

4. Bryant, D., McKenzie, A., Steel, M.: The size of a maximum agreement subtree for random binary trees. Dimacs Ser. Discrete Math. Theor. Comput. Sci. **61**, 55–66 (2003)

5. Byrka, J., Guillemot, S., Jansson, J.: New results on optimizing rooted triplets consistency. Discrete Appl. Math. **158**, 1136–1147 (2010). http://dx.doi.org/10.1016/j.dam.2010.03.004

6. Chauve, C., Jones, M., Lafond, M., Scornavacca, C., Weller, M.: Constructing a consensus phylogeny from a leaf-removal distance. http://arxiv.org/abs/1705.05295

7. Chester, A., Dondi, R., Wirth, A.: Resolving rooted triplet inconsistency by dissolving multigraphs. In: Hubert Chan, T.-H., Lau, L.C., Trevisan, L. (eds.) TAMC 2013. LNCS, vol. 7876, pp. 260–271. Springer, Heidelberg (2013). doi:10.1007/978-3-642-38236-9_24

8. Cole, R., Farach-Colton, M., Hariharan, R., Przytycka, T.M., Thorup, M.: An O(nlog n) algorithm for the maximum agreement subtree problem for binary trees. SIAM J. Comput. **30**, 1385–1404 (2000). http://dx.doi.org/10.1137/S0097539796313477

9. Deng, Y., Fernández-Baca, D.: Fast compatibility testing for rooted phylogenetic trees. In: Leibniz International Proceedings of Information, Combinatorial Pattern Matching, LIPIcs, vol. 54, pp. 12:1–12:12 (2016). http://drops.dagstuhl.de/opus/volltexte/2016/6088

10. Fernández-Baca, D., Guillemot, S., Shutters, B., Vakati, S.: Fixed-parameter algorithms for finding agreement supertrees. SIAM J. Comput. **44**, 384–410 (2015). http://dx.doi.org/10.1137/120897559

11. Guillemot, S., Mnich, M.: Kernel and fast algorithm for dense triplet inconsistency. Theoret. Comput. Sci. **494**, 134–143 (2013). http://dx.doi.org/10.1016/j.tcs.2012.12.032

12. Gusfield, D.: Algorithms on Strings, Trees and Sequences: Computer Science and Computational Biology. Cambridge University Press, Cambridge (1997)

13. Hellmuth, M., Wieseke, N., Lechner, M., Lenhof, H.P., Middendorf, M., Stadler, P.F.: Phylogenomics with paralogs. Proc. Natl. Acad. Sci. USA **112**, 2058–2063 (2015). http://dx.doi.org/10.1073/pnas.1412770112

14. Jarvis, E.D., et al.: Whole-genome analyses resolve early branches in the tree of life of modern birds. Science **346**, 1320–1331 (2014). http://dx.doi.org/10.1126/science.1253451

15. Scornavacca, C., Galtier, N.: Incomplete lineage sorting in Mammalian phylogenomics. Syst. Biol. **66**, 112–120 (2017). http://dx.doi.org/10.1093/sysbio/syw082

16. Scornavacca, C., Jacox, E., Szollösi, G.J.: Joint amalgamation of most parsimonious reconciled gene trees. Bioinformatics **31**, 841–848 (2015). http://dx.doi.org/10.1093/bioinformatics/btu728

17. Szollösi, G.J., Boussau, B., Abby, S.S., Tannier, E., Daubin, V.: Phylogenetic modeling of lateral gene transfer reconstructs the pattern and relative timing of speciations. Proc. Natl. Acad. Sci. USA **109**, 17513–17518 (2012). http://dx.doi.org/10.1073/pnas.1202997109

18. Vachaspati, P., Warnow, T.: FastRFS: fast and accurate Robinson-Foulds supertrees using constrained exact optimization. Bioinformatics **33**, 631–639 (2017). http://dx.doi.org/10.1093/bioinformatics/btw600

19. Whidden, C., Zeh, N., Beiko, R.G.: Supertrees based on the subtree prune-and-regraft distance. Syst. Biol. **63**, 566–581 (2014). http://dx.doi.org/10.1093/sysbio/syu023

Listing Maximal Independent Sets with Minimal Space and Bounded Delay

Alessio Conte[1], Roberto Grossi[1], Andrea Marino[1(✉)], Takeaki Uno[2], and Luca Versari[3]

[1] Università di Pisa, Pisa, Italy
{conte,grossi,marino}@di.unipi.it
[2] National Institute of Informatics, Tokyo, Japan
uno@nii.jp
[3] Scuola Normale Superiore, Pisa, Italy
luca.versari@sns.it

Abstract. An independent set is a set of nodes in a graph such that no two of them are adjacent. It is maximal if there is no node outside the independent set that may join it. Listing maximal independent sets in graphs can be applied, for example, to sample nodes belonging to different communities or clusters in network analysis and document clustering. The problem has a rich history as it is related to maximal cliques, dominance sets, vertex covers and 3-colorings in graphs. We are interested in reducing the delay, which is the worst-case time between any two consecutively output solutions, and the memory footprint, which is the additional working space behind the read-only input graph.

1 Introduction

Given an undirected graph $G = (V, E)$ with $|V| = n$ nodes and $|E| = m$ edges, a maximal independent set (MIS) $I \subseteq V$ does not contain any two nodes connected by an edge, and is maximal under inclusion (no other $I' \supset I$ has this property). We pose the question whether listing MISs can be achieved efficiently in small space and bounded delay.

Although this problem originated in graph theory, as MISs are related to dominance sets, vertex covers and 3-colorings in graphs, we observe that data is networked in information systems nowadays. The classical problem of looking at patterns in texts or sequences, or trees, can be translated into graphs.[1] Here the patterns are MISs, which can be seen as a way to build samples that are independent from each other, thus motivating the question.

One possible field of application is in networks analysis, such as social science, where a MIS identifies a group of persons from a tightly connected community

---

Work partially supported by University of Pisa under PRA_2017_44 project on Advanced Computational Methodologies for the Analysis of Biomedical Data.

[1] The algorithmic techniques are different, and even the simple query asking if a path occurs in a graph is NP-hard. Nevertheless, discovering patterns in sequences and patterns in graphs are quite similar tasks, and can share techniques in some cases.

© Springer International Publishing AG 2017
G. Fici et al. (Eds.): SPIRE 2017, LNCS 10508, pp. 144–160, 2017.
DOI: 10.1007/978-3-319-67428-5_13

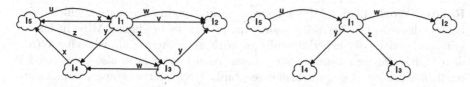

Fig. 1. Structure of the solution space defined by reverse search (left) and the solution tree defined by a PARENT function (right).

that are isolated from each other, or can be used as sample for communities, where each node of the MIS is a person from a different community.

MISs are a powerful tool for clustering: they can be used for clustering document collections (where two documents are linked if their content is similar), by using a MIS as a collection of starting points for the chosen clustering method or for clustering wireless networks to identify hierarchical structures [2]. Moreover, they are often used to build efficient indexes for answering shortest path or distance queries (see for instance [12]). MISs are applied for clustering purposes also in image segmentation, that aims at grouping image pixels into visually "meaningful" segments. In this case, the goal is to select the segments of an image that are distinct, and together partition the image area. In a graph where segments are nodes and edges correspond to the overlap of the segments, all the maximal independent sets correspond to all the non-overlapping segment partitions. [3] studied the maximum weighted independent set (MWIS) to get the maximally distinctive partitions by encoding a distinctiveness scoring of the segments into the nodes weights. This approach was also extended to clustering aggregation in general [15]. [21] modeled co-occurrences of words and documents in the web as a graph, and used MWIS's in this graph to find sets of important but distinct (i.e., rarely co-occurring) topics. However, the MWIS problem is NP-hard and hard to approximate. Listing all the MISs can also provide an exact solution for the latter problem, eventually testing different distinctiveness scoring systems.

Our Results. In this paper we describe an algorithm that lists all the MISs with $\tilde{O}(\min\{nd\Delta^2, mn\})$ delay—the $\tilde{O}$ notation ignores polylog factors—and $O(s)$ additional space, using the following parameters: d is the graph's degeneracy, that is, the minimum value d for which any induced subgraph has maximum node degree at most d; Δ is the maximum node degree; s is the maximum size of a MIS. We assume that the input graph is read-only, and the space complexity is the additional working space.

As it can be seen, the additional space is asymptotically minimal, and the delay can be as low as $\tilde{O}(n)$ (if d and Δ are $\tilde{O}(1)$), but never larger than the baseline of $O(nm)$ (ignoring logarithmic factors) given by Tskuiyama et al. [23]. We further reduce our time bound by providing a second algorithm with $\tilde{O}(\min\{d\Delta n, mn\})$ delay which increases the memory requirement to $O(n)$: this simultaneously improves both best known bounds for delay and space as $d\Delta$ is a pessimistic upper bound on the cost, which is smaller than m in practice.

Related Work. Listing MISs is a classical problem in enumeration which dates back at least to the 70s, with many results such as producing MISs in lexicographical order [16], experimentally or with guarantees [13], achieving $O(n^3)$ delay but using exponential space. Some results have been also proposed for particular classes of graphs: claw-free graphs [18], interval graphs, circular-arc graphs and chordal graphs [14,19,20], trees [14], permutation graphs [25].

In general, listing the MISs of a graph G is equivalent to listing the maximal cliques of its complement $\overline{G} = (V, \overline{E})$. However improved algorithms for maximal cliques, such as the space efficient solution that we presented in [9],[2] do not translate into improved bounds for listing MISs: the transformation from MISs to maximal cliques is not effective, especially in sparse graphs which have a dense complementary graph, but even in dense graphs, since their complementary graph can be dense too. These techniques mainly fall in the backtracking approach, as for [4], or in the reverse search paradigm introduced by [1].

In the former case, these approaches are not output sensitive for both cliques and MISs, in the sense that their guarantee on the running time is not related to the number of solutions. In the relatively recent work by Eppstein et al. [10] for cliques, the overall time $O(dn3^{d/3})$ becomes $O(n^2 \cdot 3^{n/3})$ to list all the MISs, as the degeneracy d can be $\Theta(n)$ in the complementary graph, while the delay remains exponential, as in the case of the algorithm in [22]. Moreover, the space usage, without storing the transformed graph, becomes $O(ns)$ for [22] and $O(n^2)$ for [10]. On the other hand, while adapting the reverse search for maximal cliques to MISs, the algorithms by Chiba and Nishizeki [6], by Makino and Uno [17] and Chang et al. [5] require $O(n^2 - m)$ space: recalling that arboricity, maximum degree, and degeneracy of the complementary graph can be linear, the delay bound becomes $O(n(n^2 - m))$ for [6], and $O(n^4)$ for [5,17]. Moreover, as shown next in Remark 1, the delay bound in [9] becomes $\tilde{O}(nm)$, which does not improve upon Tskuiyama et al. [23].

Also, since MISs can be considered a hereditary property or independence set system, they can be listed using the framework of Cohen et al. [7] but the resulting bounds still do not improve over those of [23]. For these reasons *ad hoc* algorithms for cliques and MISs have been proposed *separately* in the literature, and the best output sensitive bounds for MISs are $O(nm)$ delay with $O(n^2)$ space [23], or $O(n^{2.37})$ delay with $O(n^2)$ space by using matrix multiplication [17], or $O(n^{2.09})$ delay with $O(n^{4.27})$ space [8].

Our Approach. The algorithmic challenges addressed here are related to the reverse search, which is a powerful enumeration technique introduced by Avis and Fukuda [1]. Consider the graph-like structure shown in Fig. 1 (left), which we call the *solution digraph*: each "cloud", or node, corresponds to a distinct MIS, and an arrow from MIS I_i to MIS I_j with label v means that I_j can be computed from I_i through a node v, using a rule that is specific for the algorithm at hand. As in other techniques, such as divide and conquer, the algorithmic contribution is the efficient implementation of the generic step, for the problem at hand.

---

[2] This paper has been organized so as to highlight the novelties with respect to [9].

To list all the MISs, we use the rule to traverse the solution digraph and output each node/solution once. An easy way to do so is to keep track of all visited nodes. Even though such methods have been used, e.g. in [13], they are expensive as they require exponential memory. Reverse search avoids this issue by choosing a single *parent* I_i for each MIS I_j, such that $I_i < I_j$ for some given order (such as the lexicographic one), among all MISs leading to I_j. This way it induces a directed spanning forest on the solution digraph, as illustrated in Fig. 1 (right). Some MISs have no parent and are the *roots* of the spanning forest. Note that the solution digraph and directed spanning forest are for the purpose of explanation and never materialized. The roots can be easily identified and are at most n.

Traversing the solution digraph can be implicitly done by performing a DFS: each time we explore the possible children solutions and recur in just the ones whose parent is the current solution, following [17]. This visit can be made iterative, by avoiding the stack of the recursion. We can restore the state of the parent when returning from the call to a child. This strategy is particularly useful if we want to achieve sublinear additional memory, since we avoid using memory proportional to the height of the recursion tree, where a single bit per recursion level is too much. Here the techniques in [9] for maximal cliques do not translate smoothly into improved bounds for MISs, as discussed in Remark 1.

The complexity of the reverse search is dominated by the cost of applying the rule to the current MIS in the directed spanning forest. Computing the rule is expensive as the time spent checking not fruitful candidate children is completely charged on the delay of the algorithm. Thus we introduce a novel technique that allows us to apply the rule only to the children, rather than to *all* the out-neighbors in the solution digraph. We check a necessary condition, which is lighter to compute than the rule, so that the rule is actually applied to selected out-neighbors. During this task, we use a small amount of space.

2   Preliminaries

Let $G = (V, E)$ be an undirected and connected graph, represented as adjacency lists. In this work, we will use the following notation: $N(x)$ is the neighborhood of node x, and $\overline{N}(x) = V \setminus (N(x) \cup \{x\})$ the complementary-neighborhood; for a set of nodes A, $\overline{N}(A) = \bigcap_{x \in A} \overline{N}(x)$ (and we consider $\overline{N}(\emptyset) = V$).

We assume the nodes labeled as $v_1 < v_2 < \cdots < v_n$, in a *reversed degeneracy ordering*, i.e., so that $v_n < v_{n-1} < \cdots < v_1$ is a degeneracy ordering (see, e.g. [11]). It is easy to see that this ordering can be obtained with $O(1)$ additional space if it is not given.

We define $V_{<v_i}$ as $\{v_1, v_2, \ldots, v_{i-1}\}$. Given a set of nodes A, we then define $A_{<v_i}$ as respectively $A \cap V_{<v_i}$; for brevity, let $N_{<v_i}(v_i)$ be $N_<(v_i)$. $V_{>v_i}$, $A_{>v_i}$ and $N_>(v_i)$ are similarly defined. Note that in a degeneracy ordering $|N_>(v)| \leq d$, so as we are using a *reversed* degeneracy ordering, we have $|N_<(v)| \leq d$.

Given an independent set I and a vertex $v \in V \setminus I$, we denote as I_v' the set $I_{<v} \cap \overline{N}(v)$.

Given any two independent sets I_i and I_j, we say that $I_i < I_j$ if I_i is lexicographically smaller than I_j as node sets, thus inducing a lexicographic order on the independent sets. Given an independent set $I \subseteq V$, COMPLETE(I) is defined as the lexicographically smallest MIS that contains I, and can be computed by iteratively adding the smallest element that can be added to I, obtaining the following lemma.

Lemma 1. COMPLETE(I) *can be computed in* $\tilde{O}(m)$ *time.*

3   Listing MISs

Given an independent set I and a node $v \in V \setminus I$ such that $I_{<v} \neq \emptyset$, formula (1) generates a new maximal independent set.

$$F(I, v) = \text{COMPLETE}(I_{<v}' \cup \{v\}) \tag{1}$$

In the solution digraph illustrated in Fig. 1, there is an arrow $I_i \to I_j$ labeled with v if and only if $I_j = F(I_i, v)$. The parent-child relationship, which defines the directed spanning forest, is as follows.

$$\text{PARENT}(I) = \text{COMPLETE}(I_{<\text{PI}(I)}) \tag{2}$$

where PI(I), the *parent index* of I, is the smallest element $v \in I$ for which COMPLETE($I_{\leq v}$) $= I$. Note that if $I_i = \text{PARENT}(I_j)$ and $v = \text{PI}(I_j)$, then I_i, I_j, v satisfy formula (1).

The *roots*, which have no parent, can be found as COMPLETE($\{v\}$), for any $v \in V$ such that $\min\{\text{COMPLETE}(\{v\})\} = v$; the number of roots is at most n.

During the traversal of the solution digraph, in the current MIS I_j we compute its parent I_i and the parent index v, thus restoring the state of the traversal when returning from the call to I_j. Keeping this in mind, the delay per listed MIS is bounded by the maximum amount of time spent in the current MIS, say I, observing that this time is intermixed with the calls to its children.

The delay can be bounded by the cost of (i) computing I from its parent using formula (1); (ii) checking each candidate child to see if a call with formula (1) should be applied; finally (iii) if I is not a root, restoring the state to parent of I using formula (2). Indeed, once we get the costs (i)–(iii), we can employ the well-known alternative output technique in [24], so that the delay is bounded by the costs (i)–(iii) times a constant. We recall that in the alternative output technique, when the level (i.e. the distance from the root) is odd the output is done before exploring the children, otherwise it is done soon after.

Algorithm 1: BASE, Enumeration of Maximal Independent Sets

Assume $\min(\emptyset) = $ `null`, and recall that $I'_v \equiv I_{<v} \cap \overline{N}(v)$.
For function CHILD-EXISTS refer to Algorithm 2

Function ITERATIVE-SPAWN *(I)*
  $v \leftarrow$ PI(I)
  while *true* **do**
    childless $\leftarrow$ *true*
    while
    $v \leftarrow$ GET-NEXT-CAND$(I, v) \neq$`null` **do**
      if CHILD-EXISTS (I, v) **then**
        $I \leftarrow$ COMPLETE$(I'_v \cup \{v\})$
        childless $\leftarrow$ *false*
        break
    if *childless* **then**
      if IS-ROOT *(I)* **then return**
      else
        $\langle I, v \rangle \leftarrow$ PARENT-STATE(I)

Function IS-ROOT *(I)*
  return PI$(I) = \min(I)$

Function PARENT-STATE *(I)*
  $v \leftarrow$ PI(I)
  return $\langle$COMPLETE$(I_{<v})$, $v\rangle$

Function GET-NEXT-CAND *(I,v)*
  return
    $\min\{w \in \bigcup_{u \in I} \overline{N}_>(u) \setminus I :$
        $w > v\}$

Function COMPLETE *(I)*
  while $\overline{N}(I) \neq \emptyset$ **do**
    $I \leftarrow I \cup \min\{\overline{N}(I)\}$
  return I

Function PI *(I)*
  return $\min\{v \in I :$
      COMPLETE$(I_{\leq v}) = I\}$

In the rest of the paper we give the details for our new two algorithms for listing MISs using the above notions. The first algorithm is presented in Sect. 4 and achieves $O(s)$ additional memory and $\tilde{O}(\min\{d\Delta^2 n, mn\})$ delay. The second algorithm is presented in Sect. 5 and reduces the delay to $\tilde{O}(\min\{d\Delta n, mn\})$, albeit using $O(n)$ space.

One of the core ideas for both algorithms is the efficient computation of the test in point *(ii)* above. For the sake of simplicity, this behavior is encapsulated by the function CHILD-EXISTS, which is executed for each possible candidate. Our algorithms minimize the space usage by implementing some efficient implicit iterators that avoid building sets explicitly. For instance, the set $I'_v = I_{<v} \cap \overline{N}(v)$ in formula (1) is never materialized, as its explicit computation is expensive both in terms of time and space.

Remark 1. Using the above ideas, a listing algorithm for MISs can be immediately obtained by adapting those for maximal cliques in [9] to MISs, using them on the complementary graph $\overline{G}$ explicitly (see Sect. 1) or implicitly by using the complementary neighborhood $\overline{N}()$ in place of the neighborhood $N()$ whenever the latter is needed. We refer to the resulting algorithm to list the MISs using this simple modification of [9] as BASE. This is shown in Algorithm 1 and uses the implementation of function CHILD-EXISTS provided by Algorithm 2.

We further remark that some important optimizations in [9] for cliques are not useful as they do not bring any benefit for BASE. Indeed, while in [9] we have $|N_>(x)| \leq d$ thanks to the degeneracy ordering and $|N(x)| \leq \Delta$, these bounds do not hold for complementary neighborhoods. Hence, the improvements done to check the existence of a child (see Algorithm 2 in [9]) does not improve upon the basic child conditions of Makino-Uno based approach [17], which is reported in Algorithm 2 (see also Algorithm 1 in [9]). Indeed, one of the most important benefit of [9] was the speed up and the memory improvements of this function thanks to the definition of B_K (see Algorithm 2 in [9]), which can be stored in a $O(d)$ and allows to discard candidates. In the case of MISs, dealing with B_K can be costly, as its size can be $\Theta(n)$ for a generic K in $\overline{G}$. For this reason we need to use a more basic check and the function CHILD-EXISTS is replaced with the equivalent, more basic check used in Algorithm 1 in [9]. As a result, unfortunately, BASE has no benefit as shown next. The size of the CAND set increases to $\Theta(n)$, thus the cost per solution, that is the cost of a recursive call, is bounded by n times the cost of a COMPLETE call. As the cost of COMPLETE takes $\tilde{O}(m)$ (as shown in Lemma 1), this gives us a total time cost per solution $\tilde{O}(nm)$ which does not improve upon the one by Tsukiyama et al [23] (its additional space usage is $O(n)$).

Algorithm 2: CHILD-EXISTS check as in [9]

Input : A maximal independent set I and a node $v > $ PI(I)
Output: *true* if COMPLETE$(I'_v \cup \{v\})$ is a child of I, *false* otherwise

1 **Function** CHILD-EXISTS (I, v)
2 | $I'_v \leftarrow I_{<v} \cap \overline{N}(v)$
3 | **return** COMPLETE$(I'_v) = I$ *and* COMPLETE$(I'_v \cup \{v\})_{<v} = I'_v$

In the following, in order to bound our costs, we will use the lemma below.

Lemma 2. PI(I) *and* PARENT(I) *can be computed in* $\tilde{O}(m)$ *time.*

Proof. Given a MIS I, with $x = $ PI(I), we have PARENT$(I) = $ COMPLETE$(I_{<x})$. Furthermore, we know that COMPLETE$(I_{<y})$ is equal to I iff $y > x$. Thus by computing COMPLETE$(I_{<y})$ we know whether y is larger than x or not. We can thus look for x in a binary search-like fashion. We can thus find x by performing $O(\log |I|)$ times a COMPLETE call, to then compute COMPLETE$(I_{<x})$. The cost follows. □

4 Using Minimal Space $O(s)$

In this section we present our first algorithm, whose focus is minimizing the additional memory: the algorithm will only store $O(s)$ information on top of the input graph while keeping the performance competitive with state of the art approaches. This algorithm aims at improving the cost of CHILD-EXISTS of Algorithm 2 using $O(s)$ space. The improvements are due to two factors.

On one hand we identify stricter theoretical conditions to determine whether CHILD-EXISTS will succeed or not, which are used in place of CHILD-EXISTS; Lemmas 3 and 4 prove the correctness of these conditions, allowing us to prove the equivalence of Algorithms 2 and 3 in Lemma 5.

On the other hand, we provide non-trivial techniques which allow us to compute our theoretical conditions quickly and using only $O(s)$ additional space: in detail, we provide fast implicit iterators for sets which are too costly to compute, and simulate the behavior of COMPLETE, stopping it prematurely when suitable conditions are met.

Lemma 3. COMPLETE$(I'_v \cup \{v\})_{<v} = I'_v$ *is equivalent to* $\min\{\overline{N}(I'_v \cup \{v\})\} > v$.

Proof. Recalling its definition (see Sect. 2), we know that COMPLETE (I) adds nodes to I in increasing order: indeed, at a given step we select the smallest node x in $\overline{N}(I)$ and add it to I; in the following step $\overline{N}(I)$ will shrink because we added x to I, and its minimum cannot be smaller than (or equal to) x.

Let y be the first node selected by COMPLETE$(I'_v \cup \{v\})$, that is, $y = \min\{\overline{N}(I'_v \cup \{v\})\}$. If $y < v$, then COMPLETE$(I'_v \cup \{v\})_{<v} \neq I'_v$ as the earlier set contains y while the latter does not. Otherwise, if $y > v$ all other nodes selected by the COMPLETE function will too be greater than v; since $I'_v = I_{<v} \cap \overline{N}(v)$ we thus have COMPLETE$(I'_v \cup \{v\})_{<v} = I'_v$. □

Algorithm 3: Improved CHILD-EXISTS-MS check with $O(s)$ additional memory ($I'_v \equiv I_{<v} \cap \overline{N}(v)$ is actually not computed explicitly, see Lemma 9)

> **Input** : A maximal independent set I and a node $v > \text{PI}(I)$
> **Output**: *true* if COMPLETE$(I'_v \cup \{v\})$ is a child of I, *false* otherwise
> **1 Function** CHILD-EXISTS-MS (I, v)
> **2**   **if** *not* $\min\{\overline{N}(I'_v \cup \{v\})\} > v$ **then return** *false*
> **3** $A \leftarrow I'_v$
> **4**   **while** $\overline{N}(A) \neq \emptyset$ **do**
> **5** $x \leftarrow \min\{\overline{N}(A)\}$
> **6**   **if** $x \in I_{<v}$ **then** $A \leftarrow A \cup \{x\}$
> **7**   **else return** $x \in I$

Lemma 4. *If* $v > \text{PI}(I)$, *Algorithm 3 line 7 returns true iff* COMPLETE$(I'_v) = I$.

Proof. Lines 4–7 of Algorithm 3 correspond to simulating COMPLETE(I'_v) until the node x that is selected to be added to I'_v is not in $I_{<v}$. Then two cases are possible: either $x \notin I_{>v}$ or $x \in I_{>v}$. In the first case, COMPLETE$(I'_v) \neq I$ since $x \in$ COMPLETE(I'_v) and $x \notin I$, so Algorithm 3 returns *false*. Otherwise, if $x \in I_{>v}$ we show that all nodes in $I_{<v}$ that were not in I'_v have been added to it: since I is an independent set, whose nodes are not adjacent to each other, any node in $I_{<v} \setminus I'_v$ must be in $\overline{N}(I'_v)$. As so far we only added nodes in $I_{<v} \setminus I'_v$ (line 6), any other node in $I_{<v}$ that was in $\overline{N}(I'_v)$, and was not added to I'_v, is still in it. However, we have that $x = \min\{\overline{N}(I'_v)\} > v$, thus all and only nodes in $I_{<v} \setminus I'_v$ have been added to I'_v, making the set equal to $I_{<v}$. As COMPLETE$(I_{<v}) = I$, it must be that COMPLETE$(I'_v) = I$ thus the algorithm returns *true*. □

We show that, as a result of Lemmas 3 and 4, we can conclude the following.

Lemma 5. CHILD-EXISTS-MS *in Algorithm 3 can be used in place of* CHILD-EXISTS *in* BASE.

Proof. By Lemma 3 we have that CHILD-EXISTS-MS will return *false* on line 2 iff COMPLETE$(I'_v \cup \{v\})_{<v} \neq I'_v$. Otherwise, by Lemma 4, CHILD-EXISTS-MS will return *true* if COMPLETE$(I'_v) = I$, and *false* otherwise. Thus CHILD-EXISTS-MS will return the same result as CHILD-EXISTS. □

Space and Time Cost of Algorithm 3

In the following we provide space and time bounds for Algorithm 3, by firstly fixing some useful properties in Lemmas 6, 7, and 8.

Notice that $I_{<v} \setminus I_v' = N_<(v) \cap I_{<v}$. Since $\overline{N}(I_v' \cup \{v\}) \subseteq \overline{N}(I_v')$, if there exists a node $x \in \overline{N}(I_v' \cup \{v\})$ smaller than v, then x satisfies the properties shown in Lemma 6. We show that this lemma follows from the definition of parent index and it is useful to efficiently perform the computation in line 2 in Algorithm 3.

Lemma 6. *Let I be a MIS, and v a node s.t. $v \notin I$ and $v > \mathrm{PI}(I)$. Then $\overline{N}(I_{<v})_{<v} = \emptyset$, and for each node x in $\overline{N}(I_v')_{<v}$ we have that either x is in $I \cap N_<(v)$ or x has a neighbor in $I \cap N_<(v)$.*

Proof. Since $v \notin I$ and $v > \mathrm{PI}(I)$, we have that $\mathrm{COMPLETE}(I_{<v}) = I$ by definition of PI. If $\overline{N}(I_{<v})$ does contain a node x smaller than v, we could use one of such nodes to extend $I_{<v}$ and we would have $\mathrm{COMPLETE}(I_{<v}) \neq I$, a contradiction.

Consider now $\overline{N}(I_v')_{<v}$: As $I_v' \subseteq I_{<v}$, we have $\overline{N}(I_v')_{<v} \supseteq \overline{N}(I_{<v})_{<v}$. Since $\overline{N}(I_{<v})_{<v} = \emptyset$, however, we have $\forall x \in \overline{N}(I_v')_{<v}, x \notin \overline{N}(I_{<v})$, thus either x is in $I_{<v}$ has a neighbor in it by definition of $\overline{N}()$. As $x \in \overline{N}(I_v')_{<v}$, if x is in $I_{<v}$, it is actually in $I_{<v} \setminus I_v' \subseteq N_<(v)$. The statement follows.   □

Hence, we have to verify the conditions of Lemma 6 for the nodes $x \in \overline{N}(I_v' \cup \{v\})$. However, it is worth noting that the cost of storing $\overline{N}(I_v' \cup \{v\})$ is $O(n)$ which exceeds our memory requirements. To overcome this issue, we show in the following lemma how to build a heap-based iterator, that iterates over $\overline{N}(I_v' \cup \{v\})$ without computing it.

Lemma 7. *Let $X \subseteq V$ be a set of nodes and $Y = \bigcup_{x \in X} N(x)$. We can iterate over every $y \in Y$ in increasing order (without explicitly storing Y) in $\tilde{O}(\min\{|X|\Delta, m\})$ time using $O(|X|)$ additional space.*

Proof. Allocate a heap and add to it, for each node x in X, its smallest neighbor y (saving the x responsible for its addition). We can use this heap to iterate in order all nodes with a neighbor in X as follows: iteratively remove the minimum element y of the heap, recover the node x responsible for the addition of y, and insert in the heap the smallest neighbor of x larger than y. This way the smallest neighbor that we did not extract yet will always be on top of the heap. It is possible that the same node is extracted more than once; however we can trivially ignore duplicates as they appear contiguously, since nodes are extracted in increasing order. Adding/removing an element to/from the heap costs $\tilde{O}(1)$, so the total cost is bounded by $\tilde{O}(1)$ times the sum of all degrees of nodes in X, that is $\tilde{O}(\min\{|X|\Delta, m\})$.   □

By Lemma 6, to answer the check at line 2, we can consider nodes y belonging to $I \cap N_<(v)$ or $N(I \cap N_<(v))$. In particular, for each of them, we will have to check that $y \notin N(v)$ and $N(y) \cap I_v' \neq \emptyset$. To this aim, we use the following lemma.

Lemma 8. *Let I be a MIS, $v \notin I$ a node such that $v > \mathrm{PI}(I)$, and y any node. We have $N(y) \cap I_v' \neq \emptyset$ iff there exists $z \in N(y)$ such that $z < v$ and $z \in I$ and $z \notin N_<(v)$.*

Proof. Recall that $I'_v = I_{<v} \cap \overline{N}(v) = I_{<v} \setminus N_{<}(v)$, so all and only nodes in I'_v are smaller than v, in I, and not in $N_{<}(v)$. As $N(y) \cap I'_v \neq \emptyset$ iff any node in $N(y)$ is in I'_v, and $z \in I'_v$ iff ($z < v$ *and* $z \in I$ *and* $z \notin N_{<}(v)$) the statement follows.   □

We are now ready to prove the overall cost of Algorithm 3.

Lemma 9. CHILD-EXISTS-MS *can be computed in* $\tilde{O}(\min\{d\Delta^2, m\})$ *time with* $O(s)$ *space.*

Proof. Consider line 2: since $\overline{N}(I'_v \cup \{v\}) \subseteq \overline{N}(I'_v)$, by Lemma 6, if there exists a node $x \in \overline{N}(I'_v \cup \{v\})$ smaller than v, then x is a neighbor of a node in $I \cap N_{<}(v)$ (note that x cannot be in $I \cap N_{<}(v)$ since it is in $\overline{N}(I'_v \cup \{v\})$). Thus, instead of computing I'_v and its complementary-neighborhood, we iterate over node y which has a neighbor in the set $X = I \cap N_{<}(v)$ using Lemma 7. For each y, we have to check that $y \notin N(v)$ and $N(y) \cap I'_v \neq \emptyset$; for this latter check we use Lemma 8. If any y fails the check, then we return *false*, otherwise $\overline{N}(I'_v \cup \{v\})_{<v} = \emptyset$ and we can continue. We have $|I \cap N_{<}(v)| \leq d$ (due to the reversed degeneracy ordering), thus the neighbors y that we have to test can be at most $d\Delta$. It follows that the iteration will cost $\tilde{O}(\min\{d\Delta, m\})$ time by Lemma 7. Furthermore, testing each node y as in Lemma 8 takes $\tilde{O}(|N(y)|)$ time as we can perform binary searches on I, thus the total cost of testing is bounded by $\tilde{O}(\min\{d\Delta^2, m\})$.

Consider now lines 4–7: Again, using Lemma 6 we know that all nodes $x \in \overline{N}(I'_v)_{<v}$ are either in $I \cap N_{<}(v)$, or have a neighbor in it. We can rewrite this condition as: x has a neighbor in $X' = (I \cap N_{<}(v)) \cup \{v\}$.

In order to compute x in line 5, since $\overline{N}(A)_{<v} \subseteq \overline{N}(I'_v)_{<v}$, we use Lemma 7 to iterate over all the neighbors of nodes in X'; this iteration will yield in increasing order all nodes at any point in $\overline{N}(A)_{<v}$. We actually do not store A, but only the nodes that are added to A during the while, which we will here call A'. Thus to check that a node x belongs to $\overline{N}(A)$, we check $N(x) \cap I'_v = \emptyset$ and $N(x) \cap A' = \emptyset$; the earlier part can be done with Lemma 8, while the latter in $\tilde{O}(A')$ time by using binary searches.

Once we found $x = \min\{\overline{N}(A)_{<v}\}$, if it passes the check on line 6 we add it to A and repeat the loop, otherwise we return the result of the check.

Note that, as we are only iterating over $\overline{N}(I'_v)_{<v}$, we will not find among them any node in $I_{>v}$. However, this is easily fixed by saving the node $\min\{I_{>v}\}$: if at any point we have $x > \min I_{>v}$, or we finish the iteration on X', we return *true* since in both cases the candidate to be added to A would have been $\min\{I_{>v}\}$.

As $|X'| \leq \min\{d+1, s\}$, and the number of nodes with a neighbor in X are bounded by $O(\min\{d\Delta, n\})$, similarly to above we can bound the cost of the iteration with $\tilde{O}(\min\{d\Delta, m\})$, and the total cost of testing with $\tilde{O}(\min\{d\Delta^2, m\})$. Furthermore, note that the condition in line 6 can only succeed up to $\min\{d, s\}$ times, as each time x is in $I_{<v} \setminus I'_v$, and $|I_{<v} \setminus I'_v| = |I \cap N_{<}(v)| \leq \min\{d, s\}$; this means that $|A'| \leq \min\{d, s\}$.

Thus the total cost of CHILD-EXISTS-MS is $\tilde{O}(\min\{d\Delta^2, m\})$, using additional space $O(|X| + |X'| + |A'|) = O(\min\{d, s\})$ by Lemma 7.   □

By using Lemma 9, we are now able to prove the following result.

Theorem 1. *There exists an algorithm that enumerates all maximal independent sets with $\tilde{O}(\min\{nd\Delta^2, mn\})$ delay and $O(s)$ additional space.*

Proof. By using the structure described in Sect. 3, we can create an algorithm that enumerates all MISs (that is Algorithm 1 where CHILD-EXISTS is replaced by CHILD-EXISTS-MS), that is complete and correct by Lemma 5. Its delay is bounded by the costs of (i) the generation function $F(I, v) =$ COMPLETE$((I_{<v} \cap \overline{N}(v)) \cup \{v\})$ (ii) testing each candidate with CHILD-EXISTS-MS, and (iii) PARENT-STATE to return to the parent solution. These costs are respectively (i) $\tilde{O}(m)$ (as shown in Lemma 1), (ii) $\tilde{O}(n \cdot \min\{d\Delta^2, m\})$ as we apply Lemma 9 to each of the $O(n)$ candidates, and (iii) $\tilde{O}(m)$ (as shown in Lemma 2). Since $m \leq n\Delta$, this gives a total cost of $\tilde{O}(m + \min\{nd\Delta^2, mn\}) = \tilde{O}(\min\{nd\Delta^2, mn\})$.

As we have no recursion stack, the additional space is simply storing I and v, and the space required by CHILD-EXISTS-MS, that is $O(s)$.   □

5   Faster Version Using $O(n)$ Additional Memory

In this section, we propose a new algorithm which achieves a smaller time cost per solution by exploiting properties of the search space and an additional data structure of size $O(n)$, which mainly stores the amount of neighbors in $I_{<v}$ of each node in the graph. We use a function CHILD-EXISTS-FAST which improves the time cost of Algorithm 3, by constructing and maintaining this data structure. This is fundamental to improve the running time since it allows us to reduce the search space of the nodes considered by CHILD-EXISTS (and the corresponding iterations), as just nodes with zero neighbors in $I_{<v}$ need to be considered. Since v varies among all the possible candidates, even the ones not leading to a solution, this data structure cannot be rebuilt from scratch each time $I_{<v}$ changes, but needs to be properly updated and restored wherever possible. We will prove that we can cover these costs.

For the sake of completeness, the final pseudo-code is shown in Algorithm 4. The functions IS-ROOT and PARENT-STATE are the same as in BASE (see Algorithm 1). We will now analyze the difference between BASE and Algorithm 4, to show that they are equivalent, and that, hence, Algorithm 4 is correct.

The first difference we can notice is that we use a new function GET-NEXT-CAND with respect to the one in BASE. The new one is faster to compute, since the sum of the costs of all the calls done with the same I takes just $O(n)$ time but returns a superset of the one of BASE. This fact increases the number of candidate nodes to test but, on the other hand, testing them will be faster here due to an improved version of CHILD-EXISTS (see Lemma 12).

Algorithm 4: Fast enumeration of maximal independent sets

1 Assume $\min(\emptyset) = \texttt{null}$.

2 **Function** ITERATIVE-SPAWN(I)

3 $\quad v \leftarrow \text{PI}(I); \; prev \leftarrow v$

4 $\quad \text{BUILD}(\text{WS}, I_{<v})$

5 $\quad$ **while** $true$ **do**

6 $\quad\quad childless \leftarrow true$

7 $\quad\quad$ **while** $v \leftarrow \text{GET-NEXT-CAND}(I, v) \neq\texttt{null}$ **do**

8 $\quad\quad\quad \text{UPDATE}(\text{WS}, (I_{<v} \setminus I_{<prev}))$

9 $\quad\quad\quad prev \leftarrow v$

10 $\quad\quad\quad$ **if** CHILD-EXISTS-FAST(I, v, WS) **then**

11 $\quad\quad\quad\quad I \leftarrow \text{COMPLETE}(I'_v \cup \{v\})$

12 $\quad\quad\quad\quad childless \leftarrow false$

13 $\quad\quad\quad\quad \text{BUILD}(\text{WS}, I_{<v})$

14 $\quad\quad\quad\quad$ **break**

15 $\quad\quad$ **if** $childless$ **then**

16 $\quad\quad\quad$ **if** IS-ROOT(I) **then return**

17 $\quad\quad\quad$ **else**

18 $\quad\quad\quad\quad \langle I, v \rangle \leftarrow \text{PARENT-STATE}(I)$

19 $\quad\quad\quad\quad prev \leftarrow v$

20 $\quad\quad\quad\quad \text{BUILD}(\text{WS}, I_{<v})$

Algorithm 5: Fast check of the existence of a child and other auxiliary functions

1 **Function** CHILD-EXISTS-FAST(I, v, WS)

2 $\quad$ **for** $x \in I \cap N_<(v)$ **do**

3 $\quad\quad$ **for** $y \in N(x)$ **do** $\text{WS}[y] - = 1$

4 $\quad C \leftarrow \{x : \text{WS}[x] = 0\}$

5 $\quad$ **if** $not \; \min\{\overline{N}(I'_v \cup \{v\})\} > v$ **then return** $false$

6 $\quad$ **while** $C \; not \; empty$ **do**

7 $\quad\quad c \leftarrow \min\{C\}$

8 $\quad\quad$ **if** $c \in (I \setminus I'_v)$ **then**

9 $\quad\quad\quad C \leftarrow C \setminus (N(c) \cup \{c\})$

10 $\quad\quad$ **else**

11 $\quad\quad\quad \text{UPDATE}(\text{WS}, I \cap N_<(v))$

12 $\quad\quad\quad$ **return** $c \in I$

13 **Function** BUILD(WS, A)

14 $\quad \forall i \in V : \text{WS}[i] \leftarrow |N(i) \cap A|$

15 **Function** UPDATE(WS, A)

16 $\quad \forall i \in V : \text{WS}[i] + = |N(i) \cap A|$

17 **Function** GET-NEXT-CAND (I, v)

18 $\quad$ **return** $\min\{(V \setminus I)_{>v}\}$

Lemma 10. *We can use function* GET-NEXT-CAND *of Algorithm 5 in place of* GET-NEXT-CAND *in* BASE.

Proof. GET-NEXT-CAND of Algorithm 5 iterates over $(V \setminus I)_{>v}$, while GET-NEXT-CAND in BASE iterates over $\{w \in \bigcup_{u \in I} \overline{N}(u) \setminus I : w > v\}$. As the latter is a subset of the former, Algorithm 5 will iterate over all the candidates that will lead to a child. Furthermore, nodes in $(V \setminus I)_{>v}$ are still greater than PI(I), thus the conditions for CHILD-EXISTS are met, and the nodes that do not lead to a child will fail the check.   □

Notice that the candidate set size is $\Theta(n)$, since a single complementary neighborhood has size $\Theta(n)$. Another difference with respect to BASE, is that we use function CHILD-EXISTS-FAST instead of CHILD-EXISTS function to improve its computational time. To this aim, we use an additional data structure WS (for *weights*), which we keep suitably updated in order to satisfy the following invariant.

Lemma 11. *When* CHILD-EXISTS-FAST(I, v, WS) *is called in Algorithm 4, for each node $i \in V$, we have* WS$[i] = |N(i) \cap I_{<v}|$.

Proof. We first remark that for any A, B s.t. $A \cap B = \emptyset$, if $\forall i \in V$ WS$[i] = |N(i) \cap A|$ and we call UPDATE(WS, B) we obtain $\forall i \in V$ WS$[i] = |N(i) \cap (A \cup B)|$. To prove the lemma, it is thus sufficient to show that just before line 8 is executed, $\forall i \in V$ WS$[i] = |N(i) \cap I_{<prev}|$ (for the value of *prev* at that point).

Let us consider when WS was last modified when line 8 is executed: If this is the first time that the while loop in line 7 is executed, then WS was last modified in either lines 4, 13 or 20 by calling BUILD(WS, $I_{<v}$). Indeed, we have $\forall i \in V$ WS$[i] = |N(i) \cap I_{<prev}|$ by definition of BUILD, as we set *prev* $= v$ in lines 3, 9, and 20 respectively, and *prev* remained unchanged until line 8. Otherwise, note that CHILD-EXISTS-FAST leaves WS unchanged (the changes at Line 2 are canceled out by Line 11), thus WS was last modified by the previous execution of line 8 in the while loop (line 7). We prove this case by induction: Let us refer to the values of v and *prev* at line 8 in the j-th iteration of the loop as v_j and $prev_j$. Assume that $\forall i \in V$ WS$[i] = |N(i) \cap I_{<prev_j}|$ was true at line 8 in the j-th iteration. As $v_j = prev_{j+1}$ (see line 9), after the line is executed, by the remark at the beginning of the proof, we have $\forall i \in V$ WS$[i] = |N(i) \cap I_{<v_j}| = |N(i) \cap I_{<prev_{j+1}}|$. Since the condition is true for the first iteration, it is true for any iteration, thus the statement holds in each case.   □

By Lemma 11, the hypothesis on the WS data structure in the following lemmas are met, so that we can use the new CHILD-EXISTS-FAST instead of CHILD-EXISTS and CHILD-EXISTS-MS.

Lemma 12. *Suppose that* WS$[x] = |I_{<v} \cap N(x)|$ *for each $x \in V$. Then* CHILD-EXISTS-FAST *(I,v,WS) in Algorithm 5 can be used instead of* CHILD-EXISTS *(I,v) and* CHILD-EXISTS-MS *(I,v).*

Proof. Line 5 in Algorithm 5 is the same as line 2 in Algorithm 3. The loop at line 2 decrements $\mathrm{ws}[y]$ once for each neighbor of y in $I \cap N_<(v)$. After the loop we have that for each $x \in V$, $\mathrm{ws}[x] = |(I_{<v} \setminus N_<(v)) \cap N(x)| = |I'_v \cap N(x)|$, thus $x \in \overline{N}(I'_v)$ iff $\mathrm{ws}[x] = 0$. It follows that C is initialized to exactly $\overline{N}(I'_v)$. Thus, the loop in lines 6–10 will have the same outcome as the corresponding loop in lines 4–7 of Algorithm 3: when a node c is selected in line 8, C is updated as if c was added to I'_v, thus the following iterations will select the same nodes that would be selected in Algorithm 3, until finally line 10 is executed, which will give the same outcome as line 7 in Algorithm 3. $\qquad\square$

The function ITERATIVE-SPAWN has been modified only with the addiction of the function UPDATE, which has effect only on the variable WS which is used by GET-NEXT-CAND. Thus since the functions GET-NEXT-CAND and CHILD-EXISTS-FAST used by Algorithm 4 are equivalent to, respectively, GET-NEXT-CAND and CHILD-EXISTS of BASE by Lemmas 10, 11, and 12, then the function SPAWN too is equivalent to the one of BASE, obtaining the following lemma.

Lemma 13. *Algorithm 4 correctly computes all maximal independent sets.*

Space and Time Cost of Algorithm 4

In the following, we analyze the complexity of Algorithm 4. We have already discussed the cost of the new GET-NEXT-CAND function. In particular, we analyze the cost of maintaining the counters and the cost of CHILD-EXISTS-FAST.

Lemma 14. *For any set $A \subseteq V$, UPDATE(WS, A) takes $O(\min\{|A|\Delta, m\})$ time.*

Proof. We can obtain the cost above by iterating over all nodes in A and for each node x incrementing by 1 the counter of its neighbors. This is bounded by $O(|A|\Delta)$, and by $O(m)$ too as it is a sum of the degrees of distinct nodes. $\qquad\square$

The cost for BUILD is simply $O(n + \min\{|A|\Delta, m\})$, since we can set to zero each $\mathrm{ws}[x]$ for each $x \in V$ and then apply UPDATE(WS, A).

Lemma 15. CHILD-EXISTS-FAST *takes $O(d\Delta)$ time and $O(n)$ space.*

Proof. Recall from the proof of Lemma 9 that, as $v \notin I$ and $v > \mathrm{PI}(I)$, we have $\min\{\overline{N}(I_{<v})\} > v$, thus $\forall x \in (V_{<v} \setminus I)$ we have $\mathrm{ws}[x] > 0$.

Thus we compute C by simply adding to it any node y whose counter $\mathrm{ws}[y]$ is set to 0 during the loop at line 2. This is only guaranteed to add nodes which are smaller than v, but this will be enough. Recalling the proof of Lemma 12, we thus have that $C = \overline{N}(I'_v)_{<v}$. This costs us $O(\min\{d\Delta, m\})$ time, as it is the sum of the degrees of $|I \cap N_<(v)| \leq d$ distinct nodes. Line 5 takes $O(\Delta)$. Indeed, we can compute $\overline{N}(I'_v \cup \{v\})_{<v}$ as $C \setminus N(v)$. If this set is not empty, then the check fails and we return *false*.

Let us now consider the cost of the loop at line 6. Keeping C in a dynamic dictionary, lines 7 and 8 take both $\tilde{O}(1)$ time and 9 takes $\tilde{O}(|N(c)|)$ time. As the loop is executed a maximum of $|I_{<v} \setminus I'_v| + 1 \leq |N_<(v)| + 1 \leq d + 1$ times and c is different every time, this takes $\tilde{O}(\min\{d\Delta, m\})$ time. As in Lemma 9 we should store $\min\{I_{>v}\}$: since initially C only contains $\overline{N}(I'_v)_{<v}$ rather than $\overline{N}(I'_v)$, we return *true* if C actually becomes empty or if $c > \min\{I_{>v}\}$, as in both these cases $\min\{I_{>v}\}$ would have been the candidate actually selected in line 9, that would result in the algorithm returning *true*. Finally, before returning the result, we restore the data structure WS by calling UPDATE(WS, $I \cap N_<(v)$). This takes $O(\min\{d\Delta, m\})$ time by Lemma 14.

Since the additional space used is $O(|C|) = O(\min\{d\Delta, n\})$, CHILD-EXISTS-FAST can be computed in $\tilde{O}(\min\{d\Delta, m\})$ time, using $O(n)$ space. $\square$

By plugging the results of Lemmas 14 and 15 into the analysis of Theorem 1, we conclude the following.

Theorem 2. *Algorithm 4 lists all the maximal independent sets with a delay of $\tilde{O}(\min\{nd\Delta, nm\})$, and $O(n)$ additional space.*

Proof. Using Theorem 1 with the costs of CHILD-EXISTS-FAST given by Lemma 15 we obtain a total cost of $\tilde{O}(\min\{nd\Delta, nm\})$. We however need to add to steps (i) and (iii) the cost of BUILD(WS, $I_{<v}$) which takes $\tilde{O}(\min\{n\Delta, m\})$. Furthermore, we add to step (ii) the cost of UPDATE(WS, ($I_{<v} \setminus I_{<prev}$) for each candidate v. We argue that for any specific I, any node $i \in I$ is in $I_{<v} \setminus I_{<prev}$ only once, since v is never decreasing for I and *prev* keeps track of the previous value of v. The total cost is thus the same as UPDATE(WS, I), i.e., $\tilde{O}(\min\{|I|\Delta, m\})$ by Lemma 14. As $|I| \leq n$, neither of these additions affects the total cost of $\tilde{O}(\min\{nd\Delta, m\})$.

Space usage is given by the size of WS and C stored in CHILD-EXISTS-FAST, i.e., $O(n)$. $\square$

6 Conclusions

In this paper we studied the enumeration of maximal independent sets (MISs) in graphs, introducing new ideas to check efficiently which neighbors in the reverse search should be explored, as this task is time- and space-consuming. For a read-only input graph, our results are the first algorithm with minimal additional space, proportional to the size of the largest MIS, and an algorithm which improves both delay and space usage of known approaches. We remark that a MIS can indeed have linear size: in this case, due to the modular nature of our algorithms, the execution of the minimal space version can switch on-the-fly to the faster version which uses $O(n)$ space without increasing the asymptotic space usage.

References

1. Avis, D., Fukuda, K.: Reverse search for enumeration. Discrete Appl. Math. **65**(1–3), 21–46 (1996)
2. Basagni, S.: Finding a maximal weighted independent set in wireless networks. Telecommun. Syst. **18**(1), 155–168 (2001)

3. Brendel, W., Todorovic, S.: Segmentation as maximum-weight independent set. In: Advances in Neural Information Processing Systems, pp. 307–315 (2010)
4. Bron, C., Kerbosch, J.: Finding all cliques of an undirected graph (algorithm 457). Commun. ACM **16**(9), 575–576 (1973)
5. Chang, L., Yu, J.X., Qin, L.: Fast maximal cliques enumeration in sparse graphs. Algorithmica **66**(1), 173–186 (2013)
6. Chiba, N., Nishizeki, T.: Arboricity and subgraph listing algorithms. SIAM J. Comput. **14**(1), 210–223 (1985)
7. Cohen, S., Kimelfeld, B., Sagiv, Y.: Generating all maximal induced subgraphs for hereditary and connected-hereditary graph properties. JCSS **74**(7), 1147–1159 (2008)
8. Comin, C., Rizzi, R.: An improved upper bound on maximal clique listing via rectangular fast matrix multiplication. CoRR, abs/1506.01082 (2015)
9. Conte, A., Grossi, R., Marino, A., Versari, L.: Sublinear-space bounded-delay enumeration for massive network analytics: maximal cliques. In: ICALP, vol. 148, pp. 1–15 (2016)
10. Eppstein, D., Löffler, M., Strash, D.: Listing all maximal cliques in large sparse real-world graphs. ACM J. Exp. Algorithmics **18** (2013). Article No. 3.1
11. Eppstein, D., Strash, D.: Listing all maximal cliques in large sparse real-world graphs. In: Pardalos, P.M., Rebennack, S. (eds.) SEA 2011. LNCS, vol. 6630, pp. 364–375. Springer, Heidelberg (2011). doi:10.1007/978-3-642-20662-7_31
12. Fu, A.W.-C., Wu, H., Cheng, J., Wong, R.C.-W.: IS-LABEL: an independent-set based labeling scheme for point-to-point distance querying. Proc. VLDB Endow. **6**(6), 457–468 (2013)
13. Johnson, D.S., Yannakakis, M., Papadimitriou, C.H.: On generating all maximal independent sets. Inf. Proc. Lett. **27**(3), 119–123 (1988)
14. Leung, J.Y.-T.: Fast algorithms for generating all maximal independent sets of interval, circular-arc and chordal graphs. J. Algorithms **5**(1), 22–35 (1984)
15. Li, N., Latecki, L.J.: Clustering aggregation as maximum-weight independent set. In: Advances in Neural Information Processing Systems, pp. 782–790 (2012)
16. Loukakis, E., Tsouros, C.: A depth first search algorithm to generate the family of maximal independent sets of a graph lexicographically. Computing **27**(4), 349–366 (1981)
17. Makino, K., Uno, T.: New algorithms for enumerating all maximal cliques. In: Hagerup, T., Katajainen, J. (eds.) SWAT 2004. LNCS, vol. 3111, pp. 260–272. Springer, Heidelberg (2004). doi:10.1007/978-3-540-27810-8_23
18. Minty, G.J.: On maximal independent sets of vertices in claw-free graphs. J. Comb. Theor. Ser. B **28**(3), 284–304 (1980)
19. Okamoto, Y., Uno, T., Uehara, R.: Linear-time counting algorithms for independent sets in chordal graphs. In: Kratsch, D. (ed.) WG 2005. LNCS, vol. 3787, pp. 433–444. Springer, Heidelberg (2005). doi:10.1007/11604686_38
20. Okamoto, Y., Uno, T., Uehara, R.: Counting the number of independent sets in chordal graphs. J. Discrete Algorithms **6**(2), 229–242 (2008)
21. Olteanu, A., Castillo, C., Diaz, F., Vieweg, S.: CrisisLex: a lexicon for collecting and filtering microblogged communications in crises. In: ICWSM (2014)
22. Tomita, E., Tanaka, A., Takahashi, H.: The worst-case time complexity for generating all maximal cliques and computational experiments. TCS **363**(1), 28–42 (2006)
23. Tsukiyama, S., Ide, M., Ariyoshi, H., Shirakawa, I.: A new algorithm for generating all the maximal independent sets. SIAM J. Comput. **6**(3), 505–517 (1977)

24. Uno, T.: Two general methods to reduce delay and change of enumeration algorithms. National Institute of Informatics (in Japan) (2003). TR E, 4
25. Yu, C.-W., Chen, G.H.: Generate all maximal independent sets in permutation graphs. Int. J. Comput. Math. **47**(1–2), 1–8 (1993)

Fast Label Extraction in the CDAWG

Djamal Belazzougui[1] and Fabio Cunial[2(✉)]

[1] DTISI-CERIST, 16306 Algiers, Algeria
dbelazzougui@cerist.dz
[2] MPI-CBG, Pfotenhauerstr. 108, 01307 Dresden, Germany
cunial@mpi-cbg.de

Abstract. The compact directed acyclic word graph (CDAWG) of a string T of length n takes space proportional just to the number e of right extensions of the maximal repeats of T, and it is thus an appealing index for highly repetitive datasets, like collections of genomes from similar species, in which e grows significantly more slowly than n. We reduce from $O(m \log \log n)$ to $O(m)$ the time needed to count the number of occurrences of a pattern of length m, using an existing data structure that takes an amount of space proportional to the size of the CDAWG. This implies a reduction from $O(m \log \log n + \mathsf{occ})$ to $O(m + \mathsf{occ})$ in the time needed to locate all the occ occurrences of the pattern. We also reduce from $O(k \log \log n)$ to $O(k)$ the time needed to read the k characters of the label of an edge of the suffix tree of T, and we reduce from $O(m \log \log n)$ to $O(m)$ the time needed to compute the matching statistics between a query of length m and T, using an existing representation of the suffix tree based on the CDAWG. All such improvements derive from extracting the label of a vertex or of an arc of the CDAWG using a straight-line program induced by the reversed CDAWG.

Keywords: CDAWG · Suffix tree · Maximal repeat · Straight-line program · Count query · Locate query · Matching statistics · Minimal absent words

1 Introduction

Large, highly repetitive datasets of strings are the hallmark of the post-genomic era, and locating and counting all the exact occurrences of a pattern in such collections has become a fundamental primitive. Given a string T of length n, the compressed suffix tree [15,18] and the compressed suffix array can be used for such purpose, and they achieve an amount of space bounded by the k-th order empirical entropy of T. However, such measure of redundancy is known not to be meaningful when T is very repetitive [10]. The space taken by such compressed data structures also includes an $o(n)$ term which can be a practical bottleneck when T is very repetitive. Conversely, the size of the compact directed acyclic word graph (CDAWG) of T is proportional just to the number of maximal repeats of T and of their right extensions (defined in Sect. 2.2): this is a natural

© Springer International Publishing AG 2017
G. Fici et al. (Eds.): SPIRE 2017, LNCS 10508, pp. 161–175, 2017.
DOI: 10.1007/978-3-319-67428-5_14

measure of redundancy for very repetitive strings, which grows sublinearly with n in practice [2].

In previous work we described a data structure that takes an amount of space proportional to the size e_T of the CDAWG of T, and that counts all the occ occurrences in T of a pattern of length m in $O(m \log \log n)$ time, and reports all such occurrences in $O(m \log \log n + \text{occ})$ time [2]. We also described a representation of the suffix tree of T that takes space proportional to the CDAWG of T, and that supports, among other operations, reading the k characters of the label of an edge of the suffix tree in $O(k \log \log n)$ time, and computing the matching statistics between a pattern of length m and T in $O(m \log \log n)$ time. In this paper we remove the dependency of such key operations on the length n of the uncompressed, highly repetitive string, without increasing the space taken by the corresponding data structures asymptotically. We achieve this by dropping the run-length-encoded representation of the Burrows-Wheeler transform of T, used in [2], and by exploiting the fact that the reversed CDAWG induces a context-free grammar that produces T and only T, as described in [1]. A related grammar, already implicit in [6], has been concurrently exploited in [21] to achieve similar bounds to ours. Note that in some strings, for example in the family T_i for $i \geq 0$, where $T_0 = 0$ and $T_i = T_{i-1} i T_{i-1}$, the length of the string grows exponentially in the size of the CDAWG, thus shaving an $O(\log \log n)$ term is identical to shaving an $O(\log e_T)$ term.

This work can be seen as a continuation of the research program, started in [1,2], of building a fully functional, repetition-aware representation of the suffix tree based on the CDAWG.

2   Preliminaries

We work in the RAM model with word length at least $\log n$ bits, where n is the length of a string that is implicit from the context. We index strings and arrays starting from one. We call *working space* the maximum amount of memory that an algorithm uses in addition to its input and its output.

2.1   Graphs

We assume the reader to be familiar with the notions of tree and of directed acyclic graph (DAG). In this paper we only deal with *ordered* trees and DAGs, in which there is a total order among the out-neighbors of every node. The i-th leaf of a tree is its i-th leaf in depth-first order, and to every node v of a tree we assign the compact integer interval $[\text{sp}(v)..\text{ep}(v)]$, in depth-first order, of all leaves that belong to the subtree rooted at v. In this paper we use the expression DAG also for directed acyclic *multigraphs*, allowing distinct arcs to have the same source and destination nodes. In what follows we consider just DAGs with exactly one source and one sink. We denote by $\mathcal{T}(G)$ the tree generated by DAG G with the following recursive procedure: the tree generated by the sink of G consists of a single node; the tree generated by a node v of G that is not the sink, consists of a node whose children are the roots of the subtrees generated by the out-neighbors of v in G, taken in order. Note that: (1) every node of $\mathcal{T}(G)$ is generated by exactly one node of G; (2) a node of G different from the sink generates one or more internal nodes of $\mathcal{T}(G)$, and the subtrees of $\mathcal{T}(G)$ rooted at all such nodes are isomorphic; (3) the sink of G can generate one or more leaves of $\mathcal{T}(G)$; (4) there is a bijection, between the set of root-to-leaf paths in $\mathcal{T}(G)$ and the set of source-to-sink paths in G, such that every path $v_1, \ldots, v_k$ in $\mathcal{T}(G)$ is mapped to a path $v_1', \ldots, v_k'$ in G.

2.2   Strings

Let $\Sigma = [1..\sigma]$ be an integer alphabet, let $\# = 0 \notin \Sigma$ be a separator, and let $T = [1..\sigma]^{n-1}\#$ be a string. Given a string $W \in [1..\sigma]^k$, we call the *reverse of* W the string $\overline{W}$ obtained by reading W from right to left. For a string $W \in [1..\sigma]^k\#$ we abuse notation, denoting by $\overline{W}$ the string $\overline{W[1..k]}\#$. Given a substring W of T, let $\mathcal{P}_T(W)$ be the set of all starting positions of W in T. A *repeat* W is a string that satisfies $|\mathcal{P}_T(W)| > 1$. We conventionally assume that the empty string occurs $n + 1$ times in T, before the first character of T and after every character of T, thus it is a repeat. We denote by $\Sigma_T^\ell(W)$ the set of *left extensions* of W, i.e. the set of characters $\{a \in [0..\sigma] : |\mathcal{P}_T(aW)| > 0\}$. Symmetrically, we denote by $\Sigma_T^r(W)$ the set of *right extensions* of W, i.e. the set of characters $\{b \in [0..\sigma] : |\mathcal{P}_T(Wb)| > 0\}$. A repeat W is *right-maximal* (respectively, *left-maximal*) iff $|\Sigma_T^r(W)| > 1$ (respectively, iff $|\Sigma_T^\ell(W)| > 1$). It is well known that T can have at most $n - 1$ right-maximal repeats and at most $n - 1$ left-maximal repeats. A *maximal repeat* of T is a repeat that is both left- and right-maximal. Note that the empty string is a maximal repeat. A *near-supermaximal repeat* is a maximal repeat with at least one occurrence that is not contained in an occurrence of another maximal repeat (see e.g. [13]). A *minimal absent word* of T is a string W that does not occur in T, but such that any substring of W occurs in T. It is well known that a minimal absent word W can be written as aVb, where a and b are characters and V is a maximal repeat of T [8]. It is also well known that a maximal repeat $W = [1..\sigma]^m$ of T is the equivalence class of all the right-maximal strings $\{W[1..m], \ldots, W[k..m]\}$ such that $W[k + 1..m]$ is left-maximal, and $W[i..m]$ is not left-maximal for all $i \in [2..k]$ (see e.g. [2]). By *matching statistics* of a string S with respect to T, we denote the array $\mathsf{MS}_{S,T}[1..|S|]$ such that $\mathsf{MS}_{S,T}[i]$ is the length of the longest prefix of $S[i..|S|]$ that occurs in T.

For reasons of space we assume the reader to be familiar with the notion of *suffix trie* of T, as well as with the related notion of *suffix tree* $\mathsf{ST}_T = (V, E)$ of T, which we do not define here. We denote by $\ell(\gamma)$, or equivalently by $\ell(u, v)$, the label of edge $\gamma = (u, v) \in E$, and we denote by $\ell(v)$ the string label of node $v \in V$. It is well known that a substring W of T is right-maximal iff $W = \ell(v)$ for some internal node v of the suffix tree. Note that the label of an edge of ST_T is itself a right-maximal substring of T, thus it is also the label of a node of ST_T. We assume the reader to be familiar with the notion of *suffix link* connecting a node v with $\ell(v) = aW$ for some $a \in [0..\sigma]$ to a node w with $\ell(w) = W$. Here we just recall that inverting the direction of all suffix links yields the so-called *explicit Weiner links*. Given an internal node v and a symbol $a \in [0..\sigma]$, it might happen that string $a\ell(v)$ does occur in T, but that it is not right-maximal, i.e. it is not the label of any internal node: all such left extensions of internal nodes that end in the middle of an edge or at a leaf are called *implicit Weiner links*. The *suffix-link tree* is the graph whose edges are the union of all explicit and implicit Weiner links, and whose nodes are all the internal nodes of ST_T, as well as additional nodes corresponding to the destinations of implicit Weiner links. We call *compact suffix-link tree* the subgraph of the suffix-link tree induced by maximal repeats.

We assume the reader to be familiar with the notion and uses of the Burrows-Wheeler transform of T. In this paper we use BWT_T to denote the BWT of T, and we use $\mathtt{range}(W) = [\mathtt{sp}(W)..\mathtt{ep}(W)]$ to denote the lexicographic interval of a string W in a BWT that is implicit from the context. For a node v (respectively, for an edge e) of ST_T, we use the shortcut $\mathtt{range}(v) = [\mathtt{sp}(v)..\mathtt{ep}(v)]$ (respectively, $\mathtt{range}(e) = [\mathtt{sp}(e)..\mathtt{ep}(e)]$) to denote $\mathtt{range}(\ell(v))$ (respectively, $\mathtt{range}(\ell(e))$). We denote by r_T the number of runs in BWT_T, and we call *run-length encoded BWT* (denoted by RLBWT_T) any representation of BWT_T that takes $O(r_T)$ words of space, and that supports rank and select operations (see e.g. [16,17,20]).

Finally, in this paper we consider only context-free grammars in which the right-hand side of every production rule consists either of a single terminal, or of at least two nonterminals. We denote by $\pi(F)$ the sequence of characters produced by a nonterminal F of a context-free grammar. Every node in the parse tree of F corresponds to an interval in $\pi(F)$. Given a nonterminal F and an integer interval $[i..j] \subseteq [1..|\pi(F)|]$, let a node of the parse tree from F be marked iff its interval is contained in $[i..j]$. By *blanket* of $[i..j]$ in F we denote the set of all marked nodes in the parse tree of F. Clearly the blanket of $[i..j]$ in F contains $O(j - i)$ nodes and edges.

2.3   CDAWG

The *compact directed acyclic word graph* of a string T (denoted by CDAWG_T in what follows) is the minimal compact automaton that recognizes all suffixes of T [5,9]. We denote by e_T the number of arcs in CDAWG_T, and by h_T the length of a longest path in CDAWG_T. We remove subscripts when string T is implicit from the context. The CDAWG of T can be seen as the minimization of ST_T, in which all leaves are merged to the same node (the sink) that represents T itself, and in which all nodes except the sink are in one-to-one correspondence with the maximal repeats of T [19]. Every arc of CDAWG_T is labeled by a substring of T, and the out-neighbors $w_1, \ldots, w_k$ of every node v of CDAWG_T are sorted according to the lexicographic order of the distinct labels of arcs $(v, w_1), \ldots, (v, w_k)$. We denote again with $\ell(v)$ (respectively, with $\ell(\gamma)$) the label of a node v (respectively, of an arc γ) of CDAWG_T.

Since there is a bijection between the nodes of CDAWG_T and the maximal repeats of T, and since every maximal repeat of T is the equivalence class of a set of roots of isomorphic subtrees of ST_T, it follows that the node v of CDAWG_T

with $\ell(v) = W$ is the equivalence class of the nodes $\{v_1, \ldots, v_k\}$ of ST_T such that $\ell(v_i) = W[i..m]$ for all $i \in [1..k]$, and such that $v_k, v_{k-1}, \ldots, v_1$ is a maximal unary path in the suffix-link tree. The subtrees of ST_T rooted at all such nodes are isomorphic, and $\mathcal{T}(\mathsf{CDAWG}_T) = \mathsf{ST}_T$. It follows that a right-maximal string can be identified by the maximal repeat W it belongs to, and by the length of the corresponding suffix of W. Similarly, a suffix of T can be identified by a length relative to the sink of CDAWG_T.

The equivalence class of a maximal repeat is related to the equivalence classes of its in-neighbors in the CDAWG in a specific way:

Property 1 ([2]). Let w be a node in the CDAWG with $\ell(w) = W \in [1..\sigma]^m$, and let $\mathcal{S}_w = \{W[1..m], \ldots, W[k..m]\}$ be the right-maximal strings that belong to the equivalence class of node w. Let $\{v^1, \ldots, v^t\}$ be the in-neighbors of w in CDAWG_T, and let $\{V^1, \ldots, V^t\}$ be their labels. Then, $\mathcal{S}_w$ is partitioned into t disjoint sets $\mathcal{S}_w^1, \ldots, \mathcal{S}_w^t$ such that $\mathcal{S}_w^i = \{W[x^i+1..m], W[x^i+2..m], \ldots, W[x^i+|\mathcal{S}_{v^i}|..m]\}$, and the right-maximal string $V^i[p..|V^i|]$ labels the parent of the locus of the right-maximal string $W[x^i+p..m]$ in the suffix tree, for all $p \in [1..|\mathcal{S}_{v^i}|]$.

Property 1 partitions every maximal repeat of T into left-maximal factors, and applied to the sink w of CDAWG_T, it partitions T into t left-maximal factors, where t is the number of in-neighbors of w, or equivalently the number of near-supermaximal repeats of T. Moreover, by Property 1, it is natural to say that in-neighbor v^i of node w is smaller than in-neighbor v^j of node w iff $x^i < x^j$, or equivalently if the strings in $\mathcal{S}_w^i$ are longer than the strings in $\mathcal{S}_w^j$. We call $\overline{\mathsf{CDAWG}}_T$ the ordered DAG obtained by applying this order to the reversed CDAWG_T, i.e. to the DAG obtained by inverting the direction of all arcs of CDAWG_T, and by labeling every arc (v, w), where w is the source of CDAWG_T, with the first character of the string label of arc (w, v) in CDAWG_T. Note that some nodes of $\overline{\mathsf{CDAWG}}_T$ can have just one out-neighbor: for brevity we denote by $\overline{\mathsf{CDAWG}}_T$ the graph obtained by collapsing every such node v, i.e. by redirecting to the out-neighbor of v all the arcs directed to v, propagating to such arcs the label of the out-neighbor of v, if any.

The source of $\overline{\mathsf{CDAWG}}_T$ is the sink of CDAWG_T, which is the equivalence class of all suffixes of T in string order. There is a bijection between the distinct paths of $\overline{\mathsf{CDAWG}}_T$ and the suffixes of T; thus, the i-th leaf of $\mathcal{T}(\overline{\mathsf{CDAWG}}_T)$ in depth-first order corresponds to the i-th suffix of T in string order. Moreover, the last arc in the source-to-sink path of $\overline{\mathsf{CDAWG}}_T$ that corresponds to suffix $T[i..|T|]$ is labeled by character $T[i]$. It follows that:

Property 2 ([1]). $\overline{\mathsf{CDAWG}}_T$ is a context-free grammar that generates T and only T, and $\mathcal{T}(\overline{\mathsf{CDAWG}}_T)$ is its parse tree. Let v be a node of CDAWG_T with t in-neighbors, and let $\ell(v) = VW$, where W is the longest proper suffix of $\ell(v)$ that is a maximal repeat (if any). Then, v corresponds to a nonterminal F of the grammar such that $\pi(F) = V = \pi(F_1) \cdots \pi(F_t)$, and F_i are the nonterminals that correspond to the in-neighbors of v, for all $i \in [1..t]$.

Note that the nonterminals of this grammar correspond to unary paths in the suffix-link tree of T, i.e. to edges in the suffix tree of $\overline{T}$. This parallels the grammar implicit in [6] and explicit in [21], whose nonterminals correspond to unary paths in the *suffix trie* of T, i.e. to edges in the suffix tree of T.

2.4 Counting and Locating with the CDAWG

CDAWG_T can be combined with RLBWT_T to build a data structure that takes $O(e_T)$ words of space, and that counts all the occ occurrences of a pattern P of length m in $O(m \log \log n)$ time, and reports all such occurrences in $O(m \log \log n + \text{occ})$ time [2].

Specifically, for every node v of the CDAWG, we store $|\ell(v)|$ in a variable $v.\text{length}$. Recall that an arc (v, w) in the CDAWG means that maximal repeat $\ell(w)$ can be obtained by extending maximal repeat $\ell(v)$ to the right *and to the left*. Thus, for every arc $\gamma = (v, w)$ of the CDAWG, we store the first character of $\ell(\gamma)$ in a variable $\gamma.\text{char}$, and we store the length of the right extension implied by γ in a variable $\gamma.\text{right}$. The length $\gamma.\text{left}$ of the left extension implied by γ can be computed by $w.\text{length} - v.\text{length} - \gamma.\text{right}$. For every arc of the CDAWG that connects a maximal repeat W to the sink, we store just $\gamma.\text{char}$ and the starting position $\gamma.\text{pos}$ of string $W \cdot \gamma.\text{char}$ in T. The total space used by the CDAWG is $O(e_T)$ words, and the number of runs in BWT_T can be shown to be $O(e_T)$ as well [2].

We use the RLBWT to count the number of occurrences of P in T, in $O(m \log \log n)$ time: if this number is not zero, we use the CDAWG to report all the occ occurrences of P in $O(\text{occ})$ time, using a technique already sketched in [7]. Specifically, since we know that P occurs in T, we perform a *blind search* for P in the CDAWG, as follows. We keep a variable i, initialized to zero, that stores the length of the prefix of P that we have matched so far, and we keep a variable j, initialized to one, that stores the starting position of P inside the last maximal repeat encountered during the search. For every node v in the CDAWG, we choose the arc γ such that $\gamma.\text{char} = P[i+1]$ in constant time using hashing, we increment i by $\gamma.\text{right}$, and we increment j by $\gamma.\text{left}$. If the search leads to the sink by an arc γ, we report $\gamma.\text{pos} + j - 1$ and we stop. If the search ends at a node v that is associated with a maximal repeat W, we determine all the occurrences of W in T by performing a depth-first traversal of all nodes reachable from v in the CDAWG, updating variables i and j as described above, and reporting $\gamma.\text{pos} + j - 1$ for every arc γ that leads to the sink. Clearly the total number of nodes and arcs reachable from v is $O(\text{occ})$.

Note that performing the blind search for a pattern in the CDAWG is analogous to a descending walk on the suffix tree, thus we can compute the BWT interval of every node of ST_T that we meet during the search, by storing in every arc of the CDAWG a suitable offset between BWT intervals, as described in the following property:

Property 3 ([2]). Let $\{W[1..m], \ldots, W[k..m]\}$ be the right-maximal strings that belong to the equivalence class of maximal repeat $W \in [1..\sigma]^m$ of string T, and let $\text{range}(W[i..m]) = [p_i..q_i]$ for $i \in [1..k]$. Then $|q_i - p_i + 1| = |q_j - p_j + 1|$ for all i and j in $[1..k]$. Let $c \in [0..\sigma]$, and let $\text{range}(W[i..m]c) = [x_i..y_i]$ for $i \in [1..k]$. Then, $x_i = p_i + x_1 - p_1$ and $y_i = p_i + y_1 - p_1$.

Algorithm 1. Reading the first k characters of the string produced by a nonterminal F of a straight-line program represented as a DAG G. F corresponds to node u' of G. Notation follows Lemma 4.

```
 1  S ← empty stack;
 2  S.push((u', 0, 0));
 3  extracted ← 0;
 4  repeat
 5      t ← S.top;
 6      if t.lastChild < |t.node.outNeighbors| then
 7          t.lastChild ← t.lastChild + 1 ;
 8          v' ← t.node.outNeighbors[t.lastChild];
 9          if v' = G.sink then
10              print(label(t.node, v'));
11              extracted ← extracted + 1;
12          else if t.lastChild = 1 then
13              t.depth ← 1;
14              S.push((levelAncestor(t.node, t.depth), 0, t.depth));
15          else S.push((v', 0, 0)) ;
16      else
17          S.pop;
18          if S = ∅ then return extracted ;
19          t ← S.top;
20          if t.depth < t.node.depth then  t.depth ← t.depth + 1 ;
21          if t.depth < t.node.depth then
                 S.push((levelAncestor(t.node, t.depth), 1, t.depth)) ;
22      end
23  until extracted = k;
24  return k;
```

Properties 1 and 3, among others, can be used to implement a number of suffix tree operations in $O(1)$ or $O(\log \log n)$ time, using data structures that take just $O(e_T)$ or $O(e_T + e_{\overline{T}})$ words of space [1,2]. Among other information, such data structures store a pointer, from each node v of the CDAWG, to the longest proper suffix of $\ell(v)$ (if any) that is a maximal repeat. Note that such *suffix pointers* can be charged to suffix links in ST_T, thus they take overall $O(e_T)$ words of space.

3 Faster Count and Locate Queries in the CDAWG

In this paper we focus on deciding whether a pattern P occurs in T, a key step in the blind search of Sect. 2.4. Rather than using the RLBWT for such decision, we exploit Property 2 and use the grammar induced by $\overline{\mathsf{CDAWG}}_T$.

Our methods will require a data structure, of size linear in the grammar, that extracts in $O(k)$ time the first k characters of the string produced by a nonterminal. Previous research described an algorithm that extracts the whole string produced by a nonterminal in linear time, using just constant working space, by manipulating pointers in the grammar [12]. This solution does not guarantee linear time when just a prefix of the string is extracted. A linear-size data structure with the stronger guarantee of constant-time extraction per character has also been described [11], and this solution can be used as a black box in our methods. However, since we just need amortized linear time, we describe a significantly simpler alternative that needs just a level ancestor data structure (an idea already implicit in [14]) and that will be useful in what follows:

Lemma 4. *Let $G = (V, E)$ be the DAG representation of a straight-line program. There is a data structure that: (1) given an integer k and a nonterminal F, allows one to read the first k characters of $\pi(F)$ in $O(k)$ time and $O(\min\{k, h\})$ words of working space, where h is the height of the parse tree of F; (2) given a string S and a nonterminal F, allows one to compute the length k of the longest prefix of S that matches a prefix of $\pi(F)$, in $O(k)$ time and $O(\min\{k, h\})$ words of working space. Such data structure takes $O(|V|)$ words of space.*

Proof. We mark the arc of G that connects each node v' to its first out-neighbor. The set of all marked arcs induces a spanning tree τ of G, rooted at the sink and arbitrarily ordered [11]. In what follows we identify the nodes of τ with the corresponding nodes of G. We build a data structure that supports *level ancestor queries* on τ: given a node v and an integer d, such data structure returns the ancestor u of v in τ such that the path from the root of τ to u contains exactly d edges. The level ancestor data structure described in [3,4] takes $O(|V|)$ words of space and it answers queries in constant time. To read the first k characters of string $\pi(F) = W$, we explore the blanket of $W[1..k]$ in F recursively, as described in Algorithm 1. The tuples in the stack used by the algorithm have the following fields: (node, lastChild, depth), where node is a node of G, u'.outNeighbors is the sorted list of out-neighbors of node u' in G, u'.depth is the depth of u' in τ, and function label(u', v') returns the character that labels arc (u', v') in G. Algorithm 1 returns the number of characters read, which might be smaller than k. A similar procedure can be used for computing the length of the longest prefix of $\pi(F)$ that matches a prefix of a query string. Every type of operation in Algorithm 1 takes constant time, it can be charged to a distinct character in the output, and it pushes at most one element on the stack. Thus, the stack contains $O(k)$ tuples at every step of the algorithm. It is also easy to see that the stack never contains more elements than the length of the longest path from the node of G that corresponds to F to the sink.   □

If necessary, Algorithm 1 can be modified to take constant time per character:

Corollary 5. *Let $G = (V, E)$ be the DAG representation of a straight-line program. There is a data structure that takes $O(|V|)$ words of space and that, given a nonterminal F, allows one to read the characters of $\pi(F)$, from left to right, in constant time per character and in $O(\min\{k, h\})$ words of working space, where h is the height of the parse tree of F.*

Proof. After having printed character i of $\pi(F)$, the time Algorithm 1 has to wait before printing character $i + 1$ is always bounded by a constant, except when the procedure repeatedly pops tuples from the stack. This can be avoided by preventively popping a tuple t for which $t.\texttt{lastChild}$ has reached $|t.\texttt{node.outNeighbors}|$ after Line 6 is executed, before pushing new tuples on the stack.   □

Moreover, Lemma 4 can be generalized to weighted DAGs, by storing in each node of τ the sum of weights of all edges from the node to the root of τ, by saving sums of weights in the tuples on the stack, and by summing and subtracting the weights of the arcs of the DAG:

Corollary 6. *Let $G = (V, E)$ be an ordered DAG with a single sink and with weights on the arcs, and let the weight of a path be the sum of weights of all its arcs. There is a data structure that, given an integer k and a node v, reports the weights of the first k paths from v to the sink in preorder, in constant time per path and in $O(\min\{k, h\})$ words of working space, where h is the length of a longest path from v to the sink. Such data structure takes $O(|V|)$ words of space.*

Lemma 4 is all we need to verify in linear time whether a pattern occurs in the indexed text:

Theorem 7. *Let $T \in [1..\sigma]^n$ be a string. There is a data structure that takes $O(e_T)$ words of space, and that counts (respectively, reports) all the $\texttt{occ}$ occurrences of a pattern $P \in [1..\sigma]^m$ in $O(m)$ time (respectively, in $O(m + \texttt{occ})$ time) and in $O(\min\{m, h_T\})$ words of working space.*

Proof. We assume that every node v' of CDAWG_T stores in a variable $v'.\texttt{freq}$ the number of occurrences of $\ell(v')$ in T. Recall that, for a node v' of CDAWG_T, $\ell(v') = \pi(F_1)\pi(F_2)\cdots\pi(F_k) \cdot W$, where F_p for $p \in [1..k]$ are nonterminals of the grammar, and W is the maximal repeat that labels the node w' of CDAWG_T that is reachable from v' by a suffix pointer. For each arc (u', v') of CDAWG_T, we store a pointer to the nonterminal F_p of v' that corresponds to u'. We perform a blind search for P in CDAWG_T as described in Sect. 2.4: either the search is unsuccessful, or it returns a node v' of CDAWG_T and an integer interval $[i..j]$ such that, if P occurs in T, then $P = V[i..j]$ where $V = \ell(v')$, and the number of occurrences of P in T is $v'.\texttt{freq}$. To decide whether P occurs in T, we reconstruct the characters in $V[i..j]$ as follows (Fig. 1a). Clearly i belongs to a $\pi(F_p)$ for some p, and such F_p can be accessed in constant time using the pointers described at the beginning of the proof. If i is the first position of $\pi(F_p)$, we extract all characters of $\pi(F_p)$ by performing a linear-time traversal of the parse tree of F_p. Otherwise, we extract the suffix of $\pi(F_p)$ in linear time using Lemma 4. Note that j must belong to $\pi(F_q)$ for some $q > p$, since the search reaches v' after right-extending a suffix of an in-neighbor u' of v' that belongs to the equivalence class of u' (recall Property 1). We thus proceed symmetrically, traversing the entire parse tree of $F_{p+1} \ldots F_{q-1}$ and finally extracting either the entire $\pi(F_q)$ or a prefix. Finally, j could belong to W, in which case we traverse the entire parse tree of $F_{p+1} \ldots F_k$ and we recur on w', resetting j to $j - \sum_{x=1}^{k} |\pi(F_x)|$. If the verification is successful, we proceed to locate all the occurrences of P in T as described in Sect. 2.4.   □

Note that the data structure in Theorem 7 takes actually $O(\min\{e_T, e_{\overline{T}}\})$ words of space, since one could index either T or $\overline{T}$ for counting and locating. Lemma 4 can also be used to report the top k occurrences of a pattern P in T, according to the popularity of the right-extensions of P in the corpus:

Corollary 8. *Let P be a pattern, let $\mathcal{P} = \{p_1, p_2, \ldots, p_m\}$ be the set of all its starting positions in a text T. Let sequence $Q = q_1, q_2, \ldots, q_m$ be such that $q_i \in \mathcal{P}$ for all $i \in [1..m]$, $q_i \neq q_j$ for all $i \neq j$, and $i < j$ iff $T[q_i..|T|]$ is lexicographically smaller than $T[q_j..|T|]$. Let sequence $S = s_1, s_2, \ldots, s_m$ be such that $s_i \in \mathcal{P}$ for all $i \in [1..m]$, $s_i \neq s_j$ for all $i \neq j$, and $i < j$ iff the frequency of $T[s_i..s_i + x]$ in T is not smaller than the frequency of $T[s_j..s_j + x]$ in T (with ties broken lexicographically), where x is the length of the longest common prefix between $T[s_i..|T|]$ and $T[s_j..|T|]$. There is a data structure that allows one to return the first k elements of sequence Q or S in constant time per element and in $O(\min\{k, h_T\})$ words of working space. Such data structure takes $O(e_T)$ words of space.*

Proof. Recall that Theorem 7 builds the spanning tree τ of Lemma 4 on the reversed CDAWG that represents a straight-line program of T. To print Q, we build τ and the corresponding level-ancestor data structure on CDAWG$_T$, connecting each vertex of the CDAWG to its lexicographically smallest out-neighbor, and storing in each node of τ the sum of lengths of all edges from the node to the root of τ. Given the locus v' of P in CDAWG$_T$, we can print the first k elements of Q in $O(k)$ time and in $O(\min\{k, h\})$ words of space, where h is the length of a longest path from v' to the sink of CDAWG$_T$, by using Corollary 6. To print S we add to each node of CDAWG$_T$ an additional list of children, sorted by nondecreasing frequency with ties broken lexicographically, and we build the spanning tree τ by connecting each vertex of CDAWG$_T$ to its first out-neighbor in such new list.   □

Finally, Theorem 7 allows one to reconstruct the label of any arc of the CDAWG, in linear time in the length k of such label. This improves the $O(k \log \log n)$ bound described in [2], where n is the length of the uncompressed text, and it removes the $e_{\overline{T}}$ term from the space complexity, since RLBWT$_{\overline{T}}$ is not needed.

Theorem 9. *There is a data structure that allows one to read the k characters of the label of an arc (v', w') of CDAWG$_T$, in $O(k)$ time and in $O(\min\{k, h_T\})$ words of working space. Such data structure takes $O(e_T)$ words of space.*

Proof. Recall that every arc (v', w') that does not point to the sink of CDAWG$_T$ is a right-maximal substring of T. If it is also a maximal repeat, then we can already reconstruct it as described in Theorem 7, storing a pointer to such maximal repeat, starting extraction from the first nonterminal of the maximal repeat,

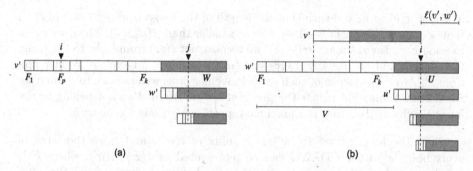

Fig. 1. (a) The verification step of pattern search, implemented with the CDAWG. Notation follows Theorem 7. (b) Reconstructing the label of an arc of the CDAWG. Notation follows Theorem 9.

and recurring to the maximal repeat reachable from its suffix pointer. Otherwise, let $W = \ell(w') = VU$, where U is the maximal repeat that corresponds to the node u' reachable from the suffix pointer of w', and let $V = \pi(F_1) \cdots \pi(F_k)$ where F_p for $p \in [1..k]$ are nonterminals in the grammar. The label of (v', w') coincides with suffix $W[i..|W|]$, and its length is stored in the index.

If $i \leq |V|$, let $V[i..|V|] = X \cdot \pi(F_{p+1}) \cdots \pi(F_k)$ for some p. To reconstruct U, we traverse the whole parse tree of $F_k, F_{k-1}, \ldots, F_{p+1}$, and we reconstruct the suffix of length $|X|$ of $\pi(F_p)$ using Lemma 4. Otherwise, if $i > |V|$, we could recur to U, resetting i to $i - |V|$ (Fig. 1b). Let $U = V'U'$, where U' is the maximal repeat that corresponds to the node reachable from the suffix pointer of u'. Note that it could still happen that $i > |V'|$, thus we might need to follow a sequence of suffix pointers. During the construction of the index, we store with arc (v', w') a pointer to the first maximal repeat t', in the sequence of suffix pointers from w', such that $|\ell(t')| \geq |\ell(v', w')|$, and such that the length of the longest proper suffix of $\ell(t')$ that is a maximal repeat is either zero or smaller than $|\ell(v', w')|$. To reconstruct $\ell(v', w')$, we just follow such pointer and proceed as described above.

Reading the label of an arc that is directed to the sink of CDAWG_T can be implemented in a similar way: we leave the details to the reader. □

We can also read the label of an arc (v', w') *from right to left*, with the stronger guarantee of taking constant time per character:

Corollary 10. *There is a data structure that allows one to read the k characters of the label of an arc (v', w') of* CDAWG_T, *from right to left, in constant time per character and in $O(\min\{k, h_T\})$ words of working space. Such data structure takes $O(e_T)$ words of space.*

Proof. We proceed as in Theorem 9, but we also keep the tree τ of explicit Weiner links from every node of CDAWG_T, imposing an arbitrary order on the children of every node t of τ, and we build a data structure that supports level ancestor queries on τ. As in Theorem 9, we move to a maximal repeat u' such that

$|\ell(u')| \geq |\ell(v', w')|$, and such that the length of the longest proper suffix of $\ell(u')$ that is a maximal repeat is either zero or smaller than $|\ell(v', w')|$. Then, we move to node $x' = \texttt{levelAncestor}(u', 1)$, we reconstruct $\ell(x')$ from right to left using Corollary 5, and we use $\texttt{levelAncestor}(u', 2)$ to follow an explicit Weiner link from x'. After a sequence of such explicit Weiner links we are back to u', and we reconstruct from right to left the prefix of $\ell(v', w')$ that does not belong to the longest suffix of $\ell(u')$ that is a maximal repeat, using again Corollary 5.   □

Since the label of arc (v', w') is a suffix of $\ell(w')$, and since the label of every node w' of the CDAWG can be represented as $\pi(F) \cdot \ell(u')$, where F is a nonterminal of the grammar and u' is the longest suffix of $\ell(w')$ that is a maximal repeat, we could implement Corollary 10 by adding to the grammar the nonterminals W' and U' and a new production $W' \rightarrow FU'$ for nodes w' and u', and by using Corollary 5 for extraction. This does not increase the size of the grammar asymptotically. Note that the subgraph induced by the new nonterminals in the modified grammar is the reverse of the compact suffix-link tree of T.

4   Faster Matching Statistics in the CDAWG

A number of applications, including matching statistics, require reading the label of an arc *from left to right*: this is not straightforward using the techniques we described, since the label of an arc (v', w') can start e.g. in the middle of one of the nonterminals of w' rather than at the beginning of one such nonterminal (see Fig. 1b). We circumvent the need for reading the characters of the label of an arc from left to right in matching statistics, by applying the algorithm in Theorem 7 to prefixes of the pattern of exponentially increasing length:

Lemma 11. *There is a data structure that, given a string S and an arc (v', w') of CDAWG_T, allows one to compute the length k of the longest prefix of S that matches a prefix of the label of (v', w'), in $O(k)$ time and in $O(\min\{k, h_T\})$ words of working space. Such data structure takes $O(e_T)$ words of space.*

Proof. Let $\gamma = (v', w')$. If $\ell(\gamma)$ is a maximal repeat of T, we can already read its characters from left to right by applying Theorem 7. Otherwise, we perform a doubling search over the prefixes of S, testing iteratively whether $S[1..2^i]$ matches a prefix of $\ell(\gamma)$ for increasing integers i, and stopping when $S[1..2^i]$ does not match a prefix of $\ell(\gamma)$. We perform a linear amount of work in the length of each prefix, thus a linear amount of total work in the length of the longest prefix of S that matches a prefix of $\ell(\gamma)$.

We determine whether $S[1..2^i]$ is a prefix of $\ell(\gamma)$ as follows. Recall that an arc of CDAWG_T (or equivalently of ST_T) is a right-maximal substring of T, therefore it is also a node of ST_T. We store for each arc γ of CDAWG_T the interval $\texttt{range}(\gamma)$ of the corresponding string in BWT_T. Given $S[1..2^i]$, we perform a blind search on the CDAWG, simulating a blind search on ST_T and using Property 3 to keep the BWT intervals of the corresponding nodes of ST_T that we meet. We stop at the node v of the suffix tree at which the blind search fails, or at the first node whose interval does not contain $\mathbf{range}(\gamma)$ (in which case we reset v to its parent), or at the last node reached by a successful blind search in which the BWT intervals of all traversed nodes contain $\mathbf{range}(\gamma)$. In the first two cases, we know that the longest prefix of S that matches $\ell(\gamma)$ has length smaller than 2^i. Then, we read (but don't explicitly store) the label of v in linear time as described in Theorem 7, finding the position of the leftmost mismatch with $S[1..2^i]$, if any.   □

Lemma 11 is all we need to implement matching statistics with the CDAWG:

Theorem 12. *There is a data structure that takes $O(e_T)$ words of space, and that allows one to compute $\mathsf{MS}_{S,T}$ in $O(|S|)$ time and in $O(\min\{\mu, h_T\})$ words of working space, where μ is the largest number in $\mathsf{MS}_{S,T}$.*

Proof. We fill array $\mathsf{MS}_{S,T}$ from left to right, by implementing with CDAWG_T the classical matching statistics algorithm based on suffix link and child operations on the suffix tree. Assume that we have computed $\mathsf{MS}_{S,T}[1..i]$ for some i. Let $c = S[i + \mathsf{MS}_{S,T}[i]]$ and let $U = S[i..i + \mathsf{MS}_{S,T}[i] - 1] = VX$, where V is the longest prefix of U that is right-maximal in T, and v is the node of ST_T with label V. Assume that we know v and the node v' of CDAWG_T that corresponds to the equivalence class of v. Let w' be the node of CDAWG_T that corresponds to the longest suffix of $\ell(v')$ that is a maximal repeat of T. If $|\ell(v)| > |\ell(w')| + 1$, then $\mathsf{MS}_{S,T}[i + 1] = \mathsf{MS}_{S,T}[i] - 1$, since no suffix of U longer than $|\ell(w')| + |X|$ can be followed by character c. Otherwise, we move to w' in constant time by following the suffix pointer of v', and we perform a blind search for X from w'. Let $\ell(w')X = ZX'$, where $Z = \ell(z)$ is the longest prefix of $\ell(w')X$ that is right-maximal in T, and let z' be the node of the CDAWG that corresponds to the equivalence class of z. If $|X'| > 0$, or if no arc from z' is labeled by c, then again $\mathsf{MS}_{S,T}[i + 1] = \mathsf{MS}_{S,T}[i] - 1$. Otherwise, we use Lemma 11 to compute the length of the longest prefix of $S[i + \mathsf{MS}_{S,T}[i]..|S|]$ that matches a prefix of the arc from z' labeled by c. The claimed time complexity comes from Lemma 11 and from standard amortization arguments used in matching statistics.   □

Note that the data structure in Theorem 12 takes actually $O(\min\{e_T, e_{\overline{T}}\})$ words of space, since one could index either T or $\overline{T}$ for computing the matching statistics vector (in the latter case, S is read from right to left).

Another consequence of Property 2 is that we can compute the minimal absent words of T using an index of size proportional just to the number of maximal repeats of T and of their extensions:

Lemma 13. *There is a data structure that takes $O(e_T + e_{\overline{T}})$ words of space, and that allows one to compute the minimal absent words of T in $O(e_T + e_{\overline{T}} + \text{out})$ time and in $O(\lambda_T + \min\{\mu_T, h_T\})$ words of working space, where out is the size of the output, λ_T is the maximum number of left extensions of a maximal repeat of T, and μ_T is the length of a longest maximal repeat of T.*

Proof. For every arc $\gamma = (v', w')$ of CDAWG$_T$, we store in a variable γ.order the order of v' among the in-neighbors of w' induced by Property 1 and used in $\overline{\text{CDAWG}}_T$ (see Sect. 2.3), and we store in a variable γ.previousChar the character a, if any, such that $a\ell(v')b$ is a substring of $\ell(w')$ and $b = \gamma$.char is the first character of $\ell(\gamma)$.

Then, we traverse every node v' of CDAWG$_T$, and we scan every arc $\gamma = (v', w')$. If γ.order > 1, then $\ell(v')b$, where $b = \gamma$.char, is always preceded by γ.previousChar in T, thus we print $a\ell(v')b$ to the output for all a that label explicit and implicit Weiner links from v' and that are different from γ.previousChar. If γ.order $= 1$ then $\ell(v')b$ is a left-maximal substring of T, so we subtract the set of all Weiner links of w' from the set of all Weiner links of v' by a linear scan of their sorted lists, and we print $a\ell(v')b$ to the output for all characters a in the resulting list. Note that the same Weiner link of v' could be read multiple times, for multiple out-neighbors w' of v'. However, every such access can be charged either to the output or to a corresponding Weiner link from w', and each w' takes part in at most one such subtraction. It follows that the time taken by all list subtractions is $O(e_{\overline{T}} + \text{out})$.

We reconstruct each $\ell(v')$ in linear time as described in Theorem 7.   □

Acknowledgements. We thank the anonymous reviewers for simplifying some parts of the paper, for improving its overall clarity, and for suggesting references [11,12,14] and the current version of Lemma 13.

References

1. Belazzougui, D., Cunial, F.: Representing the suffix tree with the CDAWG. In: CPM 2017. Leibniz International Proceedings in Informatics (LIPIcs), vol. 78, pp. 7:1–7:13. Schloss Dagstuhl-Leibniz-Zentrum fuer Informatik (2017)

2. Belazzougui, D., Cunial, F., Gagie, T., Prezza, N., Raffinot, M.: Composite repetition-aware data structures. In: Cicalese, F., Porat, E., Vaccaro, U. (eds.) CPM 2015. LNCS, vol. 9133, pp. 26–39. Springer, Cham (2015). doi:10.1007/978-3-319-19929-0_3

3. Bender, M.A., Farach-Colton, M.: The level ancestor problem simplified. Theor. Comput. Sci. **321**(1), 5–12 (2004)

4. Berkman, O., Vishkin, U.: Finding level-ancestors in trees. J. Comput. Syst. Sci. **48**(2), 214–230 (1994)

5. Blumer, A., Blumer, J., Haussler, D., McConnell, R., Ehrenfeucht, A.: Complete inverted files for efficient text retrieval and analysis. J. ACM **34**(3), 578–595 (1987)

6. Crochemore, M., Epifanio, C., Grossi, R., Mignosi, F.: Linear-size suffix tries. Theor. Comput. Sci. **638**, 171–178 (2016)

7. Crochemore, M., Hancart, C.: Automata for matching patterns. In: Rozenberg, G., Salomaa, A. (eds.) Handbook of Formal Languages, pp. 399–462. Springer, Heidelberg (1997). doi:10.1007/978-3-662-07675-0_9

8. Crochemore, M., Mignosi, F., Restivo, A.: Automata and forbidden words. Inf. Proc. Lett. **67**(3), 111–117 (1998)

9. Crochemore, M., Vérin, R.: Direct construction of compact directed acyclic word graphs. In: Apostolico, A., Hein, J. (eds.) CPM 1997. LNCS, vol. 1264, pp. 116–129. Springer, Heidelberg (1997). doi:10.1007/3-540-63220-4_55

10. Gagie, T.: Large alphabets and incompressibility. Inf. Proc. Lett. **99**(6), 246–251 (2006)
11. Gasieniec, L., Kolpakov, R.M., Potapov, I., Sant, P.: Real-time traversal in grammar-based compressed files. In: DCC 2005, p. 458 (2005)
12. Gasieniec, L., Potapov, I.: Time/space efficient compressed pattern matching. Fundam. Informaticae **56**(1–2), 137–154 (2003)
13. Gusfield, D.: Algorithms on strings, trees and sequences: computer science and computational biology. Cambridge University Press, New York (1997)
14. Lohrey, M., Maneth, S., Reh, C.P.: Traversing grammar-compressed trees with constant delay. In: DCC 2016, pp. 546–555 (2016)
15. Russo, L.S., Navarro, G., Oliveira, A.L.: Fully-compressed suffix trees. ACM Trans. Algorithms **7**(4), 53 (2011)
16. Mäkinen, V., Navarro, G.: Succinct suffix arrays based on run-length encoding. In: Apostolico, A., Crochemore, M., Park, K. (eds.) CPM 2005. LNCS, vol. 3537, pp. 45–56. Springer, Heidelberg (2005). doi:10.1007/11496656_5
17. Mäkinen, V., Navarro, G., Sirén, J., Välimäki, N.: Storage and retrieval of highly repetitive sequence collections. J. Comput. Biol. **17**(3), 281–308 (2010)
18. Navarro, G., Russo, L.M.: Fast fully-compressed suffix trees. In: DCC 2014, pp. 283–291. IEEE (2014)
19. Raffinot, M.: On maximal repeats in strings. Inf. Proc. Lett. **80**(3), 165–169 (2001)
20. Sirén, J., Välimäki, N., Mäkinen, V., Navarro, G.: Run-length compressed indexes are superior for highly repetitive sequence collections. In: Amir, A., Turpin, A., Moffat, A. (eds.) SPIRE 2008. LNCS, vol. 5280, pp. 164–175. Springer, Heidelberg (2008). doi:10.1007/978-3-540-89097-3_17
21. Takagi, T., Goto, K., Fujishige, Y., Inenaga, S., Arimura, H.: Linear-size CDAWG: new repetition-aware indexing and grammar compression. In: SPIRE (2017, to appear). arXiv:1705.09779

Lightweight BWT and LCP Merging
via the Gap Algorithm

Lavinia Egidi[1(✉)] and Giovanni Manzini[1,2(✉)]

[1] Computer Science Institute, DiSIT University of Eastern Piedmont,
Viale Teresa Michel, 11, 15100 Alessandria, Italy
{lavinia.egidi,giovanni.manzini}@uniupo.it
[2] Institute of Informatics and Telematics CNR, Via Moruzzi, 1, 56124 Pisa, Italy

Abstract. Recently, Holt and McMillan [Bioinformatics 2014, ACM-BCB 2014] have proposed a simple and elegant algorithm to merge the Burrows-Wheeler transforms of a collection of strings. In this paper we show that their algorithm can be improved so that, in addition to the BWTs, it also merges the Longest Common Prefix (LCP) arrays. Because of its small memory footprint this new algorithm can be used for the final merge of BWT and LCP arrays computed by a faster but memory intensive construction algorithm.

Keywords: Document collections · String indexing · Data compression

1 Introduction and Related Works

The Burrows Wheeler transform (BWT) is a fundamental component of many compressed indices and it is often complemented by the Longest Common Prefix (LCP) array and a sampling of the Suffix Array [9,21]. Because of the sheer size of the data involved, the construction of such data structures is a challenging problem in itself. Although the final outcome is a *compressed* index, construction algorithms can be memory hungry and the necessity of developing *lightweight*, i.e. space economical, algorithms was recognized since the very beginning of the field [4,19,20]. When even lightweight algorithms do not fit in RAM, one has to resort to external memory construction algorithms (see [5,7,13,17] and references therein).

Many construction algorithms are designed for the case in which the input consists of a single sequence; yet in many applications the data to be indexed consist of a collection of distinct items: documents, web pages, NGS reads, proteins, *etc.*. One can concatenate such items using (distinct) end-of-file separators and index the resulting sequence. However, using distinct separators is possible only

Partially supported by the University of Eastern Piedmont projects KITE and *Behavioural Types for Dependability Analysis with Bayesian Networks*, PRIN grant 201534HNXC, and INdAM-GNCS Project *Efficient algorithms and techniques for the organization, management and analysis of biological Big Data*.

© Springer International Publishing AG 2017
G. Fici et al. (Eds.): SPIRE 2017, LNCS 10508, pp. 176–190, 2017.
DOI: 10.1007/978-3-319-67428-5_15

for small collections and from the algorithmic point of view it makes no sense to "forget" that the input consists of distinct items: this additional information should be exploited to run faster.

Recently, Holt and McMillan [10,11] have presented a new approach for computing the BWT of a collection of sequences based on the concept of merging: first the BWTs of the individual sequences are computed (by any single-string BWT algorithm) and then they are merged, possibly in multiple rounds as in the standard mergesort algorithm. The idea of BWT-merging is not new [6,23] but Holt and McMillan's merging algorithm is simpler than the previous approaches. For a constant size alphabet their algorithm merges the BWTs of two sequences t_0, t_1 in $\mathcal{O}(n \cdot \mathsf{avelcp}_{01})$ time where $n = |t_0| + |t_1|$ and avelcp_{01} is the average length of the longest common prefix between suffixes of t_0 and t_1. The average length of the longest common prefix is $\mathcal{O}(n)$ in the worst case but $\mathcal{O}(\log n)$ for random strings and for many real world datasets [14]. Note that even when $\mathsf{avelcp}_{01} = \mathcal{O}(\log n)$ the algorithm is not optimal since BWT merging can be done in linear time if there are no constraints on the space usage.

In this paper we show that the H&M (Holt and McMillan) merging algorithm can be modified so that, in addition to the BWTs, it merges the LCP arrays as well. The new algorithm, called Gap because of how it operates, has the same asymptotic cost as H&M and uses additional space only for storing its additional output, i.e. the LCP values. In our implementation, the Gap' algorithm uses only ≈ 1.5 bytes per symbol of workspace in addition to the input and the output, making it interesting when the overall size of the collection is close to the available RAM.

Our contribution in context. For a collection of documents of total size n over a constant alphabet, the BWT and LCP arrays, as well as many compressed indices, can be computed in $\mathcal{O}(n)$ time by first computing the Suffix Array (SA) of the collection. The construction of the suffix array is a well studied problem and there exist time/space optimal algorithms that work well in practice. The problem with this approach is that the SA takes $n \log n$ bits of space while a compressed index takes $\mathcal{O}(n)$ bits. Hence, going through the SA we can only build indices much smaller than the available RAM. This implies that, in practice, either we build multiple "small" indices, which must be queried independently, or we use a larger machine for the construction of the index. Note that the construction of compressed indices in linear time and $\mathcal{O}(n)$ bits of space is a challenging and active area of research, see [1] and references therein, but at the moment it has produced no practical algorithms.

Given this state of affairs, we propose the following practical approach for the construction of the BWT and LCP arrays of a collection of documents. We split the input collection into subcollections $C_1, \ldots, C_k$ of roughly equal size which are sufficiently small so that we can compute the BWT and LCP arrays via the SA. Then, we merge all the BWTs and LCPs using the Gap algorithm described in this paper. Since space is the main bottleneck, to compute the SA of the subcollections we use the recently proposed gSACA-K algorithm by Louza et al. [15,16] which runs in linear time, is extremely fast in practice, and uses only 2 KB in addition to the space of the input and the output (gSACA-K is based on the SACA-K algorithm from [22]). As we will see, this approach allows us to fully exploit all the available RAM and to take advantage of the optimal and highly engineered gSACA-K algorithm to do most of the job.

Among the construction algorithms proposed in the literature, the one most similar to our approach is the one described by Sirén in [24] where a compressed index is maintained in RAM and new collections are incrementally merged to it. The two approaches share the idea that building index should not require a specialized machine with a lot of RAM. The approach in [24] is specific for that particular compressed index (which doesn't use the LCP array), while ours, providing the plain BWT and LCP arrays, can be more easily adapted to build different flavors of compressed indices.

Another related result is the algorithm proposed in [2,3] which computes (from scratch) the multi-string BWT and LCP in *external memory*. Given a collection of m strings of the same length k, the algorithm first computes the BWT of all length-ℓ suffixes for $\ell = 1, 2, \ldots, k$ and then, using an approach inspired by the H&M algorithm, merges them to obtain the multi-string BWT and LCP arrays. The algorithm accesses disk data sequentially and the reported I/O volume is $\mathcal{O}(mk\,\mathsf{maxlcp})$ where maxlcp is the maximum of the length of all common prefixes (for the same input the I/O volume of the algorithm in [5] is $\mathcal{O}(mk^2)$). Although our Gap algorithm is designed only to merge BWTs and LCPs in internal memory, it also accesses its main data structures sequentially. This feature suggests that it could be engineered to work in external memory as well. Compared to [2,3] an external memory version of Gap would have the advantages of supporting also strings of different lengths, and of exploiting any available RAM to do some of the work with the highly efficient, indeed optimal, internal memory algorithm gSACA-K. We plan to pursue this line of research in a future work.

2 Notation

Let $t[1, n]$ denote a string of length n over an alphabet Σ of size σ. As usual, we assume $t[n]$ is a symbol not appearing elsewhere in t and lexicographically smaller than any other symbol. We write $t[i, j]$ to denote the substring $t[i]t[i + 1] \cdots t[j]$. If $j \geq n$ we assume $t[i, j] = t[i, n]$. If $i > j$ or $i > n$ then $t[i, j]$ is the empty string. Given two strings t and s we write $t \preceq s$ ($t \prec s$) to denote that t is lexicographically (strictly) smaller than s. We denote by $\mathsf{LCP}(t, s)$ the length of the longest common prefix between t and s.

The *suffix array* $\mathsf{sa}[1, n]$ associated to t is the permutation of $[1, n]$ giving the lexicographic order of t's suffixes, that is, for $i = 1, \ldots, n - 1$, $t[\mathsf{sa}[i], n] \prec t[\mathsf{sa}[i + 1], n]$. The *longest common prefix* array $\mathsf{lcp}[1, n+1]$ is defined for $i = 2, \ldots, n$ by

$$\mathsf{lcp}[i] = \mathsf{LCP}(t[\mathsf{sa}[i-1], n], t[\mathsf{sa}[i], n]); \tag{1}$$

the lcp array stores the length of the longest common prefix between lexicographically consecutive suffixes. For convenience we define $\mathsf{lcp}[1] = \mathsf{lcp}[n + 1] = -1$.

lcp	bwt	context
-1	b	$
0	c	ab$
2	$	abcab$
0	a	b$
1	a	bcab$
0	b	cab$
-1		

lcp	bwt	context
-1	c	•
0	•	aabcabc•
1	c	abc•
3	a	abcabc•
0	a	bc•
2	a	bcabc•
0	b	c•
1	b	cabc•
-1		

id	lcp_{01}	bwt_{01}	context
0	-1	b	$
1	0	c	•
1	0	•	aabcabc•
0	1	c	ab$
1	2	c	abc•
0	3	$	abcab$
1	5	a	abcabc•
0	0	a	b$
1	1	a	bc•
0	2	a	bcab$
1	4	a	bcabc•
1	0	b	c•
0	1	b	cab$
1	3	b	cabc•
	-1		

Fig. 1. LCP array and BWT for t_0 = abcab$ and t_1 = aabcabc•, and multi-string BWT and corresponding LCP array for the same strings. Column id shows, for each entry of bwt_{01} = bc•cc$aaaabbb whether it comes from t_0 or t_1.

The *Burrows-Wheeler transform* $bwt[1, n]$ of t is defined by

$$bwt[i] = \begin{cases} t[n] & \text{if } sa[i] = 1 \\ t[sa[i] - 1] & \text{if } sa[i] > 1. \end{cases}$$

$bwt[1, n]$ is the permutation of t in which the position of $t[j]$ coincides with the lexicographic rank of $t[j + 1, n]$ (or of $t[1, n]$ if $j = n$) in the suffix array. We call such string the *context* of $t[j]$. See Fig. 1 for an example.

The longest common prefix (LCP) array, and Burrows-Wheeler transform (BWT) can be generalized to the case of multiple strings [5,18]. Let $t_0[1, n_0]$ and $t_1[1, n_1]$ be such that $t_0[n_0] = \$_0$ and $t_1[n_1] = \$_1$ where $\$_0 < \$_1$ are two symbols not appearing elsewhere in t_0 and t_1 and smaller than any other symbol. Let $sa_{01}[1, n_0 + n_1]$ denote the suffix array of the concatenation $t_0 t_1$. The *multi-string* BWT of t_0 and t_1, denoted by $bwt_{01}[1, n_0 + n_1]$, is defined by

$$bwt_{01}[i] = \begin{cases} t_0[n_0] & \text{if } sa_{01}[i] = 1 \\ t_0[sa_{01}[i] - 1] & \text{if } 1 < sa_{01}[i] \leq n_0 \\ t_1[n_1] & \text{if } sa_{01}[i] = n_0 + 1 \\ t_1[sa_{01}[i] - n_0 - 1] & \text{if } n_0 + 1 < sa_{01}[i]. \end{cases}$$

In other words, $bwt_{01}[i]$ is the symbol preceding the i-th lexicographically larger suffix, with the exception that if $sa_{01}[i] = 1$ then $bwt_{01}[i] = \$_0$ and if $sa_{01}[i] = n_0 + 1$ then $bwt_{01}[i] = \$_1$. Hence, $bwt_{01}[i]$ always comes from the string (t_0 or t_1) containing the i-th largest suffix (see again Fig. 1). The above notion of multi-string BWT can be immediately generalized to define $bwt_{1\ldots k}$ for a family of distinct strings $t_1, t_2, \ldots, t_k$. Essentially $\mathsf{bwt}_{1 \ldots k}$ is a permutation of the symbols in $t_1, \ldots, t_k$ such that the position in $\mathsf{bwt}_{1 \ldots k}$ of $t_i[j]$ is given by the lexicographic rank of its context $t_i[j+1, n_i]$ (or $t_i[1, n_i]$ if $j = n_i$).

Given the concatenation $t_0 t_1$ and its suffix array $\mathsf{sa}_{01}[1, n_0 + n_1]$, we consider the corresponding LCP array $\mathsf{lcp}_{01}[1, n_0 + n_1 + 1]$ defined as in (1) (see again Fig. 1). Note that, for $i = 2, \ldots, n_0 + n_1$, $\mathsf{lcp}_{01}[i]$ gives the length of the longest common prefix between the contexts of $\mathsf{bwt}_{01}[i]$ and $\mathsf{bwt}_{01}[i-1]$. This definition can be immediately generalized to a family of k strings to define the LCP array $\mathsf{lcp}_{12 \ldots k}$ associated to the multi-string BWT $\mathsf{bwt}_{12 \ldots k}$.

3   The H&M Algorithm Revisited

In [11] Holt and McMillan introduced a simple and elegant algorithm, we call it the H&M algorithm, to merge multi-string BWTs as defined above.

Given $\mathsf{bwt}_{1 \ldots k}$ and $\mathsf{bwt}_{k+1\,k+2 \ldots h}$ the algorithm computes $\mathsf{bwt}_{1 \ldots h}$. The computation does not explicitly need $t_1, \ldots, t_h$ but only the (multi-string) BWTs to be merged. For simplicity of notation we describe the algorithm assuming we are merging two single-string BWTs $\mathsf{bwt}_0 = \mathsf{bwt}(t_0)$ and $\mathsf{bwt}_1 = \mathsf{bwt}(t_1)$; the algorithm does not change in the general case where the input are multi-string BWTs. Note also that the algorithm can be easily adapted to merge more than two (multi-string) BWTs at the same time.

Computing bwt_{01} amounts to sorting the symbols of bwt_0 and bwt_1 according to the lexicographic order of their contexts, where the context of symbol $\mathsf{bwt}_0[i]$ (resp. $\mathsf{bwt}_1[i]$) is $t_0[\mathsf{sa}_0[i], n_0]$ (resp. $t_1[\mathsf{sa}_1[i], n_1]$). By construction, the symbols in bwt_0 and bwt_1 are already sorted by context, hence to compute bwt_{01} we only need to merge bwt_0 and bwt_1 without changing the relative order of the symbols within the two input sequences.

The H&M algorithm works in successive phases. After the h-th phase the entries of bwt_0 and bwt_1 are sorted on the basis of the first h symbols of their context. More formally, the output of the h-th phase is a binary vector $Z^{(h)}$ containing $n_0 = |t_0|$ **0**'s and $n_1 = |t_1|$ **1**'s and such that the following property holds.

Property 1. For $i = 1, \ldots, n_0$ and $j = 1, \ldots n_1$ the i-th **0** precedes the j-th **1** in $Z^{(h)}$ if and only if

$$t_0[\mathsf{sa}_0[i], \mathsf{sa}_0[i] + h - 1] \preceq t_1[\mathsf{sa}_1[j], \mathsf{sa}_1[j] + h - 1] \tag{2}$$

(recall that according to our notation if $\mathsf{sa}_0[i] + h - 1 > n_0$ then $t_0[\mathsf{sa}_0[i], \mathsf{sa}_0[i] + h - 1]$ coincides with $t_0[\mathsf{sa}_0[i], n_0]$, and similarly for t_1). $\square$

Following Property 1 we identify the i-th **0** in $Z^{(h)}$ with $\mathsf{bwt}_0[i]$ and the j-th **1** in $Z^{(h)}$ with $\mathsf{bwt}_1[j]$ so that to $Z^{(h)}$ corresponds to a permutation of bwt_{01}. Property 1 is equivalent to state that we can logically partition $Z^{(h)}$ into $b(h) + 1$ blocks

$$Z^{(h)}[1, \ell_1], Z^{(h)}[\ell_1 + 1, \ell_2], \ldots, Z^{(h)}[\ell_{b(h)} + 1, n_0 + n_1] \tag{3}$$

such that each block corresponds to a set of bwt_{01} symbols whose contexts are prefixed by the same length-h string (the symbols with a context of length less than h are contained in singleton blocks). Within each block the symbols of bwt_0 precede those of bwt_1, and the context of any symbol in block $Z^{(h)}[\ell_j + 1, \ell_{j+1}]$ is lexicographically smaller than the context of any symbol in block $Z^{(h)}[\ell_k + 1, \ell_{k+1}]$ with $k > j$.

The H&M algorithm initially sets $Z^{(0)} = \mathbf{0}^{n_0} \mathbf{1}^{n_1}$: since the context of every bwt_{01} symbol is prefixed by the same length-0 string (the empty string), there is a single block containing all bwt_{01} symbols. At phase h the algorithm computes $Z^{(h+1)}$ from $Z^{(h)}$ using the procedure in Fig. 2. For completeness we report in the Appendix the proof of the following lemma which is a restatement of Lemma 3.2 in [11] using our notation.

```
 1: Initialize array F[1, σ]
 2: k₀ ← 1; k₁ ← 1                          ▷ Init counters for bwt₀ and bwt₁
 3: for k ← 1 to n₀ + n₁ do
 4:     b ← Z^(h−1)[k]                          ▷ Read bit b from Z^(h−1)
 5:     if b = 0 then                ▷ Get symbol from bwt₀ or bwt₁ according to b
 6:         c ← bwt₀[k₀++]
 7:     else
 8:         c ← bwt₁[k₁++]
 9:     end if
10:     j ← F[c]++                    ▷ Get destination for b according to symbol c
11:     Z^(h)[j] ← b                            ▷ Copy bit b to Z^(h)
12: end for
```

Fig. 2. Main loop of algorithm H&M for computing $Z^{(h)}$ given $Z^{(h-1)}$. Array F is initialized so that $F[c]$ contains the number of occurrences of symbols smaller than c in bwt_0 and bwt_1 plus one. Hence, the bits stored in $Z^{(h)}$ immediately after reading symbol c are stored in positions from $F[c]$ to $F[c+1] - 1$ of $Z^{(h)}$.

Lemma 2. *For $h = 0, 1, 2, \ldots$ the bit vector $Z^{(h)}$ satisfies Property 1.*   □

We now show that with a simple modification to the H&M algorithm it is possible to compute, in addition to bwt_{01} also the LCP array lcp_{01} defined in Sect. 2. Our strategy consists in keeping explicit track of the logical blocks we have defined for $Z^{(h)}$ and represented in (3). We maintain an integer array $B[1, n_0 + n_1 + 1]$ such that at the end of phase h it is $B[i] \neq 0$ if and only if a block of $Z^{(h)}$ starts at position i. The use of such integer array is shown in Fig. 3. Note that: (*i*) initially we set $B = 1 \, 0^{n_0 + n_1 - 1} \, 1$ and once an entry in B becomes nonzero it is never changed, (*ii*) during phase h we only write to B the value h, (*iii*) because of the test at Line 4 the values written during phase h influence the algorithm only in subsequent phases. We maintain also an array $Block\_id[1, \sigma]$ such that $Block\_id[c]$ is the id of the block of $Z^{(h-1)}$ to which the last seen occurrence of symbol c belonged.

1: Initialize arrays $F[1, \sigma]$ and Block_id$[1, \sigma]$
2: $k_0 \leftarrow 1$; $k_1 \leftarrow 1$ ▷ Init counters for bwt$_0$ and bwt$_1$
3: **for** $k \leftarrow 1$ **to** $n_0 + n_1$ **do**
4:     **if** $B[k] \neq 0$ **and** $B[k] \neq h$ **then**
5:         id $\leftarrow k$ ▷ A new block of $Z^{(h-1)}$ is starting
6:     **end if**
7:     $b \leftarrow Z^{(h-1)}[k]$ ▷ Read bit b from $Z^{(h-1)}$
8:     **if** $b = 0$ **then**   ▷ Get symbol from bwt$_0$ or bwt$_1$ according to b
9:         $c \leftarrow$ bwt$_0[k_0{+}{+}]$
10:     **else**
11:         $c \leftarrow$ bwt$_1[k_1{+}{+}]$
12:     **end if**
13:     $j \leftarrow F[c]{+}{+}$ ▷ Get destination for b according to symbol c
14:     $Z^{(h)}[j] \leftarrow b$ ▷ Copy bit b to $Z^{(h)}$
15:     **if** Block_id$[c] \neq$ id **then**
16:         Block_id$[c] \leftarrow$ id   ▷ Update block id for symbol c
17:         **if** $B[j] = 0$ **then**
18:             $B[j] = h$ ▷ A new block of $Z^{(h)}$ will start here
19:         **end if**
20:     **end if**
21: **end for**

Fig. 3. Main loop of the H&M algorithm modified for the computation of the lcp values. At Line 1 for each symbol c we set Block_id$[c] = -1$ and $F[c]$ as in Fig. 2. At the beginning of the algorithm we initialize the array $B[0, n_0 + n_1]$ as $B = 1\,0^{n_0+n_1-1}\,1$.

The following lemma shows that the nonzero values of B at the end of phase h mark the boundaries of $Z^{(h)}$'s logical blocks.

Lemma 3. *For any $h \geq 0$, let ℓ, m be such that $1 \leq \ell \leq m \leq n_0 + n_1$ and*

$$\mathsf{lcp}_{01}[\ell] < h, \quad \min(\mathsf{lcp}_{01}[\ell+1], \ldots, \mathsf{lcp}_{01}[m]) \geq h, \quad \mathsf{lcp}_{01}[m+1] < h. \quad (4)$$

Then, at the end of phase h the array B is such that

$$B[\ell] \neq 0, \quad B[\ell+1] = \cdots = B[m] = 0, \quad B[m+1] \neq 0 \quad (5)$$

and $Z^{(h)}[\ell, m]$ is one of the blocks in (3).   □

Proof. We prove the result by induction on h. For $h = 0$, hence before the execution of the first phase, (4) is only valid for $\ell = 1$ and $m = n_0 + n_1$ (recall we defined $\mathsf{lcp}_{01}[1] = \mathsf{lcp}_{01}[n_0 + n_1 + 1] = -1$). Since initially $B = 1\,0^{n_0+n_1-1}\,1$ our claim holds.

Suppose now that (4) holds for some $h > 0$. Let $s = \mathsf{t}_{01}[\mathsf{sa}_{01}[\ell], \mathsf{sa}_{01}[\ell]+h-1]$; by (4) s is a common prefix of the suffixes starting at positions $\mathsf{sa}_{01}[\ell]$, $\mathsf{sa}_{01}[\ell+1]$, ..., $\mathsf{sa}_{01}[m]$, and no other suffix of t_{01} is prefixed by s. By Property 1 the 0s and 1s in $Z^{(h)}[\ell, m]$ corresponds to the same set of suffixes That is, if $\ell \leq v \leq m$ and $Z^{(h)}[v]$ is the ith 0 (resp. jth 1) of $Z^{(h)}$ then the suffix starting at $\mathsf{t}_0[\mathsf{sa}_0[i]]$ (resp. $\mathsf{t}_1[\mathsf{sa}_1[j]]$) is prefixed by s.

To prove (5) we start by showing that, if $\ell < m$, then at the end of phase $h-1$ it is $B[\ell+1] = \cdots = B[m] = 0$. To see this observe that the range $\mathsf{sa}_{01}[\ell, m]$ is part of a (possibly) larger range $\mathsf{sa}_{01}[\ell', m']$ containing all suffixes prefixed by the length $h-1$ prefix of s. By inductive hypothesis, at the end of phase $h-1$ it is $B[\ell'+1] = \cdots = B[m'] = 0$ which proves our claim since $\ell' \le \ell$ and $m \le m'$.

To complete the proof, we need to show that during phase h: (i) we do not write a nonzero value in $B[\ell+1, m]$ and (ii) we write a nonzero to $B[\ell]$ and $B[m+1]$ if they do not already contain a nonzero. Let $c = s[0]$ and $s' = s[1, h-1]$ so that $s = cs'$. Consider now the range $\mathsf{sa}_{01}[e, f]$ containing the suffixes prefixed by s'. By inductive hypothesis at the end of phase $h-1$ it is

$$B[e] \neq 0, \quad B[e+1] = \cdots = B[f] = 0, \quad B[f+1] \neq 0. \tag{6}$$

During iteration h, the bits in $Z^{(h)}[\ell, m]$ are possibly changed only when we are scanning the region $Z^{(h-1)}[e, f]$ and we find an entry $b = Z^{(h-1)}[k]$, $e \le k \le f$, such that the corresponding value in bwt_b is c. Note that by (6) as soon as k reaches e the variable id changes and becomes different from all values stored in Block_id. Hence, at the first occurrence of symbol c the value h will be stored in $B[\ell]$ (Line 18) unless a nonzero is already there. Again, because of (6), during the scanning of $Z^{(h-1)}[e, f]$ the variable id does not change so subsequent occurrences of c will not cause a nonzero value to be written to $B[\ell+1, m]$. Finally, as soon as we leave region $Z^{(h-1)}[e, f]$ and k reaches $f+1$, the variable id changes again and at the next occurrence of c a nonzero value will be stored in $B[m+1]$. If there are no more occurrences of c after we leave region $Z^{(h-1)}[e, f]$ then either $\mathsf{sa}_{01}[m+1]$ is the first suffix array entry prefixed by symbol $c+1$ or $m+1 = n_0 + n_1 + 1$. In the former case $B[m+1]$ gets a nonzero value at phase 1, in the latter case $B[m+1]$ gets a nonzero value when we initialize array B.

This completes the proof. □

Corollary 4. *For $i = 2, \ldots, n_0 + n_1$, if $\mathsf{lcp}_{01}[i] = \ell$, then starting from the end of phase $\ell+1$ it is $B[i] = \ell+1$.*

Proof. By Lemma 3 we know that $B[i]$ becomes nonzero only after phase $\ell+1$. Since at the end of phase ℓ it is still $B[i] = 0$ during phase $\ell+1$ $B[i]$ gets the value $\ell+1$ which is never changed in successive phases. □

The above corollary suggests the following algorithm to compute bwt_{01} and lcp_{01}: repeat the procedure of Fig. 3 until the phase h in which all entries in B become nonzero. At that point $Z^{(h)}$ describes how bwt_0 and bwt_1 should be merged to get bwt_{01} and for $i = 2, \ldots, n_0 + n_1$ $\mathsf{lcp}_{01}[i] = B[i] - 1$. The above strategy requires a number of iterations, each one taking $\mathcal{O}(n_0 + n_1)$ time, equal to the maximum of the lcp values, for an overall complexity of $\mathcal{O}((n_0+n_1)\mathsf{maxlcp}_{01})$, where $\mathsf{maxlcp}_{01} = \max_i \mathsf{lcp}_{01}[i]$. In the next section we describe a much faster algorithm that avoids to re-process the portions of B and $Z^{(h)}$ which are no longer relevant for the computation of the final result.

4   The Gap Algorithm

Definition 5. *If $B[\ell] \neq 0$, $B[m+1] \neq 0$ and $B[\ell+1] = \cdots = B[m] = 0$, we say that block $Z^{(h)}[\ell, m]$ is* monochrome *if it contains only 0's or only 1's.* $\square$

Since a monochrome block only contains suffixes from either t_0 or t_1, whose relative order and LCP's are known, it does not need to be further modified. This intuition is formalized by the following lemmas.

Lemma 6. *If at the end of phase h bit vector $Z^{(h)}$ contains only monochrome blocks we can compute bwt_{01} and lcp_{01} in $\mathcal{O}(n_0 + n_1)$ time.*

Proof. By Property 1, if we identify the i-th 0 in $Z^{(h)}$ with $bwt_0[i]$ and the j-th 1 with $bwt_1[j]$ the only elements which could be not correctly sorted by context are those within the same block. However, if the blocks are monochrome all elements belong to either bwt_0 or bwt_1 so their relative order is correct.

To compute lcp_{01} we observe that if $B[i] \neq 0$ then by (the proof of) Corollary 4 it is $lcp_{01}[i] = B[i] - 1$. If instead $B[i] = 0$ we are inside a block hence $sa_{01}[i-1]$ and $sa_{01}[i]$ belong to the same string t_0 or t_1 and their LCP is directly available in lcp_0 or lcp_1. $\square$

Lemma 7. *Suppose that, at the end of phase h, $Z^{(h)}[\ell, m]$ is a monochrome block. Then (i) for $g > h$, $Z^{(g)}[\ell, m] = Z^{(h)}[\ell, m]$, and (ii) processing $Z^{(h)}[\ell, m]$ during phase $h + 1$ creates a set of monochrome blocks in $Z^{(h+1)}$.*

Proof. The first part of the Lemma follows from the observation that subsequent phases of the algorithm will only reorder the values within a block (and possibly create new sub-blocks); but if a block is monochrome the reordering will not change its actual content.

For the second part, we observe that during phase $h + 1$ as k goes from ℓ to m the algorithm writes to $Z^{(h+1)}$ the same value which is in $Z^{(h)}[\ell, m]$. Hence, a new monochrome block will be created for each distinct symbol encountered (in bwt_0 or bwt_1) as k goes through the range $[\ell, m]$. $\square$

The lemma implies that, if block $Z^{(h)}[\ell, m]$ is monochrome at the end of phase h, starting from phase $g = h + 2$ processing the range $[\ell, m]$ will not change $Z^{(g)}$ with respect to $Z^{(g-1)}$. Indeed, by the lemma the monochrome blocks created in phase $h + 1$ do not change in subsequent phases (in a subsequent phase a monochrome block can be split in sub-blocks, but the actual content of the bit vector does not change). The above observation suggests that, after we have processed block $Z^{(h+1)}[\ell, m]$ in phase $h+1$, we can mark it as *irrelevant* and avoid to process it again. As the computation goes on, more and more blocks become irrelevant. Hence, in the generic phase h instead of processing the whole $Z^{(h-1)}$ we process only the blocks which are still "active" and skip irrelevant blocks. Adjacent irrelevant blocks are merged so that among two active blocks there is at most one irrelevant block (the *gap* that gives the name to the algorithm). The overall structure of a single phase is shown in Fig. 4. The algorithm terminates

---

```
1:  if (next block is irrelevant) then
2:      skip it
3:  else
4:      process block
5:      if (processed block is monochrome) then
6:          mark it irrelevant
7:      end if
8:  end if
9:  if (last two blocks are irrelevant) then
10:     merge them
11: end if
```

Fig. 4. Main loop of the Gap algorithm. The processing of active blocks at Line 4 is done as in Lines 7–20 of Fig. 3.

when there are no more active blocks since this implies that all blocks have become monochrome and by Lemma 6 we are able to compute bwt_{01} and lcp_{01}.

We point out that at Line 2 of the Gap algorithm we cannot simply skip an irrelevant block ignoring its content. To keep the algorithm consistent we must correctly update the global variables of the main loop, i.e. the array F and the pointers k_0 and k_1 in Fig. 3. To this end a simple approach is to store for each irrelevant block the number of occurrences o_c of each symbol $c \in \Sigma$ in it and the pair (r_0, r_1) providing the number of **0**'s and **1**'s in the block (recall an irrelevant block may consist of adjacent monochrome blocks coming from different strings). When the algorithm reaches an irrelevant block, F, k_0, k_1 are updated setting $k_0 \leftarrow k_0 + r_0$, $k_1 \leftarrow k_1 + r_1$ and $\forall c \ F[c] \leftarrow F[c] + o_c$.

The above scheme for handling irrelevant blocks is simple and probably effective in most cases. However, using $\mathcal{O}(\sigma)$ time to skip an irrelevant block is not competitive for large alphabets. A better alternative is to build a wavelet tree for bwt_0 and bwt_1 at the beginning of the algorithm. Then, for each irrelevant block we store only the pair (r_0, r_1). When we reach an irrelevant block we use such pair to update k_0 and k_1. The array F is not immediately updated: Instead we maintain two global arrays $L_0[1, \sigma]$ and $L_1[1, \sigma]$ such that $L_0[c]$ and $L_1[c]$ store the value of k_0 and k_1 at the time the value $F[c]$ was last updated. At the *first* occurrence of a symbol c inside an active block we update $F[c]$ adding to it the number of occurrences of c in $bwt_0[L_o[c] + 1, k_0]$ and $bwt_1[L_1[c] + 1, k_1]$ that we compute in $\mathcal{O}(\log \sigma)$ time using the wavelet trees. Using this lazy update mechanism, handling irrelevant blocks adds a $\mathcal{O}(\min(\ell, \sigma) \log \sigma)$ additive slowdown to the cost of processing an active block of length ℓ.

Theorem 8. *Given* bwt_0, lcp_0 *and* bwt_1, lcp_1 *the* Gap *algorithm computes* bwt_{01} *and* lcp_{01} *in* $\mathcal{O}(\log(\sigma)(n_0 + n_1)avelcp_{01})$ *time, where* $avelcp_{01} = (\sum_i lcp_{01}[i])/(n_0 + n_1)$ *is the average LCP of the string* t_{01}.

Proof. The correctness follows from the above discussion. For the analysis of the running time we reason as in [10] and observe that the sum, over all phases, of the length of all active blocks is bounded by $\mathcal{O}(\sum_i \mathsf{lcp}_{01}[i]) = \mathcal{O}((n_0 + n_1)\mathsf{avelcp}_{01})$. In any phase, using the lazy update mechanism, the cost of processing an active block of length ℓ is bounded by $\mathcal{O}(\ell \log(\sigma))$ and the time bound follows. $\square$

We point out that our Gap algorithm is related to the H&M algorithm as described in [10, Sect. 2.1]: Indeed, the sorting operations are essentially the same in the two algorithms. The main difference is that Gap keeps explicit track of the irrelevant blocks while H&M keeps explicit track of the active blocks (called buckets in [10]): this difference makes the non-sorting operations completely different. An advantage of working with irrelevant blocks is that they can be easily merged, while this is not the case for the active blocks in H&M. Of course, the main difference is that Gap merges simultaneously BWT *and* LCP values.

If we are simultaneously merging k BWTs, the only change in the algorithm is that the arrays $Z^{(h)}$ must now store integers in $[1, k]$; the overall running time is still $\mathcal{O}(n \log(\sigma)\mathsf{avelcp})$ where $n = \sum_i n_i$ is the size of the merged BWT and avelcp is the average of the values in the merged LCP array.

We now analyze the space usage of Gap when merging k BWTs. Let n denote the size of the merged BWTs. The arrays $\mathsf{bwt}_1, \ldots, \mathsf{bwt}_k$ take overall $n\lceil \log \sigma \rceil$ bits. At the end of the computation, in $\mathcal{O}(n)$ time using $Z^{(h)}$ the merged BWT can be written directly to disk or, using an in-place merging algorithm [8], overwritten to the space used by $\mathsf{bwt}_1, \ldots, \mathsf{bwt}_k$. The array B stores lcp values hence it can be represented in $n\lceil \log L \rceil$ bits, where $L = \max_i n_i$. Note that B takes the same space as the final merged LCP array, which indeed, at the end of the computation, could be overwritten to it using $Z^{(h)}$ (the merged LCP can also be written directly to the output file). In addition to the space used for BWT and LCP values, the algorithm uses $2n\lceil \log k \rceil$ bits for the arrays $Z^{(h)}$ (we only need 2 of them), and $\mathcal{O}(\sigma \log n)$ bits for the arrays F and Block_id.

The overall space usage so far is therefore $n(\lceil \log \sigma \rceil + \lceil \log L \rceil + 2\lceil \log k \rceil) + \mathcal{O}(\sigma \log n)$ bits. The only additional space used by the algorithm is the one used to keep track of the irrelevant blocks, which unfortunately cannot be estimated in advance since it depends on the maximum number of such blocks. In the worst case we can have $\Theta(n)$ blocks and the additional space can be $\Theta(nk \log n)$ bits. Although this is a rather unlikely possibility, it is important to have some form of control on this additional space. We use the following simple heuristic: we choose a threshold s and we keep track of an irrelevant block only if its size is at least s. This strategy introduces a $\mathcal{O}(s)$ time slowdown but ensures that there are at most $n/(s+1)$ irrelevant blocks simultaneously. In the next section we experimentally measure the influence of s on the space and running time of the algorithm and show that in practice the space used to keep track of irrelevant blocks is less than 10% of the total.

Note that also in [10] the authors faced the problem of limiting the memory used to keep track of the active blocks. They suggested the heuristic of keeping track of active blocks only after the h-th iteration ($h = 20$ for their dataset).

Table 1. Collections used in our experiments sorted by average LCP. Columns 4 and 5 refer to the lengths of the single documents. Pacbio are NGS reads from a *D.melanogaster* dataset. Illumina are NGS reads from Human ERA015743 dataset. Wiki-it are pages from Italian Wikipedia. Proteins are protein sequences from Uniprot. Collections and source files are available on https://people.unipmn.it/manzini/gap.

Name	Size GB	σ	Max Len	Ave Len	Max LCP	Ave LCP
Pacbio	6.24	5	40212	9567.43	1055	17.99
Illumina	7.60	6	103	102.00	102	27.53
Wiki-it	4.01	210	553975	4302.84	93537	61.02
Proteins	6.11	26	35991	410.22	25065	100.60

Table 2. For each collection we report the number k of subcollections, the average running time of gSACA-K+Φ in μsecs per symbol, and the running time (μsecs) and space usage (bytes) per symbol for Gap for different values of the s parameter.

Name	k	gSACA-K+Φ	$s = 50$		$s = 100$		$s = 200$	
			time	space	time	space	time	space
Pacbio	7	0.46	0.41	4.35	0.46	4.18	0.51	4.09
Illumina	4	0.48	0.93	3.31	1.02	3.16	1.09	3.08
Wiki-it	5	0.41	—	—	—	—	3.07	6.55
Proteins	4	0.59	3.90	4.55	5.18	4.29	7.05	4.15

5   Experimental Results

We have implemented the Gap algorithm in C and tested it on a desktop with 32 GB RAM and eight Intel-I7 3.40 GHz CPUs. All tests used a single CPU. We used the collections shown in Table 1. We represented LCP values using 1 byte for Illumina, 2 bytes for Pacbio and Proteins, and 4 bytes for Wiki-it. We always used 1 byte for each BWT value. We used n bytes to represent a pair of $Z^{(h)}$ arrays using 4 bits for each entry so that our implementation can merge simultaneously up to 16 BWTs. We used the simple strategy for skipping irrelevant blocks, i.e. we did not use wavelet trees to represent the input BWTs.

Referring to Table 2, we split each collection into k subcollections of size less than 2 GB and we computed the multi-string SA of each subcollection using gSACA-K [15]. From the SA we computed the multi-string BWT and LCP arrays using the Φ algorithm [12] (implemented in gSACA-K). This computation used 13 bytes per input symbol. Then, we merged the subcollections multi-string BWTs and LCPs using Gap with different values of the parameter s which determines the size of the smallest irrelevant block we keep track of. Note that for Wiki-it s has no influence since the algorithm never keeps track of a block smaller than $\sigma + k$. The rationale is that in our implementation skipping a block takes $\mathcal{O}(\sigma + k)$ time, so there is no advantage in skipping a block smaller than that size.

From the results in Table 2 we see that Gap running time is indeed roughly proportional to the average LCP. For example, Pacbio and Illumina collections both consist of DNA reads but, despite Pacbio reads being longer and having a larger maximum LCP, Gap is twice as fast on them because of the smaller average LCP. Similarly, Gap is faster on Wiki-it than on Proteins despite the latter collection having a smaller alphabet and shorter documents. gSACA-K running time is not significantly influenced by the average LCP. If we compare Gap with gSACA-K we see that only in one instance, Pacbio with $s = 50$, Gap is faster than gSACA-K in terms of μsecs per input symbol. However, since Gap is designed to post-process gSACA-K output, the comparison of the running time is only important to the extent Gap is not a bottleneck in our two-step strategy to compute the multi-string BWT and LCP arrays: the experiments show this is not the case. We point out that on our 32 GB machine, gSACA-K cannot compute the multi-string SA for any of the collections since for inputs larger that 2 GB it uses 9 bytes per input symbol.

As expected, the parameter s offers a time-space tradeoff for the Gap algorithm. In the space reported in Table 2, the fractional part is the peak space usage for irrelevant blocks, while the whole value is the space used by the arrays bwt_i, B and $Z^{(h)}$. For example, for Wiki-it we use n bytes for the BWTs, $4n$ bytes for the LCP values (the B array), n bytes for $Z^{(h)}$, and the remaining $0.55n$ bytes are mainly used for keeping track of irrelevant blocks. This is a relatively high value since in our current implementation the storage of a block grows linearly with the alphabet size. For DNA sequences and $s = 200$ the cost of storing blocks is less than 3% of the total without a significant slowdown in the running time.

For completeness, we tested the H&M implementation from [10] on the Pacbio collection. The running time was 14.57 μsecs per symbol and the space usage 2.28 bytes per symbol. These values are only partially significative for several reasons: (i) H&M computes the BWT from scratch, hence doing also the work of gSACA-K, (ii) H&M doesn't compute the LCP array, hence the lower space usage, (iii) the algorithm is implemented in Cython which makes it easier to use in a Python environment but is not as fast and space efficient as C.

Appendix

Proof of Lemma 2: We prove the result by induction. For $h = 0$, $\delta = 0, 1$ $t_\delta[\mathsf{sa}_\delta[i], \mathsf{sa}_\delta[i] - 1]$ is the empty string so (2) is always true and Property 1 is satisfied by $Z^{(0)} = \mathbf{0}^{n_0}\mathbf{1}^{n_1}$.

To prove the "if" part, let $h > 0$ and let $1 \leq v < w \leq n_0 + n_1$ denote two indexes such that $Z^{(h)}[v]$ is the i-th $\mathbf{0}$ and $Z^{(h)}[w]$ is the j-th $\mathbf{1}$ in $Z^{(h)}$. We need to show that under these assumptions inequality (2) on the lexicographic order holds.

Assume first $t_0[\mathsf{sa}_0[i]] \neq t_1[\mathsf{sa}_1[j]]$. The hypothesis $v < w$ implies $t_0[\mathsf{sa}_0[i]] < t_1[\mathsf{sa}_1[j]]$ hence (2) certainly holds.

Assume now $t_0[\mathsf{sa}_0[i]] = t_1[\mathsf{sa}_1[j]]$. We preliminarily observe that it must be $\mathsf{sa}_0[i] \neq n_0$ and $\mathsf{sa}_1[i] \neq n_1$: otherwise we would have $t_0[\mathsf{sa}_0[i]] = \$_0$ or $t_1[\mathsf{sa}_1[j]] = \$_1$ which is impossible since these symbols appear only once in t_0 and t_1.

Let v', w' denote respectively the value of the main loop variable k in the procedure of Fig. 2 when the entries $Z^{(h)}[v]$ and $Z^{(h)}[w]$ are written (hence, during the scanning of $Z^{(h-1)}$). The hypothesis $v < w$ implies $v' < w'$. By construction $Z^{(h-1)}[v'] = 0$ and $Z^{(h-1)}[w'] = 1$. Say v' is the i'-th 0 in $Z^{(h-1)}$ and w' is the j'-th 1 in $Z^{(h-1)}$. By the inductive hypothesis on $Z^{(h-1)}$ we have

$$t_0[\mathsf{sa}_0[i'], \mathsf{sa}_0[i'] + h - 2] \preceq t_1[\mathsf{sa}_1[j'], \mathsf{sa}_1[j'] + h - 2], \tag{7}$$

The fundamental observation is that, being $\mathsf{sa}_0[i] \neq n_0$ and $\mathsf{sa}_1[i] \neq n_1$, it is

$$\mathsf{sa}_0[i'] = \mathsf{sa}_0[i] + 1 \quad \text{and} \quad \mathsf{sa}_1[j'] = \mathsf{sa}_1[j] + 1.$$

Since

$$t_0[\mathsf{sa}_0[i], \mathsf{sa}_0[i] + h - 1] = t_0[\mathsf{sa}_0[i]]t_0[\mathsf{sa}_0[i'], \mathsf{sa}_0[i'] + h - 2] \tag{8}$$

$$t_1[\mathsf{sa}_1[j], \mathsf{sa}_1[j] + h - 1] = t_1[\mathsf{sa}_1[j]]t_1[\mathsf{sa}_1[j'], \mathsf{sa}_1[j'] + h - 2] \tag{9}$$

combining $t_0[\mathsf{sa}_0[i]] = t_1[\mathsf{sa}_1[j]]$ with (7) gives us (2).

For the "only if" part assume (2) holds. We need to prove that in $Z^{(h)}$ the i-th 0 precedes the j-th 1. If $t_0[\mathsf{sa}_0[i]] < t_1[\mathsf{sa}_1[j]]$ the proof is immediate. If $t_0[\mathsf{sa}_0[i]] = t_1[\mathsf{sa}_1[j]]$, we must have

$$t_0[\mathsf{sa}_0[i] + 1, \mathsf{sa}_0[i] + h - 1] \preceq t_1[\mathsf{sa}_1[j] + 1, \mathsf{sa}_1[j] + h - 1].$$

By induction, if $\mathsf{sa}_0[i'] = \mathsf{sa}_0[i] + 1$ and $\mathsf{sa}_1[j'] = \mathsf{sa}_1[j] + 1$ in $Z^{(h-1)}$ the i'-th 0 precedes the j'-th 1. During phase h, the i'-th 0 in $Z^{(h)}$ is written when processing the i'-th 0 of $Z^{(h-1)}$, and the j-th 1 in $Z^{(h)}$ is written when processing the j'-th 1 of $Z^{(h-1)}$. Since in $Z^{(h-1)}$ the i'-th 0 precedes the j'-th 1 and

$$\mathsf{bwt}_0[i'] = t_0[\mathsf{sa}_0[i]] = t_1[\mathsf{sa}_1[j]] = \mathsf{bwt}_1[j']$$

in $Z^{(h)}$ their relative order does not change and the i-th 0 precedes the j-th 1 as claimed. $\qquad\qquad\qquad\qquad\qquad\qquad\qquad\qquad\qquad\qquad\qquad\qquad\qquad\square$

References

1. Belazzougui, D.: Linear time construction of compressed text indices in compact space. In: STOC, pp. 148–193. ACM (2014)
2. Bonizzoni, P., Vedova, G.D., Nicosia, S., Previtali, M., Rizzi, R.: A new lightweight algorithm to compute the BWT and the LCP array of a set of strings. CoRR abs/1607.08342 (2016)
3. Bonizzoni, P., Vedova, G.D., Pirola, Y., Previtali, M., Rizzi, R.: Computing the BWT and LCP array of a set of strings in external memory. CoRR abs/1705.07756 (2017)
4. Burkhardt, S., Kärkkäinen, J.: Fast lightweight suffix array construction and checking. In: Baeza-Yates, R., Chávez, E., Crochemore, M. (eds.) CPM 2003. LNCS, vol. 2676, pp. 55–69. Springer, Heidelberg (2003). doi:10.1007/3-540-44888-8_5

5. Cox, A.J., Garofalo, F., Rosone, G., Sciortino, M.: Lightweight LCP construction for very large collections of strings. J. Discrete Algorithms **37**, 17–33 (2016)
6. Ferragina, P., Gagie, T., Manzini, G.: Lightweight data indexing and compression in external memory. In: López-Ortiz, A. (ed.) LATIN 2010. LNCS, vol. 6034, pp. 697–710. Springer, Heidelberg (2010). doi:10.1007/978-3-642-12200-2_60
7. Ferragina, P., Gagie, T., Manzini, G.: Lightweight data indexing and compression in external memory. Algorithmica (2011)
8. Geffert, V., Gajdos, J.: Multiway in-place merging. Theor. Comput. Sci. **411**(16–18), 1793–1808 (2010)
9. Gog, S., Ohlebusch, E.: Compressed suffix trees: efficient computation and storage of LCP-values. ACM J. Exp. Algorithmics **18** (2013). http://doi.acm.org/10.1145/2444016.2461327
10. Holt, J., McMillan, L.: Constructing Burrows-Wheeler transforms of large string collections via merging. In: BCB, pp. 464–471. ACM (2014)
11. Holt, J., McMillan, L.: Merging of multi-string BWTs with applications. Bioinformatics **30**(24), 3524–3531 (2014)
12. Kärkkäinen, J., Manzini, G., Puglisi, S.J.: Permuted longest-common-prefix array. In: Kucherov, G., Ukkonen, E. (eds.) CPM 2009. LNCS, vol. 5577, pp. 181–192. Springer, Heidelberg (2009). doi:10.1007/978-3-642-02441-2_17
13. Kärkkäinen, J., Kempa, D.: LCP array construction in external memory. ACM J. Exp. Algorithmics **21**(1), 1.7:1–1.7:22 (2016)
14. Léonard, M., Mouchard, L., Salson, M.: On the number of elements to reorder when updating a suffix array. J. Discrete Algorithms **11**, 87–99 (2012). http://dx.doi.org/10.1016/j.jda.2011.01.002
15. Louza, F.A., Gog, S., Telles, G.P.: Induced suffix sorting for string collections. In: DCC, pp. 43–52. IEEE (2016)
16. Louza, F.A., Gog, S., Telles, G.P.: Inducing enhanced suffix arrays for string collections. Theor. Comput. Sci. **678**, 22–39 (2017)
17. Louza, F.A., Telles, G.P., Ciferri, C.D.A.: External memory generalized suffix and LCP arrays construction. In: Fischer, J., Sanders, P. (eds.) CPM 2013. LNCS, vol. 7922, pp. 201–210. Springer, Heidelberg (2013). doi:10.1007/978-3-642-38905-4_20
18. Mantaci, S., Restivo, A., Rosone, G., Sciortino, M.: An extension of the Burrows-Wheeler transform. Theor. Comput. Sci. **387**(3), 298–312 (2007)
19. Manzini, G.: Two space saving tricks for linear time LCP computation. In: Proceedings of 9th Scandinavian Workshop on Algorithm Theory (SWAT 2004), pp. 372–383. Springer-Verlag, LNCS n. 3111 (2004)
20. Manzini, G., Ferragina, P.: Engineering a lightweight suffix array construction algorithm. In: Möhring, R., Raman, R. (eds.) ESA 2002. LNCS, vol. 2461, pp. 698–710. Springer, Heidelberg (2002). doi:10.1007/3-540-45749-6_61
21. Navarro, G., Mäkinen, V.: Compressed full-text indexes. ACM Comput. Surv. **39**(1), Article no. 2 (2007). doi:10.1145/1216370.1216372
22. Nong, G.: Practical linear-time O(1)-workspace suffix sorting for constant alphabets. ACM Trans. Inf. Syst. **31**(3), Article no. 15 (2013). doi:10.1145/2493175.2493180
23. Sirén, J.: Compressed suffix arrays for massive data. In: Karlgren, J., Tarhio, J., Hyyrö, H. (eds.) SPIRE 2009. LNCS, vol. 5721, pp. 63–74. Springer, Heidelberg (2009). doi:10.1007/978-3-642-03784-9_7
24. Sirén, J.: Burrows-wheeler transform for Terabases. In: IEEE Data Compression Conference (DCC), pp. 211–220 (2016)

Practical Evaluation of Lempel-Ziv-78 and Lempel-Ziv-Welch Tries

Johannes Fischer and Dominik Köppl[(✉)]

Department of Computer Science, TU Dortmund, 44221 Dortmund, Germany
{johannes.fischer,dominik.koeppl}@cs.tu-dortmund.de

Abstract. We present the first thorough practical study of the Lempel-Ziv-78 and the Lempel-Ziv-Welch computation based on trie data structures. With a careful selection of trie representations we can beat well-tuned popular trie data structures like Judy, m-Bonsai or Cedar.

Keywords: Lempel-Ziv compression · Dynamic tries · Hashing

1 Introduction

The LZ78-compression scheme [41] is an old compression scheme that is still in use today, e.g., in the Unix `compress` utility, in the GIF-standard, in string dictionaries [2], or in text indexes [1]. Its biggest advantage over LZ77 [40] is that LZ78 allows for an easy construction *within compressed space* and in *near-linear time*, which is (to date) not possible for LZ77. Still, although LZ77 often achieves marginally better compression rates, the output of LZ78 is usually small enough to be used in practice, e.g. in the scenarios mentioned above [1,5].

While the construction of LZ77 is well studied both in theory [5,14, e.g.] and in practice [18,19, e.g.], only recent interest in LZ78 can be observed: just in 2015 Nakashima et al. [31] gave the first (theoretical) linear time algorithm for LZ78. On the practical side, we are not aware of any systematic study.

We present the first thorough study of LZ78-construction algorithms. Although we do not present any new theoretical results, this paper shows that if one is careful with the choices of tries, hash functions, and the handling of dynamic arrays, one can beat well-tuned out-of-the-box trie data structures like Judy[1], m-Bonsai [34], or the Cedar-trie [39].

Related Work. An LZ78 factorization of size z can be stored in two arrays with $z \lg \sigma$ and $z \lg z$ bits to represent the character (belonging to an alphabet of size σ) and the referred index, respectively, of each factor. This space bound has not yet been achieved by any efficient trie data structure. Closest to this bound is the approach of Arroyuelo and Navarro [1, Lemma 8], taking $2z \lg z + z \lg \sigma + \mathcal{O}(z)$ bits and $\mathcal{O}(n(\lg \sigma + \lg \lg n))$ time for the LZ78 factorization. Allowing $\mathcal{O}(z \lg z)$ bits, $\mathcal{O}\left(n + z\frac{\lg^2 \lg \sigma}{\lg \lg \lg \sigma}\right)$ time is possible [13]. Another

---

[1] http://judy.sourceforge.net.

© Springer International Publishing AG 2017
G. Fici et al. (Eds.): SPIRE 2017, LNCS 10508, pp. 191–207, 2017.
DOI: 10.1007/978-3-319-67428-5_16

option is the dynamic trie of Jansson et al. [17] using $\mathcal{O}(n(\lg\sigma + \lg\lg_\sigma n)/\lg_\sigma n)$ bits of working space and $\mathcal{O}\big(n\lg^2\lg n/(\lg_\sigma n\lg\lg\lg n)\big)$ time. All these tries are favorable for small alphabet sizes (achieving linear or sub-linear time when $\lg\sigma = o(\lg n\lg\lg\lg n/\lg^2\lg n)$). If the alphabet size σ becomes large, the upper bounds on the time get unattractive. Up to $\lg\sigma = o(\lg n)$, we can use a linear time solution taking $\mathcal{O}(n\lg\sigma)$ bits of space [22,30]. Finally, for large σ, there is a linear time approach taking $(1+\epsilon)n\lg n + \mathcal{O}(n)$ bits of space [14]. Further *practical* trie implementations are mentioned in Sect. 4.

2   Preliminaries

Let T be a text of length n over an alphabet $\Sigma = \{1,\ldots,\sigma\}$ with $|\Sigma| \le n^{\mathcal{O}(1)}$. Given $X, Y, Z \in \Sigma^*$ with $T = XYZ$, then X, Y and Z are called a **prefix**, **substring** and **suffix** of T, respectively. We call $T[i..]$ the i-th suffix of T, and denote a substring $T[i]\cdots T[j]$ with $T[i..j]$. A **factorization** of T of size z partitions T into z substrings (**factors**) $F_1\cdots F_z = T$. In this article, we are interested in the LZ78 and LZW factorization. If we stipulate that F_0 and $F_{z+1}[1]$ are the empty string, we get:

A factorization $F_1\cdots F_z = T$ is called the **LZ78 factorization** [41] of T iff $F_x = F_y c$ with $F_y = \operatorname{argmax}_{S\in\{F_{y'}:0\le y'<x\}} |S|$ and $c \in \Sigma$ for all $1 \le x \le z$; we say that y is the **referred index** of the factor F_x.

A factorization $F_1\cdots F_z = T$ is called the **LZW factorization** [38] of T iff $F_x = F_y F_{y+1}[1]$ with $F_y = \operatorname{argmax}_{S\in\{F_{y'}:1\le y'<x\}} |S|$, or $F_x = c \in \Sigma$ if no such F_y exists, for all $1 \le x < z$. If $F_x = F_y F_{y+1}[1]$ for a y with $1 \le y < x$, we call y the **referred index** of the factor F_x. Otherwise, $F_x = c$ for a $c \in \Sigma$; we set its referred index to $-c < 0$.

The factors can be represented in a trie, the so-called **LZ trie**. Each factor F_x (except the last factor in LZW) is represented by a trie node v labeled with x ($1 \le x \le z$) such that the parent u of v is labeled with y if y is the referred index of F_x. The edge (u, v) is then labeled with the last character of the factor F_x (or the first character of F_{x+1} for LZW).

Output. We transform the list of factors to a list of integer values as follows: We linearly process each factor F_x for $1 \le x \le z$. If F_x's referred index is not positive, F_x is equal to a character c that is output (we output $-c$ in case of LZW). A factor F_x with a referred index $y > 0$ is processed as follows:

LZ78: If $F_x = F_y c$ for a $c \in \sigma$, we output the tuple (y, c).
LZW: If $F_x = F_y F_{y+1}[1]$ (or $F_x = F_y$ for $x = z$), we output y.

Algorithm. The folklore algorithm computing LZ78 and LZW uses a dynamic LZ trie that grows linearly in the number of processed factors. The dynamic LZ trie supports the creation of a node, the navigation from a node to one of its children, and the access to the labels.

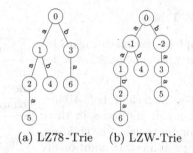

(a) LZ78-Trie   (b) LZW-Trie

Fig. 1. LZ78 trie and LZW trie. Given the text $T =$ aaababaaaba, LZ78 factorizes T into a | aa | b | ab | aaa | ba , where the vertical bars separate the factors. The LZ78 factorization is output as: a | (1, a) | b | (1, b) | (2, a) | (3, a). This output is represented by the left trie (a). The LZW factorization of the same text is a | aa | b | a | ba | aab | a. We output it as -1 | 1 | -2 | -1 | 3 | 2 | -1. This output induces the right trie (b).

Given that z is the number of LZ78 or LZW factors, the algorithm performs z searches of a prefix of a given suffix of the text. It inserts z times a new leaf in the LZ trie. It takes n times an edge from a node to one of its children.

3   LZ-Trie Representations

In this section, we show five representations, each providing different trade-offs for computation speed and memory consumption. All representations have in common that they work with dynamic arrays.

Resize Hints. The usual strategy for dynamic arrays is to double the size of an array when it gets full. To reduce the memory consumption, a hint on how large the number of factors z might get is advantageous to know for a dynamic LZ trie data structure. We provide such a hint based on the following lemma:

Lemma 1 [4, 41]. *The number of LZ78 factors z is in the range $\sqrt{2n + 1/4} - 1/2 \leq z \leq cn/\lg_\sigma n$, for a fixed constant $c > 0$.*

At the beginning of the factorization, we let a dynamic trie reserve enough space to store at least $\sqrt{2n}$ elements without resizing. On enlarging a dynamic trie, we usually double its size. However, if the number of remaining characters r to parse is below a certain threshold, we try to scale the data structure up to a value for which we expect that all factors can be stored without resizing the data structure again. Let z' be the currently computed number of factors. If $r > n/2$ we use $z' + 3r/\lg r$ as an estimate (the number 3 is chosen empirically[2]), derived from $z - z' = \mathcal{O}(r/\lg_\sigma r)$ based on Lemma 1, otherwise we use $z' + z'r/(n - r)$ derived from the expectation that the ratio between z' and $n - r$ will be roughly the same as between z and n (interpolation).

---

[2] There are artificial texts like a^n for which we overestimate the number of factors.

3.1 Deterministic LZ Tries

We first recall two trie implementations using arrays to store the node labeled with x at position x, for each x with $1 \leq x \leq z$.

Binary Search Trie. The first-child next-sibling representation binary maintains its nodes in three arrays. A node stores a pointer to one of its children, and a pointer to one of its siblings. It additionally stores the label (i.e., a character) of the edge to its parent. The trie binary takes $2z \lg z + z \lg \sigma$ bits when storing z nodes. We do not sort the nodes in the trie according to the character on their incoming edge, but store them in the order in which they are inserted. (We found this faster in our experiments.) Figure 2 gives an example. To navigate from a node v to its child with label $c \in \Sigma$, we take the first child of v and then sequentially scan all its next siblings until finding a node storing the character c.

index	1 2 3 4 5 6
first child	2 5 6
next sibling	3 4
character	a a b b a a

Fig. 2. Array data structures of binary built on the example given in Fig. 1

Ternary Search Trie. The Ternary Search Trie [6] ternary differs from binary in that a ternary node stores one more pointer to a sibling: A node of ternary stores a character, a pointer to one of its children, a pointer to one of its smaller siblings, and a pointer to one of its larger siblings. The trie ternary takes $3z \lg z + z \lg \sigma$ bits when storing z nodes. Similar to binary, we do not rearrange the nodes. To navigate from a node v to its child with label $c \in \Sigma$, we take the pointer to one of its children and then binary search for the sibling storing the character c (given that we are at a node storing a character d, we take its smaller sibling if $c < d$, otherwise its larger sibling).

3.2 LZ Tries with Hashing

We use a hash table $H[0..M-1]$ for a natural number M, and a hash function h to store key-value pairs. We determine the position of a pair (k, v) in H by the *initial address* $h(k) \mod M$; we handle collisions with linear probing. We enlarge H when the maximum number of entries $m := \alpha M$ is reached, where α is a real number with $0 < \alpha < 1$.

A hash table can simulate a trie as follows: Given a trie edge (u, v) with label c, we use the unique key $c + \sigma \ell$ to store v, where ℓ is the label (factor index) of u (the root is assigned the label 0). This allows us to find and create nodes in the trie by simulating top-down-traversals. This trie implementation is called hash in the following.

Table Size. We choose the hash table size M to be a power of two. Having $M = 2^k$ for $k \in \mathbb{N}$, we can compute the remainder of the division of a hash value by the hash table size with a bitwise-AND operation, i.e., $h(x) \mod 2^k = h(x) \& (2^k - 1)$, which is practically faster[3].

---

[3] http://blog.teamleadnet.com/2012/07/faster-division-and-modulo-operation.html.

If the aforementioned resize hint suggests that the next power of two is sufficient for storing all factors, we set $\alpha = 0.95$ before enlarging the size (if necessary). We also implemented a hash table variant that will change its size to fit the provided hint. This variant then cannot use the fast bit mask to simulate the operation mod M. Instead, it uses a practical alternative that scales the hash value by M and divides this value by the largest possible hash value [4], i.e., $Mh(k)/(\max_{k'} h(k'))$. We mark those hash table variants with a plus sign, e.g., hash+ is the respective variant of hash.

Reasons for Linear Probing. Linear probing inserts a tuple with key k at the first free entry, starting at the initial address. It is cache-efficient if the keys have a small bit length (i.e., fitting in a computer word). Using large hash tables and small keys, the cache-efficiency can compensate the chance of higher collisions [3,16]. Linear probing excels if the load ratio is below 50%, and it is still competitive up to a load ratio of 80% [7,27]. Nevertheless, its main drawback is *clustering*: Linear probing creates runs, i.e., entries whose hash values are equal. With a sufficient high load, it is likely that runs can merge such that long sequence of entries with different hash values emerge. When trying to look up a key k, we have to search the sequence of succeeding elements starting at the initial address until finding a tuple whose key is k, or ending at an empty entry. Fortunately, the expected time of a search is rather promising for an α not too close to one: Given that the used hash function h distributes the keys independently and uniformly, we get $\mathcal{O}\big(1/(1-\alpha)^2\big)$ expected time for a search [21]. In practice, even weak hash functions (like we use in this article) tend to behave as truly independent hash functions [9]. These properties convinced us that linear probing is a good candidate for our representations of the LZ trie using a hash table.

Compact Hashing. In terms of memory, hash is at a disadvantage compared to binary, because the key-value pairs consist of two factor indices and a character; for an $\alpha < 1$, hash will always take more space than binary. To reduce the size of the stored keys, we introduce the representation cht using compact hashing.

The idea of compact hashing [12,21] is to use a bijective hash function such that when storing a tuple with key k in H, we only store the value and the quotient $\lfloor h(k)/M \rfloor$ in the hash table. The original key of an entry of H can be restored by knowing the initial address $h(k)$ mod M and the stored quotient $\lfloor h(k)/M \rfloor$. To address collisions and therefore the displacement of a stored entry due to linear probing, Cleary [10] adds two bit vectors with which the initial address can be restored. (One bit vector marks the initial addresses of all stored elements, and the other marks the boundaries of groups of elements having the same initial address.)

For the bijective hash function h, we consider two classes:

The class of linear congruential generators (LCGs). The class of LCGs [8] contains all functions $\mathsf{lcg}_{a,b,p} : [0..p-1] \to [0..p-1], x \mapsto (ax+b) \bmod p$

---

[4] http://www.idryman.org/blog/2017/05/03/writing-a-damn-fast-hash-table-with-tiny-memory-footprints/.

with $p \in \mathbb{N}, 0 < a < p, 0 \leq b < p$. If p and a are relative prime, then there exists a unique inverse $a^{-1} \in [1..p-1]$ of a such that $aa^{-1} \mod p = 1$. Then $\mathsf{lcg}_{a,b,p}^{-1} : y \mapsto (y-b)a^{-1} \mod p$ is the inverse of $\mathsf{lcg}_{a,b,p}$. If p is prime, then $a^{-1} = a^{p-2} \mod p$ due to Fermat's little theorem.

The class of xorshift functions. The xorshift hash function class [28] contains functions that use shift- and exclusive or (xor) operations. Let $\oplus$ denote the binary xor-operator and w the number of bits of the input integer. For an integer $j < -\lfloor w/2 \rfloor$ or $j > \lfloor w/2 \rfloor$, the xorshift operation $\mathsf{sxor}_{w,j} : [0..2^w - 1] \to [0..2^w - 1], x \mapsto (x \oplus (\lfloor 2^j x \rfloor \mod 2^w)) \mod 2^w$ is inverse to itself: $\mathsf{sxor}_{w,j} \circ \mathsf{sxor}_{w,j} = \mathsf{id}$.

It is possible to create a bijective function that is a concatenation of functions of both families[5].

A compact hash table can use less space than a traditional hash table if the size of the keys is large: If the largest integer key is u, then all keys can be stored in $\lceil \lg u \rceil$ bits, whereas all quotients can be stored in $\lceil \lg(\max_u h(u)/M) \rceil$ bits. By choosing a hash function h with $M \leq \max_u h(u) \leq cM$ for a constant $c > 1$, it is possible to store the quotients in a number of bits independent of the number of the keys.

Enlarging the hash table. On enlarging the hash table, we choose a new hash function, and rebuild the entire table with the new size and a newly chosen hash function. We first choose a hash function h out of the aforementioned bijective hash classes and adjust h's parameters such that h maps from $[0..2m\sigma - 1]$ to $[0..2m\sigma - 1]$ (m has already its new size). This means that

- we select a function $\mathsf{lcg}_{a,b,p}$ with a prime $m\sigma < p < 2m\sigma$ (such a prime exists [37] and can be precomputed for all $M = 2^k$, $1 \leq k \leq \lg n$) and $0 < a, b \leq p$ randomly chosen, or that
- we select a function $\mathsf{sxor}_{w,j}$ with $\lg(m\sigma) \leq w \leq \lg(2m\sigma)$ and j arbitrary.

Note that although the domain of h is $[0..2m\sigma - 1]$, we apply h only to keys belonging to $[0..m\sigma - 1]$.

The hash table always stores trie nodes with labels that are at most m; this is an invariant due to the following fact: before inserting a node with label $m + 1$ we enlarge the hash table and hence update m. Therefore, the key of a node can be represented by a $\lceil \lg(m\sigma) \rceil$-bit integer (we map the key to a single integer with $[0..m-1] \times [0..\sigma - 1] \to [0..m\sigma - 1], (y, c) \mapsto \sigma y + c$). Since h is a bijection, the function $[0..m\sigma-1] \to [0..M-1] \times [0..\lfloor(2m\sigma - 1)/M\rfloor], i \mapsto (h_1(i), h_2(i)) := (h(i) \mod M, \lfloor h(i)/M \rfloor)$ is injective. We use h_1 to find the locations of the entries in our hash table H. When we want to store a node with label x and key $y\sigma + c$ in the hash table, we put x and $h_2(\sigma y + c)$ in an entry of the hash table. The entry is determined by h_1, the linear probing strategy, and a re-arrangement with the bit vectors. It stores x using $\lg m$ bits and $h_2(\sigma y + c)$ using $\lg(2\alpha\sigma)$ bits. In total, we

---

[5] Popular hash functions like MurmurHash 3 (https://github.com/aappleby/smhasher) use a post-processing step that applies multiple LCGs $\mathsf{lcg}_{a,0,2^{64}}$ with a as a predefined odd constant, and some xorshift-operations.

Trie	Space Best Case (bits)	Space Worst Case (bits)
binary	$3z(\lg(z^2\sigma) - 2/3)/2$	$3z(\lg(z^2\sigma) + 4/3)$
ternary	$3z(\lg(z^3\sigma) - 1)/2$	$3z(\lg(z^3\sigma) + 2)$
hash	$3z(\lg(z^2\sigma) - 2/3)/2\alpha$	$6z(\lg(z^2\sigma) + 4/3)/\alpha$
cht	$3z(\lg(\alpha z\sigma) + 8/3)/2\alpha$	$3z(\lg(\alpha z\sigma) + 11/3)/\alpha$
rolling	$3z(w + \lg(z\sigma) - 1/3)/2\alpha$	$6z(w + \lg(z\sigma) + 2/3)/\alpha$

Fig. 3. Upper and lower bound of the maximum memory used during an LZ78/LZW factorization with z factors. The size of a fingerprint is w bits.

need $M (\lg(2\alpha\sigma) + \lg m) + 2M$ bits to store m elements in a compact hash table of size M. Since $m \leq 2z-1$, there is a power of two such that $M = 2^{\lfloor \lg(z/\alpha)\rfloor+1} \leq (2z-1)/\alpha$. On termination, the compact hash table takes at most $M(2 + \lg(2\alpha\sigma m)) \leq (2z - 1)(3 + \lg(\alpha\sigma z))/\alpha$ bits. The memory peak is reached when we have to copy the data from the penultimate table to the final hash table with the above size. The memory peak is at most $M(3 + \lg(m\alpha\sigma)) + M/2(2 + \lg(m\alpha\sigma)) \leq (2z - 1)(11 + 3\lg(z\alpha\sigma))/2\alpha$.

If we compare this peak with the approach using a classic hash table (where we need to store the full key), we get a size of $M(\lg m + \lg m + \lg\sigma) + M/2(\lg(m/2) + \lg(m/2) + \lg\sigma) \leq 3(2z - 1)(4/3 + \lg(\sigma z^2))/\alpha$ bits.

This gives the following theorem:

Theorem 2. *We can compute the LZ78 and LZW factorization online using linear time with high probability and at most $z(3\lg(z\sigma\alpha) + 11)/\alpha$ bits of working space, for a fixed α with $0 < \alpha < 1$.*

For the evaluation, we use a preliminary version of the implementation of Poyias et al. [33] that is based on [10] with the difference that Cleary uses bidirectional probing ([33] uses linear probing).

Rolling Hashing. Here, we present an alternative trie representation with hashing, called rolling. The idea is to maintain the Karp-Rabin fingerprints [20] of all computed factors in a hash table such that the navigation in the trie is simulated by matching the fingerprint of a substring of the text with the fingerprints in the hash table. Given that the fingerprint of the substring $T[i..i + \ell - 1]$ matches the fingerprint of a node u, we can compute the fingerprint of $T[i..i + \ell]$ to find the child of u that is connected to u by an edge with label $T[i + \ell]$. To compute the fingerprints, we choose one of the two rolling hash function families:

- a function of the randomized Karp-Rabin *ID37* family [24][6], and

---

[6] https://github.com/lemire/rollinghashcpp. The function is $ID37(T) = \sum_{i=1}^{|T|} h(T[i])37^{|T|-i} \bmod 2^w$, where w is the word size and h is a hash function that maps the alphabet uniformly to the range $[0..2^{32} - 1]$.

Table 1. Properties of the text collections and their factorizations. Each column |output| shows the size of the respective (compressed) output. The sizes $z \lceil \lg(z\sigma) \rceil \leq z \lceil \lg z \rceil + z \lceil \lg \sigma \rceil$ bits, $z \lceil \lg(z + \sigma) \rceil$ bits and $2z \lg n$ bits are the output size of the LZ78, LZW and LZ77 factorization for the respective number of factors z when storing the output in arrays of fixed width.

Collection	σ	LZ78			LZW			LZ77	
		z	$z \lceil \lg(z\sigma) \rceil$	|output|	z	$z \lceil \lg(z + \sigma) \rceil$	|output|	z	$2z \lg n$
PC-ENGLISH	226	21.4 M	83.8 MiB	80.2 MiB	23.5 M	70.1 MiB	66.1 MiB	14.0 M	93.3 MiB
PCR-CERE	6	15.8 M	50.0 MiB	58.2 MiB	17.1 M	50.9 MiB	46.9 MiB	1.4 M	9.7 MiB
PC-DNA	17	16.4 M	54.8 MiB	60.5 MiB	17.8 M	52.9 MiB	48.9 MiB	13.9 M	92.1 MiB
HASHTAG	179	18.9 M	73.4 MiB	70.6 MiB	21.1 M	62.9 MiB	58.9 MiB	13.7 M	90.4 MiB

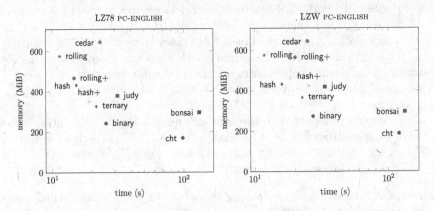

Fig. 4. Evaluation of LZ78 (*left*) and LZW (*right*) on PC-ENGLISH.

– the function $fermat(T) = \sum_{i=1}^{|T|} (T[i] - 1)(\sigma + 1)^{|T|-i} \mod 2^w$, where the modulo by the word size w surrogates the integer overflow, and $T[i] - 1$ is in the range $[0..\sigma - 1]$. In the case of a byte alphabet, $\sigma + 1 = 2^8 + 1 = 257$ is a Fermat prime [35]. We compute $fermat(T)$ with Horner's rule.

Both rolling hash functions discard the classic modulo operation with a prime number in favor of integer overflows due to performance reasons; this trick was already suggested in [15]. The LZ78/LZW computation using rolling is a Monte Carlo algorithm, since the computation can produce a wrong factorization if the computed fingerprints of two different strings are the same (because the fingerprints *are* the hash table keys).

Summary. We summarize the description of the trie data structures in this and the previous section by Fig. 3 showing the maximum space consumption of each described trie. The maximum memory consumption is due to the peak at the last enlargement of the dynamic trie data structure, i.e., when the trie enlarges its space such that $z \leq m \leq 2z - 1$ (where m is the number of elements it can maintain).

4   Experiments and Conclusion

We implemented the LZ tries in the tudocomp framework [11][7]. The framework provides the implementation of an LZ78 and an LZW compressor. Both compressors are parameterized by an LZ trie and a coder. The coder is a function that takes the output of the factorization and generates the final binary output. We selected the coder `bit` that stores the referred index y (with $y > 0$) of a factor F_x in $\lceil \lg x \rceil$ bits. That is because the factor F_x can have a referred index y only with $y < x$. We can restore the coded referred index on decompression since we know the index of the factor that we currently process and hence the number of bits used to store its referred index (if we coded it)[8]. This yields $\sum_{i=1}^{z} \lceil \lg i \rceil = z \lceil \lg z \rceil - (\lg e)z + \mathcal{O}(\lg z)$ bits for storing the (positive) referred indices.

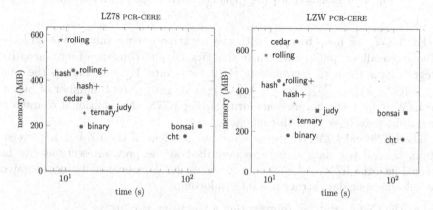

Fig. 5. Evaluation of LZ78 (*left*) and LZW (*right*) on PCR-CERE.

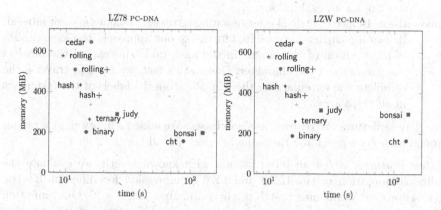

Fig. 6. Evaluation of LZ78 (*left*) and LZW (*right*) on PC-DNA.

---

[7] The source code of our implementations is freely available at https://github.com/tudocomp, except for cht and bonsai due to copyright restrictions.

[8] This approach is similar to http://www.cplusplus.com/articles/iL18T05o.

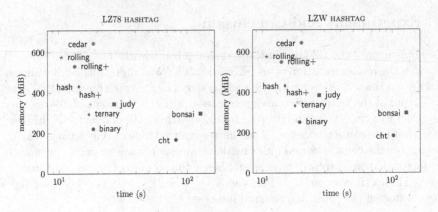

Fig. 7. Evaluation of LZ78 (*left*) and LZW (*right*) on HASHTAG.

For LZW, we have to cope with the negative integer values: We add the value σ to all output values such that its output consists of non-negative integers. Now the x-th factor costs $\lceil \lg(x + \sigma) \rceil$ bits. By splitting up the sum $\sum_{i=1}^{z} \lceil \lg(i + \sigma) \rceil = \sum_{i=1}^{z+\sigma} \lceil \lg i \rceil - \sum_{i=1}^{\sigma} \lceil \lg i \rceil$ we get the total number of bits of the LZW output by the previous formula. For LZ78, the additional characters are output naively as $\lceil \lg \sigma \rceil$-bit integers.

The LZ78 and LZW compressor are independent of the LZ trie implementation, i.e., all trie data structures described in the previous sections can be plugged into the LZW or LZ78 compressor easily. We additionally incorporated the following trie data structures into tudocomp:

cedar: the Cedar trie [39], representing a trie using two arrays.
judy: the Judy array, advertised to be optimized for avoiding CPU cache misses (cf. [26] for an evaluation).
bonsai: the m-Bonsai (γ) trie [34] representing a trie whose nodes are not labeled. It uses a compact hash table, but unlike our approach, the key consists of the position of the parent in the hash table (instead of the label of the parent) and the character. Due to this fact, we need to traverse the complete trie for enlarging the trie. We store the labels of the trie nodes in an extra array.

The data structures are realized as C++ classes. We added a lightweight wrapper around each class providing the same interface for all tries.

Online Feature. Given an input stream with known length, we evaluate the online computation of the LZ78 and LZW compression for different LZ trie representations. We assume that Σ is a byte alphabet, i.e., $\sigma = 2^8$. On computing a factor, we encode it and output it instantaneously. This makes our compression program a *filter* [29], i.e., it processes the input stream and generates an output stream, buffering neither the input nor the output.

Implementation Details. The keys stored by hash are 40-bit integers, the fingerprints of rolling are 64-bit integers, and the values stored by hash, rolling and bonsai are 32-bit integers. For all variants working with hash tables, we initially set α to 0.3.

Hash Function. We use cht with a hash function of the LCG family. Our hash table for hash uses a xorshift hash function[9] derived from [36]. It is slower than simple multiplicative functions, but more resilient against clustering. Alternatives are sophisticated hash functions like CLHash [25] or Zobrist hashing [23,42]. These are even more resilient against clustering, but have practical higher computation times in our experiments.

Setup. The experiments were conducted on a machine with 32 GB of RAM, an Intel Xeon CPU E3-1271 v3 and a Samsung SSD 850 EVO 250GB. The operating system was a 64-bit version of Ubuntu Linux 14.04 with the kernel version 3.13. We used a single execution thread for the experiments. The source code was compiled using the GNU compiler g++ 6.2.0 with the compile flags -O3 -march=native -DNDEBUG.

Datasets. We evaluated the combinations of the aforementioned tries with the LZW and LZ78 algorithms on the 200MiB text collections provided by tudocomp. We assume that the input alphabet is the byte alphabet ($\sigma = 2^8$). The indices of the factors are represented with 32-bit integers. We chose four text collections:

- PC-ENGLISH: an English text,
- PCR-CERE: a highly-repetitive DNA sequence with small alphabet size,
- PC-DNA: a non-highly-repetitive DNA sequence with small alphabet size,
- HASHTAG: a tab-spaced-version data dump with integer keys and hash tags.

Table 1 shows the number of factors produced by LZ78, LZW and LZ77 (we used the variant with overlapping) on each text collection. We plotted the memory consumption against the time (in logarithmic scale) for all datasets in Figs. 4, 5, 6 and 7. To avoid clutter, we selected one hash function per rolling hash table: We chose *fermat* with rolling and *ID37* with rolling+ for the plots.

Overall Evaluation. The evaluation shows that the fastest option is rolling. The size of its fingerprints is a trade-off between space and the probability of a correct output. When space is an issue, rolling with 64-bit fingerprints is no match for more space saving trie data structures. hash is the second fastest LZ trie in the experiments. With 40-bit keys it uses less memory than rolling, but is slightly slower. Depending on the quality of the resize hint, the variants hash+ and rolling+ take 50% up to 100% of the size of hash and rolling, respectively. hash+ and rolling+ are always slower than their respective standard variants, sometimes slower than the deterministic data structures ternary and binary. binary's speed excels at texts with very small alphabets, while ternary usually outperforms binary. Only cht can compete with binary in terms of space, but is magnitudes slower than most alternatives. The third party data structures cedar, bonsai and judy could not make it to the Pareto front.

---

[9] http://xorshift.di.unimi.it/splitmix64.c.

Table 2. Detailed evaluation of the tries using hashing. We evaluated the number of collisions and the final table size M for the LZ78 factorization of 200 MiB PC-ENGLISH. An entry in rolling costs $64 + 32$ bits, an entry in hash $40 + 32$ bits.

Trie	#Collisions	M	Memory	Time
rolling with				
- *ID37*	36 M	33.6 M	576.0 MiB	11.6 s
- *fermat*	137 M	33.6 M	576.0 MiB	11.4 s
- *fermat*⊕	36 M	33.6 M	576.0 MiB	11.8 s
rolling+ with				
- *ID37*	140 M	24.0 M	466.9 MiB	14.7 s
- *fermat*	938 M	24.0 M	466.9 MiB	21.0 s
- *fermat*⊕	142 M	24.0 M	466.9 MiB	15.8 s
hash	36 M	33.6 M	432.0 MiB	15.3 s
hash+	137 M	24.0 M	350.2 MiB	19.1 s

Evaluation of rolling. The hash table with the rolling hash function *fermat* is slightly faster than with a function of the *ID37* family, but the hash table with *fermat* tends to have more collisions (cf. Table 2). It is magnitudes slower at less compressible texts like PC-PROTEINS due to the high occurrence of collisions. The number of collisions can drop if we post-process the output of *fermat* with a hash function that is more collision resistant. Applying an evenly distributing hash function on *fermat* speeds up the computation only if the number of collisions is sufficiently high (e.g., rolling+ with *fermat* in Table 2). In the experiments, we apply the xorshift hash function used by hash (see Footnote 9) to the output of *fermat* for determining the initial address. We denote this variant with a ⊕ as suffix of either *fermat*⊕ or rolling⊕.

According to the birthday paradox, the likelihood that the fingerprints of two different substrings match is anti-correlated to the number of bits used for storing the fingerprint if we assume that the used rolling hash function distributes uniformly. This means that the domain of the Karp-Rabin fingerprints can be made large enough to be robust against collisions when hashing large texts. In our case, we used 64-bit fingerprints because, unlike 32-bit and 40-bit fingerprints, the factorization produced by rolling are correct for all test instances and all tested rolling hash functions. Nevertheless, this bit length can be considered as too weak for processing massive datasets: Given that the used rolling hash function is uniform, the probability of a collision is $1/2^{64}$. Although this number is very small, processing 10^9 datasets, each 200 MiB large, would give a collision probability of roughly 1%. This probability can be reduced by enlarging the bit length, and hence improving the correctness probability by sacrificing working space. We reran our experiments with 64-bit and 128-bit fingerprints, and measured time and space usage in Table 3. There, we can see that switching to a higher bit length slightly degrades the running time, but severely degrades the space usage.

Another option to sustain a correct computation is to check the output factorization. This check can be done by reconstructing the text with the output and the built LZ trie. However, a compression with rolling combined with a decompression step takes more time than other approaches like hash or binary. Hence, a Las Vegas algorithm based on rolling is practically not interesting.

Variations of Hash Tables. The trie representation hash can be generalized to be used with any associative container. The easiest implementation is to use the balanced binary tree `std::map` or the hash table `std::unordered_map` provided by the standard library of C++11. `std::unordered_map` is conform to the interface of the C++ standard library, but therefore sacrifices performance. It uses separate chaining that tends to use a lot of small memory allocations affecting the overall running time (see Table 4). Another pitfall is to use the

Table 3. Performance comparison of 64-bit and 128-bit fingerprints generated by *fermat.*

	LZ78				LZW			
	64 bit		128 bit		64 bit		128 bit	
	Time	Space	Time	Space	Time	Space	Time	Space
PC-ENGLISH (see also Fig. 4)								
rolling	11.4 s	576.0 MiB	12.1 s	960.0 MiB	11.8 s	576.0 MiB	12.7 s	960.0 MiB
rolling⊕	11.9 s	576.0 MiB	13.7 s	960.0 MiB	12.3 s	576.0 MiB	14.1 s	960.0 MiB
rolling+	21.0 s	466.9 MiB	24.1 s	778.1 MiB	68.8 s	565.1 MiB	52.6 s	984.6 MiB
rolling+⊕	15.8 s	466.9 MiB	18.3 s	778.1 MiB	24.9 s	565.1 MiB	22.5 s	984.6 MiB
PCR-CERE (see also Fig. 5)								
rolling	9.0 s	576.0 MiB	9.5 s	960.0 MiB	9.2 s	576.0 MiB	9.8 s	960.0 MiB
rolling⊕	9.5 s	576.0 MiB	10.8 s	960.0 MiB	9.6 s	576.0 MiB	11.2 s	960.0 MiB
rolling+	11.1 s	443.9 MiB	12.6 s	739.7 MiB	11.4 s	450.9 MiB	13.8 s	751.6 MiB
rolling+⊕	11.2 s	443.9 MiB	13.9 s	739.7 MiB	11.7 s	450.9 MiB	15.0 s	751.6 MiB
PC-DNA (see also Fig. 6)								
rolling	9.4 s	576.0 MiB	10.0 s	960.0 MiB	9.5 s	576.0 MiB	10.2 s	960.0 MiB
rolling⊕	9.8 s	576.0 MiB	11.5 s	960.0 MiB	10.0 s	576.0 MiB	11.6 s	960.0 MiB
rolling+	11.6 s	509.3 MiB	13.5 s	745.3 MiB	12.0 s	518.4 MiB	14.5 s	756.7 MiB
rolling+⊕	11.7 s	509.3 MiB	14.7 s	745.3 MiB	12.2 s	518.4 MiB	15.6 s	756.7 MiB
HASHTAG (see also Fig. 7)								
rolling	13.4 s	576.0 MiB	15.6 s	960.0 MiB	19.8 s	576.0 MiB	25.3 s	960.0 MiB
rolling⊕	10.8 s	576.0 MiB	12.6 s	960.0 MiB	11.1 s	576.0 MiB	12.9 s	960.0 MiB
rolling+	15.4 s	530.9 MiB	18.0 s	766.3 MiB	21.8 s	549.7 MiB	25.6 s	779.6 MiB
rolling+⊕	14.1 s	530.9 MiB	17.2 s	766.3 MiB	15.8 s	549.7 MiB	18.9 s	779.6 MiB

standard C++11 hash function for integers that is just the identity function. Although this is the fastest available hash function, it performs poorly in the experiments. There are two reasons. The first is that $k \mapsto k \bmod M$ badly distributes the tuples if M is not a prime. The second is that the input data is not independent: In the case of LZ78 and LZW, the composed key $c + \ell\sigma$ of a node v connected to its parent with label ℓ by an edge with label c holds information about the trie topology: all nodes whose keys are $\ell\sigma + d$ for a $d \in \Sigma$ are the siblings of v. Since ℓ is smaller than the label of v (ℓ is the referred index of the factor corresponding to v), larger keys depend on the existence of some keys with smaller values. Both problems can be tackled by using a hash function with an avalanche effect property, i.e., flipping a single bit of the input changes roughly half of the bits of the output. In Table 4 we evaluated the identity and the xorshift hash function (see Footnote 9) as hash functions for the hash table `flathash`, which seems to be very sensitive for hash collisions. We selected the LZ trie of the LZ-index [32] as an external competitor in Table 4: We terminated the execution of the LZ-index algorithm after producing the LZ trie of the LZ78 factorization. We did not integrate this data structure into tudocomp. The only interesting configuration is hash with the hash table `sparsehash`, since it takes 4.1MB less space than binary while still being faster than cht, at the LZ78-factorization of PCR-CERE.

Outlook

An interesting option is to switch from the linear probing scheme to a more sophisticated scheme whose running time is stable for high loads, too [27]. This could be especially beneficent if the resize hint provides a more accurate bounds on the number of factors.

Table 4. hash with different hash tables, and the LZ-index.

Trie	PC-ENGLISH				PCR-CERE			
	LZ78		LZW		LZ78		LZW	
	Time	Space	Time	Space	Time	Space	Time	Space
hash with hash table								
std::unordered_map	51.0 s	856.6 MiB	54.0 s	937.9 MiB	42.3 s	703.2 MiB	44.1 s	760.8 MiB
std::map	161.2 s	980.2 MiB	167.2 s	1.1 GiB	98.8 s	722.5 MiB	104.6 s	781.6 MiB
rigtorp[a]	14.9 s	960.0 MiB	15.2 s	960.0 MiB	12.0 s	960.0 MiB	12.3 s	960.0 MiB
flathash[b]	33.5 s	24 GiB	24.5 s	24 GiB	18.5 s	6 GiB	19.2 s	6 GiB
flathash[c]	15.1 s	1.3 GiB	15.7 s	1.3 GiB	12.4 s	1.3 GiB	13.0 s	1.3 GiB
densehash[d]	23.0 s	576.0 MiB	24.4 s	576.0 MiB	29.4 s	576.0 MiB	30.8 s	576.0 MiB
sparsehash[d]	49.1 s	255.7 MiB	52.2 s	280.0 MiB	68.6 s	191.3 MiB	72.4 s	206.1 MiB
LZ-index [32]	24.6 s	1047 MiB			14.5 s	817.3 MiB		

[a] https://github.com/rigtorp/HashMap, $\alpha = 0.5$ hard coded
[b] https://probablydance.com/2017/02/26/i-wrote-the-fastest-hashtable/, it uses the identity as a hash function and doubles its size when experiencing too much collisions
[c] See Footnote b, but with the xorshift hash function (see Footnote 9)
[d] https://github.com/sparsehash/sparsehash

Speaking of novel hash tables, we could combine the compact hash table [10] with the memory management of Google's sparse hash table[10] leading to an even more memory friendly trie representation.

Acknowledgments. We are grateful to Marvin Löbel for providing the basement of the LZ78/LZW framework in tudocomp. Further, we thank Andreas Poyias for sharing the source code of the m-Bonsai trie [34] and the compact hash table [33].

References

1. Arroyuelo, D., Navarro, G.: Space-efficient construction of Lempel-Ziv compressed text indexes. Inf. Comput. **209**(7), 1070–1102 (2011)
2. Arz, J., Fischer, J.: LZ-compressed string dictionaries. In: Proceedings of the DCC, pp. 322–331. IEEE Press (2014)
3. Askitis, N.: Fast and compact hash tables for integer keys. In: Proceedings of the ACSC. CRPIT, vol. 91, pp. 101–110. Australian Computer Society (2009)
4. Bannai, H., Inenaga, S., Takeda, M.: Efficient LZ78 factorization of grammar compressed text. In: Calderón-Benavides, L., González-Caro, C., Chávez, E., Ziviani, N. (eds.) SPIRE 2012. LNCS, vol. 7608, pp. 86–98. Springer, Heidelberg (2012). doi:10.1007/978-3-642-34109-0_10
5. Belazzougui, D., Puglisi, S.J.: Range predecessor and Lempel-Ziv parsing. In: Proceedings of the SODA, pp. 2053–2071. SIAM (2016)
6. Bentley, J.L., Sedgewick, R.: Fast algorithms for sorting and searching strings. In: Proceedings of the SODA, pp. 360–369. ACM/SIAM (1997)
7. Black, J.R., Martel, C.U., Qi, H.: Graph and hashing algorithms for modern architectures: design and performance. In: Proceedings of the WAE, pp. 37–48. Max-Planck-Institut für Informatik (1998)
8. Carter, L., Wegman, M.N.: Universal classes of hash functions. J. Comput. Syst. Sci. **18**(2), 143–154 (1979)
9. Chung, K., Mitzenmacher, M., Vadhan, S.P.: Why simple hash functions work: exploiting the entropy in a data stream. Theor. Comput. **9**, 897–945 (2013)
10. Cleary, J.G.: Compact hash tables using bidirectional linear probing. IEEE Trans. Comput. **33**(9), 828–834 (1984)
11. Dinklage, P., Fischer, J., Köppl, D., Löbel, M., Sadakane, K.: Compression with the tudocomp framework. In: Proceedings of the SEA. LIPIcs, vol. 75, pp. 13:1–13:22 (2017)
12. Feldman, J.A., Low, J.R.: Comment on Brent's scatter storage algorithm. Commun. ACM **16**(11), 703 (1973)
13. Fischer, J., Gawrychowski, P.: Alphabet-dependent string searching with wexponential search trees. In: Cicalese, F., Porat, E., Vaccaro, U. (eds.) CPM 2015. LNCS, vol. 9133, pp. 160–171. Springer, Cham (2015). doi:10.1007/978-3-319-19929-0_14
14. Fischer, J., I, T., Köppl, D.: Lempel Ziv computation in small space (LZ-CISS). In: Cicalese, F., Porat, E., Vaccaro, U. (eds.) CPM 2015. LNCS, vol. 9133, pp. 172–184. Springer, Cham (2015). doi:10.1007/978-3-319-19929-0_15
15. Gonnet, G.H., Baeza-Yates, R.A.: An analysis of the Karp-Rabin string matching algorithm. Inf. Process. Lett. **34**(5), 271–274 (1990)

---

[10] https://github.com/sparsehash/sparsehash.

16. Heileman, G.L., Luo, W.: How caching affects hashing. In: Proceedings of the ALENEX, pp. 141–154. SIAM (2005)
17. Jansson, J., Sadakane, K., Sung, W.K.: Linked dynamic tries with applications to LZ-compression in sublinear time and space. Algorithmica **71**(4), 969–988 (2015)
18. Kärkkäinen, J., Kempa, D., Puglisi, S.J.: Lazy Lempel-Ziv factorization algorithms. ACM J. Exp. Algorithmics **21**(1), 2.4:1–2.4:19 (2016)
19. Kärkkäinen, J., Kempa, D., Puglisi, S.J.: Lightweight Lempel-Ziv parsing. In: Bonifaci, V., Demetrescu, C., Marchetti-Spaccamela, A. (eds.) SEA 2013. LNCS, vol. 7933, pp. 139–150. Springer, Heidelberg (2013). doi:10.1007/978-3-642-38527-8_14
20. Karp, R.M., Rabin, M.O.: Efficient randomized pattern-matching algorithms. IBM J. Res. Dev. **31**(2), 249–260 (1987)
21. Knuth, D.: Sorting and Searching, the Art of Computer Programming, vol. III. Addison-Wesley, Reading (1973)
22. Köppl, D., Sadakane, K.: Lempel-Ziv computation in compressed space. In: Proceedings of the DCC, pp. 3–12. IEEE Press (2016)
23. Lemire, D.: The universality of iterated hashing over variable-length strings. Discrete Appl. Math. **160**(4–5), 604–617 (2012)
24. Lemire, D., Kaser, O.: Recursive n-gram hashing is pairwise independent, at best. Comput. Speech Lang. **24**(4), 698–710 (2010)
25. Lemire, D., Kaser, O.: Faster 64-bit universal hashing using carry-less multiplications. J. Cryptographic Eng. **6**(3), 171–185 (2016)
26. Luan, H., Du, X., Wang, S., Ni, Y., Chen, Q.: J^+-Tree: a new index structure in main memory. In: Kotagiri, R., Krishna, P.R., Mohania, M., Nantajeewarawat, E. (eds.) DASFAA 2007. LNCS, vol. 4443, pp. 386–397. Springer, Heidelberg (2007). doi:10.1007/978-3-540-71703-4_34
27. Maier, T., Sanders, P.: Dynamic Space Efficient Hashing. ArXiv CoRR 1705.00997 (2017)
28. Marsaglia, G.: Xorshift RNGs. J. Stat. Softw. **8**(14), 1–6 (2003)
29. McIlroy, M.D.: A research UNIX reader: annotated excerpts from the programmer's manual, 1971–1986. Technical report CSTR 139, AT&T Bell Laboratories (1987)
30. Munro, J.I., Navarro, G., Nekrich, Y.: Space-efficient construction of compressed indexes in deterministic linear time. In: Proceedings of the SODA, pp. 408–424. SIAM (2017)
31. Nakashima, Y.: I, T., Inenaga, S., Bannai, H., Takeda, M.: Constructing LZ78 tries and position heaps in linear time for large alphabets. Inform. Process. Lett. **115**(9), 655–659 (2015)
32. Navarro, G.: Implementing the LZ-index: theory versus practice. ACM J. Exp. Algorithmics **13**(2), 2:1.1–2:1.49 (2008)
33. Poyias, A., Puglisi, S.J., Raman, R.: Compact dynamic rewritable (CDRW) arrays. In: Proceedings of the ALENEX, pp. 109–119. SIAM (2017)
34. Poyias, A., Raman, R.: Improved practical compact dynamic tries. In: Iliopoulos, C., Puglisi, S., Yilmaz, E. (eds.) SPIRE 2015. LNCS, vol. 9309, pp. 324–336. Springer, Cham (2015). doi:10.1007/978-3-319-23826-5_31
35. Robinson, R.M.: Mersenne and Fermat numbers. Proc. Amer. Math. Soc. **5**(5), 842–846 (1954)
36. Steele Jr., G.L., Lea, D., Flood, C.H.: Fast splittable pseudorandom number generators. In: Proc. OOPSLA. pp. 453–472. ACM (2014)
37. Tchebychev, P.: Mémoire sur les nombres premiers. J. de mathématiques pures et appliquées **1**, 366–390 (1852)
38. Welch, T.A.: A technique for high-performance data compression. IEEE Computer **17**(6), 8–19 (1984)

39. Yoshinaga, N., Kitsuregawa, M.: A self-adaptive classifier for efficient text-stream processing. In: Proceedings of the COLING, pp. 1091–1102. ACL (2014)
40. Ziv, J., Lempel, A.: A universal algorithm for sequential data compression. IEEE Trans. Inform. Theory **23**(3), 337–343 (1977)
41. Ziv, J., Lempel, A.: Compression of individual sequences via variable length coding. IEEE Trans. Inform. Theory **24**(5), 530–536 (1978)
42. Zobrist, A.L.: A new hashing method with application for game playing. Technical report 88, Computer Sciences Department, University of Wisconsin (1970)

Regular Abelian Periods and Longest Common Abelian Factors on Run-Length Encoded Strings

Szymon Grabowski[(✉)]

Institute of Applied Computer Science, Lodz University of Technology, Łódź, Poland
sgrabow@kis.p.lodz.pl

Abstract. Two strings are considered Abelian equivalent if one is a permutation of the other. We deal with two problems from Abelian stringology: computing regular Abelian periods of a given string and computing the longest common Abelian factor (LCAF) of two given strings. For the former problem our solution works in $O(n \log m)$ time, where m is the length of the run-length encoded string, which improves the $O(nm)$-time result from [5]. For LCAF we propose two solutions, one working in $O(n + m^4)$ time and $O(n)$ space, the other requiring $O(n^{3/2}\sigma\sqrt{m \log n})$ time and $O(n\sigma)$ space (for $m = O(n/\log n)$).

1 Introduction

Abelian stringology has received considerable attention in theoretical computer science in the last decade, see, e.g., [1] and references therein. Two strings S_1 and S_2 are *Abelian equivalent* if S_1 is a permutation of S_2.

In this work we consider two problems, of finding all *regular Abelian periods* of a given string and of computing *longest common Abelian factors* (LCAF) of two given strings, with one presented algorithm for the former and two algorithms for the latter problem. Following [5], our algorithms make use of run-length compressibility of the input string(s). We simply assume that string S of length n can be decomposed into m, $m \leq n$, substrings S_i, $1 \leq i \leq m$, such that the number of distinct symbols in each S_i is one and the number of distinct symbols in every concatenation $S_i S_{i+1}$ is two. The symbols of S are over an integer alphabet $\Sigma = \{1, 2, \ldots, \sigma\}$, where we can safely assume that $\sigma \leq m$. Indeed, were it not the case, we could initially remap the distinct symbols from S into (at most) $\{1, 2, \ldots, m\}$, using a balanced binary search tree in $O(n + m \log m)$ time. All algorithms proposed in this work need $\Omega(n + m \log m)$ time and thus are not dominated by this (optional) preprocessing step. As creating the RLE representation of the given input takes $O(n)$ time, all our results contain such an additive term.

If a string w can be factorized into a sequence $v_1, \ldots, v_s$, $s > 1$, such that $v_1, \ldots, v_{s-1}$ are all Abelian equivalent and v_s is Abelian equivalent to some subsequence of v_1, then we say w has a regular Abelian period p. In general terms, the best algorithm for the problem of finding all regular Abelian periods of a string of length n was given by Kociumaka et al. [4] and it works in

© Springer International Publishing AG 2017
G. Fici et al. (Eds.): SPIRE 2017, LNCS 10508, pp. 208–213, 2017.
DOI: 10.1007/978-3-319-67428-5_17

$O(n(\log \log n + \log \sigma))$, where σ is the alphabet size. Recently, Sugimoto et al. [5] presented an $O(nm)$-time algorithm.

The LCAF problem is defined for two input strings, u and w. The goal is to find two Abelian equivalent substrings, one from u and the other from w, such that their length is maximized. When linear space is required, the problem can be solved either in $O(n^2\sigma)$ [2] or $O(nm^2)$ time [5]. If we can sacrifice $O(n \log^2 n)$ space, an $O(n^2 \log^2 n \log^* n)$-time algorithm [2] is known.

We use standard notation. Let $S = S[1 \ldots n]$ be a string of length n over an integer alphabet Σ of size $\sigma = |\Sigma|$. $S[i]$ denotes the ith symbol of S, and $S[i \ldots j] = S[i]S[i+1] \ldots S[j]$ the contiguous sequence of symbols (or *factor* or *substring*) of length $j - i + 1$. We will use the same notation for arrays. The *Parikh vector* for string S, denoted as $\mathcal{P}_S[1 \ldots \sigma]$, is defined as a vector (array) of size σ storing the number of occurrences of each alphabet symbol in S. The two Parikh vectors are equal, i.e., $\mathcal{P}_S = \mathcal{P}_T$, when $\mathcal{P}_S[c] = \mathcal{P}_T[c]$ for all symbols c.

All our algorithms are deterministic and work in the word-RAM model.

2   Computing All Regular Abelian Periods

There exist two prior algorithms for this problem. Kociumaka et al. [4] achieved $O(n(\log \log n + \log \sigma))$ time. Sugimoto et al. [5] gave an $O(nm)$-time solution, where m is the length of the run-length encoded input. We combine both solutions to obtain $O(n \log m)$ time.

To this end, we first note that thanks to a rather sophisticated $O(n \log \sigma)$ deterministic time preprocessing technique from [4, Lemma 12] we can tell in constant time if two substrings of S, $S[1 \ldots j]$ and $S[1 + kj \ldots (k+1)j]$, for arbitrary valid j and k, are Abelian equivalent[1]. We divide all possible period lengths into those not greater than some K (whose value will be settled later) and those that exceed this value. For simplicity, we will refer to the corresponding candidate periods as *short* and *long*. Sugimoto et al. consider each candidate period value separately; handling such a candidate takes $O(m)$ time in their algorithm. We apply their technique for short candidate periods. For long candidate periods we ignore the RLE representation and check if all $\lfloor n/p \rfloor$ corresponding factors of length p are Abelian equivalent, each factor checked in $O(1)$ time due to the aforementioned preprocessing technique. (Note that handling the suffixes of S of length $n \bmod p$, takes $O(n)$ time in total, see [4, Lemma 10].) Testing long candidate periods takes thus $O(n \sum_{i=K+1}^{n} 1/i) = O(n \log(n/K))$ time, as it is well known that partial sums of the harmonic series have logarithmic growth. Now, testing all short candidate periods clearly takes $O(Km)$ time and in total, including the preprocessing, we have $O(n \log \sigma + Km + n(\log(n/K)))$ time. By setting $K = (n/m) \log m$ we obtain

---

[1] More precisely, their lemma allows to check in constant time if two prefixes of the given string w have proportional Parikh vectors, assuming that both prefixes contain all symbols from the alphabet for w. In our setting, in $O(n \log \sigma)$ time we can compute the maximum q over the first positions of each alphabet symbol in S, and if $j < q$, then j cannot be a period of S and is immediately discarded.

$O(n(\log m + \log \sigma))$ time. Recall that if the assumption that $\sigma \leq m$ is not fulfilled, we can remap the alphabet in $O(n + m \log m)$ time, which is absorbed in our main formula. Taking all these into account, we obtain $O(n \log m)$ time for computing all regular Abelian periods. This significantly improves the result of Sugimoto et al. and dominates over the Kociumaka et al. algorithm (whose time complexity can be written as $O(n(\log \log n + \log(\min(\sigma, m))))$ in our setting) when $\log m = o(\log \log n)$.

3   Computing Longest Common Abelian Factors of Two Strings

We solve the following problem: for two given strings, S of lengths n_1 and m_1 in standard and RLE form, respectively, and T of lengths n_2 and m_2 in standard and RLE form, respectively, compute the length $maxlen = \max\{d \in [1 \ldots \min(n_1, n_2)] | \exists i : 1 \leq i \leq n_1, \exists j : 1 \leq j \leq n_2$ s.t. $\mathcal{P}_S[i \ldots i + d - 1] = \mathcal{P}_T[j \ldots j + d - 1]\}$ of the longest common Abelian factors of S and T, together with a pair (i, j) satisfying this condition. To facilitate notation, we set $n = n_1 + n_2$ and $m = m_1 + m_2$.

In the following subsections we present two algorithms for this problem.

3.1   LCAF in $O(n + m^4)$ Time and $O(n)$ Space

Let S (respectively T) be decomposed into the concatenation $s_1 s_2 \ldots s_{m_1}$ (respectively $t_1 t_2 \ldots t_{m_2}$), where each s_i (respectively t_i) is a run of equal symbols obtained from the RLE compression.

Let $startpos(S)$ be an array of size m_1 such that $startpos(S)[i] = 1 + \sum_{j=1}^{i-1} |s_j|$. For instance, if $S = abbbcbbaaa$, then $startpos = [1, 2, 5, 6, 8]$. Similarly we define $startpos(T)$.

Our algorithm basically consists of four nested loops, with $m_1^2 m_2^2 = O(m^4)$ iterations, where the innermost loop iteration is performed in constant time. The variables of the first two outer loops are associated with the first and the last run of currently inspected intervals from S; similarly the two inner loops are related to the boundaries of the current intervals from T.

The algorithm is listed in Fig. 1. The indexes i and k (line 4 and 11) are 'rough' boundaries of the current interval in S, and j and l (lines 20 and 24) have a similar function with respect to T. More precisely, the left boundary of the current interval in S is one of the symbols in the run s_i and the right boundary is one of the symbols in the run s_{k-1}. In other words, the current interval in S is nested in the half-open (left-closed, right-open) interval $[startpos(S)[i] \ldots startpos(S)[k])$. (We skip an analogous explanation for T.)

Apart from the Parikh vectors for S and T ($\mathcal{P}_S$ and $\mathcal{P}_T$), we maintain two more structures. The vector $\mathcal{D}$ of differences between the two Parikh vectors is initialized to all zeros (line 10) and increases one of its slots whenever the current span of S is extended on the right with a run (line 15), and similarly decreases one slot value when the current span of T is extended (line 28).

LCAF(S, n_1, m_1, T, n_2, m_2)
Precondition: $n_1 = |S|$, $m_1 = |RLE(S)|$, $S = s_1 s_2 \ldots s_{m_1}$,
$\qquad\qquad\quad n_2 = |T|$, $m_2 = |RLE(T)|$, $T = t_1 t_2 \ldots t_{m_2}$

---

(1)   Remap the alphabet to size $\min(m, \sigma)$. /* $O(n + m \log m)$ time */
(2) $NE \leftarrow NIL$ /* doubly-linked list of symbols c s.t. $\mathcal{P}_S[c] \neq \mathcal{P}_T[c]$ */
(3) $maxlen \leftarrow 0$
(4)   **for** $i \leftarrow 1$ **to** m_1 **do**
(5) $\qquad \mathcal{P}_S \leftarrow [0, \ldots, 0]$ /* Parikh vector for the current span of S */
(6) $\qquad \mathcal{P}_T \leftarrow [0, \ldots, 0]$ /* Parikh vector for the current span of T */
(7) $\qquad$ Re-initialize NE (with de-allocations).   /* $O(\min(m, \sigma))$ time */
(8) $\qquad R \leftarrow [NIL, \ldots, NIL]$ /* array of $\min(m, \sigma)$ pointers to elements of NE */
(9) $\qquad df \leftarrow 0$ /* number of symbols c s.t. $\mathcal{P}_S[c] \neq \mathcal{P}_T[c]$; $df = |NE|$ */
(10) $\qquad \mathcal{D} \leftarrow [0, \ldots, 0]$ /* vector of differences between $\mathcal{P}_S$ and $\mathcal{P}_T$ */
(11) $\qquad$ **for** $k \leftarrow i + 1$ **to** $m_1 + 1$ **do**
(12) $\qquad\qquad c \leftarrow s_{k-1}[1]$
(13) $\qquad\qquad equal \leftarrow (\mathcal{P}_S[c] = \mathcal{P}_T[c])$ /* true or false */
(14) $\qquad\qquad \mathcal{P}_S[c] \leftarrow \mathcal{P}_S[c] + |s_{k-1}|$
(15) $\qquad\qquad \mathcal{D}[c] \leftarrow \mathcal{D}[c] + |s_{k-1}|$
(16) $\qquad\qquad$ **if** $equal = true$ **then**   /* $\mathcal{P}_S[c] \neq \mathcal{P}_T[c]$ after line 14 */
(17) $\qquad\qquad\qquad df \leftarrow df + 1$; $\ p \leftarrow NE.append(c)$; $\ R[c] \leftarrow p$
(18) $\qquad\qquad$ **if** $equal = false$ **and** $\mathcal{P}_S[c] = \mathcal{P}_T[c]$ **then**
(19) $\qquad\qquad\qquad df \leftarrow df - 1$; $\ p \leftarrow R[c]$; $\ NE.delete(*p)$; $\ R[c] \leftarrow NIL$
(20) $\qquad\qquad$ **for** $j \leftarrow 1$ **to** m_2 **do**
(21) $\qquad\qquad\qquad \mathcal{P}_T \leftarrow [0, \ldots, 0]$ /* Parikh vector for the current span of T */
(22) $\qquad\qquad\qquad \mathcal{D} \leftarrow \mathcal{P}_S$
(23) $\qquad\qquad\qquad$ Update NE, R, df.   /* $O(\min(m, \sigma))$ time */
(24) $\qquad\qquad\qquad$ **for** $l \leftarrow j + 1$ **to** $m_2 + 1$ **do**
(25) $\qquad\qquad\qquad\qquad c \leftarrow t_{l-1}[1]$
(26) $\qquad\qquad\qquad\qquad equal \leftarrow (\mathcal{P}_T[c] = \mathcal{P}_S[c])$ /* true or false */
(27) $\qquad\qquad\qquad\qquad \mathcal{P}_T[c] \leftarrow \mathcal{P}_T[c] + |t_{l-1}|$
(28) $\qquad\qquad\qquad\qquad \mathcal{D}[c] \leftarrow \mathcal{D}[c] - |t_{l-1}|$
(29) $\qquad\qquad\qquad\qquad$ **if** $equal = true$ **then**   /* $\mathcal{P}_S[c] \neq \mathcal{P}_T[c]$ after line 27 */
(30) $\qquad\qquad\qquad\qquad\qquad df \leftarrow df + 1$; $\ p \leftarrow NE.append(c)$; $\ R[c] \leftarrow p$
(31) $\qquad\qquad\qquad\qquad$ **if** $equal = false$ **and** $\mathcal{P}_T[c] = \mathcal{P}_S[c]$ **then**
(32) $\qquad\qquad\qquad\qquad\qquad df \leftarrow df - 1$; $\ p \leftarrow R[c]$; $\ NE.delete(*p)$; $\ R[c] \leftarrow NIL$
(33) $\qquad\qquad\qquad\qquad$ **if** $df \leq 4$ **then**
(34) $\qquad\qquad\qquad\qquad\qquad$ Check if (possibly empty) substrings of s_i, s_{k-1}, t_j, t_{l-1}
$\qquad\qquad\qquad\qquad\qquad\qquad$ can be removed to have $df = 0$ (use NE first to find
$\qquad\qquad\qquad\qquad\qquad\qquad$ the mismatching symbols), update $maxlen$ if needed.
$\qquad\qquad\qquad\qquad\qquad\qquad$ /* $O(1)$ time */
(35) **return** $maxlen$

Fig. 1. Finding the length of an LCAF (the algorithm from Sect. 3.1)

NE (line 2), whose name stands for Non-Equal, is a doubly-linked list of symbols for which $\mathcal{P}_S$ and $\mathcal{P}_T$ differ. New elements will always be appended to this list (line 17), but we must also efficiently remove from it elements at arbitrary positions. This is made possible due to array R (line 8) of pointers to elements on list NE. Every time a symbol is appended to NE, the corresponding slot of R is written (line 17), and whenever we want to remove an element from NE, the pointer to it is read from R, which allows to update the list, and then the corresponding slot of R is set to NIL (line 19).

The key operations are in lines 33–34: if the current Parikh vectors differ for at most four symbols, we check if the boundary runs of the current spans of S and T can be truncated in such a way that the corresponding Parikh vectors will be equal; if there is more than one way to do it, the one which maximizes the intervals (that is, common Abelian factors) is chosen. All this can be done in $O(1)$ time, making use of the NE list and simple arithmetics. Note that for clarity the algorithm in Fig. 1 returns only the length of a longest common Abelian factor, without the start positions of the two matching factors. Adding the start positions is trivial, without compromising the time complexity.

The presented algorithm works in $O(n + m \log m + m^4) = O(n + m^4)$ time.

It is also very simple to find *all* longest common Abelian factors. We first run the code from Fig. 1, to find $maxlen$, and then basically run the procedure again, but now maintaining a list of common Abelian factors of length $maxlen$. In this way the time becomes $O(n + m^4 + occ)$, where occ is the output size. Since however $occ \leq n$, the actual time complexity is unchanged.

3.2   LCAF in (Essentially) $O(n^{3/2}\sigma\sqrt{m \log n})$ Time and $O(n\sigma)$ Space

The starting point for the algorithm from the current subsection is a simple technique from [2] with $O(\sigma n^2)$ time and $O(\sigma n)$ space. It is based on a generalized suffix tree (GST), capable to find the LCF for a pair of strings of length n in $O(n)$ time [3]. In [2, Sect. 3] this algorithm was used n times, for each factor length ℓ, replacing each ℓ-length factor by its Parikh vector followed with a unique terminator, to prevent matches longer than σ. If there exists an LCF of length exactly σ, it must correspond to a pair of factors, one from S and one from T, of length ℓ. This takes $O(\sigma n)$ time for one value of ℓ, and requires $O(\sigma n)$ space, hence the promised overall time and space complexities (we build and discard the generalized suffix trees one at a time).

Let us now refine this technique for RLE-compressible strings. We use a parameter k, whose value will be settled later. We are going to process sampled values of ℓ, namely, $\ell = 1, 1+k, 1+2k, 1+3k, \ldots$. For a given ℓ, all lengths from $[\ell \ldots \ell + k - 1]$ will be handled.

To this end, in a pass, we consider all factors from $S\#T$ of length ℓ, but in the leaves of the resulting GST, which are terminators, we also store extra data telling if the corresponding factor is followed by at least k identical symbols (and if so, this symbol is also stored). Assume now that the answer is positive. If the GST can find an LCF (in the Parikh vector domain) of length exactly σ and both respective strings (one from S, the other from T) are followed by a run of at least k copies of some symbol c, then we have a match of length $\ell + k$. All this takes (for one particular value of ℓ) $O(n\sigma)$ time and $O(n\sigma)$ space.

If this is not the case, however, we must somehow handle the factors which are not followed by a run of at least k identical symbols. Clearly, there are at most km such factors (for a given ℓ). First we notice that we can compute their Parikh vectors in $O(\sigma)$ time each after an $O(n\sigma)$ time and space preprocessing (this is done once for all values of ℓ). To this end, we calculate (in an incremental manner) the Parikh vectors for all the prefixes of $S\#T$. Then, for a given factor of $S\#T$, we subtract two Parikh vectors element-wise. Now, we find the LCAF among the candidates. We sort the (at most) km Parikh vectors, in $O(\sigma km \log(km))$ time, e.g. via heap sort. Then, in $O(\sigma km)$ time we check if there is at least one pair of equal Parikh vectors and if so, we have a candidate for the LCAF. We repeat the same procedure k times, each time appending one symbol to all considered factors, i.e., updating the corresponding Parikh vectors. All this takes $O(k^2 \sigma m \log(km))$ time.

Let us now estimate the overall time, for all n/k values of ℓ. The time is $O(n\sigma + (n/k)(n\sigma + k^2 \sigma m \log(km))) = O(n\sigma + n^2\sigma/k + kn\sigma m \log(km))$. This is minimized for $k = \sqrt{n/(m \log n)}$, provided that $m = O(n/\log n)$. For the case of $m = \omega(n/\log n)$ we set k to 1. This gives $O(n^{3/2}\sigma\sqrt{m \log n})$ time for $m = O(n/\log n)$ and $O(n\sigma m \log m)$ time for $m = \omega(n/\log n)$. The required space is $O(n\sigma)$.

Let us compare this result to existing ones. For example, for $m = \Omega(n^{0.4286+\varepsilon})$ and $m = O(n^{1-\varepsilon})$, for any $0 < \varepsilon < 0.5714$, and the alphabet size polylogarithmic in n, this algorithm dominates over the solution from [5, Sect. 5] and the algorithm from the previous subsection, not to say about $\Omega(n^2)$-time algorithms not working in terms of m, the size of the run-length encoding of the input strings.

References

1. Amir, A., Apostolico, A., Hirst, T., Landau, G.M., Lewenstein, N., Rozenberg, L.: Algorithms for jumbled indexing, jumbled border and jumbled square on run-length encoded strings. Theor. Comput. Sci. **656**, 146–159 (2016)
2. Badkobeh, G., Gagie, T., Grabowski, S., Nakashima, Y., Puglisi, S.J., Sugimoto, S.: Longest common Abelian factors and large alphabets. In: Inenaga, S., Sadakane, K., Sakai, T. (eds.) SPIRE 2016. LNCS, vol. 9954, pp. 254–259. Springer, Cham (2016). doi:10.1007/978-3-319-46049-9_24
3. Hui, L.C.K.: Color set size problem with applications to string matching. In: Proceedings of the 3rd Annual Symposium on Combinatorial Pattern Matching, pp. 230–243. LNCS 644 (1992)
4. Kociumaka, T., Radoszewski, J., Rytter, W.: Fast algorithms for abelian periods in words and greatest common divisor queries. J. Comput. Syst. Sci. **84**, 205–218 (2017)
5. Sugimoto, S., Noda, N., Inenaga, S., Bannai, H., Takeda, M.: Computing Abelian regularities on RLE strings. CoRR abs/1701.02836, accepted to IWOCA (2017)

Mining Bit-Parallel LCS-length Algorithms

Heikki Hyyrö[✉]

Faculty of Natural Sciences, University of Tampere, Tampere, Finland
heikki.hyyro@uta.fi

Abstract. Some of the most efficient algorithms for computing the length of a longest common subsequence (LLCS) between two strings are based on so-called "bit-parallelism". They achieve $O(\lceil m/w \rceil n)$ time, where m and n are the string lengths and w is the computer word size. The first such algorithm was presented by Allison and Dix [3] and performs 6 bit-vector operations per step. The number of operations per step has later been improved to 5 by Crochemore et al. [5] and to 4 by Hyyrö [6]. In this short paper we explore whether further improvement is possible. We find that under fairly reasonable assumptions, the LLCS problem requires at least 4 bit-vector operations per step. As a byproduct we also present five new 4-operation bit-parallel LLCS algorithms.

1   Introduction

Let A and B be input strings of lengths m and n. Finding LLCS(A, B), the length of a longest common subsequence (LCS) between the strings A and B, is a classic and much studied problem in computer science. A fundamental $O(mn)$ dynamic programming solution was given by Wagner and Fischer [9], and this quadratic worst-case complexity cannot be improved by any algorithm that uses individual equal/nonequal comparisons between characters [2]. Furthermore a recent conjecture [1] claims that the LLCS problem requires at least $O(n^{2-\lambda})$ time for two strings of equal length $m = n$, for any choice of a constant $\lambda > 0$.

Numerous further LLCS algorithms have been proposed over the last few decades. Breaking the quadratic complexity bound has proven elusive, but significant practical improvements have been achieved. A comprehensive survey of LLCS algorithms by Bergroth et al. [4] found the algorithms of Kuo and Cross (KC) [7], Rick [8] and Wu et al. (WMMM) [10] to be the fastest in practice. This survey, however, did not include the already existing so-called "bit-parallel" algorithm of Allison and Dix [3]. The bit-parallel approach has been later found to be very practical. For example Hyyrö [6] reported that his improved bit-parallel algorithm (Hyy) dominates over KC. In order to explore this further, we performed a comparison between Hyy, KC, WMMM and basic dynamic programming (DP)[1]. We tested first with random strings of lengths $m = n = 50$ and then with random strings of lengths $m = n = 2000$. The alphabet size varied from

---

[1] The algorithm of Rick, as recommended in [4], was omitted as it was not competitive in our experiments. This was probably due to its high $O(\sigma m)$ preprocessing cost.

© Springer International Publishing AG 2017
G. Fici et al. (Eds.): SPIRE 2017, LNCS 10508, pp. 214–220, 2017.
DOI: 10.1007/978-3-319-67428-5_18

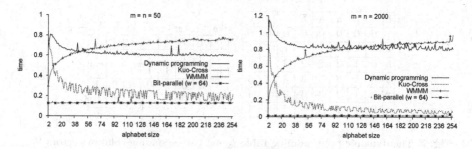

Fig. 1. LLCS algorithm tests with $m = n = 50$ (left) and $m = n = 2000$ (right).

2 to 256. The methods were implemented in C and compiled with GNU gcc using the -O3 switch. The test computer had 64-bit Ubuntu Linux 16.04, 16 GB RAM and a 2.3 GHz Intel i7-3651QM CPU. The results are shown in Fig. 1 and seem to confirm the very good performance of the bit-parallel approach.

The first bit-parallel LLCS algorithm by Allison and Dix performs 6 bit-vector operations per each character of B. Later Crochemore et al. [5] improved this to 5 and finally Hyyrö [6] to 4 operations per character, the latter being the most efficient currently known bit-parallel LLCS algorithm. In this paper we explore whether a bit-parallel algorithm that requires only 3 operations exists.

2   Preliminaries

We assume that strings consist of characters from an alphabet Σ with alphabet size σ. S_i denotes the ith character of S and $S_{i..j}$ denotes the substring of S that starts at the ith character and ends at the jth character. A string C is a subsequence of a string A if and only if A can be transformed into C by removing zero or more characters from A. C is a longest common subsequence (LCS) of strings A and B if it is both a subsequence of A and a subsequence of B, and no longer string with this property exists. We denote the unique length of an LCS between A and B by LLCS(A,B). For example LLCS("chart", "chatter") = 4, and both "chat" and "char" are corresponding LCSs of length 4.

The fundamental dynamic programming solution for LLCS computation uses Recurrence 1 to fill an $(m + 1) \times (n + 1)$ dynamic programming matrix L with values $L[i,j] = \text{LLCS}(A_{1..i}, B_{1..j})$. The following Observations 1 and 2 are well-known and easy to derive from Recurrence 1.

Recurrence 1. When $0 \leq i \leq m$ and $0 \leq j \leq n$:

$$L[i,0] = 0, \ L[0,j] = 0, \ \text{and} \ L[i,j] = \begin{cases} L[i-1,j-1] + 1, \text{ if } A_i = B_j. \\ \max(L[i-1,j], L[i,j-1]), \text{ otherwise.} \end{cases}$$

Observation 1. $L[i,j] \in \{L[i-1,j], L[i-1,j] + 1\}$.

Observation 2. *The values in a column j of L may be described by recording all rows $i \in 1, \ldots, m$ where $L[i,j] = L[i-1,j] + 1$.*

L		c	h	a	t	t	e	r
	0	0	0	0	0	0	0	0
c	0	1	1	1	1	1	1	1
h	0	1	2	2	2	2	2	2
a	0	1	2	3	3	3	3	3
r	0	1	2	3	3	3	3	4
t	0	1	2	3	4	4	4	4

V_0	V_1	V_2	V_3	V_4	V_5	V_6	V_7
0	1	1	1	1	1	1	1
0	0	1	1	1	1	1	1
0	0	0	1	1	1	1	1
0	0	0	0	0	0	0	1
0	0	0	0	1	1	1	0

Fig. 2. The dynamic programming table L and corresponding column vectors V_j.

We use the following notation with bit-vectors: '&' denotes bitwise "and", '|' denotes bitwise "or", '$\wedge$' denotes bitwise "xor", '$\sim$' denotes bit complementation, and '$<<$' and '$>>$' denote shifting the bit-vector left and right, respectively, using zero padding at both ends. The ith bit of the bit vector V is $V[i]$ and bit positions grow from right to left. For example the bits values of a bit-vector $V = 1011001$ are $V[1] = V[4] = V[5] = V[7] = 1$ and $V[2] = V[3] = V[6] = 0$.

Bit-parallel algorithms take advantage of the fact that digital computers perform operations on chunks of w bits, where w is the computer word size (in most recent computers $w = 64$). In case of LLCS computation, Observations 1 and 2 permit us to represent the m row values of column j of L by a length-m bit-vector V_j whose ith bit is 1 if and only if $L[i, j] = L[i-1, j]+1$. Now the actual value $L[m, j]$ is given by the sum $\sum_{k=1}^{m} V_j[k]$, and V_j fits into $\lceil m/w \rceil$ computer words. Figure 2 shows an example of a dynamic programming table L and its representation by V_j vectors. Clearly also other bit encodings are possible: we may e.g. define a complemented variant $V_j' = \sim V_j$, where the ith bit of V_j' is 0 if and only if $L[i, j] = L[i-1, j] + 1$. Note that the overall value LLCS(A, B) = $L[m, n]$ is given by the number of 1-bits in V_n (or the number of 0-bits in V_n'). The column vector V_j (or V_j') can be computed from the previous column vector V_{j-1} (or V_{j-1}') by a constant number of bit-vector operations. The computation requires knowledge of all rows i that have a match between the current column character $B[j]$ and the row character $A[i]$. This is facilitated by precomputing for each different character c a length-m match bit-vector $M[c]$ whose ith bit is 1 if and only if $A[i] = c$.

The 6-operation bit-parallel LLCS algorithm of Allison and Dix encodes the columns of L by V_j, and the 5-operation algorithm of Crochemore et al. and the 4-operation algorithm of Hyyrö use the complemented vectors V_j'. These three algorithms, together with the preprocessing of the match vectors $M[c]$, are described in Fig. 3. See the original articles [3,5,6] for details about the algorithms' logic. The algorithms run in $O(\lceil m/w \rceil n)$ time, as a bit-vector operation on length-m bit-vectors can be done in $O(\lceil m/w \rceil)$ time.

PreprocessM($A_{1...m}$)
1. **For** $c \in \Sigma$ **Do**
2. $\quad M[c] \leftarrow 0$
3. **For** $i \in 1 \ldots m$ **Do**
4. $\quad M[A_i] \leftarrow M[A_i] \mid (1 << (i-1))$

AD($A_{1...m}, B_{1...n}$)
1. $V_0 \leftarrow 0$
2. **For** $j \in 1 \ldots n$ **Do**
3. $\quad P \leftarrow M[B_j] \mid V_{j-1}$
4. $\quad V_j \leftarrow P \;\&\; ((P - ((V_{j-1} << 1) \mid 1)) \;^\wedge\; P)$
5. **Return countOnebits**(V_n)

CIPR($A_{1...m}, B_{1...n}$)
1. $V_0' \leftarrow \sim 0$
2. **For** $j \in 1 \ldots n$ **Do**
3. $\quad V_j' \leftarrow (V_{j-1}' + (V_{j-1}' \;\&\; M[B_j]))$
$\qquad\qquad \mid (V_{j-1}' \;\&\; (\sim M[B_j]))$
4. **Return countZerobits**(V_n')

Hyy($A_{1...m}, B_{1...n}$)
1. $V_0' \leftarrow \sim 0$
2. **For** $j \in 1 \ldots n$ **Do**
3. $\quad P \leftarrow M[B_j] \;\&\; V_{j-1}'$
4. $\quad V_j' \leftarrow (V_{j-1}' - P) \mid (V_{j-1}' + P)$
5. **Return countZerobits**(V_n')

Fig. 3. The bit-parallel LLCS algorithms of Allison and Dix (**AD**), Crochemore et al. (**CIPR**) and Hyyrö (**Hyy**). Also preprocessing of the M-vectors is shown.

3   A Lower Bound for the Bit-Vector Operations

Given the progress from 6 to 4 bit-vector operations, a natural question is whether further improvement to 3 operations is possible. In order to make this problem approachable, we make the following four fairly reasonable assumptions:

1. Generality: the algorithm must work with all bit-vector lengths w.
2. Input: a length-m bit-vector representing the increment positions in column $j - 1$ and a length-m bit vector representing the matching rows for B_j.
3. One-to-one correspondence between rows and bit-positions: each bit position in the bit-vectors corresponds to a certain row i.
4 Universality: the algorithm uses only commonly available operations.

These assumptions seem fairly reasonable as we in practice can afford to use only 1 bit per row: a scheme that uses k bits per row needs km/w computer words per column, and hence the number of operations should be less than $4/k$ in order to improve on the best current bit-parallel algorithm.

We tackled the problem by enumerating and testing all possible 3-operation bit-parallel algorithms that fulfill the preceding assumptions. This was feasible as the number of operations is so small. The enumeration proceeded roughly as follows and more or less corresponds to a 10-level deep nested for/while-loop:

1. Enumerate over all ways to select operands for 3 operations. Below the values C_1 and C_2 are constants (more than two would be redundant) and R_i refers to the result of the ith operation. Each operation selects operands as follows:
   - The 1st operation selects 2 operands from $\{V_{j-1}, C_1, C_2, M[c]\}$.
   - The 2nd operation selects 2 operands from $\{V_{j-1}, C_1, C_2, M[c], R_1\}$.
   - The 3rd operation selects 2 operands from $\{V_{j-1}, C_1, C_2, M[c], R_1, R_2\}$.

2. Under step 1, iterate over all permutations of $1, \ldots, w$, where each defines one possible mapping from bits to rows in the column and match vectors: which bit position corresponds to which row.
3. Under step 2, iterate over all 2^w length-w bit vectors, where each defines one possible set of bit roles for the column vectors: the ith bit defines whether an increment $L[i,j] = L[i-1,j] + 1$ is recorded as a 1 or 0 bit.
4. Under step 3, iterate over all 2^w length-w bit vectors, where each defines one possible set of bit roles for the match vectors: the ith bit defines whether a match $A[i] = c$ is recorded into $M[c]$ as a 1 or 0 bit.
5. Under step 4, iterate over all possible constant values (i.e. all 2^w possible values for C_1 and C_2, independent of each other).
6. Under step 5, iterate over all possible ways to select 3 operations out of the set of permitted operations.
   (a) For each selection of 3 operations, check whether the formula is correct by checking if the formula produces correct result (into R_3) with all inputs (combinations of previous column vector and current match vector).
      i. The result is verified by comparing R_3 with the result of basic dynamic programming (permuting the row positions and inverting bit values where necessary).

Although this exceeds the typical assumptions of bit-parallel algorithms, the search allowed each operation to be (1) any of the 16 possible binary logical operations, (2) an arithmetic operator $+$, $-$, $*$ or $/$, or (3) a left or right shift that uses either 1-bits or the left/rightmost bit for padding (allowed shift lengths are $1, \ldots, w-1$). Note that 0-padding shifts are expressed by multiplication and division (with one of the constants, such as C_1, specifying the multiplier).

We ran the exhaustive search using a fixed small length $w = 4$. The computation took roughly 50 min and was unable to find a working 3-operation formula. This provides support for a claim that the existing 4-operation bit-parallel LLCS algorithm is optimal within the constraints described before. In order to gain confidence in the correctness of the procedure, we modified the implementation to do an exhaustive search over all 4-operation combinations. As this would have otherwise taken too much time, the 4-operation test was restricted to consider only two linear mappings from bits to rows: the basic order, where the ith bit corresponds to row i, and a reverse order, where the ith bit corresponds to the row $m - i + 1$. The other parts of the implementations were left intact. The 4-operation run took roughly 1 h and found dozens of correct 4-operation algorithms. Many of these used non-standard logical bit-vector operations, but a total of 6 essentially different algorithms used only the universally supported C-style arithmetic and logical operations. One of these was the algorithm Hyy of Hyyrö [6] and the rest were new. We note that the search also found the CIPR algorithm of Crochemore et al. [5], as that algorithm makes only 4 operations when the non-standard logical "X and not Y"-operation counts as one operation. Finding these formulas provides some further confidence that the search procedure works correctly.

Figure 4 shows the five new 4-operation bit-parallel LLCS algorithms. All use the natural top-down mapping between bits and rows, where the ith bit corresponds to row i, and uniform bit roles (the meaning of 0 and 1 bits is the same in all rows of the same vector). Some use complemented match vectors: we define $M'[c]$ as a match vector whose ith bit is 0 if and only if $A[i] = c$. The names 11a, 11b, 10, 00a and 00b reflect the bit roles. The first letter is 1 if the algorithm uses M and 0 if it uses the complemented M' match vectors, respectively. The second letter is 1 if the algorithm uses the V_j and 0 if it uses the complemented V'_j column vectors. According to our preliminary experiments, all these 4-operation variants have virtually identical practical performance.

11a$(A_{1...m}, B_{1...n})$
1. $V_0 \leftarrow 0$
2. **For** $j \in 1 \ldots n$ **Do**
3. $\quad P \leftarrow M[B_j] \mid V_{j-1}$
4. $\quad V_j \leftarrow P \mathbin{\&} (V_{j-1} + V_{j-1} - P)$
5. **Return countOnebits**(V_n)

11b$(A_{1...m}, B_{1...n})$
1. $V_0 \leftarrow 0$
2. **For** $j \in 1 \ldots n$ **Do**
3. $\quad P \leftarrow M[B_j] \mid V_{j-1}$
4. $\quad V_j \leftarrow P \mathbin{\&} (V_{j-1} - (V_{j-1} \mathbin{\wedge} P))$
5. **Return countOnebits**(V_n)

10$(A_{1...m}, B_{1...n})$
1. $V'_0 \leftarrow \sim 0$
2. **For** $j \in 1 \ldots n$ **Do**
3. $\quad P \leftarrow M[B_j] \mathbin{\&} V'_{j-1}$
4. $\quad V'_j \leftarrow (V'_{j-1} \mathbin{\wedge} P) \mid (V'_{j-1} + P)$
5. **Return countZerobits**(V'_n)

PreprocessM'$(A_{1...m})$
1. **For** $c \in \Sigma$ **Do**
2. $\quad M'[c] \leftarrow \sim 0$
3. **For** $i \in 1 \ldots m$ **Do**
4. $\quad M'[A_i] \leftarrow M'[A_i] \mathbin{\&} \sim (1 << (i-1))$

00a$(A_{1...m}, B_{1...n})$
1. $V'_0 \leftarrow \sim 0$
2. **For** $j \in 1 \ldots n$ **Do**
3. $\quad P \leftarrow M'[B_j] \mathbin{\&} V'_{j-1}$
4. $\quad V'_j \leftarrow P \mid (V'_{j-1} + V'_{j-1} - P)$
5. **Return countZerobits**(V'_n)

00b$(A_{1...m}, B_{1...n})$
1. $V'_0 \leftarrow \sim 0$
2. **For** $j \in 1 \ldots n$ **Do**
3. $\quad P \leftarrow M'[B_j] \mathbin{\&} V'_{j-1}$
4. $\quad V'_j \leftarrow P \mid (V'_{j-1} + (V'_{j-1} \mathbin{\wedge} P))$
5. **Return countZerobits**(V'_n)

Fig. 4. The five new 4-operation bit-parallel LLCS algorithms found by our exhaustive search. Also preprocessing the complemented M'-vectors is shown.

References

1. Abboud, A., Backurs, A., Williams, V.V.: Tight hardness results for LCS and other sequence similarity measures. In: Proceedings of 56th Annual IEEE Symposium on Foundations of Computer Science, pp. 59–78 (2015)
2. Aho, A.V., Hirschberg, D.S., Ullman, J.D.: Bounds on the complexity of the longest common subsequence problem. J. ACM **23**(1), 1–12 (1976)
3. Allison, L., Dix, T.L.: A bit-string longest common subsequence algorithm. Inf. Process. Lett. **23**, 305–310 (1986)
4. Bergroth, L., Hakonen, H., Raita, T.: A survey of longest common subsequence algorithms. In: Proceedings of 7th International Symposium on String Processing and Information Retrieval, pp. 39–48 (2000)

5. Crochemore, M., Iliopoulos, C.S., Pinzon, Y.J., Reid, J.F.: A fast and practical bit-vector algorithm for the longest common subsequence problem. Inf. Process. Lett. **80**, 279–285 (2001)
6. Hyyrö, H.: Bit-parallel LCS-length computation revisited. In: Proceedings of 15th Australasian Workshop on Combinatorial Algorithms, pp. 16–27 (2004)
7. Kuo, S., Cross, G.R.: An improved algorithm to find the length of the longest common subsequence of two strings. ACM SIGIR Forum **23**(3–4), 89–99 (1989)
8. Rick, C.: A new flexible algorithm for the longest common subsequence problem. In: Galil, Z., Ukkonen, E. (eds.) CPM 1995. LNCS, vol. 937, pp. 340–351. Springer, Heidelberg (1995). doi:10.1007/3-540-60044-2_53
9. Wagner, R.A., Fischer, M.J.: The string-to-string correction problem. J. ACM **21**(1), 168–173 (1974)
10. Wu, S., Manber, U., Myers, G., Miller, W.: An $O(NP)$ sequence comparison algorithm. Inf. Process. Lett. **35**, 317–323 (1990)

Practical Implementation of Space-Efficient Dynamic Keyword Dictionaries

Shunsuke Kanda[1,2(✉)] ⓘD, Kazuhiro Morita[1], and Masao Fuketa[1]

[1] Graduate School of Advanced Technology and Science, Tokushima University,
Minamijosanjima 2-1, Tokushima 770-8506, Japan
shnsk.knd@gmail.com,
{kam,fuketa}@is.tokushima-u.ac.jp
[2] Japan Society for the Promotion of Science, Tokyo, Japan

Abstract. A keyword dictionary is an associative array with string keys. Although it is a classical data structure, recent applications require the management of massive string data using the keyword dictionary in main memory. Therefore, its space-efficient implementation is very important. If limited to static applications, there are a number of very compact dictionary implementations; however, existing dynamic implementations consume much larger space than static ones. In this paper, we propose a new practical implementation of space-efficient dynamic keyword dictionaries. Our implementation uses path decomposition, which is proposed for constructing cache-friendly trie structures, for dynamic construction in compact space with a different approach. Using experiments on real-world datasets, we show that our implementation can construct keyword dictionaries in spaces up to 2.8x smaller than the most compact existing dynamic implementation.

Keywords: Keyword dictionaries · Compact data structures · Tries · Path decomposition

1 Introduction

In modern computer science, managing massive string data in main memory is a fundamental problem. Many researchers have investigated space-efficient data structures for string processing. In this paper, we focus on the practical implementation of *keyword dictionaries* that are an associative array with string keys. Although the keyword dictionary is a classical data structure used in natural language processing and information retrieval, many recent applications require space-efficient implementations to store large string datasets, as reported in [16]. For example, Mavlyutov et al. [17] considered URIs of 14 GB for RDF data management systems.

As for static keyword dictionaries, very compact implementations have been proposed recently. For example, Martínez-Prieto et al. [16] proposed and practically evaluated compact implementations using some techniques. Grossi and Ottaviano [8] proposed a cache-friendly compact implementation using an

© Springer International Publishing AG 2017
G. Fici et al. (Eds.): SPIRE 2017, LNCS 10508, pp. 221–233, 2017.
DOI: 10.1007/978-3-319-67428-5_19

ordered labeled tree structure known as a *trie* [14]. For the implementations, Kanda et al. [13] empirically evaluated some compression strategies. Also, Kanda et al. [12] proposed a fast and compact implementation using an improved double-array trie. While those implementations can store large datasets in compact space, their applications are limited because key insertion and deletion are not supported.

As for dynamic keyword dictionaries, there are some space-efficient implementations such as the HAT-trie [1], adaptive radix tree (ART) [15], Judy [3], and Cedar [22]. While those implementations attempt to improve the space efficiency by reducing pointer overheads, they still consume much larger space than the static implementations. For example, to store a geographic name dataset, the HAT-trie uses space 7.2x larger than the static implementation by Grossi and Ottaviano [8], from the experimental results in this paper and [12]. On the other hand, a number of practical compact dynamic trie representations have been presented. Darragh et al. [5] proposed the *Bonsai* tree, which is a compact hash-based trie representation. Recently, Poyias and Raman [19] improved the Bonsai tree, namely, *m-Bonsai*. The m-Bonsai tree can represent a trie in asymptotically information-theoretically optimal space while supporting basic tree operations in constant expected time. Takagi et al. [20] also proposed an efficient data structure for online string processing. However, there has been no discussion or evaluation about keyword dictionary implementation. Therefore, we must address the engineering of more space-efficient implementations.

In this paper, we propose a new implementation of space-efficient dynamic keyword dictionaries. Our implementation is based on a trie formed by *path decomposition* [6], which is a trie transformation technique. The path decomposition was proposed for constructing cache-friendly trie structures and was utilized in static applications [8,11]; however, we use it for dynamic dictionary construction with a different approach. We implement space-efficient dictionaries by applying the m-Bonsai representation to this approach. From experiments using read-world datasets considering various applications, we show that our implementation is much more compact than existing dynamic implementations.

2   Preliminaries

2.1   Basic Notations and Definitions

A sequence A with n entries, $A[0]A[1]\ldots A[n-1]$, is denoted by $A[0,n)$. For a sequence $A[0,n)$, $|A|$ denotes the length n. A *keyword* is a byte character string that always has a special terminator drawn by \$, that is, $\$ \notin w[0, n-1)$ and $w[n-1] = \$$ for a keyword $w[0,n)$. The base of the logarithm is 2 throughout this paper.

2.2   Path Decomposition

A trie [14] is an ordered labeled tree to store a set of strings, and is constructed by merging common prefixes. Path decomposition [6] is a technique that transforms the trie as follows. It first chooses a root-to-leaf path in the original trie, and then associates the path with a root of the new trie. Children of the new root are recursively defined as the roots of new subtries corresponding to original subtries hanging off the path.

The existing purpose of path decomposition is to reduce the number of node-to-node traversals by lowering the height of the resulting tree. Although the height depends on a strategy of choosing a path, any strategy can guarantee that the height is not greater than that of the *Patricia tree* [18]; therefore, some improvement in cache efficiency can be expected for all strategies. The following fact is important for our data structure:

Fact 1. Each node of a path-decomposed trie corresponds to some node-to-leaf path of the original trie; therefore, the number of path-decomposed trie nodes is the same as that of registered keywords because the original trie has the same number of leaf nodes owing to the special keyword terminator.

2.3 m-Bonsai

The m-Bonsai tree [19] is a compact dynamic trie representation that defines nodes on hash table Q with m slots using open addressing. Let n denote the number of trie nodes. We refer to $\alpha = n/m$ $(0 \leq \alpha \leq 1)$ as a *load factor*. We assume that n and m are pre-given. As each node is located at some slot, we denote node IDs using slot addresses. That is, a node with ID v (or node v) is located on $Q[v]$. Defining a new child from node v with symbol c is implemented in three steps, assuming that the alphabet size of symbols is σ. The first step creates a hash key $\langle v, c \rangle$ of the child. The second step obtains an *initial address* of the child, $u = h(\langle v, c \rangle)$, where h is a hush function such that $h : \{0, \ldots, m \cdot \sigma - 1\} \to \{0, \ldots, m - 1\}$. The third step locates the child on $Q[u']$, where u' is the first empty slot address from the initial address u using linear probing. In other words, the new child ID is defined as u'.

If we simply store the hash key $\langle v, c \rangle$ in $Q[u']$ to check for membership, each slot uses large space of $\lceil \log(m \cdot \sigma) \rceil$ bits. To reduce this space to $\lceil \log \sigma \rceil$ bits, m-Bonsai uses the *quotienting* technique [14, Exercise 6.13], while additionally introducing *displacement array* D such that $D[u']$ stores the distance of u' and u, that is, the number of collisions. The displacement array D can be represented in compact space since the average value is small from [19, Proposition 1].

Practical Implementation. Although Poyias and Raman [19] proposed two types of displacement array representation, we adopt a simply modified version of the practical one. In our representation, we first try to store values of D in an array D_0 with each entry using Δ_0 bits. If $D[i] < 2^{\Delta_0} - 1$, we set $D_0[i] = D[i]$. Otherwise, we set $D_0[i] = 2^{\Delta_0} - 1$ and store $D[i]$ to an auxiliary associative array implemented using a standard data structure. The original representation uses a small hash table based on the original Bonsai method as an additional second data structure; however, our version omits the hash table because it is difficult to estimate the predefined length of the table when adopted for our implementation. From preliminary experiments, we obtained the best parameter $\Delta_0 = 6$ for $\alpha = 0.8$. We provide the details and source code at https://github.com/kamp78/bonsais.

3 New Implementation

This section presents a new dynamic keyword dictionary implementation through path decomposition, namely, the *dynamic path-decomposed trie (DynPDT)*.

3.1 Basic Idea: Incremental Path Decomposition

We present a basic idea called *incremental path decomposition*. This idea constructs a path-decomposed trie by incrementally defining nodes corresponding to each keyword in insertion order. We show the data structure of the path-decomposed trie while describing the insertion procedure for a keyword w as follows:

- If the dictionary is empty, a root labeled with w is defined. In this paper, we denote such a label on node v by L_v.
- If the dictionary is not empty, a keyword search is started from the root with two steps by setting v to the root ID. The first step compares w with L_v. If $w = L_v$, the procedure terminates because the keyword is already registered; otherwise, the second step finds a child with symbol $\langle i, w[i] \rangle$ such that $w[i] \neq L_v[i]$ and $w[0, i) = L_v[0, i)$. If not found, the keyword is inserted by adding a new edge labeled with the symbol $\langle i, w[i] \rangle$ and a new child labeled with the remaining suffix $w[i+1, |w|)$. If found, the procedure returns to the first step after updating v to the child ID and w to the remaining suffix.

That is to say, the path-decomposed trie has node labels representing some suffixes of keywords. Additionally, it has edge labels composed of a node label position and a byte character. A keyword search is also performed by that procedure. The feature of the incremental path decomposition is to locate nodes corresponding to early inserted keywords near the root. In other words, the search cost for such keywords is low. However, Sect. 4 evaluates the performance of DynPDT for random-ordered keywords without considering the feature.

3.2 Implementation with m-Bonsai

To obtain high space efficiency, DynPDT represents the path-decomposed trie using m-Bonsai; however, this representation has the following problem. As the edge label is a pair $\langle i, c \rangle$ composed of node label position i and byte character c, the edge labels are drawn from an alphabet of size $\sigma = 256 \cdot \Lambda$, where Λ denotes the maximum length of the node labels. The m-Bonsai representation requires the fixing of the σ parameter to predefine the allocation size of each Q slot and the hash function, but Λ, or σ, is an unfixed parameter in dynamic applications registering unknown keywords.

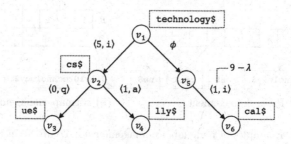

Fig. 1. Example of DynPDT when $\lambda = 8$.

To solve this problem, we forcibly fix the alphabet size as $\sigma = 256 \cdot \lambda$ by introducing a new parameter λ. If position i on L_v is greater than or equal to λ, we create virtual nodes called *step nodes* with a special symbol ϕ by repeating to add child u from node v with symbol ϕ, to set v to u, and to decrement i by λ, until $i < \lambda$. This solution creates additional step nodes depending on λ. When λ is too small, many step nodes are created. When λ is too large, the space usage of Q becomes large because each slot uses $\lceil \log(256 \cdot \lambda) \rceil$ bits. Therefore, it is necessary to define a proper λ. Section 4.1 shows such parameters obtained from experiments using read-world datasets.

Examples. Fig. 1 shows an example of DynPDT constructed by inserting keywords `technology$`, `technics$`, `technique$`, `technically$`, and `technological$` in this order, setting $\lambda = 8$. The nodes are defined in order of $v_1, v_2, \ldots, v_6$. We show how to search `technically$` using the example. First, we set w to the query keyword and compare w with L_{v_1}. As $w[0,5) = L_{v_1}[0,5) =$ `techn`, we move to v_2 using symbol $\langle 5, w[5] \rangle = \langle 5, \text{i} \rangle$ and update w to the remaining suffix `cally$`. Next, we compare w with L_{v_2}. As $w[0,1) = L_{v_2}[0,1) =$ `c`, we move to v_4 using symbol $\langle 1, w[1] \rangle = \langle 1, \text{a} \rangle$ and update w to the remaining suffix `lly$`. Finally, we can see that the query keyword is registered from $w = L_{v_4}$.

We also show how to search `technological$`. In the same manner as above, we set w to the query keyword and compare w with L_{v_1}. The result is $w[0,9) = L_{v_1}[0,9) =$ `technolog`, but we cannot create symbol $\langle 9, \text{i} \rangle$ because this symbol exceeds the alphabet size from $\lambda \le 9$. Therefore, we move to step node v_5 using symbol ϕ. From $9 - \lambda < \lambda$, i.e., $1 < \lambda$, we can create symbol $\langle 1, \text{i} \rangle$ and move to node v_6 using the symbol. Finally, we can see that the query keyword is registered because the remaining suffix `cal$` is the same as L_{v_6}.

Implementation Remarks. Arbitrary values associated with each keyword can be maintained using the space of each node label. Keyword deletion can be simply implemented by introducing flags for each node (i.e., for each keyword) in a manner similar to open address hashing.

To use the m-Bonsai representation, it is necessary to predefine the number of Q slots depending on the number of nodes and the load factor. In other words, it is necessary to estimate the number of nodes expected for a dataset. Fortunately,

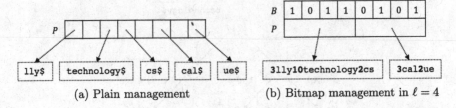

(a) Plain management   (b) Bitmap management in $\ell = 4$

Fig. 2. Examples of node label management for DynPDT in Fig. 1.

we can roughly estimate the number of nodes of DynPDT easier than a plain trie because this is the same as the number of keywords (from Fact 1) and some step nodes depending on a proper λ.

3.3   Node Label Management

The node labels are stored separately from the m-Bonsai structure (i.e., the hash table and the displacement array) because these labels are variable-length strings. The plainest implementation uses pointer array P of length m such that $P[i]$ stores a pointer to L_i. This implementation can perform to access and append a node label in constant time, but it uses large space with m pointers. We call this implementation *plain management*. Figure 2a shows an example of plain management.

We present an alternative compact implementation that reduces the pointer overhead in a manner similar to *sparsetable* of Google Sparse Hash at https://github.com/sparsehash/sparsehash. This implementation divides node labels into *groups* of ℓ labels over the IDs. That is, the first group consists of $L_0 \ldots L_{\ell-1}$, the second group consists of $L_\ell \ldots L_{2\ell-1}$, and so on. Moreover, we introduce bitmap B such that $B[i] = 1$ if L_i exists. The implementation concatenates node labels L_i such that $B[i] = 1$ in each group, while keeping the ID order. The length of P becomes $\lceil m/\ell \rceil$ by maintaining pointers to the concatenated label strings for each group. We call this implementation *bitmap management*.

Using array P and bitmap B, accessing L_i is performed as follows. If $B[i] = 0$, L_i does not exist; otherwise, we obtain the target concatenated label string from $P[g]$, where $g = \lfloor i/\ell \rfloor$. We also obtain bit chunk $B_g = B[g \cdot \ell, (g+1) \cdot \ell)$ over the target group. Let j be the number of occurrences of 1s in $B_g[0, i \bmod \ell + 1)$. L_i is the j-th node label of the concatenated label string. As ℓ is constant, counting the bit occurrences in chunk B_g is supported in constant time using the *popcount* operation [7]. Therefore, the access time is the same as the time of scanning the concatenated label string until the j-th node label.

By simply concatenating node labels (e.g., the second group in Fig. 2a is cal\$ue\$ in $\ell = 4$), the scan is performed by sequentially counting terminators in $O(\ell \cdot \Lambda)$ time, where Λ again denotes the maximum length of the node labels. We shorten the scan time using the *skipping* technique used in *array hashing* [2]. This technique puts its length in front of each node label using *VByte* encoding [21].

Note that we can omit the terminators of each node label. The skipping technique allows us to jump ahead to the start of the next node label; therefore, the scan is supported in $O(\ell)$ time. Figure 2b shows an example of the bitmap management with the skipping technique.

Comparison of Space Usage. We compare plain and bitmap management in terms of space usage, assuming a 64-bit memory address architecture. In plain management, the pointer array P uses $64m$ bits. The space usage of storing node labels is $8N$ bits, where N denotes the total length, i.e., $N = \sum_{i<m} |L_i|$. In bitmap management, the pointer array P uses $64\lceil m/\ell \rceil$ bits, and the bitmap B uses m bits. The total length of the node labels using VByte encoding becomes equal to N if all node labels are shorter than 128 because such a code length is 1 byte. Fortunately, almost 100% of the node labels were shorter than 128 in all datasets in Sect. 4. Therefore, the VByte encoding does not become a significant overhead.

For simplicity, we assume that there are no overheads related to the VByte encoding and memory allocation. The overall space usage of plain management is $64m + 8N$ bits. The overall space usage of bitmap management is $64\lceil m/\ell \rceil + m + 8N$ bits. That is, in roughly $\ell > 1.02$, the space usage of bitmap management is smaller than that of plain management. Moreover, bitmap management works more efficiently when N is small because the pointer overhead of $64m$ bits becomes relatively large over $8N$ bits in plain management.

4   Experimental Evaluation

This section analyzes the practical performance of DynPDT. The source code of our implementation is available at https://github.com/kamp78/dynpdt.

4.1   Settings

We carried out experiments on an Intel Xeon E5540 @2.53 GHz with 32 GB of RAM (L2 cache: 1 MB, L3 cache: 8 MB), running Ubuntu Server 16.04 LTS. The data structures were implemented in C++ and compiled using g++ (version 5.4.0) with optimization -O9. We used `/proc/<PID>/statm` to measure the resident set size. We used `std::chrono::duration_cast` to measure the runtimes of operations.

Datasets. We selected six real-world datasets:

Geonames is composed of geographic names in the *asciiname* column of the GeoNames dump, available at http://download.geonames.org/export/dump/.

Wiki is page titles of English Wikipedia in February 2015, available at https://dumps.wikimedia.org/enwiki/.

UK is URLs obtained from a 2005 crawl of the .uk domain performed by Ubi-Crawler [4], available at http://law.di.unimi.it/webdata/uk-2005/.

Table 1. Information concerning datasets.

Dataset	Size	Keywords	Nodes	NPK	BPK	BPNL
Geonames	101.2	6,784,722	48,240,884	7.1	15.6	10.1
Wiki	227.2	11,519,354	110,962,030	9.6	20.7	12.6
UK	2,723.3	39,459,925	748,571,709	19.0	72.4	22.0
WebBase	6,782.1	118,142,155	1,426,314,849	12.1	60.2	15.1
LUBM	3,194.1	52,616,588	247,740,552	4.7	63.7	7.7
DNA	189.3	15,265,943	36,223,473	2.4	13.0	5.4

WebBase is URLs of a 2001 crawl performed by the WebBase crawler [10], available at http://law.di.unimi.it/webdata/webbase-2001/.

LUBM is URIs extracted from the dataset generated by the Lehigh University Benchmark [9] for 1,600 universities, from DS5 available at https://exascale. info/projects/web-of-data-uri/.

DNA is substrings of 12 characters found in the DNA dataset from Pizza&Chili corpus, available at http://pizzachili.dcc.uchile.cl/texts/dna/.

Table 1 summarizes relevant statistics for each dataset, where *Size* is the total length of keywords in MiB, *Keywords* is the number of distinct keywords, *Nodes* is the number of nodes in a plain trie, *NPK* is the average number of plain trie nodes per keyword, *BPK* is the average number of bytes per keyword, and *BPNL* is the average number of bytes per node label in DynPDT.

Dictionary Data Structures. We compared the performance of DynPDT with that of m-Bonsai. For DynPDT, we tested plain and bitmap management denoted by *Plain* and *Bitmap-ℓ*, respectively. For Bitmap-ℓ, we considered that ℓ is 8, 16, 32, and 64. We set the `int` data type to associated values in DynPDT. We tested m-Bonsai based on a plain trie without maintaining associated values. For both DynPDT and m-Bonsai, we implemented the auxiliary associative array using `std::map`.

We also compared some existing dynamic dictionary implementations. We selected five space-efficient ones as follows: *Sparsehash* is Google Sparse Hash that is an associative array with keys and values of arbitrary data types, *Judy* is a trie implementation developed at Hewlett-Packard Research Labs [3], *HAT-trie* is a keyword dictionary implementation with the combination of a trie and a cache-conscious hash table [1], *ART* is a trie implementation designed for efficient main-memory database systems [15], and *Cedar* is a state-of-the-art double-array prefix trie implementation [22]. In common with DynPDT, we set the `int` data type to associated values. For HAT-trie and ART, we used the implementations available at https://github.com/dcjones/hat-trie and https:// github.com/armon/libart, respectively. As Cedar uses 32-bit integers to represent trie nodes, we could not run the test on WebBase.

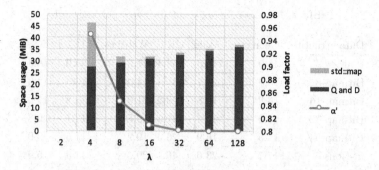

Fig. 3. Result of parameter test for λ on Wiki.

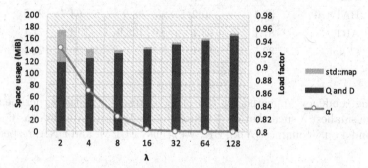

Fig. 4. Result of parameter test for λ on LUBM.

Parameters. Both DynPDT and m-Bonsai have two parameters α and Δ_0. We set $\alpha = 0.8$ in common with previous settings [5,19]. We set the number of Q slots to that of keywords divided by 0.8 in DynPDT. Note that the resulting load factor α' in DynPDT is increased from α, depending on the number of step nodes. In m-Bonsai, we set the number of Q slots to that of plain trie nodes divided by 0.8. Note that the difference of the number of Q slots between DynPDT and m-Bonsai closes with decreasing NPK. We set $\Delta_0 = 6$ from the preliminary experiments in Sect. 2.3.

DynPDT also has parameter λ, which involves α' and the space usage of hash table Q and the auxiliary associative array. When λ is large, the allocation size of Q becomes large. When λ is small, the number of step nodes, or α', is increased. The latter poses slow operations and a large auxiliary associative array because the average value of D is increased. To search a proper λ, we pretested $\lambda = 2^x$ in $2 \leq x \leq 7$ for each dataset. Figures 3 and 4 show the results on Wiki and LUBM, respectively. The figures show the sum space usage of Q, D, and the auxiliary std::map. The parameter α' is also shown. We could not construct the dictionary for $\lambda = 2$ on Wiki because α' became too large. From the results, α' closes 0.8, and the space usage is moderately increased from some λ.

Table 2. Results of space usage in bytes per keyword.

Data structure	Geonames	Wiki	UK	WebBase	LUBM	DNA
Plain	46.0	46.6	54.4	47.5	45.0	44.8
Bitmap-8	18.7	21.2	31.3	24.0	15.5	13.0
Bitmap-16	16.8	18.8	28.2	21.0	13.8	11.0
Bitmap-32	15.0	17.4	27.1	19.8	12.1	9.8
Bitmap-64	14.5	16.9	26.4	19.2	11.5	9.0
m-Bonsai	17.7	23.6	46.1	29.3	11.4	5.9
Sparsehash	62.3	71.1	131.0	119.0	122.0	43.4
Judy	47.6	50.5	60.3	53.5	33.9	24.3
HAT-trie	35.4	40.2	82.3	68.9	64.7	28.9
ART	87.1	93.1	140.9	126.9	118.9	71.1
Cedar	30.5	41.1	58.4	–	29.7	22.1

The same tendency appeared for the other datasets.[1] In the experiments, we chose the smallest λ such that $\alpha' \leq 0.81$ for each dataset. We set λ to 16, 16, 64, 32, 16, and 4 on Geonames, Wiki, UK, WebBase, LUBM, and DNA, respectively.

4.2   Results

We constructed the dictionaries by inserting keywords in random order. We measured the resident set size required for the construction. We measured the insertion and search runtimes without I/O overheads. The insertion time was averaged on 3 runs. To measure the search time, we chose 1 million random keywords from each dataset. The search time was averaged on 10 runs.

Space Usage. Table 2 shows the results. It is obvious that bitmap management can reduce the pointer overhead of plain management. Bitmap-64 is up to 5x smaller than Plain on DNA. When BPNL is small, the compression rate is high based on the comparison analysis in Sect. 3.3. Compared with m-Bonsai, Bitmap-64 is 1.2–1.7x smaller except for LUBM and DNA. Bitmap-64 is 1.5x larger on DNA because the difference of the Q lengths is small from NPK. Note that m-Bonsai did not maintain associated values of the int type. If m-Bonsai maintained those values ideally without any overhead, 4 bytes (i.e., sizeof(int)) are added per keyword. That is, Bitmap-64 becomes smaller than m-Bonsai on all the datasets. In the existing dictionaries, Cedar is basically small although 32-bit integers are used to represent node pointers. In Wiki and WebBase, HAT-trie and Judy are the smallest. Compared with the smallest existing dictionaries, Bitmap-64 is 2.1–2.8x smaller. On UK and WebBase whose BPNL is large, Plain is also smaller than the existing dictionaries because the pointer overhead is relatively small over the overall space usage.

---

[1] All the results are provided at https://github.com/kamp78/dynpdt/wiki.

Table 3. Results of insertion time in microseconds per keyword.

Data structure	Geonames	Wiki	UK	WebBase	LUBM	DNA
Plain	1.00	1.14	1.65	2.37	1.65	1.35
Bitmap-8	1.25	1.38	1.99	2.64	1.91	1.58
Bitmap-16	1.37	1.57	2.29	2.93	1.99	1.66
Bitmap-32	1.69	1.93	2.91	3.47	2.29	1.91
Bitmap-64	2.13	2.65	4.12	4.60	2.87	2.30
m-Bonsai	1.62	2.22	7.13	7.69	4.80	1.03
Sparsehash	4.31	5.15	9.13	11.32	8.72	1.99
Judy	0.93	1.06	2.15	2.94	1.53	0.90
HAT-trie	0.96	1.13	1.63	1.75	2.58	0.84
ART	1.07	1.19	2.20	2.98	1.44	0.87
Cedar	1.05	1.07	2.56	–	2.50	0.90

Table 4. Results of search time in microseconds per keyword.

Data structure	Geonames	Wiki	UK	WebBase	LUBM	DNA
Plain	1.01	1.13	1.53	2.20	1.12	1.08
Bitmap-8	1.22	1.38	2.15	2.40	1.26	1.26
Bitmap-16	1.38	1.61	2.47	2.74	1.43	1.38
Bitmap-32	1.71	2.06	3.25	3.72	1.61	1.83
Bitmap-64	2.31	3.01	4.88	5.29	2.16	2.18
m-Bonsai	1.47	2.06	6.69	8.30	3.08	0.86
Sparsehash	0.34	0.44	0.67	0.80	0.67	0.29
Judy	0.70	0.88	2.02	2.42	0.79	0.44
HAT-trie	0.31	0.35	0.61	0.80	0.51	0.22
ART	0.81	1.03	1.84	2.68	0.67	0.63
Cedar	0.42	0.69	2.51	–	0.69	0.22

Insertion Time. Table 3 shows the results. In DynPDT, Plain is the fastest and Bitmap-64 is the slowest essentially, but Bitmap-8 is not much slower than Plain. We compare Bitmap-8 for the following. Compared with m-Bonsai, Bitmap-8 is faster except for DNA. In particular, the difference is very large on datasets whose BPK is large owing to the path decomposition. Bitmap-8 is 3.6x, 2.9x and 2.5x faster than m-Bonsai on UK, WebBase, and LUBM, respectively. Bitmap-8 is 1.5x slower than m-Bonsai on DNA. Compared with the existing dictionaries, Bitmap-8 is not the fastest but is very competitive on UK, WebBase, and LUBM; however, Bitmap-8 is the slowest on the other datasets except for Sparsehash.

Search Time. Table 4 shows the results. Like the insertion time results, Plain is the fastest in DynPDT, and Bitmap-8 is faster than m-Bonsai except for DNA. On the other hand, DynPDT is basically slower compared with the existing dictionaries. Bitmap-8 is up to 5.7x slower than the fastest HAT-trie. On UK and WebBase, Bitmap-8 is close to Judy, ART, and Cedar.

5   Conclusion and Future Work

In this paper, we presented DynPDT, which is a new practical implementation of space-efficient dynamic keyword dictionaries through incremental path decomposition. Our experimental results showed that DynPDT uses much smaller space than existing keyword dictionary implementations, but its time performance is not very high. The main cause is that the node-to-node traversal using m-Bonsai is slow compared with pointer-based representations. Another disadvantage is that the hash table cannot be easily resized owing to open addressing. Therefore, we will improve upon those disadvantages by engineering an alternative trie representation in the future. Moreover, we will address more compression because DynPDT still consumes a larger space compared with existing static compact implementations. For example, the static data structure by Grossi and Ottaviano [8] can implement a dictionary in space 2.9x smaller than DynPDT for the geographic name dataset.

We have discussed dictionary structures supporting only search operations for a given keyword as a basic associative array. On the other hand, dictionary structures supporting invertible mapping between strings and unique IDs, known as *string dictionaries*, are also important in many applications [16]. In principle, DynPDT can provide such invertible mapping because m-Bonsai supports leaf-to-root traversal operations. Therefore, we will propose and evaluate DynPDT structures adapting to the string dictionaries.

Acknowledgments. This work was supported by JSPS KAKENHI Grant Number 17J07555. We would like to thank Editage (www.editage.jp) for English language editing.

References

1. Askitis, N., Sinha, R.: Engineering scalable, cache and space efficient tries for strings. VLDB J. **19**(5), 633–660 (2010)
2. Askitis, N., Zobel, J.: Cache-conscious collision resolution in string hash tables. In: Consens, M., Navarro, G. (eds.) SPIRE 2005. LNCS, vol. 3772, pp. 91–102. Springer, Heidelberg (2005). doi:10.1007/11575832_11
3. Baskins, D.: Judy IV Shop Manual (2002)
4. Boldi, P., Codenotti, B., Santini, M., Vigna, S.: Ubicrawler: a scalable fully distributed web crawler. Softw. Pract. Exp. **34**(8), 711–726 (2004)
5. Darragh, J.J., Cleary, J.G., Witten, I.H.: Bonsai: a compact representation of trees. Softw. Pract. Exp. **23**(3), 277–291 (1993)
6. Ferragina, P., Grossi, R., Gupta, A., Shah, R., Vitter, J.S.: On searching compressed string collections cache-obliviously. In: Proceedings of 27th Symposium on Principles of Database Systems (PODS), pp. 181–190 (2008)

7. González, R., Grabowski, S., Mäkinen, V., Navarro, G.: Practical implementation of rank and select queries. In: Poster Proceedings of 4th Workshop on Experimental and Efficient Algorithms (WEA), pp. 27–38 (2005)
8. Grossi, R., Ottaviano, G.: Fast compressed tries through path decompositions. ACM J. Exp. Algorithmics **19**(1) (2014). Article 1.8
9. Guo, Y., Pan, Z., Heflin, J.: LUBM: a benchmark for OWL knowledge base systems. Web Semant. Sci. Serv. Agents World Wide Web **3**(2), 158–182 (2005)
10. Hirai, J., Raghavan, S., Garcia-Molina, H., Paepcke, A.: WebBase: a repository of web pages. Comput. Netw. **33**(1), 277–293 (2000)
11. Hsu, B.J.P., Ottaviano, G.: Space-efficient data structures for top-k completion. In: Proceedings of 22nd International Conference on World Wide Web (WWW), pp. 583–594 (2013)
12. Kanda, S., Morita, K., Fuketa, M.: Compressed double-array tries for string dictionaries supporting fast lookup. Knowl. Inf. Syst. **51**(3), 1023–1042 (2017)
13. Kanda, S., Morita, K., Fuketa, M.: Practical string dictionary compression using string dictionary encoding. In: Proceedings of 3rd International Conference on Big Data Innovations and Applications (Innovate-Data), pp. 1–8 (2017)
14. Knuth, D.E.: The Art of Computer Programming: Volume 3: Sorting and Searching, 2nd edn. Addison Wesley, Redwood City (1998)
15. Leis, V., Kemper, A., Neumann, T.: The adaptive radix tree: ARTful indexing for main-memory databases. In: Proceedings of IEEE 29th International Conference on Data Engineering (ICDE), pp. 38–49 (2013)
16. Martínez-Prieto, M.A., Brisaboa, N., Cánovas, R., Claude, F., Navarro, G.: Practical compressed string dictionaries. Inf. Syst. **56**, 73–108 (2016)
17. Mavlyutov, R., Wylot, M., Cudre-Mauroux, P.: A comparison of data structures to manage URIs on the web of data. In: Gandon, F., Sabou, M., Sack, H., d'Amato, C., Cudré-Mauroux, P., Zimmermann, A. (eds.) ESWC 2015. LNCS, vol. 9088, pp. 137–151. Springer, Cham (2015). doi:10.1007/978-3-319-18818-8_9
18. Morrison, D.R.: PATRICIA: practical algorithm to retrieve information coded in alphanumeric. J. ACM **15**(4), 514–534 (1968)
19. Poyias, A., Raman, R.: Improved practical compact dynamic tries. In: Iliopoulos, C., Puglisi, S., Yilmaz, E. (eds.) SPIRE 2015. LNCS, vol. 9309, pp. 324–336. Springer, Cham (2015). doi:10.1007/978-3-319-23826-5_31
20. Takagi, T., Inenaga, S., Sadakane, K., Arimura, H.: Packed compact tries: a fast and efficient data structure for online string processing. In: Mäkinen, V., Puglisi, S.J., Salmela, L. (eds.) IWOCA 2016. LNCS, vol. 9843, pp. 213–225. Springer, Cham (2016). doi:10.1007/978-3-319-44543-4_17
21. Williams, H.E., Zobel, J.: Compressing integers for fast file access. Comput. J. **42**(3), 193–201 (1999)
22. Yoshinaga, N., Kitsuregawa, M.: A self-adaptive classifier for efficient text-stream processing. In: Proceedings of 24th International Conference on Computational Linguistics (COLING), pp. 1091–1102 (2014)

Faster Practical Block Compression
for Rank/Select Dictionaries

Yusaku Kaneta[✉]

Rakuten Institute of Technology, Rakuten, Inc., Tokyo, Japan
yusaku.kaneta@rakuten.com

Abstract. This paper presents faster practical encoding and decoding procedures for block compression that underlies both static and dynamic compressed rank/select bitmaps based on the RRR (Raman, Raman, and Rao) scheme. Our procedures use a novel combination of universal tables for chunkwise processing. Experimental results showed that our procedures were faster than existing ones on 64-bit blocks.

Keywords: Compact data structures · Rank/select queries · Compression

1 Introduction

Many compact data structures for strings [3,9], trees [2,7], graphs [4,7], full-text indexes [9,11], inverted indexes [3,11], etc. are built on top of *rank/select* queries on bitmaps. Because the performance of the queries can have a significant impact on the data structures, practical rank/select queries have been extensively studied [3–6,8,12,14].

Block compression [1] is a technique used by static compressed rank/select bitmaps [13] (known as RRR) and dynamic compressed ones [4]. This technique represents an input block B of t bits as a pair (c, o) of integers: the *class* c (stored in $\lceil \log(t+1) \rceil$ bits[1]) is the number of 1's in B and the *offset* o (stored in $\lceil \log \binom{t}{c} \rceil$ bits) is the lexicographical rank of B among all blocks of class c. There are two practical approaches to implement block compression: Claude and Navarro [3] implemented $\mathcal{O}(1)$-time block compression using universal tables of $\mathcal{O}(2^t t)$ bits. Although this approach is quite fast, it suffers from a considerable space overhead because the tables limit use of large blocks. To reduce the overhead, Navarro and Providel [12] proposed bitwise block compression using precomputed binomial coefficients of $\mathcal{O}(t^3)$ bits. This works very well on sparse bitmaps whose blocks are likely to contain a few 1's or 0's because such blocks can be encoded and decoded immediately. However, its $\mathcal{O}(t)$ worst-case time is not preferable especially for dynamic bitmaps because their density is difficult to know in advance. This can cause unexpected performance degradation due to unexpected dense

---

[1] The base of the logarithm is 2 throughout this paper.

© Springer International Publishing AG 2017
G. Fici et al. (Eds.): SPIRE 2017, LNCS 10508, pp. 234–240, 2017.
DOI: 10.1007/978-3-319-67428-5_20

blocks. Even worse, practical dynamic compressed bitmaps, recently proposed by Cordova and Navarro [4], can require more blocks to be encoded and decoded than static ones. Thus, efficient block compression is critical in dynamic settings.

In this paper, we present faster implementation of block compression. For any integer $1 \le s \le t$, our encoding and decoding procedures run in $\mathcal{O}(t/s)$ and $\mathcal{O}((t/s) \log s)$ time, respectively, using $\mathcal{O}(t^3 + 2^s s)$ bits of space. The key is a novel combination of universal tables for chunkwise processing. Table 1 shows the time and space of existing and our methods: blockwise [3], bitwise [12], and our chunkwise. Our method generalizes the existing ones [3,12]: ours with $s = t$ and $s = 1$ derives blockwise [3] and bitwise [12], respectively. Interestingly, our idea can also derive $\mathcal{O}(t)$-time block compression using $\mathcal{O}(t^3/s + 2^s s)$ bits of space. This reduces the space of bitwise [12] with, for example, $s = \log t$ by sampling precomputed binomial coefficients.

Table 1. The encoding time, decoding time, and space (in bits) of three block compression methods for the block length t and a time-space trade-off parameter $s \in [1, t]$.

Method	Encoding time	Decoding time	Space (in bits)
blockwise [3]	$\mathcal{O}(1)$	$\mathcal{O}(1)$	$\mathcal{O}(2^t t)$
bitwise [12]	$\mathcal{O}(t)$	$\mathcal{O}(t)$	$\mathcal{O}(t^3)$
chunkwise (this work)	$\mathcal{O}(t/s)$	$\mathcal{O}((t/s) \log s)$	$\mathcal{O}(t^3 + 2^s s)$

Related Work. Rank/Select queries have been extensively studied both in theory and practice. Jacobson [7] showed that rank queries on bitmaps of length n can be supported in constant time using $o(n)$ bits of extra space. Clark [2] and Munro [10] proved that select queries can also be supported in the same time and space. Raman *et al.* [13] presented a compressed representation of bitmaps, called RRR, supporting both rank and select queries in constant time using $o(n)$ bits of extra space. González *et al.* [6] presented practical rank/select bitmaps based on theoretical solutions [2,7,10]. Vigna [14] introduced broadword computation for practical rank/select queries. Claude and Navarro [3] implemented RRR [13] based on tabulation. Navarro and Providel [12] significantly improved the compression ratio of RRR in practice by introducing bitwise implementation of block compression. This was further improved by Gog and Petri [5] with practical optimization. Very recently, Klitzke and Nicholson [8] experimentally evaluated dynamic rank/select bitmaps. Following the work, Cordova and Navarro [4] proposed another practical implementation of dynamic compressed bitmaps based on theoretical work [9]. This stores blocks of bits in the leaves of an AVL tree using block compression. We refer the reader to [11] for a more comprehensive list of references on both static and dynamic rank/select bitmaps.

2   Faster Block Compression

This section presents our encoding and decoding procedures for block compression. The idea is to split an input block of length t into smaller *chunks* of length

$s \in [1, t]$ and to process it in a chunkwise manner, instead of blockwise or bitwise as in [3, 12]. Our main theorem is stated as follows:

Theorem 1. *Block encoding and decoding can be implemented in $\mathcal{O}(t/s)$ and $\mathcal{O}((t/s) \log s)$ time, respectively, using $\mathcal{O}(t^3 + 2^s s)$ bits of space after $\mathcal{O}(t^2 + 2^s s)$-time preprocessing, where t is the block length and s is any integer with $s \leq t$.*

For simplicity, we assume that s divides t. Let $m = t/s$ be the number of chunks in a block. Let $\Sigma = \{0, 1\}^s$ be the set of all chunks. We view blocks $B \in \Sigma^m$ as strings of length m over Σ. $B[i] \in \Sigma$ denotes the i-th chunk of B. For $i \leq j$, $B[i, j]$ denotes $B[i] \cdots B[j]$. For any block or chunk x, $\mathsf{lex}(x)$, $\mathsf{class}(x)$, and $\mathsf{offset}(x)$ denote its standard lexicographical rank, class and offset, respectively. For any chunk x, we assume that $\mathsf{offset}(x)$ is induced by $\mathsf{lex}(x)$.

For our chunkwise block compression, we define an ordering of chunks x and y given by $x \prec y$ iff (1) $\mathsf{class}(x) < \mathsf{class}(y)$ or (2) $\mathsf{class}(x) = \mathsf{class}(y) \wedge \mathsf{offset}(x) < \mathsf{offset}(y)$. For blocks B, we define $\mathsf{offset}(B)$ as the lexicographical rank induced by $\prec$ instead of the standard one. The first three columns of Table 2 show blocks of class 2, their standard lexicographical ranks, and their ranks induced by $\prec$ for $t = 6$ and $s = 3$. For $i \in [0, m]$, $c \in [0, t]$, and $c' \in [0, s]$, we define $\mathsf{binom}(i, c) = \binom{s \times i}{c}$ to return the number of strings of i chunks with c 1's and $\mathsf{count}(i, c, c') = \sum_{k \in [0, c')} \mathsf{binom}(1, k) \times \mathsf{binom}(i - 1, c - k)$ to returns the number of strings of i chunks with c 1's in total and less than c' 1's in the first chunk.

The functions $\mathsf{binom}(i, c)$ and $\mathsf{count}(i, c, c')$ can be computed in $\mathcal{O}(1)$ time using universal tables of $\mathcal{O}(t^3/s)$ and $\mathcal{O}(t^3)$ bits, respectively, because their values are bounded by 2^t and thus t bits are sufficient to store each entry. For any chunk x, $\mathsf{class}(x)$ and $\mathsf{offset}(x)$ can also be computed in $\mathcal{O}(1)$ time using universal tables of $\mathcal{O}(2^s s)$ bits of space as in [3]. In what follows, we explain how to compute $\mathsf{class}(B)$ and $\mathsf{offset}(B)$ from $\mathsf{class}(B[i])$ and $\mathsf{offset}(B[i])$ and vice versa.

Block Encoding. Given block $B = B[1] \cdots B[m]$ as input, our encoding procedure first computes $\mathsf{class}(B)$ and then $\mathsf{offset}(B)$ both in $\mathcal{O}(t/s)$ time. During encoding, we maintain a pair (c_i, o_i) of integers, where c_i stores the number of 1's in the i-th prefix of B and o_i stores the number of blocks $B' \in \Sigma^m$ satisfying $B'[1, i] \prec B[1, i]$. Note that $\mathsf{class}(B) = c_m$ and $\mathsf{offset}(B) = o_m$ hold. The class is easy to compute in a chunkwise manner: we start with $c_0 = 0$ and then recursively update c_i by $c_i = \mathsf{class}(B[i]) + c_{i-1}$ for $i = 1, \ldots, m$. The offset can also be computed in a similar manner: we start with $o_0 = 0$ and then recursively update o_i by

$$o_i = \mathsf{count}(m - i + 1, \mathsf{class}(B) - c_{i-1}, \mathsf{class}(B[i]))$$
$$+ \ \mathsf{offset}(B[i]) \times \mathsf{binom}(m - i, \mathsf{class}(B) - c_i) + o_{i-1}.$$

Note that the first and second terms correspond to (1) and (2) in our definition of ordering $\prec$. They add the number of blocks B' with $B'[1, i] \prec B[1, i]$. Each update of c_i and o_i takes $\mathcal{O}(1)$ time using the universal tables. Thus, our encoding takes in $\mathcal{O}(t/s)$ time in total.

For example, $B = 010\ 100$ in Table 2 can be encoded as follows: we first compute $\mathsf{class}(B)$ by $\mathsf{class}(B[1]) + \mathsf{class}(B[2]) = 1 + 1 = 2$ and then $\mathsf{offset}(B)$ by $(\mathsf{count}(2,2,1) + \mathsf{offset}(B[1]) \times \mathsf{binom}(1,1)) + (\mathsf{count}(1,1,1) + \mathsf{offset}(B[2]) \times \mathsf{binom}(0,0)) = (3 + 1 \times 3) + (0 + 2 \times 1) = 8$. Note that $\mathsf{count}(2,2,1) = 3$ adds the number of blocks prefixed by the chunk 000 of class less than $\mathsf{class}(B[1]) = 1$, and $\mathsf{offset}(B[1]) \times \mathsf{binom}(1,1)$ adds the number of blocks prefixed by the chunk 001 of class equal to $\mathsf{class}(B[1])$ and offset less than $\mathsf{offset}(B[1]) = 1$.

Block Decoding. Given $\mathsf{class}(B)$ and $\mathsf{offset}(B)$ of block B, our decoding procedure first computes $\mathsf{class}(B[i])$ and $\mathsf{offset}(B[i])$ and then restores $B[i]$ for $i \in [1, m]$. During encoding, we maintain the same pair (c_i, o_i) of integers as encoding. We start with $c_0 = 0$ and $o_0 = 0$. For $i \in [1, m]$, we first determine $\mathsf{class}(B[i])$ from c_{i-1} and o_{i-1} as follows:

$$\mathsf{class}(B[i]) = \min\Big\{c' \,\Big|\, \mathsf{count}(m - i + 1, \mathsf{class}(B) - c_{i-1}, c' + 1) \geq \mathsf{offset}(B) - o_{i-1}\Big\}$$

Table 2. The standard lexicographical rank $\mathsf{lex}(B)$ and our offset $\mathsf{offset}(B)$ of blocks B with $\mathsf{class}(B) = 2$ for $t = 6$ and $s = 3$. The table also includes $\mathsf{class}(B[i])$ and $\mathsf{offset}(B[i])$ of possible chunks $B[i]$ for $i \in \{1, 2\}$. The bold numbers indicate the differences between $\mathsf{lex}(B)$ and $\mathsf{offset}(B)$ of blocks. The solid and dashed horizontal lines show the boarders of $\mathsf{class}(B[i])$ and $\mathsf{offset}(B[i])$ of chunks, respectively.

$B = B[1]B[2]$	$\mathsf{lex}(B)$	$\mathsf{offset}(B)$	$\mathsf{class}(B[1])$	$\mathsf{offset}(B[1])$	$\mathsf{class}(B[2])$	$\mathsf{offset}(B[2])$
000 011	0	0	0	0	2	0
000 101	1	1	0	0	2	1
000 110	2	2	0	0	2	2
001 001	3	3	1	0	1	0
001 010	4	4	1	0	1	1
001 100	5	5	1	0	1	2
010 001	6	6	1	1	1	0
010 010	7	7	1	1	1	1
010 100	8	8	1	1	1	2
100 001	**10**	9	1	2	1	0
100 010	**11**	10	1	2	1	1
100 100	**12**	11	1	2	1	2
011 000	**9**	12	2	0	0	0
101 000	13	13	2	1	0	0
110 000	14	14	2	2	0	0

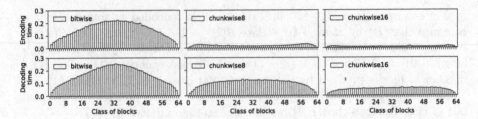

Fig. 1. The average elapsed times (in microseconds) for encoding (top) and decoding (bottom) of bitwise [3] (left), our chunkwise-8 (middle), and our chunkwise-16 (right).

Because the left-hand side of the above in equation is monotonically increasing for $c' \in [0, s)$, we can find $\mathsf{class}(B[i])$ in $\mathcal{O}(\log s)$ time. We then compute $\mathsf{offset}(B[i])$ as follow:

$$\mathsf{offset}(B[i]) = \left\lfloor \frac{\mathsf{offset}(B) - (o_{i-1} + \mathsf{count}(m - i + 1, \mathsf{class}(B) - c_{i-1}, \mathsf{class}(B[i])))}{\mathsf{binom}(m - i, \mathsf{class}(B) - c_i)} \right\rfloor$$

The numerator represents the number of blocks B' with $B'[1, i-1] = B[1, i-1]$ and $\mathsf{class}(B'[i]) = \mathsf{class}(B[i])$. Note that there are $\mathsf{binom}(m - i, \mathsf{class}(B) - c_i)$ blocks per such $B'[i]$. Thus, our decoding takes $\mathcal{O}((t/s) \log s)$ time in total.

For example, $B = 010\ 100$ in Table 2 can be decoded from its $\mathsf{class}(B) = 2$ and $\mathsf{offset}(B) = 8$ as follows: we first compute $\mathsf{class}(B[1])$ by $\min\{c' \mid \mathsf{count}(2, 2, c' + 1) \geq 8\} = 1$ and then $\mathsf{offset}(B[1])$ by $\lfloor (8 - (0 + 3))/3 \rfloor = 1$, because $\mathsf{count}(2, 2, 1) = 3$ and $\mathsf{count}(2, 2, 2) = 12$. Finally, we compute $\mathsf{class}(B[2])$ by $\min\{c' \mid \mathsf{count}(1, 1, c' + 1) \geq 2\} = 1$ and then $\mathsf{offset}(B[2])$ by $\lfloor (8 - (6 + 0))/1 \rfloor = 2$, because $\mathsf{count}(1, 1, 1) = 0$ and $\mathsf{count}(1, 1, 2) = 3$.

3 Experiments

This section presents experimental results that compare bitwise [12], which is most commonly used in practice, with our chunkwise methods. First, we measured their time and space for encoding and decoding. Then, we evaluated their performance in compressed rank/select queries. All the methods were implemented in C++ and compiled with g++ 7.1.0 using -Ofast and -march=native options. All our experiments were run on MacBook Pro with 2.5 GHz Intel Core i7 and 16 GB memory. We denote by chunkwise-8, chunkwise-16, and bitwise our method with $s = 8$, our method with $s = 16$, and one by [12], respectively. The block length t was fixed to 64 throughout our experiments.

Block Compression. For each class $c \in [0, t]$, we generated one million of (possibly duplicated) random blocks of class c and then measured the average encoding and decoding times over them. Figure 1 shows the measured times (that do not include that for precomputing the universal tables). Compared to bitwise, our chunkwise-16 was up to 23 and 4 times faster in encoding and decoding, respectively. Even for sparse blocks (with $c \in [0, 8]$, for example), our chunkwise-16 was up to 9 and 2 times faster in encoding and decoding, respectively. Furthermore, our methods were less dependent on c than bitwise. Our chunkwise-8 and chunkwise-16 used 37 KB and 362 KB, respectively, for universal tables, while bitwise used 34 KB. Finally, chunkwise-16 is about 2 times faster than chunkwise-8, as expected from their construction.

Rank/Select Queries. To evaluate how our chunkwise block compression improves the overall performance of compressed rank/select bitmaps, we implemented three variants of RRR [13], each of which uses bitwise [12], our chunkwise-8, or our chunkwise-16 for block compression. In addition to $rank_1$ and $select_1$, our RRR supported appending a bit (denoted by append) using a 64-bit buffer. We used superblocks of 64 and 128 blocks for $rank_1$ and $select_1$, respectively. As input, we randomly generated bitmaps of length 2^{28} with densities 5%, 10%, and 20%. We measured the average time over one million of random queries. Table 3 shows the average times. Although our improvement over bitwise was smaller than that in our first experiment, our chunkwise-8 and chunkwise-16 improved the performance of compressed rank/select bitmaps.

Table 3. The elapsed time (in microseconds) for each combination of methods and operations, and densities on an input bitmap of length 2^{28}.

Density	5%			10%			20%		
Operation	$rank_1$	$select_1$	append	$rank_1$	$select_1$	append	$rank_1$	$select_1$	append
bitwise [12]	0.226	0.276	0.004	0.288	0.310	0.005	0.375	0.417	0.006
chunkwise8	0.212	0.288	0.003	0.270	0.312	0.003	0.297	0.321	0.003
chunkwise16	0.187	0.250	0.003	0.219	0.254	0.003	0.235	0.265	0.003

4   Conclusion

This paper has presented a practical implementation of block compression, which offers a more flexible time-space trade-off for compressed rank/select bitmaps in practice. Experiments with dynamic bitmaps and more comprehensive configurations of block and chunk lengths on real datasets are important future work.

Acknowledgments. The author would like to thank anonymous reviewers and Shirou Maruyama for their valuable comments that greatly improved this paper.

References

1. Brodnik, A., Munro, J.I.: Membership in constant time and almost-minimum space. SIAM J. Comput. **28**(5), 1627–1640 (1999)
2. Clark, D.R.: Compact PAT trees. Ph.D. thesis, University of Waterloo (1996)
3. Claude, F., Navarro, G.: Practical rank/select queries over arbitrary sequences. In: Amir, A., Turpin, A., Moffat, A. (eds.) SPIRE 2008. LNCS, vol. 5280, pp. 176–187. Springer, Heidelberg (2008). doi:10.1007/978-3-540-89097-3_18

4. Cordova, J., Navarro, G.: Practical dynamic entropy-compressed bitvectors with applications. In: Goldberg, A.V., Kulikov, A.S. (eds.) SEA 2016. LNCS, vol. 9685, pp. 105–117. Springer, Cham (2016). doi:10.1007/978-3-319-38851-9_8

5. Gog, S., Petri, M.: Optimized succinct data structures for massive data. Softw. Pract. Exper. **44**(11), 1287–1314 (2014)

6. González, R., Grabowski, S., Mäkinen, V., Navarro, G.: Practical implementation of rank and select queries. In: Poster Proceedings of WEA 2005, pp. 27–38. CTI Press and Ellinika Grammata (2005)

7. Jacobson, G.: Space-efficient static trees and graphs. In: Proceedings of FOCS 1989. pp. 549–554. IEEE Computer Society (1989)

8. Klitzke, P., Nicholson, P.K.: A general framework for dynamic succinct and compressed data structures. In: Proceedings of ALENEX 2016, pp. 160–173 (2016)

9. Mäkinen, V., Navarro, G.: Dynamic entropy-compressed sequences and full-text indexes. ACM Trans. Algorithms **4**(3), 32:1–32:38 (2008)

10. Munro, J.I.: Tables. In: Chandru, V., Vinay, V. (eds.) FSTTCS 1996. LNCS, vol. 1180, pp. 37–42. Springer, Heidelberg (1996). doi:10.1007/3-540-62034-6_35

11. Navarro, G.: Compact Data Structures: A Practical Approach, 1st edn. Cambridge University Press, Cambridge (2016)

12. Navarro, G., Providel, E.: Fast, small, simple rank/select on bitmaps. In: Klasing, R. (ed.) SEA 2012. LNCS, vol. 7276, pp. 295–306. Springer, Heidelberg (2012). doi:10.1007/978-3-642-30850-5_26

13. Raman, R., Raman, V., Satti, S.R.: Succinct indexable dictionaries with applications to encoding k-ary trees, prefix sums and multisets. ACM Trans. Algorithms **3**(4) (2007)

14. Vigna, S.: Broadword implementation of rank/select queries. In: McGeoch, C.C. (ed.) WEA 2008. LNCS, vol. 5038, pp. 154–168. Springer, Heidelberg (2008). doi:10.1007/978-3-540-68552-4_12

Optimal Skeleton Huffman Trees

Shmuel T. Klein[1(✉)], Tamar C. Serebro[2], and Dana Shapira[2]

[1] Department of Computer Science, Bar Ilan University, 52900 Ramat Gan, Israel
`tomi@cs.biu.ac.il`
[2] Department of Computer Science, Ariel University, 40700 Ariel, Israel
`ytserebro@gmail.com, shapird@ariel.ac.il`

Abstract. A skeleton Huffman tree is a Huffman tree from which all complete subtrees of depth $h \geq 1$ have been pruned. Skeleton Huffman trees are used to save storage and enhance processing time in several applications such as decoding, compressed pattern matching and Wavelet trees for random access. However, the straightforward way of basing the construction of a skeleton tree on a canonical Huffman tree does not necessarily yield the least number of nodes. The notion of *optimal skeleton trees* is introduced, and an algorithm for achieving such trees is investigated. The resulting more compact trees can be used to further enhance the time and space complexities of the corresponding algorithms.

1 Introduction

One of the most popular static data compression methods is still Huffman coding [8], even more than sixty years after its invention. A Huffman code is a minimum redundancy code, subject to the constraint that each codeword is composed of an integral number of bits. Given is an alphabet $\Sigma = \{a_1, \ldots, a_n\}$ and a probability distribution $P = \{p_1, \ldots, p_n\}$ for the occurrences of its characters. Huffman's algorithm assigns lengths $\{\ell_1, \ldots, \ell_n\}$ to the codewords, so that the average codeword length $\sum_{i=1}^{n} p_i \ell_i$ is minimized. The algorithm for the construction of the code repeatedly combines the two smallest probabilities and may be implemented in time $O(n \log n)$. A useful way to represent the code is by means of a binary tree called a *Huffman Tree*. The leaves of the tree are associated with the elements of the alphabet. Edges in the tree pointing to the left or right child are labeled by 0 or 1, respectively, and the concatenation of the labels on the path from the root to a given leaf yields the corresponding codeword. In a more general setting, integer frequencies or even arbitrary positive numbers called *weights* $W = \{w_1, \ldots, w_n\}$ are used instead of probabilities, and it is the weighted average $\sum_{i=1}^{n} w_i \ell_i$ that is minimized. The algorithm remains the same. A tree minimizing this sum is called *optimal*; Huffman's method produces optimal trees, but not all optimal trees can be obtained directly by the Huffman algorithm.

A new data structure, called a *Skeleton tree*, or *sk-tree* for short, has been introduced in [10], which is especially suited for fast decoding of Huffman encoded texts. The storage requirements of sk-trees are much lower than those

© Springer International Publishing AG 2017
G. Fici et al. (Eds.): SPIRE 2017, LNCS 10508, pp. 241–253, 2017.
DOI: 10.1007/978-3-319-67428-5_21

of traditional Huffman trees. The latter have $2n - 1$ nodes, whereas the former need only $O(\log^2 n)$ nodes for trees of depth $O(\log n)$. The idea is to process the compressed file, one bit at a time, until a leaf of the sk-tree is reached, where the length of the current codeword w is already determined. This will often be the case before having read all the bits of w. Then several bits, from the one following the current position to the end of the codeword w, are processed in a single operation. Decoding may be faster since a part of the bit-comparisons and manipulations necessary for the conventional Huffman decoding may be saved. Empirical results on large real-life distributions show an average reduction of up to half and more in the number of bit operations [10].

There are several applications for which Huffman trees may be replaced by sk-trees in order to speed up processing time and/or save space, for example to accelerate compressed pattern matching, as shown in [16]. Another application for which sk-trees are used to improve the time and space complexities is *Wavelet Trees*. A Wavelet tree (WT), suggested by Grossi et al. [7], is a data structure which reorders the bits of the compressed file into an alternative form, thereby enabling direct access, as well as other efficient operations. WTs can be defined for any prefix code, and the tree structure associated with this code is inherited by the WT.

The internal nodes of the WT are annotated with bitmaps. The root of the WT holds the bitmap obtained by concatenating the first bit of each of the sequence of codewords in the order they appear in the compressed text. The left and right children of the root hold, respectively, the bitmaps obtained by concatenating, again in the given order, the second bit of each of the codewords starting with 0 and with 1, respectively. This process is repeated similarly on the next levels: the grand-children of the root hold the bitmaps obtained by concatenating the third bit of the sequence of codewords starting, respectively, with 00, 01, 10 or 11, if they exist at all, etc.

Various manipulations on the bitmaps of the WT are based on fast implementations of operations known as rank and select. These are defined for any bit $b \in \{0, 1\}$ as

rank$_b(B, i)$ – number of occurrences of b in B up to and including position i; and

select$_b(B, i)$ – position of the ith occurrence of b in B.

Efficient implementations for rank and select are due to Jacobson [9], Raman et al. [14], Okanohara and Sadakane [13], Barbay et al. [1] and Navarro and Providel [12], to list only a few. WTs can be seen as extensions of rank and select operations to a general alphabet.

Recently, Baruch et al. [2] suggested to replace a Huffman shaped WT by a skeleton tree shaped WT in order to support faster random access and save storage, at the price of less effective rank and select operations. The general idea is to apply some pruning strategy on the internal nodes of the WTs, so that the overhead of the additional storage, used by the data structures for processing the stored bitmaps, is reduced. Moreover, the average path lengths corresponding to the codewords is also decreased, and so is also the average time spent for traversing the paths from the root to the desired leaf, which is the basic processing component used to evaluate random access. The suggestion of [2], combining Wavelet with skeleton trees has been extended in [4], where it was empirically shown that reordering the sk-tree may enhance the direct access via WTs.

The current paper is organized as follows. We recall the details of sk-trees in Sect. 2. In Sect. 3, we develop our method for designing enhanced sk-trees with a minimal number of nodes, and prove its optimality. Finally, Sect. 4 presents preliminary experimental results.

2   Skeleton Trees

A *full* tree is a tree all of whose leaves are on the same level, as in Fig. 3(a). A *complete* tree is a (binary) tree in which every internal node has exactly two children, a left and a right one. The trees in Fig. 1 are complete, but not full. A compact way to describe a complete tree is by means of its *quantized source* $\langle n_1, n_2, \ldots, n_k \rangle$ or *q-source* for short, as defined in [5], where n_i is the number of codewords of length i, for $1 \leq i \leq k$, and k is the longest codeword length. Note that $\sum_{i=1}^{k} n_i = n$. The q-source does not uniquely identify a given tree, for example, the q-source of both trees in Fig. 1 is $\langle 0, 2, 4 \rangle$, as for both there are no codewords of length 1, two codewords of length 2, and four codewords of length 3. Nevertheless, it is convenient to use the q-source for Huffman trees, since their shape is generally of no matter, and all trees belonging to same q-source share the same codeword lengths.

A well-known property of complete trees is that they satisfy the *Kraft equality*, see, e.g., [11, Chap. 4]: if $\ell_1, \ell_2, \ldots, \ell_n$ are the lengths of the codewords, or equivalently, the depths of the leaves in the tree, then

$$\sum_{j=1}^{n} 2^{-\ell_j} = \sum_{i=1}^{k} n_i 2^{-i} = 1. \tag{1}$$

In fact, the Kraft equality is often used as a characteristic of a complete code, in the sense that if a sequence of numbers $\ell_1, \ell_2, \ldots, \ell_n$ satisfies Eq. (1), then a complete tree can be constructed whose leaves are at the given depths.

Given a complete binary tree T, *pruning* a subtree T' of T is a process that can be applied if T' is a full subtree. It consists of eliminating all the nodes of T' except its root. For example, in Fig. 1(b), the rightmost subtree of depth 2 could be pruned, leaving only its root (labeled 9) in the tree.

LEMMA 1: *Pruning a subtree from a complete binary tree results in a complete binary tree itself.*

PROOF: Actually, an even stronger property could be claimed, namely, that the replacement by its root of *any* subtree of a complete tree, not just for full subtrees, does not change the fact that all internal nodes still have two children. Thus the resulting tree is also complete.   □

We may thus repeatedly prune subtrees from a given Huffman tree, and this will not affect the completeness the remaining tree. Our goal is to prune several subtrees from optimal trees for some given weight distribution, so that the number of nodes remaining in the tree is minimal. An sk-tree is what remains after having pruned all the possible subtrees of a complete binary tree. The size and shape of an sk-tree does, however, depend on the shape of the complete tree we started from. The trees in Fig. 1 show different sk-trees derived from trees with different shapes, yet both optimal. As mentioned, Huffman trees are optimal, however, not all optimal trees can be attained directly via Huffman's algorithm. Consider for example the sequence of frequencies $\{7, 5, 3, 3, 2, 2\}$, yielding the Huffman tree in Fig. 1(a). The tree in Fig. 1(b) is still optimal as the codeword lengths remain the same as the ones in Fig. 1(a), but it is not a Huffman tree: Huffman's algorithm would not combine the weights 6 and 4, since there is a weight 5 between them, and the algorithm adds the two smallest weights in each iteration.

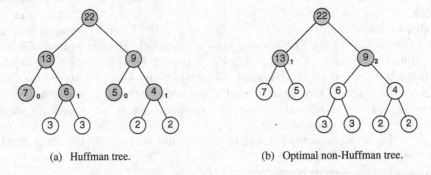

(a) Huffman tree.   (b) Optimal non-Huffman tree.

Fig. 1. Optimal trees for weights $\{7, 5, 3, 3, 2, 2\}$.

For a given set of weights, there may be many equivalent Huffman trees, as it is possible to build up to 2^{n-1} different Huffman trees by interchanging the left and right subtrees of some internal node. The number of different Huffman trees can be even larger in case the set of weights W contains ties, or even when the sequence of weight sums, that are considered during Huffman's algorithm, contains ties.

A tree is called *canonical* [15] if, when scanning its leaves from left to right, they appear in non-decreasing order of their depth. Thus the tree in Fig. 1(b) is canonical, but that in Fig. 1(a) is not. An equivalent way for defining canonicity is that when the codewords are sorted by the frequencies of their corresponding symbols, they are ordered lexicographically. To build a canonical tree, Huffman's algorithm is only used for generating the optimal lengths ℓ_i of the codewords, and then the i-th codeword is defined as the first ℓ_i bits immediately to the right of the "binary point" in the infinite binary expansion of $\sum_{j=1}^{i-1} 2^{-\ell_j}$, for $1 \leq i \leq n$ [6]. Turpin and Moffat [17] use canonical codes, with a symmetrically equivalent definition, to enhance decoding in Huffman encoded texts, so that more than a single bit can be processed in one machine operation.

Canonical trees gather all codewords of the same length consecutively, motivating the idea of pruning such trees. Although canonical trees reduce the number of different Huffman trees dramatically, there are still weight distributions for which even the canonical tree is not unique. For example, consider the frequencies $\{2,1,1,1\}$, yielding the Huffman trees in Fig. 2. Huffman's algorithm does not impose any strict order on the nodes in each level, nor any preference on connections between equal values and specific nodes. In the penultimate step of the construction of the Huffman tree for our example, the tree has 3 leaves, with weights 1, 2 and 2. The value 2 thus appears both on level 1 (the level of the root being defined as 0) and on level 2. The last step of the construction is then to create two new nodes with weight 1 each, and define them as being the children of one of the leaves with weight 2. Choosing the leaf on the lowest level yields the tree in Fig. 2(a), choosing the leaf on level 1 yields the tree in Fig. 2(b). Both choices give the weighted sum $2+2+3+3 = 2+2+2+4 = 10$, so both trees are Huffman trees and thus optimal.

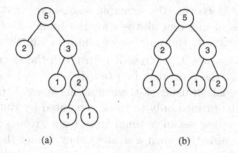

(a)   (b)

Fig. 2. Different optimal canonical trees for the frequencies $\{2,1,1,1\}$.

Figure 3 generalizes this example to show that weight distributions giving more than a single canonical Huffman tree may be found for every alphabet size. Consider the set of $n = 2^h$ frequencies $\{2,1,\ldots,1\}$, for $h \geq 2$. As in the previous example, there are two choices for splitting a node with weight 2 in the

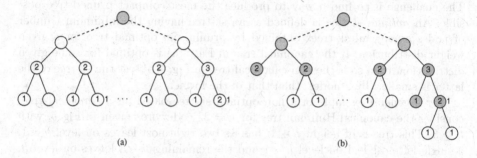

(a)   (b)

Fig. 3. Canonical trees are not unique.

last step of the construction. While Fig. 3(a) chooses to locate this node on level $h - 1$ of the tree, Fig. 3(b) selects the only node with value 2 on level h.

The original definition of the skeleton tree in [10] uses an underlying *canonical Huffman tree*, which here and below, refers to a canonical tree built for optimal codeword lengths for a given probability distribution, even if the specific canonical layout can not be obtained directly by Huffman's algorithm, as, for example, the tree in Fig. 1(b). Formally, an sk-tree is a canonical Huffman tree from which all full subtrees of depth $h \geq 1$ have been pruned. Thus, a path from the root to a leaf of an sk-tree may correspond to a prefix of several codewords of the original Huffman tree. The prefix is the shortest necessary in order to identify the length of the current codeword. A leaf, v, of the sk-tree contains the height, $h(v)$, of the subtree that has been pruned ($h(v) = 0$ for leaves that were also leaves in the original Huffman tree), as well as a list of symbols belonging to that subtree. In the examples in Fig. 1, as well as in the subsequent ones, we shall follow the convention that the nodes of the sk-trees appear in gray. The values $h(v)$ appear in boldface to the right of the leaves of the sk-trees in Fig. 1.

Figure 3 shows that different canonical trees constructed for the same set of weights may result in different sk-trees, as can be seen by inspecting the nodes highlighted in gray. Moreover, the example also shows that the difference in the number of nodes of different sk-trees for the same set of weights may not be bounded by a constant: the number of nodes in the sk-tree of Fig. 3(b) is $2 + \sum_{i=0}^{h-1} 2^i = 2^h + 1 = n + 1$, whereas it is just 1 in the sk-tree of Fig. 3(a), as the entire tree, except the root, may be pruned.

Since one of the goals of using sk-trees is saving space, it makes sense not to restrict the trees to be pruned only to those generated by Huffman's algorithm, but to consider the larger set of optimal trees for a given weight distribution. Figure 1(b) is an example that such a strategy may reduce the number of nodes in the sk-tree, from 7 to 3 in this example. Intuitively, canonical Huffman trees seem then to be a good choice in order to achieve smaller sk-trees, because the canonical structure collects all the leaves appearing on the same level together. However, we show in the following section that this intuition may be misleading.

3 Optimal Pruned Trees

The challenge is to find a way to produce the most compact pruned tree possible. An *optimal sk-tree* is defined as an sk-tree having the minimum number of nodes among all sk-trees obtained by pruning an optimal tree for a given weight distribution. If the canonical tree in Fig. 4(a) is optimal for some given distribution, then so is the non-canonical tree in Fig. 4(b); yet the sk-tree of the latter is smaller, by 2 nodes, than that of the former.

For a general example of a non optimal sk-tree based on a canonical tree, consider the canonical Huffman tree for $n = 2^h$ codewords given in Fig. 5, with $h \geq 3$. This tree is of height $h + 1$, has its two rightmost leaves on level $h + 1$, a single leftmost leaf on level $h - 1$ and the remaining $n - 3$ leaves on level h. Figure 4(a) is the particular case $h = 3$. As a result, every node (except the

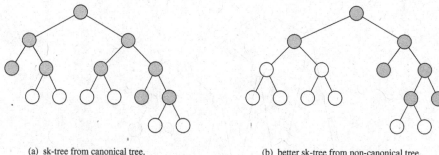

(a) sk-tree from canonical tree.   (b) better sk-tree from non-canonical tree.

Fig. 4. Optimal pruned tree.

two lowest) on the rightmost path, that from the root to the rightmost leaf, is the root of an asymmetric subtree which is not full: its right subtree is one level deeper than its left one. Similarly, the same is true also for the nodes of the leftmost path. In particular, the roots of the two largest full subtrees, which appear in the center of the figure, are not children of the same node. The number of nodes in the corresponding sk-tree is $4h - 3$: four nodes on each level, except for that of the root (with a single node), and the first and lowest level having two nodes each.

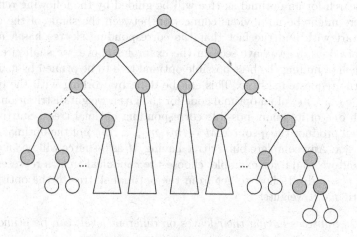

Fig. 5. A non optimal sk-tree for $n \geq 8$ codewords.

On the other hand, the tree given in Fig. 6 has the same codeword lengths as that in Fig. 5, but the locations of the nodes are different, resulting in a non canonical tree. Nevertheless, there are fewer nodes in the corresponding pruned tree. There are now two nodes on each level, except that of the root, which has only one node, for a total of $1 + 2(h - 1)$ nodes. The difference between the number of nodes in the two sk-trees is thus $2(h - 1)$, therefore this example

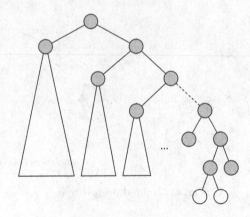

Fig. 6. Optimal pruned tree for the tree of Fig. 5.

shows that sk-trees of canonical Huffman trees might produce $\Omega(\log n)$ extra nodes as compared to pruning some non-canonical optimal tree. Therefore, not only does a canonical tree fail to provide the best possible sk-tree for n leaves, but moreover, the difference in the number of nodes between an sk-tree based on pruning a canonical tree and the best possible sk-tree might not even be bounded by a constant.

Our search for an optimal sk-tree will be guided by the following reflexions. Since there might be no obvious connection between the shape of the optimal tree to start with and the fact that the corresponding sk-tree has a minimal number of nodes, as we have seen in the examples above, we shall circumvent the problem of finding the best possible optimal tree to be pruned by generating directly the requested sk-tree. This can be done by working with the q-source $N = \langle n_1, n_2, \ldots, n_k \rangle$ of an optimal code for the given weight distribution, rather than with one of its many possible corresponding optimal trees. Starting with N, we shall produce the q-source $M = \langle m_1, m_2, \ldots, m_{k'} \rangle$ of the optimal sk-tree, where $k' \leq k$. Any complete binary tree having M as q-source will be an optimal sk-tree, and we could, for example, choose the canonical tree as representative. We shall also indicate how to get from the optimal sk-tree to the optimal tree for the original n weights.

LEMMA 2: *Subtrees having their leaves on different levels can be pruned independently.*

PROOF: Full subtrees involve only leaves appearing on the same level. In other words, if a subtree has leaves on different levels, it cannot possibly be a full subtree and is therefore not a candidate for being pruned. Any pruning may thus be applied to the leaves of a given level, without taking leaves on other levels into consideration.   □

Consider level i and suppose there are n_i leaves on this level. The largest possible savings for this level can obviously be attained when n_i is a power of 2, say,

$n_i = 2^h$, in which case, an entire full subtree of height h, having its leaves on level i, may be pruned. That is, it seems at first sight that an additional constraint has to be fulfilled, namely that the 2^h leaves all belong to the same subtree of height h, or in other words, they should all be adjacent. Referring to Fig. 1(a), there are $n_3 = 4 = 2^2$ leaves on level 3, but they do not belong to a single subtree of height 2. Nevertheless, we show that the additional constraint is not needed.

LEMMA 3: *If the number n_i of leaves on level i is a power of 2, say, $n_i = 2^h$ for some $h \geq 1$, then an entire subtree of height h may be pruned.*

PROOF: Consider the Kraft sum $\sum_{j=1}^{k} n_j 2^{-j}$. According to Lemma 1, removing the n_i leaves on level i and adding a leaf on level $i - h$ yields a new q-source that also satisfies the Kraft equality. The new q-source thus corresponds to a complete binary tree R. One can therefore choose any leaf on level $i - h$ of R and turn it to the root of a subtree of height h. The resulting tree has n_i leaves on level i belonging all to the same subtree.   □

It follows from Lemma 3 that even though the 2^h do not always belong to the same subtree, as in Fig. 1(a), it is still true that *there exists* an optimal tree for which these nodes are clumped together, as in the example of Fig. 1(b).

If n_i is not a power of 2, the best we can expect is to prune a subtree with 2^k leaves, where 2^k is the largest power of 2 still smaller than n_i, that is, $k = \lfloor \log_2 n_i \rfloor$. As in the case treated in Lemma 3, one can show that such a pruning is always possible. For example, the tree in Fig. 4(a) has $n_3 = 5$, but does not allow the pruning of a subtree of height 2; but there exists an equivalent tree with leaves on the same levels, e.g., the tree in Fig. 4(b), for which four of the leaves on level 3 are consecutive and part of the same subtree rooted at level 1.

The effect of the pruning on the q-source is materialized by updating the value of n_i to $n_i - 2^h$ and incrementing n_{i-h} by 1, reflecting the fact that 2^h leaves have been removed from the tree and a new leaf has been added. According to Lemma 1, the current q-source is again one of a complete tree, so the same argument as above can be repeated for the new value of n_i. Ultimately, what one gets is a decomposition of n_i into a sum of powers of 2, that is, the standard binary representation of n_i. For example, if $n_i = 47$, one could prune consecutively subtrees with 32, 8, 4 and 2 leaves on level i, after which, a single leaf will remain on this level.

While the different levels can be treated independently, the order by which to process them should not be arbitrary. Care has to be taken that only original leaves are considered when looking for a subtree to prune, and not newly added leaves resulting from a previous pruning action. This suggests to consider the levels top down, from level 1 to level k. Since when treating level i, nodes are only added at levels $i - h$, for $h \geq 1$, the additional nodes are inserted at levels that have been treated in previous iterations and will thus not be processed any more.

Summarizing, we propose a greedy algorithm that considers, in order for every $1 \leq i \leq k$, the n_i leaves corresponding to each codeword length i individually, and repeatedly prunes full trees having their number of leaves equal to 2^h, for the largest possible $h \geq 1$. The construction in [4] is similar, but presented as a heuristic improving the use of Wavelet trees.

Algorithm 1 gets as input parameter the q-source $\langle n_1, n_2, \ldots, n_k \rangle$ of an optimal code for a given weight distribution and constructs a corresponding optimal sk-tree after having generated its q-source $\langle m_1, m_2, \ldots, m_{k'} \rangle$. We have chosen here the canonical form for this optimal sk-tree, but any other form could be used. The algorithm maintains a list $\mathcal{L}$ in which the pairs (i, h) are inserted, each identifying a pruned subtree T, with i being the index of the level of the leaves of T, and h being its height, implying that the number of its leaves is 2^h. Once the optimal sk-tree is constructed, the elements in $\mathcal{L}$ are used to assign the correct values $h(v)$ to its leaves v. The list $\mathcal{L}$ can be implemented as queue or stack or any other way, as long as it permits to process all of its elements in some order.

Algorithm 1. *Optimal Pruning Algorithm*

OPTIMALPRUNING($\langle n_1, n_2, \ldots, n_k \rangle$)
  for $i \leftarrow 1$ **to** k **do**
    $m_i \leftarrow n_i$
    while $m_i \geq 2$ **do**
      $h \leftarrow \lfloor \log_2 m_i \rfloor$
      $m_i \leftarrow m_i - 2^h$
      $m_{i-h} \leftarrow m_{i-h} + 1$
      add the pair (i, h) to the list $\mathcal{L}$

  $k' \leftarrow \max\{i \mid 1 \leq i \leq k, m_i > 0\}$
  build canonical tree for $\langle m_1, m_2, \ldots, m_{k'} \rangle$ and set $h(v) \leftarrow 0$ to all its leaves v
  for each pair $(i, h) \in \mathcal{L}$ **do**
    choose a leaf v on level $i - h$ for which $h(v) = 0$
    $h(v) \leftarrow h$

The algorithm can also be adapted to produce an optimal tree for the given weight distribution, whose corresponding sk-tree is optimal. All one needs to do is to replace the last line by

> replace the leaf v by the root of a full subtree of height h

THEOREM: *The sk-tree constructed by Algorithm 1 is optimal.*

PROOF: The claim follows from the above discussion. Lemma 1 implies that the structure of a complete tree may be maintained after each pruning action. Lemma 2 justifies that each level is treated separately and Lemma 3 suggests the greedy approach. Since at each step, the number of eliminated nodes is the largest possible, the size of the remaining tree at the end of the process is minimal. □

Applying Algorithm 1 on the q-source $\langle 0, 1, 5, 2 \rangle$ results in the q-source $\langle 1, 1, 2 \rangle$; a possible optimal tree yielding this optimal sk-tree is the one in Fig. 4. Applying Algorithm 1 on the h-tuple q-source $\langle 0, \ldots, 0, 1, n-3, 2 \rangle$ corresponding to Fig. 5 results in the $(h-1)$-tuple q-source $\langle 1, \ldots, 1, 2 \rangle$; a possible optimal tree yielding this optimal sk-tree is the one in Fig. 6.

4 Experimental Results

We considered four texts of different languages and alphabet sizes. *ebib* is the Bible (King James version) in English, in which the text was stripped of all punctuation signs; *ftxt* is the French version of the European Union's JOC corpus, a collection of pairs of questions and answers on various topics used in the ARCADE evaluation project [18]; *sources* is formed by C/Java source codes obtained by concatenating all the .c, .h and .java files of the linux-2.6.11.6 distributions; and *English* is the concatenation of English text files selected from etext02 to etext05 collections of the Gutenberg Project, from which the headers related to the project were deleted so as to leave just the real text.

Table 1 presents some information on the data files involved. The second and third columns present the original file sizes in MB and millions of words, and the fourth column gives the size of the encoded alphabet, $|\Sigma|$.

Table 1. Information about the used datasets.

File	Size (MB)	# of words (in millions)	$|\Sigma|$
ebib	3.5	0.6	53
ftxt	7.6	1.2	127
sources	200.0	25.8	208
English	200.0	37.0	217

The experimental results are summarized in Table 2. Columns 2, 3 and 4 list, respectively, the number of nodes in a Huffman tree, in an sk-tree based on pruning a canonical Huffman tree, as advocated in [10], and in an optimal sk-tree, according to Algorithm 1. There is a gain of 12–23% for the given example files. The last three columns of the table give the average number of necessary bit comparisons for the decoding of a single codeword. This is the average codeword length for a Huffman tree, and for the two skeleton trees, these numbers are smaller since no additional bit comparisons are needed once the codeword length is known, that is, a leaf of the sk-tree has been reached. Since decoding time should be roughly proportional to the number of processed bits, these averages can be seen as estimates for the average decoding times. The improvement in the average number of bit comparisons of the optimal over the canonical sk-tree is, for our examples, of about 4–11%. We see that in spite of the already significant savings in both time and space of the canonical sk-tree versus Huffman trees, passing to the non-intuitive optimal sk-trees may still yield some additional gain.

Table 2. Comparing tree sizes and average codeword lengths.

File	Number of nodes			Average codeword length		
	Huffman	Canonical	Optimal	Huffman	Canonical	Optimal
ebib	105	57	47	4.22	3.35	2.97
ftxt	253	89	77	4.59	3.14	3.02
English	433	129	113	4.48	3.22	3.00
sources	415	93	71	5.55	3.42	3.17

5 Conclusion

Skeleton trees have been introduced as a data structure improving both the space and time complexities of the decoding of texts encoded by optimal prefix codes such as Huffman's. The construction of skeleton trees is based on canonical Huffman trees, clustering leaves on each level together, according to the assumption that this should increase the number of nodes in the pruned subtrees. This paper shows, however, that this intuition is misleading, as pruning a canonical tree does not always yield a tree with a minimal number of nodes. An algorithm for creating such an optimal skeleton tree is presented.

Note that sk-trees are just one of the possibilities to enhance decoding: while some prefix of each codeword is processed bit by bit, several bits forming its suffix may be dealt with as a single unit. Alternatively, other methods use lookup tables prepared in a preprocessing stage, to decode prefixes or other substrings of codewords, or even several codewords together, as a bulk [3].

References

1. Barbay, J., Gagie, T., Navarro, G., Nekrich, Y.: Alphabet partitioning for compressed rank/select and applications. In: Cheong, O., Chwa, K.-Y., Park, K. (eds.) ISAAC 2010. LNCS, vol. 6507, pp. 315–326. Springer, Heidelberg (2010). doi:10. 1007/978-3-642-17514-5_27
2. Baruch, G., Klein, S.T., Shapira, D.: A space efficient direct access data structure. J. Discrete Algorithms **43**, 26–37 (2017)
3. Bergman, E., Klein, S.T.: Fast decoding of prefix encoded texts. In: 2005 Data Compression Conference (DCC 2005), Snowbird, UT, USA, 29–31 March 2005, pp. 143–152 (2005)
4. Dubé, D.: Leaner skeleton trees for direct-access compressed files. In: Proceedings of IEEE International Symposium on Information Theory and its Applications (ISITA), Monterey, pp. 122–130 (2016)
5. Ferguson, T.J., Rabinowitz, J.H.: Self-synchronizing Huffman codes. IEEE Trans. Inf. Theory **30**(4), 687–693 (1984)
6. Gilbert, E.N., Moore, E.F.: Variable-length binary encodings. Bell Syst. Tech. J. **38**, 933–968 (1959)
7. Grossi, R., Gupta, A., Vitter, J.S.: High-order entropy-compressed text indexes. In: Proceedings of the 14th Annual SIAM/ACM Symposium on Discrete Algorithms (SODA), pp. 841–850 (2003)

8. Huffman, D.: A method for the construction of minimum redundancy codes. In: Proceedings of the IRE, pp. 1098–1101 (1952)
9. Jacobson, G.: Space efficient static trees and graphs. In: Proceedings of Foundations of Computer Science (FOCS), pp. 549–554 (1989)
10. Klein, S.T.: Skeleton trees for the efficient decoding of Huffman encoded texts. J. Inf. Retrieval **3**, 7–23 (2000). Special issue on Compression and Efficiency in Information Retrieval of the Kluwer
11. Klein, S.T.: Basic Concepts in Data Structures. Cambridge University Press, Cambridge (2016)
12. Navarro, G., Providel, E.: Fast, small, simple rank/select on bitmaps. In: Klasing, R. (ed.) SEA 2012. LNCS, vol. 7276, pp. 295–306. Springer, Heidelberg (2012). doi:10.1007/978-3-642-30850-5_26
13. Okanohara, D., Sadakane, K.: Practical entropy-compressed rank/select dictionary. In: Proceedings of ALENEX. SIAM (2007)
14. Raman, R., Raman, V., Satti, S.R.: Succinct indexable dictionaries with applications to encoding k-ary trees, prefix sums and multisets. ACM Trans. Algorithms **3**(4), 43 (2007)
15. Schwartz, E.S., Kallick, B.: Generating a canonical prefix encoding. Commun. ACM **7**, 166–169 (1964)
16. Shapira, D., Daptardar, A.: Adapting the Knuth-Morris-Pratt algorithm for pattern matching in Huffman encoded texts. Inf. Process. Manag. **42**(2), 429–439 (2006)
17. Turpin, A., Moffat, A.: Fast file search using text compression. In: Australian Computer Science Conference, pp. 1–8 (1997)
18. Véronis, J., Langlais, P.: Evaluation of parallel text alignment systems: The arcade project. In: Véronis, J. (ed.) Parallel Text Processing, vol. 13, pp. 369–388. Springer, Dordrecht (2000). doi:10.1007/978-94-017-2535-4_19

Detecting One-Variable Patterns

Dmitry Kosolobov[2]([⊠]), Florin Manea[1], and Dirk Nowotka[1]

[1] Institut für Informatik, Christian-Albrechts-Universität zu Kiel, Kiel, Germany
{flm,dn}@informatik.uni-kiel.de
[2] Institute of Mathematics and Computer Science, Ural Federal University,
Ekaterinburg, Russia
dkosolobov@mail.ru

Abstract. Given a pattern $p = s_1 x_1 s_2 x_2 \cdots s_{r-1} x_{r-1} s_r$ such that $x_1, x_2, \ldots, x_{r-1} \in \{x, \overline{x}\}$, where x is a variable and $\overline{x}$ its reversal, and $s_1, s_2, \ldots, s_r$ are strings that contain no variables, we describe an algorithm that constructs in $O(rn)$ time a compact representation of all P instances of p in an input string of length n over a polynomially bounded integer alphabet, so that one can report those instances in $O(P)$ time.

Keywords: Patterns with variables · Matching · Repetitions · Pseudo-repetitions

1 Introduction

A *pattern* is a string consisting of *variables* (e.g., x, y, z) and *terminal letters* (e.g., a, b, c). The terminal letters are treated as constants, while the variables are letters to be uniformly replaced by strings over the set of terminals (i.e., all occurrences of the same variable are replaced by the same string); by such a replacement, a pattern is mapped to a terminal string. Patterns with variables appeared in various areas of computer science, e.g., stringology and pattern matching [1], combinatorics on words [20], language and learning theory [2], or regular expressions with back references [10,24], used in programming languages like Perl, Java, Python. In such applications, patterns are used to express string searching questions such as testing whether a string contains regularities.

Here, we consider the so-called *one-variable patterns* $p = s_1 x_1 \cdots s_{r-1} x_{r-1} s_r$ such that, for all z, $x_z \in \{x, \overline{x}\}$, where x is a variable and $\overline{x}$ its reversal, and s_z is a string over a set Σ of terminals. An *instance* of p in a text t is a substring $s_1 w_1 \cdots s_{r-1} w_r s_r$ of t, with $w_z = w$ if $x_z = x$ and $w_z = \overline{w}$ if $x_z = \overline{x}$, for a non-empty $w \in \Sigma^*$ called *substitution* of x. We address the problem of efficiently finding instances of such patterns in texts.

For example, let $p = ax ab x bc \overline{x}$. An instance of this pattern, if the alphabet of terminals is $\{a, b, c\}$, is $a\,abc\,ab\,abc\,bc\,cba$, where x is substituted by abc (and, consequently, $\overline{x}$ by cba). Another instance is $a\,aaabbb\,ab\,aaabbb\,bc\,bbbaaa$ if x is substituted by $aaabbb$. Both these instances occur in the text $t = aabcababcbccbaaaabbbabaaabbbbcbbbaaa$: the former instance starts at position 1 and the later starts at position 14. These two instances overlap at position 14.

© Springer International Publishing AG 2017
G. Fici et al. (Eds.): SPIRE 2017, LNCS 10508, pp. 254–270, 2017.
DOI: 10.1007/978-3-319-67428-5_22

Our motivation for studying such patterns is two-fold. Firstly, the efficient matching of several classes of restricted patterns was analyzed in [9] and connected to algorithmic learning theory [8]. Generally, matching patterns with variables to strings is NP-complete [7], so it seemed an interesting problem to find structurally restricted classes of patterns for which the matching problem is tractable. As such, finding all occurrences of a one-variable pattern in a word occurred as basic component in the matching algorithms proposed in [9] for patterns with a constant number of repeated variables or for non-cross patterns (patterns that do not have the form $..x..y..x..$).

Secondly, our work extends the study of pseudo-repetitions (patterns from $\{x, \overline{x}\}^*$). The concept of pseudo-repetitions (introduced in [6], studied from both combinatorial [22] and algorithmic [13,25] points of view) draws its original motivations from important biological concepts: tandem repeat, i.e., a consecutive repetition of the same sequence of nucleotides; inverted repeat, i.e., a sequence of nucleotides whose reversed image occurred already in the longer DNA sequence we analyze, both occurrences (original and reversed one) encoding, essentially, the same genetic information; or, hairpin structures in the DNA sequences, which can be modeled by patterns of the form $s_1 x s_2 \overline{x} s_3$. More interesting to us, from a mathematical point of view, pseudo-repetitions generalize both the notions of repetition and of palindrome, central to combinatorics on words and applications. The one-variable pattern model we analyze generalizes naturally the mathematical model of pseudo-repetition by allowing the repeated occurrences of the variable to be separated by some constant factors.

Thus, we consider the next problem, aiming to improve the detection of pseudo-repetition [13], as well as a step towards faster detection of occurrences of restricted patterns [8,9].

Problem 1. Given a string $t \in \Sigma^*$ of length n and a pattern $p = s_1 x_1 \cdots s_{r-1} x_{r-1} s_r$ such that, for $1 \leq z \leq r - 1$, $x_z \in \{x, \overline{x}\}$ where $x \notin \Sigma$ is a variable and $\overline{x}$ its reversal, and $s_z \in \Sigma^*$ for $1 \leq z \leq r$, report all P instances of p in t (in a form allowing their retrieval in $O(P)$ time).

We assume that t and all strings s_z, for $z = 1, \ldots, r$, are over an integer alphabet $\Sigma = \{0, 1, \ldots, n^{O(1)}\}$, and that we use the word RAM model with $\Theta(\log n)$-bit machine words[1] (w.l.o.g., assume that $\log n$ is an integer). In this setting, we propose an algorithm that reports in $O(rn)$ time all instances of p in t in a compactly encoded form, which indeed allows us to retrieve them in $O(P)$ time. Our approach is based on a series of deep combinatorics on words observations, e.g., regarding the repetitive structure of the text, and on the usage of efficient string-processing data structures, combining and extending in novel and nontrivial ways the ideas from [9,13,17].

If the pattern contains only a constant number of variables (e.g., generalized squares or cubes with terminals between the variables), our algorithm is asymptotically as efficient as the algorithms detecting fixed exponent (pseudo-)repetitions. For arbitrary patterns, our solution generalizes and improves the results of [13],

---

[1] Hereafter, log denotes the logarithm with base 2.

where an $O(r^2 n)$-time solution to the problem of finding one occurrence of a one-variable pattern with reversals (without terminals) was given. Here, compared to [13], we work with patterns that contain both variables and terminals and we detect, even faster, all their instances. Also, we improve the results of [9] in several directions: as said, we find all instances of a one-variable pattern (in [9] such a problem was solved as a subroutine in the algorithm detecting non-cross patterns, and only some instances of the patterns were found), our algorithm is faster by a $\log n$ factor, and our patterns also contain reversed variables.

In this paper, we omit most of the technicalities of the solution to Problem 1 from the main part, and prefer to keep the presentation at an intuitive level; the full proofs are available in the full version of this paper [18].

2 Preliminaries

Let w be a string of length n. Denote $|w| = n$. The *empty string* is denoted by ϵ. We write $w[i]$ for the ith letter of w and $w[i..j]$ for $w[i]w[i+1]\cdots w[j]$. A string u is a *substring* of w if $u = w[i..j]$ for some $i \leq j$. The pair (i, j) is not necessarily unique; we say that i specifies an *occurrence* of u in w. A substring $w[1..j]$ (resp., $w[i..n]$) is a *prefix* (resp. *suffix*) of w. The *reversal of* w is the string $\bar{w} = w[n]\cdots w[2]w[1]$; w is a *palindrome* if $w = \bar{w}$. For any $i, j \in \mathbb{R}$, denote $[i..j] = \{k \in \mathbb{Z}: i \leq k \leq j\}$, $(i..j] = [i..j] \setminus \{i\}$, $[i..j) = [i..j] \setminus \{j\}$, $(i..j) = [i..j) \cap (i..j]$. Our notation for arrays is similar to that for strings, e.g., $a[i..j]$ denotes an array indexed by the numbers $[i..j]$: $a[i], a[i+1], \ldots, a[j]$.

In Problem 1 we are given an input string (called text) t of length n and a pattern $p = s_1 x_1 s_2 x_2 \cdots s_{r-1} x_{r-1} s_r$ such that, for $z \in [1..r)$, $x_z \in \{x, \bar{x}\}$ and $s_1, s_2, \ldots, s_r$ are strings that contain no x nor $\bar{x}$. For the simplicity of exposure, we can assume $x_1 = x$. An *instance of* p in the text t is a substring $t[i..j] = s_1 w_1 s_2 w_2 \cdots s_{r-1} w_{r-1} s_r$ such that, for $z \in [1..r)$, $w_z = w$ if $x_z = x$, and $w_z = \bar{w}$ if $x_z = \bar{x}$, where w is a string called a *substitution* of x; $\bar{w}$ is called a *substitution of* $\bar{x}$. We want to find all instances of p occurring in t.

An integer $d > 0$ is a *period* of a string w if $w[i] = w[i+d]$ for all $i \in [1..|w|-d]$; w is *periodic* if it has a period $\leq \frac{|w|}{2}$. For a string w, denote by $\mathrm{pre}_d(w)$ and $\mathrm{suf}_d(w)$, respectively, the longest prefix and suffix of w with period d. A *run* of a string w is a periodic substring $w[i..j]$ such that both substrings $w[i-1..j]$ and $w[i..j+1]$, if defined, have strictly greater minimal periods than $w[i..j]$. A string w is *primitive* if $w \neq v^k$ for any string v and any integer $k > 1$.

Lemma 2 (see [5]). *A primitive string v occurs exactly twice in the string vv.*

Lemma 3. *Let R be the set of all runs of t, whose period is at least three times smaller than the length of the run (such runs are called cubic). Then $\sum_{s \in R} |s| \in O(n \log n)$.*

Proof. Consider a run $t[i..j] \in R$ with the minimal period p. Since a primitively rooted square of length $2p$ occurs at any position $k \in [i..j-2p+1]$, the sum $\sum_{s \in R} |s|$ is upper bounded by three times the number of primitively rooted squares occurring in t. At each position of t, at most $2\lceil \log n \rceil$ primitively rooted squares may occur (see, e.g., [5]), so the result follows.   □

In solving Problem 1, we use a series of preprocessing steps. First, we find all runs in t in $O(n)$ time using the algorithm of [3] and, using radix sort, construct lists R_d, for $d = 1, 2, \ldots, n$, such that R_d contains the starting positions of all runs with the minimal period d in increasing order. We produce from R_d two sublists R'_d and R''_d containing only the runs with the lengths $\geq \log n$ and $\geq \log\log n$, respectively (so that R'_d is a sublist of R''_d). The following lemma provides us fast access to the lists R_d, R'_d, R''_d from periodic substrings of t.

Lemma 4 ([15, Lemma 6.6]). *With $O(n)$ time preprocessing, we can decide in $O(1)$ time for any substring $t[i..j]$ of t whether it is periodic and, if so, compute its minimal period d and find in R_d, R'_d, or R''_d the run containing $t[i..j]$.*

For $i, j \in [1..n]$, let $\mathsf{lcp}(i, j)$ and $\overleftarrow{\mathsf{lcp}}(i, j)$ be the lengths of the longest common prefixes of the strings $t[i..n]$, $t[j..n]$ and $\overleftarrow{t[1..i]}$, $\overleftarrow{t[1..j]}$, respectively. In $O(n)$ time we build for the string $t\overleftarrow{t}$ the *longest common prefix* data structure (for short, called the lcp *structure*) that allows us retrieving the values $\mathsf{lcp}(i, j)$ and $\overleftarrow{\mathsf{lcp}}(i, j)$ for any $i, j \in [1..n]$ in $O(1)$ time (see [5,14]). Thus, to check if the substrings of length ℓ starting (resp., ending) at positions i and j in the string t are equal, we just check whether $\mathsf{lcp}(i, j) \geq \ell$ (resp., $\overleftarrow{\mathsf{lcp}}(i, j) \geq \ell$). As a side note, we essentially use that we can compare the reversed image of two substrings of t using the lcp structure built for $t\overleftarrow{t}$.

With the lcp structure, it is easy to solve Problem 1 in $O(rn^2)$ time: we first apply any linear pattern matching algorithm to find in $O(rn)$ time all occurrences of the strings $s_1, s_2, \ldots, s_r$ in t and then, for every position $i \in [1..n]$ of t and every $\ell \in [0..n]$, we check in $O(r)$ time whether an instance $s_1 w_1 \cdots s_{r-1} w_{r-1} s_r$ of the pattern p, with $\ell = |w_1| = \cdots = |w_{r-1}|$, occurs at position i.

General Strategy. For each $z \in [1..r]$, using a pattern matching algorithm (see [5]), we fill in $O(n)$ time a bit array $D_z[1..n]$ where, for $i \in [1..n]$, $D_z[i] = 1$ iff s_z occurs at position i. Assume that p contains at least two occurrences of the variable, i.e., $p \notin \{s_1 x s_2\}$ (in the case $p = s_1 x s_2$ each instance of p is given by an occurrence of s_1, stored in D_1, followed by an occurrence of s_2, stored in D_2).

Let $\alpha = \frac{4}{3}$. For each $k \in [0.. \log_\alpha n]$, our algorithm finds all instances of p that are obtained by the substitution of x with strings of lengths from $(\frac{3}{2}\alpha^k .. 2\alpha^k]$. Clearly, the intervals $(\frac{3}{2}\alpha^k .. 2\alpha^k]$ do not intersect and their union covers the interval $[2..n]$. In this manner, our algorithm obtains all instances of p with substitutions of x of length at least two. The remaining instances, when the string substituting x has length one or zero, can be easily found in $O(rn)$ time using the arrays $\{D_z\}_{z=1}^r$.

So, let us fix $k \in [0.. \log_\alpha n]$ and explain our strategy for this case. Suppose that, for $i, j \in [1..n]$, $t[i..j] = s_1 w_1 s_2 w_2 \cdots s_{r-1} w_{r-1} s_r$ is an instance of p and $\frac{3}{2}\alpha^k < |w_1| = \cdots = |w_{r-1}| \leq 2\alpha^k$; then w_1 contains a substring v of length $\lceil \alpha^k \rceil$ starting, within t, either at position $q_1 = h\lceil \alpha^k \rceil + 1$ or at position $q_1 =$

$h\lceil\alpha^k\rceil + \lfloor\frac{\lceil\alpha^k\rceil}{2}\rfloor$ for some integer $h \geq 0$. Based on this observation, we consider all choices of a substring v of t, with length $\lceil\alpha^k\rceil$, starting at positions $h\lceil\alpha^k\rceil + 1$ and $h\lceil\alpha^k\rceil + \lfloor\frac{\lceil\alpha^k\rceil}{2}\rfloor$ for $h \geq 0$. Such a string v acts as a sort of anchor: it restricts (in a strong way, because of its rather large length with respect to $|w_1|$) the positions where w_1 may occur in t, and copies of either v or $\bar{v}$ should also occur in all $w_2, \ldots, w_{r-1}$, thus restricting the positions where these strings may occur in t, as well. Based on a series of combinatorial observations regarding the way such substrings v occur in t, and using efficient data structures to store and manipulate these occurrences, we find all corresponding instances of p that contain v in the substitution of x_1 in $O(r + \frac{r|v|}{\log n})$ time plus $O(\frac{\log n}{\log\log n})$ time if $\frac{\log n}{16\log\log n} \leq |v| \leq \log n$. We discuss two cases: v is non-periodic or periodic.

In the first case, distinct occurrences of v (or $\bar{v}$) in t do not have large overlaps, so we can detect them rather fast, as described in Lemma 6: for $\lambda = |s_2|$, we preprocess a data structure that allows us to efficiently find all occurrences of v or $\bar{v}$ at the distance λ to the right of v and these occurrences serve as additional anchors inside the substitution w_2; note that the case of very short v requires a separate discussion. Hence, the distinct instances of p where the substitution of x contains a certain non-periodic v also do not have large overlaps (which means, as well, that they are not too many), and they can be identified (and stored, as described in Lemma 7) by trying to align occurrences of the strings $s_1, \ldots, s_r$ in a correct manner around the found v's.

Then we consider the case when v is periodic. Then, the occurrences of v or $\bar{v}$ corresponding to different instances of p might have large overlaps and form runs, so we analyze the runs structure of t. Consider, for the simplicity of exposure, a typical example: $t = (abc)^m$ contains $\Theta(|t|^2)$ instances of $p = xcxcabcxcxcxca$ with substitutions $x = ab(cab)^k$, for different k. The point in this example is that almost all substitutions are periodic and are contained in one run with the same minimal period. We can encode these instances by an arithmetic progression: for all $0 \leq h \leq m - 7$, $0 \leq k \leq m - h - 7$, there is an instance of p starting at position $1+3h$ of t with substitution of length $2 + 3k$. It turns out, as described in Lemmas 13 and 15, that, for any pattern p, all instances of p whose substitutions are periodic substrings of one run with the same minimal period can be encoded by similar arithmetic progressions.

Consider now another relevant example: $t = (abc)^{\ell}d(abc)^m$ contains $\Theta(|t|)$ instances of $p = xxdxabcxx$ with substitutions $x = (abc)^k$. All these instances can be encoded as follows: for all $k = 0, 1, \ldots, \min\{\ell, m\}$, there is an instance of p starting at position $1 + 3\ell - 3k$ with substitution of length $3k$. So, the letter d "separates" the image of p into two runs, breaking the period of the first run. As shown in Lemmas 11 and 12, there might exist only a constant number of such "separators" in a general p and all instances of p, with the image x periodic, and which lie in two runs with the same minimal period, split by a given "separator", can be encoded by similar arithmetic progressions (the analysis of this case is similar to the analysis of in-a-run instances, so, it is moved in the full version [18]).

If the substitutions in an instance of p lie in three or more runs (so, also there are more points where the period breaks inside each instance of p), then we can find the possible occurrences of v (which are periodic, so they must avoid period-breaking points that separate the runs contained in p) and, consequently, find the instances of p. The combinatorics of such instances of the pattern is discussed in Lemmas 8 and 9: the essential idea is that the occurrences of v and $\bar{v}$ in p and the substrings connecting them form runs, separated by substrings which break the periodicity; these substrings should correspond to substrings that interrupt runs in t. The actual algorithm identifying and storing these instances of the pattern follows from Lemmas 10, 11 and 12 (and the comments connecting them).

Finally, since there are $O(\frac{n}{\alpha^k})$ such substrings v and at most $O(n/\frac{\log n}{\log \log n})$ of them (for all $k = 0, 1, \ldots$ in total) are such that $\frac{\log n}{16 \log \log n} \leq |v| \leq \log n$, the overall time is $O(\sum_{k=0}^{\log_\alpha n} \frac{n}{\alpha^k}(r + \frac{r\alpha^k}{\log n}) + (n/\frac{\log n}{\log \log n})\frac{\log n}{\log \log n}) = O(rn)$.

The details of all the cases considered in our approach are given in Sects. 3 and 4, following the general strategy described above. Summing up, we get:

Theorem 5. *Problem 1 can be solved in $O(rn)$ time.*

3 Non-periodic Anchor Substring v

As described in the *General Strategy* paragraph, we first choose an anchor string v occurring in w_1 and then try to construct an instance of the pattern p around this v. So, let v be a substring of t of length $\lceil \alpha^k \rceil$ starting at position $q_1 = h|v| + 1$ for some integer $h \geq 0$ (the case of position $h|v| + \lfloor \frac{|v|}{2} \rfloor$ is similar). As explained before, we will iterate through all possible values of h, which allows us to identify all instances of the pattern. For a fixed v, using Lemma 4, we check whether it is periodic. In this section, we suppose that v is not periodic; the case of periodic v is considered in Sect. 4.

Our aim is to find all instances $t[i..j] = s_1 w_1 s_2 w_2 \cdots s_{r-1} w_{r-1} s_r$ of p in which w_1 contains v and has length close to $|v|$, i.e., i and j must be such that $i + |s_1| \leq q_1 < q_1 + |v| \leq i + |s_1 w_1|$ and $\frac{3}{2}|v| < |w_1| = \cdots = |w_{r-1}| \leq 2|v|$.

Let $t[i..j]$ be such a substring. It follows from the inequality $\frac{3}{2}|v| < |w_1| \leq 2|v|$ that we can compute a relatively small interval of t where the v (or $\bar{v}$) corresponding to w_2 may occur. More precisely, if $w_1 = w_2$ (resp., $w_1 = \bar{w}_2$), then the string v (resp., $\bar{v}$) has an occurrence starting at a position from the interval $[q_1 + |vs_2|..q_1 + |vvs_2v|]$. Since v is not periodic, the length of the overlap between any two distinct occurrences of v is less than $\frac{|v|}{2}$. Hence, there are at most four occurrences of v (resp., $\bar{v}$) starting in $[q_1 + |vs_2|..q_1 + |vvs_2v|]$. To find these occurrences, our algorithm applies the following general lemma for $\lambda = |s_2|$.

Lemma 6. *Let $\lambda \geq 0$ be an integer. We can preprocess the text t of length n in $O(n)$ time to produce data structures allowing us to retrieve, for any given non-periodic substring $v = t[q..q'-1]$, all occurrences of v and $\bar{v}$ starting in the substring $t[q' + \lambda..q' + \lambda + 2|v|]$ in:*

- *$O(\frac{|v|}{\log n})$ time if $|v| > \log n$,*

– $O(\frac{\log n}{\log \log n})$ *time if* $\frac{\log n}{16 \log \log n} \leq |v| \leq \log n$, *and*

– $O(1)$ *time otherwise.*

Proof. For $i \in [1..n]$, let $t_i = t[i..i+\log n - 1]$ be the substring of length $\log n$ starting at position i in t. Let S be the set of all distinct strings t_i. Using the suffix array of t, its lcp structure, and radix sort, we construct in $O(n)$ time the set of arrays $\{A_s\}_{s \in S}$ such that, for any $s \in S$, A_s contains the starting positions of all occurrences of s in t in ascending order. Essentially, for each $s \in S$, we locate an occurrence of s in t and then produce a "cluster" of the suffix array of t with the suffixes starting with s, then we radix sort (simultaneously) the positions in these "clusters" (all numbers between 1 and n, keeping track of the "cluster" from where each position came), to obtain the arrays A_s. Further, using the suffix array of the string $t\overleftarrow{t}$, its lcp structure, and radix sort, we build in $O(n)$ time arrays of pointers $B[1..n]$ and $\overleftarrow{B}[1..n]$ such that, for $i \in [1..n]$, $B[i]$ (resp., $\overleftarrow{B}[i]$) points to the element of A_{t_i} (resp., $A_{\overleftarrow{t_i}}$) storing the leftmost position j with $j \geq i + \lambda$ and $t_i = t_j$ (resp., $\overleftarrow{t_i} = t_j$); $B[i]$ (resp., $\overleftarrow{B}[i]$) is undefined if there is no such j.

The case $|v| > \log n$. In this case, to find all required occurrences of v, we note that $v = t[q..q' - 1]$ starts with t_q. Thus, we first find all occurrences of t_q starting within the segment $[q + \lambda..q' + \lambda + 2|v|]$. The sequence of all such occurrences forms a contiguous subarray in A_{t_q} and $B[q]$ points to the beginning of this subarray.

In a first case, suppose that the distance between any two consecutive positions stored in this subarray is greater than $\frac{|t_q|}{2}$. Then there are at most $O(\frac{|v|}{|t_q|}) = O(\frac{|v|}{\log n})$ such occurrences of t_q. Some of these occurrences may be extended to form an occurrence of v, and they must be identified. To check in constant time whether v occurs indeed at a given position ℓ of the subarray we use the lcp structure and verify whether $\text{lcp}(\ell, q) \geq |v|$.

The case of the string $\overleftarrow{v}$ is analogous but involves $\overleftarrow{t_q}$ and $\overleftarrow{B}$ instead of t_q and B. Hence, we find all required occurrences of v and $\overleftarrow{v}$ in $O(\frac{|v|}{\log n})$ time.

Suppose that the aforementioned subarray of A_{t_q} (resp., $A_{\overleftarrow{t_q}}$), containing the positions of t_q (resp., $\overleftarrow{t_q}$) in the desired range, contains two consecutive occurrences of t_q (resp., $\overleftarrow{t_q}$) whose starting positions differ by at most $\frac{|t_q|}{2}$. Then t_q is periodic. Using Lemma 4, we compute the minimal period d of t_q and find, in $O(1)$ time, the run $t[i'..j']$ (in the list R'_d) containing t_q. Recall now that v is not periodic, so we must have that $t[q..j']$ is $\text{pre}_d(v)$, the maximal d-periodic prefix of v, and $|\text{pre}_d(v)| < |v|$. We now focus on finding the occurrences of t_q in the range $[q' + \lambda..q' + \lambda + 2|v|]$. Since R'_d contains only runs of length $\geq \log n$ and any two runs with period d cannot overlap on more than $d-1$ letters, there are at most $O(\frac{|v|}{\log n})$ runs in R'_d that overlap with the segment $[q+\lambda..q'+\lambda+2|v|]$. These runs can be all found in $O(\frac{|v|}{\log n})$ time. Some of them may end with $\text{pre}_d(v)$ and may be extended to the right to obtain an occurrence of v (resp., $\overleftarrow{v}$). If $t[i''..j'']$

is one of the runs we found, then there might be an occurrence of v starting at position $j'' - j' + q$ or an occurrence of $\overleftarrow{v}$ ending at position $i'' + j' - q$. So, using the lcp structure, in a similar way as before, we find all required occurrence of v (resp., $\overleftarrow{v}$) in $O(\frac{|v|}{\log n})$ time.

It remains to consider how to find all occurrences of $v = t[q..q' - 1]$ (resp., $\overleftarrow{v}$) starting in the segment $[q'+\lambda..q'+\lambda+2|v|]$ in the case $\frac{\log n}{16 \log \log n} \leq |v| \leq \log n$ and $|v| < \frac{\log n}{16 \log \log n}$.

The case $\frac{\log n}{16 \log \log n} \leq |v| \leq \log n$. This case is similar to the case $|v| > \log n$. For $i \in [1..n - \lfloor \log \log n \rfloor]$, define $t'_i = t[i..i+\lfloor \log \log n \rfloor]$. Let S' be the set of all distinct strings t'_i. In the same way as in the case $|v| > \log n$, using the suffix array of t, its lcp structure, and radix sort, we construct in $O(n)$ time the set of arrays $\{A'_{s'}\}_{s' \in S'}$ such that, for any $s' \in S'$, $A'_{s'}$ contains the starting positions of all occurrences of s' in t in ascending order. Further, using the suffix array of the string $t\overleftarrow{t}$, its lcp structure, and radix sort, we build in $O(n)$ time arrays of pointers $B'[1..n]$ and $\overleftarrow{B}'[1..n]$ such that, for $i \in [1..n]$, $B'[i]$ (resp., $\overleftarrow{B}'[i]$) points to the element of $A'_{t'_i}$ (resp., $A'_{\overleftarrow{t'_i}}$) storing the leftmost position j with $j \geq i + \lambda$ and $t'_i = t'_j$ (resp., $\overleftarrow{t'_i} = t'_j$); $B'[i]$ (resp., $\overleftarrow{B}'[i]]$) is undefined if there is no such j. Now we proceed like in the case $|v| > \log n$ but use t'_q instead of t_q, the arrays $A'_{t'_q}$, B', $\overleftarrow{B}'$ instead of A_{t_q}, B, $\overleftarrow{B}$, and the list R''_d instead of R'_d. The processing takes $O(\frac{|v|}{\log \log n}) = O(\frac{\log n}{\log \log n})$ time.

The case $|v| < \frac{\log n}{16 \log \log n}$. Using radix sort, we can reduce the alphabet of t to $[0..n)$ in $O(n)$ time; let $\$$ be a new letter. For $h \in [0..\frac{n}{\log n})$, let $e_h = t[h \log n+1..h \log n+2 \log n]$ and $f_h = t[h \log n+\lambda..h \log n+\lambda+5 \log n]$ assuming $\$ = t[n+1] = t[n+2] = \ldots$, so that e_h and f_h are well defined. Note that v is a substring of e_h for $h = \lfloor \frac{q-1}{\log n} \rfloor$ and, if there is an occurrence of v (resp., $\overleftarrow{v}$) starting in the segment $[q' + \lambda..q' + \lambda + 2|v|]$, then this occurrence is a substring of f_h.

For each $h \in [0..\frac{n}{\log n})$, our algorithm constructs a string $g_h = e_h\$f_h$ and reduces the alphabet of g_h to $[1..|g_h|]$ as follows. Let $E[0..n]$ be an array of integers filled with zeros. While processing g_h, we maintain a counter c; initially, $c = 0$. For $i = 1, 2, \ldots, |g_h|$, we check whether $E[g_h[i]] = 0$ and, if so, assign $c \leftarrow c + 1$ and $E[g_h[i]] \leftarrow c$. Regardless of the result of this check, we perform $g_h[i] \leftarrow E[g_h[i]]$. Once the alphabet of g_h is reduced, we clear all modified elements of E using an unmodified copy of g_h and move on to g_{h+1}. Thus, the reductions of the alphabets of all g_h take $O(n + \sum_{h=0}^{\lfloor n/\log n \rfloor} |g_h|) = O(n)$ overall time.

Each letter in a string g_h fits in $\lceil \log(|g_h| + 1) \rceil \leq 2\lceil \log \log n \rceil$ bits. Hence, the substrings of g_h corresponding to the substrings $v = t[q..q' - 1]$ and $t[q' + \lambda..q' + \lambda + 3|v|]$ together fit in $8|v|\lceil \log \log n \rceil \leq \frac{\log n}{2}$ bits. Thus, we can perform the searching of v (resp., $\overleftarrow{v}$) in $t[q' + \lambda..q' + \lambda + 3|v|]$ in $O(1)$ time using a precomputed table of size $O(2^{\frac{\log n}{2}}) = O(\sqrt{n})$. $\square$

Recall that q_1 was the starting point of v (for simplicity, assume that $v = t[h_1..h_2]$, where h_1 is an alias of q_1 that is only used for the uniformity of the notation). Let $q_2 \in [q_1 + |vs_2|..q_1 + |vs_2vv|]$ be the starting position of an occurrence of v (or $\bar{v}$) found by Lemma 6. We now want to see whether there exists an instance of the pattern that has the anchor v from w_1 occurring at position q_1 and the corresponding v (resp., $\bar{v}$) from w_2 occurring at q_2.

If $x_1 = x_2$ (and, consequently, $w_1 = w_2$), then $\beta = q_2 - q_1 - |s_2|$ is the length of substitution w_1 of x that could produce the occurrence of v at position q_2. Once the length β is computed, we get that w_1 can start somewhere between $h_2 - \beta - |s_1|$ and $q_1 - |s_1| = h_1 - |s_1|$, so all corresponding instances of p will start in the interval $[h_2 - \beta - |s_1|+1..h_1 - |s_1|]$. These instances (determined by $h_1 = q_1$, $|v|$, and β) can be found by the following lemma (see the case $x_1 \neq x_2$ in [18]).

For a given β, let $L_p(\beta) = |s_1 s_2 \cdots s_r| + (r - 1)\beta$, that is, the length of the image of the pattern p when x is substituted by a variable of length β.

Lemma 7. *Given a substring $t[h_1..h_2] = v$ and an integer $\beta \geq |v|$, we can compute a bit array $occ[h_2 - \beta - |s_1|+1..h_1 - |s_1|]$ such that, for any i, we have $occ[i] = 1$ iff the string $t[i..i+L_p(\beta) - 1]$ is an instance of p containing v in its substring that corresponds to w_1 (i.e., $i + |s_1| \leq h_1 < h_2 < i + |s_1| + \beta$). This computation takes $O(r + \frac{r\beta}{\log n})$ time, to which we add $O(\frac{\log n}{\log \log n})$ time when $\frac{\log n}{16 \log \log n} \leq |v| \leq \log n$.*

Proof. The general idea of the proof is as follows. Knowing where v (which anchors w_1, which substitutes x) starts and knowing the length $|w_1|$, we know, if $x_1 = \cdots = x_{r-1}$, where the corresponding occurrences of v from $w_2, \ldots, w_{r-1}$ should be positioned (the case when $x_i \neq x_j$, for some $i \neq j$, is analyzed using more complicated ideas, e.g., from [4]; see the full version [18]). We check, in $O(r)$ time, if they indeed occur at those positions. Suppose this checking succeeds. These v's might correspond to more instances of p as in Fig. 1. We further check where the w_z's corresponding to occurrences of x in p may occur.

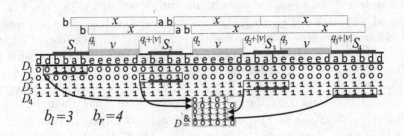

Fig. 1. Two instances of the pattern $p = bxabxx$.

To this end, we measure how much can we extend simultaneously, with the same string to the left (respectively, to the right), the occurrences of v corresponding to these w_i's. This will give us ranges of the same length, around each of the v's, that contain all possible w_i's. We follow a similar strategy for the

w_j's corresponding to $\bar{x}$ in p (see the details below). Now, all it remains is to see whether we can glue together some occurrences of $w_1, w_2, \ldots, w_r$ from the respective ranges, by identifying between them exactly the strings $s_1, s_2, \ldots, s_r$. This is be done efficiently using the arrays storing the occurrences of the s_i's, and standard bitwise operations. Let us formalize this explanation.

For $z \in [1..r)$, denote $q_z = h_1 + |s_2 s_3 \cdots s_z| + (z-1)\beta$. Denote by Z (resp., $\bar{Z}$) the set of all $z \in [1..r)$ such that $x_z = x$ (resp., $x_z = \bar{x}$). If there is an instance $t[i..j] = s_1 w_1 s_2 w_2 \cdots s_{r-1} w_{r-1} s_r$ of p such that $|w_1| = \cdots = |w_{r-1}| = \beta$ and $i + |s_1| \leq h_1 < h_2 < i + |s_1 w_1|$, then, for any $z, z' \in Z$ (resp., $z, z' \in \bar{Z}$), $t[q_z..q_z+|v|-1] = t[q_{z'}..q_{z'}+|v|-1]$. We check these equalities in $O(r)$ time using the lcp structure. Suppose this checking succeeds. There might exist many corresponding instances of p as in Fig. 1.

We can immediately calculate the numbers $b_\ell = \min\{\overleftarrow{\mathsf{lcp}}(q_z-1, q_{z'}-1): (z, z') \in (Z \times Z) \cup (\bar{Z} \times \bar{Z})\}$ and $b_r = \min\{\mathsf{lcp}(q_z+|v|, q_{z'}+|v|): (z, z') \in (Z \times Z) \cup (\bar{Z} \times \bar{Z})\}$ in $O(r)$ time. Assume that $t[i..j] = s_1 w_1 s_2 w_2 \cdots s_{r-1} w_{r-1} s_r$ is an instance of p with $|w_1| = \cdots = |w_{r-1}| = \beta$ and $i + |s_1| \leq h_1 < h_2 < i + |s_1 w_1|$. By the definition of b_ℓ and b_r, we then necessarily have $q_z - \delta \geq q_z - b_\ell$ and $q_z - \delta + \beta \leq q_z + |v| + b_r$ for all $z \in [1..r]$, where $\delta = h_1 - (i + |s_1|)$.

Thus, the next segments are non-empty (see Fig. 1):

$$S_z = [q_z - |s_z| - b_\ell .. q_{z-1} + |v| + b_r] \cap [q_{z-1} + |v| .. q_z - |s_z|] \text{ for } z \in (1..r),$$
$$S_1 = [q_1 - |s_1| - b_\ell .. q_1 - |s_1|] \cap [q_1 + |v| - |s_1| - \beta .. q_1 - |s_1|],$$
$$S_r = [q_{r-1} + |v| .. q_{r-1} + |v| + b_r] \cap [q_{r-1} + |v| .. q_{r-1} + \beta].$$

Further, if such instance $t[i..j]$ exists, then there is a sequence of positions $\{i_z\}_{z=1}^{r}$ such that $i_z \in S_z$, $D_z[i_z] = 1$ for $z \in [1..r]$ and $i_{z+1} - i_z = |s_z| + \beta$ for $z \in [1..r)$ (namely, $i_1 = i$). If $x_1 = \cdots = x_{r-1}$, then the converse is also true: if a sequence $\{i_z\}_{z=1}^{r}$ satisfies all these conditions, then $t[i_1..i_r+|s_r|-1] = s_1 w s_2 w \cdots s_{r-1} w s_r$, where $|w| = \beta$ and $i + |s_1| \leq h_1 < h_2 < i + |s_1| + \beta$. The bit arrays $\{D_z\}_{z=1}^{r}$ help us to find all such sequences.

Let $D'_1 = D_1[q_1 + |v| - |s_1| - \beta .. q_1 - |s_1|]$, $D'_r = D_r[q_{r-1} + |v| .. q_{r-1} + \beta]$ and $D'_z = D_z[q_{z-1} + |v| .. q_z - |s_z|]$ for $z \in (1..r)$. For each $z \in [1..r]$, we clear in the array D'_z all bits corresponding to the regions that are not covered by the segment S_z and then perform the bitwise "and" of $D'_1, \ldots, D'_r$; thus, we obtain a bit array $D[0..\beta-|v|]$ (see Fig. 1). If $x_1 = \cdots = x_{r-1}$, then, for any $i \in [0..\beta-|v|]$, we have $D[i] = 1$ iff there is a string $s_1 w s_2 w \cdots s_{r-1} w s_r$ starting at $i' = h_2 - \beta - |s_1| + i + 1$ such that $|w| = \beta$ and $i' + |s_1| \leq h_1 < h_2 < i' + |s_1 w|$. Obviously, one can put $occ[h_2 - \beta - |s_1| + 1..h_1 - |s_1|] = D[0..\beta-|v|]$. Since the length of each of the arrays $D'_1, \ldots, D'_r$ does not exceed β, all these calculations can be done in $O(r + \frac{r\beta}{\log n})$ time by standard bitwise operations on the $\Theta(\log n)$-bit machine words.

If p contains both x and $\bar{x}$, it is not clear how to check whether the substitutions of x and $\bar{x}$ corresponding to a given $D[i] = 1$ respect each other. The case when p contains both x and $\bar{x}$ turns out to be much more difficult; see [18]. □

4   Periodic Anchor Substring v

In this section we suppose v is periodic. Recall that v starts at q_1 and we also know its length. By Lemma 4, we find in $O(1)$ time the minimal period d of v and a run $t[i'..j']$ with period d containing v (i.e., $i' \le q_1 < q_1 + |v| - 1 \le j'$).

Just like before, we are searching for instances $t[i..j] = s_1 w_1 \cdots s_{r-1} w_{r-1} s_r$ of p such that $\frac{3}{2}|v| < |w_1| \le 2|v|$ and v occurs in w_1, so at least $|s_1|$ symbols away from i (in other words, $i + |s_1| \le q_1 < q_1 + |v| \le i + |s_1 w_1|$). Let us assume that $t[i..j]$ is such an instance. Then, either w_1 has period d or one of the strings $v' = t[q_1..j'+1]$ or $v'' = t[i'-1..q_1+|v|-1]$ is a substring of w_1 (that is, the run containing v ends or, respectively, starts strictly inside w_1).

Suppose first that w_1 contains v' as a substring (the case of v'' is similar); note that v' is the suffix of the run $t[i'..j']$ starting at position q_1, to which a letter that breaks the period was added. One can show that, since the minimal period of $t[q_1..j']$ is d, $2d \le j' - q_1 + 1$, and $t[j'+1] \ne t[j'+1-d]$, the string v' is not periodic. Hence, v' can be processed in the same way as v in Sect. 3, and get the instances of p that occur around it. A similar conclusion is reached when w_1 contains v'', so we assume in the following that w_1 is periodic.

Suppose that w_1 has period d. Periodic substitutions of x (such as w_1) can produce a lot of instances of p: e.g., a^n contains $\Theta(n^2)$ instances of xx. However, it turns out that when such multiple instances really occur, they have a uniform structure that can be compactly encoded and appear only when all substitutions of x and $\bar{x}$ lie either within one or two runs. Before the discussion of this case, let us first consider the case when three or more runs contain $w_1, \ldots, w_{r-1}$. Due to space constraints, some proofs are moved to the full version [18].

Three and More Runs. Let $t[i..j]$ be an instance of p with a substitution of $x_1 = x$ denoted by $w_1 = w$ and such that w has period d. Moreover, for our chosen v starting at position q_1, we still have $\frac{3}{2}|v| < |w| \le 2|v|$ and v occurs inside w_1 (i.e., $i + |s_1| \le q_1 < q_1 + |v| \le i + |s_1 w_1|$). Since $|v| \ge 2d$, we have $|w| \ge \frac{3}{2}|v| \ge 3d$. Clearly, each substitution of x or $\bar{x}$ in $t[i..j]$ is contained in some run with period d (some of these runs may coincide). It turns out that if all substitutions of x and $\bar{x}$ in $t[i..j]$ are contained in at least three distinct runs with period d, then there are only constantly many possibilities to choose the length $|w|$, and these possibilities can be efficiently found and then processed by Lemma 7 to find the instances of the pattern. To begin with, let us introduce several lemmas; in their statements w and s are strings (extensions for reversals are given in [18]).

Lemma 8. *Let ws be a substring of t such that w has period d, $|w| \ge 3d$, and ws does not have period d. Let $t[i..j]$ be a run with period d containing w and let h be the starting position of s. Then, either $h = j - |\mathrm{pre}_d(s)| + 1$ or $h \in (j+1-d..j+1]$.*

Proof. Suppose that $h \le j + 1 - d$. Then, $|\mathrm{pre}_d(s)| \ge j - h + 1 \ge d$. Thus, since $t[j+1] \ne t[j+1-d]$, $|\mathrm{pre}_d(s)|$ must be equal to $j - h + 1$ and hence $h = j - |\mathrm{pre}_d(s)| + 1$. $\square$

Lemma 9. *Let wsw (resp., $\bar{w}sw$) be a substring of t such that w has period d, $|w| \geq 3d$, and wsw (resp., $\bar{w}sw$) does not have period d. Let $t[i..j]$ be a run with period d containing the first occurrence of w (resp., $\bar{w}$) in wsw (resp., $\bar{w}sw$). Denote by h the starting position of s. Then, we have $h = j - |\mathrm{pre}_d(s)| + 1$ or $h \in (j+1-d..j+1]$ or $h \in (j-|s|-d..j-|s|]$.*

Proof. If $h + |s| > j$, then, by Lemma 8, either $h = j - |\mathrm{pre}_d(s)| + 1$ or $h \in (j+1-d..j+1]$. Suppose that $h + |s| \leq j$. Let $t[i'..j']$ be a run with period d containing the last occurrence of w in wsw (resp., $\bar{w}sw$). Clearly, $i' \leq h + |s|$. Hence, since $t[i..j]$ and $t[i'..j']$ cannot overlap on d letters, we obtain $j - d + 1 < h + |s|$. Therefore, $h \in (j-|s|-d..j-|s|]$. □

As the string w is periodic, but the whole image of p is not (it extends over three or more runs), some of the strings s_z must break the period induced by w. If we can identify the s_z's which break the period, Lemmas 8 and 9 allow us to locate their occurrences which, together with the v we considered, might lead to finding corresponding instances of p. The next lemma formalizes these ideas (its proof, especially for the patterns containing both x and $\bar{x}$, is rather non-trivial and uses results from [11,12,19,21,23]; see the full version [18]).

Lemma 10. *Let $v = t[h_1..h_2]$ be a string with the minimal period $d \leq \frac{|v|}{2}$. Given z, z' such that $1 < z < z' < r$, we can find all instances $t[i..j] = s_1 w_1 s_2 w_2 \cdots s_{r-1} w_{r-1} s_r$ of p such that $\frac{3}{2}|v| < |w_1| \leq 2|v|$, v is contained in w_1, $w_1 s_2 w_2 \cdots s_{z-1} w_{z-1}$ and $w_z s_{z+1} w_{z+1} \cdots s_{z'-1} w_{z'-1}$ both have period d, and $w_{z-1} s_z w_z$ and $w_{z'-1} s_{z'} w_{z'}$ both do not have period d, in $O(r + \frac{r|v|}{\log n})$ time. To this we add $O(\frac{\log n}{\log\log n})$ time if $\frac{\log n}{16\log\log n} \leq |v| \leq \log n$.*

It remains to explain how to identify the s_z's that break the period inside the instances of p, and show that their number is $O(1)$. Let Z (resp., Z', Z'') be the set of all numbers $z \in (1..r)$ such that $x_{z-1} = x_z$ (resp., $\bar{x}_{z-1} = x_z = \bar{x}$, $x_{z-1} = \bar{x}_z = \bar{x}$). By Lemma 2, as $w_z \in \{w, \bar{w}\}$ for $z \in [1..r]$, the next lemma follows:

Lemma 11. *For any numbers $z_1, z_2 \in Z$ (resp., Z', Z''), if the strings $w_{z_1-1} s_{z_1} w_{z_1}$ and $w_{z_2-1} s_{z_2} w_{z_2}$ both have period d, then the next properties hold:*

$$|s_{z_1}| \equiv |s_{z_2}| \pmod{d}, \quad s_{z_1} \text{ and } s_{z_2} \text{ both have period } d,$$
$$\text{one of } s_{z_1} \text{ and } s_{z_2} \ (s_{z_1} \text{ and } \bar{s}_{z_2} \text{ if } x_{z_1} \neq x_{z_2})\text{is a prefix of another.} \quad (1)$$

In the following sense, the converse is also true: if $|s_{z_1}| \geq d$, $w_{z_1-1} s_{z_1} w_{z_1}$ has period d, and z_1 and z_2 satisfy (1), then $w_{z_2-1} s_{z_2} w_{z_2}$ necessarily has period d.

We call a pair of numbers (z, z') such that $z \leq z'$ and $z, z' \in Z$ a *separation* in Z if all numbers $z_1, z_2 \in ((1..z) \cup (z..z')) \cap Z$ satisfy (1) and all numbers $z_1 \in ((1..z)\cup(z..z'))\cap Z$ and $z_2 \in \{z, z'\}$ either do not satisfy (1) or satisfy $|s_{z_1}| < d \leq |s_{z_2}|$; separations in Z' and Z'' are defined analogously. Informally, a pair (z, z') is a separation in Z (resp., Z', Z'') if $w_1 s_2 \cdots s_{z-1} w_{z-1}$ and $w_z s_{z+1} \cdots s_{z'-1} w_{z'-1}$ both have period d, and $w_{z-1} s_z w_z$ and $w_{z'-1} s_{z'} w_{z'}$ both do not have period d.

In other words, such a pair indicates exactly the first two s_z's where the period breaks in an instance of p. Accordingly, if we will apply Lemma 10 for all pairs (z, z') such that z and z' occur in some separations in Z or Z' or Z'', then we will find all instances $t[i..j] = s_1 w_1 s_2 w_2 \cdots w_{r-1} s_r$ of p such that $w_1, \ldots, w_{r-1}$ lie in at least three distinct runs with period d, $\frac{3}{2}|v| < |w_1| \leq 2|v|$, and v occurs in w_1. So, it suffices to show that there are at most $O(1)$ possible separations in Z (resp., Z', Z'') and, to reach the complexity announced in the *General Strategy* section, all such separations can be found in $O(r)$ time.

We describe how to find all separations in Z (the cases of Z', Z'' are similar). Clearly, if (z, z') is a separation, then (z, z) is also a (degenerate) separation. We find all separations $(z, z) \in Z$ applying the following general lemma with $Z_0 = Z$.

Lemma 12. *For any subset $Z_0 \subseteq Z$ (resp., $Z_0 \subseteq Z'$, $Z_0 \subseteq Z''$), there are at most three numbers $z \in Z_0$ satisfying the following property (2):*

$$\begin{aligned} &\text{any } z_1, z_2 \in (1..z) \cap Z_0 \text{ satisfy (1),} \\ &\text{any } z_1 \in (1..z) \cap Z_0, z_2 = z \text{ either do not satisfy (1) or } |s_{z_1}| < d \leq |s_{z_2}|. \end{aligned} \quad (2)$$

All such z can be found in $O(r)$ time.

Proof. Let $z' = \min Z_0$. Clearly, $z = z'$ satisfies (2). Using the lcp structure on the string $p\bar{p}$, we find in $O(r)$ time the smallest number $z'' \in Z_0$ such that any $z_1, z_2 \in [z'..z''] \cap Z_0$ satisfy (1) and some $z_1, z_2 \in [z'..z''] \cap Z_0$ do not satisfy (1); assume $z'' = +\infty$ if there is no such z''. Obviously, if $z'' \neq +\infty$, then $z = z''$ satisfies (2). Any $z \in (z''..+\infty) \cap Z_0$ does not satisfy (2) because in this case $z'' \neq +\infty$ and some $z_1, z_2 \in [z'..z''] \cap Z_0$ do not satisfy (1). In $O(r)$ time we find the minimal $z''' \in [z'..z''] \cap Z_0$ such that $|s_{z'''}| \geq d$; assume $z''' = z''$ if there is no such z'''. By the definition, we have $s_{z_1} = s_{z_2}$ and $|s_{z_1}| = |s_{z_2}| < d$ for any $z_1, z_2 \in [z'..z''') \cap Z_0$. Therefore, any $z \in (z'..z''') \cap Z_0$ does not satisfy (2). Further, any $z \in (z'''..z'') \cap Z_0$ does not satisfy (2) since in this case $z_1 = z'''$ and $z_2 = z$ satisfy (1) and $|s_{z_1}| \geq d$, which contradicts to (2). Finally, if $z''' \neq +\infty$, then $z = z'''$ obviously satisfies (2). So, z', z'', z''' are the only possible numbers in Z_0 that can satisfy (2). $\qquad \square$

Finally, for each separation $(z, z) \in Z$ we have found, we apply Lemma 12 with $Z_0 = Z \setminus \{z\}$ and obtain all separations in Z of the form (z, z') for $z' > z$. Employing Lemma 12 at most three times, we obtain at most 9 new separations in total, in $O(r)$ total time, and, besides the at most three (z, z) separations we initially had, no other separations exist. So, there are at most 12 separations in Z and they can be found in $O(r)$ time. Lemma 10 can be now employed to conclude the identification of the instances of p extending over at least three runs.

In-a-run instances of p. This case requires a different approach. More precisely, we process each run $t[i'..j']$ (only once) with period d in order to find all instances $t[i..j]$ of p satisfying the following properties (denoted altogether as (3)):

$$t[i..j] \text{ is an instance of } p \text{ with substitutions of } x \text{ and } \bar{x} \text{ of length } \geq 3d, \qquad (3)$$
$$t[i + |s_1|..j - |s_r|] \text{ is a substring of } t[i'..j'].$$

So, in this case, we no longer try to extend the string v that anchors the occurrence of w_1, but have a more global approach to finding the instances of the pattern.

To begin with, since $t[i'..j']$ has period d, we obtain the following lemma.

Lemma 13. *Let $t[i..j]$ be a string satisfying (3) such that $i' \leq i$. Then $t[i + (r-1)d..j]$ is an instance of p and, if $i - (r-1)d \geq i'$, $t[i - (r-1)d..j]$ is also an instance of p.*

Let $t[i..j]$ satisfy (3) and w be a substitution of x in $t[i..j]$. Recall that $x_1 = x$ and $r \geq 3$. We try to get some information on $|w|$, the length of the substitution of x. Suppose that $p \neq s_1 x s_2 \bar{x} s_3$ (the case $p = s_1 x s_2 \bar{x} s_3$ is considered in the full version [18]). Then, either there is $z \in (1..r)$ such that $x_{z-1} = x_z$ or there are $z', z'' \in (1..r)$ such that $x_{z'-1} s_{z'} x_{z'} = \bar{x} s_{z'} x$ and $x_{z''-1} s_{z''} x_{z''} = x s_{z''} \bar{x}$. Accordingly, we can compute the number $|w| \bmod d$ as follows.

Lemma 14. *Let $t[i..j]$ satisfy (3) and w be a substitution of x in $t[i..j]$. If, for some $z \in (1..r)$, $x_{z-1} = x_z$, then $|w| \equiv -|s_z| \pmod{d}$; if, for some $z', z'' \in (1..r)$, $x_{z'-1} s_{z'} x_{z'} = \bar{x} s_{z'} x$ and $x_{z''-1} s_{z''} x_{z''} = x s_{z''} \bar{x}$, then either $|w| \equiv \frac{d - |s_{z''}| - |s_{z'}|}{2} \pmod{d}$ or $|w| \equiv \frac{-|s_{z''}| - |s_{z'}|}{2} \pmod{d}$.*

Proof. Suppose that $x_{z-1} = x_z$. Since, by Lemma 2, the distance between any two occurrences of w (or $\bar{w}$) in $t[i'..j']$ is a multiple of d, we have $|w| \equiv -|s_z| \pmod{d}$.

Suppose that $x_{z'-1} s_{z'} x_{z'} = \bar{x} s_{z'} x$ and $x_{z''-1} s_{z''} x_{z''} = x s_{z''} \bar{x}$. Since w and $\bar{w}$ both are substrings of $t[i'..j']$ and $|w| \geq 3d$, it can be shown (see [18, Lemma 19]) that there are palindromes u and v such that $|uv| = d$, $v \neq \epsilon$, and $\bar{w}$ is a prefix of the infinite string $(vu)^\infty$. Since $w s_{z''} \bar{w}$ is a substring of $t[i'..j']$ and the strings vu and uv are primitive, it follows from Lemma 2 that $s_{z''} = u(vu)^{k'}$ for an integer k' and hence $|u| = |s_{z''}| \bmod d$, $|v| = d - |u|$. Similarly, since $\bar{w} s_{z'} w$ is a substring of $t[i'..j']$, we have $\bar{w} s_{z'} w = (vu)^{k'} v$ for an integer k' and therefore $2|w| \equiv |v| - |s_{z'}| \pmod{d}$. Thus, either $|w| \equiv \frac{|v| - |s_{z'}|}{2} \pmod{d}$ or $|w| \equiv \frac{d + |v| - |s_{z'}|}{2} \pmod{d}$. Since $|v| = (-|s_{z''}|) \bmod d$, we obtain either $|w| \equiv \frac{d - |s_{z''}| - |s_{z'}|}{2} \pmod{d}$ or $|w| \equiv \frac{-|s_{z''}| - |s_{z'}|}{2} \pmod{d}$. $\qquad \square$

We now fix the possible ends of the instances $t[i..j]$ of the pattern p, with respect to $t[i'..j']$. Consider the segments $\{(j'+1-bd..j'+1-(b-1)d]\}_{b=1}^f$, where f is the maximal integer such that $j'+1-fd \geq i'$ (i.e., f is exponent of the period in the run $t[i'..j']$). For each $b \in [1..f]$, we can find in $O(r + \frac{rd}{\log n})$ time, using Lemma 15, all strings $t[i..j]$ satisfying (3) such that

$j - |s_r| + 1 \in (j'+1-bd..j'+1-(b-1)d]$ (so with $s_1 w_1 \ldots s_{r-1} w_{r-1}$ ending in the respective segment); the parameter δ in this lemma is chosen according to Lemma 14 (see below). Adding all up, this enables us to find all instances of p satisfying (3) in $O(r(\frac{j'-i'+1}{d} + \frac{j'-i'+1}{\log n}))$ time. Since $j' - i' + 1 \geq 3d$, it follows from [16] and Lemma 3 that the sum of the values $\frac{j'-i'+1}{d} + \frac{j'-i'+1}{\log n}$ over all such runs $t[i'..j']$ is $O(n)$; hence the total time needed to find these instances of the pattern is $O(rn)$.

Technically, our strategy is given in the following lemma (which does not cover the case $p = s_1 x s_2 \overline{x} s_3$, which is present in the full version [18]). In this lemma, $\delta \in [0..d)$ is one of the possible values of $|w| \bmod d$, as obtained in Lemma 14: if $x_{z-1} = x_z$ for some $z \in (1..r)$, we use only one value $\delta = -|s_z| \bmod d$; otherwise, we use two values of δ described in Lemma 15 (the special case $p = s_1 x s_2 \overline{x} s_3$ is considered separately in [18]). For each thus computed δ, we process each segment $[b_1..b_2] = (j'+1-bd..j'+1-(b-1)d]$ and get a compact representation (in the bit arrays E, F) of the instances $s_1 w_1 \ldots s_{r-1} w_{r-1} s_r$ of p such that $s_1 w_1 \ldots s_{r-1} w_{r-1}$ ends in the respective segment and $\delta = |w| \bmod d$. The proof of Lemma 15 is moved to the full version [18].

Lemma 15. *Let $p \neq s_1 x s_2 \overline{x} s_3$, $r \geq 3$, and $\delta \leq d$. Given a run $t[i'..j']$ with period d and a segment $[b_1..b_2] \subset [i'..j'+1]$ of length d, we can compute in $O(r + \frac{rd}{\log n})$ time the numbers $d', d'', h', h'', a', a''$ and bit arrays $E[b_1..b_2]$, $F[b_1..b_2]$ such that:*

1. *for any $h \in [b_1..h']$ (resp., $h \in (h'..b_2]$), we have $E[h] = 1$ iff the strings $t[h - |s_1 s_2 \cdots s_{r-1}| - (r-1)(\delta + cd)..h + |s_r| - 1]$ for all $c \in [0..d']$ (resp., for all $c \in [0..d'']$) are instances of p and $h - |s_1 s_2 \cdots s_{r-1}| - (r-1)(\delta + cd) \geq i'$;*
2. *for any $h \in [b_1..h'']$ (resp., $h \in (h''..b_2]$), we have $F[h] = 1$ iff the string $t[h - |s_1 s_2 \cdots s_{r-1}| - (r-1)(\delta + ad)..h + |s_r| - 1]$, where $a = a'$ (resp., $a = a''$), is an instance of p and $h - |s_2 s_3 \cdots s_{r-1}| - (r-1)(\delta + ad) \geq i'$.*

In addition, we find at most one instance $t[i_0..j_0] = s_1 w_1 s_2 w_2 \cdots w_{r-1} s_r$ of p satisfying (3) and such that $j_0 - |s_r| + 1 \in [b_1..b_2]$, $|w_1| \equiv \delta \pmod{d}$, and it is guaranteed that if a string $t[i..j] = s_1 w_1 s_2 w_2 \cdots w_{r-1} s_r$ satisfies (3), $j - |s_r| + 1 \in [b_1..b_2]$, and $|w_1| \equiv \delta \pmod{d}$, then either $t[i..j]$ is encoded in one of the arrays E, F or $i = i_0$ and $j = j_0$.

The only case left is of in-two-runs instances of p. To solve this case we combine (in a rather technical way) the ideas of the previous cases. Instances of p extending over two runs are determined by separators (as the period breaks once inside these instances), but the prefix and suffix of each instance, occurring before, resp. after, the separator can be extended just as in the case of instances occurring inside a single run, discussed above. The details are given in [18].

References

1. Amir, A., Nor, I.: Generalized function matching. J. Discrete Algorithms **5**, 514–523 (2007)
2. Angluin, D.: Finding patterns common to a set of strings. J. Comput. Syst. Sci. **21**, 46–62 (1980)
3. Bannai, H., I, T., Inenaga, S., Nakashima, Y., Takeda, M., Tsuruta, K.: The "runs" theorem. arXiv preprint arXiv:1406.0263v4 (2014)
4. Crochemore, M., Iliopoulos, C., Kubica, M., Radoszewski, J., Rytter, W., Waleń, T.: Extracting powers and periods in a string from its runs structure. In: Chavez, E., Lonardi, S. (eds.) SPIRE 2010. LNCS, vol. 6393, pp. 258–269. Springer, Heidelberg (2010). doi:10.1007/978-3-642-16321-0_27
5. Crochemore, M., Rytter, W.: Jewels of Stringology. World Scientific Publishing Co., Pte. Ltd., Singapore (2002)
6. Czeizler, E., Czeizler, E., Kari, L., Seki, S.: An extension of the Lyndon Schützenberger result to pseudoperiodic words. In: Diekert, V., Nowotka, D. (eds.) DLT 2009. LNCS, vol. 5583, pp. 183–194. Springer, Heidelberg (2009). doi:10.1007/978-3-642-02737-6_14
7. Ehrenfeucht, A., Rozenberg, G.: Finding a homomorphism between two words is NP-complete. Inform. Proc. Lett. **9**, 86–88 (1979)
8. Fernau, H., Manea, F., Mercaş, R., Schmid, M.L.: Revisiting Shinohara's algorithm for computing descriptive patterns. Theor. Comput. Sci. (to appear)
9. Fernau, H., Manea, F., Mercaş, R., Schmid, M.L.: Pattern matching with variables: fast algorithms and new hardness results. In: Schloss Dagstuhl - Leibniz-Zentrum für Informatik, STACS 2015, LIPIcs, vol. 30, pp. 302–315 (2015)
10. Friedl, J.E.F.: Mastering Regular Expressions, 3rd edn. O'Reilly, Sebastopol (2006)
11. Galil, Z., Seiferas, J.: A linear-time on-line recognition algorithm for "palstar". J. ACM **25**(1), 102–111 (1978)
12. Gawrychowski, P., Lewenstein, M., Nicholson, P.K.: Weighted ancestors in suffix trees. In: Schulz, A.S., Wagner, D. (eds.) ESA 2014. LNCS, vol. 8737, pp. 455–466. Springer, Heidelberg (2014). doi:10.1007/978-3-662-44777-2_38
13. Gawrychowski, P., Manea, F., Nowotka, D.: Testing generalised freeness of words. In: Schloss Dagstuhl - Leibniz-Zentrum für Informatik, STACS 2014, LIPIcs, vol. 25, pp. 337–349 (2014)
14. Kärkkäinen, J., Sanders, P., Burkhardt, S.: Linear work suffix array construction. J. ACM **53**, 918–936 (2006)
15. Kociumaka, T., Radoszewski, J., Rytter, W., Waleń, T.: Internal pattern matching queries in a text and applications. In: SODA 2015, pp. 532–551. SIAM (2015)
16. Kolpakov, R., Kucherov, G.: Finding maximal repetitions in a word in linear time. In: FOCS 1999, pp. 596–604. IEEE (1999)
17. Kosolobov, D.: Online detection of repetitions with backtracking. In: Cicalese, F., Porat, E., Vaccaro, U. (eds.) CPM 2015. LNCS, vol. 9133, pp. 295–306. Springer, Cham (2015). doi:10.1007/978-3-319-19929-0_25
18. Kosolobov, D., Manea, F., Nowotka, D.: Detecting one-variable patterns. arXiv preprint arXiv:1604.00054 (2016)
19. Kosolobov, D., Rubinchik, M., Shur, A.M.: Pal^k is linear recognizable online. In: Italiano, G.F., Margaria-Steffen, T., Pokorný, J., Quisquater, J.-J., Wattenhofer, R. (eds.) SOFSEM 2015. LNCS, vol. 8939, pp. 289–301. Springer, Heidelberg (2015). doi:10.1007/978-3-662-46078-8_24

20. Lothaire, M.: Algebraic Combinatorics on Words. Cambridge University Press, Cambridge (2002). Chap. 3
21. Manacher, G.: A new linear-time on-line algorithm finding the smallest initial palindrome of a string. J. ACM **22**(3), 346–351 (1975)
22. Manea, F., Müller, M., Nowotka, D., Seki, S.: Generalised Lyndon-Schützenberger equations. In: Csuhaj-Varjú, E., Dietzfelbinger, M., Ésik, Z. (eds.) MFCS 2014. LNCS, vol. 8634, pp. 402–413. Springer, Heidelberg (2014). doi:10.1007/978-3-662-44522-8_34
23. Rubinchik, M., Shur, A.M.: EERTREE: an efficient data structure for processing palindromes in strings. In: Lipták, Z., Smyth, W.F. (eds.) IWOCA 2015. LNCS, vol. 9538, pp. 321–333. Springer, Cham (2016). doi:10.1007/978-3-319-29516-9_27
24. Schmid, M.L.: Characterising REGEX languages by regular languages equipped with factor-referencing. Inf. Comput. **249**, 1–17 (2016)
25. Xu, Z.: A minimal periods algorithm with applications. In: Amir, A., Parida, L. (eds.) CPM 2010. LNCS, vol. 6129, pp. 51–62. Springer, Heidelberg (2010). doi:10.1007/978-3-642-13509-5_6

Order Preserving Pattern Matching
on Trees and DAGs

Temma Nakamura$^{(\boxtimes)}$, Shunsuke Inenaga, Hideo Bannai, and Masayuki Takeda

Department of Informatics, Kyushu University, Fukuoka, Japan
{temma.nakamura,inenaga,bannai,takeda}@inf.kyushu-u.ac.jp

Abstract. The *order preserving pattern matching* (*OPPM*) problem is, given a pattern string p and a text string t, find all substrings of t which have the same relative orders as p. In this paper, we consider two variants of the OPPM problem where a set of text strings is given as a *tree* or a *DAG*. We show that the OPPM problem for a single pattern p of length m and a text tree T of size N can be solved in $O(m+N)$ time with $O(m)$ working space if the characters of p are drawn from an integer alphabet of polynomial size. The time complexity becomes $O(m \log m + N)$ if the pattern p is over a general ordered alphabet. We then show that the OPPM problem for a single pattern and a text DAG is NP-complete.

1 Introduction

The *order preserving pattern matching* (*OPPM*) problem is, given a pattern string p and a text string t, find all substrings of t which have the same relative orders as p. For instance, let $p = (22, 41, 35, 37)$ and $t = (63, 18, 48, 29, 42, 56, 25, 51)$. The relative orders of the characters in p is $1, 4, 2, 3$. A substring $t[2..5] = (18, 48, 29, 42)$ have the same relative orders $1, 4, 2, 3$ as p, and hence the occurrence of this substring is reported. OPPM captures structural isomorphism of strings, and thus has potential applications in the analysis of times series such as stock prices, and in melody matching of musical sequences [7, 10].

Let m and n be the lengths of the pattern string p and the text string t, respectively. Kim et al. [10] proposed an $O(m \log m + n)$-time algorithm for the OPPM problem. Independently, Kubica et al. [11] proposed an $O(\text{sort}(p) + n)$-time algorithm, where $\text{sort}(p)$ denotes the time complexity to sort the elements in p; $\text{sort}(p) = O(m \log m)$ for general ordered alphabets and $\text{sort}(p) = O(m)$ for integer alphabets of size $m^{O(1)}$. These algorithms are based on the Morris-Pratt algorithm [12]. Kubica et al.'s algorithm works when the input strings do not contain same characters. Cho et al. [7] showed how Kubica et al.'s algorithm can be modified when there are same characters in the input strings, retaining the same efficiency. Other types of algorithms for the OPPM problem have also been proposed (e.g., see [6, 7, 9, 10]).

This paper considers two natural extensions to the OPPM problem, where a set of text strings is given as a tree or a DAG. We show that the OPPM

© Springer International Publishing AG 2017
G. Fici et al. (Eds.): SPIRE 2017, LNCS 10508, pp. 271–277, 2017.
DOI: 10.1007/978-3-319-67428-5_23

problem for a single pattern p and a text tree T of size N can be solved in $O(\text{sort}(p)+N)$ time. Our method uses a Morris-Pratt type of (non-deterministic) pattern matching automaton, and generalizes the existing results for the OPPM problem on a single text string. We then show that the OPPM problem for a single pattern and a text DAG is NP-complete.

Related work. The exact pattern matching problem on a single pattern string and a tree was first considered by Dubiner et al. [8]. Their algorithm is based on a (non-deterministic) Morris-Pratt automaton.

Amir and Navarro [3] considered the *parameterized pattern matching* (*PPM*) problem on trees. Let σ be the alphabet size. They showed that the PPM problem on trees can be solved in $O(N \log(\min\{\sigma, m\}))$ time, provided that the *deterministic* version of a Morris-Pratt type automaton is available. However, the size of the deterministic version of such an automaton can be as large as $O(m^2)$. Hence, their algorithm takes $O(m^2 + N(\min\{\sigma, m\}))$ time in the worst case[1].

Recall that the running time per text character of a *non-deterministic* Morris-Pratt automaton depends on the number of failure transitions used per text character. The key analysis of a total linear running time of this method on a single text string is that this number is amortized constant. The same amortization argument holds for its OPPM and PPM variants on a single text string.

The difficulty in using a non-deterministic Morris-Pratt automaton for a tree text is that if we simply run the automaton on the tree as is, then the above amortization argument does not hold. It seems that this point was overlooked even in the exact pattern matching problem on trees (see the proof of Lemma 2.2 of the work by Dubiner et al. [8]).

Still, we will show that a small trick permits us to bound the number of failure transitions per character to amortized constant, achieving our result for the OPPM problem on trees. We here emphasize that the same trick can be employed in *any* variant of a non-deterministic Morris-Pratt type automaton. This implies that it is actually possible to solve the exact pattern matching problem on trees in $O(m + N)$ time using the Morris-Pratt automaton, and the PPM problem on trees in $O((m+N) \log(\min\{\sigma, m\}))$ time. Both of these results are optimal; the former is clear, and the latter matches the lower bound of the PPM problem in the comparison model [3].

Several results for the exact pattern matching problem with a single pattern string and a labeled graph are known (e.g. [1,13]). See a survey [2] for other schemes of pattern matching on graph texts.

Amir and Navarro [3] showed the PPM problem on DAGs is NP-complete. Coupled with their afore-mentioned results on trees, we can observe that the PPM and OPPM problems have similar complexities on trees and DAGs.

---

[1] Simon [14] proposed an $O(m)$-space Morris-Pratt automaton for exact pattern matching, however, it is unclear if this can be extended to PPM or OPPM.

2   Preliminaries

Let Σ be a totally ordered alphabet. An element of Σ^* is called a *string*. The length of a string w is denoted by $|w|$. The empty string ε is a string of length 0. For a string $w = xyz$, x, y and z are called a *prefix*, *substring*, and *suffix* of w, respectively. The length of a string w is denoted by $|w|$. The i-th character of a string w is denoted by $w[i]$ for each $1 \leq i \leq |w|$. For a string w and two integers $1 \leq i \leq j \leq |w|$, let $w[i..j]$ denote the substring of w that begins at position i and ends at position j. For convenience, let $w[i..j] = \varepsilon$ when $i > j$.

Any strings $x, y \in \Sigma^*$ of equal length m are said to be *order-isomorphic* [11] if the relative orders of the characters of x and y are the same, i.e., $x[i] \leq x[j] \iff y[i] \leq y[j]$ for any $1 \leq i, j \leq m$. A non-empty pattern string p is said to *order-preserving match* (*op-match* in short) a non-empty text string t iff there is a position i in t such that $p \approx t[i - |p| + 1..i]$. The *order-preserving pattern matching* (*OPPM*) problem is to find all such text positions.

For any string x of length m, an integer i $(1 \leq i < m)$ is said to be an *order-preserving border* of x if $x[1..i] \approx x[m - i + 1..m]$.

We consider the following two variants of the OPPM problem: Assume that the set of text strings is given as a tree T or a DAG G where each edge is labeled by a character from Σ. A pattern string p of length m is said to op-match a tree T (resp. a DAG G) if p op-matches the label of a path in T (resp. in G). In this paper, we consider the locating version of the OPPM on trees and the decision version of the OPPM on DAGs, which are respectively defined as follows.

Problem 1 (The OPPM problem on trees).   Given a pattern string p and an edge-labeled tree T, report the final node of every path in T that p op-matches.

Problem 2 (The OPPM problem on DAGs).   Given a pattern string p and an edge-labeled DAG G, determine whether p op-matches G or not.

3   Order Preserving Pattern Matching on Trees

Our algorithm for order preserving pattern matching on a text tree is inspired by the algorithms for order preserving pattern matching on a text string [7,11]. We will utilize the following tools in our algorithm.

For any string x let $LMax_x$ be an array of length $|x|$ such that $LMax_x[i] = j$ if $x[j] = \max\{x[k] \mid 1 \leq k < i, x[k] \leq x[i]\}$. Similarly, let $LMin_x$ be an array of length $|x|$ such that $LMin_x[i] = j$ if $x[j] = \min\{x[k] \mid 1 \leq k < i, x[k] \geq x[i]\}$. If there is no such j, then let $LMax_x[i] = 0$ and $LMin_x[i] = 0$, respectively. If there are several such j's, then we select the rightmost one among them.

Lemma 1 ([11]).   *Given a string x, we can compute the $LMax_x$ and $LMin_x$ arrays in $O(\mathrm{sort}(x))$ time, where $\mathrm{sort}(x)$ is the time to sort the elements of x.*

Lemma 2 ([7]).   *For strings x and y, assume $x[1..i] \approx y[1..i]$ for $1 \leq i < \min\{|x|, |y|\}$. Let $a = LMax_x[i+1]$ and $b = LMin_x[i+1]$. Let α be the condition*

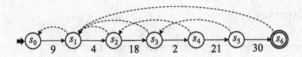

Fig. 1. The MP-style automaton $\mathcal{A}_p$ for pattern string $p = (9, 4, 18, 2, 21, 30)$. The solid arcs denote the goto transitions, and the broken arcs do the failure transitions.

that $y[a] < y[i+1]$ and β be the condition that $y[i+1] < y[b]$. Then, $x[1..i+1] \approx y[1..i+1] \iff (\alpha \wedge \beta) \vee (\neg\alpha \wedge \neg\beta)$. In case a or b is equal to 0, we assume the respective condition α or β is true.

Let p be a pattern string of length m. We compute the *order-preserving border array* B_p of length m such that $B_p[1] = 0$ and $B_p[i] = \max\{j \mid j < i, p[1..j] \approx p[i-j+1..i]\}$ for $2 \leq i \leq m$. Namely, $B_p[i]$ stores the largest order-preserving border of the prefix $p[1..i]$. Suppose that $LMin_p$ and $LMax_p$ have already been computed using Lemma 1. Kubica et al. [11] showed that using a variant of the Morris-Pratt (MP) algorithm [12] based on Lemma 2, the B_p array can be computed in $O(m)$ time. Then, given a text string t of length n, all positions i in t where $p \approx t[i-m+1..i]$ can be computed in $O(n)$ time.

We will extend the above algorithm to the case where the text strings are given as a tree T of size N. It is convenient to consider an MP-style automaton $\mathcal{A}_p$ based on the op border array B_p such that the set of states is $\{s_0, \ldots, s_m\}$; the initial state is s_0; the only accepting state is s_m; for each $1 \leq i \leq m$ there is a goto transition from s_{i-1} to s_i with character $c = p[i]$; and there is a failure transition from s_i to s_j iff $B_p[i] = j$. See Fig. 1 for a concrete example of $\mathcal{A}_p$. We run $\mathcal{A}_p$ over the text tree T in depth first manner. Let v be any node in T. For any $1 \leq i \leq m$, let v_i denote the ith ancestor of v (if it exists), and $path(v_i, v)$ the path label from v_i to v. At each node v visited during the DFS, we compute the length $\ell(v)$ of the longest path $v_{\ell(v)}, \ldots, v$ such that $p[1..\ell(v)] \approx path(v_{\ell(v)}, v)$. We report every node v with $\ell(v) = m$. If $\ell(v) < m$, then we store a pointer to state $s_{\ell(v)}$ at node v, and otherwise we store a pointer to state s' at node v, where s' is the state pointed by the failure transition of $s_{\ell(v)}$.

Suppose we have just visited node v. Initially, let $\ell \leftarrow \ell(v)$. Let u be any child of v and let c be the edge label from v to u. We proceed to node u and find $\ell(u)$. We test if the characters $path(v_\ell, u)[a]$ and $path(v_\ell, u)[b]$ satisfy one of the conditions in Lemma 2, where $a = LMax_p[\ell + 1]$ and $b = LMin_p[\ell + 1]$. If they do, then we let $\ell(u) = \ell + 1$ and proceed with the DFS. Otherwise, then let $\ell \leftarrow B_p[\ell]$, and repeat the above procedure until we find the largest ℓ with which one of the conditions in Lemma 2 is satisfied. For each candidate ℓ above, accessing the character $path(v_\ell, u)[a]$ from the currently visited node u means accessing the $(\ell - a + 1)$th ancestor of u. Let L be the length of the longest path in T. During the DFS, we store the edge labels of the current path from the root into an array of length L. Using this array we can access $path(v_\ell, u)[a]$ (and $path(v_\ell, u)[b]$) in $O(1)$ time. It is easy to update this array during the DFS, in total $O(N)$ time. When we come back to node v after a back track, then we resume pattern matching from state $s_{\ell(v)}$ of $\mathcal{A}_p$ using a pointer stored at v, and proceed to the next child of v. This pointer is used after a back track.

One delicacy remains. For a single text string the number of candidate ℓ's, which is the same as the number of failure transitions used per text character, can be amortized constant. This amortization argument is based on the fact that the total number of times the failure transitions are used for the whole text cannot exceed the total number of times the goto transitions are used in the automaton $\mathcal{A}_p$, which is bounded by the length of the single text string. However, in our tree case, this amortization argument does not hold if we carelessly continue the DFS at branching nodes that are close to leaves, leading to $O(mN)$ worst case time. To avoid this, at each node u of the tree T we store the distance D_u between u and a furthest leaf in the subtree rooted at u. Namely, D_u is the length of the longest path from u and a leaf below u. Suppose that we are currently visiting a node u during the DFS with $D_u \geq m - \ell$, and that the respective state of the automaton $\mathcal{A}_p$ is s_ℓ (Notice that if $D_u < m - \ell$, then clearly the pattern p does not op-match any path ending in the subtree under u, and thus we need not search the subtree under u in this case). Let v be any child of u. If at least one of the conditions of Lemma 2 is satisfied, then we let $\ell \leftarrow \ell + 1$ and the DFS proceeds to v. Otherwise, we let $\ell \leftarrow B_p[\ell]$ and check if $D_u \geq m - \ell$ holds each time the value of ℓ gets updated. We stop updating ℓ as soon as we encounter ℓ for which $D_u < m - \ell$, and the DFS immediately starts a back track from this child v. This permits us to charge the cost for amortization to the length D_u of this longest path under u. Thus, this method correctly finds all locations in the tree T where p op-matches. We can easily precompute D_u for all nodes u in T in $O(N)$ total time by a standard traversal on T.

Theorem 1. *Given a pattern p of length m and a text tree T of size N, the OPPM problem on trees (Problem 1) can be solved in $O(\text{sort}(p) + N)$ time.*

$\text{sort}(p)$ is respectively $O(m \log m)$, $O(m)$, and $O(m + N)$ for general ordered alphabets, integer alphabets of size $m^{O(1)}$, and integer alphabets of size $N^{O(1)}$.

4   Order Preserving Pattern Matching on DAGs

A string x is said to be a *subsequence* of another string t if there exists an increasing sequence of positions $1 \leq i_1 < \cdots < i_{|x|} \leq |t|$ of t such that $x = t[i_1] \cdots t[i_{|x|}]$. Intuitively, x is a subsequence of t if x can be obtained by removing zero or more characters from t.

The *order-preserving subsequence matching problem* (*OPSM* in short) is, given a pattern string p and a text string t, to determine whether there is a subsequence s of t such that $p \approx s$. This problem is known to be NP-complete [5].

Theorem 2. *The OPPM problem on DAGs (Problem 2) is NP-complete.*

Proof. It is clear that the OPPM problem on DAGs is in NP. The proof for NP-completeness is via the above OPSM problem. Suppose p is a given pattern string and t is a given text string for the OPSM problem. Consider the *directed acyclic*

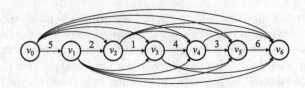

Fig. 2. The DASG G_t of string $t = (5, 2, 1, 4, 3, 6)$. At each node, every in-coming edge is labeled with the same character.

subsequence graph (*DASG* in short) [4] $G_t = (V, E)$ such that $V = \{v_0, \ldots, v_{|t|}\}$ and $E = \{(v_i, c, v_j) \mid c = t[j] \text{ and } t[k] \neq c \text{ for } i < \forall k < j\}$. The DASG G_t represents all subsequences of t, i.e., s is a subsequence of t if and only if there is a path in G_t of which label coincides with s (see Fig. 2 for an example). Hence, if we can solve the op-matching problem for the given pattern string p and the DASG G_t, then we can immediately solve the OPSM problem. The size of DASG G_t is clearly polynomial in the length of the given text t and G_t can be easily constructed in polynomial time. This completes the proof. □

References

1. Amir, A., Lewenstein, M., Lewenstein, N.: Pattern matching in hypertext. In: Dehne, F., Rau-Chaplin, A., Sack, J.-R., Tamassia, R. (eds.) WADS 1997. LNCS, vol. 1272, pp. 160–173. Springer, Heidelberg (1997). doi:10.1007/3-540-63307-3_56
2. Amir, A., Lewenstein, M., Lewenstein, N.: Hypertext searching - a survey. In: Language, Culture, Computation. Computing - Theory and Technology - Essays Dedicated to Yaacov Choueka on the Occasion of his 75th Birthday, Part I, pp. 364–381 (2014)
3. Amir, A., Navarro, G.: Parameterized matching on non-linear structures. Inf. Process. Lett. **109**(15), 864–867 (2009)
4. Baeza-Yates, R.A.: Searching subsequences. Theor. Comput. Sci. **78**(2), 363–376 (1991)
5. Bose, P., Buss, J.F., Lubiw, A.: Pattern matching for permutations. In: Dehne, F., Sack, J.-R., Santoro, N., Whitesides, S. (eds.) WADS 1993. LNCS, vol. 709, pp. 200–209. Springer, Heidelberg (1993). doi:10.1007/3-540-57155-8_248
6. Chhabra, T., Tarhio, J.: A filtration method for order-preserving matching. Inf. Process. Lett. **116**(2), 71–74 (2016)
7. Cho, S., Na, J.C., Park, K., Sim, J.S.: A fast algorithm for order-preserving pattern matching. Inf. Process. Lett. **115**(2), 397–402 (2015)
8. Dubiner, M., Galil, Z., Magen, E.: Faster tree pattern matching. J. ACM **41**(2), 205–213 (1994)
9. Faro, S., Külekci, M.O.: Efficient algorithms for the order preserving pattern matching problem. In: Dondi, R., Fertin, G., Mauri, G. (eds.) AAIM 2016. LNCS, vol. 9778, pp. 185–196. Springer, Cham (2016). doi:10.1007/978-3-319-41168-2_16
10. Kim, J., Eades, P., Fleischer, R., Hong, S., Iliopoulos, C.S., Park, K., Puglisi, S.J., Tokuyama, T.: Order-preserving matching. Theor. Comput. Sci. **525**, 68–79 (2014)
11. Kubica, M., Kulczynski, T., Radoszewski, J., Rytter, W., Walen, T.: A linear time algorithm for consecutive permutation pattern matching. Inf. Process. Lett. **113**(12), 430–433 (2013)

12. Morris, J.H., Pratt, V.R.: A linear pattern-matching algorithm. Technical report, 40, University of California, Berkeley (1970)
13. Park, K., Kim, D.K.: String matching in hypertext. In: Galil, Z., Ukkonen, E. (eds.) CPM 1995. LNCS, vol. 937, pp. 318–329. Springer, Heidelberg (1995). doi:10.1007/3-540-60044-2_51
14. Simon, I.: String matching algorithms and automata. In: Karhumäki, J., Maurer, H., Rozenberg, G. (eds.) Results and Trends in Theoretical Computer Science. LNCS, vol. 812, pp. 386–395. Springer, Heidelberg (1994). doi:10.1007/3-540-58131-6_61

A Self-index on Block Trees

Gonzalo Navarro$^{(\boxtimes)}$

Department of Computer Science, University of Chile, Beauchef 851, Santiago, Chile
gnavarro@dcc.uchile.cl

Abstract. The Block Tree is a recently proposed data structure that reaches compression close to Lempel-Ziv while supporting efficient direct access to text substrings. In this paper we show how a self-index can be built on top of a Block Tree so that it provides efficient pattern searches while using space proportional to that of the original data structure. More precisely, if a Lempel-Ziv parse cuts a text of length n into z non-overlapping phrases, then our index uses $O(z \lg(n/z))$ words and finds the *occ* occurrences of a pattern of length m in time $O(m^2 \lg n + occ \lg^\epsilon n)$ for any constant $\epsilon > 0$.

1 Introduction

The Block Tree (BT) [1] is a novel data structure for representing a sequence, which reaches a space close to its LZ77-compressed [25] space. Given a string $S[1..n]$ over alphabet $[1..\sigma]$, on which the LZ77 parser produces z phrases (and thus an LZ77 compressor uses $z \lg n + O(z \lg \sigma)$ bits, where lg denotes the logarithm in base 2), the BT on S uses $O(z \lg(n/z) \lg n)$ bits (also said to be $O(z \lg(n/z))$ space). This is also the best asymptotic space obtained with grammar compressors [4,14,15,23,24]. In exchange for using more space than LZ77 compression, the BT offers fast extraction of substrings: a substring of length ℓ can be extracted in time $O((1 + \ell/\lg_\sigma n) \lg(n/z))$. In this paper we consider the LZ77 variant where sources and phrases do not overlap, thus $z = \Omega(\lg n)$.

Kreft and Navarro [17] introduced a *self-index* based on LZ77 compression, which proved to be extremely space-efficient on highly repetitive text collections [6]. A self-index on S is a data structure that offers direct access to any substring of S (and thus it replaces S), and at the same time offers indexed searches. Their self-index uses $3z \lg n + O(z \lg \sigma) + o(n)$ bits (that is, about 3 times the size of the compressed text) and finds all the *occ* occurrences of a pattern of length m in time $O(m^2 h + (m + occ) \lg z)$, where $h \leq n$ is the maximum number of times a symbol is successively copied along the LZ77 parsing. A string of length ℓ is extracted in $O(h\ell)$ time.

Experiments on repetitive text collections [6,17] show that this LZ77-index is smaller than any other alternative and is competitive when searching for patterns, especially on the short ones where the term $m^2 h$ is small and *occ* is large, so that the low time to report each occurrence dominates. On longer patterns,

Funded in part by Fondecyt Grant 1-170048.

© Springer International Publishing AG 2017
G. Fici et al. (Eds.): SPIRE 2017, LNCS 10508, pp. 278–289, 2017.
DOI: 10.1007/978-3-319-67428-5_24

however, the index is significantly slower. The term h can reach the hundreds on repetitive collections, and thus it poses a significant penalty (and a poor worst-case bound).

In this paper we design the *BT-index*, a self-index that builds on top of BTs instead of on LZ77 compression. Given a BT of $w = O(z \lg(n/z))$ leaves (which can be represented in $w \lg n + O(w)$ bits), the BT-index uses $3w \lg n + O(w)$ bits, and it searches for a pattern of length m in time $O((m^2 \lg(n/z) \lg \lg z + m \lg z \lg \lg z + occ(\lg(n/z) \lg \lg n + \lg z))$, which is in general a better theoretical bound than that of the LZ77-index. If we allow the space to be any $O(w) = O(z \lg(n/z))$ words, then the time can be reduced to $O(m^2 \lg(n/z) + m \lg^\epsilon z + occ(\lg \lg n + \lg^\epsilon z))$ for any constant $\epsilon > 0$. In regular texts, the $O(\lg(n/z))$ factor is around 3–4, and it raises to 8–10 on highly repetitive texts; both are much lower than the typical values of h. Thus we expect the BT-index to be faster than the LZ77-index especially for longer patterns, where the $O(m^2)$ factor dominates.

The self-indexes that build on grammar compression [7,8] can use the same asymptotic space of our BT-index, and their best search time is $O(m^2 \lg \lg n + m \lg z + occ \lg z)$. Belazzougui et al. [1], however, show that in practice BTs are faster to access S than grammar-compressed representations, and use about the same space if the text is highly repetitive. Thus we expect that our self-index will be better in practice than those based on grammar compression, again especially when the pattern is long and there are no too many occurrences to report.

There are various other indexes in the literature using $O(z \lg(n/z))$ bits [2,11] or slightly more [2,10,21] that offer better time complexities. However, they have not been implemented as far as we know, and it is difficult to predict how will they behave in practice.

2   Block Trees

Given a string $S[1..n]$ over an alphabet $[1..\sigma]$, whose LZ77 parse produces z phrases, a Block Tree (BT) is defined as follows. At the top level, numbered $l = 0$, we split S into z blocks of length $b_0 = n/z$. Each block is then recursively split into two, so that if b_l is the length of the blocks at level l it holds $b_{l+1} = b_l/2$, until reaching blocks of one symbol after $\lg(n/z)$ levels. At each level, every pair of consecutive blocks $S[i..j]$ that does not appear earlier as a substring of $S[1..i-1]$ is *marked*. Blocks that are not marked are replaced by a pointer *ptr* to their first occurrence in S (which, by definition, must be a marked block or overlap a pair of marked blocks). For every level $l \geq 0$, a bitvector D_l with one bit per block sets to 1 the positions of marked blocks. In level $l + 1$ we consider and subdivide only the blocks that were marked in level l. In this paper, this subdivision is carried out up to the last level, where the marked blocks store their corresponding symbol.

We can regard the BT as a binary tree (with the first $\lg z$ levels chopped out), where the internal nodes are the marked nodes and have two children, and the leaves are the unmarked nodes. Thus we store one pointer *ptr* per leaf. We also spend one bit per node in the bitvectors D_l. If we call w the number of unmarked blocks (leaves), then the BT has $w - z$ marked blocks (internal nodes), and it uses $w \lg n + O(w)$ bits.

To extract a single symbol $S[i]$, we see if i is in a marked block at level 0, that is, if $D_0[\lceil i/b_0 \rceil] = 1$. If so, we map i to a position in the next level, which only contains the marked blocks of this level:

$$i \leftarrow (rank_1(D_0, \lceil i/b_0 \rceil) - 1) \cdot b_0 + ((i - 1) \mod b_0) + 1.$$

Function $rank_c(D, p)$ counts the number of occurrences of bit c in $D[1..p]$. A bitvector D can be represented in $|D| + o(|D|)$ bits so that $rank_c$ can be computed in constant time [5]. Therefore, if i falls in a marked block, we translate the problem to the next level in constant time. If, instead, i is not in a marked block, we take the pointer ptr stored for that block, and replace $i \leftarrow i - ptr$, assuming ptr stores the distance towards the first occurrence of the unmarked block. Now i is again on a marked block, and we can move on to the next level as described. The total time to extract a symbol is then $O(\lg(n/z))$.

3   A Self-index

Our self-index structure is made up of two main components: the first finds all the pattern positions that cross block boundaries, whereas the second finds the positions that are copied onto unmarked blocks. The main property that we exploit is the following. We will say that a block is *explicit* in level l if all the blocks containing it in lower levels are marked. Note that the explicit blocks in level l are either marked or unmarked, and the descendants of those unmarked are not explicit in higher levels.

Lemma 1. *The occurrences of a given string P of length at least 2 in S either overlap two explicit blocks at some level, or are completely inside an unmarked block at some level.*

Proof. We proceed by induction on the BT block size. Consider the level $l = 0$, where all the blocks are explicit. If the occurrence overlaps two blocks or it is completely inside an unmarked block, we are done. If, instead, it is completely inside a marked block, then this block is split into two blocks that are explicit in the next level. Consider that we concatenate all the explicit blocks of the next level. Then we have a new sequence where the occurrence appears, and we use a smaller block size, so by the inductive hypothesis, the property holds. The base case is the leaf level, where the blocks are of length 1.   □

We exploit the lemma in the following way. We will define an occurrence of P as *primary* if it overlaps two consecutive blocks at some level. The occurrences that are completely contained in an unmarked block are *secondary* (this idea is a variant of the classical one used in all the LZ-based indexes [16]). Secondary occurrences are found by detecting primary or other secondary occurrences within the area from where an unmarked block is copied. We will use a data structure to find the primary occurrences and another to detect the copies.

Lemma 2. *The described method correctly identifies all the occurrences of a string P in S.*

Proof. We proceed again by induction on the block length. Consider level $l = 0$. If a given occurrence overlaps two explicit blocks at this level, then it is primary and will be found. Otherwise, if it is inside a marked block at this level, then it also appears at the next level and it will be found by the inductive hypothesis. Finally, if it is inside an unmarked block, then it points to a marked block at the same level and will be detected as a copy of the occurrence already found in the source. The base case is the last level, where all the blocks are of length 1.   □

3.1   The Data Strucures

We describe the data structures used by our index. Overall, they require $3w \lg n + O(w)$ bits, and replace the pointers ptr used by the original structure. We also retain the bitvectors D_l, which add up to $O(w)$ bits.

Primary Occurrences. Our structure to find the primary occurrences is a two-dimensional discrete grid G storing points (x, y) as follows. Let $B_i \cdot B_{i+1}$ be two explicit (marked or unmarked) blocks at some level l, corresponding to the substrings $S[j - b_l..j - 1] \cdot S[j..j + b_l - 1]$. Then we collect the reverse block $B_i^{rev} = S[j - 1] \cdot S[j - 2] \cdots S[j - b_l]$ in the multiset Y and the suffix $S[j..n]$ in the multiset X. If the same suffix $S[j..n]$ turns out to be paired with different preceding blocks (from different levels), we choose only the longest of those preceding blocks (they are all suffixes of one another).

We lexicographically sort X and Y, to obtain the strings $X_1, X_2, \ldots$ and $Y_1, Y_2, \ldots$. The grid then has a point at (x, y) for each $X_x Y_y$ such that Y_y is some reversed block B_i^{rev} and X_x is the suffix of S starting with B_{i+1}.

To see that there are only w points in the grid, notice that a suffix $S[j..n]$ is stored only once, even if it starts blocks at different levels of the BT. Therefore, it can be charged to the lowest common ancestor v of the nodes that represent $S[j - b_l..j - 1]$ and $S[j..j + b_l - 1]$. Since the tree is binary and the second child of v starts at position j, the only pairs of blocks that charge v are those associated with the suffix $S[j..n]$. Therefore, v is charged only once. If such node v exists, it is an internal node (of which there are $w - z$), otherwise the suffix $S[j..n]$ starts a block of level $l = 0$ (of which there are z). We then have w different suffixes in the grid G, which is of size $w \times w$.

We represent G using a wavelet tree [12,13,20], so that it takes $w \lg w + o(w)$ bits and can report all the y-coordinates of the p points lying inside any rectangle of the grid in time $O((p + 1) \lg w)$. We spend other $w \lg n$ bits in an array $T[1..w]$ that gives the position j in S corresponding to each point (x, y), sorted by y-coordinate.

Secondary Occurrences. Let $S_l[1..n_l]$ be the subsequence of S formed by the explicit blocks at level l. If an unmarked block $B_i[1..b_l]$ at level l points to its first occurrence at $S_l[k..k + b_l - 1]$, we say that $[k..k + b_l - 1]$ is the *source* of B_i.

Algorithm 1. Extracting symbols from our encoded BT.

---

1 **Proc** *Extract(i)*
2     $l \leftarrow 0$
3     $b \leftarrow n/z$
4   **while** $b > 1$ **do**
5        $j \leftarrow \lceil i/b \rceil$
6   **if** $D_l[j] = 0$ **then**
7           $r \leftarrow rank_0(D_l, j)$
8           $p \leftarrow select_1(F_l, \pi_l(r))$
9           $s \leftarrow (j - 1) \cdot b + 1$
10          $i \leftarrow (p - \pi_l(r)) + (i - s)$
11          $j \leftarrow \lceil i/b \rceil$
12       $i \leftarrow (rank_1(D_l, j) - 1) \cdot b + ((i - 1) \bmod b) + 1$
13       $l \leftarrow l + 1$
14       $b \leftarrow b/2$
15   Return the symbol stored at position i in the last level

---

For each level l with w_l unmarked blocks, we store two structures to find the secondary occurrences. The first is a bitvector $F_l[1..n_l + w_l]$ built as follows: We traverse from $S_l[1]$ to $S_l[n_l]$. For each $S_l[k]$, we add a 0 to F_l, and then as many 1s as sources start at position k. The second structure is a permutation π_l on $[w_l]$ where $\pi_l(i) = j$ iff the source of the ith unmarked block of level l is signaled by the jth 1 in F_l.

Each bitvector F_l can be represented in $w_l \lg(n_l/w_l) + O(w_l)$ bits so that operation $select_1(F_l, r)$ can be computed in constant time [22]. This operation finds the position of the rth 1 in F_l. On the other hand, we represent π_l using a structure [19] that uses $w_l \lg w_l + O(w_l)$ bits and computes any $\pi_l(i)$ in constant time and any $\pi_l^{-1}(j)$ in time $O(\lg w_l)$. Added over all the levels, since $\sum_l w_l = w$, these structures use $w \lg n + O(w)$ bits.

3.2 Extraction

Let us describe how we extract a symbol $S[i] = S_0[i]$ using our representation. We first compute the block $j \leftarrow \lceil i/b_0 \rceil$ where i falls. If $D_0[j] = 1$, we are already done on this level. If, instead, $D_0[j] = 0$, then the block j is not marked. Its rank among the unmarked blocks of this level is $r_0 = rank_0(D_0, j)$. The position of the 1 in F_0 corresponding to its source is $p_0 = select_1(F_0, \pi_0(r_0))$. This means that the source of the block j starts at $S_0[p_0 - \pi_0(r_0)]$. Since block j starts at position $s_0 = (j - 1) \cdot b_0 + 1$, we set $i \leftarrow (p_0 - \pi_0(r_0)) + (i - s_0)$ and recompute $j \leftarrow \lceil i/b_0 \rceil$, knowing that the new symbol $S_0[i]$ is the same as the original one.

Now that i is inside a marked block j, we move to the next level. To compute the position of i in the next level, we do $i \leftarrow (rank_1(D_0, j) - 1) \cdot b_0 + ((i - 1) \bmod b_0) + 1$, and continue in the same way to extract $S_1[i]$. In the last level we find the symbol stored explicitly. The total time to extract a symbol is $O(\lg(n/z))$.

Algorithm 2. General search procedure.

```
1  Proc Search(P, m)
2     if m = 1 then
3        m ← 2
4        P = P[1]*
5     for k = 1 to m − 1 do
6        [x₁, x₂] ← binary search for P[k + 1..m] in X₁,..., Xw
                    (or [1, w] if P[k + 1..m] = *)
7        [y₁, y₂] ← binary search for P[1..k]ʳᵉᵛ in Y₁,..., Yw
8        for (x, y) ∈ G ∩ [x₁, x₂] × [y₁, y₂] do
9           Primary(T[y] − k, m)
```

Algorithm 1 gives the pseudocode.

3.3 Queries

Primary Occurrences. To search for a pattern $P[1..m]$, we first find its primary occurrences using G as follows. For each partition $P_< = P[1..k]$ and $P_> = P[k + 1..m]$, for $1 \le k < m$, we binary search Y for $P_<^{rev}$ and X for $P_>$. To compare $P_<^{rev}$ with a string Y_i, since Y_i is not stored, we extract the consecutive symbols of $S[T[i] − 1]$, $S[T[i] − 2]$, and so on, until the lexicographic comparison can be decided. Thus each comparison requires $O(m \lg(n/z))$ time. To compare $P_>$ with a string X_i, since X_i is also not stored, we extract the only point of the range $[i, i] \times [1, w]$ (or, in terms of the wavelet tree, we extract the y-coordinate of the ith element in the root sequence), in time $O(\lg w)$. This yields the point Y_j. Then we compare $P_>$ with the successive symbols of $S[T[j]]$, $S[T[j] + 1]$, and so on. Such a comparison then costs $O(\lg w + m \lg(n/z))$. The m binary searches require $m \lg w$ binary search steps, for a total cost of $O(m^2 \lg w \lg(n/z) + m \lg^2 w)$.

Each couple of binary searches identifies ranges $[x_1, x_2] \times [y_1, y_2]$, inside which we extract every point. The m range searches cost $O(m \lg w)$ time. Further, each point (x, y) extracted costs $O(\lg w)$ and it identifies a primary occurrence at $S[T[y] − k..T[y] − k + m − 1]$. Therefore the total cost with occ_p primary occurrences is $O(m^2 \lg w \lg(n/z) + m \lg^2 w + occ_p \lg w)$.

Algorithm 2 gives the general search procedure, using procedure *Primary* to report the primary occurrences and all their associated secondary ones.

Patterns P of length $m = 1$ can be handled as $P[1]*$, where $*$ stands for any character. Thus we take $[x_1, x_2] = [1, w]$ and carry out the search as a normal pattern of length $m = 2$. To make this work also for the last position in S, we assume as usual that S is terminated by a special character $.

To speed up the binary searches, we can sample one out of $\lg w$ strings from Y and insert them into a Patricia tree [18], which would use $O(w)$ extra space. The up to σ children in each node are stored in perfect hash functions, so that in $O(m)$ time we can find the Patricia tree node v representing the pattern prefix or suffix sought. Then the range $[y_1, y_2]$ includes all the sampled leaves descending from v, and up to $\lg w$ strings preceding and following the range. The search is then completed with binary searches in $O(\lg \lg w)$ steps. In case the pattern prefix or suffix is not found in the Patricia tree, we end up in a node v that does not have the desired child and we have to find the consecutive pair of children v_1 and v_2 that surround the nonexistent child. A predecessor search structure per node finds these children in time $O(\lg \lg \sigma) = O(\lg \lg z) = O(\lg \lg w)$. Then we finish with a binary search between the rightmost leaf of v_1 and the leftmost leaf of v_2, also in $O(\lg \lg w)$ steps. Each binary search step takes $O(m \lg(n/z))$ time to read the desired substring from S. At the end of the Patricia search, we must also read one string and verify that the range is correct, but this cost is absorbed in the binary searches. Overall, the search for each cut of the pattern costs $O(m \lg(n/z) \lg \lg w)$. We proceed similarly with X, where there is an additional cost of $O(\lg w \lg \lg w)$ to find the position where to extract each string from. The total cost over all the $m - 1$ searches is then $O(m(m \lg(n/z) + \lg w) \lg \lg w)$.

Secondary Occurrences. Let $S[i..i + m - 1]$ be a primary occurrence. This is already a range $[i_0..i_0 + m - 1] = [i..i + m - 1]$ at level $l = 0$. We track the range down to positions $[i_l..i_l + m - 1]$ at all the levels $l > 0$, using the position tracking mechanism described in Sect. 3.2 for the case of marked nodes:

$$i_{l+1} = (rank_1(D_l, \lceil i_l/b_l \rceil) - 1) \cdot b_l + ((i_l - 1) \mod b_l) + 1.$$

Note that we only need to consider levels l where the block length is $b_l \geq m$, as with shorter blocks there cannot be secondary occurrences. So we only consider the levels $l = 0$ to $l = \lg(n/z) - \lg m$. Further, we should ensure that the block or the two blocks where $[i_l..i_l + m - 1]$ lies are marked before projecting the range to the next level, that is, $D_l[\lceil i_l/b_l \rceil] = D_l[\lceil (i_l + m - 1)/b_l \rceil] = 1$. Still, note that we can ignore this test, because there cannot be sources spanning concatenated blocks that were not contiguous in the previous levels.

For each valid range $[i_l..i_l + m - 1]$, we determine the sources that contain the range, as their target will contain a secondary occurrence. Those sources must start between positions $k = i_l + m - b_l$ and $k' = i_l$. We find the positions $p = select_0(F_l, k)$ and $p' = select_0(F_l, k' + 1)$, thus the blocks of interest are $\pi_l^{-1}(t)$, from $t = p - k + 1$ to $t = p' - k' - 1$. Since F_l is represented as a sparse bitvector [22], operation $select_0$ is solved with binary search on $select_1$, in time $O(\lg w_l) = O(\lg w)$. This can be accelerated to $O(\lg \lg n_l)$ by sampling one out of $\lg n_l$ 1s in F_l, building a predecessor structure on the samples, and then completing the binary search within two samples. The extra space of the predecessor structures adds up to $O(w)$ bits.

To report the occurrence inside each such block $q = \pi_l^{-1}(t)$, we first find its position in the corresponding unmarked block in its level. The block starts at $S_l[(select_0(D_l, q) - 1) \cdot b_l + 1]$, and the offset of the occurrence inside the block is $i_l - (select_1(F_l, t) - t)$ (operation $select_c$ on D_l is answered in constant time using $o(|D_l|)$ further bits [5]). Therefore, the copied occurrence is at $S_l[i_l'..i_l' + m - 1]$, where

$$i_l' = ((select_0(D_l, q) - 1) \cdot b_l + 1) + (i_l - (select_1(F_l, t) - t)).$$

Algorithm 3. Reporting primary and secondary occurrences.

```
 1  Proc Primary(i, m)
 2  │   l ← 0
 3  │   b ← n/z
 4  │   while b/2 ≥ m and D_l[⌈i/b⌉] = D_l[⌈(i + m − 1)/b⌉] = 1 do
 5  │   │   i ← (rank_1(D_l, ⌈i/b⌉) − 1) · b + ((i − 1) mod b) + 1
 6  │   │   l ← l + 1
 7  │   └   b ← b/2
 8  └   Secondary(l, i, m)

 9  Proc Secondary(l, i, m)
10  │   b ← (n/z)/2^l
11  │   while l ≥ 0 do
12  │   │   k ← i + m − b
13  │   │   k′ ← i
14  │   │   p ← select_0(F_l, k)
15  │   │   p′ ← select_0(F_l, k′)
16  │   │   for t ← p − k + 1 to p′ − k′ − 1 do
17  │   │   │   q ← π_l^{−1}(t)
18  │   │   │   i′ ← ((select_0(D_l, q) − 1) · b + 1) + (i − (select_1(F_l, t) − t))
19  │   │   └   Secondary(l, i′, m)
20  │   │   b ← 2 · b
21  │   │   l ← l − 1
22  │   │   if l ≥ 0 then
23  │   │   │   j ← ⌈i/b⌉
24  │   │   └   i ← (select_1(D_l, j) − 1) · b + ((i − 1) mod b) + 1
25  └   Report occurrence at position i
```

We then project the position i'_l upwards until reaching the level $l = 0$, where the positions correspond to those in S. To project $S_l[i'_l]$ to S_{l-1}, we compute the block number $j = \lceil i'_l / b_{l-1} \rceil$, and set

$$i'_{l-1} \leftarrow (select_1(D_{l-1}, j) - 1) \cdot b_{l-1} + ((i'_l - 1) \mod b_{l-1}) + 1.$$

Each new secondary occurrence we report at $S[i..i + m - 1]$ must be also processed to find further secondary occurrences at unmarked blocks copying it at any level. This can be done during the upward tracking to find its position in S, as we traverse all the relevant ranges $[i'_l..i'_l + m - 1]$.

Algorithm 3 describes the procedure to report the primary occurrence $S[i..i + m - 1]$ and all its associated secondary occurrences.

Considering the time to compute π_l^{-1} at its source, the upward tracking to find its position in S, and the tests to find further secondary occurrences at each level of the upward tracking, each secondary occurrence is reported in time $O(\lg(n/z) \lg \lg n)$. Each primary occurrence, in turn, is obtained in time $O(\lg w)$ and then we spend $O(\lg(n/z) \lg \lg n)$ time to track it down to all the levels to find possible secondary occurrences. Therefore, the *occ* primary and secondary occurrences are reported in time $O(occ(\lg(n/z)\lg\lg n + \lg w))$.

Total Query Cost. As described, the total query cost to report the *occ* occurrences is $O(m^2\lg(n/z)\lg\lg w + m\lg w\lg\lg w + occ(\lg(n/z)\lg\lg n + \lg w))$. Since $w = O(z\lg(n/z))$ and $z = \Omega(\lg n)$, it holds $\lg w = \Theta(\lg z)$. A simplified formula is $O(m^2\lg n\lg\lg z + occ\lg n\lg\lg n)$. The space is $3w\lg n + O(w)$ bits.

Theorem 3. *Given a string $S[1..n]$ that can be parsed into z non-overlapping Lempel-Ziv phrases and represented with a BT of $w = O(z\lg(n/z))$ pointers, there exists a data structure using $3w\lg n + O(w)$ bits that so that any substring of length ℓ can be extracted in time $O(\ell\lg(n/z))$ and the occ occurrences of a pattern $P[1..m]$ can be obtained in time $O(m^2\lg(n/z)\lg\lg z + m\lg z\lg\lg z + occ(\lg(n/z)\lg\lg n + \lg z))$. This can be written as $O(m^2\lg n\lg\lg z + occ\lg n\lg\lg n)$.*

If we are interested in a finer space result, we can see that the space is actually $2w\lg n + w\lg w + O(w)$ bits. This can be reduced to $w\lg n + 2w\lg w + O(w)$ by storing the array $T[1..w]$ in $w\lg w + O(w)$ bits as follows. We have shown that each such position is either the start of a block at level $l = 0$ or the middle of a marked block. If we store the bitvectors D_0 to $D_{\lg(n/z)}$ concatenated into $D = 1^z D_0 \cdots D_{\lg(n/z)}$, then the first z 1s represent the blocks at level $l = 0$ and the other 1s represent the marked blocks of each level. We can therefore store $T[k] = p$ to refer to the pth 1 in D, so that T uses $w\lg w$ bits. From the position $select_1(D, p)$ in D, we can determine in constant time if it is among the first z, which corresponds to a level-0 block, or that it corresponds to some $D_l[i]$ (by using *rank* on another bitvector of $O(w)$ bits that marks the $\lg(n/z)$ starting positions of the bitvectors D_l in D, or with a small fusion tree storing those positions). If $T[k]$ points to $D_l[i]$, we know that the suffix starts at $S_l[i_l]$, for $i_l = (i - 1/2) \cdot b_l + 1$. We then project this position up to S. Thus we obtain any position of T in time $O(\lg(n/z))$, which does not affect the complexities.

4   Using Linear Space

If we do not care about the constant multiplying the space, we can have a BT-index using $O(w\lg n)$ bits and speed up searches in various ways. First, we can build the Patricia trees over all the strings in X and Y, so that the search time is not $O(m\lg(n/z)\lg\lg w)$ but just $O(m\lg(n/z))$. To obtain this time we also explicitly store the array of positions T associated with the set X, instead of obtaining it through the wavelet tree.

Third, we can use faster two-dimensional range search data structures that still require linear space [3] to report the p points in time $O((p + 1)\lg^\epsilon w)$ for any constant $\epsilon > 0$ [3]. This reduces the cost per primary occurrence to $O(\lg(n/z)\lg\lg n + \lg^\epsilon w)$.

Finally, we can replace the predecessor searches that implement $select_0$ on the bitvectors F_l by a completely different mechanism. Note that all those searches we perform in our upward or downward path refer to the same occurrence position $S[i..i + m - 1]$, because we do not find unmarked blocks in the path. Thus, instead of looking for sources covering the occurrence at every step in the path, we use a single structure where all the sources from all the levels l are mapped to S. Such sources $[j..j + b_l - 1]$ are sorted by their starting positions j in an array $R[1..w]$. We create a range maximum query data structure [9] on R, able to find in constant time the maximum endpoint $j + b_l - 1$ of the blocks in any range of R. A predecessor search structure on the j values gives us the rightmost position $R[r]$ where the blocks start at i or to its left. A range maximum query on $R[1..r]$ then finds the block $R[k]$ with the rightmost endpoint in $R[1..r]$. If even $R[k]$ does not cover the position $j + b_l - 1$, then no source covers the occurrence. If it does, we process it as a secondary occurrence and recurse on the ranges $R[1..k - 1]$ and $R[k + 1..r]$. It is easy to see that each valid secondary occurrence is identified in $O(1)$ time.

Note that, if we store the starting position j' of the target of source $[j..j + b_l - 1]$, then we directly have the position of the secondary occurrence in S, $S[i'..i' + m - 1]$ with $i' = j' + (i - j)$. Thus we do not even need to traverse paths upwards or downwards, since the primary occurrences already give us positions in S. The support for inverse permutations π_l^{-1} becomes unnecessary. Then the cost per secondary occurrence is reduced to a predecessor search. A similar procedure is described for the LZ77-index [17].

The total time then becomes $O(m^2 \lg(n/z) + m \lg^\epsilon z + occ(\lg \lg n + \lg^\epsilon z))$.

Theorem 4. *A string $S[1..n]$ where the LZ77 parse produces z non-overlapping phrases can be represented in $O(z \lg(n/z))$ space so that any substring of length ℓ can be extracted in time $O(\ell \lg(n/z))$ and the occ occurrences of a pattern $P[1..m]$ can be obtained in time $O(m^2 \lg(n/z) + m \lg^\epsilon z + occ(\lg \lg n + \lg^\epsilon z))$, for any constant $\epsilon > 0$. This can be written as $O(m^2 \lg n + (m + occ) \lg^\epsilon n)$.*

5   Conclusions

We have proposed a way to build a self-index on the Block Tree (BT) [1] data structure, which we call BT-index. The BT obtains a compression related to the LZ77-parse of the string. If the parse uses z non-overlapping phrases, then the BT uses $O(z \lg(n/z))$ space, whereas an LZ77-compressor uses $O(z)$ space. Our BT-index, within the same asymptotic space of a BT, finds all the occ occurrences of a pattern $P[1..m]$ in time $O(m^2 \lg n + occ \lg^\epsilon n)$ for any constant $\epsilon > 0$.

The next step is to implement the BT-index, or a sensible simplification of it, and determine how efficient it is compared to current implementations [6–8,17]. As discussed in the Introduction, there are good reasons to be optimistic about the practical performance of this self-index, especially when searching for relatively long patterns.

Acknowledgements. Many thanks to Simon Puglisi and an anonymous reviewer for pointing out several fatal typos in the formulas.

References

1. Belazzougui, D., Gagie, T., Gawrychowski, P., Kärkkäinen, J., Ordóñez, A., Puglisi, S.J., Tabei, Y.: Queries on LZ-bounded encodings. In: Proceedings of 25th Data Compression Conference (DCC), pp. 83–92 (2015)
2. Bille, P., Ettienne, M.B., Gørtz, I.L., Vildhøj, H.W.: Time-space trade-offs for Lempel-Ziv compressed indexing. In: Proceedings of 28th Annual Symposium on Combinatorial Pattern Matching (CPM). LIPIcs, vol. 78, pp. 16:1–16:17 (2017)
3. Chan, T.M., Larsen, K.G., Pătraşcu, M.: Orthogonal range searching on the RAM. In: Proceedings of 27th ACM Symposium on Computational Geometry (SoCG), pp. 1–10 (2011)
4. Charikar, M., Lehman, E., Liu, D., Panigrahy, R., Prabhakaran, M., Sahai, A., Shelat, A.: The smallest grammar problem. IEEE Trans. Inf. Theory 51(7), 2554–2576 (2005)
5. Clark, D.: Compact PAT trees. Ph.D. thesis, University of Waterloo, Canada (1996)
6. Claude, F., Fariña, A., Martínez-Prieto, M., Navarro, G.: Universal indexes for highly repetitive document collections. Inf. Syst. 61, 1–23 (2016)
7. Claude, F., Navarro, G.: Self-indexed grammar-based compression. Fundamenta Informaticae 111(3), 313–337 (2010)
8. Claude, F., Navarro, G.: Improved grammar-based compressed indexes. In: Calderón-Benavides, L., González-Caro, C., Chávez, E., Ziviani, N. (eds.) SPIRE 2012. LNCS, vol. 7608, pp. 180–192. Springer, Heidelberg (2012). doi:10.1007/978-3-642-34109-0_19
9. Fischer, J., Heun, V.: Space-efficient preprocessing schemes for range minimum queries on static arrays. SIAM J. Comput. 40(2), 465–492 (2011)
10. Gagie, T., Gawrychowski, P., Kärkkäinen, J., Nekrich, Y., Puglisi, S.J.: A faster grammar-based self-index. In: Dediu, A.-H., Martín-Vide, C. (eds.) LATA 2012. LNCS, vol. 7183, pp. 240–251. Springer, Heidelberg (2012). doi:10.1007/978-3-642-28332-1_21
11. Gagie, T., Gawrychowski, P., Kärkkäinen, J., Nekrich, Y., Puglisi, S.J.: LZ77-based self-indexing with faster pattern matching. In: Pardo, A., Viola, A. (eds.) LATIN 2014. LNCS, vol. 8392, pp. 731–742. Springer, Heidelberg (2014). doi:10.1007/978-3-642-54423-1_63
12. Golynski, A., Raman, R., Rao, S.S.: On the redundancy of succinct data structures. In: Gudmundsson, J. (ed.) SWAT 2008. LNCS, vol. 5124, pp. 148–159. Springer, Heidelberg (2008). doi:10.1007/978-3-540-69903-3_15
13. Grossi, R., Gupta, A., Vitter, J.S.: High-order entropy-compressed text indexes. In: Proceedings of 14th Annual ACM-SIAM Symposium on Discrete Algorithms (SODA), pp. 841–850 (2003)
14. Jez, A.: Approximation of grammar-based compression via recompression. Theor. Comput. Sci. 592, 115–134 (2015)
15. Jez, A.: A really simple approximation of smallest grammar. Theor. Comput. Sci. 616, 141–150 (2016)
16. Kärkkäinen, J., Ukkonen, E.: Lempel-Ziv parsing and sublinear-size index structures for string matching. In: Proceedings of 3rd South American Workshop on String Processing (WSP), pp. 141–155 (1996)
17. Kreft, S., Navarro, G.: On compressing and indexing repetitive sequences. Theor. Comput. Sci. 483, 115–133 (2013)
18. Morrison, D.: PATRICIA - practical algorithm to retrieve information coded in alphanumeric. J. ACM 15(4), 514–534 (1968)

19. Munro, J.I., Raman, R., Raman, V., Rao, S.S.: Succinct representations of permutations and functions. Theor. Comput. Sci. **438**, 74–88 (2012)
20. Navarro, G.: Wavelet trees for all. J. Discrete Algorithms **25**, 2–20 (2014)
21. Nishimoto, T., Tomohiro, I., Inenaga, S., Bannai, H., Takeda, M.: Dynamic index, LZ factorization, and LCE queries in compressed space. CoRR abs/1504.06954 (2015)
22. Okanohara, D., Sadakane, K.: Practical entropy-compressed rank/select dictionary. In: Proceedings of 9th Workshop on Algorithm Engineering and Experiments (ALENEX), pp. 60–70 (2007)
23. Rytter, W.: Application of Lempel-Ziv factorization to the approximation of grammar-based compression. Theor. Comput. Sci. **302**(1–3), 211–222 (2003)
24. Sakamoto, H.: A fully linear-time approximation algorithm for grammar-based compression. J. Discrete Algorithms **3**(24), 416–430 (2005)
25. Ziv, J., Lempel, A.: A universal algorithm for sequential data compression. IEEE Trans. Inf. Theory **23**(3), 337–343 (1977)

Counting Palindromes in Substrings

Mikhail Rubinchik and Arseny M. Shur[✉]

Department of Algebra and Fundamental Informatics, Ural Federal University,
pr. Lenina, 51, Ekaterinburg, Russia
mikhail.rubinchik@gmail.com, arseny.shur@urfu.ru

Abstract. We propose a data structure and an online algorithm to
report the number of distinct palindromes in any substring of an input
string. Assume that the string S of length n arrives symbol-by-symbol
and every symbol is followed by zero or more queries of the form "report
the number of distinct palindromes in $S[i..j]$". We use $O(n \log n)$ total
time to process the string plus $O(\log n)$ time per query. The required
space is $O(n \log n)$ in general and $O(n)$ in a natural particular case. As
a simple application, we describe an algorithm reporting all palindromic
rich substrings of an input string in $O(n \log n)$ time and $O(n)$ space.

Keywords: Palindrome · Counting palindromes · Eertree · String algorithm · Online algorithm

1   Introduction

Palindromes are one of the most important repetitive structures in strings.
During the last decades they were actively studied in formal language theory,
combinatorics on words and stringology. Recall that a palindrome is any string
$S = a_1 a_2 \cdots a_n$ equal to its reversal $\overleftarrow{S} = a_n \cdots a_2 a_1$.

Active studies on palindrome algorithmics began with the problem of online
recognition of palindromes by (multi-tape) Turing machines. Slisenko in a huge
paper [20] presented a 6-tape machine recognizing palindromes in real time;
using Slisenko's ideas, Galil described a much simpler construction [9]. In the
more powerful RAM model, a big variety of fast algorithms was developed for
palindrome-related problems since then. Manacher [18] came up with a linear-
time algorithm capturing all palindromic substrings of a string. The problem of
counting distinct palindromes in a string was solved offline in [12] and online
in [16]. Knuth, Morris, and Pratt [15] gave a linear-time algorithm for checking
whether a string is a product of even-length palindromes. Galil and Seiferas [10]
asked for such an algorithm for the *k-factorization* problem: decide whether or
not a given string can be factored into exactly k non-empty palindromes, where
k is an arbitrary constant. They presented an online algorithm for $k = 1, 2$ and
an offline one for $k = 3, 4$. An $O(kn)$ time online algorithm for the length n

This work was Partially supported by the grant 16-01-00795 of the Russian Foundation of Basic Research.

© Springer International Publishing AG 2017
G. Fici et al. (Eds.): SPIRE 2017, LNCS 10508, pp. 290–303, 2017.
DOI: 10.1007/978-3-319-67428-5_25

string and any k was designed in [17]. Close to the k-factorization problem is the problem of finding the *palindromic length* of a string, which is the minimal k in its k-factorization. This problem was solved by Fici et al. and independently by Tomohiro et al. in $O(n \log n)$ time [7,14]. Simpler algorithms with the same asymptotics for counting and factorization problems were proposed in [19] on the base of a new data structure called "eertree". Note that hard palindromic-related problems also exist: thus, it is NP-complete to check whether a string can be factorized into distinct palindromes [1].

In this paper we study a generalization of the palindrome counting problem: *in a string arriving online, report at any moment the number of distinct palindromes in any given substring*. Thus, if for $S = aabcac \cdots$ a request for $S[2..6]$ comes, the algorithm should quickly report "4" (a, b, c, cac, the empty string does not count) no matter of whether the request comes after the 6th or the 1006th letter of S. Clearly, an algorithm precomputing the answers to all requests has at least quadratic complexity. As usual in the online setting, we seek for an algorithm working in $O(n \operatorname{polylog}(n))$ time. Our main result is the algorithm processing the length n input string in $O(n \log n)$ time and space into a data structure which returns the number of distinct palindromes in any substring in $O(\log n)$ time.

We also consider a restricted version of the above counting problem, in which the requested substring must be a suffix of the current input. In this case the processing and query time remain the same, while the linear space suffices. Finally, we apply the obtained solutions to the offline version of the counting problem: given a string and a set of pairs of indices, output the number of distinct palindromes in each substring specified by such a pair.

A length n string contains at most n distinct palindromes [5]. The "rich" strings with the maximum number of palindromes are studied in many papers, see, e.g., [2,11,13]. We apply our technique to the problem of finding all rich substrings of an input string and solve it in $O(n \log n)$ time and $O(n)$ space.

The main theorem, construction and data structure are presented in Sect. 2. Section 3 contains the proof of the main theorem. In Sect. 4, we consider the offline counting problem and the problem on rich substrings.

1.1   Definitions and Notation

We study finite strings, viewing them as arrays of symbols: $S = S[1..n]$. The notation σ stands for the number of distinct symbols of the processed string. We write ε for the empty string, $|S|$ for the length of a string S, and $S[i..j]$ for $S[i]S[i+1]\ldots S[j]$, where $S[i..i-1] = \varepsilon$ for any i. The same $[i..j]$ notation is used for ranges in arrays and integers. A *period* of a string $S = S[1..n]$ is any p, $0 < p \leq n$ such that $S[1..n-p] = S[p+1..n]$. The minimal period of S is denoted by $\operatorname{per}(S)$. A string T is a *substring* of S (or *contained in* S) if $T = S[i..j]$ for some i and j; we say that T *occurs in* S *at position* i and order the occurrences of T in S by their position (e.g., "last" occurrence is the one with maximum j). A substring $S[1..j]$ (resp., $S[i..n]$) is a *prefix* (resp. *suffix*) of S. If a substring (prefix, suffix) of S is a palindrome, it is called a *subpalindrome* (resp. *prefix-palindrome*, *suffix-palindrome*). The number of distinct subpalindromes of S is denoted by #Pal(S). A subpalindrome $S[l..r]$ has *center* $(l+r)/2$. Throughout the paper we do not count ε as a palindrome.

Fact 1 ([5]). *For a string S and a symbol b, the string Sb (resp., bS) contains at most one palindrome which is not contained in S; this palindrome is the longest suffix-palindrome of Sb (resp., the longest prefix-palindrome of bS).*

Problem SUB-PCOUNT

Input: a sequence of queries append(b) (b is a symbol) and return(i, j) ($i \leq j$ are integers such that j is at most the number of append's in the preceding input). *Processing/output (online)*: let S be the current string (initially $S = \varepsilon$). For each append(b) query, assign Sb to S, output nothing; for each return(i, j) query, output #Pal($S[i..j]$).

In the *Restricted* SUB-PCOUNT, j in the input is always equal to the current length of S; thus, all requests are about the suffixes of the current string.

2   Main Result, Construction, and Data Structure

Theorem 1. *For an input sequence consisting of n append queries and some return queries,*

(1) SUB-PCOUNT *can be solved in $O(n \log n)$ time for all append queries plus $O(\log n)$ time per return query using $O(n \log n)$ space;*
(2) restricted SUB-PCOUNT *can be solved in the same time using $O(n)$ space.*

For a string $S = S[1..n]$ consider the *difference array* $A_n = A_n[1..n]$ such that $A_n[k] = \#Pal(S[k..n]) - \#Pal(S[k+1..n])$. By Fact 1, $A_n[k] \in \{0, 1\}$. Note that $\#Pal(S[k..n]) = \sum_{i=k}^{n} A_n[k]$. So if we can efficiently

- build the difference arrays A_j for the prefixes $S[1..j]$ of S online
- retrieve the sums of bits from A_j,

we obtain a solution to the restricted SUB-PCOUNT. If we further show how to store all arrays A_j simultaneously in a compact form, we solve SUB-PCOUNT. We store and update difference arrays using some versions of *segment trees*.

2.1   Segment Tree

Segment tree is a data structure of probably folklore origin, which is popular in the ACM-ICPC community and allows fast computation of different symmetric functions (sums, minima, etc.) on all ranges of an integer array (see e.g., http://wcipeg.com/wiki/Segment_tree)[1]. Segment tree is an alternative to Fenwick's tree [6] and admits both lazy and persistent versions. Below we describe the version for sums which allows the upgrade to a persistent structure.

---

[1] Unfortunately, there is one more data structure with this name, see, e.g., Wikipedia.

I. For an *ordinary segment tree* storing an array of length n, where $2^{d-1} < n \leq 2^d$, take a fully balanced binary tree with 2^d leaves and delete the $2^d - n$ rightmost leaves together with all internal vertices having no remaining leaves in their subtrees; see Fig. 1. Each vertex has weight; the weight of ith (from the left) leaf is the ith element of the array, and the weight of an internal vertex is the sum of weights of its children (and thus, the total weight of all leaves in its subtree).

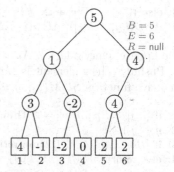

Fig. 1. Example of an ordinary segment tree. Numbers in vertices are weights. Some parameters of the blue vertex are shown. (Color figure online)

For each vertex v we store its children $L[v], R[v]$ ($L[v] = $ null for leaves only; internal vertices may have $R[v] = $ null), the boundaries $B[v], E[v]$ of the range spanned by the leaves in its subtree, and the weight $W[v]$. We want to perform three types of queries to the stored array A, each in $O(\log n)$ time:

1) add(i, Δ): adds Δ to the element $A[i]$;
2) sum(i, j): requests the sum of all elements of the subarray $A[i..j]$;
3) push: extends A to the right by a zero element.

To adjust weights, we descend from the root to the leaf i, adding Δ to the weight of each vertex. To push a new (nth) element, we descend from the root following the binary expansion of n, setting $E[v] = n$ for existing vertices and creating new vertices of zero weight on the way; if n is a power of 2, we start with creating a new root and making the existing tree its left subtree. For sums, the recursive function $SUM(i, j, v)$ is used:

1: **if** $[i..j] \cap [B[v]..E[v]] = \varnothing$ **then** return 0
2: **if** $[B[v]..E[v]] \subseteq [i..j]$ **then** return $W[v]$
3: **else** return $SUM(i, j, L[v]) + SUM(i, j, R[v])$

The query sum(i, j) is answered by $SUM(i, j, root)$.

For add and push the $O(\log n)$ time bound is obvious. For sum the bound follows from the observation that at most 4 vertices on each level are touched by the recursive procedure.

II. *Lazy segment tree* supports an extended form add(i, j, Δ) of the update query: adding Δ to all $A[k]$ such that $i \leq k \leq j$. To perform such queries in $O(\log n)$ time, a new parameter δ is assigned to each vertex. For any v, the sum of the elements of $A[B[v]..E[v]]$ is $W[v] + (E[v] - B[v] + 1) \cdot \sum_{u \in pred[v]} \delta[u]$, where $pred[v]$ is the set of all predecessors of v including v itself. For an add query, the recursive operation $ADD(i, j, \Delta, v)$ is used:

1: **if** $[i..j] \cap [B[v]..E[v]] = \varnothing$ **then** stop
2: **if** $[B[v]..E[v]] \subseteq [i..j]$ **then** $\delta[v] \leftarrow \delta[v] + \Delta$; stop

3: **else** $W[v] \leftarrow W[v] + \Delta \cdot \#([i..j] \cap [B[v]..E[v]])$
4: $ADD(i,j,\Delta,L[v]); ADD(i,j,\Delta,R[v]);$ stop

The update query add(i,j,Δ) is performed by $ADD(i,j,\Delta,root)$.

Pushing a new element is similar to the ordinary version. Now consider the recursive function $SUM(i,j,\eta,v)$, where η accumulates δ's from $pred[v]$:

1: **if** $[i..j] \cap [B[v]..E[v]] = \varnothing$ **then** return 0
2: $\eta \leftarrow \eta + \delta[v]$
3: **if** $[B[v]..E[v]] \subseteq [i..j]$ **then** return $W[v] + \eta \cdot (E[v] - B[v] + 1)$
4: **else** return $SUM(i,j,\eta,L[v]) + SUM(i,j,\eta,R[v])$

The query sum(i,j) is answered by $SUM(i,j,0,root)$. Clearly, both add and sum queries take the same time as the sum query in the ordinary version. Note that both ordinary and lazy versions use linear (in the size of A) space.

Maintaining the current difference array in either ordinary or lazy version of the segment tree suits as a part of solution of restricted SUB-PCOUNT. Indeed, each request return(i,j) to the difference array A_j is answered by the sum of the range $A_j[i..j]$ in $O(\log n)$ time, while the segment tree itself requires $O(n)$ space. However, to solve SUB-PCOUNT we need access to all arrays A_j simultaneously. Storing them in a naive way would mean an $\Omega(n^2)$ lower bound on the space and time used; to avoid this, we define a *persistent* segment tree. (For the basics on persistent structures see [4].)

III. *Persistent segment tree* stores a lazy segment tree with *all its previous versions* and answers the same queries as the lazy segment tree, but addressed to *any* version. In a persistent tree, we never change the parameters of an existing vertex; a clone of this vertex is created each time a change is needed, and the change is performed in the clone. Note that if we clone a vertex, all its predecessors must be cloned: they now have a new vertex as a child. In particular, a root is cloned on each change in the tree. Thus, the version of the tree is uniqely identified by the root; the array of pointers to the roots can be stored explicitly.

Consider the modification of the ADD procedure (pushing is done in a similar way, while SUM does not change the tree). Now $ADD(i,j,\Delta,v)$ returns a vertex instead of just stopping; in line 1 this is vertex v, and in remaining lines this is a clone v' of v, created if the condition in line 1 fails. In line 4 the results of recursive calls are assigned to $L[v']$ and $R[v']$.

Every update affects $O(\log n)$ vertices, so the memory used is $O((a+n)\log n)$ (for a add's and n push'es). For difference arrays, a push followed by a group of add's updates A_j to A_{j+1}; after this, a group of sum queries come. Thus, there is no need to store links to all versions of the tree; n links to the versions after each group of add's is enough, reducing the memory cost to $O(n\log n)$.

3   Combinatorics of Difference Arrays

In this section we describe how to process append queries, updating the difference array (stored as a segment tree) and auxiliary data structures. By "iteration" we mean processing of one query (changing the input string from $S[1..j]$ to $S[1..j+1]$). Let $T, b, A[1..|T|]$ be a string, a symbol, and an integer array. Consider the function $UPDATE(Tb, A)$ which uses queries to the segment tree of A:[2]

```
1: push; t ← number of suffix-palindromes of Tb
2: for (i = 1; i ≤ t; i++) do
3:     uᵢ ← ith longest suffix-palindrome of Tb
4:     kᵢ ← position of the suffix uᵢ in Tb
5:     lᵢ ← position of last occurrence of uᵢ in T
6:     add(kᵢ, 1); add(lᵢ, −1)
7: return A
```

Lemma 2. *Let A_j, A_{j+1} be the difference arrays of the prefixes $S[1..j]$ and $S[1..j+1]$ of a string S. Then $A_{j+1} = UPDATE(S[1..j+1], A_j)$.*

Proof. First note that for each $i = 1, \ldots, t$ one has $A_{j+1}[k_i] = 1$ ($S[k_i..j+1]$ is a palindrome not contained in $S[k_i+1..j+1]$) and $A_j[l_i] = 1$ (the palindrome u_i is contained in $S[l_i..j]$ but not in $S[l_i+1..j]$). Now we check that $A_{j+1}[k]$ was computed correctly in all cases.

- $A_j[k] = A_{j+1}[k] = 0$: $k \notin \{k_i, l_i\}$ for any i, so there was no $\mathsf{add}(k, \Delta)$ query.
- $A_j[k] = 0$, $A_{j+1}[k] = 1$: $k \neq l_i$ for any i, so there was no $\mathsf{add}(k, -1)$ query. By definition of a difference array, all prefix-palindromes of $S[k..j]$ have other occurrences in $S[k..j]$, while some prefix-palindrome of $S[k..j+1]$ has not; hence $S[k..j+1]$ is a palindrome (say, u_i), $k = k_i$, and thus $\mathsf{add}(k, 1)$ was performed.
- $A_j[k] = 1$, $A_{j+1}[k] = 0$: $k \neq k_i$ for any i, no $\mathsf{add}(k, 1)$ query. Further, some prefix-palindrome u of $S[k..j]$ has no other occurrences in $S[k..j]$ but occurs in $S[k..j+1]$; hence u is a suffix-palindrome of $S[1..j+1]$ (say, u_i), $k = l_i$, and thus $\mathsf{add}(k, -1)$ was performed.
- $A_j[k] = 1$, $A_{j+1}[k] = 1$: let u (resp., v) be the prefix-palindrome of $S[k..j]$ (resp., $S[k..j+1]$) having no other occurences in this substring. Then either $v = u$ or $v = S[k..j+1]$. In the latter case, $k \in \{k_1, \ldots, k_t\}$. Since v is a palindrome, its prefix-palindrome u is its suffix-palindrome; so u is a suffix-palindrome of $S[1..j+1]$ and $k \in \{l_1, \ldots, l_t\}$. Hence both queries $\mathsf{add}(k, 1)$ and $\mathsf{add}(k, -1)$ were performed. In the former case, $S[k..j+1]$ is not a palindrome (otherwise v would occur as its suffix), so $k \notin \{k_1, \ldots, k_t\}$. Further, a palindrome at position k either is not a suffix of $S[1..j+1]$ or has a later occurrence in $S[k..j]$ as a suffix of v, so $k \notin \{l_1, \ldots, l_t\}$. Hence there was no $\mathsf{add}(k, \Delta)$ query.

Thus we proved that $UPDATE(S[1..j+1], A_j)$ correctly computes the number $A_{j+1}[k]$ for $k = 1, \ldots, j$. Finally, $k_t = j+1$, so $\mathsf{add}(k_t, 1)$ sets the correct value $A_{j+1}[j+1] = 1$. □

Due to Lemma 2, to update A_j to A_{j+1} one can iterate through suffix-palindromes of $S[1..j+1]$ preparing the lists $\{k_i\}_1^t$ and $\{l_i\}_1^t$ for add queries.

---

[2] By Fact 1, only l_1 can be undefined; if so, we assume that $\mathsf{add}(l_1, -1)$ is ignored.

To optimize this process, we rule out some of the positions which appear in two lists simultaneously. We need some special notions.

Let $u_1, \ldots, u_t$ be all non-empty suffix-palindromes of a string S in the order of decreasing length. Since u_j is a suffix of u_i for any $i < j$, the sequence of minimal periods of $u_1, \ldots, u_t$ is non-increasing. The sets of suffix-palindromes with the same minimal period are *series of palindromes* (for S):

$$\underbrace{u_1, \ldots, u_{i_1}}_{p_1}, \underbrace{u_{i_1+1}, \ldots, u_{i_2}}_{p_2}, \ldots, \underbrace{u_{i_{r-1}+1}, \ldots, u_t}_{p_r}.$$

We refer to the longest and the shortest palindrome in a series as its *head* and *baby* respectively (they coincide in the case of a 1-element series). A crucial observation [7,14,17] is that the length of a head is multiplicatively smaller than the length of the baby from the previous series, and thus every string of length n has $O(\log n)$ series. The following lemma on the structure of series is easily implied by [17, Lemmas 2,3,7].

Lemma 3. *Let U be a series of palindromes with period p for a string S. There exist $k \geq 1$ and unique palindromes u, v with $|uv| = p$, $v \neq \varepsilon$ such that U equals one of the following sets:*

(1) $U = \{(uv)^{k+1}u, (uv)^k u, \ldots, (uv)^2 u\}$ and the next series' head is uvu,
(2) $U = \{(uv)^k u, (uv)^{k-1}u, \ldots, uvu\}$ and the next series' head is u,
(3) $U = \{v^k, v^{k-1}, \ldots, v\}$, $p = 1$, $|v| = 1$, $u = \varepsilon$, and U is the last series for S.

We need some further properties.

Lemma 4.

(1) If v is a baby in some series of palindromes, then it is a baby of any series containing v (in any string).
(2) If a palindrome v satisfies $\mathsf{per}(v) > |v|/2$, then v is a baby.
(3) Let subpalindromes u, v of S share the same center. If $|u| = |v| - 2$, u is a baby and v is not, then $\mathsf{per}(u) = \mathsf{per}(v)$.

Proof. Let v' be the longest suffix-palindrome of a palindrome v.

(1) "v is a baby" is equivalent to $\mathsf{per}(v) > \mathsf{per}(v')$ and thus depends on v only.
(2) We have $\mathsf{per}(v') \leq |v'| = |v| - \mathsf{per}(v) < \mathsf{per}(v)$, so v is a baby.
(3) Assume $\mathsf{per}(u) < \mathsf{per}(v)$. By statement 2, $\mathsf{per}(v) \leq |v|/2$. Then $\mathsf{per}(u) + \mathsf{per}(v) \leq |u| + 1$. Since both $\mathsf{per}(u), \mathsf{per}(v)$ are periods of u, by the Fine–Wilf theorem [8] u has the period $\gcd(\mathsf{per}(u), \mathsf{per}(v))$. Since $\mathsf{per}(u)$ is the minimal period of u, it divides $\mathsf{per}(v)$. Lemma 3 implies $u = xyxyx$, $\mathsf{per}(u) = |xy|$, $\mathsf{per}(v) = |xyxy|$. Then $v = y[1] \cdot xyxyx \cdot y[1]$, implying that $\mathsf{per}(u)$ is a period of v. This contradiction proves statement 3. $\qquad\square$

Now return to difference arrays.

Lemma 5. *Let $u_1, \ldots, u_r$ $(r > 1)$ be a series of suffix-palindromes of $S[1..j+1]$ occurring at positions $k_1 < \ldots < k_r$, respectively. Then for any $i = 1, \ldots, r-1$ the function $UPDATE(S[1..j+1], A_j)$ performs both* add$(k_i, 1)$ *and* add$(k_i, -1)$.

Proof. The suffix-palindrome u_i occurs at position k_i, so add$(k_i, 1)$ is performed when processing u_i. Note that u_{i+1} occurs in $S[1..j+1]$ at position k_{i+1} as a suffix and also at position k_i as a prefix of u_i; by definition of a series, $|u_{i+1}| = |u_i| - p > p$, where p is the period of the series. Hence these two occurrences of u_{i+1} overlap. Then u_{i+1} cannot occur at position l such that $k_i < l < k_{i+1}$ (the occurrences of u_{i+1} at positions l and k_{i+1} would overlap, implying that $S[l..j+1]$ is a palindrome; but this is impossible, since u_i has no suffix-palindromes which are longer than u_{i+1}). Hence k_i is the position of the last occurrence of u_{i+1} in $S[1..j]$, and add$(k_i, -1)$ is performed when processing u_{i+1}. □

According to Lemma 5, the statement of Lemma 2 remains true if we replace $UPDATE$ with the following function $UPDATE'(Tb, A)$:

1: push
2: Inc ← list of positions of babies in all series for Tb
3: Dec ← list of positions of last occurrences in T of heads in all series for Tb
4: **for each** $k \in$ Inc **do** add$(k, 1)$
5: **for each** $l \in$ Dec **do** add$(l, -1)$
6: **return** A

Lists Inc and Dec have length equal to the number of series, which is $O(\log n)$. Moreover, the following lemma holds.

Lemma 6. *The lists* Inc *and* Dec *can be built in* $O(\log n)$ *time.*

We store the information about palindromes in S in the *eertree* data structure [19]. Below we briefly describe the version of eertree used here.

Eertree is a tree-like data structure consisting of vertices, labeled edges, and two types of suffix links. Each vertex is identified with a unique subpalindrome of S; two special vertices correspond to ε and to "imaginary" palindrome -1. An edge with a label a leads from a vertex v to ava (from -1 to a). The suffix link link$[v]$ points to the longest suffix-palindrome of v; the series link serieslink$[v]$ points to the baby of the series to which v belongs; see Fig. 2 for an example. (In [19] the related version of eertree used series links to the head of the next series; the described version is built in almost the same way. We use it because it is convenient to

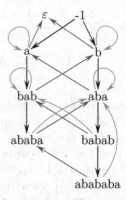

Fig. 2. Eertree for $S = ababab a$ (with black edges, blue suffix links and orange series links; edge labels are omitted). No edges from ε means no even-length palindromes (Color figure online)

store additional information in the babies.) Each vertex v contains: the length len$[v]$ of the palindrome; the list go$[v]$ of children (as a binary search tree); the links link$[v]$ and serieslink$[v]$. The eertree requires $O(n)$ space and can be built online in $O(n \log \sigma)$ time with at most $O(\log n)$ time per symbol appended to the string. Each iteration either finds or creates the vertex corresponding to the longest suffix-palindrome maxPal of the updated string, so we have free access to maxPal. Note that we also have an $O(1)$ access to the smallest period of any palindrome v: $per(v) = len[v] - len[link[v]]$, and to the position of v as a suffix-palindrome: $pos(v) = |S| - len[v] + 1$.

Proof (of Lemma 6). Given the eertree of $S[1..j{+}1]$, it is easy to build the list Inc in $O(\log n)$ time. Starting from maxPal, we visit all babies in the order of decreasing length (the longest baby is $v =$ serieslink[maxPal], the next is serieslink[link$[v]$], and so on) and append their positions to Inc.

For Dec, first recall that a palindrome v is a baby iff $per(v) > per(link[v])$; we refer to any series with the baby v as v-*series*. Creating a vertex v in the eertree, we will check whether v is a baby; if yes, we will create a new stack for the occurrences of all v-series and point to this stack from v. An element of a stack is a pair $(U.\text{card}, U.\text{pos})$ consisting of the cardinality of the v-series U and the position of its head. The maintenance of stacks and the array Dec is as follows (top2 is the second element of a stack, the function pop2 pops it):

1: $u \leftarrow$ head of the current series; $v \leftarrow$ serieslink$[u]$
2: **if** $u \neq v$ **then** top.card $\leftarrow$ top.card $+ 1$ **else** push$(1, pos(u))$
3: **if** top2 $\neq$ null **then** add $(\text{top2.pos} + (\text{top2.card} - \text{top.card}) \cdot per(v))$ to Dec
4: **if** top.card $=$ top2.card **then** pop2
5: $u \leftarrow$ link$[v]$ ▷ proceed to the next series

Example 7. Let us follow the evolution of the stack of the baby aba:

```
      1 2  3  4  5  6  7  8 9 10 11 12 13 14  15   16   17   18   19
S =  a b  a  b  a  b  a  c a  b  a  d  a  b   a    b    a    b    a   ···
      ↓    ↓    ↓              ↓              ↓     ↓    ↓    ↓
     1,1  2,1  3,1            1,9            1,13  2,13 3,13
                             3,1            3,1   3,1
```

The stack is created when processing $S[1..3]$; for $S[1..5]$, the head of the aba-series is $ababa \neq aba$, so we increase top.card; the same applies to $S[1..7]$. For $S[1..11]$ aba is the head, so we push a new element to the stack; then we add the position of the last occurrence of aba in $S[1..10]$, which is $5 = 1 + (3 - 1) \cdot 2$, to Dec. Processing $S[1..15]$, we push a new series, add 9 to Dec, and pop the series $(1, 9)$. For $S[1..17]$ we increase top.card and add the position $3 = 1 + (3 - 2) \cdot 2$ of the occurrence of $ababa$ to Dec. Finally, for $S[1..19]$ we increase top.card, add 1 to Dec and pop the series $(3, 1)$.

Consider a baby $v = xyx$ with $per(v) = p = |xy|$ (for a baby of the form $xyxyx$ the same argument works). If v ends in S at position j, its next occurrence ends at position $j{+}p$ or later; otherwise, v would have a smaller period. If it ends at $j{+}p$, the occurence ending at j extends to $xyxyx$ and all palindromes from this v-series also extend. Hence at $j{+}p$ we also have a v-series; compared to the v-series at j, it has one more element and the same position of the head. If the next occurrence of v ends at some $j' > j+p$, it becomes a new v-series of length 1. Thus, the line 2 correctly maintains the last v-series.

The **if** in line 4 ensures that the lengths of the stored v-series are in strictly decreasing order and the previous occurrence of the head of the top v-series is in the series contained in top2. Since in a k-element v-series the head has the length $|v| + (k-1)p$, the **if** in line 3 correctly identifies the position of this previous occurrence. Overall, each head is processed in $O(1)$ time, so the time to build Dec is $O(\log n)$. □

Remark 8. All series stored simultaneously in stacks have different heads. Hence all stacks together contain $O(n)$ elements (which is the number of distinct palindromes in S).

Storing difference arrays in a standard segment tree, we update it $O(n \log n)$ times while processing the whole string S. Thus, we can solve the restricted SUB-PCOUNT in $O(n \log^2 n)$ time and linear space. To improve working time, we use the lazy segment tree and update its segments in a lazy manner also. Note that in the proof of Lemma 6 we process suffix-palindromes in the order of decreasing length; so both lists Inc and Dec are sorted in increasing order.

We use two lists of "postponed" updates, iInc and iDec; their elements are pairs of the form (l, r), $1 \le l \le r \le n$, sorted by the first coordinate in increasing order. After building Inc and Dec, we do not update the segment tree immediately; instead, we add new updates to iInc/iDec and perform some of the earlier postponed updates. We store all postponed increments in iInc. On each iteration, after building Inc we "merge" iInc and Inc: for each $k \in$ Inc, if iInc contains a pair of the form $(k+1, r)$, we replace it with (k, r); if no such pair exists, we add the pair (k, k) to iInc; all pairs which were not changed, are deleted; deleting a pair (l, r) from iInc, we apply add$(l, r, 1)$ to the lazy segment tree. Note that after merging the size of iInc equals the size of Inc (and hence is $O(\log n)$). Since both lists are sorted, the merging takes $O(\log n)$ time. The lists iDec and Dec are processed in the same way. Thus we have

Lemma 9. *On each iteration, the lists* iInc *and* iDec *are updated in* $O(\log n)$ *time.*

To retrieve the sum of a range $[i..j]$ of A_j, we request the sum of $[i..j]$ from the segment tree and correct it checking the intersections of $[i..j]$ with all intervals stored in iInc and iDec. Note that even if some leaves of the segment tree contain integers different from 0,1 (the order of updates may be violated due to laziness), the sum is computed correctly. Since these lists are of logarithmic size, we get

Lemma 10. *A lazily updated lazy segment tree returns the sum of any range of the stored array in* $O(\log n)$ *time.*

Now we prove the property which is key for our time bound.

Lemma 11. *The total number of pairs deleted from the lists* iInc *and* iDec *during* n *iterations is* $O(n)$.

Proof. Assume that a pair (l, r) is deleted from iInc at $(j+1)$th iteration. This means that l is in Inc after jth iteration and $l-1$ is not in Inc after $(j+1)$th iteration; so we need to estimate the number of pairs (l, j) with this property. The same applies to the lists iDec and Dec.

We begin with the study of Inc. By definition, $u = S[l..j]$ is a baby palindrome, while $v=S[l-1..j+1]$ is not. The center of u is $c = (j-l)/2$. There are two cases for v.

Case Inc.1: v is not a palindrome. Then $S[1..j+1]$ and all longer prefixes of S have no suffix-palindrome with the center c, while $S[1..j]$ has; we say that the center c *dies* at $(j+1)$th iteration. Clearly, each center dies at most once and the centers of suffix-palindromes of the same string are different, so the number of pairs (l, j) falling into this case is bounded by the number of possible centers, which is $2n$.

Case Inc.2: v is a palindrome, but not a baby. By Lemma 4(3), $\text{per}(v) = \text{per}(u)$. For the case $|u| = 1$, there are at most n pairs of the form (j, j), so we assume $|u| > 1$ below. Let $u' = \text{link}[u] = S[l'..j]$, $v' = \text{link}[v]$. Since $|v'| = |v| - \text{per}[v] = |u| + 2 - \text{per}[u] = |u'| + 2$, we have $v' = S[l'-1..j+1]$. Then u' and v' share the center $c' = (j-l')/2$. In addition, $\text{per}(u') < \text{per}(u)$ and $\text{per}(v') = \text{per}(v)$ since u is a baby and v is not. Hence $|\text{link}[u']| = |u'| - \text{per}(u')$ and $|\text{link}[v']| = |v'| - \text{per}(v) < |u'| - \text{per}(u') + 2$. Thus, the center c'' of $\text{link}[u']$ dies at $(j+1)$th iteration. Different suffix-palindromes u points to different centers c'' (including the case $u' = S[j]$, $u'' = S[j+1..j] = \varepsilon$; the center $c'' = j+1/2$ also dies at the $(j+1)$th iteration), so the number of pairs (l, j) falling into this case is at most $2n$, as in the previous paragraph. Overall, the number of pairs (l, j) for all the lists Inc is $O(n)$.

Consider the array Dec. The pair (l, j) is such that (a) for some i, k, u one has $u = S[l..i] = S[k..j]$, u is the head of some series at jth iteration, and $S[l..i]$ is the last occurrence of u in $S[1..j-1]$; (b) the property (a) fails for the pair $(l-1, j+1)$. Consider $v = S[k-1..j+1]$ and $w = S[l-1..i+1]$. If v is a palindrome and $\text{per}(v) = \text{per}(u)$, then v is the head of some series at $(j+1)$th iteration. Indeed, if v is not a head, then $S[k-1-\text{per}[v]..j+1]$ is a palindrome from the same series as v; hence $S[k-\text{per}(v)..j]$ is a palindrome from the same series as u, so u is not a head, contradicting (a). Further, if $v = w$, then $S[l-1..i+1]$ is the last occurrence of w in $S[1..j]$; hence the pair $(l-1, j+1)$ satisfies (a), thus contradicting (b). Therefore, either v is not a palindrome, or $\text{per}(v) > \text{per}(u)$, or w is not a palindrome, or $\text{per}(w) > \text{per}(u)$. Below we prove a linear upper bound on the number of pairs (l, j) falling into each case.

Case Dec.1: v is not a palindrome. Same as Case Inc.1.

Case Dec.2: v is a palindrome, $\text{per}(v) > \text{per}(u)$. This is a simplified version of Case Inc.2: the center c' of $u' = \text{link}[u] = S[k'..j]$ dies at the $(j+1)$th iteration (including the case $u' = \varepsilon$), and we have the number $2n$ of centers as the upper bound.

Case Dec.3: w is not a palindrome. This means death of the center $d = (i - l)/2$ at the $(i+1)$th iteration. At each iteration, starting with the $(j+1)$th, building

Dec one does not refer to palindromes with the center d because they have later occurrences inside the suffix u of $S[1..j]$. Thus, no other pair falling into this case can be related to d; again the number $2n$ of centers is the upper bound.

Case Dec.4: w is a palindrome, $\mathsf{per}(w) > \mathsf{per}(u)$. Similar to Case Dec.2, the center d' of $u' = \mathsf{link}[u] = S[l'..i]$ dies at the $(i+1)$th iteration. As in Case Dec.3, subsequent iterations do not refer to palindromes with the center d, because they occur later inside the suffix u of $S[1..j]$. So the $2n$ upper bound works here as well. Thus, we get $O(n)$ pairs (l, j) for all lists Dec.   □

Proof (of Theorem 1). Let us process each query $\mathsf{append}(b)$ as follows:

1: push   ▷ into a lazy segment tree
2: update $eertree(S)$ to $eertree(Sb)$
3: **if** a vertex v is created and v is a baby **then** create a stack for v-series
4: build Inc; update stacks; build Dec   ▷ using $eertree(Sb)$; see Lemma 6
5: merge Inc and iInc; **for** each deleted pair (l, r) **do** add$(l, r, 1)$
6: merge Dec and iDec; **for** each deleted pair (l, r) **do** add$(l, r, -1)$

The segment tree (by definition), the eertree (see [19]), and auxiliary stacks (Remark 8) require $O(n)$ space; other data uses less space. The working time is: $O(n \log \sigma)$ for eertree [19]; $O(\log n)$ per iteration for the Inc/Dec lists (Lemma 6) and for the iInc/iDec lists (Lemma 9); $O(\log n)$ per add query (Sect. 2.1). Since the number of add queries is $O(n)$ (Lemma 11), we spend $O(n \log n)$ time for n append's, as required.

The answer to $\mathsf{return}(i, j)$ is

$$\mathsf{sum}(i, j) + \sum_{(l,r)\in\text{iInc}} \#([i..j] \cap [l..r]) - \sum_{(l,r)\in\text{iDec}} \#([i..j] \cap [l..r]).$$

This query for restricted SUB-PCOUNT is answered in $O(\log n)$ time by Lemma 10. For SUB-PCOUNT, this query is answered within the same time bound using the versions of the segment tree and the lists iInc, iDec after appending of $S[j]$. All versions of the segment tree are available from the persistent segment tree (which uses $O(n \log n)$ space); all versions of iInc/iDec can be stored explicitly, in $O(n \log n)$ space as well. Thus, both statements of the theorem are proved.   □

4   Some Applications

First we describe all rich substrings of a given string. Since substrings of rich strings are rich, it is enough to list all maximal (not extendable) rich substrings.

Theorem 12. *All maximal rich substrings of a length n string S can be found in $O(n \log n)$ time and $O(n)$ space.*

Proof. The substring $S[i..j]$ is the longest rich suffix of the prefix $S[1..j]$ of S iff the difference array A_j contains 1's in all positions from $[i..j]$ and 0 in position

$i-1$ (if $i > 1$). Let $S[i..j]$ and $S[i'..j+1]$ be the longest rich suffixes of $S[1..j]$ and $S[1..j+1]$ respectively; then $S[i..j]$ is a maximal rich substring of S iff $i' > i$.

We process S online using the eertree and build the lists Inc and Dec on each iteration. To keep track of the longest rich suffixes, we do not need to store difference arrays. The procedure is as follows. After the first iteration, the longest rich suffix is $S[1..1]$. Assume that $S[i..j]$ is such a suffix after the jth iteration. On the $(j+1)$th iteration we compare the new lists Inc and Dec to find the maximum k which belongs to Dec but not to Inc; then $A_{j+1}[k] = 0$ and $A_{j+1}[l] = 1$ for all $l > \max\{i, k\}$. So if $k \geq i$, the new longest rich suffix is $S[k+1..j+1]$ and $S[i..j]$ is reported as a maximal rich substring; otherwise, the longest rich suffix is $S[i..j+1]$ and nothing is reported.

Since Inc and Dec have $O(\log n)$ length and are ordered, k can be found in $O(\log n)$ time (e.g., during the mergesort of Inc and Dec). By Lemma 6, the lists are built in $O(\log n)$ time also. So the whole string is processed in $O(n \log n)$ time. The space usage is dominated by the linear space for the eertree.   □

Now consider the offline analog of SUB-PCOUNT: *given a string $S[1..n]$ and a set of intervals from $[1..n]$, report the number of distinct palindromes in each interval.* Using Theorem 1, we suggest the following solution.

- If the total length L of intervals is $O(n \log n)$, build an eertree for each interval separately and obtain the number of distinct palindromes from the size of the eertree; an eertree can be built offline in linear time [19, Proposition 11]. So we need $O(L)$ time and $O(l)$ space, where l is the maximum length of an interval.
- If the number k of intervals is $O(n \log n)$, we sort them by the right end in $O(k)$ time and solve the problem as restricted SUB-PCOUNT in $O((n+k) \log n)$ time and $O(n)$ space.
- If k is not $O(n \log n)$, we solve the problem as SUB-PCOUNT in $O(k \log n)$ time and $O(n \log n)$ space.

Finally, an interesting open question is the optimality of the solutions presented in this paper. As was pointed by one of the referees, since we compute sums only for suffixes of difference arrays, we might use Dietz's construction [3] to report such sums in $O(\log n / \log \log n)$ time. However, this works only if we update individual elements of arrays, so we should spend $\Omega(n \log^2 n / \log \log n)$ time processing $\Omega(n \log n)$ updates. So it remains open whether one can improve the time bounds of Theorem 1.

References

1. Bannai, H., Gagie, T., Inenaga, S., Kärkkäinen, J., Kempa, D., Piatkowski, M., Puglisi, S.J., Sugimoto, S.: Diverse palindromic factorization is NP-complete. In: Potapov, I. (ed.) DLT 2015. LNCS, vol. 9168, pp. 85–96. Springer, Cham (2015). doi:10.1007/978-3-319-21500-6_6
2. Brlek, S., Hamel, S., Nivat, M., Reutenauer, C.: On the palindromic complexity of infinite words. Int. J. Found. Comput. Sci. 15(2), 293–306 (2004)

3. Dietz, P.F.: Optimal algorithms for list indexing and subset rank. In: Dehne, F., Sack, J.-R., Santoro, N. (eds.) WADS 1989. LNCS, vol. 382, pp. 39–46. Springer, Heidelberg (1989). doi:10.1007/3-540-51542-9_5

4. Driscoll, J.R., Sarnak, N., Sleator, D.D., Tarjan, R.E.: Making data structures persistent. J. Comput. Syst. Sci. **38**(1), 86–124 (1989)

5. Droubay, X., Justin, J., Pirillo, G.: Episturmian words and some constructions of de Luca and Rauzy. Theoret. Comput. Sci. **255**, 539–553 (2001)

6. Fenwick, P.M.: A new data structure for cumulative frequency tables. Soft. Pract. Experience **24**(3), 327–336 (1994)

7. Fici, G., Gagie, T., Kärkkäinen, J., Kempa, D.: A subquadratic algorithm for minimum palindromic factorization. J. Discrete Algorithms **28**, 41–48 (2014)

8. Fine, N.J., Wilf, H.S.: Uniqueness theorems for periodic functions. Proc. Am. Math. Soc. **16**, 109–114 (1965)

9. Galil, Z.: Real-time algorithms for string-matching and palindrome recognition. In: Proceedings of 8th Annual ACM Symposium on Theory of Computing (STOC 1976), pp. 161–173. ACM, New York, USA (1976)

10. Galil, Z., Seiferas, J.: A linear-time on-line recognition algorithm for "Palstar". J. ACM **25**, 102–111 (1978)

11. Glen, A., Justin, J., Widmer, S., Zamboni, L.: Palindromic richness. Eur. J. Comb. **30**(2), 510–531 (2009)

12. Groult, R., Prieur, E., Richomme, G.: Counting distinct palindromes in a word in linear time. Inform. Process. Lett. **110**, 908–912 (2010)

13. Guo, C., Shallit, J., Shur, A.M.: Palindromic rich words and run-length encodings. Inform. Process. Lett. **116**(12), 735–738 (2016)

14. Tomohiro, I., Sugimoto, S., Inenaga, S., Bannai, H., Takeda, M.: Computing palindromic factorizations and palindromic covers on-line. In: Kulikov, A.S., Kuznetsov, S.O., Pevzner, P. (eds.) CPM 2014. LNCS, vol. 8486, pp. 150–161. Springer, Cham (2014). doi:10.1007/978-3-319-07566-2_16

15. Knuth, D.E., Morris, J., Pratt, V.: Fast pattern matching in strings. SIAM J. Comput. **6**, 323–350 (1977)

16. Kosolobov, D., Rubinchik, M., Shur, A.M.: Finding distinct subpalindromes online. In: Proceedings of Prague Stringology Conference, PSC 2013, pp. 63–69. Czech Technical University in Prague (2013)

17. Kosolobov, D., Rubinchik, M., Shur, A.M.: Pal^k is linear recognizable online. In: Italiano, G.F., Margaria-Steffen, T., Pokorný, J., Quisquater, J.-J., Wattenhofer, R. (eds.) SOFSEM 2015. LNCS, vol. 8939, pp. 289–301. Springer, Heidelberg (2015). doi:10.1007/978-3-662-46078-8_24

18. Manacher, G.: A new linear-time on-line algorithm finding the smallest initial palindrome of a string. J. ACM **22**(3), 346–351 (1975)

19. Rubinchik, M., Shur, A.M.: EERTREE: an efficient data structure for processing palindromes in strings. In: Lipták, Z., Smyth, W.F. (eds.) IWOCA 2015. LNCS, vol. 9538, pp. 321–333. Springer, Cham (2016). doi:10.1007/978-3-319-29516-9_27

20. Slisenko, A.: Recognition of palindromes by multihead Turing machines. In: Proceeding of the Steklov Institute of Mathematics, vol. 129, pp. 30–202 (1973). In Russian, English translation by Silverman, R.H., American Mathematical Society, Providence, R.I. (1976), 25–208

Linear-Size CDAWG: New Repetition-Aware Indexing and Grammar Compression

Takuya Takagi[1](✉), Keisuke Goto[2], Yuta Fujishige[3], Shunsuke Inenaga[3], and Hiroki Arimura[1]

[1] Graduate School of IST, Hokkaido University, Sapporo, Japan
{tkg,arim}@ist.hokudai.ac.jp
[2] Fujitsu Laboratories Ltd., Kawasaki, Japan
goto.keisuke@jp.fujitsu.com
[3] Department of Informatics, Kyushu University, Fukuoka, Japan
{yuta.fujishige,inenaga}@inf.kyushu-u.ac.jp

Abstract. In this paper, we propose a novel approach to combine *compact directed acyclic word graphs* (*CDAWGs*) and grammar-based compression. This leads us to an efficient self-index, called *Linear-size CDAWGs* (*L-CDAWGs*), which can be represented with $O(\tilde{e}_T \log n)$ bits of space allowing for $O(\log n)$-time random and $O(1)$-time sequential accesses to edge labels, and $O(m \log \sigma + occ)$-time pattern matching. Here, $\tilde{e}_T$ is the number of all extensions of maximal repeats in T, n and m are respectively the lengths of the text T and a given pattern, σ is the alphabet size, and occ is the number of occurrences of the pattern in T. The repetitiveness measure $\tilde{e}_T$ is known to be much smaller than the text length n for highly repetitive text. For constant alphabets, our L-CDAWGs achieve $O(m + occ)$ pattern matching time with $O(e_T^r \log n)$ bits of space, which improves the pattern matching time of Belazzougui et al.'s run-length BWT-CDAWGs by a factor of $\log \log n$, with the same space complexity. Here, e_T^r is the number of right extensions of maximal repeats in T. As a byproduct, our result gives a way of constructing a straight-line program (SLP) of size $O(\tilde{e}_T)$ for a given text T in $O(n + \tilde{e}_T \log \sigma)$ time.

1 Introduction

Background: Text indexing is a fundamental problem in theoretical computer science, where the task is to preprocess a given text so that subsequent pattern matching queries can be answered quickly. It has wide applications such as information retrieval, bioinformatics, and big data analytics [10,14]. There have been a lot of recent research on *compressed text indexes* [1,4,9–11,13,14,16] that store a text T supporting extract and find operations in space significantly smaller than the total size n of texts. Operation extract returns any substring $T[i..j]$ of the text. Operation find returns the list of all occ occurrences of a given pattern P in T. For instance, Grossi, Gupta, and Vitter [9] gave a compressed text index based on compressed suffix arrays,

© Springer International Publishing AG 2017
G. Fici et al. (Eds.): SPIRE 2017, LNCS 10508, pp. 304–316, 2017.
DOI: 10.1007/978-3-319-67428-5_26

which takes $s = nH_k + O(n \log \log n \log \sigma / \log n)$ bits of space and supporting $O(m \log \sigma + \text{polylog}(n))$ pattern match time, where H_k is the k-th order entropy of T and m is the length of the pattern P.

Compression measures for highly repetitive text: Recently, there has been an increasing interest in indexed searches for highly repetitive text collections. Typically, the compression size of such a text can be described in terms of some measure of repetition. The followings are examples of such repetitiveness measures for T:

- the *number g_T of rules in a grammar (SLP)* representing T,
- the *number z_T of phrases in the LZ77 parsing* of T,
- the *number r_T of runs in the Burrows-Wheeler transform* of T, and
- the *number $\tilde{e}_T = e_T^r + e_T^\ell$ of right- and left-extensions of maximal repeats* of T.

Belazzougui *et al.* [1] observed close relationship among these measures. Specifically, the authors empirically observed that all of them showed similar logarithmic growth behavior in $|T|$ on a real biological sequence, and also theoretically showed that both z_T and r_T are upper bounded by $\tilde{e}_T$. These repetitive texts are formed from many repeated fragments nearly identical. Therefore, one can expect that compressed index based on these measures such as g_T, z_T, r_T, and $\tilde{e}_T$ can effectively capture the redundancy inherent to these highly repetitive texts than conventional entropy-based compressed indexes [14].

Repetition-aware indexes: There has been extensive research on a family of *repetition-aware indexes* [1,4,10,11] since the seminal work by Claude and Navarro [4]. They proposed the first compressed self-index based on grammars, which takes $s = g \log n + O(g \log g)$ bits supporting $O((m^2 + h(m + occ)) \log g)$ pattern match time, where $g = g_T$ and h are respectively the size and height of a grammar. Kreft and Navarro [10] gave the first compressed self-index based on LZ77, which takes $s = 3z \log n + 5n \log \sigma + O(z) + o(n)$ bits supporting $O(m^2 d + (m + occ) \log z)$ pattern match time. Here, d is the height of the LZ parsing. Makinen, Navarro, Siren, and Valimaki [11] gave a compressed index based on RLBWT, which takes $s = r \log \sigma \log(2n/r)(1 + o(1)) + O(r \log \sigma \log \log(2n/r)) + O(\sigma \log n)$ bits supporting $O(m f(r \log \sigma, n \log \sigma))$ pattern match time, where $f(b, u)$ is the time for a binary searchable dictionary which is $O((\log b)^{0.5})$ and $o((\log \log u)^2)$ for example [11].

Previous approaches: Considering the above results, we notice that in compression ratio, all indexes above achieve good performance depending on the repetitive measures, while in terms of operation time, most of them except the RLBWT-based one [11] have quadratic dependency in pattern size m. Hence, a challenge here is to develop repetition-aware text indexes to achieve good compression ratio for highly repetitive texts in terms of repetition measures, while supporting faster `extract` and `find` operations. Belazzougui *et al.* [1] proposed a repetition-aware index which combines *CDAWGs* [3,7] and the run-length encoded BWT [11], to which we refer as *RLBWT-CDAWGs*. For a given text T

of the length n and a pattern P of the length m, their index uses $O(e_T^r \log n)$ bits of space and supports find operation in $O(m \log \log n + occ)$ time.

Main results: In this paper, we propose a new repetition-aware index based on combination of CDAWGs and grammar-based compression, called the *Linear-size CDAWG* (L-CDAWG, for short). The L-CDAWG of a text T of length n is a self-index for T which can be stored in $O(\tilde{e}_T \log n)$ bits of space, and support $O(\log n)$-time random access to the text, $O(1)$-time sequential character access from the beginning of each edge label, and $O(m \log \sigma + occ)$-time pattern matching. For constant alphabets, our L-CDAWGs use $O(e_T^r \log n)$ bits of space and support pattern matching in $O(m + occ)$ time, hence improving the pattern matching time of Belazzougui *et al.*'s RLBWT-CDAWGs by a factor of $\log \log n$. We note that RLBWT-CDAWGs use hashing to retrieve the first character of a given edge label, and hence RLBWT-CDAWGs seem to require $O(m \log \log n + occ)$ time for pattern matching even for constant alphabets.

From the context of studies on *suffix indices*, our L-CDAWGs can be seen as a successor of the *linear-size suffix trie* (*LSTries*) by Crochemore *et al.* [5]. The LSTrie is a variant of the suffix tree [6], which need not keep the original text T by elegant scheme of linear time decoding using suffix links and a set of auxiliary nodes. However, it is a challenge to generalize their result for the CDAWG because the paths between a given pair of endpoints are not unique. By combining the idea of LSTries, an SLP-based compression with direct access [2,8], we successfully devise a text index of $O(\tilde{e}_T \log n)$ bits by improving functionalities of LSTries. As a byproduct, our result gives a way of constructing an SLP of size $O(\tilde{e}_T \log \tilde{e}_T)$ bits of space for a text T. Moreover, since the L-CDAWG of T retains the topology of the original CDAWG for T, the L-CDAWG is a compact representation of all maximal repeats [15] that appear in T.

2   Preliminaries

In this section, we give some notations and definitions to be used in the following sections. In addition, we recall string data structures such as suffix tries, suffix trees, CDAWGs, linear-size suffix tries and straight-line programs, which are the data structures to be considered in this paper.

2.1   Basic Definitions and Notations

Strings: Let Σ be a general ordered alphabet of size $\sigma \geq 2$. An element $T = t_1 \cdots t_n$ of Σ^* is called a *string*, where $|T| = n$ denotes its length. We denote the empty string by ε which is the string of length 0, namely, $|\varepsilon| = 0$. Let $\Sigma^+ = \Sigma^* \setminus \{\varepsilon\}$. If $T = XYZ$, then X, Y, and Z are called a *prefix*, a *substring*, and a *suffix* of T, respectively. Let $T = t_1 \cdots t_n \in \Sigma^n$ be any string of length n. For any $1 \leq i \leq j \leq n$, let $T[i..j] = t_i \cdots t_j$ denote the substring of T that begins and ends at positions i and j in T, and let $T[i] = t_i$ denote the ith character of T. For any string T, we denote by $\overline{T}$ the reversed string of T,

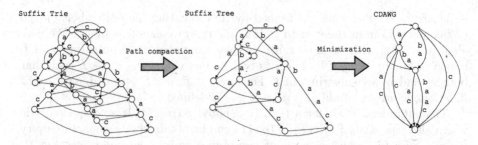

Fig. 1. Illustration of $STrie(T)$, $STree(T)$, and $CDAWG(T)$ with $T = $ ababaac. The solid arrows and broken arrows represent the edges and the suffix links of each data structure, respectively.

i.e., $\overline{T} = T[n] \cdots T[1]$. Let $Suffix(T)$ denote the set of suffixes of T. For a string x, the number of occurrences of x in T means the number of positions where x is a substring in T.

Maximal repeats and other measures of repetition: A substring w of T is called a *repeat* if the number of occurrences of w in T more than one. A *right extension* (resp. a *left extension*) of w of T is any substring of T with the form wa (resp. aw) for some letter $a \in \Sigma$. A repeat w of T is a *maximal repeat* if both left- and right-extensions of w occur strictly fewer times in T than w. In what follows, we denote by μ_T, e_T^r, e_T^ℓ, and $\tilde{e}_T = e_T^r + e_T^\ell$ the numbers of maximal repeats, right-extensions, left-extensions, and all extensions of maximal repeats appearing in T, respectively. Recently, it has been shown in [1] that the number $\tilde{e}_T$ is an upper bound on the number r_T of runs in the Burrows-Wheeler transform for T and the number z_T of factors in the Lempel-Ziv parsing of T. It is also known that $\tilde{e}_T \leq 4n - 4$ and $\mu_T < n$, where $n = |T|$ [3,15].

Notations on graphical indexes: All index structures dealt with in this paper, such as suffix tries, suffix trees, CDAWGs, linear-size suffix tries (LSTries), and linear-size CDAWGs (L-CDAWGs), are *graphical indexes* in the sense that an index is a pointer-based structure built on an underlying DAG $G_L = (V(L), E(L))$ with a root $r \in V(L)$ and mapping $lab : E(L) \rightarrow \Sigma^+$ that assign a label $lab(e)$ to each edge $e \in E(L)$. For an edge $e = (u, v) \in E(L)$, we denote its *end points* by $e.hi := u$ and $e.lo := v$, respectively. The *label string* of e is $lab(e) \in \Sigma^+$. The *string length* of e is $slen(e) := |lab(e)| \geq 1$. An edge is called *atomic* if $slen(e) = 1$, and thus, $lab(e) \in \Sigma$. For a path $p = (e_1, \ldots, e_k)$ of length $k \geq 1$, we extend its *end points*, *label string*, and *string length* by $p.hi := e_1.hi$, $p.lo := e_k.lo$, $lab(p) := lab(e_1) \ldots lab(e_k) \in \Sigma^+$, and $slen(p) := slen(e_1) + \cdots + slen(e_k) \geq 1$, respectively.

2.2   Suffix Tries and Suffix Trees

The *suffix trie* [6] for a text T of length n, denoted $STrie(T)$, is a trie which represents $Suffix(T)$. The size of $STrie(T)$ is $O(n^2)$. The path label of a node v

is the string $str(v) := lab(\pi_v)$ formed by concatenating the edge labels on the unique path π_v from the root to v. If $x = str(v)$, we denote v by $[x]$. We may identify $v = [x]$ with its label x if it is clear from context. A substring x of T is said to be *branching* if there exists two distinct characters $a, b \in \Sigma$ such that both xa and xb are substrings of T. For any $a \in \Sigma$, $x \in \Sigma^*$, we define the *suffix link* of node $[ax]$ by $slink([ax]) = [x]$ if $[ax]$ is defined.

The *suffix tree* [6,17] for a text T, denoted $STree(T)$, is a compacted trie which also represents $Suffix(T)$. $STree(T)$ can be obtained by compacting every path of $STrie(T)$ which consists of non-branching internal nodes (see Fig. 1). Since every internal node of $STree(T)$ is branching, and since there are at most n leaves in $STree(T)$, the numbers of edges and nodes are $O(n)$. The edges of $STree(T)$ are labeled by non-empty substrings of T. By representing each edge label α with a pair (i, j) of integers such that $T[i..j] = \alpha$, $STree(T)$ can be stored in $O(n \log n)$ bits of space.

2.3   CDAWGs

The *compact directed acyclic word graph* [3,6] for a text T, denoted $CDAWG(T)$, is the minimal compact automaton which represents $Suffix(T)$. $CDAWG(T)$ can be obtained from $STree(T\$)$ by merging isomorphic subtrees and deleting associated endmarker $\$ \notin \Sigma$. Since $CDAWG(T)$ is an edge-labeled DAG, we represent a directed edge from node u to v with label string $x \in \Sigma^+$ by a triple $f = (u, x, v)$. For any node u, the label strings of out-going edges from u start with mutually distinct characters.

Formally, $CDAWG(T)$ is defined as follows. For any strings x, y, we denote $x \equiv_L y$ (resp. $x \equiv_R y$) iff the beginning positions (resp. ending positions) of x and y in T are equal. Let $[x]_L$ (resp. $[x]_R$) denote the equivalence class of strings w.r.t. $\equiv_L$ (resp. $\equiv_R$). All strings that are *not* substrings of T form a single equivalence class, and in the sequel we will consider only the substrings of T. Let $\overrightarrow{x}$ (resp. $\overleftarrow{x}$) denote the longest member of the equivalence class $[x]_L$ (resp. $[x]_R$). Notice that each member of $[x]_L$ (resp. $[x]_R$) is a prefix of $\overrightarrow{x}$ (resp. a suffix of $\overleftarrow{x}$). Let $\overleftrightarrow{x} = (\overrightarrow{\overleftarrow{x}}) = (\overleftarrow{\overrightarrow{x}})$. We denote $x \equiv y$ iff $\overleftrightarrow{x} = \overleftrightarrow{y}$, and let $[x]$ denote the equivalence class w.r.t. $\equiv$. The longest member of $[x]$ is $\overleftrightarrow{x}$ and we will also denote it by $value([x])$. We define $CDAWG(T)$ as an edge-labeled DAG (V, E) such that $V = \{[\overrightarrow{x}]_R \mid x$ is a substring of $T\}$ and $E = \{([\overrightarrow{x}]_R, \alpha, [\overrightarrow{x}\alpha]_R) \mid \alpha \in \Sigma^+, \overrightarrow{x} \neq \overrightarrow{x}\alpha\}$. The $\overrightarrow{\cdot}$ operator corresponds to compacting non-branching edges (like conversion from $STrie(T)$ to $STree(T)$) and the $[\cdot]_R$ operator corresponds to merging isomorphic subtrees of $STree(T)$. For simplicity, we abuse notation so that when we refer to a node of $CDAWG(T)$ as $[x]$, this implies $x = \overrightarrow{x}$ and $[x] = [\overrightarrow{x}]_R$.

Let $[x]$ be any node of $CDAWG(T)$ and consider the suffixes of $value([x])$ which correspond to the suffix tree nodes that are merged when transformed into the CDAWG. We define the *suffix link* of node $[x]$ by $slink([x]) = [y]$, iff y is the longest suffix of $value([x])$ that does not belong to $[x]$.

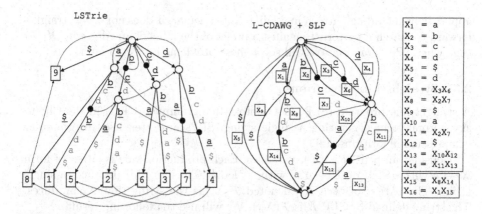

Fig. 2. Illustration of $LSTrie(T)$ and our index structure L-$CDAWG(T)$ with SLP for text $T = \mathtt{abcdbcda\$}$. Solid and broken arrows represent the edges and suffix links, respectively. Underlined and shaded characters attached to each edge are the first (real) and the following (virtual) characters of the original edge label . The expression X_i at the edge indicates the i-th variable of the SLP for T.

It is shown that all nodes of $CDAWG(T)$ except the sink correspond to the maximal repeats of T. Actually, $value([x])$ is a maximal repeat in T [15]. Following this fact, one can easily see that the numbers of edges of $CDAWG(T)$ and $CDAWG(\overline{T})$ coincide with the numbers e_T^r and e_T^ℓ of right- and left- extensions of maximal repeats of T, respectively [1,15].

By representing each edge label α with pairs (i, j) of integers such that $T[i..j] = \alpha$, $CDAWG(T)$ can be stored in $O(e_T^r \log n + n \log \sigma)$ bits of space.

2.4 LSTrie

Recently, Crochemore et al. [5] proposed a compact variant of a suffix trie, called *linear-size suffix trie* (or LSTrie, for short), denoted $LSTrie(T)$. It is a compacted tree with the topology and the size similar to $STree(T)$, but has no indirect references to a text T (See Fig. 2). $LSTrie(T)$ is obtained from $STree(T)$ by adding all nodes v such that their suffix links $slink(v)$ appear also in $STree(T)$. Unlike $STree(T)$, each edge (u, v) of $LSTrie(T)$ stores the first character and the length of the corresponding suffix tree edge label (see Fig. 2). Using auxiliary links called the *jump pointers* the following theorem is proved.

Proposition 1 (Crochemore et al. [5]). *For a text T of length n, the linear-size suffix trie $LSTrie(T)$ for T can be stored in $O(n \log n)$ bits of space supporting reconstruction of the label of a given edge in $O(\ell)$ time, where ℓ is the length of the edge label.*

Crochemore et al.'s method [5] does not regard the order of decoding characters on an edge label. This implies that $LSTrie(T)$ needs $O(\ell)$ worst case time to read any prefix of an edge label of length ℓ. This may cause troubles in some applications including pattern matching. In particular, it does not seem straight-forward to match a pattern P against a prefix of the label of an edge e in $O(|P|)$ time when $|P| < |lab(e)|$. We will solve these problems in Sect. 3 later.

2.5   Straight-Line Programs

A straight-line program (SLP) is a context-free grammar (CFG) in the Chomsky normal form generating a single string. SLPs are often used in grammar compression algorithms [14].

Consider an SLP R with n variables. Each production rule is either of form $X \to a$ with $a \in \Sigma$ or $X \to YZ$ without loops. Thus an SLP produces a single string. The *phrase* of each X_i, denoted $\mathcal{F}(X_i)$, is the string that X_i produces. The string defined by SLP R is $\mathcal{F}(X_n)$. We will use the following results.

Proposition 2 (Gasieniec et al. [8]). *For an SLP R of size g for a text of length n, there exist a data structure of $O(g \log n)$ bits of space which supports expansion of a prefix of $\mathcal{F}(X_i)$ for any variable X_i in $O(1)$ time per character, and can be constructed in $O(g)$ time.*

Proposition 3 (Bille et al. [2]). *For an SLP R of size g representing a text of length n, there exists a data structure of $O(g \log n)$ bits of space which supports to access consecutive m characters at arbitrary position of $\mathcal{F}(X_i)$ for any variable X_i in $O(m + \log n)$ time, and can be constructed in $O(g)$ time.*

3   The Proposed Data Structure: L-CDAWG

In this section, we present *the Linear-size CDAWG* (*L-CDAWG*, for short). The L-CDAWG can support CDAWG operations in the same time complexity without holding the original input text and can reduce the space complexity from $O(e_T^r \log n + n \log \sigma)$ bits of space to $O(\tilde{e}_T \log n)$ bits of space, where $\tilde{e}_T = e_T^r + e_T^\ell$ is the number of extensions of maximal repeats. From now on, we assume that an input text T terminates with a unique character \$ which appears nowhere else in T.

3.1   Outline

The *Linear-size CDAWG* for a text T of length n, denoted $L\text{-}CDAWG(T)$, is a DAG whose edges are labeled with single characters. $L\text{-}CDAWG(T)$ can be obtained from $CDAWG(T)$ by the following modifications. From now on, we refer to the original nodes appearing in $CDAWG(T)$ as *type-1 nodes*, which are always branching except the sink.

1. First, we add new non-branching nodes, called *type-2 nodes* to $CDAWG(T)$. Let $u = value([x])$ for any type-1 node $[x]$ of $CDAWG(T)$. If au is a substring of T but the path spelling out au ends in the middle of an edge, then we introduce a type-2 node v representing au. We add the suffix link $u = slink(v)$ as well. Adding type-2 nodes splits an edge into shorter ones. Note that more than one type-2 nodes can be inserted into an edge of $CDAWG(T)$.

2. Let (u, x, v) be any edge after all the type-2 nodes are inserted, where $x \in \Sigma^+$. We represent this edge by $e = (u, c, v)$ where c is the first character $c = x[1] \in \Sigma$ of the original label. We also store the original label length $slen(e) = |x|$.
3. We will augment $L\text{-}CDAWG(T)$ with a set of SLP production rules whose nonterminals correspond to edges of $L\text{-}CDAWG(T)$. The definition and construction of this SLP will be described later in Sect. 3.3.

If non-branching type-2 nodes are ignored, then the topology of $L\text{-}CDAWG(T)$ is the same as that of $CDAWG(T)$. For ease of explanation, we denote by $lab(e)$ the original label of edge e. Namely, for any edge $e = (u, c, v)$, $lab(e) = x$ iff (u, x, v) is the original edge for e.

The following lemma gives an upper bound of the numbers of nodes and edges in $L\text{-}CDAWG(T)$. Recall that μ_T is the number of maximal repeats in T, e_T^ℓ and e_T^r are respectively the number of left- and right-extensions of maximal repeats in T, and $\tilde{e}_T = e_T^\ell + e_T^r$.

Lemma 1. *For any string T, let $L\text{-}CDAWG(T) = (V, E)$, then $|V| = O(\mu_T + e_T^\ell)$ and $|E| = O(\tilde{e}_T)$.*

Proof. Let $CDAWG(T) = (V_0, E_0)$ and $CDAWG(\overleftarrow{T}) = (\overline{V_0}, \overline{E_0})$. It is known that $|V_0| = |\overline{V_0}| = \mu_T$, $|E_0| = e_T^r$ and $|\overline{E_0}| = e_T^\ell$ (see [3] and [15]). Let V_1 and V_2 be the set of type-1 and type-2 nodes in $L\text{-}CDAWG(T)$, respectively. Clearly, $V_1 \cap V_2 = \emptyset$, $V = V_1 \cup V_2$, and $V_1 = V_0$. Let $[x] \in V_1$ and $u = value([x])$. Note that u is a maximal repeat of T. For any character $a \in \Sigma$ such that au is a substring of T, clearly au is a left-extension of u. By the definition of $L\text{-}CDAWG(T)$, it always has a (type-1 or type-2) node which corresponds to au. Hence $|V_2| \leq e_T^\ell$. This implies $|V| = |V_1| + |V_2| = O(\mu_T + e_T^\ell)$. Since each type-2 node is non-branching, clearly $|E| = O(e_T^r + e_T^\ell) = O(\tilde{e}_T)$. $\qquad\square$

Corollary 1. *For any string of T over a constant alphabet, $|V| = O(\mu_T + e_T^r)$ and $|E| = O(e_T^r)$, where $L\text{-}CDAWG(T) = (V, E)$.*

Proof. It clearly holds that $\mu_T \geq e_T^\ell / \sigma$ and $e_T^r \geq \mu_T$. Thus we have $e_T^\ell \leq \sigma e_T^r$. The corollary follows from Lemma 1 when $\sigma = O(1)$. $\qquad\square$

3.2 Constructing Type-2 Nodes and Edge Suffix Links

Lemma 2. *Given $CDAWG(T)$ for a text T, we can compute all type-2 nodes of $L\text{-}CDAWG(T)$ in $O(\tilde{e}_T \log \sigma)$ time.*

Proof. We create a copy G of $CDAWG(T)$. For each edge (u, x, v) of $CDAWG(T)$, we compute node $u' = slink(u)$ and the path Q that spells out x from u'. The number of type-1 nodes in this path Q is equal to the number of type-2 nodes that need to be inserted on edge (u, x, v), and hence we insert these nodes to G. After the above operation is done for all edges, G contains all type-2 nodes of $L\text{-}CDAWG(T)$. Since there always exists such a path Q, to find Q it suffices to check the first characters of out-going edges. Hence we need only $O(\log \sigma)$ time for each node in Q. Overall, it takes $O(\tilde{e}_T \log \sigma)$ time. $\qquad\square$

The above lemma also indicates the notion of the following *edge suffix links* in *L-CDAWG(T)* which are virtual links, and will not be actually created in the construction.

Definition 1 (Edge suffix links). For any edge e with $slen(e) \geq 2$, $e\text{-}suf(e) = (e_1, \ldots, e_k)$ is the path, namely a list of edges, from $e_1.hi = slink(e.hi)$ to $e_k.lo$ that can be reachable from $e_1.hi$ by scanning $lab(e)$.

Edge suffix links have the following properties.

Lemma 3. *For any edge e such that $slen(e) \geq 2$ and its edge suffix link $e\text{-}suf(e) = (e_1, \ldots, e_k)$, (1) both $e_1.hi$ and $e_k.lo$ are type-1 nodes, and (2) all nodes in the path $e_1.lo = e_2.hi, \ldots, e_{k-1}.lo = e_k.hi$ are type-2 nodes.*

Proof. From the definition of edge suffix links, we have $e_1.hi = slink(e.hi)$ and the path from $e_1.hi$ to $e_k.lo$ spells out $lab(e)$. (1) By the definitions of type-2 nodes and edge suffix links, $e_1.hi$ is always of type-1. Hence it suffices to show that $e_k.lo$ is of type-1. There are two cases: (a) If $e.lo$ is a type-2 node, then by the definition of type-2 nodes, $e_k.lo$ must be the node pointed by $slink(e.lo)$. Therefore, $e_k.lo$ is a type-1 node. (b) If $e.lo$ is a type-1 node, then let ax be the shortest string represented by $e.hi$ with $a \in \Sigma$ and $x \in \Sigma^*$. Then, string $x \cdot lab(e)$ is spelled out by a path from the source to $e_1.hi, \ldots, e_k.lo$, where either $e_k.lo = e.lo$ or $e_k.lo = slink(e.lo)$. Since $e.lo$ is of type-1, $slink(e.lo)$ is also of type-1. (2) If there is a type-1 node u in the path $e_2.hi, \ldots, e_{k-1}.lo$, then there has to be a (type-1 or type-2) node v between $e.hi$ and $e.lo$, a contradiction. $\square$

Lemma 3 says that the label of any edge $e = (u, c, v)$ with $slen(e) \geq 2$ can be represented by a path $p = (e_1, \ldots, e_k) = e\text{-}suf(e)$. In addition, since the path p includes type-1 nodes only at the end points and since type-2 nodes are non-branching, p is uniquely determined by a pair of $(slink(u), c)$. We can compute all edges $e_i \in p$ for $1 \leq i \leq k$ in $O(k + \log \sigma)$ per query, as follows. Firstly, we compute $p.hi = slink(u)$ and then select the out-going edge e_1 starting with the character c in $O(\log \sigma)$ time. Next, we blindly scan the downward path from e_1 while the lower end of the current edge e_i has type-2. This scanning terminates when we reach an edge e_k such that $e_k.lo$ is of type-1.

3.3   Construction of the SLP for L-CDAWG

We give an SLP of size $O(\tilde{e}_T)$ which represents T and all edge labels of $L = L\text{-}CDAWG(T)$ based on the jump links.

Jumping from an edge to a path: First, we define *jump links*, by which we can jump from a given edge e with $slen(e) \geq 2$ to the path consisting of at least two edges, and having the same string label. Although our jump link is based on that of LSTries [5], we need a new definition since a path in $CDAWG(T)$ (and hence in $L\text{-}CDAWG(T)$) cannot be uniquely determined by a pair of nodes, unlike $STree(T)$ (or $LSTrie(T)$).

Definition 2 (Jump links). For an edge e with $slen(e) \geq 2$ and $e\text{-}suf(e) = (e_1, \ldots, e_k)$, $jump(e)$ is recursively defined as follows:

1. $jump(e) := jump(e_1)$ if $k = 1$ (thus $e\text{-}suf(e) = (e_1)$), and
2. $jump(e) := (e_1, \ldots, e_k)$ if $k \geq 2$.

Note that $lab(e)$ equals $lab(e_1) \cdots lab(e_k)$ for $jump(e) = (e_1, \ldots, e_k)$.

Lemma 4. *For any edge e with $slen(e) \geq 2$, $jump(e)$ consists of at least two edges.*

Proof. Assume on the contrary that $jump(e) = e'$ for some edge e'. This implies $slen(e') \geq 2$. By definition, $e'.hi$ is a proper suffix of $e.hi$, namely, there exists an integer $k \geq 1$ such that $slink^k(e.hi) = e'.hi$. For any character c which appears in T, there is a (type-1 or type-2) node which represents c as a child of the source of $L\text{-}CDAWG(T)$. This implies that there is an out-going edge e'' of length 1 from the source representing the first character of $e.hi$. This contradicts that $jump(e)$ only contains a single edge e' with $slen(e') \geq 2$.   □

Theorem 1. *For a given $L\text{-}CDAWG(T)$, there is an algorithm that computes all jump links in $O(\tilde{e}_T \log \sigma)$ time.*

Proof. We explain how to obtain $jump(e)$ for an edge e with $slen(e) \geq 2$. For all edge e with $slen(e) \geq 2$, we manage a pointer to the first edge e' of $jump(e)$ by $P[e] = e'$. We initially set $P[e] = \epsilon$ for all e. For all nodes e with $slen(e) \geq 2$, let u be an outgoing edge of $slink(e.hi)$ with the same label character of e. We check whether $P[e] = \epsilon$ and, if so, we recursively compute $P[u]$, and then set $P[e] = P[u]$. In this way all $P[e]$ can be computed in $O(\tilde{e}_T \log \sigma)$ time in total, where the $\log \sigma$ is needed for selecting the out going edge. From Lemma 3, since there does not exist branching edge on each jump link, $jump(e)$ can be easily obtained from $P[e]$ by traversing the path until encountered a type-1 node.   □

An SLP for the L-CDAWG: We build an SLP which represents all edge labels in $L\text{-}CDAWG(T) = (V, E)$ based on jump links. For each edge e, let $X(e)$ denote the variable which generates the string label $lab(e)$. Let $E = \{e_1, \ldots, e_s\}$. For any $e_i \in E$ with $slen(e_i) = 1$, we construct a production $X(e_i) \rightarrow c$ where $c \in \Sigma$ is the label. For any $e_i \in E$ with $slen(e_i) \geq 2$, let $jump(e_i) = (e'_1, \ldots, e'_k)$. We construct productions $X(e_i) \rightarrow X(e'_1)Y_1, Y_1 \rightarrow X(e'_2)Y_2, \ldots, Y_{k-3} \rightarrow X(e'_{k-2})Y_{k-2}$, and $Y_{k-2} \rightarrow X(e'_{k-1})X(e'_k)$. We call a production whose left-hand size is Y_i an *intermediate* production. It is clear that $X(e_i)$ generates $lab(e)$ and we introduced $k - 1$ productions. If there is another edge e_j ($i \neq j$) such that $jump(e_j) = (e'_1, \ldots, e'_k)$, then we construct a new production $X(e_j) \rightarrow X(e'_1)Y_1$ and reuse the other productions. Let p be the path that spells out the text T.

We create productions which generates T using the same technique as above for this path p. Overall, the total number of intermediate productions is linear in the number of type-2 nodes in $L\text{-}CDAWG(T)$. Since there are $O(|E|)$ non-intermediate productions, this SLP consists of $O(\tilde{e}_T)$ productions.

Now, we have the main result of this subsection.

Theorem 2. *For a given $L\text{-}CDAWG(T)$, there is an algorithm that constructs an SLP which represents all edge labels in $O(\tilde{e}_T \log \sigma)$ time.*

Proof. By the above algorithm, if jump links are computed, we can obtain an SLP which represents all edge labels in $O(\tilde{e}_T)$ time. From Theorem 1, we can compute all jump links in $O(\tilde{e}_T \log \sigma)$ times. Overall, the total time of this algorithm is $O(\tilde{e}_T \log \sigma)$. □

Fig. 2 shows $LSTrie(T)$ and $L\text{-}CDAWG(T)$ enhanced with the SLP for string $T = abcdbcda\$$.

We associate to each edge label the corresponding variable of the SLP. By applying algorithms of Gasieniec *et al.* [8] (in Proposition 2) and Bille *et al.* [2] (in Proposition 3), we can show the following theorems.

Theorem 3. *For a text T, $L\text{-}CDAWG(T)$ can support pattern matching for a pattern P of length m in $O(m \log \sigma + occ)$ time.*

Proof. From Proposition 2, any consecutive m characters from the beginning of an edge in $L\text{-}CDAWG(T)$ can be sequentially read in $O(m)$ time. $CDAWG(T)$ can support pattern matching by traversing the path from the source with P in $O(m \log \sigma + occ)$ time [3]. Since $L\text{-}CDAWG(T)$ contains the topology of $CDAWG(T)$, it can also support pattern matching in $O(m \log \sigma + occ)$ time. □

Theorem 4. *For a text T of length n, $L\text{-}CDAWG(T)$ has an SLP that derives T. In addition, we can read any substring $T[i..i+m]$ can be read in $O(m + \log n)$ time.*

Proof. The text T of $L\text{-}CDAWG(T)$ is represented by the longest path p from the source to the sink. Remembering p makes it possible to read any position of T by using the Proposition 3. □

3.4   The Main Result

It is known that for a given string T of length n over an integer alphabet of size $n^{O(1)}$, $CDAWG(T)$ can be constructed in $O(n)$ time [12]. Combining this with the preceding discussions, we obtain the main result of this paper.

Theorem 5. *For a text T of length n, $L\text{-}CDAWG(T)$ supports pattern matching in $O(m \log \sigma + occ)$ time for a given pattern of length m and substring extraction in $O(m + \log n)$ time for any substring of length m, and can be stored in $O(\tilde{e}_T \log n)$ bits of space (or $O(\tilde{e}_T)$ words of space). If $CDAWG(T)$ is already constructed, then $L\text{-}CDAWG(T)$ can be constructed in $O(\tilde{e}_T \log \sigma)$ total time. If T is given as input, then $L\text{-}CDAWG(T)$ can be constructed in $O(n + \tilde{e}_T \log \sigma)$ total time for integer alphabets of size $n^{O(1)}$. After $L\text{-}CDAWG(T)$ has been constructed, the input string T can be discarded.*

4   Conclusions and Further Work

In this paper, we presented a new repetition-aware data structure called Linear-size CDAWGs. $L\text{-}CDAWG(T)$ takes linear space in the number of the left- and right-extensions of the maximal repeats in T, which is known to be small for highly repetitive strings. The key idea is to introduce type-2 nodes following LSTries proposed by Crochemore et al. [5]. Using a small SLP induced from edge-suffix links that is enhanced with random access and prefix extraction data structures, our $L\text{-}CDAWG(T)$ supports efficient pattern matching and substring extraction. This SLP is repetition-aware, i.e., its size is linear in the number of left- and right-extensions of the maximal repeats in T. We also showed how to efficiently construct $L\text{-}CDAWG(T)$.

Our future work includes implementation of $L\text{-}CDAWG(T)$ and evaluation of its practical efficiency, when compared with previous compressed indexes for repetitive texts. An interesting open question is whether we can efficiently construct $L\text{-}CDAWG(T)$ in an *on-line manner* for growing text.

References

1. Belazzougui, D., Cunial, F., Gagie, T., Prezza, N., Raffinot, M.: Composite repetition-aware data structures. In: Cicalese, F., Porat, E., Vaccaro, U. (eds.) CPM 2015. LNCS, vol. 9133, pp. 26–39. Springer, Cham (2015). doi:10.1007/978-3-319-19929-0_3
2. Bille, P., Landau, G.M., Raman, R., Sadakane, K., Satti, S.R., Weimann, O.: Random access to grammar-compressed strings and trees. SIAM J. Comput. **44**(3), 513–539 (2015)
3. Blumer, A., Blumer, J., Haussler, D., McConnell, R., Ehrenfeucht, A.: Complete inverted files for efficient text retrieval and analysis. J. ACM (JACM) **34**(3), 578–595 (1987)
4. Claude, F., Navarro, G.: Self-indexed grammar-based compression. Fundamenta Informaticae **111**(3), 313–337 (2011)
5. Crochemore, M., Epifanio, C., Grossi, R., Mignosi, F.: Linear-size suffix tries. Theor. Comput. Sci. **638**, 171–178 (2016)
6. Crochemore, M., Rytter, W.: Jewels of Stringology: Text Algorithms. World Scientific, Singapore (2003)
7. Crochemore, M., Vérin, R.: Direct construction of compact directed acyclic word graphs. In: Apostolico, A., Hein, J. (eds.) CPM 1997. LNCS, vol. 1264, pp. 116–129. Springer, Heidelberg (1997). doi:10.1007/3-540-63220-4_55
8. Gasieniec, L., Kolpakov, R.M., Potapov, I., Sant, P.: Real-time traversal in grammar-based compressed files. In: Data Compression Conference, p. 458 (2005)
9. Grossi, R., Gupta, A., Vitter, J.S.: High-order entropy-compressed text indexes. In: ACM-SIAM Symposium on Discrete Algorithms, Society for Industrial and Applied Mathematics, pp. 841–850 (2003)
10. Kreft, S., Navarro, G.: On compressing and indexing repetitive sequences. Theor. Comput. Sci. **483**, 115–133 (2013)
11. Mäkinen, V., Navarro, G., Sirén, J., Välimäki, N.: Storage and retrieval of highly repetitive sequence collections. J. Comput. Biol. **17**(3), 281–308 (2010)

12. Narisawa, K., Inenaga, S., Bannai, H., Takeda, M.: Efficient computation of sub-string equivalence classes with suffix arrays. Algorithmica (2016)
13. Navarro, G.: A self-index on block trees. arXiv preprint arXiv:1606.06617 (2016)
14. Navarro, G., Mäkinen, V.: Compressed full-text indexes. ACM Comput. Surv. (CSUR) **39**(1), 2 (2007)
15. Raffinot, M.: On maximal repeats in strings. Inf. Process. Lett. **80**(3), 165–169 (2001)
16. Takabatake, Y., Tabei, Y., Sakamoto, H.: Improved ESP-index: a practical self-index for highly repetitive texts. In: Gudmundsson, J., Katajainen, J. (eds.) SEA 2014. LNCS, vol. 8504, pp. 338–350. Springer, Cham (2014). doi:10.1007/978-3-319-07959-2_29
17. Weiner, P.: Linear pattern-matching algorithms. In: IEEE Annual Symposium on Switching and Automata Theory, pp. 1–11 (1973)

Author Index

Printed in the United States
By Bookmasters

Printed in the United States
By Bookmasters